GUARDIANS OF THE SEA

GUARDIANS OF THE SEA

HISTORY OF
THE UNITED STATES COAST GUARD,
1915 TO THE PRESENT

by
Robert Erwin Johnson

NAVAL INSTITUTE PRESS   **Annapolis, Maryland**

Library of Congress Cataloging-in-Publication Data

Johnson, Robert Erwin.
  Guardians of the sea.

  Bibliography: p.
  Includes index.
  1. United States. Coast Guard—History—20th
century. I. Title.
VG53.J64 1987   359.9′7′0973   87-11193
ISBN 0-87021-720-8

With the following exceptions, all illustrations are official
United States Coast Guard or United States Navy photographs.

Page 75.   Photograph in author's possession.
Page 112.   Drawing made for author by Ms. B. A. Peterson
Page 134.   Photograph in author's possession.
Page 137.   Joe Williamson photograph. Reproduced from James A. Gibbs, Jr.,
            Pacific Graveyard (Portland, Ore.: Binfords and Mort, Publishers, 1950)
Page 163.   Photograph in author's possession.
Page 216.   Reproduced from R. S. Crenshaw, Jr., *Naval Shiphandling* (Annapolis,
            Md.: U.S. Naval Institute, 1955).

Book design by Moira Megargee

Printed in the United States of America

For John Haskell Kemble

CONTENTS

PREFACE

My association with the United States Coast Guard began almost forty-five years ago and ended, or so I thought, five years later. I spent nearly all of that five-year period as a cutter sailor—a term expanded to include service in a frigate and a destroyer-escort of World War II vintage—and this experience with only one of the Coast Guard's branches may be reflected in this book. But I was aware, even before I read Admiral Willard J. Smith's apt comment that the Coast Guard is a collection of different but related functions, that there were other, perhaps equally important, sections, and I have tried to explain how these came to be Coast Guard responsibilities and how it has executed them.

My selection of rescue and other operations was determined largely by the availability of information, which for the post–World War II period proved to be increasingly difficult to obtain. I must admit, however, that shiphandling and seamanship have always fascinated me—I am reminded of a line from the musical "Brigadoon" to the effect that a poet always writes about the things he cannot do!—and this fascination is probably discernible in the following pages.

This work is, in a sense, a sequel to the late Rear Admiral Stephen Hadley Evans's *United States Coast Guard, 1790–1915: A Definitive History,* which was published by the U.S. Naval Institute in 1949. For the benefit of those who are not familiar with Evans's book, my first two chapters trace briefly the development of the U.S. Revenue-Cutter and Life-Saving services, which were merged in 1915 to form the Coast Guard, writing whose history has been the most interesting and the most difficult work that I have undertaken.

Among those who have assisted me with research for this book, I am especially indebted to Paul H. Johnson, librarian and curator at the U.S. Coast Guard Academy; Sheila Lamb and Mary McKenzie of the Academy Library staff; Robert L. Scheina, historian at U.S. Coast Guard Headquarters; Teresa F. Matchette and William Sherman of the Fiscal and Judicial Branch, National Archives and Records Service; Catherine T. Jones, Sarah B. Reeves, William A. Henderson, and others at the University of Alabama's Amelia Gayle Gorgas Library; the staffs of the Southern Historical Collection, the Library of the University of North Carolina at Chapel Hill, and the Manuscript Collections of the University of Virginia; and those at the James Madison Library of the Library of Congress.

I wish to thank the following retired Coast Guard officers: Rear Admiral William B. Ellis, the late Captain Earl K. Rhodes, and Captains William F. Adams, William K. Earle, and Clifford R. MacLean for responding to my requests for information, and Admiral Chester R. Bender for allowing me to use a portion of his Reminiscences. I appreciate James A. Gibbs, Jr.'s, permission to reproduce the picture of the *Redwing*.

I undertook this work at the urging of Jan Snouck-Hurgronje, then acquisitions editor at the Naval Institute Press, and Thomas F. Epley, the Press director, has subsequently served as project "shepherd." I am grateful to both, as I am to Ruth M. Kibbey and Emily Ellis, who typed the manuscript, and to Carol Swartz for her editorial assistance. The University of Alabama provided support through a Research Stimulation Grant and a semester of sabbatical leave, without which this book would have been delayed even further.

Finally, words cannot express my gratitude to Vivian. She and Mr. Jefferson, our cocker, have spent almost eight years with the Coast Guard. This book owes much to her patience as well as to her assistance as critic and proofreader.

GUARDIANS OF THE SEA

CHAPTER ONE

THE UNITED STATES
REVENUE-CUTTER SERVICE

On 16 January 1912, Ellsworth P. Bertholf, captain commandant of the United States Revenue-Cutter Service, might very well
have been a badly worried man. A scant six months after his appointment to the service's highest position, he had been handed a
portion of the report of the President's Commission on Economy and
Efficiency that recommended that the Revenue-Cutter Service be
abolished and its duties and vessels be distributed among other
governmental agencies. Moreover, President William H. Taft would
support the recommendation. Yet Bertholf was not unduly discouraged by this development; both he and his service had overcome
adversity before.

The Revenue-Cutter Service traced its origin to an act of Congress
that became law on 4 August 1790, authorizing President George
Washington to have built and fitted out "so many boats or cutters,
not exceeding ten, as may be necessary to be employed for the
protection of the revenue."[1] Secretary of the Treasury Alexander
Hamilton, on whose recommendation this measure had been enacted, was less successful with regard to the status of the officers
appointed to these cutters. He had wished them to be granted naval
commissions; there was, however, no U.S. Navy at the time, and the
Congress apparently saw no need for one. Instead, the appointees
became "officers of the customs," which, in view of the intended duty
of the cutters, seemed reasonable enough, especially since the service was placed under Treasury Department control.

The Congress authorized the president to have cutters built and
put into service; it did not authorize him to establish a cutter service
as such. Presumably the absence of an official name for the cutters
and their personnel can be attributed to this fact. At any rate, a
service they became, albeit a service lacking formal organization as
well as a name. In official correspondence, it was often referred
to as the "Revenue Service" or more frequently in the nineteenth
century, as the "Revenue-Marine." The name "Revenue-Cutter Ser-

vice" appeared in an act of Congress of 1863, but Revenue-Marine seems to have been the usual designation until the 1890s, when United States Revenue-Cutter Service won acceptance as its proper name.[2]

Its vessels gained distinguishing colors much earlier. Nine years after the service's founding, Secretary of the Treasury Oliver Wolcott informed collectors of customs that the revenue cutters would display "an ensign and pennant consisting of sixteen perpendicular stripes, alternate red and white, the Union of the Ensign to be the Arms of the United States, in dark Blue on a White field."[3] The cutters flew this ensign in lieu of the national flag in home waters, displaying both while abroad. Use of this ensign having spread to customs activities generally, President Taft ordered in 1910 that the blue and white Revenue-Cutter Service emblem—the Treasury Department seal superimposed on crossed anchors—be affixed to the fly of the ensign flown in each cutter.

With the passage of time, the revenue cutters had additional duties thrust upon them, some of which they had already performed on occasion. The first of these were of a military nature: In 1797 the threatening international situation caused the cutters to be assigned responsibility for coast defense and commerce protection in their cruising areas, and in 1799 the president was authorized to order some or all to serve under the direction of the newly established Navy Department. President John Adams had anticipated this authorization, placing the cutters at the disposal of the secretary of the navy in October 1798, and eight of them served with the Navy in the Quasi-War with France, taking fifteen armed French vessels, assisting in the capture of five others, and recovering at least ten American ships from their French captors. The Navy, however, thought most of the cutters too small and slow to be of much use. Five were returned to the Treasury Department in 1799, and of the three retained by the Navy, the *Pickering* was lost with all hands in a gale in 1800, while the others were sold in the general reduction of the naval establishment that followed the Quasi-War.[4]

Subsequent conflicts—the War of 1812, the first Seminole War, the Mexican War, the Civil War, and the Spanish-American War—brought cutters under Navy Department control, but in none were these small ships with their light armaments of major importance. Nonetheless, the Revenue-Cutter Service treasured its naval tradition, even exaggerating it somewhat, as witness the attention given the role of the *McCulloch* in the Spanish-American War. The cutter did serve with Commodore George Dewey's Asiatic Squadron, but her role during the Battle of Manila Bay was that of an interested spectator who hoped in vain that her participation might be required. Thereafter the *McCulloch* served Dewey mainly as a dispatch boat, but her claim to fame was never questioned.

Repeatedly, however, individuals in Congress or in the Navy Department pointed out the absurdity of maintaining two establishments of armed vessels and insisted that the duties of the revenue cutters could be performed as efficiently by ships of the Navy. In 1859, even Secretary of the Treasury Howell Cobb urged that the Revenue-Cutter Service be transferred to the Navy—perhaps it was symbolic that the cutter bearing his name was stranded on the New England coast after a short career—and thirty years later 198 of the service's 206 officers, seeking to improve their prospects for promotion, pay, and retirement, petitioned Secretary of the Treasury William Windom to have their service consolidated with the Navy. Windom was agreeable, and Secretary of the Navy Benjamin F. Tracy urged Congress to enact legislation to this effect. Nonetheless, as on every other occasion, the opponents of the proposed transfer were able to prevent it, stressing the nonmilitary nature of the cutters' more important duties.[5]

Yet another of these nonmilitary duties had been added in 1799. The fear of contagious diseases that might be transmitted in vessels, especially those trading to tropical regions, had led individual states to adopt health and quarantine measures, and officers commanding revenue cutters and coastal fortifications were directed to aid in their enforcement. Periodically, this became an important responsibility, as in 1884 and 1885 when cutters imposed a virtual blockade of the Delaware and Chesapeake bays and the Gulf coast, cooperating with the Public Health and Marine-Hospital Service in an effort to prevent the introduction of cholera and yellow fever from abroad. The yellow-fever epidemic that afflicted New Orleans in 1905 led to the imposition of a quarantine zealously enforced by personnel of the Revenue-Cutter and Public Health services together with officials of the state of Mississippi. Six cutters and seven chartered craft manned by the service, all under the direct supervision of Captain Worth G. Ross, chief of the Revenue-Cutter Service Division, patrolled the waters contiguous to the Gulf coast, boarding some 1,500 vessels, of which more than 250 were fumigated and quarantined. In addition to the risk of yellow fever inherent in boarding infected ships, the oppressive heat, swarms of mosquitoes, and frequent storms—two of which attained hurricane strength—the cutter force had to endure the enmity of Louisiana officials, who denounced it for supporting Mississippi's "invasion" of their state's waters and had one of the chartered launches "captured" by the Louisiana militia. When the quarantine was lifted after three months, the Revenue-Cutter Service boasted that "not one case of yellow fever has been reported to have entered by water."[6]

Prevention of another evil, the foreign slave trade, became a duty of the cutters when it was prohibited in 1807, although this duty seems not to have elicited any unusual effort on their part. In December 1807 they joined the Navy's gunboats to enforce the unpopular embargo, by which President Thomas Jefferson hoped to compel warring European powers to show greater regard for American rights. This was short-lived, as were the acts that empowered the president to utilize revenue cutters in antipiratical operations in 1819 and 1820, although the cutters *Louisiana* and *Alabama* made considerable reputations by their forays against Gulf Coast buccaneers. Enforcement of neutrality laws, dating from 1818, and protection of live-oak forests on public lands against the depredations of illegal loggers under a law of 1833, extended to other trees later, were responsibilities lasting into the twentieth century.

Until 1832, rendering assistance to vessels in distress was not a specific obligation of revenue cutters. Should they encounter such in the course of their usual cruising, cutter sailors would offer whatever aid they could, in accordance with the time-honored practice of those who use the sea. In 1832, however, Secretary of the Treasury Louis McLane directed several cutters to cruise actively during winter months solely for this purpose, and the custom seems to have been followed generally until December 1837, when Congress authorized the president "to cause any suitable number of public vessels, adapted to the purpose, to cruise upon the coast, in the severe portion of the season, when the public service will allow of it, and to afford such aid to distressed navigators as their circumstances and necessities may require; and such public vessels shall go to sea prepared fully to render such assistance."[7] The law's phraseology permitted the use of naval vessels as well as cutters, but those naval vessels assigned to the task proved to be unsuitable. Thus, winter cruising came to be the responsibility of the revenue cutters alone, and over the years the importance of this aspect of their duties came to eclipse even that of enforcing payment of customs and tonnage duties, at least in the public mind. Needless to say, this function was not limited to waters of the Atlantic seaboard; the task of assisting distressed vessels on the Great Lakes was specifically assigned to cutters stationed thereon in 1870, while those on the Gulf and Pacific coasts seem to have undertaken it as a matter of course.

The service's concern with saving life and property from the perils of the sea quite naturally brought it into association with rescue from the shore. A few private organizations—most notably the Massachusetts Humane Society founded in 1786—along with state-appointed wrecking personnel and those engaged by underwriters, had carried on such lifesaving activity as there was until the mid-nineteenth century, by which time the Massachusetts group operated eighteen stations with lifeboats and line-throwing equipment at dangerous locations on the state's coastline. In 1847, the appropriations for the nation's lighthouses included $4,000 for equipping "lighthouses and other exposed places where vessels are liable to be driven on shore, with boats and other suitable means of equipment." This money, the government's response to the increasing number of shipwrecks occurring off American shores, was not used, and a year later, largely as the result of efforts by New Jersey Congressman William A. Newell, the sum of $10,000 was authorized to be spent for lifesaving equipment for the New Jersey coast, "to be expended under the supervision of such officers of the Revenue Marine Corps as may be detached for this duty by the Secretary of the Treasury." This time the appropriation was not ignored; at Secretary Robert J. Walker's request, the New York Board of Underwriters formed a committee to work with Captain Douglas Ottinger in organizing stations between Sandy Hook and Little Egg Harbor. The Massachusetts Humane Society, to which the money appropriated in 1847 had just been allotted, provided information on the equipment and practices it had evolved to guide those involved in this endeavor.[8]

Thus began the movement that in due course would grow into the U.S. Life-Saving Service. Captain Ottinger was deeply interested in his work and within a year had eight boathouses built and equipped in addition to carrying out continuing experiments with various types of equipment, with the occasional assistance of a revenue cutter. A $20,000 appropriation in 1849 led the New York legislature to give official status to the Life-Saving Benevolent Association of New York, while the Philadelphia underwriters also evinced interest. The cooperation of these groups facilitated the establishment of further stations, so that a series of boathouses, twenty-four in all, soon lined the Long Island and New Jersey coasts. Appropriations forthcoming in succeeding years brought the total number of government-supported stations to fifty-six, located between Watch Hill, Rhode Island, and Cape May, New Jersey, while surfboats were furnished to various coastal points from Maine to Texas and on the Great Lakes.

This rapidly evolving lifesaving system had one obvious deficiency—it had no provision for personnel. Captain Ottinger was able to do no more than to leave each boathouse and its contents in the care of a reputable person in the vicinity. But he was too realistic to think this an adequate assurance that all would be cared for, and recommended that commanding officers of cutters within the limits of whose stations they were located visit them at bimonthly intervals to inspect the equipment. No such inspections seem to have been made, however, for several years.

The lack of responsible personnel notwithstanding, the system soon brought results. When the British bark *Ayrshire* was stranded on Squan Beach, New Jersey, in 1850, heavy snow driven by a gale from the northeast made rescue of the 202 persons on board unlikely before she broke up. Yet volunteers using the nearby station's surfcar saved all but one, and this person would have been saved had he obeyed instructions and not tried to ride to shore on top of the surfcar. Perhaps 2,900 more were rescued from ships wrecked on the shores of Long Island and New Jersey during the next five years by men using boats and equipment furnished by the government. On the other hand, some 700 lives were lost in the wrecks of the *Powhattan* and the *New Era*—163 of about 500 were saved from the latter—in 1854, showing the inadequacies of equipment and maintenance. As a result, Congress authorized the employment of su-

The Life-Saving Service. Surfboat drill at the Orleans, Massachusetts, station in 1908.

perintendents for the Long Island and New Jersey coasts and of a salaried keeper for each station. Even when these positions were filled in 1856, the system remained inadequate: no funds were provided for maintenance, keepers had no regulations to guide them, and in the absence of paid crews, they could not hold regular drills.[9]

Perhaps because of the growing tension between North and South over the extension of slavery within the United States and because of the Civil War in which it culminated, the Treasury Department showed little interest in the matter of saving life after 1854. It ignored the reports of Revenue Marine officers inspecting the stations and left unspent the moneys appropriated by Congress from time to time. The establishment of a Division of Revenue Marine, responsible for lifesaving stations as well as revenue cutters, steamboat inspection, and marine hospitals, indicated a change of attitude in 1869; the following years brought authorization to man alternate stations, and when this proved inadequate, the secretary of the treasury was empowered to "employ crews of experienced surfmen at such stations and for such periods as he may deem necessary." Nor was this all—Congress voted $200,000 for the purchase and maintenance of equipment and ordered that all stations henceforth be built under Revenue Marine supervision.[10] Sumner I. Kimball, who became chief of the Revenue Marine Division in 1871, was a vigorous administrator who took full advantage of his opportunity, and ten years later the lifesaving section of his division

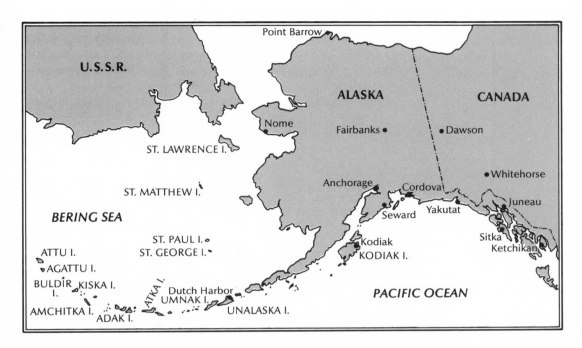

Alaska and the Aleutian Islands.

comprised 189 stations—139 on the Atlantic coast, seven on the Pacific coast, five on the Gulf coast, thirty-seven on the Great Lakes, and one at the Falls of the Ohio. By this time, it was a separate service; at Kimball's behest, Congress established the U.S. Life-Saving Service in 1878, with Sumner I. Kimball as its first and only general superintendent.

The connection between lifesavers ashore and afloat remained close, however, for officers of the cutter service, who had overseen the rapid growth of the shore lifesaving establishment and helped to draw up its regulations, remained responsible for its general efficiency. A senior officer served as inspector with nine juniors as assistant inspectors, while two captains supervised the construction and repair of stations, and another saw to the building of lifeboats, surfboats, and other equipment. In addition, revenue cutters and lifesaving stations regularly cooperated in rescue efforts and the like.

The immediate post–Civil War period had brought a considerable expansion of revenue cutter activity in another direction. Acquisition of Russian America, soon to be known as Alaska, meant a vast territory to be policed, and while the U.S. Army had the principal responsibility during the first decade of United States ownership, revenue cutters based on the Pacific coast regularly cruised in Alaskan waters. Indeed, the schooner *Reliance* was stationed at Sitka from 1868 to 1875, sailing thence into the Gulf of Alaska and the Bering Sea in the summers. Thereafter, a naval vessel was based at Sitka until the turn of the century to maintain law and order in southeastern Alaska.

From the beginning, the cutters' duties in Alaskan waters were extensive, and they were added to as time passed. The *Lincoln*, the first cutter sent north in 1867, had orders to reconnoiter the coast contiguous to the Gulf of Alaska, seeking coaling station and light-house sites, fishing banks, and points at which customhouses might be established and where smugglers might congregate. She embarked a Coast Survey party to make local surveys, and Captain W. A. Howard was enjoined to collect information as to tides, currents, and subsurface water temperatures, marking the service's entry into the field of oceanography. And when not otherwise employed, the *Lincoln*'s surgeon would collect specimens of flora and fauna for the Smithsonian Institution. This was a large order for an under-powered 165-footer, yet Captain Howard gathered a considerable amount of useful information in the course of his four-month cruise, while the cutter *Wayanda*, sailing later in 1867 and in the two succeeding years, carried out a reconnaissance of the coast from the Alaska Panhandle to the Aleutian Islands and thence to the Bering Strait. These early voyages added a good deal to the knowledge of Alaskan waters, although it should be noted that American whaling vessels had been seeking their prey in the Gulf of Alaska and the Bering Sea for two decades and more and had sailed through the Bering Strait into the Arctic Ocean as early as 1848. European explorers, mainly Russian and English, had preceded them, so these waters were hardly unknown.[11]

Regular cutter cruises into the Arctic Ocean began in 1879, when the 145-foot *Corwin*, an "unusually strong" vessel built four years earlier, was ordered to search for two whalers and the exploring steamer *Jeannette*. Although the search was unsuccessful—all three had been crushed by the ice—the little *Corwin* set the pattern for cruises that became an annual occurrence. She continued this duty for the next five years, when the Revenue Marine obtained the larger—and slower—*Bear*, a sometime sealer two years older than the *Corwin* but more suitable for lengthy cruises in icy seas.

In the course of these cruises, the service enhanced its reputation by giving aid to whaling crews whose vessels were trapped in the ice—Lieutenants David H. Jarvis and Ellsworth P. Bertholf and Public Health Surgeon Samuel J. Call were awarded gold medals by Congress for driving reindeer herds some 1,500 miles to Barrow at Alaska's northern extremity in 1897–98. In addition, of course, medical and other assistance was offered those at points where the cutters touched, and they regularly transported scientists and others gathering information in a variety of areas.[12]

Protection of the Bering Sea fur seal and sea otter herds became a cutter responsibility in part because of a recommendation by the *Wayanda*'s Captain John W. White that the Pribilof Islands be made a federal reservation in order to prevent the extinction of the animals who bred there and the exploitation of the Aleuts hired to kill them. This was done in 1870, with the Alaska Commercial Company of San Francisco gaining the sole right to sealing. Thereupon, other sealers,

American and foreign, were forced into pelagic sealing, a practice that seemingly posed the threat of more immediate extinction of the herds because of the impossibility of determining the sex of the seals—the killing of a cow seal usually meant death by starvation for her pup. Whether this was an immediate danger is perhaps open to question; the Alaska Commercial Company has been accused of exaggerating the extent of pelagic sealing in order to eliminate its competition, making the revenue cutters charged with protection of the herds from "poachers" the agents of a monopoly.[13]

The extension of this protection to waters beyond the territorial limits could possibly bring the United States into conflict with foreign powers, especially Britain, a possibility diminished by a *modus vivendi* whereby warships of the U.S. and Royal navies were sent to the Bering Sea in 1891 to keep vessels flying their respective flags from illegal activity. Revenue cutters shared the duty with the Navy's gunboats, and in 1895 the cutters so engaged were formally organized as the Bering Sea Patrol Fleet, based at Unalaska. After 1900, the Navy's participation became increasingly sporadic, while the summer Bering Sea Patrol came to rank with winter cruising off the Atlantic coast as one of the Revenue-Cutter Service's major activities.

Nor did the Alaskan duties end there. Prevention of the illegal traffic in firearms, ammunition, and liquor; protection of salmon fisheries, later extended to other types of fish and game; assistance to personnel of the Bureau of Education and later the Office of Indian Affairs; introduction of domestic reindeer from Siberia into north-western Alaska; exploration of the Kowak and Noatak rivers; maintenance of order on the Yukon River during the Klondike gold rush—these were among the duties thrust on the Revenue-Cutter Service by the government or assumed by cutter personnel on their own initiative.[14]

Elsewhere, the harbor cutter *Manhattan* was detailed to enforce anchorage regulations in New York Harbor in 1888, while other cutters were given a similar function on Michigan's St. Mary's River in 1896. The latter year also saw the service's duties extended to include the patrol of regattas and marine parades, a development prompted by the dangerous overcrowding of excursion steamers attending many of these events.

Derelicts—partially submerged hulks that had been abandoned voluntarily or involuntarily—were a perennial maritime hazard that became greater as the speed of ships increased, and revenue cutters undertook the elimination of this danger as a matter of course whenever it was encountered. Methods of coping with derelicts varied: Some had potential value and were towed into port for salvage if possible, others might be beached, and those that could neither be towed in nor beached had to be destroyed, usually by gunfire or by demolition charges known as mines, occasionally by ramming.

Towing was difficult enough, for a hawser had to be secured to the derelict, which most often meant putting men on board—no simple task if a sea were running—and not every hulk had a fitting readily available to which a line could be made fast. Destruction by gunfire would have been easier, but for the fact that except in wartime no revenue cutter carried guns heavier than 6-pounders, and a hulk of wooden construction or laden with a fairly buoyant cargo was unlikely to sink when struck by such light projectiles. So demolition mines were much used. A boat crew would secure the mines where they would do the greatest damage, which usually required boarding, and if the hulk had capsized, they would chop holes in her planking. Swinging an axe while balancing on a slippery surface and lurching in even a slight swell required skill of no ordinary kind, but one or another of the boat crew must have possessed it. Back in their boat, the sailors would pull away from the derelict while the gunner paid out the electrical firing cable until, at a safe distance, the mines were exploded. Obviously, destroying derelicts was not a job for the novice, and even the most experienced seamen might find themselves "hoist by their own petard" if any one of a number of possible mishaps were to occur.[15]

Convinced of the importance of derelict destruction, Congress voted in 1906 to authorize the secretary of the treasury "to have constructed . . . a steam vessel especially fitted for and adapted to service at sea in bad weather, for the purpose of blowing up or otherwise destroying or towing into port wrecks, derelicts, and other floating dangers to navigation."[16] Christened the *Seneca* on her launching in 1907, this cutter was alleged to be the only vessel ever designed primarily as a derelict destroyer. In fact, however, she was to gain a notable reputation in a variety of roles, and subsequent cutters were usually designed with derelict destruction among their capabilities.

As the foregoing discussion of its multifarious duties must indicate, the Revenue-Cutter Service, under whatever name it may have been operating at the time, was primarily an organization of vessels, whether seagoing or harbor cutters. Its force varied considerably over the years, and one doubts that a truly complete list of cutters and their characteristics can ever be compiled. Suffice it to say that early cutters were built of wood and rigged for sail—sloops, schooners, and brigs. They were small vessels, whatever their date, and while the steam-propelled iron cutters introduced to the service in 1844 were considerably larger, they were generally unsuccessful. So smaller vessels of wood and canvas, shapely brigs and topsail schooners, composed the cutter force in the 1850s, with the beautiful wooden side-wheeler *Harriet Lane* of 1857 its only steamer and at 180 feet and 674 tons, by far its largest ship.

A number of smaller vessels, including both screw-steamers and side-wheelers, were acquired during the Civil War, and Secretary of the Treasury Hugh McCulloch reported a force comprising twenty-seven steamers and nine sailers at war's end, about three times the

size of the prewar fleet. Too many of these vessels, however, had been designed with an eye toward naval use, and McCulloch thought them inefficient and uneconomical as revenue cutters. In his opinion, "cutters should be of light draught, manned by a small crew, and able to navigate the shoal waters and penetrate the inland bays, rivers, and creeks with which our sea, lake, and gulf coasts abound, but of sufficient tonnage to enable them to perform efficiently and safely the duties of a coast guard at sea and to furnish succor to vessels in distress."[17]

The Revenue-Cutter Service. The 165-foot Perry, *built in 1884, was lost in the Pribilof Islands in 1910.*

A committee of Revenue Marine officers headed by the Coast Survey's Captain Carlisle T. Patterson repeated this recommendation to McCulloch's successor, George S. Boutwell, to greater effect; in 1873 the Revenue Marine had twenty-eight steamers, of which three were new ships and ten had been rebuilt, as well as six small sailing vessels. Three more steamers were building, and Boutwell thought that with the addition of a steam cutter for the Columbia River vicinity, "the service will be in a condition to answer the demands on it, economically and efficiently, for many years to come."[18]

By 1890, however, developments in naval architecture and marine engineering had made most of these ships obsolete. Bigger and faster cutters were authorized, mostly built of steel, although the *Manning* and the *McCulloch*, intended for use in Alaskan waters, were of composite construction, on the assumption that their wooden bottoms would be less vulnerable to the dangers of those

The cutter Seminole *soon after her completion in 1900.*

poorly charted seas. At 18 knots these vessels were thought fast enough to serve as torpedo boats in time of need, and each had a bow torpedo tube, a useless appurtenance that drenched the forward deck and bridge in heavy spray when steaming into a head sea. Three steel 205-footers so equipped were built at Cleveland, Ohio, as a result of Anglo-American tension in the mid-1890s, and had to be cut in half for transfer to the Atlantic coast in 1898. The Spanish-American War, of course, ended well before the *Algonquin, Gresham,* and *Onondaga* could be put together again.

Cutters built during the first decade of the twentieth century were generally somewhat smaller vessels, mainly because in its appropriations Congress declined to keep pace with the increasing costs of shipbuilding. The 204-foot *Seneca* and the 210-foot *Androscoggin* were exceptions, but their slower 12-knot top speeds were typical of the new cutters. Indeed, the 18 knots attained by the *Algonquin* and her near-sisters would not be equalled by any cutters for the next thirty years and more.[19]

In 1911, Captain Commandant Bertholf reported that the service had thirty-six cutters, ranging from such ancients as the *Woodbury* of 1863 to the newly completed sisters *Tahoma* and *Yamacraw.* Almost all were single-screw vessels, and the older were rigged for sail as well. Most were built of iron or steel, with the *Bear, Thetis,* and *Androscoggin* the most notable exceptions; the *Thetis* was a wooden whaler acquired from the Navy in 1900 to work with the *Bear,* while the wooden-hulled *Androscoggin* was built in 1910 for occasional icebreaking in New England waters.

Early revenue cutters had been named for notable individuals— secretaries of the treasury and others; for qualities—*Active, Alert,* etc., or for states wherein they were stationed. By the late nineteenth century, Indian names, usually associated with the stations for which the ships were designed, had gained favor. Indeed, all of the cutters built during the period 1900–1921 bore Indian names, and one cannot but regret the later departure from this practice, for the white-painted ships with buff stacks and masts, bearing names familiar to their localities, clearly struck the public fancy.

The service's reputation, of course, depended on its personnel, especially its officers. The first of these were experienced seamen, many of whom had served in the Continental Navy, the various state navies, or in privateers during the Revolutionary War. They were reputed to be men of integrity and good character, and were recommended for their positions by collectors of customs, prominent merchants, and others of importance in the various seaport localities, the president then appointing them on the advice of the secretary of the treasury. Each cutter was allotted four officers—a master and three mates—four "mariners," and two boys, which seems a very top-heavy complement. In fact, the early cutters often had fewer officers because competent individuals could earn much more sailing in merchantmen. Officers' pay and allowances and cutter complements were increased within a few years, however, and naval ranks—captain and lieutenant—replaced the unpopular master and mate in 1799.[20]

Thereafter, officer selection seems to have been largely a political process, with influential acquaintance of greater importance than professional competence. A number of junior naval officers obtained leaves of absence to accept employment in revenue cutters during the period 1821–32. Believing this practice "liable to objection," Secretary McLane ended it and also directed that vacancies in the cutter service's ranks be filled by promotion of junior officers, "having regards to fitness as well as seniority." These developments, of course, did little to decrease the importance of political influence, but perhaps the legislation of 3 March 1845, which specified that no person should be appointed a cutter officer without "competent proof of proficiency and skill in navigation and seamanship," was more effective. In 1863, Congress authorized the president to appoint the service's commissioned officers, with the advice and consent of the Senate.[21]

The quality of a number of the officers remained questionable nonetheless, and in 1869 George S. Boutwell undertook to resolve this problem by appointing an examining committee headed by Captain John Faunce. The process of testing 130 officers took some time; it was completed in 1871, and thirty-nine officers, including seven captains, were forced to resign their commissions. The vacancies thus created were filled by promotion from the next lower ranks on the basis of performance on the examination. Thereafter, all appointments and promotions were to be made as a result of competitive examinations.[22]

As before, new third lieutenants reported to cutters when commissioned and learned their profession on board ship. The resulting lack of uniformity concerned a number of senior officers, most notably Captains George W. Moore, James H. Merryman, and John A. Henriques, who urged Sumner Kimball, chief of the Revenue-Marine Division, to establish a school of instruction for officers. Kimball was sympathetic and possessed of the necessary political influence; an act of 31 July 1876 provided for the appointment of cadets to fill vacancies in the rank of third lieutenant. After two years of instruction, the cadets who passed a final examination would be commissioned third lieutenants when vacancies occurred.

The captains agreed that sail training was essential, so in 1877 the cutter *Dobbin,* a schooner built in 1853, became the school ship until a more suitable vessel could be obtained. Captain Henriques took command and welcomed nine cadets who composed the first class. They had passed an examination in arithmetic, geography, and English and had impressed the examining board by their general attitude; ten others had not been so fortunate. During their two years on board the school ship, which was moored at New Bedford, Massachusetts, from October to May and spent the summer months cruising along the Atlantic coast, cadets studied a curriculum weighted heavily toward mathematics and in the second year, law. English, French, and history were also taught, and of course seamanship and navigation received a good deal of attention. The lovely bark *Chase,* designed and built under Captain Merryman's supervision, replaced the old *Dobbin* in the late summer of 1878, providing more ample classrooms and quarters for twelve cadets.[23]

This system of providing officers for the service was a great advance; indeed, it might be said to have completed the work of revitalization begun by Secretary Boutwell. It did not escape criticism, however. Two weaknesses especially were noted: The competitive entrance examination could be taken only in Washington, thus favoring those from the Middle Atlantic states, and two years provided time for little more than elementary education in some subjects. The military and naval academies, both of which had four-year classes and far superior facilities, obviously provided better training, and the latter graduated each year more students than the Navy could commission. With the number of cadets required dwindling each year in the 1880s, it was difficult to justify the continued operation of a separate school, so the *Chase* was decommissioned in 1890, and third lieutenants were acquired from the Naval Academy's surplus, those who had graduated with marks too low to obtain Navy commissions.[24]

But the nineteenth century's final decade brought an expansion of the Navy, and by 1894 there were no officers available from that source. Thus, the training ship could embark another class of cadets, and when the selective retirement of infirm and superannuated officers—some over eighty year of age!—in 1895 led to the promotion of all third lieutenants, the *Chase* had to be lengthened 40 feet to double her cadet capacity. Eight years later, Congress extended the course of instruction to three years, and it made provision for a six-month course of training for engineer-cadets in 1906. The latter was clearly impractical in a sailing vessel, so the sometime Naval Academy practice ship and gunboat *Bancroft* was acquired. Thoroughly overhauled, with new boilers and engines, rearmed with 6-pounders, and rerigged as a hermaphrodite brig, she was commissioned as the *Itasca* in 1907 and provided cadet training under both sail and steam for the next fifteen years.[25]

After 1900, the school ship made only an occasional visit to her home base at New Bedford, for the Revenue-Cutter Service had acquired its first shore installation, and it seemed reasonable that the School of Instruction be located there. This facility was the result of dissatisfaction with the cost and quality of repair work in private shipyards. Captain Charles F. Shoemaker, the service's chief, leased an area on Curtis Bay, just south of Baltimore, and in April 1899 Lieutenant John C. Moore brought the old side-wheeler *Colfax* into the bay's Arundel Cove. Her men constructed a ship-repair and boat-building yard over the next several years, and in the summer of 1902 the cutters *Seminole* and *Algonquin* were overhauled there. Almost three years later, by which time the yard was a fully functioning facility, Congress authorized its establishment, appropriating $30,000 for the purchase of the land and necessary equipment. This made further development possible, and the yard acquired a civilian work force in addition to its service personnel.[26]

By the time the *Chase* was retired, Arundel Cove was becoming too crowded to allow expansion of the School of Instruction, and with cadets spending three years therein, expansion was necessary. Captain Worth G. Ross, Shoemaker's successor, sought funds to establish a proper academy elsewhere. These were not forthcoming, but Congress did authorize the transfer of Fort Trumbull at New London, Connecticut, and in September 1910 fifty cadets and their instructors disembarked from the *Itasca* to set up the School of Instruction in the recently abandoned Army post's buildings.[27]

As might be expected, the service's "other ranks" were obtained as needed with little regard for origin or education. Recruited from the maritime population of the cutter's station, they probably required little training, and that which they received was entirely practical in nature. Terms of enlistment seem to have varied—some men were engaged for a cruise, others for a year or more. During much of the time, discipline varied from cutter to cutter; the *Regulations,* most notably those of 1843 and 1871, were well-meant, but adherence to them seems often to have been an individual matter, and those enacted in 1894 were similarly ineffectual. Thus, Commodore Dewey thought it advisable to put a naval lieutenant and four armed sailors on board the *McCulloch* before sailing for Manila Bay, and in 1904 Secretary of the Treasury Leslie M. Shaw wrote, "The Service is suffering for the entire lack of legal authority to properly control its ships' crews in the matter of discipline and order, from which lack the morale of the Service is threatened daily."[28] Two years later, Congress passed a bill "to regulate enlistments and punishments"; this was followed in 1907 by the comprehensive *Regulations for the United States Revenue-Cutter Service,* which eliminated any uncertainties.[29]

Administration of the service had developed in similarly haphazard fashion. The collectors of customs, under whose supervision the earliest cutters were built and fitted out, came to be almost autonomous and if they wished, could exercise direct control over the cutters assigned to their districts with little interference from the secretary of the treasury. Occasionally a secretary might take an interest in the service, as did Louis McLane in the early 1830s and John C. Spencer a decade later. The latter sought to establish an effective organization by appointing Captain Alexander V. Fraser to supervise "all matters appertaining to the Revenue-Service."[30] Predictably, the captain encountered opposition from collectors and fellow-officers, especially those senior to him. But Fraser was an enterprising individual who made considerable progress with Spencer's support. Unfortunately, the iron steam-propelled cutters, whose building he advocated, turned out to be failures, and Spencer's successors held Fraser partly responsible. Moreover, eleven cutters were ordered to serve with the Navy's Gulf Squadron in the Mexican War, which obviously interfered with Fraser's efforts. Nonetheless, he left his successor, Captain Richard Evans, a promising beginning, which came to naught when Evans was transferred in 1849, after only a year in Washington.[31]

Administration of the service was then entrusted to the commissioner of customs in the Treasury Department, but in fact the collectors regained the control they had exercised before Fraser's appointment. With secretaries of the treasury such as Howell Cobb, who thought the cutters a nuisance whose duties should be performed by the Navy, no change could be expected, nor did any occur until George S. Boutwell undertook his reforms in 1869.

These were carried out initially under N. Broughton Devereux, who was succeeded by Sumner I. Kimball as chief of the Revenue Marine Bureau, comprising the cutters and the lifesaving stations, in 1871. Congress gave this organization statutory existence as the Treasury Department's Division of Revenue Marine four years later. Kimball remained in charge until 1878, when he became general superintendent of the newly formed Life-Saving Service, and his civilian successors proved not to be his equals.[32]

An apparent diminution of the service's efficiency during the decade of the 1880s, coupled with the officers' petitions pleading for transfer to the Navy Department, led Secretary William Windom to appoint Captain Leonard G. Shepard chief of the Revenue Marine Division in 1889, anticipating congressional authorization by five years. Shepard proved to be an effective leader, beginning a rejuvenation of the service in both equipment and personnel. On his death in 1895, Captain Charles F. Shoemaker continued along the same lines until he retired a decade later. Captain Worth G. Ross, a member of the School of Instruction's first class, succeeded to the position. For all of their efforts, however, neither Shepard, Shoemaker, nor Ross was able to assume operational control over the cutters. A step in that direction was taken by Shepard just before his death in 1895, when he established the Bering Sea Patrol Fleet, whose senior officer reported directly to Washington because there was no collector of customs in that area. Elsewhere, of course, the collectors retained their control.

Captains Shepard, Shoemaker, and Ross had been appointed to head the Revenue-Cutter Service without any increase in rank or pay and for no specific period. The first served until his death, the second until his statutory retirement, and the third would presumably do the same. In 1908, however, Congress authorized the appointment of a captain commandant for a four-year term, to rank with captains in the Navy. Six other captains were promoted to the new rank of senior captain, ranking with commanders, while captains continued to rank with lieutenant commanders and lieutenants with the corresponding lower naval grades. Engineer officers were treated similarly, and the position of chief engineer, ranking with a senior captain, was created. Pay and allowances were equalized with those of naval officers; since retirement at the age of 64 had been extended to the Revenue-Cutter Service in 1902, its officers had now gained everything that they could reasonably have expected.[33]

This, then, was the service that seemingly faced abolition in 1912 in the cause of economy and efficiency, a service almost as old as the nation it served, a service whose past was somewhat chequered perhaps, yet which had achieved a not inconsiderable reputation, in maritime circles at least. Over the years it had managed to survive a number of efforts to transfer it to the Navy Department, a move that almost certainly would have resulted in its eventual dissolution. Whether the Revenue-Cutter Service could survive this latest threat to its existence would depend in large part on the ability of Captain Commandant Ellsworth P. Bertholf to make a telling argument for its continuation.

CHAPTER TWO

THE LAST YEARS OF THE REVENUE-CUTTER AND LIFE-SAVING SERVICES

*W*hen Captain Commandant Worth G. Ross requested that he be retired on 1 May 1911 because of poor health, he recommended that Captain John C. Cantwell be named to succeed him. Both seem to have expected the appointment to follow as a matter of course, for the 51-year-old Cantwell had a distinguished record, principally in Pacific coast and Alaskan waters.[1] But he was not the only applicant for the position, which had become much more attractive as a result of the 1908 legislation.

Several officers thought themselves qualified, among them Captain Ellsworth P. Bertholf, who in 1909 had written his friend Godfrey L. Carden, offering to support Carden should he decide to apply and if not, asking Carden's assistance in his own quest for the position. In the latter case, "I do not intend to make a service campaign, as Ross did, for the conditions and circumstances are quite different. If I can manage to get the proper backing to make the deal, I do not need any 'service' help, and if I can not get the proper backing, then the 'service' could do me no good. Any way my efforts will be entirely outside of the Service." Carden's response was noncommittal, but he agreed that "the help must come from the outside."[2] Both officers must have been aware that Article 658 of the *Regulations* forbade them to use "political or other influence" to gain a position, and just as surely, both were aware that the use of such influence was far from unknown.

At any rate, Secretary of the Treasury Franklin MacVeagh nominated Captain Bertholf to succeed Ross, and President Taft sent his name to the Senate for confirmation. There it stayed for a time. Senators wished to know why a relatively junior captain had been selected over twenty-two officers senior to him, including Cantwell, who was fourth on the list of captains. The senators also were interested in the fact that Bertholf had been dismissed from the Naval

Academy after one year for his involvement in a hazing incident—indeed, had the 1907 *Regulations* been in effect in 1885, Bertholf could not have been admitted to the School of Instruction.[3] On the other hand, he was one of the three officers to whom Congress had awarded gold medals for their relief of the imperiled whalers in 1897–98, and he had proven himself in a variety of assignments, including command of the *Bear* on two Alaskan cruises. The record was convincing; Bertholf became captain commandant on 19 June 1911.

In fairness to Bertholf, one must note that Secretary MacVeagh had some reason to choose him over Captain Cantwell. The latter's record bore two blemishes: In 1905 he had given his wife and some relatives and friends passage from Sausalito, California, to Portland, Oregon, in the *McCulloch* without seeking permission to do so, and more important, he had "forgotten" to have their presence on board the cutter noted in her logbook. An official reprimand for this negligence was followed by another two years later when he ran the *Manning* aground in Alaska's Prince William Sound. The subsequent investigation cleared him of any responsibility for the mishap, but it revealed that he had failed to give adequate attention to assuring the accuracy of the cutter's logbooks and navigation record.[4] His biographer concluded that "Cantwell's difficulties arose, not from want of nautical ability or poor judgment, but from his apparent disinterest in administrative chores."[5] This would hardly seem to be a desirable quality in an officer seeking his service's highest administrative position. Subsequent events would confirm MacVeagh's good judgment in choosing Ellsworth P. Bertholf to head the Revenue-Cutter Service.

The Commission on Economy and Efficiency, which recommended the service's abolition, was headed by Professor Frederick A. Cleveland, a highly respected economist who served as President Taft's financial adviser. At the president's behest, the commission had been appointed to study "the methods of transacting the public business of the various executive departments and other governmental establishments" in order to suggest changes to bring about greater economy and efficiency. Among other things, the commission recommended that the Life-Saving Service be transferred to the Department of Commerce and Labor to be merged with the Bureau of Lighthouses, and its report on the Revenue-Cutter Service began:

Ellsworth Price Bertholf, captain-commandant of the Revenue-Cutter Service, 1911–15, and of the Coast Guard, 1915–19.

> In the consideration which the commission has given to the organization and activities of the services of the Government having to do with maritime affairs special attention has been given to the Revenue-Cutter Service. After a careful study of the work now being performed by this service the commission is convinced that the service has not a single duty or function that can not be performed by some other existing service, and be performed by the latter at much smaller expense on its part.

Noting that the annual cost of the Revenue-Cutter Service was nearly

$2,500,000, the commission anticipated a saving of at least $1,000,000 each year were the service abolished. "This economy . . . will be effected not at the expence of efficiency, but that, on the contrary, all the duties now being performed by the service will be equally, if not more efficiently discharged by other services."[6] A later statement to the effect that the commission assumed that the Revenue-Cutter Service was being operated efficiently can have been little solace to MacVeagh and Bertholf.

The commission recommended, however, that the opinions of the three departments most interested be sought before Taft submitted his own views to Congress. First to respond was Secretary Charles Nagel of Commerce and Labor, who was quite willing to have the combined Bureau of Lighthouses and Life-Saving Service under his control. Nor was he opposed to the abolition of the Revenue-Cutter Service, believing that the seagoing cutters would be just as useful as naval vessels as they were at present. He added that some of the cutters would have to be transferred to his department for the purpose of aiding ships in distress off the American coasts.[7]

Secretary of the Navy George von L. Meyer had some reservations: "It is true that the chief functions of the Revenue-Cutter Service can be performed by the Navy, but this can not be done as stated in the Cleveland report in the regular performance of their military duties. All duties which interfere with the training of personnel for war are irregular and in a degree detrimental to the efficiency of the fleet." On the other hand, Meyer professed to believe that the smaller service's abolition would be a measure of economy, and he thought it imperative that the cutters be transferred to the Navy, which had too few small vessels. The enlisted personnel would be welcome as well; transfer of the 390 (actually 290) officers and cadets, however, "would be of no possible advantage to the Navy, but a serious menace to the harmony of the personnel."[8]

Nagel's response was positive and Meyer's ambiguous; that of Franklin MacVeagh can best be described as indignant:

> The recommendation to abolish the Revenue-Cutter Service . . . came out of a clear sky. No one connected with the service or with the Treasury Department . . . knew that the project was being considered. And it never had been considered before. It had been suggested a good while ago that the Revenue-Cutter Service should be transferred to the Navy Department; but the thought of abolishing it is new, and the recommendation by the commission has been keenly felt by the revenue-cutter officers and men. It came at a time when the service was performing conspicuous and heroic work and its fit equipment and its high usefulness were in immediate and conspicuous evidence.

The treasury secretary went on to present a mildly emotional defense of the service and its situation, and added a copy of laudatory remarks that he had made a week earlier at the launching of the cutters *Miami* and *Unalga.* Perhaps his most telling argument was to question the commission's view that abolition of the service would result in greater economy.[9] Here he referred to the captain commandant's comments on the commission report.

Bertholf asserted that without revenue cutters to assist them, the Departments of the Treasury, Justice, the Interior, Agriculture, and Commerce and Labor would have to acquire their own individual maritime forces in order to meet certain parts of their responsibilities. Even the Navy, which would of course assume most of the duties, could not operate the cutters without additional officers and men. Economy was hardly likely to result from a proliferation of forces afloat or from transfer of cutters to the Navy, for the annual expense of maintaining and operating a gunboat similar in size and characteristics to a cutter was 53.2 percent higher, mainly because of the larger crew needed to man the warship's heavier battery.

The captain commandant also produced figures to prove that his service was becoming more efficient: During the period 1898–1901 $2.39 worth of marine property had been saved for each dollar appropriated for the Revenue-Cutter Service and for 1908–11 the value of property saved had risen to $4.43 per dollar investment. Bertholf went on to make his own prediction of the monetary cost of abolishing the service—$1,125,000 more would have to be expended annually to provide the services traditionally performed by revenue cutters.[10]

President Taft was not convinced. He sent the commission report to Congress on 4 April 1912, recommending passage of the legislation necessary to put its various sections into effect. But the president's relationship with a significant section of his own Republican party had deteriorated markedly as his administration progressed; anything that he urged was certain to be subjected to the most searching scrutiny in Congress.

Meanwhile, the proposal to abolish a service of such antiquity had attracted a good deal of public attention. The press played its part, reviewing the service's record and reporting the cutters' rescue activities in some detail, while editorial comment was almost uniformly favorable to it. As Bertholf wrote a friend, the Revenue-Cutter Service received "an enormous amount of free advertising . . . which has done us . . . no harm at all but a great deal of good."[11] The sinking of the White Star liner *Titanic* with the loss of some 1,500 of the more than 2,200 persons on board only ten days after Taft had sent his message to Congress, focused even more attention on a service that listed the saving of life and property at sea among its principal duties, a service that had no foreign counterpart and was even then threatened with dissolution.

Secretary MacVeagh was by no means resigned to the loss of either the Revenue-Cutter Service or the Life-Saving Service. He, like almost everyone else in the Treasury Department, was convinced that the two should have an even closer connection. "Indeed, I think it might be very well a little later to make the Life-Saving Service a part of the Revenue-Cutter Service, and I believe that will be done."[12] Whether Sumner I. Kimball shared this view is not clear. A year earlier he had urged that district superintendents of the Life-Saving Service take over the duties then performed by Revenue-Cutter Service captains serving as assistant inspectors, which would seem to imply that he wished to diminish the connection.[13] At any rate, an individual who had spent fifty-one years in the Treasury Department was unlikely to wish to leave it for another so late in his career.

With the Taft administration nearing its end and the split in the Republican party rendering the president's nomination for a second term doubtful, MacVeagh had little time in which to bring about a consolidation of the two services. He directed their heads to draft a measure to this effect for his approval, and the 78-year-old Kimball and Bertholf, thirty-two years his junior, set to work.

The basic problem confronting them was that of merging a group of civilians, most of whom—those on the Atlantic and Gulf coasts and the Great Lakes—were employed only for a part of the year, into a full time military organization without damaging the morale of the former and at as little cost to the government as possible. Moreover, Kimball's future had to be considered. His age excluded him from consideration as head of the combined service, yet he could hardly be expected to serve as a civilian department head under a much younger captain commandant.

They solved these problems in a fashion to be described later, to MacVeagh's satisfaction, but the Taft administration left office before Congress could act on the proposal. President Woodrow Wilson's extensive legislative program caused further delay, so two years elapsed before the bill was passed.

By that time, the Revenue-Cutter Service had assumed yet another responsibility, that of preventing a recurrence of the *Titanic* tragedy. The British liner had foundered after colliding with an iceberg off the coast of Newfoundland. This was not an isolated occurrence; each spring bergs calved by Greenland's glaciers drifted southward into the tracks of steamships on passage between Europe and North America, and especially in the periods of low visibility not infrequent in those waters, they were a serious menace to vessels. Soon after the *Titanic*'s loss, concerned New Yorkers proposed that revenue cutters be sent "to observe movements of icebergs and warn shipping."[14] The same thought had occurred to Captain John J. Knapp, hydrographer of the navy, and in mid-May 1912, little more than a month after the *Titanic* sinking, the scout cruiser *Birmingham* was ordered to the tail (the southern corner) of the Grand Banks of Newfoundland to seek out and report the positions of icebergs in the vicinity of the transatlantic shipping lanes. Relieved early in June by her sister *Chester*, the cruiser replenished her fuel and provisions and granted liberty to her company at Halifax, Nova Scotia, before returning to the patrol. On 6 July, by which time the ice danger had passed, the *Birmingham* departed for Philadelphia. Although both ships had experienced difficulty in maintaining contact with icebergs in the dense fog that blanketed the station much of the time, their work was judged to have been of great benefit to shipping, and Captain George F. Cooper, Knapp's successor in the Hydrographic Office, recommended that it be continued in 1913 by older cruisers commissioned from the reserve fleet. His superior in the Bureau of Navigation concurred, although he thought that a more suitable vessel should be acquired for the patrol.[15]

Early in 1913, Captain Commandant Bertholf prepared a memorandum for Assistant Secretary of the Treasury Sherman Allen, in which he pointed out that the North Atlantic ice patrol was markedly similar to one of the duties annually performed by the old cutter *Bear*—that of reconnoitering the Bering Sea ice fields and recommending safe routes for steamers plying those waters. Revenue cutters could perform the same function in the North Atlantic more economically than the much larger cruisers, so Bertholf believed that the Revenue-Cutter Service should assume the responsibility.[16] Allen passed the memorandum on to Secretary MacVeagh, who responded that he knew nothing of the ice patrol or of any authority by which the Revenue-Cutter Service might undertake it. Moreover, he wondered at Bertholf's assertion that no additional vessels would be needed for the patrol; this implied a surplus of cutters that might be difficult to explain to Congress, especially since the secretary had assured that body that the service was in dire need of four additional cruising cutters.[17]

The captain commandant was equal to the occasion, informing MacVeagh that authority existed in the 1906 legislation whereby Congress had authorized the construction of the derelict-destroyer *Seneca*. This act directed that all revenue cutters destroy or remove floating dangers to navigation that they encountered in the course of their usual patrols. Icebergs were the greatest floating dangers to navigation known, and while they could neither be destroyed nor towed away from the shipping lanes, warnings of their proximity would minimize their menace. Thus, Congress itself had by implication made the Revenue-Cutter Service responsible for the ice patrol.

As far as the availability of cutters was concerned, Bertholf explained that the ice patrol would require the services of two vessels for five months each year at most, from 1 April, by which time the major storm danger in the Western Ocean had passed, until 1 September at the latest. He planned to use the *Seneca* and the new *Miami* because of their ability to stay at sea for at least twenty days without replenishing their bunkers. The cruising areas of the *Yamacraw*, *Mohawk*, *Onondaga*, and *Seminole* would be extended to include that normally patrolled by the *Miami*, and the *Androscoggin*, which assisted the *Seneca* in the destruction of derelicts, could assume the latter's duties for the duration of the ice season. The captain commandant added that the patrol's benefit to life and property at sea would amply justify any temporary slighting of the Revenue-Cutter Service's less important police functions.[18]

The treasury secretary seemed to be persuaded, but the Navy's announced intention to renew the ice patrol with the two scout cruisers remained a potential obstacle. Late in February 1913, however, the Navy Department informed MacVeagh that the necessity to keep both warships available for service in Mexican and West Indian waters had caused it to abandon plans for the patrol.[19]

Franklin MacVeagh was not destined to give final approval for the Revenue-Cutter Service's assumption of the ice patrol. He and his fellows of the Taft administration left office early in March, so a new secretary of the treasury, William G. McAdoo, had to be won over to Bertholf's proposal. The boards of directors of the Maritime Association of New York and the Philadelphia Maritime Exchange gave their support, and McAdoo seemed amenable—until he learned that the steam-whaler *Scotia,* formerly with the Scott Antarctic expedition, was fitting out at Dundee, Scotland, for an ice-reconnaissance mission. Anxious to avoid duplication of effort, the secretary decided that the Revenue-Cutter Service should forgo the ice patrol.

But the captain commandant was not yet ready to give up. Scrutinizing a copy of the *Scotia*'s sailing orders provided by a representative of His Majesty's Board of Trade, which would finance her cruise jointly with the leading British steamship lines, he found that the duplication cited by McAdoo would be more apparent than real. While the whaler was to radio information regarding the amount of ice that could be expected in the vicinity of the shipping lanes, she would simply steer the customary courses from the British Isles to the tail of the Grand Banks and then proceed to St. John's, Newfoundland, whence her track would lead northward so that the scientists embarked could study the movement of bergs in the Labrador Current.[20] Thus, the *Scotia* would be unable to warn shipping of the proximity of icebergs during most of her cruise. Learning of McAdoo's decision, the New York and Philadelphia maritime groups renewed their efforts to have the Revenue-Cutter Service take over the ice patrol, and the treasury secretary issued the necessary orders on 29 March 1913.

On the same day, the *Seneca* at New York was directed to prepare for patrol duty, and the *Miami* was summoned from her home port, Key West, for the same purpose. The latter's departure did not escape notice: a Florida senator joined the Key West Chamber of Commerce in urging that another cutter be sent to take her place promptly. And when the *Yamacraw* stood out of Savannah bound for Key West, the Georgia city's chamber of commerce and a congressman voiced their objections. Bertholf's assurance that the *Miami* and the *Yamacraw* would return to their regular stations at the end of the ice season seems to have satisfied the complainants.[21]

Captain Charles E. Johnston, designated senior officer of the ice

patrol, took his *Seneca* to sea within a week after receipt of the preparatory order. She reached the Grand Banks on 8 April and began to solicit ice information from steamers plying the transatlantic routes. One such radioed the cutter that two large icebergs were in the vicinity of the shipping lane some distance to the eastward. The *Seneca* sighted them on 13 April, and her position reports enabled vessels to give these and other dangers a wide berth until the *Miami* reported for duty. Johnston turned the patrol over to her commanding officer, Captain Aaron L. Gamble, and set a course for Halifax. After ten days of rest and replenishment, the *Seneca* steamed out to relieve the *Miami* so that the latter could enjoy a period of respite in the Nova Scotia harbor.

The Miami. *Renamed the* Tampa, *she was lost in 1918. The* Unalga *was her sister.*

The two cutters alternated on patrol through May and into June, by which time it was obvious that the ice danger was diminishing rapidly. On 8 June, Captain Johnston recommended that the patrol be terminated for the year. Bertholf thought the suggestion premature, but two weeks later, after discussing the matter with Captain Cooper, whose Hydrographic Office received the cutters' ice reports, he decided that the *Miami* should make a final search of an area about 950 miles ESE of Cape Race, Newfoundland. If she encountered no bergs, she would depart the station for New York, to which the *Seneca* was directed to proceed when the *Miami* acknowledged her orders. The reconnaissance indicated that the area was devoid of ice, so the 1913 patrol was formally ended on 1 July.

By general accord, the Revenue-Cutter Service had conducted its first North Atlantic ice patrol in exemplary fashion. No vessels had been sunk or damaged by collision with icebergs, and the timely warnings provided by the cutters' daily broadcasts elicited the praise of mariners and shipping executives. Copies of Captain Johnston's

Drift of icebergs from their source into the North Atlantic. (Official U.S.C.G. Publication)

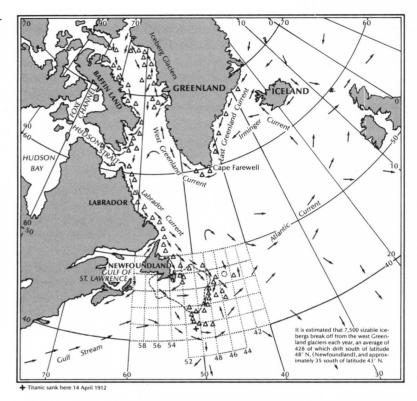

It is estimated that 7,500 sizable icebergs break off from the west Greenland glaciers each year, an average of 428 of which drift south of latitude 48° N, (Newfoundland), and approximately 35 south of latitude 43° N.

✛ Titanic sank here 14 April 1912

patrol report were in considerable demand and furnished material for articles published in the *New York Times, Scientific American,* and *Popular Mechanics* within the next few months. A British trade journal contrasted the *Scotia*'s cruise—"a dismal failure"—with those of the *Seneca* and the *Miami,* which it thought the only possible pattern for the patrol.[22]

Nonetheless, the Revenue-Cutter Service had no assurance that the ice patrol would continue to be numbered among its duties. Assistant Secretary Allen and Captain Bertholf had to appear before the House of Representatives committee on appropriations in mid-July to support a request for nearly $5,000 to defray the expenses of the ice patrol cutters, and Secretary McAdoo, noting that the United States had borne the burden virtually alone for two years, stated unequivocally that "the patrol should be discontinued." He urged that the steamship companies be made to route their vessels via more southerly and safer, albeit longer, transatlantic tracks during the period of ice danger or to maintain an annual ice patrol themselves. Realizing that neither of these solutions to the problem was likely to be adopted, McAdoo mentioned a third option—that each of the leading maritime countries contribute to the maintenance of the ice patrol.[23]

The means for implementing the treasury secretary's recommendation were at hand, for, as another result of the *Titanic* disaster, fourteen of the principal maritime nations were appointing delegates to the International Conference on the Safety of Life at Sea, which assembled in London on 12 November 1913. The twelve-man United States delegation included Captains Bertholf and Cooper, both of whom became members of the committee on the safety of navigation.

Bertholf obviously took a leading part in the committee's deliberations, for its report recognized the work of the Revenue-Cutter Service in derelict destruction and the ice patrol, recommending that the United States be asked to continue these activities. In addition, the committee believed that the investigation of ice conditions in the Labrador Sea and Davis Strait, which the *Scotia* had begun, ought to be carried on each year and that the United States should be requested to provide this service as well.[24]

These recommendations became Articles 6 and 7 of the International Convention Relating to the Safety of Life at Sea that the conference approved before adjourning on 20 January 1914. Article 7 specified that two ships be assigned to ice patrol during the ice season and to derelict destruction in the North Atlantic Ocean for the remainder of the year, except that "the study and observation of ice conditions shall be effectively maintained, in particular from the beginning of February to the opening of the ice season." Article 7 invited the United States government to undertake the conduct of all three services, with the thirteen signatories dividing the expense among themselves according to their degrees of interest. Great Britain was to contribute 30 percent of the total cost; France, Germany, and the United States 15 percent each; and the others lesser amounts. This too followed the committee report, which estimated the annual expense to be about $200,000 and suggested that the United States pay $30,000.[25]

Since the convention would not become effective until 1 July 1915, some arrangement had to be made if there were to be ice patrols in 1914 and 1915. To this end, Great Britain, on behalf of the other contracting powers, inquired on 31 January 1914 if the United States would be willing to commence the ice observation cruise as described in the yet unratified convention as soon as possible.[26]

President Woodrow Wilson responded affirmatively, issuing the necessary orders on 7 February, and the *Seneca* stood out of New York two weeks later to begin the investigation of ice conditions in the area to the north of the shipping lanes. So the ice patrol was begun, with the *Miami* and the *Seneca* relieving one another at fifteen-day intervals until the end of June when the patrol was terminated.

The 1914 ice patrol was even more successful than its predecessor, or so it must have seemed to four British seamen from the Leyland steamer *Columbian.* Bound from Antwerp to Boston with a highly inflammable cargo, their vessel caught fire and exploded just to the west of Sable Island on the night of 3 May. Her distress signals attracted nearby ships, which picked up two of her boats, but the gale-whipped snow falling at the time masked the third from the rescuers' sight. By the time the *Seneca* sighted it two weeks later, eleven of the boat's fifteen occupants had perished of starvation and exposure. The four survivors, who must soon have shared their fellows' fate, gradually regained their strength in the cutter's sick bay.[27]

Well before the next year's ice cruises were scheduled to begin, events in Europe assured that most of the contracting powers, including the United States, would never ratify the International Convention Relating to the Safety of Life at Sea. Nonetheless, the *Seneca* cast off her lines early in February 1915 to begin the ice-observation cruise, and the *Miami* joined her for the ice patrol nearly two months later. This patrol differed from its predecessors in that few merchant steamers plying the North Atlantic routes chose to break radio silence to report ice—thus, virtually all iceberg warnings originated with the cutters themselves.

Owing to World War I, several of the signatories to the convention, most notably Austria-Hungary, Germany, and France, failed to contribute their shares to the maintenance of the 1914 and 1915 ice patrols. Thus, it was as well that derelict destruction was never undertaken on the scale required by Article 6, for expenses of the patrol—salaries and wages, operation and maintenance, administration, and depreciation of the cutters—were considerably less than half the $200,000 annual estimate, small enough so that there seems to have been no thought that it should be discontinued in 1916.

As before, the *Seneca* sailed on the ice-observation cruise early in February, and her consort, now renamed the *Tampa*, steamed north from Florida in March to prepare for the ice patrol, which passed without noteworthy incident. But the 1916 patrol was the last for some years, for the severance of diplomatic relations between the United States and Germany on 3 February 1917 presaged another type of employment for the *Seneca* and the *Tampa*, one that the latter and her company would fail to survive.

The four years during which first the Revenue-Cutter Service and then the Coast Guard had been responsible for the ice patrol were sufficient to establish it as a traditional duty, which was resumed in 1919 and which has been maintained by the service ever since, with the exception of the World War II years. The "temporary" financing arrangement of 1914 remained in force until another International Conference on the Safety of Life at Sea met in London in 1929. The delegates agreed that the United States should continue the ice-observation and ice-patrol cruises described in the earlier convention's Article 6 and adjusted the scale of contributions by signatories to reflect their involvement in transatlantic shipping, a scale that has been readjusted several times subsequently.[28]

In its 124 years of existence, the Revenue-Cutter Service lost at least fourteen of its vessels to hazards of the sea. The last of these, the 191-foot *Tahoma*, ran onto an uncharted reef south of Buldir

Island in the western Aleutians during the night of 20 September 1914. Efforts to free her failed, and with his ship pounding heavily in a moderate swell, Captain Richard O. Crisp had distress signals sent. These were acknowledged by St. Paul Island in the Pribilofs, which relayed them to Unalaska, and the next afternoon Crisp decided that the *Tahoma* must break up soon unless she could be settled firmly on the reef. Sea valves and air ports were opened to speed the flooding, but as she sank, the cutter began to list dangerously, so she had to be abandoned. The boats had been prepared for this eventuality and got off without difficulty. During the night, however, they became separated, and three made Semichi Island, whence their crews were rescued several days later by the SS *Cordova*. Three other boats landed on Agattu, where the Coast and Geodetic Survey's *Patterson* found them. Captain Crisp's own gig was most fortunate to be sighted by the *Cordova* at sea, for owing to a 40° compass error—one of the sailors had stowed two rifles under the magnetic compass!—the boat would have missed Agattu by a wide margin.[29]

Ironically, the only member of the *Tahoma*'s company who lost his life did so in an unrelated mishap three weeks later. Because her coxswain was familiar with the Cape Sarichef landing, he was assigned to the *Manning* when she sailed to provide medical care for a lighthouse keeper there. Returning to the cutter, the whaleboat was swamped and capsized, with the loss of the surgeon, the sick man, and four of the boat crew.[30]

This second cutter wreck in Alaskan waters—the old *Perry* had grounded on St. Paul Island in a dense fog in July 1910—was considered unavoidable. Captain Commandant Bertholf, himself no stranger to the Bering Sea, wrote that "not a single island west of Unimak Pass is correctly charted; the positions of the islands themselves are incorrectly shown, the coast lines are incorrect, and the soundings and outlying dangers are, for the most part, left to the conjecture of the navigator . . . it is not surprising that the *Tahoma* struck an uncharted reef; indeed, the surprising thing is that the cutters have navigated those waters these many years with so few mishaps."[31] Nor would this situation change rapidly. Some of the best charts of the western Aleutians used by American forces thirty years later were those made by the Japanese.

A shipwreck later in 1914 attracted a good deal of public attention and initially at least, criticism of the Life-Saving Service as well. The steam schooner *Hanalei* bound from Eureka, California, to San Francisco with a cargo of shingles and railroad ties and with sixty-six persons on board, grounded on a reef off Bolinas Point soon after noon on 23 November. Unfortunately, her master thought that she had struck Duxbury Reef, three miles to the southward, and her distress call gave that position. Power lifeboats from the Fort Point and Point Bonita stations were sent to the *Hanalei*'s assistance, and the *McCulloch* got underway as well. Meanwhile, the fog that had contributed to the mishap was thickening, and as the boats approached the scene, visibility was almost nil. They groped their way inshore, inside the line of breakers, and finally located the wreck. A heavy swell was running, and each time a lifeboat tried to go alongside the *Hanalei*, its engine stopped in the "high, short-footed, and angry surf," forcing its crew to pull seaward again.[32] On the third attempt, the Fort Point boat capsized, and although it righted itself quickly, Keeper John S. Clark and a surfman were washed away. Clark shouted to his men to head offshore and directed the surfman to swim to the wreck while he himself swam ashore to inform San Francisco of the situation and the need for beach apparatus. Two and a half hours later, Clark was pulled from the surf, unconscious but still living. Meanwhile, Keeper Joseph L. Nutter in the Point Bonita boat decided that nothing could be accomplished in the darkness and took both lifeboats alongside the *McCulloch*, which was anchored nearby, to await the morrow.

The *Hanalei*'s true position became known in San Francisco, and a newspaper provided a truck to transport the Golden Gate station's beach apparatus to the scene. After crossing the bay to Sausalito, the station crew drove off in the foggy darkness on a mountain road noted for its crookedness. The steepest inclines could be ascended only by backing the truck up hill, and seldom could any speed be attained. Nonetheless, the 60-mile drive ended at 2 A.M. The Lyle gun was set on the bluff above the wreck and began shooting lines across it. None was secured by those on board the *Hanalei*, however, and when it became apparent that she was going to pieces, the surfmen descended to the beach. There they did their best to save those struggling amid the wreckage in the heavy surf.

> Joining hands and forming a living chain the rescuers rushed into the water wherever a living form was seen struggling, sometimes beaten back by the force of the surf or battered by floating wreckage, sometimes entirely submerged, and again taking desperate risks by crawling over the larger portions of the flotsam in the surf, they held valiantly to their work for nearly four hours until every soul had been saved that could be reached . . . With the coming of daylight . . . the lifesavers themselves were found to be in a pitiable condition, their clothing stripped to tatters and their bodies covered with bruises and cuts from head to foot.[33]

Twenty-nine survivors were pulled from the surf in this fashion, and personnel of the nearby radio station rescued another.

At dawn, Keeper Nutter took his lifeboat through the fog-shrouded, wreckage-strewn passage between the reefs, and his men pulled thirteen more from the water. These were taken to the *Mc-Culloch* for treatment, and the cutter's boats joined the lifeboat in a further search, which resulted only in the recovery of fifteen bodies.

In all, forty-three of those on board the *Hanalei* were rescued, and twenty-three, including a number of women and children, lost their lives. This outcome was especially disappointing in view of the wreck's proximity to San Francisco, and the press vented its indignation against those who had failed to save everyone from the steam schooner. The official investigation, however, found no evidence of dereliction of duty. Had the lifeboat engines been equal to their task, Clark and Nutter might have taken passengers and crew to the *McCulloch;* had the wreck's true location been known immediately, beach apparatus undoubtedly could have been sent in ample time for all on board to be saved. As it was, the crews of the three stations had done all in their power, and three of their number—Clark, Nutter, and Michael Maxwell, who had jumped out of Nutter's boat to save two people—were awarded gold lifesaving medals.[34]

By this time—late November 1914—the Revenue-Cutter Service and the Life-Saving Service were nearing the end of their separate existences, and it is to their merger that attention must now be directed.

CHAPTER THREE

THE UNITED STATES COAST GUARD, 1915–17

*T*he Treasury Department's proposal to merge the Life-Saving Service into the Revenue-Cutter Service was sent to Congress in 1913 and introduced into the Senate, where it was referred to the committee on commerce. Although an effort to have it considered by the full Senate later that year failed, the bill obviously had a good deal of support, and it was adopted without a division on 12 March 1914. Consideration by the House of Representatives, however, required the personal intervention of President Woodrow Wilson, who at Secretary William G. McAdoo's request, wrote in December 1914 to ask that the bill be added to the House calendar at an early date. A few congressmen expressed concern about the expense of extending military retirement benefits to Life-Saving Service personnel, but their opposition found little favor with their fellows. The bill was passed by a vote of 212 to 79 on 20 January 1915, and President Wilson signed it into law eight days later.[1]

This act began by combining the Revenue-Cutter Service and the Life-Saving Service to form the Coast Guard, a name that obviously had its origin in European usage. Spanish vessels known collectively as the *guarda costa* had attempted to prevent illegal trade with Spain's New World colonies in the seventeenth and eighteenth centuries, and in 1822 the British government had given the name "Coastguard" to an organization of coast watchers that reported smuggling activity and vessels in distress, and acted as a naval reserve. Secretary of the Treasury Hugh McCulloch had mentioned "the duties of a coast guard" in discussing the characteristics of revenue cutters in 1865, and the term seems to have been used informally from time to time thereafter. Captain Commandant Bertholf held that "'Coast Guard['] is the logical name for the old Revenue Cutter Service as well as the new combination . . . " and it found ready acceptance with the public.[2]

The Coast Guard was to "constitute a part of the military forces of the United States . . . under the Treasury Department in time of peace and [to] operate as a part of the Navy, subject to the orders of the Secretary of the Navy, in time of war or when the President shall so direct."[3] This was almost the only part of the legislation that would have a direct effect on officers and men of the Revenue-Cutter Service. Personnel of the Life-Saving Service, on the other hand, found themselves made a part of a military organization, with district superintendents becoming commissioned officers, station keepers warrant officers, and surfmen enlisted men. The number one surfman at each station became a petty officer. Vacancies in the ranks of district superintendent and keeper were to be filled by promotions from the next lower grade, thus protecting the interests of the lifesavers and assuring that these positions would be held by experienced men. The retirement benefits enjoyed by the Revenue-Cutter Service under the act of 1902 were extended to all Coast Guardsmen, who might apply for retirement at three-quarters pay upon completion of thirty years of service.

The legislation made provision for the general superintendent, authorizing the president to retire him on three-quarters of his salary "when the organization of the Coast Guard shall have been perfected . . . and no further appointment shall be made to such office."[4] This was not the end of Sumner Kimball's long association with his service, however, for in May 1915 he was appointed president of the Board on Life-Saving Appliances that had been created in 1882 to evaluate new and improved devices for possible use by the Life-Saving Service. Despite his advanced age, Kimball presided over the board's annual meetings for the next five years. He died in 1923.

Captain Commandant Bertholf felt constrained to offer his own elucidation:

> The Coast Guard occupies a peculiar position among other branches of the Government, and necessarily so from the dual character of its work, which is both civil and military. Its organization, therefore, must be such as will best adapt it to the performance of both classes of duties, and as a civil organization would not suffice for the performance of military functions, the organization of the service must be and is by law military. More than 120 years of practical experience has demonstrated that it is by means of military drills, training, and discipline that the service is enabled to maintain that state of preparedness for the prompt performance of its most important civil duties, which . . . are largely of an emergent nature.[5]

Whatever the elation he may have felt at this successful culmination of his efforts, Bertholf was not entirely satisfied. The act did nothing to change the law whereby all surfmen except those manning stations on the Pacific coast, where summer fogs nearly equalled winter gales as hazards to shipping, were employed for no more than ten months each year. He pointed out that it was very difficult for those on the Atlantic and Gulf coasts to find employment during the months of June and July, when their stations were closed, because boat owners and masters were unwilling to engage men for such a short period. Thus, these surfmen were reduced to reliance on odd jobs and usually had exhausted their meager savings by the end of the two months of leave without pay. Moreover, the great increase in the number of "motor-propelled boats" used for pleasure and commerce during the summer months was a positive argument in favor of keeping the stations open year-round.[6] Despite the obvious merit of Bertholf's argument, Congress was not disposed to authorize additional funding for the new service, and it remained for World War I to bring the surfmen to active duty status throughout the year.

Ellsworth P. Bertholf's term as captain commandant had less than five months remaining when the Coast Guard was formed, and while he became head of the new service as a matter of course, there was a distinct possibility that a heated competition for his position might hamper the Coast Guard's initial development. With this in mind, Assistant Secretary Byron R. Newton wrote McAdoo on 6 February that while several of the officers eligible would probably do well as commandant, "there is no one of them so well equipped to carry forward the work of whipping the Coast Guard into shape as the present incumbent. I know from my intimate touch with both branches of the consolidated service, that he has the full confidence and respect of the officers and men."[7] McAdoo, President Wilson, and the Senate concurred; thus, Bertholf had another four years in which to realize his plans for the Coast Guard, plans that he had already formulated.

Organization of the Coast Guard required a short time, reflecting the fact that to a large extent it was an old service under a new name. At its head, of course, was the secretary of the treasury, under whom an assistant secretary exercised immediate supervision. The captain commandant's headquarters had five divisions—operations, materiel, construction and repair, engineering, and inspection, the first two of which were subdivided into sections—personnel and operations, ordnance and communications, law, and statistics in the first, and supplies, accounts, mail, and files in materiel. Civilians headed the divisions of operations and materiel, while senior captains directed the remainder.

The so-called field service had no less than twenty-four divisions, of which the first six comprised the cutter fleet: Northern and Southern Pacific coast divisions, Bering Sea Patrol Fleet, New York and Eastern (Boston) divisions, and independent vessels—those stationed at seaports from Pennsylvania to Texas, on the Great Lakes, and at Honolulu. Senior captains were in charge of the first five, while independent vessels were controlled directly from Washington.

The lifesaving stations were divided among thirteen coast dis-

A surfboat and its crew in 1916.

tricts, numbered consecutively from Maine-New Hampshire—the first—to the Gulf coast—the ninth. Lakes Erie and Ontario and Louisville, Kentucky, were in the tenth, Lakes Huron and Superior in the eleventh, and Lake Michigan in the twelfth. California, Oregon, Washington, and Nome, Alaska, were included in the thirteenth coast district. Each of these was headed by a district superintendent, later known as a district commander.

The remaining five divisions of the field service were the Academy (a name adopted in 1914) at Fort Trumbull, the Curtis Bay yard, and supply depots at New York, Grand Haven, Michigan, and San Francisco.[8] Implementation of this organizational structure marked the end of the customs collectors' direct authority over the cutters in their districts. That authority had been waning for some time—appointment of the first division commanders predated the Coast Guard by several years. Henceforth, cutter commanding officers would cooperate with the collectors as needed, but they looked to their division commanders for orders.

Those who had feared that the old Life-Saving Service would lose its identity as a part of the Coast Guard should have been gratified by the form of organization, for quite clearly the two services had been joined at the top only. District superintendents, keepers, and surfmen would have been out of their element on shipboard, and station complements were too small to permit the inclusion of specialist petty officers from the cutter service. Thus, there was little exchange of personnel between the two branches of the Coast Guard, and probably little feeling of unity as well. To be sure, the captain commandant was the professional head of the service; in practice, however, the chief of the operations division at Headquar-

The Algonquin *fighting a fire in a gasoline-laden schooner, San Juan, Puerto Rico, 1916.*

ters—Oliver M. Maxam, for ten years Kimball's assistant—devoted his attention to the lifesaving branch, over which he came to exert an authority rivaling that of the commandant himself. One reason for this development was, of course, that civilian division chiefs had virtually unlimited tenure, while commandants were appointed for four-year terms. The latter could be reappointed and sometimes were, but none could approach Maxam's twenty years of continuous service in one position.

Undesirable though this situation may seem to have been at first sight, it was undoubtedly wiser to proceed gradually in the direction of more complete amalgamation of personnel than to attempt it at the very beginning. Officers of both branches had to be convinced that the change was beneficial; Captain Godfrey L. Carden, for example, wrote that he "was loathe [sic] to let that title [Revenue Cutter] pass away," but Bertholf ventured to predict "that most, if not all, of the officers who had doubts as to its advisability will before long be enthusiastic in [the Coast Guard's] support."[9] Over the years, the Coast Guard would make its own reputation, and its officers and men would come to identify with it. Then further steps might be taken to bring the service's branches into a closer relationship. Meanwhile, Congress had specified that "all duties now performed by the Revenue-Cutter Service and Life-Saving Service shall continue to be performed by the Coast Guard . . ."—some 2,000 sailors and 2,300 surfmen, all Coast Guardsmen now, would go on in their accustomed ways.[10]

Early in January 1915, the *Androscoggin*, fitted as "a small hospital afloat" with Public Health Service surgeon and medical attendants embarked, sailed from Boston to undertake the duty most recently assigned, that of extending "medical and surgical aid to crews of American vessels engaged in the deep-sea fisheries."[11] After several short cruises, a schedule was worked out whereby the cutter was based at Shelburne, Nova Scotia, during the winter months, after which she accompanied the fishing fleet eastward to Sable Island and thence to the waters off Miquelon, where the schooners fished for bait before heading for the Grand Banks. Through the summer and early autumn, the *Androscoggin* cruised about, keeping a careful lookout for a union jack at a schooner's mainmast, signifying that medical assistance was needed. The cruises were deemed successful in 1915 and 1916, during which 263 fishermen were treated, and several fishing schooners assisted in a variety of ways, but the imminence of American involvement in World War I caused the medical assistance cruises to be discontinued early in 1917, nor were they resumed after the war. Instead, the ice patrol cutters, each of which had a surgeon and a reasonably well-equipped sick bay, responded to calls for medical assistance from all vessels, regardless of nationality, in their cruising area.

Cutters on Bering Sea Patrol carried surgeons and were accustomed to providing medical assistance to fishermen and others during their cruises, which of course ended in the autumn. Representatives of Seattle's fishing industry urged that a cutter provide similar service to those fishing in the Gulf of Alaska during the winter, so the *Unalga* sailed in January 1917. She touched at Ketchikan to inform the collector of customs so that he could disseminate news of her mission, and then worked northwestward, her officers boarding fishing vessels in Wrangell, Petersburg, and Juneau. The *Unalga* stopped at Sitka to investigate reports of a measles epidemic and to take on coal before standing out into the gulf. Extreme cold and squalls of hurricane force caused Captain Francis G. Dodge to suspend the coaling for two days; then the weather moderated, and the cutter sailed on 30 January.

A northeaster began to blow that evening, and by the next morning it had increased to hurricane strength. The heavy snowfall accompanying the gale stopped early on the 31st, the temperature fell to −1°, and the *Unalga* was soon shrouded in freezing vapor rising from the water's surface. Dodge had hove to in the heavy snow, but the cutter was icing up so badly as she labored in the rough sea that he decided to seek smoother water in the lee of the land, slowing to take soundings periodically to ascertain her position. After the fourth cast of the lead, the quartermaster had to be sent below, his hands and face virtually frozen.

By late afternoon, the *Unalga's* starboard whaleboat had been smashed by a heavy sea, her radio antennae had snapped under the weight of ice, and the cutter had a 20° list to starboard, the weather side. With the temperature ranging between 1° and 3° and the ship lurching in the seaway, little could be done to free her of ice. Dodge thought it best to let her drift on the starboard tack, with wind and sea helping to hold her more or less upright and oil keeping seas from breaking on board, until the weather permitted him to set a course for Yakutat. All hands spent an uneasy night, but wind and sea abated early the next day, and when the weather cleared later that morning, the *Unalga* headed for Yakutat, with her men clearing the ice from her anchors, chains, and windlass.

She anchored that afternoon—1 February—still listing 20° and drawing three feet more than her maximum draft, with an estimated 150–175 tons of ice on board. Her crew turned to with axes, coal shovels, and a hot water hose, first to free a boat for use and then to bring the cutter to an even keel. The radiomen untangled wires, rejoined them, and hoisted a partial aerial that enabled them to establish contact with Sitka before dark.

The next week brought a slow warming trend, but thick, unsettled weather kept the *Unalga* at anchor. Her officers boarded fishing schooners in the harbor, while the surgeon treated the few who required it and busied himself among the inhabitants of Yakutat, treating their assorted ailments and giving the resident missionary a brief course in medicine. Captain Dodge was assured by masters of the fishing vessels that none would sail until the weather had improved considerably, which it did on 10 February. The *Unalga* stood out to cruise on the fishing banks, and by noon the next day a full gale was blowing from the east northeast.

So it went for the remainder of the cruise—gale following gale, usually with heavy snow, but there was no recurrence of the severe icing, in part because Dodge took care to seek shelter in good time. His men must have been grateful, for they had not been provided with heavy clothing in spite of the cutter's assignment. This was not an oversight; with the exception of a few items of such clothing issued for the use of watch standers, Coast Guardsmen had to purchase their own heavy garments until Navy foul-weather apparel was issued during World War II.

When the *Unalga* received orders on 6 March to return to Seattle, she had steamed almost 3,000 miles, boarded 342 vessels, and given medical aid to nineteen persons, of whom three were fishermen.[12] Quite clearly, winter cruising in the Gulf of Alaska was not a profitable pastime.

While the *Unalga*'s company suffered nothing more than a few cases of frostbite, that of the *Yamacraw* was not so fortunate when attempting to assist the stranded steamer *Louisiana* on 4 March 1917. The last, bound from Tampico, Mexico, to Delaware Bay with a cargo of crude oil, grounded near Ocean City, Maryland, early that morning, and was sighted by the patrol from Station No. 146 when the fog lifted. A boat was launched through the high surf, only to find that the *Louisiana*'s master merely wished a telegram sent to her owners. The steamer called for assistance that afternoon, so the surfboat

went out again, under more adverse conditions. Again, the master refused to allow his crew to be taken ashore; he wanted a cutter or a tug summoned to float his ship. Seas began to break over the *Louisiana* not long thereafter, whereupon she sent out urgent distress signals. By this time, however, the surf was running too high to permit a boat to be launched from the beach.

The Yamacraw. *The Ta-homa,* lost in the Aleutians in 1914, was her sister.

The *Yamacraw* had sailed from Norfolk the preceding evening after receiving a report that the British steamer *Strathearn* was ashore on the Virginia coast. By getting underway promptly, the cutter could reach the *Strathearn* early enough the next day to pass a hawser and attempt to refloat her on the morning tide. This advantage would be lost if the *Yamacraw* waited until her liberty men had been recalled, and since all hands would not be required for a simple towing operation, her commanding officer decided to sail immediately with only two-thirds of her enlisted men on board.

Whatever the reason, the *Yamacraw* was still seeking the *Strathearn* when she received the *Louisiana*'s distress signal the following evening. The latter was urgent, so the cutter steamed northward at once. Unfortunately, the signal gave an erroneous position, so the cutter arrived well after dark. A moderate sea was running, and the moon, frequently obscured by clouds and heavy rain squalls, gave little illumination, nor could the *Yamacraw*'s searchlight beam penetrate the drizzle between squalls. Thus, her officers could not ascertain the *Louisiana*'s true plight, but her urgent distress signal and the likelihood that the weather would deteriorate before morning, led them to agree that her company should be removed by a surfboat as soon as possible.

The cutter was anchored, and a surfboat manned by an experienced crew with the gunner, "an expert boatman," at the steering oar, departed. The *Louisiana* acknowledged a request that she release oil to smooth the seas, and the gunner brought his boat under her port bow with little difficulty. Just as the first man dropped into the boat, an exceptionally large wave, invisible in the darkness, roared over the steamer's starboard quarter, surged down her deck, and filled the surfboat, which was then thrown against the ship's bow by the backlash from the beach, flinging all ten men into the sea. Recovering quickly, those on the *Louisiana*'s deck dropped lighted life buoys and informed the *Yamacraw* of the calamity by signal light.

But the short-handed cutter had too few skilled oarsmen on board to man another surfboat, so her chain was slipped and she stood inshore to do what she could. It was tragically little. One member of the boat crew was brought alongside the *Yamacraw,* only to be wrenched from the grasp of those attempting to get him on board when she rolled suddenly. The dinghy, manned by two first-class boys, was riding to its falls; its occupants tried and failed to reach the drowning man. The two then cast off and went to help another, but they were unable to pull him into the boat. Nothing daunted, they lashed him alongside—and then found their strength unequal to the task of rowing against the strong current. The dinghy was swept against fish stakes and capsized, drowning one of the boys and the seaman they had tried to save.

Meanwhile, a scratch crew manned the *Yamacraw*'s whaleboat, and it pulled off in search of survivors. None was found, and then it too proved unable to make way against the current. The cutter ordered the whaleboat to anchor until she could reach it, but being almost in the breakers, its men decided to take their chances on pulling through the surf to the beach. In this they were successful, their inexperience notwithstanding—the boat capsized, but its five occupants gained the shore, where patrols from Station No. 146 soon found them. Unaware of their safety, the *Yamacraw* stood in as close as she could, remaining as long as there was hope of saving anyone. Thereafter, the cutter steamed offshore and anchored, having too few men left on board to assist the *Louisiana.* Nor did the latter's crew require assistance. The weather improved the next day, the sea went down, and they got ashore without difficulty.

The board of inquiry and subsequent official investigation found that the loss of eleven lives, of whom ten were Coast Guardsmen, was unavoidable and that the service personnel involved had performed their duties to the fullest extent of their ability. Making the incident the subject of a special order, to be read at a general muster of every Coast Guard unit, Treasury Secretary McAdoo praised the devotion to duty and selflessness of those who had lost their lives and of their fellows who survived, stating that all had been "true to the noblest traditions of the sea."[13]

Nonetheless, one cannot escape the feeling that the *Yamacraw*'s commanding officer used poor judgment in sailing short-handed to no real purpose. The *Strathearn* can hardly have been in immediate danger, or the cutter would not have abandoned the quest for her to go to the *Louisiana*'s aid. Thus, a delay of twelve hours or so in refloating the British steamer would have been of little moment, while several lives might have been saved could the *Yamacraw* have sent a second surfboat to the assistance of the first.

A somewhat similar lack of judgment had been shown by the men of Station No. 276, Louisville, Kentucky, eight months earlier. A small flatboat had gone over the falls of the Ohio on 27 June 1916, and its two occupants were struggling in the water swirling beneath the falls. Six men of the station crew manned two boats and to save time, steered directly over the falls. Both boats were damaged badly on striking the rocks below and swamped. With eight men in urgent need of assistance, a fisherman came up from downstream and pulled the flatboat's two men into his boat, after which they helped him to save all but one of their would-be rescuers.[14] Station crews usually possessed expert knowledge of the waters in their vicinity, and these should have known that their chances of success were small. Had the unnamed fisherman not been close at hand, the loss of life might well have approached that in the *Louisiana* rescue attempt.

Little more than a month after he had signed the legislation creating the Coast Guard, President Wilson approved the Seamen's Act, which did much to improve the lot of those manning American-flag merchant vessels and to assure passenger safety. To the latter end, the act stipulated that within five years 65 percent of a passenger-carrying ship's complement must be able seamen competent to handle lifeboats, with a smaller number to be certified by 1 July 1915. The Steamboat-Inspection Service, which licensed merchant mariners, was unable to administer examinations to determine the competence of some thousands of seamen, so the secretary of commerce requested the assistance of the Coast Guard.

Five days after receiving the request, Assistant Secretary Newton announced the schedule for the examinations, which after 1 July, would be given in seaports that had Coast Guard district headquarters.[15] Whenever possible, seamen were required to demonstrate their competence on board their own ships, thus proving their familiarity with the boats they would have to use in time of need. Commissioned officers conducted the examinations initially, and within a few months warrant officers—boatswains and keepers— were authorized to do so as well. The figures reported on 30 June 1916—16,028 men examined, of whom 11,408 received certificates, in the past eight months—indicate that this was no small task and that the examiners took their duty seriously.[16] Thereafter, of course, the number declined, with about 5,000 seamen examined annually, but the Coast Guard had entered the area of licensing merchant marine personnel on a regular basis. Within thirty years, it would have the sole responsibility for doing do.

Coast Guard aviation had its uncertain beginning during this period also. In 1915, Lieutenants Elmer F. Stone and Norman B. Hall of the *Onondaga*, based at Norfolk, persuaded Captain Benjamin M. Chiswell to allow them to fly search missions for the cutter in a borrowed aircraft. Reports of their success led the captain commandant to assign three junior officers to aviation training, of whom Stone was sent to the Navy's flight school at Pensacola and Hall was ordered to study aeronautical engineering at the Curtiss Airplane and Motor Company.[17]

In addition, Assistant Secretary Newton asked Congress to authorize the construction of ten Coast Guard air stations and the acquisition of twenty aircraft. Neither Newton nor Bertholf desired a separate air corps within the service, but they wanted additional personnel—fifteen officers and forty men—for aviation duty. Their request for two instructors implied that the Coast Guard wished to train its own pilots. To support this application, Newton pointed out the difficulty experienced in finding the derelicts and distressed vessels that were invariably reported in some numbers after every onshore gale. These were almost never in the reported positions, so the cutters had to spend much time seeking them, time that could be spent to greater benefit assisting those in need or in disposing of the derelicts. Bertholf saw an additional use for the aircraft, that of carrying lines from the shore to wrecks beyond the reach of line-throwing guns when sea conditions prevented the use of surfboats. Newton, however, omitted this from his application to the Congress.[18]

A bill authorizing the construction of 156 naval vessels, including ten battleships and six battlecruisers, intended to make the U. S. Navy "second to none" may seem a strange vehicle, yet one of its provisions authorized the establishment, equipment, and maintenance of ten Coast Guard air stations, to be located on the Atlantic, Pacific, and Gulf coasts and on the Great Lakes, with a school of instruction at one. The legislation was signed into law on 29 August 1916, but the failure of Congress to appropriate money for Coast Guard aviation at a later date reduced this provision to the level of the proverbial good intention. Bertholf could do no more than to order a few more junior officers to Pensacola for flight training—six officers and nine warrant officers had completed the course, and nine others were being trained when the entry of the United States into World War I caused their assignment to more pressing duties.[19]

Enforcement of the nation's neutrality laws was among the earliest duties performed by cutters; thus, they found themselves supporting officials concerned therewith at Boston, New York, Baltimore, Norfolk, and San Juan, Puerto Rico, almost from the beginning of World War I. Noting that this required the withdrawal of cutters from their usual duties sometimes for protracted periods, the captain commandant asked that additional vessels be provided. The Congress appropriated money for the construction of five cutters in 1916 and 1917, but the expansion of the U. S. Navy and the merchant marine made it impossible to find builders. So the existing cutters had to serve, with the *Itasca* joining them between cadet practice cruises.

The requirement for neutrality enforcement ended when, on 6 April 1917, the United States declared war on the German Empire. On that day, Coast Guard units received the cryptic message "PLAN ONE ACKNOWLEDGE," which signified their transfer to the U.S. Navy.

CHAPTER FOUR

THE COAST GUARD IN WORLD WAR I

With most of the European world at war when President Wilson signed the legislation creating the Coast Guard, attention quite naturally focused on the provision that the new service would "operate as a part of the Navy, subject to the orders of the Secretary of the Navy, in time of war or when the President shall so direct."[1] Seemingly unambiguous at first sight, the language of this provision left unanswered a variety of questions about the Coast Guard's place within the Navy, nor could past experience provide useful guidance, for while individual revenue cutters had operated with naval forces in five of the nation's nineteenth century wars, the Revenue-Cutter Service itself had remained under Treasury Department control during peace and war alike.

At Secretary McAdoo's request, Secretary of the Navy Josephus Daniels appointed Captain William H. G. Bullard, head of the Navy's Radio Service, to confer with Bertholf and recommend measures necessary to facilitate the efficient functioning of the Coast Guard within the Navy. The report that the two officers submitted to their respective superiors on 20 March 1915 described the personnel and materiel of the Coast Guard and considered ways in which these might be used to greatest advantage. As far as the cutters were concerned, lack of speed and endurance would limit most to such local duties as patrol and mine laying and sweeping in coastal waters, although the larger ships might be used "as convoy vessels to merchantmen or transports" or as radio relay ships. Most of the former Life-Saving Service personnel would be retained at their peacetime stations, where they could provide useful service as coast watchers and, if properly drilled and equipped, as armed guards for coastal radio stations. A few surfmen, however, "could be profitably employed on small gunboats to take charge of landing boats through the surf."[2]

In order to prepare Coast Guardsmen for these military duties, Bullard and Bertholf recommended close cooperation between the Navy and the Coast Guard when the latter was under Treasury Department control, with special emphasis on signaling and infantry drill, in which the greatest deficiencies were thought to exist. They also suggested the temporary exchange of junior officers and even of vessels and their companies between the two services.[3]

While the close cooperation recommended seems not to have been realized, in large part because the Navy itself was being expanded rapidly and had a serious shortage of trained personnel, the Coast Guard continued to prepare for service with the Navy, compiling tactical data on its cutters and completing mobilization plans in March 1917.[4] Meanwhile, some units took part in Navy preparedness exercises, while harbor cutters helped to ensure security at the launching of new warships in the major Atlantic coast ports.

Even before Coast Guard Headquarters sent the telegraphic order "PLAN ONE ACKNOWLEDGE," which transferred the service to the Navy on 6 April 1917, several of its vessels were participating in what might be termed hostile action. At 4 A.M. that day, the collector of customs at New York ordered four harbor cutters to embark 165 soldiers at Governor's Island to support him in seizing twenty-three German vessels interned in the port. All were quickly secured without trouble, and the cutters escorted the immigration steamers conveying the German crews to detention on Ellis Island. The cutter *Apache* at Baltimore provided armed guards to assist federal marshals taking over three German vessels there; again, there was no resistance.[5]

Upon receipt of the mobilization order, most Coast Guard activities and cutters came under control of the naval districts in which they were located, but Coast Guard Headquarters retained responsibility for the Academy, depot, Supervisor of Lifeboats, and stores. Cutters assigned to Bering Sea Patrol and to cadet practice cruises likewise remained under Headquarters direction.

The most immediate problem involved personnel. The Revenue-Cutter Service had relied heavily on foreign-born seamen, many of whom had departed, by discharge or desertion, for their homelands when World War I began. Local recruitment by commanding officers had sufficed to provide a minimum of enlisted men, but when cutter complements were increased to wartime levels early in 1917, recruiting offices had to be opened. A considerable number of deserters, hoping to clear their names, volunteered for duty soon after the declaration of war—the secretary of the navy decided that they might receive honorable discharges after completing their enlistments—but only the adoption of conscription in June 1917 brought an ample number of men to meet the Coast Guard's needs. Recruits were sent to the Academy at New London for outfitting and training before assignment to ships or stations; pending their arrival, some cutter commanding officers had to request drafts of naval reservists to fill vacancies in their crews.[6] In due course, it became apparent that the usual one-year enlistments would not suffice in wartime, so enlistments for the duration of the war, not to exceed three years, were adopted instead.[7]

Initially, most of the cutters were used on coastal patrol and similar duties. On 30 July 1917, however, six of the larger vessels—the *Algonquin, Manning, Ossipee, Seneca, Tampa,* and *Yamacraw*—were ordered to be fitted out for "distant service" in an unspecified region.[8] Most had earlier received their wartime batteries of 3-inch guns; now they were provided with depth charges as well. When ready for sea in August and September, all were sent to Gibraltar for service as ocean escorts with slow convoys sailing between the United Kingdom and the Mediterranean.

Captain Commandant Bertholf had hoped that Coast Guard ships' companies could be kept together even in wartime, a hope that was dashed when Naval Reserve Force officers were assigned to cutters for training. In August the Bureau of Navigation asked that Coast Guard officers be made available for service in yachts being converted to antisubmarine vessels, and within a few months the practice became general, with Coast Guard officers serving in a variety of small combatants, transports, and auxiliary ships both at home and abroad, their places being taken by naval reservists. Although he was not officially informed of the plans of the Bureau of Navigation, Bertholf suspected that it intended to make the cutters in home waters training ships for Naval Reserve Force personnel, with only the Coast Guard commanding and executive officers and chief engineers permanently assigned.[9]

The mixing of officer personnel brought problems, for while Captains Bullard and Bertholf had agreed on the list of comparative ranks in 1915, legislation of 22 May 1917 provided for the temporary promotion of naval officers only. Thus, Coast Guard officers of extensive service and experience found themselves junior to much younger men with whom they were serving. To make matters worse, naval officers received 10 percent additional pay for sea duty, while Coast Guard officers did not. Bertholf found few supporters among his fellows when he refused to persist in his efforts to rectify this situation on the grounds that it was not essential to the war effort and could not apply to enlisted men. The discrepancy was removed in part when the Naval Appropriations Act of 1 July 1918 provided both sea pay and temporary promotions for Coast Guard officers, the former to be retroactive.[10] This experience helped to convince many Coast Guard officers that their prospects would be better could their service be amalgamated completely into the Navy.

Perhaps the Coast Guard's first loss could be attributed to the practice of using the cutters as training vessels. The *McCulloch,* the service's largest ship and one of the most famous, thanks to her Spanish-American War record, departed San Pedro, California, for San Francisco on 12 June 1917 with a trio of Naval Coast Defense Reserve ensigns embarked. Despite the fact that the *McCulloch* encountered decreasing visibility early the next morning, Senior Captain John C. Cantwell retired to his cabin after the cutter had entered the Santa Barbara Channel, leaving one of the ensigns as officer of the deck. A few hours later, while engulfed in a dense fog off Point Conception, the passenger steamer *Governor* crashed into the *McCulloch*'s starboard bow, and the latter sank in thirty-five minutes. Cantwell had ordered her abandoned in good time, and the *Governor* picked up all hands. A water-tender, fatally injured in the collision, was the only fatality.[11]

A Navy board of inquiry held Captain Cantwell solely responsible, but the reviewing authority, noting a degree of personal animosity in the finding, reprimanded the board's members and ordered another investigation. The second board noted that Cantwell should have been on the cutter's bridge during a period of poor visibility and with an officer of the deck who was unfamiliar with the vessel; it absolved the captain of blame, however, because the *Governor* had been proceeding at excessive speed—14 knots—in the fog.[12]

While one cannot deny that the passenger steamer was mainly responsible for the collision, it is worth noting that the U.S. government ultimately accepted an offer by her owners and underwriters to pay only two-thirds of the cutter's value in settlement. Government attorneys and reviewing Coast Guard officers concluded that questionable judgment shown by the *McCulloch*'s officer of the deck just before the collision, together with an allegation that her log had been altered, would cause a court to divide the responsibility equally between the *Governor* and her victim if the case came to trial.[13]

Another of the first-class cutters succumbed to collision in a heavy fog, this time on the Atlantic coast. The *Mohawk*, patrolling off Ambrose Channel on the morning of 1 October 1917, found herself in the midst of an inward-bound convoy, apparently becoming aware of her danger only when the bow of a larger vessel loomed out of the fog to strike her. As the cutter's men lowered her boats, the Navy storeship *Bridge* passed a hawser and took the sinking *Mohawk* in tow, hoping to reach shallow water where salvage might be feasible. It was a vain hope, however, for the cutter sank in deep water some 3 miles southeast of Ambrose Light little more than a hour after the collision. The *Bridge* rescued all her company.[14]

A harrowing experience of a different nature was that of the older second-class cutter *Morrill*, which patrolled waters in the vicinity of Detroit, Michigan, until ordered to the Atlantic coast in the autumn of 1917. She arrived at Halifax, Nova Scotia, on 5 December and anchored in Dartmouth Cove to await coal and fresh water. In clear weather the next morning, the Norwegian steamer *Imo*, outward bound in ballast, collided with the inward-bound French *Mont Blanc* in the Narrows, more than a mile from the *Morrill*'s anchorage. The French steamer, laden with 5,000 tons of high explosives, caught fire, and her men attempted to extinguish the flames instead of scuttling the ship immediately. Too late, they found the fire beyond control and abandoned ship. Soon afterward, as First Lieutenant George E. Wilcox reported: "A funnel-shaped gray cloud, streaked with flame and assuming the appearance of a volcano in violent eruption,

The second-class cutter Morrill.

quickly arose and spread over the sky. Almost immediately afterwards, numerous fires were observed, some assuming alarming proportions."[15] The accompanying explosions seemed almost to lift the cutter from the water, and an object thought to be a ship's boiler passed over her to splash into the cove some 200 yards away.

After ascertaining that his command had escaped serious damage, Wilcox sent a rescue party to the explosion-shattered city. While Assistant Surgeon J. H. Hardy, U.S.N.R.F., set up a temporary hospital in which to treat the injured, Second Lieutenant Henry G. Hemingway and his twenty men searched for victims and fought fires. Shore parties from HMS *Highflyer,* the USS *Tacoma,* and other vessels in the vicinity joined them later, and when Hemingway's group returned to the cutter that night, Wilcox was asked by local authorities to wait until morning to send further aid.

By that time, a distress call from the American steamer *Saranac,* adrift in the harbor in a blinding snowstorm, required the *Morrill's* attention. Failing to locate the steamer, Wilcox anchored his cutter, which sustained serious damage when another vessel ran into her after nightfall. Rendered unable to respond to any of the numerous distress calls from ships battered by the storm, the *Morrill* could only wait until the weather moderated to attempt to float the now grounded *Saranac.* Unsucceessful in this, she proceeded to Philadelphia for repairs before joining the Fourth Naval District patrol force.

The *Mont Blanc* disaster, which was estimated to have killed 1,635, injured 9,000, and destroyed or damaged property valued at $35 million, caused serious concern to U.S. authorities, for the *Mont Blanc* had sailed from New York, one of the hundreds of vessels that loaded explosive cargoes there for transport to Europe during the war. Should a similar collision occur in the congested waters of New York Harbor, the consequences would be far more catastrophic than those of the Halifax explosion.[16]

To be sure, the means for implementation of preventative measures already existed, for the Espionage Act of June 1917 had shifted responsibility for the adoption and enforcement of regulations governing the anchorages and movements of vessels in specified navigable waters of the United States from the Army Corps of Engineers to the Treasury Department. Although the Coast Guard was no longer under his jurisdiction, the treasury secretary designated senior officers of that service captains of the port to carry out these duties at New York, Philadelphia, Norfolk, and Sault Ste. Marie.

In the first, obviously the most important port, Captain Godfrey L. Carden, commander of the Coast Guard's New York Division, was named captain of the port as well. Apparently an admirable choice for the position, Carden had commanded the New York-based *Mohawk* for several years, thus gaining familiarity with local maritime conditions and the shipping community. At its peak in 1918, his division was the Coast Guard's largest single command, comprising 1,446 officers and men, four tugs loaned by the Corps of Engineers and the Navy, and five harbor cutters.[17] Under the system developed by Carden, the harbor craft placed detachments of Coast Guardsmen on board vessels arriving to load explosive cargoes, and these men remained on board to assure adherence to the regulations and to prevent unauthorized persons from boarding. Ship movements between the munitions piers on the New Jersey shore and the principal explosives anchorage in Gravesend Bay at the western end of Long Island were scheduled carefully to eliminate the danger of collision.

The most exciting occurrence involving personnel of the New York Division occurred on 4 October 1918, when an explosion ripped the T.A. Gillespie Company munitions yard at Morgan, New Jersey. A Coast Guard detachment from Perth Amboy was first on the scene, and other units arrived as quickly as possible. Further explosions hampered rescue efforts, and the resulting fires threatened to spread to a trainload of TNT in the yard. Coast Guardsmen attempting to remove the train found that they had first to repair tracks twisted by the explosions, which they did in time to prevent a greater disaster. Two Coast Guardsmen were killed while involved in the rescue work.[18]

Captain Carden had no responsibility for safety regulations ashore, so his division's record was unscathed by the Gillespie Company explosion. The captain himself, however, had become a controversial figure by this time. Irascible, dictatorial, and tactless, he had alienated civilians and service personnel alike. Master mariners especially disliked Carden's arbitrary interpretation of the ship movement regulations, which they thought hampered sailings unnecessarily, and their complaint was echoed by some of the captain's subordinates, whose lot was not made any easier by his attention to petty detail. In September 1918 a board of investigation considered charges brought against Carden by a junior officer and recommended his relief. As captain of the port, however, Carden was responsible to the Treasury Department, which had to be consulted before any action was taken, and the acting secretary—on Bertholf's advice?—responded that Carden's performance in that capacity had been satisfactory. As a result, he retained both positions. He survived another investigation a year later, but one suspects that the 1918 board was correct in its conclusion that Captain Carden was "temperamentally unfitted for his duties."[19] On the other hand, no serious marine mishap occurred in the waters under his control.

The captains of the port in Philadelphia, Norfolk, and Sault Ste. Marie met their responsibilities with equal success and less friction. Their harbors also escaped calamity, and none seems to have been as unpopular as Godfrey L. Carden.

The fear of sabotage that figured in the captain of the port activities also spurred the extension of the Coast Guard communication system. The prewar service had about 65 miles of submarine cable and 1,435 miles of overhead lines linking Coast Guard stations. Recognizing that the station and lighthouse personnel could serve effectively as coastwatchers while performing their regular duties, the Navy urged the expansion of the communication system to include all such installations on the nation's seacoasts, to be operated in conjunction with naval radio stations. Such an undertaking required full-time supervision, so First Lieutenant Russell R. Waesche was ordered to Washington to head the newly established Communication Division at Coast Guard Headquarters. Under his direction, additional lines were laid and strung, and by mid-1919 the system had 416 miles of submarine cable and 3,255 miles of overhead wire providing telephone service to 282 Coast Guard stations, 44 Coast Guard units and offices, 139 lighthouses and lightships, 22 naval radio compass stations, and 56 other governmental activities.[20]

The submarine cables proved to be the most difficult to maintain, especially along the New England coast where cables secured in accordance with the best commercial practice could not withstand "the action of heavy seas beating against rocky shores."[21] Waesche assembled a force of his men at Boston to cope with this problem, but they were unable to procure the services of lighthouse tenders or patrol boats, and the cost of hiring private vessels was prohibitive. Thereupon, Waesche turned to Bertholf, naming the former menhaden fishing steamer *J.A. Palmer, Jr.,* recently fitted for working cable in the Chesapeake Bay vicinity, among the ships suitable for his division's work. At the commandant's request, the Navy made the 155-foot *Palmer* available for Coast Guard manning and service, transferring her permanently in September 1918, when she was renamed the *Pequot.*[22]

While captain of the port and Communication Division activities were wartime extensions of the Coast Guard's role, the service's customary duties continued to be performed throughout the war as well. The International Ice Patrol, to be sure, was terminated, as was the time-honored practice of winter cruising off the Atlantic coast from Eastport, Maine, to Cape Canaveral, Florida. In the latter case, however, cutters patrolling or otherwise employed and naval vessels on passage along the coast were available to respond to distress calls. On the West Coast, the first-class cutter *Unalga* spent the spring and summer months of 1917 and 1918 on Bering Sea patrol, and the old *Bear* made her usual Arctic cruises, to Point Barrow in 1917 and as far as Wainwright in 1918, when ice conditions made it impossible for her to reach Point Barrow. Both cutters were used for training naval reservists during the autumn and winter months.[23]

John Allen Midgett as a chief boatswain.

Those at the Coast Guard stations performed their normal duties as well, rendering assistance to endangered persons and vessels on a scale quite comparable to that of peacetime. Most of the distress cases stemmed from the usual causes—weather, accident, and carelessness—but two could be attributed directly to the war.

The first of these involved the tug *Perth Amboy,* steaming southward off Cape Cod with four barges in tow on 21 July 1918. A submarine surfaced nearby and opened fire on the tug, whose crew hoisted a distress signal before abandoning her. When it was reported by the lookout at Station No. 40, East Orleans, Keeper Robert F. Pierce and his crew manned the power surfboat and headed for the *Perth Amboy.* As the unarmed surfboat approached the tug, the submarine ceased firing and submerged, whereupon the Coast Guardsmen treated slightly wounded tugboatmen and returned the crew to their vessel.

News of the submarine's presence led the nearby Chatham Naval Air Station to send two HS-1 seaplanes in search, the second piloted by Coast Guard Captain (Engineering) Philip B. Eaton, commanding officer of the station. The submarine was located and fired on the aircraft as they made bombing runs—its fire was ineffective and so were the bombs, which failed to explode. The submarine then submerged, presumably to seek a less dangerous operating area.[24]

Keeper Pierce's readiness to assist a ship under submarine attack is worthy of note, but it pales by comparison with the feat of Keeper John A. Midgett on 16 August 1918. That afternoon, the lookout at Station No. 179, Chicamacomico, North Carolina, was watching a tanker steam northward about 7 miles offshore, when the vessel's after part was suddenly obscured by a mass of water, followed by a cloud of smoke. Soon she was steering erratically, and as flames appeared above her after deck, the sound of explosions could be heard. The victim of mine or torpedo, the tanker was clearly in need of assistance, so Midgett called all hands and manned the power surfboat. A moderately heavy surf hampered the boat's departure, but a half-hour after the tanker's plight was reported, Midgett got the boat clear of the beach.

About 5 miles offshore, the Coast Guardsmen encountered a

ship's boat with seventeen men, one of whom identified himself as the master of the British tanker *Mirlo*. He reported that two other boats had been lowered, of which one had capsized with the probable loss of all its occupants. Midgett directed him to pull inshore but not to attempt a landing through the surf, and then headed his surfboat for the *Mirlo*, which by this time was a blazing wreck surrounded by a flaming sea. As the boat approached, the smoke and flames cleared momentarily, revealing the bottom of a capsized boat with six men clinging to it as the heavy swell surged over them. Running his surfboat "through the smoke, floating wreckage, and burning gas and oil," Midgett rescued these men, all of whom were burned slightly, and then sought others who had been in the boat.[25] Finding no trace of these, the keeper steered downwind in search of the third of the *Mirlo*'s boats. When sighted, this boat was drifting before the wind and sea, so overcrowded with nineteen men that it could not be rowed. The surfboat took it in tow and headed inshore where the first of the tanker's boats was waiting. Both were towed toward the Chicamacomico station, but the wind had begun to freshen and night had fallen, so Midgett decided to land through the surf 2 miles south of the station. Anchoring the *Mirlo*'s boats just outside the surf zone, he ferried her men, ten or eleven at a time, through the surf to the beach. Personnel and horses from his own station and from Station No. 180, Gull Shoal, were waiting to assist the survivors as they were landed, and on the fourth and final trip, Midgett had his surfmen bring the two ship's boats to the shore as well. By the time the boats had been hauled up on the beach and the survivors had been fed and had their burns treated, it was 11:00 P.M., just six and a half hours since the first explosion. Ten of the *Mirlo*'s men had been lost; had it not been for Keeper Midgett and his surfmen—all but one of whom were also Midgetts!—the toll might well have reached fifty-two.[26] The members of the boat crew received gold lifesaving medals—in 1924!

Unlike most of their fellows, the Coast Guardsmen serving in the six cutters that were prepared for distant service in August 1917 did actually serve in the war zone. Their ships, which formed the second squadron of the Atlantic Fleet Patrol Force's Sixth Division, did not go out together; the *Ossipee* reached Gibraltar at the end of August, the *Seneca, Manning,* and *Yamacraw* reported in September, and the *Algonquin* and the *Tampa*, both delayed by duties assigned them en route, arrived in October.

Despite their moderate speeds, the cutters were welcome additions to the escort force based at Gibraltar. When the United Kingdom–Gibraltar convoys were initiated during the summer, it was assumed that escort would be required only in the "danger zone" at either end of the passage. Experience showed, however, that at least one escort vessel should accompany each convoy all the way, to keep attackers at a distance, discourage straggling, and serve as a radio link between the convoy and the British Admiralty.[27] With

The Seneca *in postwar rig.*

suitable British warships in short supply, the cutters were assigned to ocean escort duty, as were the American scout cruisers *Birmingham* and *Chester* and four old gunboats, although the last were soon reassigned.

During the next year, the cutters plied the convoy routes between Gibraltar and Britain, usually putting in at Milford Haven on the coast of Wales after being detached from their convoys at the northern termination of the passage. Steaming in company with 7.5-knot convoys in fair weather and foul was wearing, monotonous duty with the usual danger of collision in periods of poor visibility and the constant threat of submarine attack, for the entire route was within U-boat range. All of the cutters except the *Algonquin* reported being attacked at least once, while the *Ossipee* and the *Seneca* were thought to have had torpedoes fired at them on five occasions each.[28]

The *Seneca,* commanded by Captain William J. Wheeler, gained especial recognition for her rescue work. The cutter was steaming astern of a convoy nearing Gibraltar in thick weather when, at 2 A.M. on 28 April 1918, the British sloop *Cowslip* of the danger zone escort was torpedoed. Wheeler immediately headed for the sinking ship, about a quarter-mile away, ignoring the rule that the submarine, not her victim, should be the object of other escorts' attention. Not even a blinker signal to the effect that the U-boat had been sighted from the sloop deterred the cutter, which lowered a boat as one from the *Cowslip* came alongside. Helping the Britons on board, Coast Guardsmen manned this boat as well and pulled for the sloop. The two boats rescued eighty-one officers and men, all that had survived the torpedo explosion, picking up the commanding officer just before the *Cowslip* sank.[29]

The *Seneca* was the sole escort when the merchant vessel *Queen* was torpedoed at 7:45 A.M. on 28 June 1918. The *Queen* sank in four minutes, well before the cutter could reach her, and Wheeler conned his ship through the wreckage with his men throwing life rings and lines to survivors. As the *Seneca*'s boat was lowered, one in which a few men had managed to leave the *Queen* came alongside. Captain Wheeler ordered its occupants to help to save their fellows before they themselves were taken on board. While the rescue work was proceeding, the *Seneca*'s 4-inch guns kept up a steady fire, aimed between ships of the convoy, to dissuade the submarine from attacking again, and the cutter dropped depth charges as a further deterrent when the last of the twenty-seven survivors had been pulled from the water.[30]

The *Seneca* is best remembered, however, for a salvage effort that ended in failure. On Friday, 13 September 1918, a convoy of some twenty ships sailed from Milford Haven with a local escort of British destroyers. These departed two days later, leaving the cutter to shepherd the convoy to Gibraltar. At 11 A.M. on 16 September, the British collier *Wellington* received a torpedo hit well forward. As she settled by the head, her crew took to their boats and were picked up by the *Seneca*, which had rushed to the scene, dropping depth charges to keep the submarine down. The collier's master reported that her damage was probably not fatal but that his men, fearing another torpedo, had insisted on abandoning her. Thereupon, First Lieutenant Fletcher Brown, the boat officer in the two previous rescues, obtained Captain Wheeler's permission to salve the *Wellington*. Taking one of the collier's boats, Brown and eighteen volunteers from the *Seneca* pulled over to the *Wellington*, where they were joined by her master and twelve members of her crew. As they busied themselves making emergency repairs and raising steam, the cutter bade them farewell and stood on to overtake her convoy.

At first the *Wellington*'s chances seemed good. She steamed toward Brest, distant some 300 miles, at 7 knots, stopping periodically so that water flooding #2 hold could be pumped out. But the weather worsened as night approached, and the helmsmen found it impossible to hold her on course. The collier fell off into the trough, rolling heavily. Concluding that she could not survive, Lieutenant Brown ordered distress signals sent, and the USS *Warrington*, which had been detached from a westbound convoy to assist her, responded. Conflicting reports of the *Wellington*'s position complicated the destroyer's task, but four hours later she sighted the collier, which sank soon afterward when a bulkhead collapsed.

The *Wellington*'s one serviceable boat had been cast off prematurely with only eight men embarked; the *Warrington* picked them up and, unable to lower her own boat in the heavy swell, floated rafts and life buoys toward the spot where the collier had disappeared. After daylight, she picked up eight more survivors clinging to these and to floating wreckage. In all, the abortive salvage attempt claimed the lives of eleven of the "Senecas" and five members of the *Wellington*'s crew. But for the superb seamanship of the *Warrington*'s commanding officer, Lieutenant Commander N.R. Van der Veer, and the courage of his men, several of whom plunged into the water to save survivors, most must have perished. Van der Veer, however, considered Lieutenant Brown, who survived, the true hero, praising his plucky attempt to save a badly needed collier and her cargo as well as his efforts to assure the safety of his men when the ship was sinking.[31]

The Coast Guard suffered a much more grievous loss ten days later. The cutter *Tampa* had brought a convoy from Gibraltar and was joined by British destroyers for the passage through the danger zone. As the convoy stood into the Bristol Channel during the evening of 26 September, Captain Charles Satterlee received the customary order to take the cutter to Milford Haven. Some time later, at about 8:45, the shock of an explosion was felt by several in the convoy. It seems not to have been considered important enough for the British destroyers to investigate, but when the *Tampa* failed to arrive at Milford Haven, escort vessels based there undertook a search. Three days of cruising along the cutter's probable track resulted in the recovery of two unidentified bodies and some floating wreckage, all that remained of the *Tampa* and the 111 Coast Guardsmen and four Navy men who had sailed from Gibraltar in her. German records subsequently identified her assailant as the *UB-91*, which sank a ship of the *Tampa*'s description in that position with a single torpedo at evening twilight that day.[32]

The *Tampa*'s loss was the more painful because she had been considered one of the happiest and most efficient ships of the ocean escort force. During her first eight months attached to that force, she had been under way more than half the time, escorting eighteen convoys from which only two ships had been lost. This record and her almost constant readiness for service had earned the *Tampa* a special commendation from Rear Admiral Albert P. Niblack, commanding the Atlantic Fleet Patrol Force, just before she departed Gibraltar for the last time.[33]

Hostilities ceased little more than six weeks after the sinking of the *Tampa*, and four of the remaining Coast Guard cutters sailed for the United States in December 1918. The *Seneca*, however, was too useful to be spared. Ordered to the assistance of the Navy transport *Tenadores*, which had grounded on the Ile d'Yeu off the Biscay coast of France, the cutter participated in unsuccessful efforts to refloat the stranded vessel and helped to remove her crew and a portion of her cargo. The *Seneca* then put in at Brest, where she landed her wartime armament before returning to Gibraltar to take part in salvage operations on the Navy cargo ship *Ophir*, which had burned after an internal explosion. Ordered to Britain when released from this duty, the cutter steamed to Kirkwall in the Orkney Islands, whence she towed the mine-damaged USS *Bobolink* of the North Sea Minesweeping Detachment, to Devonport on the English Channel coast for repair. The *Seneca* delivered her tow to the Royal Navy dockyard and then, finally, was allowed to return to the United States.[34]

With the *Seneca*'s arrival at New York on 1 July 1919, the Coast Guard's part in World War I may be said to have ended, although nearly two months had yet to elapse before the service was returned to Treasury Department control. At first sight, the Coast Guard's war record seems unimpressive. No Coast Guardsmen participated in any major battle; indeed, relatively few were involved in any military action against an enemy. Instead, they served in a variety of support functions, few of which gained much notice, although a number, such as the activities of the captain of the port detachments, were undoubtedly important. Properly enough, the occurrences that did attract public attention—the *Morrill*'s relief work at Halifax, the New York Division's efforts to contain the Gillespie Company fire, Keeper Midgett's rescue of the *Mirlo*'s men, and the *Seneca*'s rescue and salvage feats—were all directed toward saving life and property, in the best tradition of the Coast Guard and its predecessors.

Nor was the cost to the Coast Guard inconsiderable. The three first-class cutters sunk constituted about one-eighth of its prewar strength, and with the possible exception of the Navy collier *Cyclops*, which disappeared without a trace after leaving Barbados in March 1918, the *Tampa* sinking resulted in the Navy's greatest single loss of life caused by enemy action.

From its association with the Navy, the Coast Guard undoubtedly gained military efficiency. Its system of courts was reorganized along the lines of that of the Navy, with consequent improvement of discipline. The practice of recruit training begun during the war proved quite successful and was a useful precedent, although it was not adhered to strictly for some years thereafter.

Perhaps most important, Navy and Coast Guard had increased regard for each other as a result of their close wartime association. So great was this regard that many in both services, especially in the Coast Guard, had no desire to end the association.

CHAPTER FIVE

THE FIGHT FOR SURVIVAL, 1919–23

*H*ostilities having ended, Commodore Bertholf was eager to have his service returned to its peacetime status. As a first step toward this end, he wrote the secretary of the navy on 6 December 1918 to urge that cutters and stations be released from naval districts to operate under the direction of Coast Guard Headquarters, making the commencement of the winter cruising season the occasion for his request. Secretary Daniels, however, decided that winter cruising by Coast Guard and naval vessels could be carried on as well under naval district commandants and declined to accede to Bertholf's proposal.[1]

In fact, Josephus Daniels and Franklin D. Roosevelt, his assistant secretary, were determined that the Coast Guard should remain under the Navy Department. The secretary believed that all government vessels ought to be under his control, arguing that unnecessary duplication inevitably resulted from the existence of five "navies"—by which he meant the Coast Guard, Lighthouse Service, Coast and Geodetic Survey, and Army Transportation Service, in addition to the Navy itself.[2] Retention of the Coast Guard would be an important development toward the realization of his goal.

While a simple executive order would suffice to keep the Coast Guard under the Navy Department indefinitely, permanent transfer by legislative act was desirable lest the president be accused of thwarting the will of Congress as stated in the 1915 legislation that had created the Coast Guard. Moreover, the possibility that the service might be returned to the Treasury Department at some time in the future would remain unless Congress took definite action.

Accordingly, Pennsylvania Representative Guy E. Campbell introduced such a measure in January 1919. This bill, which Coast Guard Captain Frank L. Austin claimed to have written while serving in the Bureau of Navigation, provided for the complete amalgamation of Coast Guard personnel, vessels, and stations into the Navy and the closing of redundant shore activities such as Coast Guard Headquarters and the Academy.[3] In short, the Campbell Bill would, if enacted, terminate the Coast Guard's existence. A copy of the bill was sent to the Treasury Department for comment, and Carter Glass, the Virginia congressman who had succeeded McAdoo as secretary, responded quickly and unfavorably.

Pointing out that the Navy had attempted repeatedly to gain control of the Revenue-Cutter Service in the course of its existence, Glass noted that Congress had consistently refused to permit the two services to be merged permanently and gave as reasons the arguments that had been put forward some five years earlier when the bill to create the Coast Guard was being debated. The Treasury secretary went on to use the comparative expense figures produced for the earlier occasion to cast doubt on the allegation of economy to be realized by merging the services. Considering the Campbell Bill itself, Glass called attention to the injustice that would be done to enlisted men, especially to the personnel of the former Life-Saving Service, most of whom would have to reenlist in lower rates upon expiration of their current enlistments because the Navy had no rating equivalent to that of surfman. Indeed, the secretary believed that passage of the Campbell Bill "would utterly demoralize the enlisted personnel of the Coast Guard."[4]

Since neither increased efficiency nor economy could be cited to justify the proposed legislation, Glass suggested that its true motivation might be found in the desire of most Coast Guard officers to retain the temporary ranks to which they had been promoted since 1 July 1918. In conclusion, the Treasury secretary asked that Congress act to return the Coast Guard to his department at an early date, because the official proclamation of peace was likely to be delayed.[5]

Glass's supporters introduced resolutions to this end in both houses of Congress, and Secretary Daniels was given the opportunity to express his opinion. Predictably, he was opposed to an early return of the Coast Guard to the Treasury, holding that the duties of the Coast Guard were being carried out adequately under the existing arrangement. Two weeks later, Daniels forwarded letters from Coast Guard Captains Charles H. Dench and Philip F. Roach, both of whom favored merger, to support his view, but to no avail.[6] The joint resolution of Congress calling for the transfer of the Coast Guard to Treasury control was sent to the president late in February 1919.

Although passage of the joint resolution signified the defeat of the Campbell Bill, at least temporarily, it was not a complete victory for Carter Glass. President Wilson, who had been in Europe engaged in the negotiation of the peace treaties, returned to the United States in February. His time, however, was taken up entirely with matters pertaining to the treaties, and he sailed for France again early in March without taking any action with regard to the Coast Guard. Josephus Daniels did return more cutters to Coast Guard Headquarters control during the spring, but this is no way implied any change in his attitude. In fact, the battle for survival of the Coast Guard had just begun, and to a large extent, it was to be fought within the service itself.

The views expressed by Captains Austin, Dench, and Roach were shared by perhaps as many as 90 percent of the Coast Guard's commissioned officers, and in 1919 a number of them were working actively to keep their service within the Navy.[7] Contrary to Glass's assertions, they insisted that military efficiency and economy would be enhanced were the Navy to assume the Coast Guard's functions permanently. They cited the "unsatisfactory" record of cutter construction in prewar years as proof of the Treasury Department's lack of interest; Dench, for example, noted that the first-class cutters built since 1900 were smaller and slower than the *Manning* of 1898. The latest, the *Ossipee* and *Tallapoosa* of 1915, he considered "not capable of the best service in purely Coast Guard work . . . being too slow to quickly render assistance to vessels in distress and too small to properly and comfortably accommodate their personnel."[8] These officers could not agree, however, on the Coast Guard's proper relationship to the Navy; some supported the complete amalgamation envisioned by Austin, while others wished their service to have a place under the Navy Department analogous to that of the Marine Corps. Whatever their views in this regard, it is clear that the vast majority of Coast Guard officers expected better equipment and a brighter future under a sympathetic Navy Department than they foresaw under an apparently uninterested Department of the Treasury.

Not all agreed, however. Perhaps twenty-five officers, many of whom were on duty at Coast Guard Headquarters, were known to favor a return to the service's normal peacetime status. Ellsworth P. Bertholf, of course, was the most prominent of these, and he summed up his views admirably in a private letter:

> . . . the fundamental reasons for the two services are diametrically opposed. The Navy exists for the sole purpose of keeping itself prepared for . . . war. Its usefulness to the Government is therefore to a large degree potential. If it performs in peace time any useful function not ultimately connected with the preparation for war, that is a by-product. On the other hand, the Coast Guard does not exist solely for the purpose of preparing for war. If it did there would then be, of course, two navies—a large and a small one, and that condition, I am sure you will agree, could not long exist. The Coast Guard exists for the particular and main purpose of performing duties which have no connection with a state of war, but which, on the contrary, are constantly necessary as peace functions. It is, of course, essentially an emergency service and it is organized along military lines because that sort of an organization best enables the Coast Guard to keep prepared as an emergency service, and by organization along military lines it is invaluable in time of war as an adjunct and auxiliary to the Navy. . . . while peace time usefulness is a by-product of the Navy, it is the war time usefulness that is a by-product of the Coast Guard.

Bertholf went on to point out the fallacy of assuming that the

Coast Guard could long endure as a separate service under the Navy Department, arguing that the two services were too similar to permit that. And he brought up a matter that his fellows seem to have overlooked:

> Also I have no desire to be a mustang in the Navy or in any other service, and I cannot understand how officers can be so short-sighted as not to see what that entails. Just now as it appears that the Navy wants the Coast Guard, everything has a rosy hue and all hands are being patted on the back, told how efficient we are, and how welcome we would be in the Navy. Your experience, as well as mine, makes us know what will happen should the transfer take place. Two hundred and forty (240) officers will be lost among many thousands of officers and each will be an outsider and an interloper.

After stating his firm belief that Congress was strongly opposed to any permanent change in the Coast Guard's status, the commodore concluded with a stirring peroration:

> This is a day when humanitarianism is in the minds of most people, and the war being over, militarism is on the wane. The Coast Guard rests on the idea of humanitarianism; the Navy rests on the idea of militarism. To my mind, the best band-wagon is the former, and so I say the Coast Guard for mine and no Navy under any consideration.[9]

Bertholf, however, was nearing the end of his second term as commandant, and while he was not averse to appointment to a third four-year term, he must have known that there was little likelihood of this being offered under the circumstances. On 30 June 1919, the Coast Guard's first commandant retired to accept a position of vice president of the American Bureau of Shipping, the nation's official maritime classification agency, where he was joined by his former engineer in chief, Charles A. McAllister. Although there was no lack of candidates of Bertholf's position, Secretaries Daniels and Glass agreed that no permanent appointment should be made until the Coast Guard's future had been decided.[10] For the next few months, Coast Guard Headquarters functioned under the direction of Captain Daniel P. Foley.

Considering the attitude of most of his officers, it seems probable that few other than the small group at Headquarters were sorry to see Bertholf depart. When the Coast Guard's first commandant died after a short illness in 1921, senior officers at Headquarters served as pallbearers at his interment in Arlington National Cemetery. The service has since ignored his memory—so far as can be determined, no vessel, facility, or building of the Coast Guard has ever borne his name. This neglect can only be categorized as shameful, for Ellsworth Price Bertholf was not only the Coast Guard's first commandant; he should be ranked with Frederick Chamberlayne Billard and Russell Randolph Waesche as a great commandant.

Commodore Bertholf's retirement, which might have been a blow to those sharing his views, actually made little difference because Carter Glass had decided to press the matter of the Coast Guard's future to a decision. The Treasury secretary had become aware that certain Coast Guard officers were carrying on "a most remarkable campaign of propaganda" in favor of permanent retention of their service by the Navy Department. Terming their conduct a violation of "the most elementary rules of propriety and decorum . . . calculated to destroy the morale of the of the [Coast Guard]," Glass singled out Captain Paul H. Harrison, who as secretary of a "committee" composed of commissioned and warrant officers had solicited funds for telephone calls and correspondence as well as misrepresenting Glass's own views, which he had circulated without the secretary's permission, and Senior Captain John C. Cantwell, who had taken advantage of an official inspection tour of Coast Guard stations and bases to urge amalgamation of the two services, hoping that the Navy Department might take some action.[11]

Daniels quite naturally failed to press charges against those urging a course that he himself favored, but he agreed to join Glass in seeking an appointment with President Wilson in order to decide the issue. The Navy secretary, however, seemed unable to find time for the proposed meeting, and aware that the president was about to depart on a transcontinental tour to raise support for the peace treaties and the League of Nations, Glass broached the matter in late August, while Daniels was in Pearl Harbor to open a new dry dock. In response to the Treasury secretary's initiative, Wilson issued an executive order on 28 August 1919, ". . . it is hereby directed that the Coast Guard shall on and after this date operate under the Treasury Department."[12]

Proponents of merger with the Navy, however, refused to accept their defeat as final. They set out to rally support for a revised version of the Campbell Bill, with special emphasis on the shipping community as a whole. In this they were successful; within six months the American Steamship Owners Association of New York, the Pacific American Steamship Association, the Lake Carriers Association, the International Shipmasters Association of the Great Lakes, and several chambers of commerce in seaboard and lake cities had expressed strong support for the permanent transfer of the Coast Guard to the Navy. These cited as a principal reason the alleged inadequacy of existing Coast Guard units and personnel to provide assistance to American-flag shipping, which had been greatly expanded during the war.[13] In all likelihood, their informants were Coast Guard officers. Nor was the Navy idle; when the House Committee on Interstate and Foreign Commerce began its hearings on the revised Campbell Bill, Secretary Josephus Daniels, Assistant

Secretary Franklin D. Roosevelt, the chief of naval operations, and other high-ranking officers appeared to support the measure, as did Senior Captain John C. Cantwell, recently retired, and Captain Paul H. Harrison of the Coast Guard.[14]

The resignation of Secretary of the Treasury Carter Glass to accept appointment to a Virginia seat in the Senate in February 1920 may have given them some hope. If so, it was in vain, for the Campbell Bill again failed to emerge from committee and David F. Houston, Glass's successor at the Treasury, proved to be as insistent on retaining his department's control of the Coast Guard as Glass himself had been. Sporadic efforts to merge the two maritime services by executive order later in the year also came to nought.

Dissatisfied officers had one remaining recourse. The naval appropriation act of 1920 provided that some Coast Guard officers might be commissioned in the Navy after passing an examination. Of the ninety-seven officers eligible under the terms of this legislation, thirty-six made application to take the examination in the autumn of 1920, including twenty-three temporary captains and eleven engineer officers. They, too, were to be disappointed; their service already had sixty-five vacancies in its authorized strength of 270 commissioned officers, with only four cadets to be graduated from the Academy in 1921. Holding that further reductions "would so seriously cripple the Coast Guard as to make it impossible to officer the vessels it now has," Secretary Houston declined to approve any of the applications.[15]

Two matters concerning this controversy require further consideration: the apparent willingness of most Coast Guard officers to see their service abolished or to transfer to another, and the ability of a few Treasury Department officials and Coast Guard officers to triumph over such formidable opposition. In regard to the first, four years—almost half of which had been spent as a part of the Navy—was not enough time for the Coast Guard to win recognition from the public or to establish a sense of loyalty in its officers, some of whom had not been overjoyed to have their Revenue-Cutter Service made a part of a new organization in which they were forced to accept personnel of the former Life-Saving Service, whom they thought socially inferior, as an important component.[16] The social status of the naval officer corps was not in doubt; by becoming members of this group the Coast Guard officers could assure their own standing in addition to gaining the material benefits of better pay and more rapid promotion.

Nor was the triumph of the Treasury Department and Coast Guard Headquarters surprising. Carter Class, a respected congressman for sixteen years before becoming secretary of the treasury, was a powerful advocate, and Commodore Bertholf had had ample experience at dealing with congressional committees. They could point out that the Coast Guard had functioned quite well during the brief period of its existence, a period too short for the arguments that had led to the service's creation to have lost their force. For Josephus Daniels and his subordinates in the Navy Department, control of the Coast Guard was only one, and far from the most important, of the matters on which they wished congressional action. Moreover, Daniels was hampered by his unwillingness to take a strong stand on the issue without the president's approval, which he could not obtain because of the paralytic stroke that Wilson had suffered in October 1919.[17]

William Edward Reynolds, commandant, 1919–24.

The Coast Guard had weathered the most serious threat to its existence as a separate service, but few contemporaries, including its new commandant, can have felt much optimism as it began the second half of its first decade.

As his second term as captain commandant neared its end in mid-1919, Bertholf wrote Secretary Glass "to strongly urge and recommend" that Senior Captain William E. Reynolds be appointed his successor.[18] The 59-year-old Reynolds had a distinguished record, including service as superintendent of Construction and Repair and of the Academy, commander of the Bering Sea Patrol Fleet, and most recently chief of staff of the Twelfth Naval District. Stationed in San Francisco since 1917, he was not likely to be considered a member of the Bertholf group by his fellows, nor could any complain of being passed over were Reynolds appointed, for he was the Coast Guard's senior officer. Although one or two other officers seem to have had greater support in Congress, Glass accepted Bertholf's recommendation when the Coast Guard was returned to Treasury jurisdiction. Captain Reynolds was confirmed by the Senate in September and assumed office on 2 October 1919.

The new commandant confronted a formidable array of problems. The personnel situation was critical, for most of the men who had volunteered for war service wished to be discharged as soon as hostilities ended and few came forward to replace them, in spite of a return to one-year enlistments and greatly increased recruiting activity.[19] Enlisted men had to be retained regardless of their wishes, but the law permitted them to be held for only three months after the United States formally made peace with Germany. And when that occurred, the Coast Guard would revert to the 1908 pay scale, making it more difficult to retain trained men and to attract recruits.

Secretary Glass had addressed this problem in September 1919, urging Congress to equalize the pay and allowances of Coast Guardsmen with those of their Navy counterparts.[20] Although a measure to this effect was enacted in May 1920, the fiscal year 1920–21 seems to have witnessed the greatest amount of dissatisfaction among the enlisted men generally, for the disciplinary problem, as indicated by the number of court cases, reached its peak then. Thereafter, the discontent declined, although the next few years brought little increase in numbers, with the service having about 3,500 enlisted men, little more than three-fifths of its authorized strength.[21]

The officer situation was little brighter. With 205 commissioned officers, the Coast Guard had less than three-quarters of its authorized number, and only nineteen cadets were under instruction at the Academy in mid-1919. Legislation of June 1920 required the Coast Guard to adopt the Navy's rank terminology according to the arrangement agreed on in 1915, whereby senior captains became commanders. The slight implied by the exclusion of Coast Guard officers from the highest command rank—captain—was not mitigated by the knowledge that all temporary wartime promotions would be rescinded in 1921. To alleviate the shortage of officers in part, Treasury Secretary Houston asked the Navy Department to allow forty members of the Naval Academy class of 1922 to volunteer for Coast Guard commissions upon completion of their studies, only to be told that the Navy itself would require all of the graduates.[22] Thus, the Coast Guard had to "make do" with an officer corps that was only a little less inadequate in numbers than its enlisted strength. Not surprisingly, no officers could be spared for flight training at Pensacola in December 1920.

Lifesaving stations were less seriously affected by the personnel shortage because they could usually hire men, often former surfmen, from nearby communities for temporary service. This expedient, however, was impractical for the cutters, six of which had to be decommissioned on the Atlantic coast in the spring of 1920 so that vessels of the Bering Sea Patrol Fleet could be manned. The *Itasca* was among them, but Reynolds's aide advised that "by the time she is needed for the cadet practice cruise, conditions on the East Coast may have improved. In any event, get her to the Academy at the proper time by towing if necessary and let Captain Jacobs [the superintendent] solve the problem as regards her personnel for the cruise."[23]

The old *Itasca* did sail on the cadet cruise that summer, her last because the smaller barkentine-rigged composite gunboat *Vicksburg* was acquired from the Navy to replace her in 1921. Renamed the *Alexander Hamilton,* the slightly younger gunboat provided this service for the next decade, thereafter serving as receiving ship and barracks at Curtis Bay and the Academy.

In light of the personnel shortage, the service's plight with regard to ships was perhaps less serious than it seemed at first sight. Here, too, however, the inadequacies were considerable—in need of four first-class cutters in 1917, the Coast Guard had lost three more during the war while adding only the harbor cutter *Manhattan* and the shallow-draft stern-wheelers *Kankakee* and *Yocona* for flood relief on the Ohio and Mississippi rivers.

Both the Navy and the United States Shipping Board had many vessels surplus to their needs at the war's end. The Coast Guard was especially interested in the former's Bird-class minesweepers, sturdy 14-knot steel 188-footers with good cruising range and towing capacity. Reynolds thought that his service could use twelve of these ships to advantage, although he admitted that few, if any, could be

The newly completed Modoc.

manned immediately.[24] But the Navy did not consider the "Bird-boats" surplus; instead it offered five of the 180-foot Eagle-boats mass-produced by the Ford Motor Company and twenty-one of the 110-foot wooden submarine-chasers that had been built in large numbers during the war. Neither type proved suitable for Coast Guard service—the Eagles had poor maneuvering characteristics and sea-keeping qualities, while the submarine-chasers' gasoline engines required inordinate amounts of fuel and attention. Within a short time, all of the former and most of the latter had been returned to the Navy or sold.[25] Ten 88-foot wooden tugs, completed for the Navy in 1919, were more satisfactory, but their size limited them to harbor service.

Five steel oceangoing tugs were acquired from the Shipping Board in 1920 and 1921. Converted for Coast Guard use at Curtis Bay, these 11-knot 152-footers were commissioned as the *Cahokia*, *Kickapoo*, *Mascoutin*, *Saukee*, and *Tamaroa*, and stationed at ports from Rockland, Maine, to Eureka, California. Somewhat handicapped by their low freeboard, these vessels served for a decade and more.[26] They were not, however, first-class cutters.

Although five large cutters had been authorized in 1916 and

1917, and designs had been prepared by Construction and Repair, wartime shipbuilding programs had made it impossible to find a builder. In the summer of 1919, contracts for these vessels were let to the Norway-Pacific Construction and Dry Dock Company, which was establishing a shipyard at Everett, Washington. Unfortunately, the new company found itself in financial difficulty, in part because the Norwegian government, impatient at the delay in settlement of claims relating to vessels commandeered by the United States during the war, encouraged a boycott by Norwegian-American investors. Becoming convinced that Norway-Pacific would be unable to complete the cutters within a reasonable time, the Coast Guard cancelled the agreements in February 1920.[27] Soon thereafter, the Union Construction Company of Oakland, California, was awarded contracts for four 240-foot cutters and a 158-foot oceangoing tug, all of which were launched in 1921.

While the last of these vessels, the *Shawnee*, was simply a further development of the tug type, the larger *Tampa, Haida, Mojave,* and *Modoc* were the first true "multi-mission" cutters, designed for police work in territorial waters, ice patrol, search and rescue, derelict destruction, and towing. And because all cutters were required to be of use to the Navy in time of war, each mounted two 5-inch 51-caliber guns with provision for a third in wartime, and a 3-inch 50-caliber antiaircraft gun—the heaviest batteries carried by any Coast Guard vessels before World War II! The hull design, by Constructor Frederick A. Hunnewell, was essentially an enlarged version of the successful *Seneca*—flush-decked with plumb bow, graceful sheer, and counter stern. The compact superstructure, located amidships to provide ample working space on the weather deck, bore one mast with extensive radio antennae and a tall, slender stack, which increased natural draft to the boiler furnaces.[28]

The hull design was traditional; the engineering plant was not. Heretofore, cutters had been powered by reciprocating engines because the more efficient steam turbines lacked the responsiveness and backing power needed for maneuvering in restricted areas under difficult conditions of wind and sea. Turbo-electric drive, used in the Navy's latest battleships, eliminated these disadvantages, but an induction motor of the required power was too large for installation in a cutter. Engineer in chief Quincy B. Newman found a solution to the problem in the General Electric turbo-generator units that powered rolling mills ashore. In these plants, modified for marine use, the turbine drove an alternating current generator that produced power for the synchronous main motor, combining the turbine's efficiency with the responsiveness and backing power of the reciprocating engine in machinery of acceptable size. To Newman's chagrin, however, the delay in building the 240-footers resulted in the new machinery first going to sea in the rebuilt SS *Cuba.*[29]

Upon completion, the *Tampa* was ordered to New York and the

Modoc to Wilmington, North Carolina, while the *Haida* was based at Seattle and the *Mojave* at Honolulu. The two Atlantic coast vessels would alternate regularly on International Ice Patrol, and their sisters were intended to serve with the Bering Sea Patrol Fleet. Although their steering engines were unreliable until modified and they failed to reach their designed 16 knots in service, these cutters were successful ships. Lieutenant Commander William J. Wheeler, who commissioned the *Tampa* and commanded her on ice patrol for three years, thought them "wonderful sea boats."[30] The next big cutters would be slightly larger *Tampa*s.

Completion of the five cutters did not entirely satisfy the Coast Guard's need for new ships. Requests for money to replace the veteran *Bear* and the *Androscoggin,* whose wooden hull was beyond repair, were not heeded, however, nor were the repeated applications for funds with which to restore the *Onondaga* to useful condition. Out of commission at Curtis Bay, the last-named cutter simply deteriorated until she had to be sold for scrap.[31]

The plight of Coast Guard aviation was even worse. The service's half-dozen aviators had served competently at naval air stations during the war, and Lieutenant Elmer F. Stone added to their reputation by piloting the Navy's big flying boat *NC-4* on the first transatlantic flight in May 1919.[32] But the Coast Guard's return to the Treasury Department virtually severed this connection with aviation, and only in March 1920 was the first aviation station established, at Morehead City, North Carolina, using the facilities of an abandoned naval air station and six Curtis HS-2L single-engine flying boats borrowed from the Navy. These aircraft were utilized in accordance with a directive from Headquarters, which listed their duties in order of priority: a) Saving life in coastal regions and adjacent waters, b) saving property in the same area, c) enforcement of laws and assisting federal and state officials engaged therein, d) transportation of officials to remote areas or if time precluded the use of other means, e) assisting fishermen by spotting schools of fish, f) surveying and mapping.[33] Although the flying boats proved their worth, especially in locating vessels in distress and derelicts, no appropriation for their continued operation was forthcoming. In January 1922, all were returned to the Navy, and the Morehead City air station was closed.[34]

The Congress, however, was not entirely inattentive to the Coast Guard's needs. In response to repeated urging by Secretary of the Treasury Andrew W. Mellon, it passed a bill designed to remove most of the inequities endured by Coast Guard officers. This measure, which was signed by President Warren G. Harding in January 1923, provided that the commandant rank with the Navy's rear admirals of the lower half and authorized the promotion of seven senior officers to the rank of captain. Maximum numbers for lower ranks were adjusted accordingly, and most important, provision was made for promotions at regular and reasonable intervals.

Thus, there was some slight cause for optimism as Admiral Reynolds's term as commandant neared its end in 1923. Yet the *Annual Report* for that year reveals that the Coast Guard's problems had been endured rather than alleviated during that period. On 30 June 1923 the service had 3,496 enlisted men, 395 warrant officers, and 206 commissioned officers, very nearly the same numbers in each category that Reynolds had reported three years earlier. He could note one improvement, however: the number of cadets at the Academy had increased from twenty-three in 1920 to seventy-two in 1923. Nonetheless, Admiral Reynold's successor would obviously have the same problems to contend with—until a major change occurred in 1924.

CHAPTER SIX

OPERATIONS DURING THE LEAN YEARS, 1919–24

Considering the generally unfavorable circumstances of the period just reviewed, one might expect to find an accompanying diminution of efficiency in the Coast Guard's performance generally. This, however, does not seem to have been the case, as witness the following statistics taken from *Annual Reports*:

Fiscal Year	Lives Saved and Persons Rescued from Peril	Persons on Board Vessels Assisted	Vessels Seized or Reported for Violations of Law	Derelicts, etc., Removed or Destroyed
1919	2,081	12,044	152	10
1920	2,417	8,424	601	7
1921	1,621	14,013	340	19
1922	2,954	14,531	596	48
1923	2,792	16,253	2,106	46
1924	2,462	15,902	2,205	75

Fiscal 1922 recorded the highest number of lives saved and persons rescued from peril since the Coast Guard's creation in 1915. And the value of vessels assisted, including cargoes, ranged from almost $15 millions in 1919 to more than $65 millions in 1920 and 1921, after which it fell gradually to some $25 millions in 1924. During these years, the annual appropriation for support of the Coast Guard averaged about $10 millions.[1]

Meanwhile, the routine duties of the service continued to be performed as before. Each year saw cutters assigned to winter cruising off the Atlantic coast, after which two of their number undertook the International Ice Patrol. First-class cutters on the Pacific coast made their way northward to the Bering Sea annually, while the elderly *Bear* steamed and sailed into the Arctic Ocean and the seagoing tugs *Shawnee*, *Snohomish*, and *Cahokia* conducted a seal patrol in waters of the Pacific Northwest and southeastern Alaska.

Surfmen manned lookout towers by day and patrolled the beaches in the vicinity of their stations each night, ready to ignite red Coston signals to warn vessels offshore or to indicate to the less fortunate that their plight was known and help was on the way.

Despite the press of other duties, the commandant always found it possible to send several cutters to New London to patrol the Yale-Harvard regatta on the Thames, each of them embarking dignitaries whose positions or connections entitled them and their ladies to these vantage points. Nor was this the only regatta patrolled; the number grew from two—Yale-Harvard and Yachtsmen's Club of Philadelphia—in 1920 to thirty listed in the 1924 *Annual Report.* Most, of course, had to be satisfied with the presence of a single cutter or patrol boat, but the Gloucester fisherman's race in August 1923 had three first-class cutters, the *Alexander Hamilton,* and the boats of the Gloucester Coast Guard station in attendance, nor was this number unusual for a prestigious event.[2]

Regatta patrol was perhaps the most glamorous of the Coast Guard's duties; it may be contrasted with the service's role in coping with some other occurrences, beginning with the influenza epidemic of 1918–19.

When news that influenza had stricken the inhabitants of villages of Alaska's Seward Peninsula reached Nome, men of Coast Guard Station No. 305 loaded a dog sled with medicines and supplies, and on 6 December 1918 Surfman L. E. Ashton and an Eskimo driver departed for Cape Prince of Wales, 160 miles to the northwest. After stopping to treat the sick in eight villages on the way, Ashton reached his destination to find the epidemic far advanced, with sick and dead in almost every dwelling. The surfman set up a dispensary in the Wales post office and had the seriously ill carried to the schoolhouse, the most suitable building for hospital purposes. After almost a month of caring for the living, Ashton found time to arrange the interment of the more than 150 dead. The epidemic had run its course by late February, so Surfman Ashton returned to more usual duties in Nome.[3]

The *Unalga,* on Bering Sea Patrol, was sheltering from a storm at Akun Island in late May 1919 when her captain was advised by radio to return to Unalaska, where influenza had reached epidemic proportions. Soon after the cutter weighed anchor, he received a request for assistance to cope with a similar outbreak in the Bristol Bay area. Upon reaching Unalaska, however, Senior Captain Francis G. Dodge decided that the situation there and at nearby Dutch Harbor required his crew's full attention. Thereupon, he advised the governor of Alaska of his decision by radio, and with Public Health Surgeon F. H. Johnson and most of his ship's company, began the work of caring for the eighty sick, distributing food, making coffins, and burying the dead. Each succeeding day brought additional cases of illness and more deaths as well, until 3 June, when no new cases were reported, and the *Bear* stood in to offer additional medical assistance. Captain Dodge and several of his men became ill the next day; fortunately, all recovered in a short time. By 7 June, the epidemic was obviously on the wane, but orphans and sick continued to require care, so the *Unalga* remained at Unalaska.

Dodge's messages describing the situation had led to the dispatch of the old cruiser *Marblehead* with doctors, nurses, and medicines. She arrived at Unalaska on 16 June, and after conferring with Captain Dodge, her commanding officer transferred half of the embarked medical personnel to the *Unalga*. The cutter steamed to Bristol Bay and up the Nushagak River to Dillingham, while the *Marblehead* and the USS *Vicksburg* undertook to treat the ill in other areas adjacent to Bristol Bay.

After providing care for those stricken at Dillingham, medical and burial parties from the cutter made their way to villages in the vicinity, in each of which they found a similar situation: most of the surviving adults ill, orphans in need of care, and the dead unburied—some partially eaten by packs of ravenous dogs. The last necessitated the addition of riflemen to each party, for the starving animals did not hesitate to attack service personnel. Under the circumstances, there was no alternative to shooting the dogs.

By the end of June, the *Unalga*'s services were no longer required. Sending the remaining food and medical supplies ashore, the cutter departed for Unalaska, where she coaled, and then resumed her patrol of the Bering Sea.[4]

Atlantic coast cutters performed duties of more traditional type, including helping to salve the U.S. Army transport *Powhatan*, which had sailed for Europe with 500 persons on board in January 1920. The 10,000-ton vessel was disabled some 500 miles east of Boston, and her distress calls soon brought assistance—the transport *Northern Pacific*, two destroyers, a cargo ship, and the Canadian government's salvage steamer *Lady Laurier*. The last took the big transport in tow but could do little more than hold her in position. The cutter *Ossipee* reached the *Powhatan* during the evening of 22 January, and after conferring with the senior naval officer, her captain sent boats to transfer 102 passengers and their baggage to the *Northern Pacific*. When the cutter *Acushnet* joined the next morning, she ran a hawser from her bow to the *Powhatan*'s quarter, while the *Ossipee* took position ahead of the *Lady Laurier*, to which she sent a towing hawser. With two vessels towing and the *Acushnet* holding the big transport on course, the tow made good progress toward Halifax, although slowed occasionally when one or another of the hawsers parted. The cutter *Gresham* relieved the two destroyers standing by that evening, and the next morning a northeasterly gale buffeted the vessels. When the *Lady Laurier*'s hawser snapped, sea conditions prevented passing another, so all the ships cast off to await better weather. The *Powhatan* was lost to sight in a blinding snowstorm during the afternoon and located again a day later. By the morning of 26 January, wind and sea had gone down considerably, so the

Ossipee assumed the steering position astern of the *Powhatan* and the newly arrived salvage steamer *Relief* and the *Acushnet* took over the tow.

The weather soon deteriorated again, causing the *Powhatan* to sheer wildly despite the *Ossipee*'s efforts to hold her on course, but the vessels plodded onward, with the *Lady Laurier* and the *Gresham* in company. Their lookouts sighted the Halifax light vessel during the afternoon of 27 January, and the disabled transport let her anchors go in the harbor that evening.[5]

As so often was the case, however, the most dramatic rescue was made by surfmen—of Station No. 296 at Grand Marais, Michigan. The lake steamer *H.E. Runnels* encountered a gale in Lake Superior in November 1919 and took shelter in Grand Marais harbor. When the weather moderated, she headed to the westward early on the morning of 14 November, only to encounter another gale with heavy snow. Attempting to return to the harbor, the *Runnels* missed the entrance in the poor visibility, and a steering casualty occurred as she backed out into the lake. With a whole gale blowing and a heavy sea running, the helpless steamer was soon driven ashore broadside on, 150 yards from the outer end of one of the piers.

The keeper of Station No. 296 was away at the time; when the Coast Guard lookout reported the *Runnels*'s first approach, Surfman Alfred E. Kristofferson ordered his men to prepare boats and beach apparatus for use should she run into difficulty. He himself boarded a small Coast Guard cutter moored in Grand Marais to seek assistance from her crew. Learning that Kristofferson's superior was away, Keeper John O. Anderson, who was on board the cutter while on leave from his station in Chicago, offered to take charge of the station crew, to which the surfman promptly agreed. As they made their way to the station, they saw the *Runnels* go aground.

The conditions for rescue of her crew could hardly have been worse. It was barely daylight at 7 A.M., and gale-whipped snow obscured the steamer much of the time. Short, steep seas dashing against her soon sheathed the *Runnels* in ice—the temperature stood at 18°—and waves driving shoreward around her combined with the backwash from the pier to create a turbulent cross sea.

Nonetheless, it appeared that this would be routine breeches-buoy rescue. The first shot from the Lyle gun placed a line over the steamer's bowsprit, and her men quickly pulled the block with a whipline rove through it aboard and secured it. But the ice-coated line kinked and snarled as the surfmen hauled the hawser out, forcing the abandonment of that effort.

With the wreck already beginning to break up, there was no time to lose, yet no surfboat could be controlled by ordinary means in the sea raging between the shore and the ship. Then Kristofferson suggested a solution—if the whip were hauled taut, it could serve to guide the boat. He looped the surfboat's bow painter over the tightened line and secured it in the boat, which was then launched with

Keeper Anderson and former surfman James MacDonald supplementing its crew. Anderson decided that a stern painter over the whipline would offer even better control, as it did, and the surfboat reached the *Runnels* with little trouble. Here another difficulty arose; it was impractical to throw heaving lines from the tossing boat against the wind, and the wreck victims were reluctant to make their way out on the whipline hand over hand. Finally they were persuaded to try, but when four of them had dropped into the boat safely, the endurance of the boat crew had reached its limit. On reaching the shore, three surfmen had to be carried to their quarters. Others took their places, and thirteen more men were rescued in two more boat trips. Although only two men—the master and the chief engineer—now remained on board the *Runnels,* two more of the boat crew were in a state of collapse from cold and fatigue, and none of the spectators volunteered to take their places.

With less than a full crew in the surfboat, the last rescue effort was the most difficult, and the fact that the two men remaining to be rescued were older and less agile than their fellows added to the difficulty. Somehow heaving lines were got to them and each tied the line around his waist before leaving the wreck; each lost his grip and had to be pulled from the water. During the struggle to get them into the boat—the engineer weighed over 300 pounds!—a wave washed three of the rescuers overboard. All clambered back into the boat quickly, but Keeper Anderson, directing the work and less attentive to his own situation, endured two more immersions before the surfboat could return to the shore.

The rescue of all nineteen men from the wreck of the *H.E. Runnels* was considered a feat worthy of note even by the standards of the old Life-Saving Service, and all who took part in the operations were awarded gold lifesaving medals. For the four men who manned the surfboat throughout the rescue—Anderson, Kristofferson, Samuel Martin, and MacDonald—the awards seem hardly adequate.[6]

Bitter cold excepted, the rescue of the *Cape Horn*'s crew by the surfboat from Station No. 222 two months earlier was effected under conditions nearly as difficult as those of the *Runnels* wreck. The fishing schooner had been knocked down by a hurricane off Port Isabel, Texas, but righted herself when her masts were cut away. She drifted helplessly for two days with decks awash as her eight men labored at the pumps in what was coming to seem a vain effort to keep her afloat. A surfman at the station on the northern end of Brazos Island sighted a faint light some distance offshore during the night of 15 September 1919, and although it was thought to mark a vessel at anchor, Keeper Wallace L. Reed had his men prepare the power surfboat for use should she show signs of dragging or be in other need of assistance.

Daylight revealed the dismasted *Cape Horn* in sinking condition with no sign of life on board, and a heavy surf beating against the shore combined with large waves breaking far out in the Gulf of

Mexico presaged a trying passage for any boat attempting to reach her. The 26-foot surfboat was tossed about, rolled on its beam ends, and almost pitch-poled (turned end over end). Heavy seas broke over it repeatedly, testing its self-bailing capability to the utmost, as Reed with his steering oar and his men at the oars strove to keep the boat on course.

A struggle of two hours' duration brought the surfboat close enough to make out the exhausted men on the schooner's deck, and Keeper Reed decided that with precise timing the boat could close her from the leeward immediately after a sea had surged over her weather rail. He shouted instructions to the *Cape Horn* crew on the first approach, sheered off to await the next opportunity, ran in at full power to pull one man into the boat, retreated again, and dashed in seven times more, retiring each time with another man saved from the hulk.

With the entire crew removed from the sinking schooner, Reed had to find a landing place, for the surfboat, overloaded with fifteen men embarked, could hardly survive another crossing of the bar off Brazos Island. Standing as close in as he dared, he selected a spot where the surf appeared to be somewhat less daunting, then streamed a drogue and headed for the beach with his men at the oars again to aid in keeping the boat on course. All went well despite the heavy seas that filled the boat repeatedly until the drogue split within 100 yards of the shore; before the surfboat could broach, however, a large wave lifted it and deposited it on the beach with all hands safe. For the *Cape Horn* rescue, Wallace L. Reed and the boat crew of Station No. 222 were awarded silver lifesaving medals.[7]

The spring of 1922 brought extensive flooding to the Ohio and Mississippi valleys, the worst since the calamitous inundation of 1913. The earlier floods had led to the construction of the *Kankakee* and the *Yocona,* and the two sternwheelers were soon involved in the removal of people and livestock from imperiled locations, while personnel and boats from Stations No. 278, 279, 280, and 281, all in the Chicago vicinity, performed similar relief work farther to the northward. The *Yocona* transported some 300 persons and more than 1,000 head of livestock in the course of a cruise along the lower Mississippi, and both river cutters figured prominently in the distribution of food and supplies to those left destitute by the floods. The commandant noted with some satisfaction that the new vessels had "abundantly fulfilled their missions."[8]

The 152-foot cutter *Snohomish* left Port Angeles, Washington, on 14 February 1923 to assist a vessel reported aground off Vancouver Island. Late that afternoon, she received an SOS from the steamer *Nika* near Cape Flattery, and Lieutenant Commander Henry G. Hemingway, temporarily in command, headed the *Snohomish* seaward. As she plunged through the night, the cutter encountered increasingly rough seas, the result of a gale blowing offshore. The *Nika*'s lights were sighted early the next morning, and when the

The Haida *leaving Seward with World Flight supplies on board. The large objects on her after deck were aircraft pontoons.*

Snohomish approached, the steamer was seen to be afire. With a 75-mile wind blowing and heavy seas running, Hemingway considered it unwise to lower a boat, so he worked the cutter to within 20 feet of the *Nika*'s starboard quarter. A 3-inch line with a ring buoy attached was put on board the steamer, and Hemingway kept the *Snohomish* close aboard while the *Nika*'s entire crew, with the exception of several men who had left the burning ship in a lifeboat, was taken off by this means. When the master was brought on board, the cutter cast off her line and began a search for the lifeboat, which was soon sighted in spite of heavy rain and darkness. Again, the *Snohomish* was handled faultlessly, and the men were taken from the boat without injury. Lieutenant Commander Hemingway was awarded a gold lifesaving medal for the *Nika* rescue—in 1928.[9]

Later in 1923 the Coast Guard received a request for assistance of another sort. The postwar interest in aviation had led to an informal competition among several nations for the honor of being first to circumnavigate the world by air, and the U.S. Army Air Service entered the lists, planning a flight by four Douglas World Cruisers, single-engine biplanes that could be fitted with either wheels or floats. They were to fly westward, departing as early in the spring as possible in order that the flight be completed before bad weather set in. It was obviously impossible to station vessels along a more southerly transpacific route, so the flight would originate in Seattle, whence the aircraft were to fly to Alaska, westward along the Aleutian chain, and thence to Japan by way of the Komandorski and Kurile islands. For meteorological and other information pertaining to this portion of the route, Major General Mason M. Patrick, chief of the Air Service, turned to the Coast Guard, and the commandant designated his aide, Lieutenant Commander Stephen S. Yeandle, who combined a keen interest in aviation with Aleutian experience—he had been navigator of the *Tahoma* when she was lost in 1914—to provide the desired data. General Patrick later stated that the plan for the North Pacific section of the route was "based almost entirely on [Yeandle's] recommendations."[10]

But the matter did not end there. Spare parts and equipment for the World Cruisers were shipped to Seward, where it became apparent that the vessels available to transport them to the westward lacked deck space for spare wing panels. Thereupon, the cutters *Haida* and *Algonquin* were ordered northward to provide every possible assistance to the flyers. Both sailed on 6 April 1924, the former from Seattle to Seward to embark the supplies, and the *Algonquin* from Astoria, Oregon, directly to Unalaska. The *Haida* steamed into Unalaska on 15 April, and two days later the *Algonquin* loaded an engine and other parts for delivery to Kanatak, almost 500 miles to the eastward, where Major Frederick L. Martin, the flight leader, had been forced down. The three remaining biplanes reached Unalaska on 19 April, and their pilots and mechanics accepted the *Haida*'s hospitality while they awaited Martin.

Soon after their arrival, a blizzard set in, but the cutter's men helped to clean the aircraft, installed a new engine in one, and stood guard over them. During a heavy snowfall on the night of 25 April, a williwaw drove the aircraft toward the beach, where the fragile machines would inevitably be damaged beyond repair. The "Haidas" responded to the call for all hands at once, many not even taking time to dress, pulling on oilskins as they raced topside. They were in time; a number waded into the water despite the subfreezing temperature and stood shoulder-deep to hold the biplanes away from the shore, while their shipmates prepared to haul them onto the beach when the wind diminished, for it was obvious that they could not be anchored adequately.[11]

Meanwhile, the "Algonquins" were finding that icy winds and blizzards were hardly conducive to rapid repair of an airplane on an exposed beach. They got the engine changed nonetheless, and Major Martin managed the flight to Chignik, about halfway to Unalaska. After taking off there, the biplane simply vanished, touching off a search that involved the Coast and Geodetic Survey's *Pioneer,* the Fishery Commission's *Eider,* and all available private vessels in addition to the two cutters.[12]

Two days later, the other pilots felt that they could wait no longer, so they flew on to Atka Island, to which the *Haida* steamed after embarking the necessary supplies and gasoline. There the weather deteriorated again, causing Commander John F. Hottel to note that "duty about the planes performed this day [5 May] was probably the most arduous performed by the crew at any time during the flight."[13]

It improved a few days later, and when the *Eider* reported favorable conditions at Attu on 9 May, the aircraft took off, with the *Haida* following under forced draft. Another gale had to be weathered at the westernmost of the Aleutians; it finally blew itself out, and on the morning of the 15th the cutter headed westward along the line of flight, making smoke to guide the aircraft. They appeared soon after noon, circled at low altitude to read the latest weather report received from the Kuriles as indicated by black-painted planks in a prearranged pattern on the *Haida*'s deck, and disappeared over the horizon ahead.

Learning that the flyers had made an unscheduled landing in the Komandorski Islands, the cutter continued on to Nikol'skoye, arriving there a few hours after they had taken off for the Kurile Islands. She steamed on along their route until U.S. Navy destroyers awaiting the aviators in the Kuriles announced their safe landing there; then the *Haida* headed for Unalaska, having too little fuel to investigate the possibility of refloating a Navy lighter reported ashore at Kiska.

Return to Unalaska brought the welcome news that Major Martin and his mechanic were safe. After taking off at Chignik, they had encountered poor visibility and had flown into the side of a mountain. Fortunately, the deep snow had cushioned the impact. The two men walked into Port Moller ten days later.

Forty-three tons of Air Service parts and equipment remained at Unalaska, as did Army support personnel. Having been refueled and cleaned—routine duties on board had been neglected somewhat during the past several weeks—the *Haida* embarked all for return to Seward, whence the materiel was shipped to Newfoundland for use by the returning world flyers.[14]

And return they did. Two of the World Cruisers, piloted by Lieutenants Lowell Smith and Erik Nelson, landed at Seattle on 28 September, marking the conclusion of the first flight around the world. The third, forced down in the North Atlantic, had been irreparably damaged while being picked up by the USS *Richmond.* The U.S. Army Air Service was justifiably proud of this feat, a feat made possible only by Coast Guard and Navy support, as General Patrick readily acknowledged.

For the men of the *Haida* and the *Algonquin,* the association with the world flight had been an interesting, if sometimes trying, interlude, but the Bering Sea Patrol was their proper occupation, and to it they returned. The *Haida* was off the Bay of Waterfalls, Adak Island, on 13 July, when her radiomen copied a distress call from the Shipping Board's 5,866-ton steamer *West Jena,* which had lost her screw 350 miles south of Attu. The unfortunate's sister *West Niger,* ordered to her assistance, was 2,000 miles away, so Commander Hottel ordered steam for full speed, and the cutter churned to the southwestward. Perhaps the days of attempting to keep up with aircraft had taken their toll; boiler tubes began to sag in the intense heat generated by forced draft, and the *Haida* had to slow to her maximum speed under natural draft. The disabled steamer was sighted two days later, and after observing her drift, Hottel maneuvered within range, the shoulder line-throwing gun put a line on board with its first shot, and the *West Jena*'s windlass soon brought the end of the 12-inch towing hawser onto her forward deck. There it was secured to her port anchor chain, she veered 45 fathoms of chain while the *Haida* was paying out 200 fathoms of hawser, and the tow was ready to proceed.

What seemed likely to be an uneventful towing job became something more when the wind got up from the southwest on 17 July. It increased to force 7—a moderate gale—and the heavy seas coming up from astern caused the cutter to roll deeply. But nothing carried away, so she kept on at 80 rpm, making good about 6 knots. The weather moderated late the next day, and on 20 July the *West Jena* dropped the *Haida*'s hawser and let her anchor go in Dutch Harbor.

No doubt relieved at the successful conclusion of a five-day, 750-mile towing operation, the cutter's men made her fast to the fueling wharf. Then it became apparent that they had not yet finished with the *West Jena*. She dragged anchor in heavy squalls and was soon aground. With a gale blowing directly against the wharf, the single-screw *Haida* had difficulty in working away from it; when she was clear, she anchored to windward of the grounded steamer and sent a boat with a line. Two hours later, the *West Jena* was afloat again, and Hottel advised her master not to cast off the towing hawser prematurely. Apparently assuming that the danger had passed, the master let the hawser go thirty minutes later, whereupon a williwaw drove the *West Jena* ashore in almost the same place. This was becoming tiresome. Once more the *Haida* worked up to windward, dropped an anchor, sent a line on board, and hauled her hapless charge off the beach. By this time, it was after midnight, so the cutter simply held onto the *West Jena* until the next morning, when she was towed to a safer anchorage.[15]

The foregoing examples of Coast Guardsmen at work during the lean postwar years would seem to indicate that the problems of personnel and materiel noted in the preceding chapter were not reflected to any notable extent in the performance of the service's duties. Each mission completed successfully added something to the reputation of the Coast Guard; as it approached the tenth anniversary of its founding, the service appeared to be maintaining the traditions of its predecessors.

CHAPTER SEVEN

PROHIBITION ENFORCEMENT— MEANS AND METHODS

In June 1919, former Secretary of the Treasury William G. McAdoo wrote his successor to recommend that Captain Frederick C. Billard, "one of the most efficient men in the Coast Guard," be nominated to succeed the retiring commandant.[1] Billard, a member of the cadet class of 1896, had been superintendent of the Academy from 1914 to 1918, when he was detached to command the armed yacht *Aphrodite* in European waters. He had the endorsement of the Coast Guard Warrant Officers Association as well, but he was said to be among those who favored the permanent transfer of the service to the Navy Department and so was unacceptable to Carter Glass. When Senior Captain Reynolds was appointed commandant, however, he summoned Billard to Washington to become his aide, and the latter served in that capacity throughout Reynolds's term. In fact, Billard was more nearly an assistant commandant and exercised an authority approaching that of the commandant himself. Thus, it is not surprising that he succeeded Reynolds on 11 January 1924, advancing in rank from lieutenant commander to rear admiral. It seems to have been a popular appointment—within a few months, an officer wrote that "Admiral Billard is the man who can handle the job . . . His taking over the reins has had a wonderful effect on the Service even thus far."[2]

"The job" was that of supervising a rapid expansion of the Coast Guard and of directing its efforts to enforce the legislation against smuggling on an unprecedented scale, the direct result of the Eighteenth Amendment to the Constitution, which forbade the manufacture, sale, import, and export of intoxicating beverages after 16 January 1920. So-called "war prohibition" had been adopted after the Armistice and was continued until 1920; thus, the United States had been legally "dry" for more than a year when the Eighteenth Amendment became effective. The enforcing measure for both legislative and constitutional prohibition, the National Prohibition (Volstead) Act, placed the responsibility for enforcement on the

Frederick Chamberlayne Billard, commandant, 1924–32.

Treasury Department's Bureau of Internal Revenue, despite the plea of Secretary Houston and the commissioner that this duty be assigned elsewhere. Thereupon, Houston created a Prohibition Unit within the Bureau, charging it with enforcement of the laws regarding alcohol and narcotics generally.[3]

Perhaps the ease with which prohibition was pushed through Congress and state legislatures led authorities on every level of government to expect that enforcement would be a simple matter. At any rate, little was done to prepare any agency for this purpose, and then it became apparent that many Americans were by no means resigned to lives of absolute sobriety. By mid-1921 whiskey was being brought across the border from Canada in quantity, and somewhat smaller amounts were arriving in ships from Cuba, the Bahamas, St. Pierre and Miquelon, and Newfoundland. New York, obviously the most important market, soon had its "Rum Row" composed of liquor-laden vessels of various types and flags, moored off the Long Island and New Jersey shores just outside the 3-mile limit, ready to transfer their cargoes to smaller craft. A lesser counterpart appeared off Boston, and Delaware and Chesapeake bays, the Florida coast, and New Orleans were also points of entry.[4]

The Coast Guard's involvement in the enforcement of prohibition would seem axiomatic, yet it came about only slowly and one may assume, somewhat reluctantly. In February 1922, the commandant informed Prohibition Commissioner Roy Haynes that "the Appropriation Committees of Congress have consistently declined to increase the appropriation for the Coast Guard to enable it to maintain and operate additional vessels which could be used to assist in the enforcement of the laws relating to prohibition, a duty with which the Coast Guard is not specifically charged by law, other than that it shall assist other departments of the Government in carrying out their functions." That being the case, Reynolds suggested that the president might direct his service to loan to the Prohibition Unit some or all of its nine available 110-foot submarine-chasers, with crews and funds for their operation, of course, to be provided by the Unit.[5]

In fact, however, Coast Guard cutters had detained an occasional vessel for violating the Prohibition amendment, with the first important seizure that of the British-registered schooner *Henry L. Marshall* by the *Seneca* six months earlier. A number of other arrests were made thereafter, and in April 1922, lighthouse keepers were directed to inform the nearest Coast Guard station of suspicious vessels in their vicinity. But cutters and stations alike were involved in prohibition enforcement only in connection with their other duties; no Coast Guard activity was devoted to that purpose alone.[6]

Had it been merely a matter of quenching the nation's thirst, the government of President Warren G. Harding might have continued to ignore suggestions that more effective measures to enforce prohibition be taken. But some officials argued that continued neglect would lead to an expansion of smuggling in other commodities, and that possibility, together with evidence of increased criminal activity of a more serious nature—piracy, hijacking, murder—in connection with liquor-smuggling, led the administration to consider the use of naval vessels to bring it under control. The attorney general, however, could find no indication that an emergency justifying such action existed; another means would have to be found.

Meanwhile, the Coast Guard had been increasing its antismuggling efforts gradually, especially by intercepting small craft carrying provisions out to Rum Row, and in his *Annual Report* for 1923, Secretary of the Treasury Andrew W. Mellon recommended that the service be enlarged considerably in order to combat rum running more effectively. For this purpose, the commandant wanted 20 new cutters, about 200 cabin cruisers, and 91 motorboats, as well as 3,535 additional officers and men, all at a cost of $28,500,000. This request was transmitted to President Calvin Coolidge, who had succeeded Harding on the latter's death in August 1923, and one may assume that the frugal New Englander found the figures rather startling. Nonetheless, he included them in his annual message to Congress in December, pledging to enforce prohibition to the fullest extent.[7]

Congress, accustomed to annual appropriations of less than $10 million for the Coast Guard, thought the request excessive. New cutters could not be built in less than nine months; surely the Navy and the Shipping Board had surplus vessels that could be obtained in a shorter time at lower cost. Accordingly, the amount was slashed by more than 50 percent—to $13,853,989, of which $12,194,900 would be used to prepare twenty destroyers and two minesweepers for Coast Guard use and to build 223 cabin cruisers and 100 smaller motorboats. A bill to this effect was passed by Congress and signed into law on 2 April 1924. In addition to the vessels specified, it authorized the necessary personnel—149 commissioned officers, 418 warrant officers, and 3,789 men. But Congress had not been carried away by its generosity. The measure provided that the fifty-two officers above the rank of lieutenant and twenty-five chief warrant officers be obtained by promoting regular officers and warrant officers temporarily without increasing their pay and allowances.[8]

With passage of this legislation assured, Admiral Billard addressed a circular letter to all Coast Guard commissioned officers, informing them of the situation and adding:

> We can not, however, carry out this big undertaking to our full satisfaction unless I can count on the loyal and earnest support of each one of you. So many conditions are bound to arise to try your devotion to a successful outcome in this matter and to test your interest and indeed your loyalty. Very many officers will have to be moved, maybe frequently, and often to stations or kinds of duty that may not be agreeable to them. Tours of shore duty may have to be curtailed or eliminated. Leaves of absence may have to be restricted or deferred. In short, conditions will be far from normal

and may entail unusual discomforts and inconveniences. Furthermore, some mistakes are bound to be made, and Headquarters will probably do things that some of you think ill-advised, and experience may prove you right about them. Through it all, will you not bear in mind the big issues involved—the unsullied reputation of the Service for efficiency and devotion to duty.[9]

Personnel were clearly the most important facet of this expansion, and just as obviously the Coast Guard lacked facilities for recruiting and training thousands of men. Admiral Billard initiated informal discussions with the Navy's Bureau of Navigation and then requested officially that the Navy Recruiting Service be directed to enlist men for the Coast Guard and that these recruits be sent to a naval training station for basic training, to be kept there until their services were required. He emphasized that he desired no departure from the usual Navy training and that Coast Guard courts would deal with disciplinary problems.[10]

Recruiting began in May, and thanks to considerable unemployment in some areas, three-quarters of the number authorized had been enlisted by the end of the summer. The remainder were not urgently needed, so the Coast Guard could rely on its own recruiters thereafter. Training of the recruits at the Newport, Rhode Island, and Hampton Roads, Virginia, naval stations was equally successful—until August 1925, when the comptroller general ruled that without the permission of Congress, the use of naval facilities to train Coast Guardsmen was illegal.[11] Thus, the Coast Guard had to provide its own training at New London thereafter.

Expansion of the officer corps proceeded less rapidly. Efforts to interest students completing engineering courses at colleges and universities in Coast Guard careers had modest success—eighty-nine received temporary commissions—and the Academy class of 1925 was graduated in September 1924, leaving forty-one vacancies, a number that diminished slowly over the next several years.[12]

The selection of naval vessels for Coast Guard use presented relatively few difficulties, although the Navy, which had earlier transferred three of its minesweepers to the Coast and Geodetic Survey and turned several others over to the Shipping Board for lease to private salvage companies, was willing to make only the *Redwing* of this type available to the Coast Guard. Billard agreed to accept the smaller and slower fleet tug *Carrabasset* in lieu of the second because the Navy had been so cooperative in every other regard.[13]

The twenty destroyers were selected from those laid up at the Philadelphia Navy Yard by Commander John Q. Walton, a veteran naval constructor, and four other officers. Even with the assistance of navy yard personnel, it was not a simple task, for these were the Navy's oldest destroyers, built between 1910 and 1916, and after arduous war service, they had been consigned to "red lead row" without extensive preservative preparation. Boilers, turbines, condensers, and auxiliary machinery were inspected, and the first half-dozen were towed from the reserve anchorage to the navy yard for reconditioning while the board selected fourteen more, of which two were refitted at the New York Navy Yard.

Thirteen of these ships were of the 742-ton "flivver" class, and seven were later 1,000-tonners. All were oil-burning "broken-deckers" with raised forecastles and four stacks, except the *Roe* and the *Terry*, which were three-stackers. They were capable of 29 knots at full speed and could maintain 20 knots on two boilers with ease, an important factor in terms of manning and fuel consumption. Their batteries—five 3-inch guns in the "flivvers" and four 4-inch in the others—were reduced by removal of the after mount or mounts, unnecessary because smugglers were unlikely to pursue their pursuers, and torpedo tubes and depth-charge tracks were removed as well. A 1-pounder was mounted forward to fire warning shots and to economize on the use of ammunition, the after magazine having been converted to a provision storeroom to increase endurance.[14]

No Coast Guard officer had ever served in a destroyer, and Admiral Billard thought that younger men could acquire the skills necessary to handle such temperamental craft more readily than their elders.[15] Therefore, senior officers were ordered from shore duty to command the cutters, and the lieutenant commanders they relieved went to the destroyers. The prospective commanding and executive officers attended seminars on destroyer handling while their ships were fitting out, and engineer officers and chief water tenders and machinist's mates took the Navy's four-week course in the operation of oil-fueled boilers and turbines.

The work of reconditioning was largely performed by Coast Guard enlisted men, many of them just out of recruit training, who were sent to a receiving unit set up by Commander Harry G. Hamlet at the Philadelphia Navy Yard. It turned out to be a lengthy process, for the first of the ships, the *Henley*, was not ready for service until late summer, while the last was commissioned in 1925.

Meanwhile, construction of the smaller vessels authorized in April was proceeding. The largest of these in size and number were the 203 patrol boats, sturdy wooden 75-footers with gasoline engines driving them at 13.5 knots, mounting a 1-pounder and a .30-caliber machine gun, and providing adequate quarters for their eight-man crews. The 103 picket boats, 30 and 36 feet long, were day boats only, capable of 24 knots and carrying small arms. None of these vessels were named—the "six-bitters" were numbered consecutively from *CG 100* and the picket boats from *CG 2200*.

While personnel and vessels were being procured, officers at Coast Guard Headquarters were considering the manner of their employment. In mid-July, Admiral Billard distributed a sixteen-page confidential Doctrine for Prevention of Smuggling, which began by separating his forces into two categories—General Service units (cutters and stations) and Special Service Craft (destroyers and patrol and picket boats). The former were to "perform the regular pre-scribed work of the Coast Guard" as their main mission, while con-tinuing their antismuggling activities to the extent that they did not interfere with that mission. Special service craft, on the other hand, were assigned the primary mission of preventing smuggling into the United States from the sea, with traditional Coast Guard duties as a secondary mission. For all units, however, "the saving of life shall at all times be considered to be above and beyond any other mission of Coast Guard craft."[16]

Section 30 was a summary of the "General Plan" for the pre-vention of smuggling:

> To quickly discover newly arrived rum ships. To watch all rum ships and prevent any intercourse with them by craft from shore, thus finally starving them out. To keep them from disposing of their cargoes, thus making it unprofitable for them to remain. To "hang on" to the rum ship unceasingly, day and night, following her up when she changes positions, and wear the rum ship out.
>
> To stop, board, and seize (if circumstances warrant) all craft suspected of rum running.
>
> To prevent entrance into inlets, rivers, or bays, or landing of liquor on the beach, by rum-running craft that have eluded or escaped from our forces offshore.
>
> To harass the enemy.[17]

The destroyers would locate known rum ships, called "blacks," and summon patrol boats operating in pairs, to keep them under constant surveillance. In the course of patrolling his assigned area, each destroyer commanding officer was to ensure that the patrol boats were maintaining a proper watch and to offer assistance to the smaller vessels in time of need. And the commandant expected that the destroyers would be used aggressively, as Sections 15 and 34 indicate:

> Experience has shown that destroyers can keep the sea in the worst weather. State of weather or sea should not be considered an excuse for abandoning an important mission. When the weather is so bad that it is evident that small vessels cannot take on cargo from a rum ship, and when not on an important scouting mission, the destroyers should seek a lee and anchor. . . .
>
> . . . The destroyer captain with judgment, enthusiasm, and ingenuity should be able to render most useful service. He can see that the rum ships are closely watched. He has the speed to enable him to stop all craft sighted; he can appear at numerous points within his sphere of operation; he can occasionally lie off inlets, and, in general, make his vessel seem to be omnipresent. He has two searchlights, star shells, rockets, signal lights, etc., and at night he can so operate as to make the enemy in his area believe that the Coast Guard is present in force.[18]

Admiral Billard stated his ultimate purpose in Section 42:

The fulfillment of the general plan at which we are aiming is that there shall be no more cases before the courts of vessels or boats seized for rum running, this end to be finally attained by watching the rum ships so closely and so continuously that no boat from ashore can go alongside them. Pending this consummation, if any boat from ashore does receive liquor from a rum ship, see that that boat does not get to shore with that liquor in her. If the fleeing rum runner throws her cargo overboard, pick up only enough for evidence if required; sink the rest. Our mission is to prevent a drop of liquor from getting ashore from rum ships. Accomplish this mission and we will not have to bother about judicial processes, court decisions, attendance of witnesses, and the like.[19]

To what lengths should a commanding officer go to fulfill his mission? "The Coast Guard has no desire to shoot up people needlessly, but it intends to stop rum running at sea and it intends to make any vessel bring-to that is liable to seizure or examination.... Blow the whistle and fire a number of shots across her bow.... if she continues to flee you are fully authorized under the law, in the opinion of Headquarters, to 'fire at or into such vessel.' If, unfortunately, someone should be killed or wounded, be assured that Headquarters will do all in its power to protect you."[20]

Admiral Billard's desire to avoid court cases was quite understandable, for a good deal of time would be wasted were there many of these, and defense lawyers and courts alike had already shown a willingness to embarrass those attempting to enforce prohibition. He could be sure, however, that there would be not only court cases but a good deal of unfavorable publicity as well were many craft fired into by vessels displaying the Coast Guard ensign and pennant.

Prohibition enforcement had been hampered from the beginning by the 3-mile limit of territorial waters, although the courts had upheld some seizures made farther out on the ground that the blacks were conspiring to violate American law.[21] Needless to say, foreign governments did not agree with this interpretation, and Congress attempted to clarify the situation by providing in the Tariff Act of 1922 that ships violating the laws of the United States anywhere within 4 leagues (12 miles) of the coast might be boarded, searched, arrested, and if condemned, forfeited. But this unilateral extension of territorial waters was equally unacceptable, so negotiations to resolve this problem were begun with Britain. The resulting convention, proclaimed in May 1924, confirmed the 3-mile limit, yet permitted boarding and search within one hour's steaming distance from the American coast. If, however, the liquor was intended to be landed in another vessel, the latter's speed would be the determinant.[22] Other nations agreed to similar conventions—Norway, Denmark, Germany, Sweden, and Italy in 1924; Panama and the Netherlands in 1925; Cuba and Spain in 1926; France in 1927; and Belgium in 1928.[23] Thus, the Coast Guard would enjoy a greater freedom of action than heretofore—and its officers' task of ascertaining the

The destroyer Cassin *as fitted for Coast Guard service.*

exact positions in which seizures were made became more difficult than ever.

To implement the doctrine developed at Headquarters, the Destroyer Force was established, comprising five four-ship divisions based at Boston, New London, and New York. Each division was assigned a specific patrol area, which destroyers would traverse each day, identifying blacks, reporting their positions by radio, and checking on the activities of the patrol boats trailing them. Initially, each destroyer was expected to spend ten days on patrol, followed by ten days at her base. This schedule proved to be too ambitious. With the exception of officers and a few petty officers, the ships were manned by untrained men, and while these were more effective than had been anticipated, ten days were not enough to make good the defects, especially in the vessels' machinery, resulting from a ten-day cruise during which the ships generally steamed at 15–18 knots in daylight hours. Their deck forces often had to provide details to guard seized blacks during periods in port, and neither officers nor men could be expected to forgo liberty entirely. After some months, the Destroyer Force adopted a more realistic schedule of five-day patrols followed by ten days at the base.

Although the 1,000-tonners were reputed to be poorer seaboats than the older destroyers, Lieutenant Commander Philip F. Roach reported after riding out a moderate gale early in 1925, that his *Cassin* of the former type was "a seaworthy vessel. She rolls deeply in a seaway, but with a smooth, easy roll having a very short period. She does not snap, jerk nor vibrate when the seas hit her. She does not appear to pitch at all. She is remarkably dry forward." Like all American destroyers built before 1944, however, the *Cassin* had a very large turning circle, which was an obvious handicap when trying to maintain contact with a turning, twisting black, especially in poor visibility. Roach noted also that the destroyer could not be relied on to answer her helm at less than 8 knots, which together with

the sail area of her high bow, complicated shiphandling in confined areas. Fortunately, her twin-screws compensated for this deficiency.[24]

The Shaw *was one of the second group of destroyers transferred to the Coast Guard.*

Small-boat work presented an interesting challenge, for even in a fresh breeze the *Cassin* drifted to leeward so rapidly that a boat could not get away from her lee side. Turning the ship's head into the wind required an undesirable amount of headway but seemed more practical than backing her away from the boat. In practice, destroyer commanding officers preferred to leave the responsibility for boarding blacks at sea to the patrol boats, which could simply go alongside.

The 75-foot patrol boats, operating under warrant officers or chief petty officers, were capable craft for their size, but their performance in service was sometimes disappointing. Reporting on a cruise in late May 1925, the commanding officer of the destroyer *Beale* stated that, of ten patrol boats ordered to his area from the section base at Greenport on Long Island, one failed to appear; a second had no charts and when returning from Wood's Hole, where she had gone to refuel, she struck a rock and had to be escorted back to the base by a third, whose engines had been disabled for two days. Four of the remaining boats either had no radio equipment or it was inoperative, and two more were running on one engine each most of the time. Headquarters properly attributed this state of affairs to "the failure of personnel both aboard the patrol boat[s] and the bases" adding, rather surprisingly, that this was "not to be construed as a criticism of any particular Base."[25]

Experiences such as that of the *Beale* may help to explain Admiral Billard's decision a few weeks earlier to establish a Special Patrol Force composed of ten cutters, including the ex-minesweeper

Redwing, to put Rum Row out of business. This force was commanded by Captain William J. Wheeler in the *Mojave,* which had been transferred from Honolulu for antismuggling duty. By midsummer, when the force was disbanded, Rum Row no longer existed as such, but of course its vessels had merely been dispersed, not seized or destroyed.[26]

In a sense, this dispersal only made the rum war more difficult for the Coast Guard because the rum ships moved farther out to sea, with the result that the destroyers had to spend more of their time looking after the picketing patrol boats to the detriment of their proper search activities. Larger boats that would not be a burden on the destroyers were needed for offshore picketing and trailing, and Congress authorized the construction of forty-six of these as well as the transfer of five more 1,000-ton destroyers.

The last of the additional destroyers, the *Tucker,* was commissioned in September 1926, whereupon the Coast Guard unit at the Philadelphia Navy Yard was closed. The Destroyer Force was reorganized into four six-ship divisions, with the *Downes* attached to the training station at New London. While the doctrine for employment of the destroyers remained the same, the area that they patrolled was extended farther offshore.

The new "offshore patrol boats," all of which were named for earlier cutters or officers of the Revenue-Cutter Service, came into service in 1926 and 1927. Steel vessels with diesel engines driving twin screws, each mounting a 3-inch 23-caliber gun noted more for its loud report than for its accuracy, these were of two classes—thirteen 100-footers and thirty-three 125-footers. The smaller ships were ready first and proved to be poor seaboats, very wet in even moderately rough water. Most of them were stationed on the Gulf Coast, where they were less likely to encounter bad weather.

The more numerous 125-footers, popularly known as the "buck and a quarters," were much more successful—"unusually steady and when they roll it is with a slow, easy motion . . . they are seaworthy, heading into the sea or running before it."[27] Neither type was designed with speed in mind; their 10-knot top speed was accepted in order to gain the reliability and endurance provided by diesel engines.

The doctrine for employment of the offshore patrol boats represented a change in tactics, intended to eliminate what Admiral Billard thought "the only weak spot in the Coast Guard's line of defense," the inability of existing boats to trail blacks until the latter had to return to port. When a scout—a destroyer or a cutter—located a black outside the range of the 75-footers, she would summon an offshore patrol boat and picket the black until the smaller vessel reached her. "The offshore patrol boat should then follow the black wherever the latter may go, leaving that particular black only upon being relieved by another offshore patrol boat or when the black has been trailed into a foreign port." Should the black come within range of 75-footers, some of these might be sent to assist the offshore patrol boat, but their presence did not relieve the larger vessel of her primary responsibility to stay with that black. As before, rendering assistance to ships in distress took precedence over all else; with this exception, however, the commandant stressed that "these offshore patrol boats *are intended to trail blacks.*"[28]

With this outer cordon supported by activities of smaller patrol boats, picket boats, and stations inshore, smuggling liquor into the New England-New York area theoretically became much more difficult, and Admiral Billard professed to believe that it had.[29] Perhaps he was correct; but in practice the system was far from perfect. Even had all of the offshore boats been assigned there, they would have been too few, for only a little more than one-third of their number could have been picketing blacks at one time. And the rum-runners were not limited to 10 knots, so complaints about the patrol boats' lack of speed were frequent. Even the slower vessels often found it possible to slip away from their trailers in periods of low visibility, and storms were likely to separate pickets from their blacks.

More and faster patrol boats were obtained by acquiring seized craft having the characteristics necessary for Coast Guard use, which had the additional benefit of assuring that they would not fall into the hands of their former owners or other rum-runners. The boats taken into the Coast Guard were given CG numbers—800–999 for those over 40 feet, and 8000–9999 for smaller craft—and although a few of these were so useful that they were retained after prohibition had ended, most were too small for offshore work.[30] The courts released many arrested vessels on bond, however, with the result that a number were seized repeatedly, only to return to their former occupation within a short time.

Knowledge of smugglers' practices and plans were invaluable, and an intelligence office was established at Coast Guard Headquarters under Lieutenant Commander Charles S. Root, to gather, evaluate, and disseminate information pertaining to these. Officers of the operational commands undertook their own intelligence-gathering through various contacts in their areas, placing greater faith in these sources than in the customs and prohibition officials from whom they received occasional warnings of intended landings.[31]

The use of radio was an important facet of intelligence activity for both sides of the rum war. Blacks listening in on Coast Guard frequencies obviously could gain useful information regarding patrol boat locations and movements, so Navy codes were used until the larger service expressed concern that they might be compromised by too regular use. The Coast Guard then developed codes of its own, with the help of the noted Army cryptographer, Major William F. Friedman, and his wife. Some divisions devised their own simple ciphers for patrol boat use as well.[32]

The blacks used plain language radio transmissions at first, and when they began to use codes, the Coast Guard had to become involved in cryptanalysis. Elizabeth Friedman at Headquarters and Lieutenant Frank M. Meals in the specially equipped *CG 210* handled the intercepts at first, and radiomen showing an aptitude for such work were trained as the need increased. In December 1930, the commandant informed the Eastern Division commander that the first Field Intelligence Unit would be established in New York under Meals's direction. Four 75-footers with high-frequency radio receivers and experimental high-frequency radio direction finders were attached to the unit to aid in traffic interception and to locate the blacks and the illegal shore stations with which they were communicating.[33]

Yet another means of gaining information was the airplane, one of which was borrowed from the Navy in 1925 and operated from Gloucester, Massachusetts. This single-engine, single-float Chance Vought biplane was effective enough to convince Admiral Billard that more were needed, so he obtained an appropriation of $152,000 for the purchase of five aircraft in 1926. Three of these were Loening OL-5 amphibians, the first aircraft built specifically to Coast Guard order, and the other two were Chance Voughts.[34] Thus, Coast Guard aviation owed its renaissance to prohibition; hereafter it would become an increasingly important part of the service, although its development was very gradual.

On 21 September 1927, the commandant met with forty officers ranging in rank from captain to ensign, at the Academy to consider the smuggling situation. Inspector in Chief Wheeler, Intelligence Officer Root, and Communication Officer Edward M. Webster accompanied him from Headquarters, while the others, with the exception of the superintendent and another officer from the Academy, were all directly involved in prohibition enforcement. Admiral Billard began the meeting by praising the work that had been done: "I have got the feeling that we have got the job about nine-tenths done; what we want to do is to mop up."[35] Then the admiral listened as each of the officers described his own role and suggested changes in current practices. Unfortunately for the historian, the latter part of the discussion dealt with confidential matters, so the recorder was excused. In the absence of a complete record, one can only state that whatever Admiral Billard's expectations, little of significance seems to have resulted from this conference.

So the rum war continued, with the blacks continuing to display a good deal of ingenuity in concealing liquor in secret compartments and adopting new tactics such as the use of smoke screens to evade trailing patrol boats. This was extremely unpleasant because inhalation of the fumes often made the Coast Guardsmen violently ill, requiring hospitalization in some cases, and leading the commandant to investigate the possibility of prosecuting the owner of a boat with smoke-making apparatus installed.[36]

Even more alarming at first sight was the apparently increasing propensity of blacks to collide with trailing destroyers and patrol

The 165-foot patrol boat Hermes *not long before World War II.*

boats at night. At least seven such collisions occurred in 1930–32, but in each the Coast Guard vessel suffered only slight damage while two of the blacks sank.[37]

Meanwhile, the older destroyers were nearing the end of their useful lives, and some questioned whether they should be replaced. Captain Wheeler, whose responsibility included a study of their effectiveness, argued that the destroyers' lack of maneuverability made it impossible for them to trail blacks until patrol boats could relieve them—five blacks had been "lost after dark" by destroyers on 1 and 2 January 1930 alone. Indeed, Wheeler asserted that "there is not a single actually recorded case of a destroyer turning over a trail to an offshore patrol boat. It would appear that the present day tactics of the rumrunner have largely, if not absolutely, eliminated the usefulness of the destroyer as an anti-rum craft, in the North Atlantic."[38] To those who insisted that the destroyers' speed made them essential, the captain responded that destroyers on patrol averaged 15.2 knots, and even higher patrolling speeds would be of little value in view of their inability to turn blacks over to patrol boats. He recommended that larger patrol boats capable of at least 15 knots be built to replace the destroyers. These would be much more economical in terms of fuel and maintenance, and the destroyer complement, usually five officers and eighty-four men, could man several such vessels. Wheeler urged that commissioned officers be assigned to as many patrol boats as possible, because he was convinced that most warrant officers and chief petty officers could not be relied on to operate them efficiently.[39]

But larger patrol boats would take time to design and build, so when seven worn-out 742 tonners were returned to the Navy late in 1930, five of the larger flush-decked, four-stack destroyers, all completed after World War I, were transferred to the Coast Guard in their place. The remainder of the "flivvers" and the 1,000-ton *Downes*, decommissioned in the spring of 1931, were not replaced, but the flush-decker *Semmes* was obtained in April 1932, just before two more older ships were laid up. The end of prohibition in 1933 found the Coast Guard still operating fifteen destroyers, but seven had to be returned to the Navy within a few months for want of funds to maintain them. The remaining eight followed in the spring of 1934, marking the end of the Coast Guard's "destroyer decade."

By that time, however, a number of new cutters and eighteen of the larger patrol boats advocated by Captain Wheeler had been commissioned. A board of officers had decided on the characteristics of the latter soon after the inspector in chief had presented his first memorandum to the commandant. They thought that diesel-powered 130-footers capable of 17 knots would suffice, but the designers found it necessary to enlarge the vessels to 165 feet to obtain the required speed and endurance.[40] The first of them was christened the *Thetis* when launched in November 1931, apparently in honor of the ex-whaler stricken in 1916, and this led to the adoption of names from Greek mythology for all of her sisters, an interesting departure from the usual Coast Guard practice. Lightly built, crowded, and uncomfortable at sea, these handsome vessels— some had two stacks, others one—turned out to be effective trackers. Guided to the blacks on bearings provided by the direction finder-equipped "six-bitters," they could make contact and hold it, their twin rudders providing superior maneuverability and their powerful searchlights illuminating the blacks in any but the thickest weather.[41] Only nine of the eighteen were commissioned before the end of prohibition, however, so their contribution was small.

Faster inshore patrol boats were built as well, of which the six wooden 78-footers of 1931 were the best known. But they attained their 22-knot speeds at the expense of endurance, and the fact that no more were built implies that the fuel consumption of their gasoline engines was considered too high.

Reviewing the situation as of 30 June 1933, Headquarters reported that:

> . . . the activities of the organized international smuggling syndicates continued as in previous years on all coasts of the United States from Maine to Florida, from Florida to Texas, and from California to Washington. The continued pressure of Coast Guard preventive measures was a potent factor in reducing the volume of the smugglers' business and in bringing about a change of smuggling technique, particularly along the seacoast adjacent to contiguous foreign countries where the Coast Guard surface patrols forced the smugglers in many instances to take to the air; and

airplane smuggling along the southern seaboard and the coast of California increased by leaps and bounds.

On the eastern seaboard the liquor continued to be shipped in bond from Canadian distilleries to St. Pierre where it was loaded on foreign rumrunning vessels, mostly British, which proceeded to the coast of the United States, from Maine to Virginia, where the cargo was transferred to high-speed American contact boats, or to cargo carriers of ostensibly legitimate coast-wise steamship companies and introduced illicitly into the various United States ports. There were about 90 foreign vessels engaged exclusively in this contraband trade on the eastern seaboard. Hundreds of specially constructed high-speed motor boats, fishing vessels, and coast-wise vessels were employed in attempting to unload the cargoes of these foreign hovering vessels. . . .

On the seaboard of the southern states from Virginia to Florida, smuggling was carried on constantly between Bermuda, the Bahamas and West Indies, and the United States by foreign vessels, domestic vessels, and airplanes.

On the Gulf Coast there were 36 foreign vessels engaged exclusively in bringing contraband cargoes from Belize, British Honduras, and Cuba. . . .

On the Pacific Coast contraband cargoes were introduced . . . from mother ships anchored off the Mexican coast which transferred cargoes to high-speed Canadian vessels, which in turn transferred the cargoes to American contact boats . . . or landed the cargo directly on the United States coast.[42]

That somber appraisal described the final months of prohibition and indicates that the smuggling of liquor was continuing on a lavish scale despite a decade and more of efforts to bring it under control. No doubt this reflects in part the ineptitude of some of those attempting to suppress rum running, but with an ever-increasing number of people in the United States willing to abet the smugglers and the syndicates amassing profits that enabled them to invest in faster vessels and more sophisticated equipment, it is likely that the most efficient governmental agents could not have succeeded in coping with them.

No mere analysis of the means and methods used by the Coast Guard can give a clear understanding of the service's participation in the rum war. Perhaps a description of some of the occurrences and vicissitudes incidental to that participation may help to do so.

CHAPTER EIGHT

SOME INCIDENTS OF THE PROHIBITION ERA

*T*he Coast Guard's decade of prohibition enforcement was marked by a number of incidents, some of which reflected favorably on the service while others did not. Several of these involved loss of life, inevitable because of the authorization to fire into fleeing rum-runners. Three smugglers who refused to heave to were killed in as many separate incidents off New York in 1924, and five men died in the Miami vicinity in 1926 and 1927, one of whom was shot while trying to ram a Coast Guard boat and another in a fight on board a picket boat, in which he accidentally killed a Negro companion before he himself was shot. The sole casualty on the Pacific coast occurred in 1928 when a rum-runner, jettisoning her cargo to increase her speed, ignored the patrol boat *Imp*'s repeated orders to stop. Three fatalities were reported on the Canadian-American border, of which two were in boats and one in an automobile.[1] The last caused a public outcry.

When their cutters were inactive because of ice on the Great Lakes, armed Coast Guardsmen were detailed to patrol the frontier to intercept smugglers. Early on the morning of Sunday, 6 May 1928, Jacob D. Hanson of Lewiston, New York, refused to stop when hailed by a uniformed Coast Guardsman. The latter fired two shots into the ground, but Hanson drove on toward the border, ignoring the order of a second enlisted man farther up the road. Thereupon, the sailor aimed at a tire and fired—the bullet splintered the automobile's windshield, inflicting wounds from which Hanson died almost four months later. Telegrams and letters protesting this "unwarranted attack" on a respected citizen deluged congressmen, and some of these in turn introduced legislation that would require certain armed employees of the government to post bond to satisfy judgments against them for injuries inflicted by careless or illegal use of their firearms. Coast Guard and Treasury officials reacted strongly, with the latter pointing out that there clearly had been no intent to harm Hanson, who may have tried to run one of the men down, and that

Coast Guardsmen enforcing customs laws on the international boundary were required to use force if necessary.[2]

The next incident had international repercussions. The *Wolcott*, a 100-foot patrol boat based at Pascagoula, Mississippi, was drifting near Trinity Shoal buoy, a favorite rendezvous off the Louisiana coast for blacks and their contact boats, when she sighted a two-masted auxiliary schooner at 6 A.M. on 20 March 1929. Boatswain Frank Paul rang up full speed on both engines and closed the schooner, which displayed the British red ensign and was identified as the *I'm Alone*—the *Wolcott* had picketed her in the same vicinity some months before. The weather was hazy, but Paul reckoned that the schooner was 10.8 miles offshore—her master would later claim that she was 4 miles farther out—and ordered her to heave to. Her master refused, so the *Wolcott*'s gun crew fired three blank charges to no effect. Six of the Coast Guardsmen volunteered to board the *I'm Alone* despite her master's assurance that boarders would be shot, but Paul declined because the patrol boat was already shorthanded.

The two vessels stood seaward for several hours, during which a passing steamer was asked to log their position to confirm Paul's estimate. Finally, the schooner's master indicated that Boatswain Paul might come on board alone and unarmed. A half-hour's discussion revealed only that the master, a former Royal Navy officer, would not demean himself by "surrendering" his ship to an American under any circumstances. Repeated warnings were ineffectual, so at 2 P.M., the *Wolcott* fired blanks from her 3-inch gun and shifted to service ammunition five minutes later, while rifle and machine-gun fire kept the schooner's men below. Whether the patrol boat's gunnery was pathetically inaccurate or she was merely trying to frighten the black into submission is not apparent; at any rate, after twenty-three minutes of deliberate shooting at close range, a projectile stuck in the gun muzzle and could not be removed. Thereupon, the *Wolcott* informed her division commander of the situation and fell back to trail the *I'm Alone*.

The two ships continued to the southward through the next day, and although the schooner was said to be 2 knots faster, she seems to have made no effort to evade the patrol boat. The latter's sister *Dexter* was sighted on the morning of 22 March, and after conferring with Paul, her officer in charge, Boatswain A. W. Powell, ordered the schooner to stop. Repeated hails brought no response, so the *Dexter* opened fire while the *Wolcott* prepared to send a boarding party should the black heave to. But her master remained obdurate, and efforts to dismast the schooner proved fruitless, so the *Dexter*'s gun was depressed. A shell soon tore a large hole in the *I'm Alone*'s hull below the waterline forward, and her crew abandoned ship as she sank. All were picked up by the patrol boats, but one man was unconscious when brought on board the *Wolcott*. Artificial resuscitation was continued for almost three hours, to no avail.[3]

The sinking of the *I'm Alone* some 200 miles offshore brought immediate denunciation from Britain and Canada—and from France, because the one casualty was of French origin. After a lengthy discussion, the matter was referred to a Canadian-American joint commission, which in 1935 concluded that the internationally recognized doctrine of hot pursuit did not apply, so the sinking was illegal. The United States formally acknowledged its error and paid $25,000 to the Canadian government in restitution. The schooner's men were awarded $25,666.50, but the owners of ship and cargo received no compensation because she had been employed in violation of American law "by a group of persons acting in concert who were entirely, or nearly so, citizens of the United States."[4]

After six years of negotiation, most Americans had probably lost interest in the *I'm Alone* case, which was as well, for the terms of its settlement seem very unsatisfactory. The commissioners held that the doctrine of hot pursuit did not apply because the *Dexter*, which sank the schooner in international waters, had just come up with her. Yet the *Wolcott* had trailed the *I'm Alone* continuously from her original sighting within an hour's steaming distance of the coast and was close at hand when she sank, which would appear to be an adequate example of hot pursuit. Even less acceptable is the finding that the master and crew "were not party to the illegal conspiracy to smuggle liquor into the United States and sell the same there."[5] The American commissioner conceded a good deal in the interest of Canadian-American amity.

The notorious *Black Duck* incident occurred nine months after the *I'm Alone* sinking. The *Black Duck* was a fast motorboat that had outrun inshore patrol boats on a number of occasions before she took a cargo from a British-registered black and headed into Narragansett Bay by the East Passage during the night of 28 December 1929. Boatswain Alexander C. Cornell, who led all of his fellows in number of seizures, was guarding the East Passage that night, with his *CG 290* darkened and tied up to the Dumpling Rock bell buoy. Early the next morning, Cornell detected the sound of muffled engines and then sighted an unlighted motorboat standing in. When illuminated by the *CG 290*'s searchlight, she was recognized as the *Black Duck*, and part of her cargo was plainly visible on deck, so Cornell used the required procedure to identify his command and ordered the motorboat to stop. When she increased speed instead, the boatswain directed that a machine-gun burst be fired close aboard. As the gunner fired, the *Black Duck* turned hard left and the bullets hit her pilothouse. She disappeared into the patchy fog, only to reappear a short time afterward and bump alongside the *CG 290*.

When the Coast Guardsmen boarded, they found two men dead, a third dying, and a fourth wounded in the arm. After administering first aid and transferring a sack of liquor to his boat as evidence, Cornell sought medical assistance at nearby Fort Adams and then reported to his superior at New London's Section Base 4.[6]

The killing of three men in the *Black Duck* brought widespread public condemnation, especially in the New England area. Protest meetings were held in Boston, where recruiting had to be suspended for a time, and some Coast Guardsmen on liberty in New London were attacked by irate citizens. The Hearst newspapers demanded Admiral Billard's resignation, while Secretary of the Navy Charles F. Adams added to the furor by ill-judged remarks intended to divert public hostility from personnel of his service.[7] But a Coast Guard investigation and special grand jury proceedings in Providence, Rhode Island, found Cornell and his men blameless, and the *Black Duck* was turned over to the Coast Guard to become the *CG 808.*[8]

The *Black Duck* was not the only liquor-laden vessel at Section Base 4 on Sunday, 29 December 1929. The 125-footer *Legare* had found the *Flor del Mar* of Halifax burning and abandoned off Block Island. After searching to no avail for her small boats, the *Legare* directed streams from her fire hoses into the blazing vessel and brought the fire under control some four hours later. By that time the *Flor del Mar* was in sinking condition, so the part of her liquid cargo that could be reached was transferred to the patrol boat, which towed her into New London, where she was kept afloat by a harbor cutter's pumps.

With the eager attention of myriad newspaper reporters and others focused on Section Base 4 because of the *Black Duck*'s presence, one might expect that the Coast Guard officers in charge of the base and of the Destroyer Force, of which it was a part, would have taken every precaution to assure that nothing untoward occurred. They did not. The Destroyer Force commander and his chief of staff departed early in the afternoon, as did the base commander, who had ordered his executive officer to have the sacks of liquor removed from the *Flor del Mar,* which seemed likely to sink at any time, and from the *Legare,* where they were a temptation to pilfering. The executive officer, a young lieutenant of no great ability, posted guards adequate for daylight hours, but winter darkness comes early to Connecticut and he did not seek additional guards. Those transferring the liquor wore bulky outer garments, in which bottles could easily be concealed, and the guards were too few to scrutinize all.

Thus, working parties returning to the destroyers *Ericsson, Shaw, Davis,* and *Fanning,* moored at the base, did not return empty-handed, and within a short time the Sunday night quiet was disturbed by the raucous shouts of happy and belligerent drunken sailors. Captains and executive officers were all ashore, and the junior officers remaining on board seem to have been taken aback by the disturbance. Only Lieutenant (junior grade) Miles H. Imlay showed any initiative, posting additional petty officers at the gangway of the inboard ship to search each man coming on board and advising other ships' ensigns to telephone their seniors while he tried to locate the source of the liquor. Apparently most of the senior officers could not be reached; only the *Davis*'s executive officer returned to his ship, but with the assistance of warrant and petty officers, he was able to restore order.[9]

All in all, it was a disgraceful episode that resulted in a good deal of unfavorable publicity, especially unfortunate in view of its timing. A board of investigation found the commanding and executive officers of Section Base 4 solely responsible and recommended that they be admonished. Admiral Billard concurred, although he felt that the Destroyer Force officers and most of those on board the destroyers should have shared the blame.[10]

Several Coast Guardsmen died in the course of the rum war as well, although their deaths were seldom noticed by the public. Chief Boatswain's Mate Carl Gustafson was the first, the victim of machine-gun fire while his *CG 237* was chasing a black off Montauk Point, Long Island, in April 1925. Two men from the cable ship *Pequot* were run down by a narcotics addict near Jacksonville, Florida, early in 1927—one was killed and the other crippled for life—and two more died in the *CG 249* incident six months later.[11]

On 7 August 1927, the *CG 249*, Boatswain Sidney C. Sanderlin, was ordered to convey Secret Service agent Robert K. Webster to Bimini in the Bahamas, where counterfeit American money was being used to purchase liquor. When 35 miles out of Fort Lauderdale, the "six-bitter" encountered a suspicious motorboat, which stopped only after several shots had been fired across her bow. Sanderlin found 160 cases of whiskey on board and arrested the two-man crew, Horace Alderman and Robert W. Weech, both of Miami. Assuring himself that neither was armed, the boatswain ordered them to the patrol boat, to which his men were transferring the liquor.

Sanderlin could not spare men to take the motorboat in and he could not tow her to Bimini without undue delay, so he went to his pilothouse radio to seek instructions. As the boatswain began to transmit his message, the two suspects entered the pilothouse and Alderman shot him in the back with a pistol he had apparently picked up after being searched. At that moment, Motor Machinist's Mate Victor Lamby came up from the engine room and started aft for a gun, only to be shot down by Alderman, who then armed Weech and forced the Coast Guardsmen to return the liquor to his boat. That done, he mustered the men and Webster on the motorboat's deck, announcing his intention to kill them all and burn the patrol boat, while his companion broke the *CG 249*'s fuel lines, allowing gasoline to run into her bilges. Weech's first attempt to ignite the gasoline failed, and then Alderman decided that his boat's engine should be started before the patrol boat was set afire. Weech had trouble with the engine, distracting Alderman momentarily, and his captives attacked him. Webster was killed instantly and the ship's cook was seriously wounded, but the others beat Alderman insensible and subdued Weech when he came on deck.

The survivors used the patrol boat's radio to summon aid, and both vessels were towed into Fort Lauderdale. Alderman and Weech were tried at Miami on charges of murder and piracy; after two years of legal maneuvering, during which Weech cooperated with the prosecution in return for a prison sentence, Horace Alderman was sentenced to death by hanging. The public was infuriated by the verdict, and he had to be hanged at Section Base 6, Fort Lauderdale, because local and state officials refused to carry out the sentence.[12]

That Alderman was a desperate man cannot be doubted, but whatever the sympathy one must feel for his victims, one must also note that Boatswain Sanderlin's own carelessness led to the tragedy. Presumably he was anxious to be on his way to Bimini and so had all of his men except the unfortunate Lamby engaged in transferring the liquor cargo, yet Webster should have been willing to guard the rum runners while Sanderlin communicated with his base. And Alderman could hardly have concealed or obtained a weapon had those in the CG 249 been even relatively vigilant.

More traditional enemies—storms and floods—also took their toll during this period. Fort Lauderdale's Section Base 6 and the Biscayne Bay station were demolished by the hurricane of 18 September 1926, which killed 372 people, 250 of them in the Miami area, and drove the station ship Moccasin and patrol boats CG 247 and 248 ashore. Upon receiving news of this tragedy, Admiral Billard organized a relief force under Commander Hamlet, consisting of the Seneca and the destroyers Downes, Shaw, Cassin, and Patterson, for dispatch to Florida, ordering the Manning, Tallapoosa, Yamacraw, and Saukee to report to Hamlet for service in the devastated area as well. Personnel of stations in the vicinity joined the cutter and destroyer sailors in aiding hurricane victims, patrolling the stricken section to maintain order, improvising hospitals, searching for those still missing, and assisting local authorities in countless ways.[13]

The spring of 1927 brought the worst flooding in the valleys of the Mississippi River and its tributaries known to that time. The Coast Guard's flood relief efforts involved 674 officers and men manning 128 of the service's vessels and boats as well as forty other craft. These ferried almost 44,000 people and 11,000 head of livestock to safety, distributed food, clothing, medicine, and forage provided by the American Red Cross, transported laborers and materials for levee repair, and cruised some 5,000 miles inspecting levees. Federal, state, local, and Red Cross officials, reporters, and photographers viewed the flooded areas from Coast Guard boats, which also brought physicians to isolated villages and transported those requiring hospitalization, including twenty-two smallpox cases. Needless to say, the Coast Guardsmen were not alone in their efforts—the Army, Navy, Lighthouse Service, Coast and Geodetic Survey, Mississippi River Commission, and municipalities adjoining the inundated region sent men and equipment, but the Coast Guard's organization and experience made its contribution the more notable.

Occasionally Coast Guardsmen themselves are the objects of Coast Guard rescue efforts, as in the northeast gale that battered Cape Cod early in 1927, claiming the CG 238 and her eight-man crew. The 75-footer was patrolling 8 miles off Plymouth, Massachusetts, during the afternoon of 19 February, when rising wind and sea

A newly completed "six-bitter"—the CG 290, 249, *and* 238 *were almost identical.*

caused her to head across the bay to seek shelter in Provincetown. The officer in charge, unfamiliar with those waters, did not realize the strength of the ebb tide, which swept the patrol boat around the cape and out to sea. Attempting to regain the bay, the *CG 238* approached the outer breakers near the Highland Coast Guard Station and anchored about 3 miles offshore to await better weather. The wind continued to increase from the northeast, however, and a heavy snowfall reduced visibility. At 6 P.M. the station lookout sighted a flare and a blinker light signaling the boat's number and SOS. After burning a Coston signal in response, the station watch reported the *CG 238*'s situation to the district commander, who promptly informed Eastern Division headquarters in Boston.[14]

Four ships were immediately available: The 178-foot cutter *Tuscarora* and the 742-ton destroyers *Paulding* and *Jouett* were anchored in Boston's President Roads waiting for the weather to moderate before going on patrol, and the *Redwing* was riding out the gale about 80 miles north of Cape Cod. On receipt of radio orders, the ex-minesweeper headed for the scene, but the wind and sea increased to the extent that she had to heave to before midnight. The old *Tuscarora* was the first to leave Boston, pitching heavily as she left the sheltered roadstead, and once at sea she could make little headway against the gale. Midnight found her hove to off Minots Ledge, little more than 12 miles to the southeastward.

The destroyer crews took time to secure boats and deck fittings with extra lashings before weighing anchor. Both ships found it difficult to leave the crowded anchorage in the gale, and the *Jouett* had to anchor twice to avert collision. Once at sea, the destroyers rolled heavily, shipping green water, and ultimately they too found it impossible to proceed.

With the larger vessels experiencing such difficulty, one can hardly imagine what the night must have been like for those living through their final hours on board the *CG 238*. The patrol boat began to drag toward the beach at about 2:30 A.M., 20 February, and apparently parted her anchor chains some two hours later. She broached and capsized on the outer bar, breaking up within fifteen minutes. Two bodies were found in the mass of wreckage on the beach; there were no survivors.[15]

Sunday, 20 February, was a horrible day for those attempting to assist the doomed vessel as well. The *Tuscarora,* smallest and least powerful of the four, was hard put to avoid a fate similar to that of the *CG 238*. She lost one boat and had another smashed by the heavy seas, and she had to resort to hand-steering when a wheel rope parted later in the morning. The old cutter managed to reach Provincetown that afternoon.

The *Redwing* was less fortunate—or more. Soon after noon, a wave breaking on board threw her motor launch against her radio shack, damaging both and leaving both radio sets inoperable. Then a manhole plate on her fantail went adrift, flooding the rudder quadrant compartment, whence water poured into the after hold. Seas washing over the deck made it impossible to replace the plate, and to make matters worse, there was no provision for pumping the hold. As it filled, water entered the berthdeck, where sailors standing chest-deep labored incessantly to control the flooding by bailing. Both main and auxiliary feed pumps broke down that night, but the engineers, traditionally known as the black gang, got the first repaired in time to keep the boilers steaming. The *Redwing,* fantail awash, made Boston in the early afternoon, 21 February.

The destroyers fared even worse. The *Paulding* spent 20 February hove to in a whole gale—force 10—laboring heavily and taking green water fore and aft. In the course of the morning, her forward lifelines and anchor davit were flattened, and the jack staff was carried away, releasing the chain stoppers as it went. The anchors remained secured to the billboards, but the chains ran out to the bitter ends. Small boats were swept away or damaged, forward compartments were flooded, and that night the forward smokestack went over the side when a guy parted, doing a good deal of damage to deck fittings and the motor sailer as it fell. The deck force rigged a stay to support the number two stack and secured a tarpaulin over the gaping hole in the deck, no mean feat in that weather. Number three stack tottered when its port guy snapped, but a preventer tackle was rigged promptly to keep the stack upright, which was just as well because the after fireroom boilers were in use. The *Paulding* took advantage of a lull just before midnight to come about and ran back to Boston before the wind and sea, mooring in the navy yard at 7:20 A.M.

The *Jouett* battled wind, sea, and heavy snow to reach Cape Cod at 12:30 A.M., 20 February, when her whaleboat and both davits carried away, leaving a large hole in the deck over a fuel tank, from which oil spewed as she rolled. She hove to, but mountainous seas broke over her fore and aft, washing away deck gear and smashing a dory. Four hours later, steam pressure fell because of salt water in the fuel oil, and the old broken-decker lurched into the trough where she rolled violently. Her black gang raised steam a half-hour later, and she headed into the gale once more. After a few hours of relative respite, a stop valve gasket blew out, filling the engine room with steam. Without power, the *Jouett* fell into the trough again, pumping oil overboard with a handy billy (portable pump) in an effort to lessen the impact of the seas. Repairs required two hours, by which time she had been driven uncomfortably close to the lee shore.

Her struggle continued through the night—the chain locker filled with sea water, decks leaked copiously, the gale shredded canvas gun covers, and large hailstones smashed the bridge windows. Salt water in the fuel oil put out the boiler fires again the next morning, but the gale was diminishing by that time so the loss of power was not as serious. The *Jouett* reached Boston at 1 P.M., 21 February, drifting into the anchorage when her fuel oil pump broke down.[16]

The board investigating the loss of the *CG 238* concluded that with one exception, everyone involved in the effort to save the patrol boat and her crew had done his utmost. The Second District commander, who had accepted the opinion of the Wood End Station crew that its lifeboat could not be launched in the sea that was running in Cape Cod Bay, should have insisted that the attempt be made, because "material counts for nothing when weighted against the possibility of saving life." The board recommended that Commander Thomas A. Shanley of the *Tuscarora*, Lieutenant Commanders John S. Baylis and John Trebes, Jr., of the *Paulding* and the *Jouett* respectively, Chief Boatswain Oscar Vinje of the *Redwing*, and their officers and men "be commended for their devotion to duty, valor, and fine seamanship . . . in circumstances of great danger to themselves thus fearlessly upholding the traditions of the service."[17] One cannot but agree; the survival of the four vessels in New England's worst storm in more than a generation was due almost entirely to those sailing in them. Repairs to the *Jouett* required two months, and the *Paulding* remained in the navy yard a month longer, mainly because her surviving stacks were found to be in extremely bad condition.

Less than six months later, the *Paulding* returned to the navy yard to be repaired after a collision on 17 December 1927. She had completed a sweep of her offshore patrol area earlier that day and was identifying vessels in Cape Cod Bay during the afternoon, running at 18 knots in order to finish the task before darkness fell. It was a cold, windy day, and the destroyer's lookouts had been stationed in the pilothouse to escape the spray thrown up as she knifed through the heavy white-capped swell. Approaching Provincetown, Lieutenant Commander Baylis stepped into the chartroom and was looking at the chart when he heard the officer of the deck order the rudder right full. Running into the pilothouse, he saw "an object resembling a couple of spars or stakes close aboard under our port bow."[18] They were the periscopes of the USS *S-4*, a submarine that was crossing the *Paulding*'s bow as she surfaced. Baylis ordered the engines backed full speed and sounded the general alarm—then the destroyer's bow rose as it slashed into the submarine just forward of the latter's deck gun.

The *S-4* sank at once, and the *Paulding*, which stopped only after a third of her length had passed over the submarine, began to settle rapidly as her forward compartments filled. Sending her lifeboat to search for survivors, Baylis had the other boats prepared for lowering should it be necessary to abandon ship and backed the destroyer slowly into the harbor while her men pumped and bailed. By what he termed "almost superhuman efforts," they kept her afloat until holes had been plugged and manhole covers shored, after which the bilge pumps freed the crew's compartment of water.[19]

Meanwhile, the fleet tug *Wandank* and a boat from the Wood End Coast Guard Station had joined the *Paulding*'s lifeboat in its search—in vain, for the only survivors were trapped in the *S-4* some 100 feet below. The lifeboat returned to the destroyer three hours later with its men almost frozen; most had not taken time to don warm clothing. Divers from the submarine salvage ship *Falcon* located the sunken submarine within a short time, thanks to the anchor buoy the *Paulding* had dropped to mark her position, but the weather was so bad that nothing could be done to save the six submariners who had survived the collision itself. The *Paulding* remained at anchor in Provincetown until 22 December, when the weather moderated enough for the *Tampa* to tow her to Boston stern first. As she passed the site of the collision, the *Paulding* half-masted her colors in mourning for the forty who had died in the *S-4*.

The loss of the second American submarine in little more than two years—the *S-51* had been sunk in collision with a coastal steamer off Block Island in 1925—attracted a good deal of attention, and the Senate subcommittee on naval affairs joined the two services in investigating the tragedy. The Navy court of inquiry found that the *S-4*'s commanding officer and Lieutenant Commander Baylis were jointly responsible "and that serious blame was incurred by them," the latter because he had kept an inadequate lookout and should have been aware that submarines running trials submerged were likely to be encountered off Provincetown.[20] The secretary of the navy disapproved the finding with regard to the *S-4* commander, because no one could know what had occurred in the submarine just before the collision.

The Coast Guard board of investigation, on the other hand,

exonerated Baylis, holding that periscopes "painted in war color" were supposed to be nearly invisible in a sea condition such as that prevailing in Cape Cod Bay on 17 December. Moreover, the harbor chart merely showed a measured mile adjacent to the fairway, making no mention of its use by submarines, nor had the *Wandank* been flying the signal specified when a submerged submarine was in the vicinity. In addition, the Navy's own doctrine required submarines operating at periscope depth to keep clear of surface vessels; and if the surfacing *S-4* were considered a surface vessel, she would have been the burdened ship under the Rules of the Road. The board concluded by praising Baylis for his efforts to aid possible *S-4* survivors even as his own ship seemed likely to sink.[21]

After an exhaustive investigation, in the course of which Treasury Secretary Mellon and Admiral Billard strongly defended Lieutenant Commander Baylis—"one of the most efficient, competent, and experienced seamen" the commandant had ever known—the Senate subcommittee agreed that whatever the reasons, the submarine had been responsible for the collision.[22] In order to forestall criticism in the event of a future disaster, however, Mellon insisted that Coast Guard vessels carry lookouts aloft and that destroyers patrolling at night show the proper running lights.

The next serious collision involving a Coast Guard destroyer occurred five years later. The flush-decker *Herndon* was patrolling at reduced speed—15 knots—in a dense fog some 60 miles southwest of Montauk Point, Long Island, on 15 January 1932. She was sounding the required fog signals, and when Commander Charles G. Roemer heard a steamer's whistle blast off the destroyer's port bow at 12:44 P.M., he had her engines stopped. The next signal was much closer, so both engines were backed at full speed and the *Herndon* had considerable sternway when the bow of the collier *Lemuel Burrows* crunched into her forward fireroom, penetrating 5 feet and tearing a hole 25 feet long in the shell plating before the collier backed away and disappeared in the fog.

The fireroom and all compartments forward of it filled rapidly, but the bulkhead between the two firerooms was undamaged and the watertight door connecting them was closed at the time of the collision. Thus, the *Herndon* did not sink. Her situation was very precarious nonetheless, for she had been steaming on the forward boilers and so lost all power when the fireroom was flooded. Moreover, her radio equipment was disabled and she had no means of summoning assistance.[23]

The *Lemuel Burrows* sent a boat in search of her unknown victim and attempted to reach her by radio, to no avail. The *Herndon*'s radiomen, spurred by a report that the ship was settling, worked feverishly to repair a transmitter, and using the gasoline auxiliary power plant, they were able to send a distress signal a half-hour after the collision. The cutter *Acushnet* was ordered to the destroyer's assistance from Woods Hole, but the *Lemuel Burrows* located her

first, towing the *Herndon* to Montauk Point, whence the *Acushnet* took her to New London.[24]

Although responsibility for the collision clearly rested with the collier, almost three years passed before the Mystic Steamship Company paid the government's claim against the *Lemuel Burrows*. The delay was caused in part by the Steamboat Inspection Service investigators' finding that at the time of the collision the headway of the *Burrows* "had been almost, if not entirely stopped," a conclusion that led a Coast Guard officer to remark tartly that if such were the case, the *Herndon* must have been "traveling sidewise with sufficient speed to cause the damage, which, of course, is absurd."[25]

The Coast Guard obviously had its share of adventures with the destroyers, but on the whole the ships were handled competently, especially when one considers that few of their officers and men had any previous service and that the old vessels often kept the sea in adverse weather conditions. Although the first to be commissioned reflected the inexperience of those overhauling them—the *Henley, Jouett, Cassin,* and *Downes* required major repairs within a year—those that followed benefited from the lessons learned in the first few and were in much better condition when they entered service.[26] And while a number suffered the usual minor damages in the occasional grounding or rough landing, the only serious mishaps that can be attributed to their personnel were fires.

The destroyers had at least twelve oil fires during their first five years of operation by the Coast Guard. Some were minor and were

The flush-deck destroyer Semmes *was one of the* Herndon's *sisters. These vessels repeated the numbers of those they replaced; the* Trippe *had been the earlier CG-20.*

extinguished quickly; others endangered the ships. That in the *Ammen* in 1926 was among the more dangerous. The 742-tonner was steaming well offshore in a moderate sea when a fuel-oil line broke near a boiler furnace. The oil ignited and the flames spread so rapidly that the watch had to leave the fireroom without shutting off the fuel pump, which continued to force oil into the conflagration. Within a short time, the main deck plates over the fireroom were red hot. The remote control steam-smothering valves on deck could not be opened, either because of the heat or neglect, and efforts to seal the fireroom were thwarted by intermittent explosions that blew the stack covers off. With the hot deck plating and the state of the sea making it impossible to lower boats, members of the crew were mustered by liferafts fore and aft in the expectation that the 1,200-gallon fuel tanks on either side of the fireroom must explode. But the *Ammen* was lucky—one of the steam-smothering valves was finally forced open, and the fire was extinguished twenty minutes later. Raising steam in her after boilers, the old destroyer limped in for major repairs.[27]

The *Henley* was moored at her base in 1929 when fire broke out in a fireroom. It should have been controlled easily, but the engineering officer, a warrant machinist, and all four of his chief petty officers were ashore. None of those on board displayed any familiarity with the fire-fighting equipment, so the ship was damaged extensively before personnel from the shore put the fire out.

Reviewing the report of this occurrence, Engineer in Chief Robert B. Adams professed to be "at a loss to understand how such a state of affairs could exist on any vessel in the Coast Guard."[28] The commanding officer was relieved of his command, and the engineering officer lost his warrant. The situation was quite different when the *Patterson* had a fire a few weeks later. It was extinguished promptly, doing little damage, and Adams noted that "it is gratifying to see that some of our men know how to fight an oil fire."[29]

Part of the difficulty undoubtedly lay in the fact that the destroyers were manned on a minimum scale. Under way, the executive officer usually stood a regular watch and so had less time to devote to drills and training than would normally have been the case. To be sure, the junior watch officers alternated as officers of the deck in port so that the executive officer would be free for other duties, but too often outside matters intervened. Further, officers were shifted from one destroyer to another quite frequently, with a resulting loss of familiarity with individual ships and men. In the event of illness or leave, a vessel would simply have to operate shorthanded unless an officer were available from another ship—Lieutenant Commander Baylis, for example, made patrols in the *Wainwright* and the *Beale* while his *Paulding* was being repaired in 1927 and 1928.

Owing to the rapid expansion of the service, junior officers were promoted rapidly—for that day—spending only two years in rank before taking the examination for promotion; indeed, temporary promotion did not require an examination. And promotion brought added responsibilities, which in more normal times would not have been thrust on the officers until much later. As a result, a substantial number of admonitions, reprimands, and censures were incurred, but these seem to have had little effect on officers' subsequent careers. Nor was this peculiar to the Coast Guard. A number of naval officers—World War II Admirals Ernest J. King, Chester W. Nimitz, and Raymond A. Spruance among them—did not have unblemished records when they were promoted to flag rank.

Admiral Billard and his fellows were surely more concerned, however, about the possibility that Coast Guardsmen would succumb to the enticements offered by rum runners. They knew that customs officers had never been absolutely immune to bribery and that the profits realized from the successful landing of a liquor cargo enabled smugglers to offer sizable bribes. The service was the more vulnerable because of its expansion, although recruiters did their best to reject those likely to prove unreliable.

Corruption clearly did exist, although its extent cannot now be determined. In fiscal 1926, Coast Guard courts convicted eleven temporary warrant officers and twenty enlisted men "of corruption, or of taking bribes, or of improperly assisting liquor smugglers . . . *which is two-tenths of one per cent of the individuals in the Service."* Two more warrant officers, one a regular, and fifteen men were convicted in the next five months.[30] Reports for subsequent years were not located, and the lists of court cases in the *Annual Reports* do not indicate the offenses for which the individuals were tried. Whatever the reason, the *Annual Reports* no longer list court cases after 30 June 1928. In March 1930, Captain Wheeler, the inspector in chief, thought corruption of various types "absolutely the most serious problem," which was made worse by the inattention of officers in the field.[31] Unfortunately, his memorandum on the subject did not include detailed evidence to support his allegation.

In the absence of a thorough study of the extent of corruption in the Coast Guard during the prohibition period, which would be difficult at best because the indices to the records of courts-martial are incomplete and the records themselves are unavailable at present, one can only speculate that it came to involve more than the *"two-tenths of one percent"* of Coast Guard personnel reported in 1926. On the other hand, it was not sufficiently widespread to cause a public scandal, which those eager to embarrass the service surely would have brought about had there been an opportunity.

On that rather unsatisfactory note, this discussion of the Coast Guard's participation in the rum war must end, but one cannot take leave of Admiral Billard's period as commandant without considering occurrences therein that were not directly linked to the suppression of liquor smuggling.

CHAPTER NINE

THE COAST GUARD DURING THE BILLARD YEARS

Like most great leaders, Frederick C. Billard was sincerely interested in his men, those "who, perforce, must endure the hardships, privations, exposure, discomforts, and monotony attending the hazardous occupations and vigils of service at sea and elsewhere."[1] Realizing that the higher their morale, the more efficient they would be in performance of their duties, he initiated a "welfare" program when he became commandant, setting aside funds with which to provide a variety of types of recreational equipment to Coast Guard units. Remote stations received radios and phonographs, cutters on Bering Sea and ice patrol welcomed motion-picture projectors and films, and ships and stations alike got athletic equipment with which to field teams to compete with others in their vicinities. Through the assistance of the American Merchant Marine Library Association and private donations, libraries were established in most units.[2]

The League of Coast Guard Women, organized in November 1924 probably at the commandant's instance, was composed of service wives and mothers, other female relatives and friends of Coast Guardsmen, and those elected to membership because of their interest in the service. This group was to promote "the morale, contentment, and happiness of service personnel, by visiting and aiding the sick and distressed, by standing behind the men and being 'always ready,' in fulfillment of the motto and standards of the service with whatever form of good-fellowship, assistance, and kindliness the situation may require."[3] The admiral would express his appreciation to "these good women" each year in his *Annual Report,* considering that they made an important contribution to the maintenance of service morale.

Learning that some enlisted men had expressed an interest in educational courses, the admiral arranged with the Navy's Bureau of Navigation training division to make correspondence courses in a variety of subjects available to them. This proved to be a popular innovation, with over 1,200 courses distributed in the first year, so the commandant considered ways of enlarging it. The Marine Corps Institute extended its facilities to Coast Guardsmen in 1928 and became the model for the Coast Guard Institute established at New London under the direction of the superintendent of the Academy a year later. In its first two years, the Institute awarded 1,050 educational certificates and 299 International Correspondence School diplomas. It also assumed responsibility for grading examinations for advancement in rating of enlisted men, which provided a degree of uniformity heretofore lacking.[4] The Coast Guard certainly was not a leader in the educational field, but under Admiral Billard it began to catch up with the other armed services.

As a former superintendent of the Academy, the admiral had a good deal of interest in that institution also, and while he reported in 1924 that "the course of instruction given and the standards of discipline maintained leave little to be desired," the accommodations at Fort Trumbull were another matter—"the lack of proper buildings, good roads and walkways, and a suitable space for drills and athletics . . . is a profound discouragement to the school."[5] A number of those attending the Academy at the time would later question the adequacy of their training, but none would disagree with the commandant as to the physical facilities—they were disgraceful.

Billard had first called attention to the need for improved facilities while he was Academy superintendent in 1917, and he was to repeat his request annually after 1924, until in February 1929 Congress finally agreed that $1,750,000—a sum later increased to $2,500,000 on Secretary Mellon's recommendaticn—should be appropriated to construct a suitable Academy for the Coast Guard. The question of its location was settled when Admiral Billard joined the past and incumbent superintendents and leading Connecticut officials favoring New London, and the city purchased a tract of land adjacent to the Thames River, which it donated to the U.S. government for the school. The first buildings were designed under the direction of the supervising architect of the Treasury Department, and Mellon laid the cornerstone of Hamilton Hall on 15 May 1931.[6] Cadets returning from the summer practice cruise in September 1932 were the first to disembark at the new Academy, but Admiral Billard, who had brought its construction about, was not present to welcome them.

The acquisition of land and the construction of buildings thereon are only the first steps in the creation of an academic institution—even when as in the case of the Coast Guard Academy, it involves the transfer of an existing school. The course of instruction had been increased to four years in 1930, and perhaps most important, Captain Quincy B. Newman, the former engineer in chief, was appointed head of the Department of Engineering at the Academy. In this capacity, he revised the engineering curriculum thoroughly and designed the facilities to support it, sending his subordinates to obtain information from leading universities and industrial laboratories

Captain Quincy B. Newman.

The famous Bear.

across the country. Since all cadets had to take engineering courses—the distinction between line and engineer cadets had been abolished in 1926—a properly organized department was essential. According to one of his subordinates, however, Newman's influence went beyond engineering: "He did this for every single thing at the Coast Guard Academy. He put it together, and when we opened shop it all worked. And he's the man that did it."[7] At Newman's insistence, the engineering building was named McAllister Hall in memory of his predecessor as engineer in chief; none bears Quincy Newman's name.

Admiral Billard was also successful in obtaining new ships for the service. In addition to the offshore patrol boats built for the rum war, a replacement for the aged *Bear,* ten cruising cutters, and a smaller cutter to assist shipping on Lake Michigan were authorized, and all but the last were completed while Admiral Billard was commandant.

Whether a replacement for the *Bear* was actually required has been doubted. Engineer in chief McAllister had suspected that she was too rotten in 1909 to justify extensive alteration, and ten years later Naval Constructor Hastings at the Puget Sound Navy Yard thought her no longer safe for Arctic duty because "the wood is so old and spongy that it would be practi[c]ally impossible to put the ship in a thorough seagoing condition."[8] After the 1920 Arctic cruise, Captain Francis S. Van Boskerck reported that the *Bear* would require extensive repair annually and agreed with Hastings that she was not safe for Bering Sea and Arctic duty. Two years later, however, Commander Claude S. Cochran expressed the opposite view, believing that "the hull and machinery are in good condition and if properly cared for the vessel will be good for many years of Arctic service."[9]

As the superintendent of Construction and Repair and the engineer in chief saw it, the difference of opinion was due to the *Bear*'s massive construction, which made a thorough examination of her hull impossible except at excessive cost. But they agreed that Cochran's belief was based on "superficial knowledge" and that after fifty years of arduous service, the *Bear* must be replaced.[10] Commander Cochran responded that he had first joined the old ship in 1896 and with six years as navigator and executive officer and another six years in command, he could hardly be said to speak from "superficial knowledge." He conceded that the *Bear* had too little power to assist vessels in autumn gales, "but for ice work and the peculiar duties of the Arctic no better vessel can be found."[11]

The *Bear*'s experience in 1924 did nothing to strengthen Cochran's case, for she encountered the ice pack a week after leaving Unalaska on 31 May and spent the next five weeks trying to work her way through it to Nome. She succeeded finally, at the cost of two adjacent propeller blades and considerable rudder damage. The Arctic cruise had to be abandoned, but the crippled cutter made the passage from Unalaska to San Francisco in ten days, averaging 9 knots, which was nearly her maximum speed under any conditions.[12]

The next two years found the *Bear* performing her usual duties, reaching Barrow in August each year and experiencing no real difficulties. But her departure from Unalaska on 2 September 1926 marked the end of her forty years of Alaskan service, and the *Annual Report* included a "tribute to this distinguished ship," which ended: "The ravages of service and time have told on her. Her work is done. Her last cruise to the frozen regions of the North is made and she must go to the inactive list. This old ship will have a place always in the hearts of her shipmates and in the history of the service."[13] Nonetheless, Commander Cochran proved to be a truer prophet, for the *Bear* had an active career in future years, taking part in two Antarctic expeditions before World War II and spending almost three years with the Greenland Patrol during that conflict. She never sailed under the Coast Guard ensign after decommissioning in 1929.

Characteristics of the ship built to replace the *Bear* were determined by Construction and Repair after soliciting the views of forty-seven officers who had had considerable Arctic experience. The responses varied: most preferred steel to wood or composite construction, oil fuel to coal, and steam reciprocating engines to diesels or turbines. Six were quite emphatically opposed to sail rig, but most

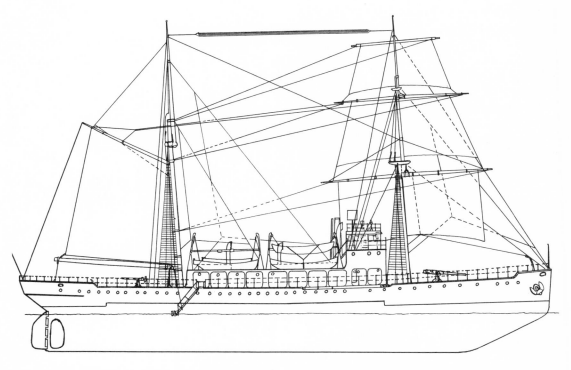

The Northland—*outboard profile.*

felt that it would be useful in an emergency. Opinions as to length ranged from 180 to 250 feet, power from 700 to 4,000 horsepower, and speed from 10 to 18 knots.[14]

The result was the *Northland,* a 216-foot steel vessel of exceptionally strong construction with hermaphrodite-brig rig. The officers' preference for reciprocating engines notwithstanding, she was propelled by two 600-horsepower diesel engines each driving a generator that provided current to turn a 1,000-horsepower motor directly connected to the single propeller shaft. This power plant, which obviously reflected Newman's predilection for electric drive, was adopted principally because of the greater cruising range made possible by diesels—there was no oil fuel to be had north of Unalaska, and no one seems to have expected much from her sail rig. A 4-inch 50-caliber single-purpose gun mounted on either side forward met the Navy's requirement for gunboat armament, but at 11 knots the *Northland* was a knot below the larger service's minimum speed for that type of vessel.

Like the *Bear,* the *Northland* was designed to navigate in heavy ice; unlike the *Bear,* she had some pretensions to being an icebreaker. Bilge keels were omitted from her design, despite her 15-foot draft, and most notably, her forefoot was cut away—from a point just above the waterline, her stem was slanted aft at a 245° angle until it joined the keel. The underwater portion of the bow was rounded, assuming a broad U shape.[15]

The *Northland* was built by Virginia's Newport News Shipbuilding and Drydock Company, the seventh and last cutter to be built there. Her construction was unusual in that electric welding was used to supplement the rivets in what was thought to be "for its size, the strongest and heaviest steel hull which has ever been projected."[16] When she was commissioned in May 1927, Commander John F. Hottel took her up the Potomac River to Washington, where her sail rig was admired by those who lamented the disappearance of sailing vessels. Then she proceeded to the Pacific coast by way of the Panama Canal, and in mid-August, the new cutter departed Seattle for her first Alaskan cruise.

The *Northland*'s performance was disappointing. She rolled deeply, due to the top weight of her heavy steel masts and spars and the absence of bilge keels; and under sail alone, she defied all efforts to hold a course, drifting to leeward whatever the wind conditions. Her staysails did serve a purpose—her spoon-shaped bow resulted in a loss of directional stability, and their steadying pressure made the ship easier to handle under power. Nor was the *Northland* successful as an icebreaker, for her bow's weight was distributed over too broad an area of ice surface when she forced her way onto it, which she lacked the power to do to any significant extent. Moreover, her diesel engines' cooling systems were often clogged by ice, with consequent delay when she was working through ice fields.[17]

But the most expensive cutter yet built for the Coast Guard—she cost $865,750—could not be dismissed as a failure; she *had* to serve. For the next decade, the *Northland* made her way northward each year, and in time she won the affection of at least some of those who sailed in her. Few, however, would have argued that she was a worthy successor to the *Bear*.

Admiral Billard had made it very clear that the acquisition of numerous naval vessels for prohibition enforcement did not satisfy the Coast Guard's need for additional cruising cutters. Secretary Mellon agreed, pointing out early in 1926 that the service had but sixteen vessels of the first class, including the *Bear* and such veterans as the *Algonquin, Gresham, Manning, Seminole,* and *Tuscarora,* all of which were well past twenty years of age. Only the four *Tampa*-class cutters were fully capable of any service that might be required of them, so the secretary urged passage of a bill to authorize the construction of ten first-class cutters to perform "important, difficult, and arduous work."[18]

Not everyone agreed that the Coast Guard should be charged with all of this work. T. A. Scott, president of the Merritt and Chapman Company, which had paid more than $1,000,000 for government salvage equipment after the war, objected that commercial salvors would be adversely affected were these ships put into service. He argued that since Coast Guard cutters towed disabled vessels free of charge, the latters' owners and masters usually refused the salvors' offers of assistance, preferring to await a cutter. Owing to this loss of business, the salvage companies had to curtail their operations, which could have serious consequences in the event of a gale in which the number of ships in distress exceeded the number of cutters available. In addition, Scott thought European underwriters the true beneficiaries of the Coast Guard's towing service; thus, the U.S. government was sponsoring a service that was driving American salvors out of business, for the ultimate benefit of foreigners.[19]

One assumes that Scott was not aware of the section of Coast Guard *Regulations* forbidding the activity of which he complained: "In extending assistance to vessels [the cutter captain] shall not interfere with private enterprise, though he may assist private effort, and it shall be his duty to do so when he deems it necessary. He shall not use his vessel for towing private craft, except in cases of distress, and not even then if there shall be other and sufficient assistance at hand; but he shall not permit undue advantage to be taken of a master whose vessel is in a perilous position or otherwise in distress."[20] Perhaps cutter commanding officers did interpret this regulation loosely on occasion, but Scott failed to provide specific examples, and his objection had no effect. Congress authorized the construction of the ten cutters in June 1926, appropriating money to begin the first three a month later.

The design of these ships reflected five years of experience with the 240-footers. Constructor Frederick A. Hunnewell cited reports that the *Tampa* and her sisters suffered heavy shocks when the steep seas typical of the waters off Newfoundland struck their counters, as a reason to provide a cruiser stern in the new design. He also abandoned the plumb bow in favor of a handsomely raked stem, which leads one to suspect that current fashion had some part in his decision. The 240-footers were rather wet when driving into a head sea, so the new vessels were to have somewhat higher freeboard with their bows flared considerably. To provide for greater power and endurance, they would be 10 feet longer and proportionately beamier than their predecessors. Their designed armament was also heavier—three 5-inch 51-caliber and two 3-inch 50-caliber guns—but they mounted only one of each in peacetime.[21]

Quincy B. Newman believed that in every important respect—initial cost, size, economy, reliability, and availability for service—his synchronous motor turbo-electric drive was most suitable for use in large cutters. Tests conducted during the *Modoc*'s trials, however, had revealed that about a third of the steam generated in the 240-footer's boilers was consumed by auxiliary machinery. This he thought "startling," so he set the Engineering Division to work seeking a way to reduce it. Newman dubbed the ultimate solution "the central electrical power station," wherein the main generator provided electrical current for most of the auxiliary machinery as well as for propulsion when it was operating at two-thirds power or more. A separate turbine-driven generator provided power to the auxiliary machinery at lower speeds or when the ship was maneuvering, cutting in automatically whenever the main generator fell below 40 cycles.[22]

The Lake-class cutter Champlain *soon after commissioning. Her 5-inch and 3-inch guns have not yet been mounted.*

At that time, some were predicting that the world's oil resources would soon be exhausted, and the use of pulverized coal to fuel marine boilers was thought to offer an economical alternative to black oil. Therefore, Hunnewell and Newman arranged fireroom and fuel tanks so that "conversion to coal would require no changes other than the installation of coaling chutes, bunker doors, and coal handling machinery."[23]

Another interesting feature of the design was the provision of a contra-propellor—horizontal fins attached to the rudder. Model tests indicated that it would increase propulsion efficiency considerably, but the contra-propeller was thought to cause the first cutter so fitted to vibrate badly when going astern, so it was removed.[24]

The first five ships were built by the Bethlehem Shipbuilding Corporation at Quincy, Massachusetts, and completed in 1928 and 1929. Named for American lakes, they were christened the *Chelan, Pontchartrain, Tahoe, Champlain,* and *Mendota.* They performed very well on trials, approaching 17 knots at 3,000 shaft horsepower, and the *Chelan* had an early opportunity to demonstrate her towing ability. While at Bermuda on her shakedown cruise in the autumn of 1928, she was ordered to assist the New York state training ship *Newport,* which had lost her screw some 1,200 miles to the eastward. Coming up with the auxiliary barkentine three days later, the new cutter sent a boatload of fresh provisions and then took her in tow, making almost 10 knots until a gale forced Commander Ralph W. Dempwolf to slow to half-speed for a time. Nonetheless, the *Chelan* towed the *Newport* 1,500 miles to New York in less than eight days.[25]

The remaining cutters were built to almost the same design, the main difference being a slightly larger fireroom. The General Engineering and Drydock Company built the *Itasca, Sebago, Saranac,* and *Shoshone* in the old Union yard at Oakland, California, while the *Cayuga*, the last to be completed, was launched from the United Drydock yard at Staten Island, New York, in October 1931.

These were very successful ships. Commander Thaddeus G. Crapster reported that the *Mendota* could maintain 17 knots almost indefinitely. She was somewhat lively when steaming at a fair rate of speed in a rough sea, but with proper handling, he thought she could be comfortable in any sea condition. "She is not perfect but so far in advance of the other ships I have been on as to preclude any comparison." And the ebullient Raymond L. Jack wrote that his *Shoshone* could "do anything but dance the tango and she would probably do that if we had the proper music."[26] With some reason, Hunnewell and Newman exchanged congratulations—the latter thought that the new "Lake-class" cutters would be "forty year ships" without requiring major expenditure and looked forward to their inspection by marine engineers in 1968.[27] For reasons that he could not foresee, however, none would reach her thirtieth birthday.

The final cutter of the Billard era was a heavier, beamier version of the 165-foot *Ossipee* and *Tallapoosa* of 1915. Intended to break ice on Lake Michigan, she had heavy plating at the bow and waterline, but with criticism of the *Northland* fresh in his memory, Hunnewell designed a more nearly conventional bow with the forefoot cut away only moderately. Probably because of her size, Newman's successor as engineer in chief, Captain Robert B. Adams, decided to try the geared turbine in this ship, which was named the *Escanaba* when launched at Bay City, Michigan, late in 1932. She was successful enough to be followed by five sisters, all named for earlier cutters—the *Algonquin*, *Comanche*, *Mohawk*, *Onondaga*, and *Tahoma*—in 1933–34, and the designs prepared for the next large cutters included geared turbines.[28]

One other matter concerning cutters was decided during the Billard period—that of fitting them into the standard list of letter-designators adopted by the Navy in 1920. The larger service seems to have wanted to use Navy designations according to the cutters' characteristics, but Admiral Billard wished to have Coast Guard units clearly distinguished from their Navy counterparts. He accepted the letter *W* for all Coast Guard vessels early in 1926.[29] Although the literal meaning of this *W* has been the subject of a good deal of speculation, it seems likely that it was chosen for no better reason than that there could be no confusion as to its meaning—its only other appearance in the Navy's list was as *YW*, district water barge! And fifteen years would pass before individual cutters were assigned *W*-number designations.

The International Ice Patrol had been reestablished in 1919, and the cruises of the *Androscoggin* and the *Tallapoosa* that year were the first to be directed by the Interdepartmental Board on International Service of Ice Observation, Ice Patrol, and Ocean Derelict Destruction established by President Wilson in the autumn of 1916.

This board, which included the Coast Guard commandant, the hydrographer of the Navy, and the heads of the Weather, Standards, and Fisheries bureaus, was to prepare a systematic program of scientific observations to be carried out by the patrol cutters and to receive and publish the reports of the observers.

The 165-foot cutter Algonquin. She and her five sisters were handsome little vessels—and among the Coast Guard's less successful.

Initially, the scientific observer (the Coast Guard hydrographer) embarked in the first cutter to sail each year and remained in her throughout the patrol period, a practice that obviously resulted in an incomplete series of observations. In 1922, however, a scientific observer and an oceanographer sailed in the *Seneca* and on completion of her ice-observation cruise, they were transferred by small boat to the *Tampa*, which began the ice patrol itself. As the cutters relieved one another, the observers were transferred, remaining at sea during the entire patrol period.[30] In succeeding years, the duties of scientist and oceanographer were performed by one Coast Guard officer, whose nerves must have been tested on those occasions when rough seas enlivened the transfers.

The establishment of the Coast Guard Oceanographic Unit, staffed by two scientists, one of whom was a civilian, and six enlisted men, at Harvard University in 1923 marked an increased interest in oceanography, as did the assignment of Lieutenant Edward H. Smith to graduate study in the subject at Harvard. On the recommendation of the Interdepartmental Board, Smith was ordered to Norway in 1924 to work with V. Bjerknes, a meteorologist whose theories were used in computing the directions and velocities of underwater ocean currents, and with Norwegian oceanographers. Returning to the United States in 1925, Smith published *A Practical Means for Determining Ocean Currents* (CG Bulletin No. 14) and then sailed as observer in the *Tampa* when she began the 1926 ice patrol, estab-

Lieutenant Commander Edward H. "Iceberg" Smith on board the Marion.

lishing new observation procedures that had been approved by the Interdepartmental Board.[31]

In 1928, Lieutenant Noble G. Ricketts took Lieutenant Commander Smith's place as scientific observer, and when the *Modoc* returned to Boston late in June, he volunteered to sail in the 125-foot patrol boat *Marion,* which Smith was preparing for an oceanographic survey of the waters between Labrador and the west coast of Greenland, seeking information on which to base predictions of iceberg movement.

With two officers, two warrant officers, and twenty-three men— six more than her normal complement—supplies and provisions for seventy days, and spare parts for every unit of machinery on board, the *Marion* was somewhat crowded even before she embarked the ice patrol cutters' oceanographic equipment. She left Boston on 11 July, paused briefly at Halifax, and put in at Sydney on Cape Breton Island's north shore where fuel and water tanks were filled and seventy-eight drums of diesel oil and gasoline were stowed on deck. At both Halifax and Sydney, Smith consulted mariners acquainted with the Labrador Sea and Davis Strait and acquired the latest charts of their coasts.

Departing Sydney on 16 July, the patrol boat stood northward through the Gulf of St. Lawrence at 6 knots, using only one engine to conserve fuel. She traversed the narrow Strait of Belle Isle between Labrador and Newfoundland in a dense fog two days later, fortunately avoiding the fifteen icebergs reported therein, and began her survey work, in which Smith and Ricketts, the only oceanographers on board, had been training their men since leaving Boston.

Basically, this consisted of pausing periodically, determining the ship's position by observation or dead reckoning and the depth by fathometer, and lowering sounding wires with water-sample bottles attached at intervals. When the wires had been paid out to the proper depth—as much as 3,450 meters—the bottles were filled and the wires were hove in by the oceanographic winches. Thermometers in the bottles indicated temperatures at the various depths, while the water samples themselves revealed the salinity. Bottom samples were obtained occasionally until the device used for this purpose was lost on 26 August. This process, which was called "taking a station," depended for its accuracy on the proper functioning of the bottles and on keeping the wires nearly vertical. The bottles caused much difficulty because there had been too little time to refurbish them after their transfer from the ice patrol cutters. The *Marion,* on the other hand, proved to be an admirable oceanographic vessel, keeping station even in bad weather by heading into the wind and going ahead on one screw or the other as necessary.

The first line of stations ended at Labrador's Battle Harbor, where her warrant machinist, whose chronic rheumatism had been aggravated by the sudden transition to cold, damp weather, was landed to await transportation to the United States. While there, her crew

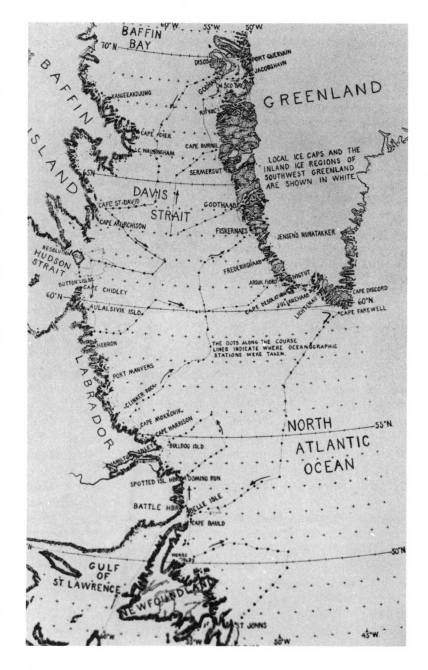

The track chart of the Marion *expedition.*

watered ship, passing buckets full on board from a stream while the ship's bow was held against the shore.

After a week working off the coast of Labrador, the *Marion* stood across Davis Strait toward the west coast of Greenland. On the night of 27 July, both winches broke down with 2,400 meters of wire in the water. This might well have terminated the expedition, for even if the equipment could be recovered, thousands of meters of wire could not be paid out repeatedly and then brought back on board without a winch. Despite the conditions—wet, dark, and rough—the wire was got to the anchor windlass, which required three hours to heave it in. Meanwhile, the spare winch was dismantled and its drum hoisted atop the deckhouse to replace that which had been broken. By the next morning, the wire had been wound back onto the drum, so one winch was operational again.

Danish officials radioed permission for the *Marion* to visit Godthaab, the capital of South Greenland, and she stood in on 31 July. Liberty was granted that night, after which a winch drum was repaired ashore while by dint of hard labor with tackles and crowbars, the sailors lifted the two-ton spare winch onto the deckhouse in place of that disabled beyond repair. They then watered ship, and the *Marion* departed Godthaab that evening.

She sounded her way north for four days, until a gale forced her to seek a sheltered anchorage just above the Arctic Circle. On 7 August, her men counted 100 icebergs in Disko Bay as the *Marion* approached Godhavn, North Greenland's capital, where the natives gave a dance for her crew while the officers were entertained by Danish officials. The last provided fresh water and—to Smith's surprise—diesel oil. Henceforth, his vessel could run at 9 knots, using both engines.

Again, one day of relative relaxation sufficed. The patrol boat crossed Disko Bay to Jacobshavn and Port Quervain, where all but a few ship keepers hiked inland to the edge of Greenland's ice cap. After completing a line of stations north of Disko Island, she returned to Godhavn to top off her fuel and water tanks while a soccer team of Danes and natives bested the "Marions" 26–0 in a pouring rain.

The *Marion*'s passage toward Baffin Island's Cape Dyer was interrupted by pack ice 30 miles offshore, and after vainly seeking a lead for two days, she turned southward in Davis Strait, making Cape St. David unexpectedly at 1 A.M. on 18 August. Fortunately, the fathometer warned of the cape's presence 20 miles northeast of its charted position. She ran a line of stations to mid-strait and then turned westward again, making Resolution Island at the entrance to Hudson Strait, which separates Baffin Island from Labrador, on 20 August. After coasting south to Rama, Labrador, the *Marion* ran a 450-mile line across Davis Strait to Arsuk Fjord, Greenland, which she ascended to Ivigtut, site of the cryolite mine that was Greenland's chief source of wealth.

The usual entertainment, diesel oil, and provisions were provided during an overnight stay, but when the *Marion* headed seaward in the evening of 29 August, she encountered a gale that kept her at anchor under Mt. Kungmat for three days. Then she stood southeast to Cape Farewell, Greenland's southern extremity, whence a 620-mile line of stations was run to Belle Isle. Deeming it unwise to enter the Strait of Belle Isle because of the bad weather, Lieutenant Commander Smith decided to put in at St. John's, Newfoundland, for

The Marion, *conducting an oceanographic survey off the Jacobshaven Glacier on 8 August 1928.*

liberty and supplies, running two unscheduled lines of stations off the Newfoundland coastal shelf on the way.

An autumn storm delayed her briefly, but the *Marion* reached Newfoundland's principal seaport and capital on 11 September. She departed the next day, running homeward before a northeast gale with both engines turning at full speed and staysails set to add their bit. The patrol boat arrived at New London 18 September, after spending a night at Vineyard Haven, her commanding officer's home town.

For those sailing in the 125-footer, the expedition had been a trying experience, for they had worked incessantly to complete the survey before autumn gales and ice made it impossible to continue. As her executive officer described it:

> The station work, coming as it does night and day, gale and calm, rain and shine, is no child's play either for those on deck or those at the motors. It requires alertness and knowledge of a ship to hold her up at a station on a dark night with the wind howling and 3,000 meters of wire out. . . . we had seen whole series of observations down to 3,100 meters repeated three times, just because waves, or other patience-trying accidents had caused the premature tripping of the instruments.[32]

To this work, repeated almost endlessly, one must add the lack of diversion on board an over-crowded small vessel and the monotony of sea rations, supplemented by whale meat, seal, polar bear steaks, and of course codfish—it is not surprising that the romance of Arctic adventure had faded somewhat by September.

In terms of scientific accomplishment, the *Marion* had traversed a 450,000-square sea mile area between St. John's and 70° North latitude, taking 191 oceanographic stations, with some 2,000 observations of temperature and salinity. Numerous bottom samples were procured, and 1,700 soundings were added to charts of the area covered.[33]

The *Marion* expedition revealed that pack ice had a direct influence on the drift of icebergs. Heavy ice in the Newfoundland and Labrador shelf waters prevented bergs from being carried inshore with the cold water currents, thus leaving them to drift southward into the shipping lanes. In the absence of a sufficient pack ice "fender," on the other hand, the current bore the icebergs toward the coast until they grounded, which rendered them harmless.[34] Smith published a report to this effect in 1931. Then, using data collected by expeditions sent to the western North Atlantic and adjacent waters by other nations—Denmark, Norway, Germany, Britain, and France among them—together with those from the *Marion* expedition and subsequent cruises by the patrol boat *General Greene,* he and two associates, Floyd M. Soule and Olav Mosby, completed a work on the physical oceanography of Davis Strait and the Labrador Sea in 1937.[35]

The oceanographic work of the ice patrol cutters and the *Marion* led the Aeroarctic Society, an international group of scientists interested in the use of aircraft for arctic exploration, to add a Coast Guard officer to the scientific staff flying from Spitsbergen to Fairbanks, Alaska, and back in the German dirigible *Graf Zeppelin* in the summer of 1931. Lieutenant Commander "Iceberg" Smith was assigned to temporary duty in the dirigible, and then the plans were changed. Ultimately, she spent a week flying northeast from Leningrad, over the Kara Sea to Severnaya Zemlaya and back over Novaya Zemlaya, covering an area without special significance for the United States or its Coast Guard.[36] But Smith had made the acquaintance of leading scientists in his field, and he looked forward to an aeronautical survey of the west coast of Greenland, hoping that it might be undertaken by the *Graf Zeppelin* in the near future.

That was not to be, but the *Marion* expedition marked the beginning of a Coast Guard involvement in Greenland waters that would culminate in its domination of the Greenland Patrol established during World War II, which in turn led to an important expansion of the service's ice-breaking activity.

Admiral Billard's success in enlarging the seagoing branch of the Coast Guard was not equalled with regard to the shore stations and their floating equipment, although not for want of effort. Station crews operated lifeboats, which had to be launched from specially constructed ways into the sheltered waters of inlets, bays, and rivers, and surfboats that could be launched directly into the surf. Both types evolved from craft used by the old Life-Saving Service; indeed, a number of its boats remained in use in the 1920s. All lifeboats were self-bailing and self-righting, and by 1924 the 34-footers—those built before 1908—and 36-footers powered by gasoline engines were most numerous, although some smaller pulling lifeboats were still in service. The lighter surfboats included 26-foot self-bailing craft with gasoline engines, self-bailing 25-footers without power, and a variety of "open" boats with neither engines nor the capacity for self-bailing. All lifeboats and surfboats were built of wood at the Curtis Bay yard, known at this time as the repair depot.[37]

Lifeboat and surfboat designs were reviewed periodically with an eye to possible improvement, and the Board on Life-Saving Appliances scrutinized new designs presented for its consideration. In its 1920 report, its members expressed their confidence in the boats then in service, suggesting that more powerful engines and radio-telephone equipment be installed when they became available and stating that 36 feet was the maximum practical length for lifeboats.[38]

In June 1928, Oliver Maxam and District Commander Martin W. Rasmussen accompanied the commandant on a month-long trip to Europe, where they attended the International Congress of Maritime Coast Life-Saving in Paris, at which groups from eighteen nations were represented. Thereafter, the Americans visited stations and facilities of various lifesaving organizations—France's Central Society for Saving the Lives of Shipwrecked and its Humane Society for the Shipwrecked, the North and South Holland Life-Saving Service, the German Life-Saving Service, and Britain's Royal National Life-Boat Institution—each of which arranged demonstrations of equipment and techniques for the visitors.

Admiral Billard and his associates concluded that their service's equipment was generally superior to that of the European stations, while "the personnel of the American service measure[d] up well to that of the foreign stations visited," all of which were manned by volunteers.[39]

Despite this apparent satisfaction, the commandant convened a board of district commanders soon after his return, providing it with information on foreign lifeboats for comparison with the Coast Guard's small craft so that it could recommend improvements in the latter. After ten days of deliberation, the board recommended that designs for a larger lifeboat be prepared—preferably a diesel-powered 50-footer, but if a satisfactory engine was not available, a 45-footer with a gasoline engine. The district commanders thought that a more powerful version of the "excellent, able" 36-footer should be built as well.[40]

A year later, Billard reported that four boats had been built to a new 36-foot design "representing the latest and most modern developments in motor lifeboats."[41] These had proven satisfactory and more would be built, but the Coast Guard continued to need a larger boat, which could put farther out to sea and provide greater space and protection for those rescued. Construction and Repair began work on the preliminary design for a 50-foot boat early in 1932, but the fiscal constraint resulting from the Great Depression—and perhaps the absence of Admiral Billard—caused its construction to be deferred indefinitely later in the year.

Like his predecessor, Billard continuously pressed for funds to maintain some 250 Coast Guard stations during the 1920s, with indifferent success, appropriations for this purpose ranging from $200,000 in 1920 to $500,000 in 1929. By that time, many of the older stations were badly in need of renovation, being "inadequate, and without the modern facilities and conveniences and sanitary arrangements enjoyed in the present day."[42] The commandant was somewhat more successful in 1931 and 1932, when Congress appropriated $764,000 and $796,000, which seems to have alleviated the worst of the conditions complained of, although those of the lifesaving branch might have contrasted the latter figure unfavorably with the $2,400,000 designated for repairs to cutters, destroyers, and patrol boats in that year.

As his second term as commandant approached its final year, Admiral Billard decided that a reorganization of the Coast Guard was overdue. The organizational structure evolved under Ellsworth Bertholf had been adequate for a small service, but Billard thought that the rapid expansion of 1924–25 had revealed several deficiencies. The press of other duties, however, had made it impossible to undertake a careful study when these became apparent. On 9 January 1931, the commandant appointed Captains Herman H. Wolf, William H. Munter, and Leon C. Covell and Commander Russell R. Waesche to a board headed by Captain Randolph Ridgely, Jr., to scrutinize "the duties, responsibilities and problems that confront the Coast Guard as a whole, and of its resources in personnel and material, and recommend the best organization for carrying out efficiently the work of the Service. . . . the organization should be efficient, practical and in accord with military principles." Members of the board were to take every opportunity to discuss the matter with their fellows "of appropriate rank and experience" before convening at Headquarters on 2 March 1931.[43] A month later, District Commanders Simon R. Sands and Martin W. Rasmussen were ordered to report to Captain Ridgely when the board convened, to advise it on matters pertaining to the Coast Guard districts.[44] They were not, however, appointed to membership on the board.

The officers composing the board began their deliberations by considering in turn the Coast Guard's mission, the conditions and problems that had to be overcome to accomplish the mission, and the means available for its accomplishment. Having defined these, they concluded that the field forces should be reorganized in accordance with certain principles: Authority and responsibility should be decentralized but clearly established, and each major function should be carried out in accordance with a basic plan under the direct control of one man. The board recommended that the land and water areas of the United States be divided into Northern, Southern, Western, and Eastern areas, each of which would be subdivided into divisions and other activities within its boundaries. The area commanders were to be primarily operations officers, responsible for the performance of the Coast Guard's mission by the forces under their command. They would meet at least twice each year with the assistant commandant and other officers appointed by the commandant and would constitute a planning board for the service. Certain activities—the Academy, the Coast Guard yard, the International Ice Patrol, the Cadet Practice Squadron, the cable ship *Pequot,* the Coast Guard Institute, and the Permanent General Court—were exempted from area control, reporting to the assistant commandant. Forces afloat in the Eastern Area—Maine to Cape Hatteras—were organized into task groups, but ships in other areas usually operated singly so no similar organization seemed practical for them. The board recommended a few changes in station and base sites and in cutter home ports, although generally it held that such matters were beyond its cognizance.[45]

Had these recommendations referred only to the cutter branch of the service, they should have caused little controversy. But the board, adhering to its principle of firmly fixed authority, recommended that the district commanders be subordinated to the officers commanding the divisions in which their districts were located. District Commanders Sands and Rasmussen demurred vigorously, pointing out that the lifesaving branch had functioned efficiently for fifteen years and that most of their fellows were satisfied with the existing situation. They did not doubt that the expansion of the seagoing branch necessitated changes in its organization, and they admitted that cooperation between divisions and districts could be improved. But they argued that

> ... the Life Saving Branch consists of personnel who are specialists in their particular line of work. For this reason command of this personnel should be kept in the hands of officers who are familiar with this duty and qualified by experience to administer the affairs of the district in a satisfactory manner. The Life Saving Branch of the Coast Guard is a humanitarian organization composed largely of an enlisted personnel native to the locality in which they are enlisted. To a considerable extent they are familiar with the coast line and have had experience with small boats before enlisting into the Service. Changing the fundamental principles of the organization will disrupt the Service and cause its primary purpose to be lost sight of.[46]

Sands and Rasmussen saw in the board's proposal the danger that the lifesaving branch would lose its separate identity, which they believed was contrary to the intent of Congress as expressed in the legislation that had created the Coast Guard. To prevent this, they urged that a board composed of district commanders be convened to consider reorganization of the lifesaving branch, should the commandant think it desirable. Meanwhile, they recommended that the pay and status of surfmen and district commanders be improved and that training schools especially for surfmen be established in the various districts.[47]

Nonetheless, the board stood by its recommendation, although it forwarded a letter containing the district commanders' views with its report, which was completed on 13 March. Admiral Billard, however, took no action to implement it, probably because he thought it unwise to undertake a major reorganization that might lead to bitter controversy in the final months of his second term as commandant. Nor was anything done after he was appointed to a third four-year term in January 1932, presumably because his health deteriorated during the spring. The fifty-eight-year-old admiral died of pneumonia on 7 May 1932.

Frederick Chamberlayne Billard must rank with the greatest commandants of the Coast Guard. He had guided his service through a very trying period, presiding over an unprecedented expansion and attempting to deal with the herculean task of prohibition enforcement without neglecting his service's traditional responsibilities. His concern for his subordinates won their affection, and he dealt effectively with the Treasury Department and Congress. Throughout, Admiral Billard was concerned lest his service's reputation be sullied by its involvement in the rum war, and he continually impressed on his officers, most of whom he knew personally, the necessity for impeccable conduct and a close attention to those serving under them. He himself seemed indefatigable; his closest associates were convinced that he had literally worked himself to death.

CHAPTER TEN

DEPRESSION, DANGER, AND DEVELOPMENT, 1932–36

Admiral Billard's unexpected death left Secretary of the Treasury Ogden L. Mills with the difficult problem of choosing a successor. Although Mills had been associated with the Treasury Department as under secretary since 1927, he had little knowledge of the Coast Guard when he succeeded Andrew Mellon in February 1932, and he had not had the opportunity to become acquainted with many senior officers since becoming secretary. Nonetheless, Mills moved quickly. He conferred with the assistant commandant, Captain Leon C. Covell, and the two senior captains, Benjamin M. Chiswell and Harry G. Hamlet, both Billard's classmates at the School of Instruction, and then nominated Hamlet to be commandant.

The 58-year-old Hamlet was an officer of distinguished appearance and record. His gunboat *Marietta* had rescued the forty-seven-man crew of the minesweeper *James* when she sank in a Bay of Biscay storm in 1919, winning him a gold lifesaving medal, and he had supervised the fitting out of the Coast Guard destroyers at the Philadelphia Navy Yard before commanding the Destroyer Force for two years. Since 1928, he had been superintendent of the Academy, overseeing the construction of its new facilities. Perhaps equally important, he had the support of the officers at New London and of a number elsewhere.

Hamlet had his opponents as well, among them Captain Chiswell, who thought him unqualified to be commandant, and not wishing the position himself, urged Mills to nominate Commander Russell R. Waesche instead.[1] Waesche shared Chiswell's opinion of Hamlet, but he agreed with other friends that his own want of rank and seniority would be a serious handicap. Thus, he backed Hamlet—and asked for a cutter command, hoping to absent himself from what might be a calamitous four years.[2] He had predicted, however, that Hamlet would surround himself with able officers, and the new commandant began by appointing Waesche his aide.

The immediate problem facing Rear Admiral Hamlet was that of

Harry Gabriel Hamlet, commandant, 1932–36, pictured as a vice admiral during World War II.

reduced appropriations resulting from the Great Depression, which led inevitably to a diminution of the Coast Guard. Much of this was carried out in accordance with the proposal for the reorganization of the field forces put forward in 1931. Hamlet submitted the proposal, slightly modified, to Secretary Mills, who gave his approval in September 1932, and it was implemented in January 1933. Six bases were closed permanently, and fifteen lifesaving stations, ten of them in the New England and New York-New Jersey area, were inactivated. Numerous prohibition-enforcement vessels—7 destroyers, 111 75-footers, and 58 picket boats—were decommissioned, and within a short time the appointments of 170 temporary warrant officers were to be revoked (most were assigned to duty with the Civilian Conservation Corps instead), and 1,600 enlisted men were discharged. Many of those retained in the service were reduced in rating. As a result, annual expenses were reduced by some 25 percent. Even after these reductions in personnel had been effected, however, the Coast Guard had more than 400 commissioned officers, 500 warrant officers, and 9,000 enlisted men.[3] Quite clearly, there would be no return to the situation of a decade earlier.

The Depression had led Congress to enact measures in 1932 and 1933 looking to the reorganization of executive departments within the government in the interest of increasing economy and efficiency and eliminating duplication and overlapping. Given the Coast Guard's unique situation, its status was bound to be scrutinized, and President Franklin D. Roosevelt was unlikely to have abandoned his earlier belief that the Coast Guard should be a part of the Navy.

The first rumors of transfer began to circulate soon after Roosevelt's inauguration on 4 March 1933, and in April Congressman Carl Vinson proposed that the Coast Guard obtain its officers from the Naval Academy henceforth and that the smaller Academy be closed. This proposal was the more startling because the new Coast Guard Academy had been opened less than a year before and the process of making it a degree-granting institution had been initiated. Treasury Secretary William H. Woodin responded sharply that the service had had its own officers' school for more than a half-century, that it had been important in establishing tradition and esprit de corps, and that its abolition would be a serious blow to morale. Woodin thought that little economy would be realized were the Coast Guard Academy closed; thus, Vinson's true purpose probably was to provide for Naval Academy graduates who could not be commissioned in the Navy.[4] Admiral William V. Pratt, chief of naval operations, showed no enthusiasm for the proposal, going beyond it to counsel caution in the whole matter of the Navy's relationship to the Coast Guard: "I believe that sometimes consolidation may work exactly to the opposite effect from what its purpose is, and I have always stood for the principle that the Services devoted to the national defense should effect their readjustments among themselves. . . ."[5] But Admiral William H. Standley, who succeeded Pratt within two months, was to show more interest in acquiring the Coast Guard, or at least part of it.

Admiral Hamlet and his subordinates at Coast Guard Headquarters did not wait for notification that the president was officially considering transfer of their service to the Navy Department. They produced memoranda on the subject early in June, restating the arguments for keeping the Coast Guard under Treasury control that Commodore Commandant Bertholf had presented so eloquently in 1919 and developing new ones as well, among them the fact that smuggling activity was clearly increasing, the approaching repeal of the Eighteenth Amendment notwithstanding, and that Coast Guard vessels would be subject to treaty limitations were the service transferred to the Navy Department. As far as economy was concerned, the Coast Guard budget was less than half that of New York City's police department, so no significant saving could result from transfer.[6]

During the autumn, Hamlet met with the president and Secretary Woodin at Hyde Park for a discussion of Coast Guard matters and then submitted another statement on the subject of transfer, reiterating earlier arguments against it together with a concise statement of the most likely danger:

> The paramount duty of the Navy, as stated in its fundamental policy, is preparation for war and maintenance of the fleet in being; all other duties are sacrificed to this end, and properly so. Should the Coast Guard and its duties be transferred to the Navy, it is obvious that this Service and its duties would be sacrificed, if necessary to maintain the Fleet in readiness for war. If appropriations were not sufficient to maintain the Fleet and carry out the duties assigned to the Navy Department, those activities which have no direct bearing on readiness for war would be sacrificed first, and the duties of the Coast Guard would fall within this category. The best officers of the Navy would properly be assigned to purely naval duties, so that the less efficient officers would be assigned to Coast Guard duties. As a result, the performance of Coast Guard duties would be on an equivalent scale.

Hamlet concluded with an assurance of loyal support by the Coast Guard whatever the president's decision.[7]

Ill health forced Secretary Woodin's resignation in November 1933, and Roosevelt appointed his close friend and associate Henry Morgenthau, Jr., to replace him. This probably benefited the Coast Guard because Morgenthau was no more desirous of giving up the service than Woodin had been and he was closer to the president personally.

Nonetheless, the transfer seemed almost assured when a committee was formed "to consider the question of administration of the Coast Guard, if the latter should be transferred to the jurisdiction of the Navy Department. . . ." This committee, which consisted of sixteen naval officers, nine Coast Guard officers, a Public Health Service surgeon, and two civilians from Coast Guard Headquarters, met on 26 December 1933 with Rear Admiral Cyrus W. Cole as senior member. A week later it presented a series of recommendations, of which the most important was that the Coast Guard have a position in the Navy Department analogous to that of the Marine Corps, with its own commandant. Owing to the short time allowed it, the committee deferred for later consideration most of the administrative problems that would be involved as well as the question of the Coast Guard Academy's future.[8]

The Coast Guard members of the committee, almost all of whom were stationed at Headquarters, must have helped to prepare Admiral Hamlet's next document on the matter, which was devoted largely to demonstrating that there would be little in the way of saving were the transfer carried out. Then the joint committee was reconvened to address this subject directly, and it predicted annual savings of not more than $46,527. On the other hand, it pointed out that the expense of moving Coast Guard Headquarters to the vicinity of "Main Navy" on Constitution Avenue would be considerable.[9]

For those at Coast Guard Headquarters, the situation must have been reminiscent of that some fifteen years earlier, when Carter Glass and Ellsworth P. Bertholf had fought successfully to bring about the Coast Guard's return to Treasury control. On that occasion, however, most of the service's officers—Harry Hamlet among them—had opposed their commandant, as had a large part of the shipping community. In 1933–34, almost no one in the Coast Guard seems to have wished to "join the Navy," while the American Steamship Owners' Association informed the president of its strong opposition to any change in the Coast Guard's status.[10] Maritime interests generally agreed, fearing lest the service's "high state of efficiency" suffer under the Navy's control.[11]

Congress also became involved, in part because of the efforts of North Carolina Congressman Lindsay C. Warren, whose district had more Coast Guard stations than any other in the country. On his election to the House of Representatives in 1924, Warren had been surprised to find that very few members had any knowledge of or interest in the Coast Guard. He soon developed a close relationship with Admiral Billard and others at Headquarters and made himself a spokesman for the service, responding to criticisms arising from prohibition enforcement and arguing the case of those in the life-saving branch especially.

On 12 January 1934, Warren headed a delegation consisting of Representatives Schuyler Otis Bland of Virginia, Stephen W. Gambrill of Maryland, and Robert L. Bacon of New York—the last a Republican—which met with President Roosevelt, and speaking for sixty fellow congressmen, urged him not to carry out the contemplated transfer. Roosevelt received the group cordially, and while he made no commitment, Warren soon concluded that the Coast Guard would remain under the Treasury Department.[12] There was no official statement to that effect to quiet rumors, however, so the transfer continued to seem inevitable.

One area of controversy between Navy and Coast Guard came up in the joint committee's discussions, and its outcome helped to prolong the suspense. This had to do with the Coast Guard communication system, which had been developed to meet the need of the rapidly expanded service. This was largely the work of Lieutenant Commander Edward M. Webster, who had served as communications officer at Headquarters since his retirement for physical disability in 1923. Lest it be thought that this was a simple task, one should note that procuring enough radiomen for ships and bases was only the beginning; it was also necessary to devise doctrine and procedures for a variety of contingencies. Webster began with a copy of the Navy's radio manual and modified it according to the dictates of experience, keeping all units informed by periodic communications bulletins and initiating a series of studies of communication aspects of distress cases in order to identify weaknesses and failures of the system. He modestly attributed his success to luck—whatever the reason, the Coast Guard communication system came to function very well, with occasional problems attributable to inexperienced personnel.[13]

The Navy showed little concern until the Coast Guard decided to install intermediate frequency transmitters at shore radio stations for emergency use on the international distress frequency. The Navy argued that this practice duplicated its own coastal radio system and that since 1904 it had been responsible for coordinating all radio traffic relating to distress cases. Webster responded that the 1904 directive had been superseded by a statement of policy prepared by the Interdepartmental Radio Advisory Committee in 1924, which left each executive department free to determine these matters according to its needs. So far as economy was concerned, the transmitters were those removed from decommissioned cutters, and personnel already assigned to the Coast Guard radio stations operated them. Thus, there was no additional cost, nor would confusion result from their use because they would transmit only when the delay necessitated by relaying messages through a naval radio station was unacceptable.[14]

There the matter stood until the joint committee took it up at the end of 1933. Naval members of a subcommittee on the subject recommended that the Navy take over control of the Coast Guard communication system to save some $32,000 annually, and the Coast Guard representative—Lieutenant Commander Webster—disagreed, anticipating that the saving would be less than half as much and asserting that the Coast Guard must be "the sole and final judge of the communication facilities it required and their locations . . ." even if it became a part of the Navy.[15]

Admiral Standley presented the Navy's view in hearings before the Director of the Budget in the spring of 1934, and Admiral Hamlet finally conceded that the Navy should have an opportunity to prove its point by taking over a section of the Coast Guard communication system and operating it for two years.[16] Hardly had the commandant agreed to this when the Treasury Department expressed its desire to postpone the experiment indefinitely, citing "certain additional duties" that might be assigned to the Coast Guard as the reason.[17] But Standley would not let the opportunity pass, and on 28 June 1934 Secretary Morgenthau decided that stations from Maine to Cape May, New Jersey—the Navy had hoped for all north of Washington, D.C.—should be transferred.[18]

The reaction among Coast Guard officers was very unfavorable. Lieutenant Frank T. Kenner, who was assigned to help with arrangements for the transfer, found it "truly a heart-breaking job. . . . It seems to me that it is just a step, toward a complete merger."[19] Less than a month after the agreement, Assistant Commandant Covell urged Morgenthau to cancel it because of the increased smuggling activity reported in the New York area, but to no avail. And in August, Randolph Ridgely, Jr., the Coast Guard's senior captain, believed that the service's transfer to the Navy Department was imminent.[20]

In all likelihood, however, the danger had already passed. Commander Waesche, who was probably as well informed as any, thought the transfer "a dead issue" in the autumn, and although rumors continued to circulate almost a year later, he wrote that the service's position had never been more secure. He continued: "The cat with nine lives is a piker compared to the Coast Guard. You can kick this old service around, tear it to pieces, scream from the house-tops that it is worthless, ought to be abolished or transferred to the Navy, have the people in it fighting among themselves and working at cross purposes and it bobs up serenely bigger and stronger than ever. What wonderful wonders could be accomplished if everybody pulled together!"[21]

Nor did the Coast Guard lose its radio stations permanently. Within a short time after the transfer, Covell reported that the Navy was having difficulty meeting its communications responsibilities, with consequent detriment to Coast Guard operations, and when the two-year trial period had expired, the larger service gladly returned the stations to the Coast Guard. Soon thereafter, Treasury and Navy departments agreed that each service should "establish, maintain, and operate such communication facilities on shore as may be necessary for efficient communication between its own units and with vessels and aircraft in distress. Where the communication facilities of the Navy or the Coast Guard can be made to serve adequately the requirements of the other, existing facilities of the Navy or Coast Guard will not be duplicated."[22] So Lieutenant Commander Webster had been vindicated—but by this time he had retired from the Coast Guard to join the Federal Communication Commission.

It should not be assumed that the relationship between Navy and Coast Guard was strained as a result of these developments. Individuals such as Webster and Kenner, who were directly involved in the communications controversy, expressed their annoyance and fears privately, and others did what they could to prevent transfer by writing congressmen and those influential in maritime circles. But the two services continued to cooperate in various areas, Coast Guardsmen were trained in Navy schools as before, and the Coast Guard's supply and repair services were coordinated with those of the larger service. A Coast Guard commander was regularly assigned to the Navy Department as liaison officer, while the Coast Guard's role under the Navy in time of war received frequent consideration.

Naval respect for the Coast Guard was enhanced by the latter's ability to handle the destroyers, an example of which had occurred in the autumn of 1933. The Coast Guard's remaining eight destroyers had gathered at Hampton Roads, Virginia, for their annual gunnery practice, when conditions in Cuba deteriorated seriously. The Cuban economy, almost entirely reliant on the American market for sugar, had been hurt badly by the Depression, and the government of President Gerardo Machado y Morales responded to growing unrest by repressive measures, which inflamed the situation further. Machado was deposed by the Cuban Army, but the violence continued, leading President Roosevelt to order the Navy's Special Service Squadron to Cuban ports to protect the lives of foreigners. The one light cruiser and two destroyers composing that force were obviously too few ships for the task, so the Coast Guard destroyers and the cutters *Gresham, Yamacraw, Unalga,* and *Tuscarora,* all stationed at southern ports, were ordered to report to Rear Admiral Charles S. Freeman in the USS *Richmond* for duty in Cuba. The unrest subsided after two months, whereupon the Coast Guard vessels were released from naval control. Admiral Freeman stated that they had "operated with the associated vessels of the Navy smoothly and efficiently" throughout the deployment period, and he commented on the "high order of administrative and professional ability among the officers in command and a commendable state of training among all of the personnel."[23]

The destroyers were decommissioned and returned to the Navy six months later, and with prohibition having ended in December 1933, the future of the offshore patrol boats had also to be considered. Two of the 100-footers were transferred to the Navy Department, and the others went to the Great Lakes, as did four of the 125-footers. The remainder of the latter class were distributed among ports around the American littoral, with the *Marion* going to the Virgin Islands, the *Reliance* and the *Tiger* to Hawaii, and the *Morris* to Seward, Alaska. Several of these assignments had been recommended by the board on reorganization in 1931, among them that of the *Pulaski* to Marshfield (now Coos Bay), Oregon, where she was the first Coast Guard vessel to be stationed between the Co-

The 125-foot patrol boat Morris *at Seward.*

lumbia River and Humboldt Bay, California—a distance of nearly 400 miles! The presence of a cutter or patrol boat had some economic value, especially to a small town such as Marshfield, in that fresh provisions for her crew and such entertainment as the sailors might enjoy on liberty were alike purchased locally. And in time, of course, families of officers and men would reside in the vicinity of the home port.

Coast Guard units were involved in a number of important rescue operations during these years, among them those of the yacht *Uvira,* the Navy's dirigible *Akron,* the Norwegian motorship *Childar,* and the Ward liner *Morro Castle.* The first of these was an auxiliary schooner with a crew of twenty-two, bound from New York to Miami with four passengers on board. She ran into a storm two days out, and when her engines failed north of Cape Hatteras, the *Uvira* was in trouble. Just before noon on 13 February 1933, a Navy destroyer relayed her distress signal to the 250-footer *Pontchartrain,* cruising offshore for just such a contingency, and the cutter headed toward the reported position. Radio direction finder bearings on the *Uvira*'s weak and fragmentary transmissions indicated a different heading, so Commander Joseph F. Farley changed course, and the *Pontchartrain* drove into the heavy seas at full speed. A merchant steamer closer to the yacht offered to assist, but her effort to get a line on board failed, so she stood by until the cutter reached the scene. Daylight was fading by that time and snow driven by a full gale hampered visibility even more, but the *Pontchartrain*'s searchlights revealed the battered yacht rolling heavily in the trough. The cutter made her initial approach from leeward, the line-throwing gun was fired, but the projectile fell short. She was then worked around to windward, and Commander Farley headed her downwind to cross the *Uvira*'s bow close aboard, a difficult feat with heavy seas smashing against the *Pontchartrain*'s stern. The line-throwing gun was fired again as the yacht came abeam—the shot was true, and the cutter came about and lay to while the *Uvira*'s men hauled the shot line, a messenger, and finally an 8-inch hawser on board. When the last had been made fast, the *Pontchartrain* went ahead slowly, barely maintaining steerage way and holding the yacht's head into the sea through the hours of darkness. The seas moderated the next day, so the cutter increased speed gradually and brought her charge into Hampton Roads on the morning of 15 February. One of the *Uvira*'s passengers had been lost overboard two days earlier. The others and her crew owed their survival to the *Pontchartrain*'s timely assistance.[24]

The crash of the dirigible *Akron* off Barnegat Lightship just after midnight on 4 April 1933 provided the Coast Guard little opportunity to carry out rescue operations, but the search for survivors occupied a number of units for some time. The *Akron,* less than two years old, was the largest airship of her day. She left the Lakehurst, New Jersey, Naval Air Station on 3 April, despite threatening weather conditions, with seventy-six officers and men on board, including Rear Admiral William A. Moffett, chief of the Navy's Bureau of Aeronautics. Dodging electrical storms, the dirigible encountered severe turbulence off the New Jersey coast, and when she attempted to gain altitude, her tail struck the water. The *Akron* fell into the sea only a few miles from the German tanker *Phoebus,* which promptly headed for her lights when they were sighted through the storm. The Navy had made little provision for a possible water landing by the airship, so those who survived the crash itself were dependent on their own swimming ability and endurance. The *Phoebus* picked up four, of whom one died soon afterward.

The *Phoebus*'s radio message announcing the crash reached Captain William H. Shea, commanding the New York Division, little more than an hour later, and he immediately ordered the nearest Coast Guard units to the scene. These included the destroyers *Hunt* at New London, *McDougal* anchored inside Sandy Hook, and *Tucker* bound from New York to Norfolk; the cutter *Mojave* about 100 miles away; and the 125-footers *Reliance* and *Vigilant*, sheltering from the storm behind the Delaware Breakwater. The Atlantic City, Barnegat, and Bonds stations were ordered to send their lifeboats, and aircraft from the Cape May Coast Guard Air Station joined the search after daybreak. The *Tucker* was the first to reach the *Phoebus;* her pharmacist's mate braved the rough seas in a small boat to treat the survivors, who were transferred to the destroyer later that morning for transportation to the Brooklyn naval hospital.

Captain Herbert Leary of the new heavy cruiser *Portland* took over direction of the search, which ultimately involved two Navy destroyers and a fleet tug in addition to no less than six Coast Guard destroyers, six patrol boats, six 75-footers, and several smaller craft. Five Coast Guard aircraft were among the more than fifty also taking part, but although the search was continued for more than a week, only a few bodies were recovered, among them that of Admiral Moffett by the 165-footer *Daphne*.[25]

Little more than a year later, on 3 May 1934, the 4,100-ton Norwegian motorship *Childar*, deeply laden with lumber for South Africa, departed Longview, Washington, and stood down the Columbia River. A southwest gale was blowing as she approached the river's treacherous mouth early the next morning, and the current, notorious for its sudden and unpredictable changes, thrust her onto Peacock Spit, "the graveyard of the Pacific." Breakers crashing over the ship snapped the chains holding her deckload of lumber, which was strewn across her decks and littered the water to leeward, while the mate and two seamen attempting to secure a lifeboat were washed overboard. Others were injured, one fatally.

The *Childar* sent a distress call before her foremast fell, carrying the radio antennae away, and this was received by the *Redwing*, stationed at Astoria in place of the old *Algonquin* since 1928. Her commanding officer was on leave, but Lieutenant Arthur W. Davis, a temporary officer who had received a regular commission, had had almost eleven months in which to familiarize himself with ship and station. Although the *Redwing* was on the usual two hours' notice, her liberty party was recalled, steam was raised in both boilers, and the duty section had her ready for sea in less than an hour and a half. Meanwhile, the Cape Disappointment and Point Adams stations, on either side of the river mouth, were directed to send their lifeboats to the *Childar*.

The Redwing, *salvor of the* Childar.

The *Redwing* put out at 8:30 A.M., crossed the heavily breaking bar about two hours later with visibility obscured by frequent rain squalls, and sighted the grounded freighter momentarily through the murk. Working the cutter as close to the breakers as he dared, Davis had a line shot on board, but without power on her winches, the *Childar's* men were unable to haul the steel wire to her deck. Retrieving it, the *Redwing* stood clear of the surf, and then, with a fog bank moving in to hamper the operation even more, she maneuvered in cautiously to shoot another line across the *Childar*. A 12-inch hawser proved more manageable; the freighter's men secured it to forward bitts, and the *Redwing* headed seaward, taking a strain on the hawser very gradually as the much larger freighter wallowed in the breakers. The seas assisted, lifting the *Childar* from the shoals as they roared inshore, and she moved seaward slowly until she was finally afloat.

By that time, the Norwegians had rigged a jury antenna, so Lieutenant Davis was able to communicate with the master, who advised him that his ship would probably remain afloat, but her injured men required medical attention. The two Coast Guard lifeboats were at hand, although Chief Boatswain's Mate Lee Woodward of the Cape Disappointment station had had several ribs broken when a heavy sea threw him against his boat's engine compartment bulkhead. He was ordered to stand by while Lars Bjelland brought his Point Adams boat under the *Childar's* stern. In a masterful display of lifeboat handling under the most difficult conditions, Bjelland kept the 36-footer close aboard as three injured men were lowered on makeshift stretchers. As soon as they were aboard, Bjelland sheered off and the lifeboats headed for Astoria while the *Redwing* continued to tow the *Childar* seaward. Whether the badly damaged, heavily listing freighter would stay afloat long enough to reach the sheltered waters of the Strait of Juan de Fuca, more than 200 miles to the northward, Davis could not know, but he agreed with her master that it was better than risking another crossing of the Columbia bar under such adverse conditions.

There was an uncomfortable moment later in the day, when the bitts tore out of the *Childar's* weakened deck plating and lodged in her bow chock. The *Redwing's* engine was stopped before the chock gave way, the freighter's men made the hawser fast to an anchor chain, and the tow continued, very slowly because the weather was worse and the *Childar,* her rudder carried away, persisted in heading westward. With Gray's Harbor abeam at 8 P.M., the freighter's master feared that she was about to break up and asked that her men be taken off. Lieutenant Davis summoned the Gray's Harbor lifeboat by radio, and with the *Redwing's* searchlight providing illumination, eighteen men jumped into the sea one after another and were pulled into the lifeboat by Boatswain Hilman J. Persson and his men. The master and four others elected to stay on board the *Childar,* so the lifeboat took the eighteen to the cutter and stood by to pick up the others if necessary.

The seas were somewhat lower the next morning, but when the *Chelan* joined from Seattle just before noon, Commander Frederick A. Zeusler and Lieutenant Davis concurred that it was still too rough for the larger cutter to take over the tow. The few men remaining in the *Childar* obviously could not haul another hawser on board, so the *Redwing* continued to tow, with the *Chelan* steaming in company. Although the Norwegian master thought that the *Childar's* leaks were worse during the afternoon and doubted that she could remain afloat, Davis saw no reason to admit failure, nor did he have to. The weather moderated during the night, and the tow rounded Cape Flattery during the morning of 6 May. The *Childar* was turned over to the commercial tug *Roosevelt* that afternoon, and the underwriters' agent, fearing that she would founder before she could reach Seattle, had her towed to Victoria, British Columbia, the nearest port at which she could be docked. The *Redwing* put in at Port Angeles for a night's rest before returning to Astoria.[26]

The salving of the *Childar* might be cited as an example of effective Coast Guard performance; not so the *Morro Castle* disaster. The *Morro Castle* was an 11,500-ton passenger liner built for the New York-Havana, Cuba, run. Completed in 1930, she was a modern vessel in every respect, with the latest safety provisions, including smoke and fire-detecting systems, fire-fighting equipment, and ample lifeboats and rafts. Periodic inspections by the Bureau of Navigation and Steamboat Inspection were intended to assure that ship and equipment were maintained in good condition and that her crew was fully competent.

The *Morro Castle* departed Havana early in September 1934, with 319 passengers and 258 crew members on board.[27] During the evening of 7 September, her master died suddenly, whereupon First Officer William F. Warms assumed command. The weather was deteriorating—rain driven by a 20-mile easterly breeze pelted the liner's decks as she steamed through choppy seas at full speed, almost 19 knots, and a hurricane was reported moving up the coast astern. But Warms was a master mariner, as were all of the deck officers, and the ship was due to reach New York on the morrow, so there seemed no cause for concern.

Early the next morning, however, smoke was reported coming from a ventilator, and an investigation revealed a fire, which spread rapidly along B deck, blocking both passenger stairways from the lower decks. Captain Warms did not call the crew to fire quarters, nor did he slow the ship or direct efforts to control the blaze. A few fire hoses and an extinguisher were put into use, to no effect. About a half-hour after the fire had been discovered, radio operators transmitted a CQ—stand by—message, apparently on their own authority, but Warms would not permit them to send an SOS until some ten or fifteen minutes later. By that time, the glare of the fire had already been seen by people on the New Jersey coast and in nearby ships. Warms finally gave up his effort to reach New York and was maneuvering the *Morro Castle* shoreward when her electrical power failed, plunging the ship into darkness and rendering the steering gear inoperative. Emergency equipment was not put into use, engines and boilers were secured when the engineering spaces had to be abandoned, and the blazing ship was anchored 2 miles east of Sea Girt, New Jersey.

Passengers awakened by the fire alarm found themselves unable to use the normal exits, and few of the ship's company seem to have made any effort to guide them to the boat deck where the lifeboats were being lowered. The six lifeboats that left the *Morro Castle* could have accommodated 408 people; they were lowered with eighty-five, mostly crew members. Although they might well have remained close aboard to pick up others, all headed for the shore at once, leaving a large number of passengers gathered on the liner's stern and some already in the water.[28]

By this time, several vessels had responded to the distress signal, among them the merchant steamers *City of Savannah*, *Monarch of Bermuda*, and *Andrea F. Luckenbach*, all of which sent boats to the *Morro Castle*, and the *President Cleveland*, which did not.[29] The fishing boat *Paramount* and small craft from the shore, some manned by Coast Guardsmen, also participated in the rescue work.

Coast Guard involvement began when the lookout at the Shark

139

River station reported a ship afire just before the *Morro Castle*'s CQ message was sent. Chief Boatswain's Mate Melvin M. Hymer telephoned the report to his district commander and then put out in the power surfboat, leaving the station's picket boat to follow at daybreak if wind and sea permitted. The Shark River surfboat was the first rescue craft on the scene and picked up some eighty survivors, taking them to the *City of Savannah* and the *Luckenbach,* although Hymer had to report that the *Monarch of Bermuda*'s master declined to cooperate in that fashion. The picket boat also put out and saved thirty-six despite very unfavorable conditions. As time passed, however, rescue came too late for an increasing number of those pulled from the water.

The Squan Beach station was next to be alerted. Unlike Shark River, it had a lifeboat, which was unfortunately under repair at the time, so the crew sailed in a picket boat. Considering sea conditions too bad, the acting station commander decided to return for the lifeboat. Several hours were spent getting it ready, during which the picket boat went out again and rescued seven. The lifeboat succeeded only in recovering several bodies. More distant stations sent men to the scene overland, where they helped to beach the *Morro Castle*'s lifeboats, pulled survivors from the surf, and helped to care for the unfortunates. Commander Stephen S. Yeandle, intelligence officer of the New York Division, was put in charge of the rescue operation and eventually had some 250 Coast Guardsmen and as many more men sent by the Army and the Navy under his command. By that time, however, there were few still living who had not been rescued.

Under the circumstances, Coast Guard vessels should also have joined in the rescue operation. Those available included the *Tampa,* moored at Staten Island on two hours' notice; several 75-footers in the New York vicinity; and the 125-footer *Cahoone,* on patrol only 25 miles from the *Morro Castle*. None of these units picked up the distress signal, nor did the Rockaway Coast Guard radio station. Instead, the New York Division commander received the information from a commercial radio station.

The *Cahoone* finally received the relayed message a half-hour later, and Boatswain Michael J. Bruce headed her for the scene at full speed, but in the prevailing sea condition that was somewhat less than her normal 10 knots. Reaching the *Morro Castle* almost four hours later, Bruce found several ships in the vicinity and another departing. Failing to establish radio contact with one of them, the *Cahoone* closed the still-burning liner to ask if a group of seamen on her forecastle wished to be taken off. One, apparently an officer, responded that they were awaiting a tow. Bruce quite reasonably— and unfortunately—took this to mean that the passengers and other crew members had been taken ashore or to other vessels, so the *Cahoone* stood by to remove those still on board should it be necessary. Had Bruce known the situation, the patrol boat could have stood inshore and possibly saved some lives, for the bridge of a 125-footer was a far better vantage point from which to spot people in the water than a surfboat or a picket boat.

The New York Division commander informed the *Tampa* of the distress signal by way of the Rockaway radio station, with the result that the cutter received the message almost an hour after the SOS had been sent. Commander Earl G. Rose lost no time in recalling her liberty party and raising steam—the *Tampa* got underway seventy-eight minutes later! Larger and faster than the *Cahoone,* she reached the *Morro Castle* soon after the patrol boat, and like Boatswain Bruce, Commander Rose assumed that the rescue operation as such had been completed, nor did those on board the *Morro Castle* enlighten him. The *Tampa* was anchored near the liner and prepared to take her in tow. Owing to the rough sea, the Sandy Hook lifeboat had to take a line from the cutter to the liner, and then it took the fourteen men on her forecastle two hours to get the 12-inch hawser on board and secured.

While this was being done, Commander Rose was surprised by a message from the New York Division—about two dozen people, perhaps half of them living, were reported to be in the water off Spring Lake Beach, several miles to the southward. Considering the difficulty that had been experienced in getting a line to the *Morro Castle* and the fact that fourteen men were still on board, Rose decided to send only the *Cahoone* and smaller craft to investigate. These recovered a number of bodies and continued the search until midafternoon, when increasing wind and sea forced the small vessels to seek shelter.

After the hawser had been secured on board the *Morro Castle,* her men found themselves unable to slip the anchor chain, so they had to cut it with hacksaws. That was a slow process—it was accomplished just before noon, when the Sandy Hook lifeboat transferred the fourteen men from the liner to the cutter and the pilot boat *Sandy Hook,* which made a line fast to the *Morro Castle*'s stern to act as a rudder while the *Tampa* towed.

The tow proceeded very slowly, with the wind increasing steadily and veering to the northwest and then to the north during the afternoon. The *Sandy Hook*'s line parted after an hour, and her master offered to run another to the *Tampa*'s bow to help in towing. The commercial salvage tug *Willet*—a Navy "Bird boat" leased to Merritt and Chapman—made the same offer, but Rose declined both, believing correctly that the *Tampa*'s hawser to the *Morro Castle* could not stand the strain. By 6 P.M., the tow had made about 10 miles, but a whole gale was blowing from the north, and the liner persisted in taking it on her starboard bow. A leadsman warned repeatedly that she was dragging the *Tampa* toward the beach, only about 3 miles away. Ordering the engine room to work up to 110 rpm—13.5 knots under normal circumstances—Commander Rose had the cutter's fantail cleared and hoped that if the hawser parted, it would do so in the *Morro Castle*'s chock. Momentarily the liner's head came into the wind; then the hawser snapped close to the *Tampa*'s stern and fouled her screw before it could be stopped. Both vessels drifted toward the beach, the *Morro Castle* grounding off Asbury Park, New Jersey, and the *Tampa* letting her anchors go in time to avoid a like fate. The *Willet* was asked to take the cutter in tow, but before she could get a line on board, the *Tampa*'s men were able to free her screw partially, and the cutter returned to New York at slow speed under her own steam.

The weather moderated the next day, so the *Cahoone* put Boatswain Bruce on board the grounded liner to ascertain that no one had been left in her. Afterward, a breeches buoy was rigged from the shore so that representatives of the press and others could visit the *Morro Castle,* which became a total loss.[30]

At first sight, the Coast Guard had little to be ashamed of, for 146 persons had been rescued by Coast Guardsmen, and they had assisted in saving 113 more, while 164 had been rescued by smaller craft, including the fishing boat *Paramount,* which plucked sixty-seven from the sea, and the boats of the *Monarch of Bermuda,* credited with forty lives saved. But the dead numbered at least 126, a figure that might have been considerably lower had various activities of the Coast Guard functioned effectively.[31]

The board of investigation singled out communications for especial criticism. The Rockaway radio station, communication center for the New York Division, was being dismantled for transfer to the Navy, but the latter had not yet assumed responsibility for handling distress traffic; thus, Rockaway's failure to communicate promptly with the *Tampa* could not be condoned. The radioman "striker" (student) standing watch in the cutter had been inattentive, contributing to her delay in getting under way. The *Cahoone* had only two inexperienced radiomen on board, and they had had trouble with her equipment; the board felt that they had done their best—the patrol boat could not have reached the *Morro Castle* much earlier in any case. The duty petty officers at the Cape May air station had failed to inform their superiors when they learned of the disaster, although they had attempted to reach the *Cahoone* by radio.

So far as others were concerned, the acting commanding officer at Cape May had flown search missions despite the foul weather later in the day, but he had erred in not seeking instructions from the New York Division and in waiting some time before having boats and aircraft prepared to take part in the rescue. The Squan Beach picket boat might have saved more lives had the acting station commander persisted in his efforts to get to sea in it instead of returning to spend precious hours working on the lifeboat, which saved no one. Neither Commander Rose nor Boatswain Bruce seems to have used much imagination, but the board held that they had acted correctly on the basis of their knowledge of the situation. Chief Boatswain's Mate Melvin M. Hymer was considered to have performed most effectively of all; "He started into action immediately upon observing the fire and in going to sea under conditions that obtained, it required great skill and seamanship in small boat handling."[32]

Quite obviously, the major responsibility for the disaster rested with those who owned and operated the *Morro Castle*. A federal court in New York found Acting Captain Warms, the chief engineer, and the Ward Line's executive vice president guilty of dereliction of duty, and the judge sentenced them to prison for varying terms, none of which were sustained on appeal, and the line itself was fined $10,000—the maximum permitted by law. The judge noted the necessity for effective enforcement of maritime law, and the Board of Supervisors of the Bureau of Navigation and Steamboat Inspection recognized that its inspections were sometimes inadequate because its personnel were too few and too poorly paid.[33] So ended the *Morro Castle* disaster, although its importance for the Coast Guard had yet to become apparent.

In spite of the financial exigencies of the early 1930s, the Coast Guard received appropriations for a number of new vessels during Admiral Hamlet's term as commandant, among them nine more 165-foot patrol boats of the *Thetis* class and the *Escanaba*'s five sisters mentioned earlier. The *Electra* of the former group served the Coast Guard for no more than a year, being transferred to the Navy for conversion to the presidential yacht *Potomac* in 1935.

Only one of the five 165-foot icebreaking cutters, the *Tahoma*, stationed at Cleveland, Ohio, remained on the Great Lakes, for which the vessels were originally designed. While the *Algonquin* at Woods Hole, Massachusetts; the *Comanche* at New York; and the *Mohawk* at Cape May were all in areas where their icebreaking capability could be of some use, the assignment of the *Onondaga* to Astoria, Oregon, in place of the *Redwing* seemed inexplicable to some. In fact, ice jams on the Columbia River had damaged vessels, bridges, and riverfront structures on occasion, and in January 1930 the *Northland* had spent a week breaking ice in the Portland-Vancouver vicinity. Both cities asked that she be kept on the Columbia during winter months thereafter—indeed, Portland offered free mooring, water, and power were she stationed there. The commandant had refused because of the arrangements for supplying the *Northland* for her Arctic cruises through the San Francisco depot.[34] With somewhat shallower draft and greater power, the *Onondaga* was more suitable for icebreaking on the river than the *Northland,* and her first commanding officer thought her "much safer and more able" for work on the Columbia River bar than the *Redwing,* which was reassigned to Port Angeles, Washington.[35]

In May 1933, the commandant submitted a list of vessels and equipment needed by the service in order to carry out its varied duties, asking that these be funded as Emergency Public Works under the National Industrial Recovery Act. Nine cruising cutters, 300 feet long, capable of carrying airplanes, and of higher speed than any then in the Coast Guard, were given the highest priority.

143

Six of these were intended to replace existing vessels, all nearing the ends of their useful lives, and the others were to be stationed in areas where large cutters were obviously needed: Unalaska; San Pedro, California; and the Panama Canal Zone. Construction of all nine was approved by the Public Works Administration, but by the time bids had been received, the cost of materials and labor had increased to the extent that only seven vessels could be built for the sum allotted. Efforts to obtain funding for the other two were unsuccessful.[36]

Constructor Hunnewell and his associates prepared a design based on that of the successful Lake-class cutters, enlarged to provide greater speed without a disproportionate increase in power and to furnish deck space to accommodate an airplane. Geared turbines and a single screw would drive the ship at 20 knots, the maximum speed permitted if the cutters were not to be included in the total tonnage allowed the United States under the Treaty of London of 1930. The Navy was preparing the design for gunboats of similar size and speed at the same time, and when it became apparent that money could be saved were the new cutters built in navy yard dry docks with underwater lines and propelling machinery identical to those of the gunboats *Charleston* and *Erie,* Hunnewell was directed to modify the Navy design to meet Coast Guard requirements. The resulting ships were quite different in appearance from the new gunboats, and they were unlike previous cutters as well—longer, slimmer, and having lighter draft for their size. Their length—327 feet—caused the constructors to adopt longitudinal framing in place of the usual transverse system, and Hunnewell also incorporated heavier scantlings—frames, girders, and plating—than were used in the gunboats. Perhaps most notable, these would be twin-screw vessels.[37] All were laid down in navy yards—two in New York, four in Philadelphia, and one in Charleston, South Carolina—in 1935, but none was commissioned during Admiral Hamlet's term as commandant.

The emphasis on airplane-carrying capability for the 327 footers reflected the great strides being made in aviation at the time. The application for funds with which to build them had noted as well that "certain cutters will require equipment of novel design to undertake rescue and assistance work for aircraft flying the ocean traffic lanes."[38] By this time, the same advances had led to a further development of Coast Guard aviation.

The service's "air wing" had hardly prospered since its modest rebirth in the 1920s. The five aircraft purchased in 1926 were operated from air stations at Gloucester and Cape May until 1931, when they were replaced by three, of which two were flying boats. These had the theoretical capability for open-water landings and takeoffs, so it was hoped that they would be especially useful for removing injured persons from vessels at sea. The smaller of the two, a single-engine Viking biplane, was less satisfactory than the Douglas Dolphin, a twin-engine monoplane, but the latter also had certain limitations. To overcome these, the Coast Guard aviation section, which

had been established at Headquarters under Commander Norman B. Hall in 1928, furnished a statement of its requirements to manufacturers:

The "flying lifeboat" Altair taking off.

> An aerial "eye," capable of extended search, radio equipped to maintain constant contact with surface, thus saving hours and possibly days of delay of search; an aerial ambulance capable of a speed of 100 miles per hour, able to land in a rough sea, equipped with hatches large enough to admit of stretcher cases and to be able to take off in rough water; a demolition outfit to effect the destruction at sea of derelicts and obstructions to navigation within a few hours after the report of location; a high speed flying patrol for observation, landing and returning with rescued crews of distressed small craft and capable of taking aboard fifteen or more passengers from distressed craft and standing by for lengthy periods on the surface, maintaining in the meantime radio communication with surface craft until transfer can be made of its passengers.[39]

Seven of these "flying lifeboats"—they might better have been called "flying cutters" in view of the multi-mission requirement!— were obtained in 1932, of which two were improved Douglas Dolphin amphibians modified for the Coast Guard and five were built by the General Aviation Corporation of Baltimore. The latter were flying boats generally similar to the Dolphins, although the engines of four were mounted atop the wing as pushers.[40] All were named

145

for stars important to navigators, which again implies that they were regarded as cutters—lifeboats were not named.

In August 1932, the Gloucester air station was notified that a fisherman in a schooner 175 miles east of Nantucket Island required medical attention. Although it was after nightfall, the new Douglas *Sirius* was dispatched at once. The aircraft failed to find the schooner in the darkness and was forced down for want of fuel the next day. When the *Sirius* did not return, the base notified Coast Guard activities by radio that it was missing. The new General Aviation *Altair*, on a test flight out of Cape May, picked up the message and after refueling began a search for both aircraft and schooner. The former was located off the Maine coast, and the destroyer *Wainwright*, standing by, informed the *Altair*'s pilot that his assistance was not needed, for the *Sirius* had directed surface craft to the schooner to remove the injured man.[41]

Further "flying lifeboat" operations proved the value of these aircraft, but it became apparent that the General Aviation flying boats had design faults that made them less useful than the Dolphins. Indeed, at the time of the *Morro Castle* disaster, the *Antares* and the *Acrux* of this type were "only to be used in case of emergency" and "grounded as unsafe" respectively.[42] And the ability of flying boats to land and take off at sea under any but favorable conditions was very limited, although on occasion there was no alternative.

Thus, when Lieutenant Commander Carl C. von Paulsen set the *Arcturus* down in a choppy sea off Cape Canaveral to pick up a boy who had drifted to sea in a skiff in January 1933, the aircraft lost its left wingtip float. Nonetheless, von Paulsen took off after getting the boy on board, but when the damaged left wing's plywood covering began to peel off soon thereafter, the *Arcturus* had to come down again, suffering hull damage in the rough water. The loss of the float made it impossible to taxi across the wind and sea to the beach, so the flying boat's crew rigged a sea anchor and awaited rescue, knowing that it would be some time in coming—von Paulsen would not have risked a landing had there been a vessel close enough to reach the skiff before nightfall. In the event, the *Arcturus* drifted through the surf onto the Florida coast early the next morning, sustaining a good deal of damage, but since neither the rescued boy nor any of the crew suffered injury, the flight was considered successful.[43]

Aircraft demonstrated their worth in other ways as well, dropping hurricane and storm-warning streamers to boats and areas that had no radio, searching for missing craft and persons, guiding cutters and patrol boats to distressed vessels and derelicts, providing ambulance service to remote areas, and helping to suppress smuggling. Secretary Morgenthau, an aviation enthusiast, supported the expansion of the Coast Guard's air activity, transferring the Customs aviation detachment to it in 1934 and helping to obtain Public Works Administration funds for the procurement of aircraft and the construction of additional air stations. By 1 July 1935, the service was operating forty aircraft from air stations at Salem, Massachusetts; Cape May, New Jersey; Miami and St. Petersburg, Florida; Biloxi, Mississippi; and Port Angeles, Washington. Air patrol detachments were stationed at San Antonio, Texas, and San Diego, California, as well. The number of Coast Guard officers receiving flight training at the Pensacola Naval Air Station rose from four in January 1932 to twelve in mid-1935,[44] and in September 1934, the aviation section at Headquarters, heretofore under the engineer in chief, was made a separate activity, with its head, Commander Lloyd T. Chalker, reporting directly to the commandant.[45] Quite clearly, Coast Guard aviation had finally "taken off"!

The Academy also continued to develop during this period. Following the occupation of its new facilities, it joined the Military and Naval academies in seeking degree-granting status, and a consideration of curriculum revision had already begun. Senior officers were asked to suggest changes, and Admiral Hamlet wrote the presidents of Columbia, Harvard, and Yale universities and the Massachusetts Institute of Technology, requesting that each appoint a faculty member to a Coast Guard Academy advisory committee. The commandant regretted that the service had no funds with which to pay committee members, but he noted that the Coast Guard Academy Alumni Association was prepared to defray their travel expenses.[46] Commander James Pine from Headquarters and Professor Chester E. Dimick, who had been teaching mathematics to cadets for twenty-eight years, during most of which he was the only civilian faculty member!, visited the two engineering deans and two professors of engineering appointed to the committee to acquaint them with the situation, and in 1934 the advisory committee met at New London. On the whole, its members were impressed by the new Academy, but they thought the faculty woefully inadequate, with which Dimick and his fellows undoubtedly agreed.[47] Implementation of the committee's recommendations on curriculum revision, which introduced a limited number of electives, was quite rapid, but not until 1937 did Congress authorize the desired enlargement of the faculty. The same legislation provided for an advisory committee similar to that of 1934 and a board of visitors composed of three senators and four congressmen.[48]

Admiral Hamlet's *Annual Reports* reveal that the service continued—indeed, it improved on—the record of achievement established under his highly respected predecessor, which would seem to indicate that the doubts of Captain Chiswell, Commander Waesche, and others were groundless. In fact, however, there was growing discontent with Hamlet's leadership, discontent that reached a peak when the commandant agreed to the trial operation of Coast Guard radio facilities in the Northeast by the Navy. Foremost among the malcontents seems to have been Commander Stephen S. Yeandle, who deplored the admiral's ineffectiveness to Congressman Warren, "the ever militant apostle of the Coast Guard," making no secret of his ambition to succeed Hamlet at an early date.[49] Both Warren and former North Carolina Governor Angus MacLean, a prominent Washington attorney, supported Yeandle strongly, the first urging Assistant Secretary of the Treasury Stephen B. Gibbons to make him commandant— "[Yeandle] has the confidence and esteem of everyone in Congress who knows him, and he is a gentleman and officer of distinction."[50] Gibbons responded noncommitally that Yeandle would be considered when the time came to make an appointment. Warren was prepared to write Secretary Morgenthau as well if the commander wished him to do so, but Yeandle feared that the secretary would react strongly to any congressional interference in a Treasury Department appointment. Admiral Hamlet suffered a heart attack during the autumn of 1934, giving Yeandle new hope. He hesitated to begin a personal campaign to oust the commandant, however, and the latter recovered fully.[51]

While one may discount Commander Yeandle's low estimate of Admiral Hamlet's leadership ability, there is ample evidence that morale declined during his term as commandant. To a degree this was inevitable, for pay cuts, stagnation in rank, demotions in rating, and discharges "for the convenience of the Government" could hardly be conducive to the happiness of those affected. On the other hand, officers had been promoted so rapidly during the Billard period that few seem to have been disaffected, and reenlistments continued at an unprecedented rate, if only because of the lack of employment opportunity for those accepting discharges.

Admiral Hamlet may justly be blamed for a growing feeling of alienation between Headquarters and the field, on which Commander Waesche commented late in 1934.[52] In part, this was due to the fact that so many of the officers at Headquarters, including Waesche himself, had been stationed in Washington for years, leading those in the field to believe that their problems were viewed with neither understanding nor sympathy by deskbound officers who were caught up in the political atmosphere of the nation's capital. Admiral Hamlet, having found—or inherited—subordinates who could administer the service effectively, had little desire to replace them with officers from the field—perhaps Captain Chiswell was correct in thinking Hamlet somewhat lazy. But succeeding a commandant as popular as Admiral Billard must have been difficult for anyone, and whatever else may be said about Rear Admiral Harry G. Hamlet, one must note that his four-year term as commandant certainly was not calamitous for the Coast Guard.

CHAPTER ELEVEN

YEARS OF EXPANSION, 1936–40

Among the papers of Russell Randolph Waesche in the Coast Guard Academy library, which bears his name, is an unsigned, undated memorandum listing six general qualifications for a commandant of the Coast Guard.

1. To have confidence of officers and their entire confidence in his fairness and sense of justice.
2. A reputation for zeal and whole-hearted enthusiasm for the welfare of the Coast Guard.
3. Executive and administrative ability.
4. Ability to present to the best advantage the needs of the Coast Guard to Committees of Congress and others in charge of its destinies.
5. Qualities of leadership and capacity to win and hold the loyal and enthusiastic support of the Service.
6. Vision and progressive ideas coupled with *balance* and *judgement.*

Had the writer of this memorandum added a lively sense of humor, a capacity for hard work, and a readiness to delegate authority, he might have been describing Waesche himself.

In view of his interest in the Coast Guard, one might expect that Lindsay Warren would have been fully informed as to whom would be appointed to succeed Rear Admiral Hamlet in 1936. Yet Warren wrote a constituent in March that no one in Congress had been able to learn anything about the appointment, and when others urged him to endorse one or another of the service's senior officers, the North Carolina congressman responded that he thought political support of no value to aspirants to the position.[1] A few days earlier, however, Representative Schuyler Otis Bland, chairman of the committee on the merchant marine and fisheries, implied strongly that Warren, who chaired the subcommittee on the Coast Guard, should join him in endorsing Waesche, which the North Carolinian did—a week after assuring his constituents that political support was of no value![2]

In all likelihood, Treasury Secretary Morgenthau had already

Russell Randolph Waesche, commandant, 1936–45.

decided to nominate Commander Waesche, who became commandant on 14 June 1936, less than a month after Warren had endorsed him. The 50-year-old Waesche was promoted over twenty captains and four commanders, which of course, was hardly unusual—both Bertholf and Billard had been relatively junior when they were appointed. Nor were many in the service likely to have been surprised, for several members of Waesche's class of 1906 had decided five years earlier that he should succeed Admiral Billard if the latter did not accept reappointment in 1932. Others, including some captains, also saw in the commander the qualities that they thought essential in a commandant. Waesche readily admitted that he desired the position, but he was willing to wait—unless someone like Yeandle, his junior, seemed likely to be appointed.[3]

Over half of Waesche's thirty years in the Coast Guard had been spent on sea duty, and while he had never commanded a large cutter, he had been commanding officer of the Eagle-boat *Bothwell*, the *Snohomish*, and the destroyers *Beale* and *Tucker*. On leaving the last, he had served briefly as Destroyer Force ordnance officer, and in March 1928 he went to Headquarters as chief ordnance officer of the Coast Guard. Thereafter, Waesche represented the Coast Guard in the Navy's war plans office for a time. As aide to Admiral Hamlet, he had additional responsibility as finance and budget officer, and he was a member of almost every board appointed by the commandant. Thus, Waesche probably had a more intimate knowledge of Coast Guard affairs generally than any other, and his acquaintance with the Treasury Department and Congress was almost equally extensive.

In his capacity as aide to Admiral Hamlet in 1935, Commander Waesche had implemented a reorganization of Headquarters in accordance with the recommendations of a board appointed two years earlier, which he modified in some respects. Basically, this amounted to combining offices and sections according to the functions they performed. Operations became the direct responsibility of the assistant commandant, under whom there were divisions of intelligence, communications, aviation, surface craft, and shore activities. The divisions of finance, inspections, procurement and supplies, and personnel reported directly to the commandant, as did the section of mail, files, and duplicating. Boards on planning, regulations, retirements, and other matters were abolished, their responsibilities being assumed by the permanent board, consisting of five officers, which also served in an advisory capacity to the commandant. The commandant's aide, a public relations officer, and a technical advisor—the last, Oliver Maxam, who was nearing the end of his decades of service at Headquarters—had desks in the commandant's office.

By the time Waesche became commandant, the new organization was functioning well, and the departure of Admiral Hamlet, who reverted to the rank of captain to serve as an advisor to the Senate committee on commerce until his retirement in 1938, seems not to have caused any disruption. Like his predecessor, Waesche kept certain officers at Headquarters for years, among them Leon C. Covell as assistant commandant, Harvey F. Johnson as engineer in chief, Joseph F. Farley as communication officer, and Frank J. Gorman as finance officer. Lloyd T. Chalker also remained at Headquarters, first as aviation officer, then as Covell's assistant, and upon the latter's retirement in December 1941, he became assistant commandant. All were very capable officers, and Waesche reposed a great deal of trust in them.

Seeking to remedy the existing alienation between Headquarters and the field, Admiral Waesche undertook a series of visits to Coast Guard activities and cutters across the country soon after becoming commandant, meeting with their officers to explain the service's situation and problems as seen by those at Headquarters, answering questions, and soliciting opinions.[4] Even Admiral Billard had never attempted personal communication with his subordinates to this degree, and Waesche, who was especially effective when dealing with small groups, was able to dispel much of the distrust felt by many in the field.

It was physically impossible for the new commandant to go to each of the stations personally, nor would his visits have reassured those in the lifesaving branch, for Waesche intended to bring them into a closer relationship with the service as a whole and to close redundant stations, wherever they might be. On the other hand, he was keenly aware of the need to avoid unnecessary alarm and alienation on the part of the officers and men.

The situation required a delicate touch, for the resentment felt by the latter at what they considered unequal treatment had led to a short-lived move to reestablish the old Life-Saving Service in 1934. Frank L. Toon, a former Coast Guardsman, had attempted to make himself the leader of this movement, assuring Congressman Lindsay Warren that the Coast Guard was "inefficient, unsatisfactory, and disliked by the personnel of the stations. A nonmilitary body of men who traditionally saved lives for the love of it are now goaded with useless military drill and discipline, transferred from home shoals to strange waters, reduced in military allowances and pay, and placed on a basis where they cannot efficiently perform their duties."[5] Warren responded that he was awaiting further information before protesting the treatment of the livesaving branch at Coast Guard Headquarters, but in fact he had no intention of undertaking anything that might be deleterious to the service as a whole, nor did Toon's effort elicit any significant response from the personnel of the lifesaving branch. Groups representing the latter did meet with Representative Robert L. Bacon of New York later in 1934, and Bacon asked Warren's assistance on their behalf.[6] The nation's economic situation, however, was largely responsible for the matters about which the lifesaving branch complained, so this effort also had little result.

Closing the redundant stations was obviously a politically sensitive matter, but it was begun after a careful study at Headquarters. By mid-1938, forty-one stations, most of which were on the coasts of New York, New Jersey, and North Carolina, and on Lakes Huron and Michigan, had been inactivated, leaving 200 fully manned. As Admiral Waesche explained to Congressman Warren, who was predictably concerned, conditions had changed markedly in the years since most of the stations had been established: Commercial sailing vessels, which had needed assistance most frequently, had almost disappeared from American coastal waters; improvements in methods of navigation and the widespread use of radio had reduced the number of craft getting into difficulty; and the employment of power boats in rescue work had extended the range of operations from individual stations, as had the replacement of horses by tractors and trucks to haul surfboats and beach apparatus to the disaster scene. Although this more mobile and effective equipment facilitated the surfmen's performance of their duties, it was more costly as well. A number of the stations still lacked adequate heating, lighting, and sanitary systems, and to provide these would require funds that the service simply did not have. Therefore, the commandant saw no alternative to closing stations.

Waesche assured Warren that each district's stations were being evaluated by the same standard and that no property was being disposed of at the time; thus, should the need for a station be demonstrated, it could be reactivated quite easily. And there would be no reduction in personnel or their ratings, for four men were to be added to the complement of each of the active stations, among them a cook, whose arrival must have led to some rejoicing—heretofore, culinary duties had been performed by the surfmen in turn, regardless of their competence.[7]

After conferring with Waesche, the congressman assured his constituents of the commandant's sincerity and deep interest in the lifesaving branch, although he continued to deplore the rapidity with which the stations were being closed. Waesche was not deterred—when Warren forwarded a petition in which 268 residents of Avon, North Carolina, protested the inactivation of the Big Kinnakeet station, he responded bluntly that "neither the increasing automobile traffic at the Cape [Hatteras] nor the thought that the salaries of the station crew act as the financial backbone of the village of Avon can possibly justify maintaining an active Coast Guard station in that vicinity."[8] The reactivation of Big Kinnakeet two years later did not indicate a change of heart on Waesche's part, for the nearby Little Kinnakeet station was closed at the same time.

Developmental work on equipment for use by the station crews continued without dramatic changes. Two 52-foot lifeboats completed in 1935 were being evaluated at Sandy Hook and Point Adams. Neither self-righting nor self-bailing, these boats were very stable and could accommodate sixty persons in watertight compartments with another 100 on deck, weather and sea conditions per-

mitting. Although the 52-footers were considered successful, they were too expensive to replace the 36-footer as the service's workhorse; no more of the larger boats were built until after World War II. Meanwhile, the 36-footer continued to evolve from the Type T of 1928, through the TR of 1931, to the TRS of 1937, each of which was a slightly improved version of its predecessor. Some experimental small craft were built as well, while Construction and Repair continued to simplify and standardize the designs of surfboats and the small boats carried on board cutters. An improved shoulder line-throwing gun was introduced in 1937, and the venerable Lyle guns were modified to enhance their performance.

A 36-foot motor lifeboat in post–World War II rig.

The middle years of the decade brought greater changes for the cutter branch, among them the decommissioning of a number of older vessels. These included the *Apache, Gresham, Seminole, Seneca, Tuscarora,* and *Yamacraw,* and all of the seagoing tugs except the *Carrabasset, Kickapoo,* and *Shawnee.* The departure of these veterans left the *Pamlico* of 1907, which spent her entire career on the North Carolina sounds, the oldest cutter on the active list; the *Unalga* of 1912 was the oldest cruising cutter. Probably never before or since have relatively new vessels made up such a large proportion of the Coast Guard's cutter force. All but four of the 100-foot patrol boats were decommissioned as well, while the 125-footers were withdrawn from service a few at a time to be re-engined, increasing their speeds to 12 or 13 knots.

153

The newly completed
George W. Campbell.

The first of the 327-foot cutters was commissioned two days after Waesche was sworn in as commandant, with her six sisters following her into service during the next nine months. They were named for secretaries of the treasury—in order of commissioning, the *George W. Campbell, William J. Duane, Samuel D. Ingham, Roger B. Taney, John C. Spencer, Alexander Hamilton,* and *George M. Bibb*—and so came to be known as the Treasury class in later years. All were reduced to surnames only in mid-1937.

Like most of the vessels designed by Frederick Hunnewell, these were good-looking ships, with nicely raked bows, cruiser sterns, and raised bulwarks fore and aft, which disguised their flush decks. Unlike the earlier large cutters, each had a short, broad stack, and king posts aft served an aircraft-handling crane, although the desired hangar could not be provided on a ship of that size. As completed, each of these cutters mounted two 5-inch 51-caliber guns and three 6-pounders, an armament that was increased considerably within a few years.

In view of these vessels' later reputations and longevity—five of them were nearing the half-century mark when decommissioned—it is interesting to note that the initial impressions of them were not entirely favorable. Some thought them too large for most cutter duties, and they lacked the towing capability of the popular Lake class. Their twin screws, which made them easier to handle, were extremely vulnerable to damage when working in ice. Commander John S. Baylis, who took the *Campbell* to the Azores and Southampton, England, on her shakedown cruise, reported that she handled much better than any other Coast Guard vessel he had served in, "riding moderate seas much easier and with an easy roll." On the other hand, she was extremely wet in a seaway, and when driven into heavy seas, the *Campbell* pitched "with a terrible pounding, shaking and quivering all over."[9] On her way back to New York, she encountered a series of gales, which delayed even the Cunard liner *Queen Mary,* one of the two largest ships of the day. Baylis had orders to return as quickly as possible, so he forced the new cutter through the storms, changing course as necessary to reduce her pounding. At the worst of a southerly gale on Friday, 13 November, with seas running to 40 feet or more, "the vessel was smashed down by a heavy sea hitting us amidship on the port side; [she] was reported rolling about 48° or 49° to starboard."[10] At that point, a number of tubes in the port condenser gave way, and the boiler feed water began to salt up. With the port engine stopped and the starboard screw turning 150 rpm to keep steerage way, the black gang plugged the damaged tubes, and the *Campbell* made New York without serious damage. Quite clearly, these would be tough ships.

Commissioning the 327-footers brought some redistribution of the large cutters. Most of the new ships went to the Pacific, where their great endurance and embarked aircraft were expected to be most useful: the *Duane* and the *Hamilton* to San Francisco, the *Ingham* to Port Angeles, the *Taney* to Honolulu, and the *Spencer* to Cordova, Alaska, the last to relieve the *Haida,* which since 1935 had been stationed at Cordova to assist ships in difficulty in the Gulf of Alaska and to enforce the Convention for the Preservation of the Halibut Fisheries. The *Bibb* was based at Norfolk and the *Campbell* at New York, while the Lake-class *Chelan* and *Tahoe* were assigned to the Boston Division, leaving the *Itasca* at San Diego and the *Shoshone* at San Francisco the only ships of their class in the Pacific. With the exception of the *Haida,* which replaced the *Tallapoosa* at Juneau, Alaska, older cutters were sent to Southern ports: the *Tallapoosa* to Savannah, the *Mojave* to Miami, the *Tampa* to Mobile, Alabama, and the *Unalga* to San Juan, Puerto Rico.

Another matter of importance to the cutter branch especially was President Roosevelt's executive order of 21 December 1936, directing that the Coast Guard assist in keeping channels and harbors open to navigation by means of icebreaking operations. The commandant was authorized to request the cooperation of suitable vessels belonging to the War, Navy, and Commerce departments, but the order left no doubt that icebreaking in American waters was primarily a Coast Guard responsibility. The Coast Guard, of course, had been involved in this activity since the time of its founding. The *Androscoggin* of 1909 had been designed for icebreaking among other duties, as had the *Ossipee* of 1915, while the smaller *Acushnet* and *Manhattan* were strengthened for ice navigation. The *Kickapoo* had been extensively rebuilt as an icebreaker during the mid-1920s, and the *Northland*'s construction has been noted. All except the last were intended for service in New England waters, but the need soon extended to New York as well.

Albany, New York, had developed port facilities at considerable expense in the 1920s, but these could be used only when the Hudson River was relatively ice-free. The city's municipal and business leaders implored the Coast Guard to keep the channel open during the winter, and in 1933 the Congress took up a bill authorizing the construction of an icebreaking cutter for work on the Hudson. Treasury Secretary Woodin doubted the necessity for such a vessel, but one of the 165-footers laid down later that year was designated for service there.[11]

Meanwhile, the increasing use of oil for heating purposes and a succession of unusually cold winters in the Northeast made the problem more acute, for unlike coal, which was transported by rail and could be stored in some quantity without special facilities, oil was shipped in barges, which could not navigate ice-clogged waterways, and required costly tanks for bulk storage. During the winter of 1933–34, several 125-foot patrol boats were pressed into service to clear channels for oil barges, and while their sturdy hulls were equal to the occasion, almost all reported propeller damage. The commandant assured the Inland Water Petroleum Carriers Association that the patrol boats' deficiencies would be overcome in the 110-foot harbor cutters for which preliminary designs had been prepared.[12]

But no one in the Coast Guard seems to have known how to design an icebreaker. No information on the *Androscoggin*'s performance has been found; in all likelihood it was limited to forcing her way through thin ice and pushing small floes aside. The *Ossipee* was said to be a better icebreaker backing down than going ahead, which may explain the rudder damage she sustained early in her career.[13] The *Kickapoo*'s alterations included cutting away her forefoot and extending her bow by some 6 feet, after which she was described as the Coast Guard's first real icebreaker, "with one of the first bows ever designed to break ice by riding up over it."[14] The nature of her bow form is not clear, but since the alterations were said to have affected her seagoing ability adversely, one suspects that her new bow resembled that of the *Northland*, which was being designed at the time the *Kickapoo* was rebuilt. The *Escanaba* and her sisters revealed no influence of a successful *Kickapoo* bow.

In May 1936, Lieutenant Dale R. Simonson of Construction and Repair published a paper entitled "Bow Characteristics for Ice Breaking," in which he stated: "It may be found in some vessels that the stem is cut away so much that a reverse curve is necessary to obtain a proper draft and displacement forward."[15] One assumes that Simonson referred to the draft necessary for directional stability as well as to the weight necessary to break ice, and the drawing accompanying the paper depicts a closer approach to a proper bow form than any the Coast Guard had yet developed. He made no mention of the desirable cross section, however, nor does the drawing include one. Given time, Simonson probably would have developed an effective icebreaking bow, but he was transferred to the staff of the San Francisco District in 1937 and so had no part in designing the service's first successful icebreakers.

President Roosevelt's executive order gave the whole matter of icebreaker design immediate importance, although quite naturally the order did not include funds to finance research and development. Engineer in Chief Harvey F. Johnson nonetheless ordered a study of the subject begun, and to gain information on current European practice, he resorted to a typical Coast Guard expedient. One of his subordinates, Lieutenant Edward H. Thiele, was married to a Danish girl whom he had met on a cadet cruise while he was an instructor at the Academy some years earlier. Thiele and his wife and children were visiting her family in Denmark when Captain Johnson became interested in icebreakers, and the lieutenant's leave was interrupted by telegraphic orders to visit northern European nations to study icebreaker design. Thiele had to make his own arrangements through the various American embassies and legations, and while his travel expenses within Europe were paid by the Coast Guard, he was not reimbursed for his transportation to and from Europe.

Edward H. Thiele as a rear admiral.

Lieutenant Thiele went first to Sweden and then on to Finland, Latvia, Denmark, Norway, and the Netherlands. He found officials and officers in all quite willing to discuss icebreakers and to demonstrate their vessels, but the Swedes and the Finns seem to have had the most to offer. Thiele was especially interested in the formers' triple-screw, 258-foot *Ymer* of 1932, and the head of the Swedish icebreaking service must have been amused when he explained that she combined the bow form of the Great Lakes car ferry *Ste. Marie* with Quincy B. Newman's diesel-electric drive. The Swedes had added trim tanks that could be filled and emptied rapidly to induce an artificial rolling motion, helping the vessel to free herself from the ice, and other refinements, but the basic information that Thiele sought was readily available in the United States!

The lieutenant visited the Netherlands principally to investigate the "ice plows" about which Captain Johnson had read before sending his telegram. These were detachable bows that could be fitted to tugs during the winter months in order to keep inland waterways open to navigation. There were two types, one of which projected under the water and broke the ice from beneath, while the more conventional utilized its weight and the boat's power to break the ice from above. Thiele was impressed by the latter, but its adoption by the Coast Guard had to await World War II.[16]

On his return to the United States, Thiele joined Hunnewell and Lieutenant Commander Rutherford B. Lank, Jr., in designing 110-foot icebreaking tugs, four of which were completed in 1939. Although this design had its origin in four 110-foot harbor cutters built almost five years before, these vessels—the *Hudson, Calumet, Navesink,* and *Tuckahoe*—had bows like that of the *Escanaba,* and they had suffered hull damage while breaking ice. Thus, the *Raritan, Naugatuck, Arundel,* and *Mahoning* were modified considerably, with heavier framing and plating, more powerful diesel-electric power plants, and most important, properly designed icebreaking bows. Any doubt as to their ability disappeared when the *Arundel* and the 165-foot *Comanche* were tested against one another on the

157

Hudson River in January 1940. The larger, more powerful cutter chiseled away at 12-inch sheet ice, making slow progress, while the 110-footer combined power and bow weight to break the ice without resorting to backing and ramming, leaving no doubt as to her superiority.[17] Nor did the icebreaking bow result in any lack of directional stability, such as afflicted the *Northland.* Within the next five years, nine more vessels were built to virtually the same design, and although icebreaking is obviously strenuous duty, nine of the thirteen were still in service almost forty years later. The Coast Guard had finally learned to design an icebreaker. As events would show, it was none too soon.

Three legislative acts of 1936 were important to the Coast Guard. The first provided for the enforcement of the international convention for the regulation of whaling. For the next several years, Coast Guard officers served as inspectors on board the two American whale factory vessels operating in the Indian and Antarctic oceans and at whaling stations on the Alaska and California coasts. Others accompanied the American delegation to the international conference on whaling held in London in 1937 and represented the United States at conferences in Oslo and London during the next year.

It seems to have been taken for granted that Coast Guard officers had full authority to board vessels under U.S. jurisdiction and to take whatever steps were necessary to enforce the nation's laws. The decision in the 1927 case of *Maul* v. *the U.S.,* however, had been appealed to the Supreme Court, and while that body upheld the seizure of the vessel involved, the majority thought it necessary to find a specific statute authorizing the Coast Guard to act. Realizing the alarming implications of this opinion, the Treasury Department prepared a bill to rectify the situation. It was enacted on 22 June 1936, and thereafter, commissioned, warrant, and petty officers were empowered "to make inquiries, examinations, inspections, searches, seizures, and arrests upon the high seas . . . for the prevention, detection, and suppression of violations of the laws of the United States, under certain limitations."[18] To realize the maximum benefit from this extensive authority, Headquarters urged division commanders to set up regular boarding schedules for vessels frequenting their areas, making sure that none was overlooked. Consideration for those operating the ships was also important: "Courtesy by boarding officers should be stressed together with thoroughness. No vessel, if legitimately operated, should be harassed by boarding with unreasonable frequency or at inappropriate times."[19]

By the mid-1930s, the situation of the American merchant marine was causing concern. The over-optimistic expectation that the post–World War I merchant fleet would be able to compete with foreign shipping in overseas trade had long since disappeared, and legislation of 1928 had provided subsidies for ships carrying the mails, weighted according to the size and speed of the vessel, and construction loans to encourage the building of ships that could be operated more efficiently, thus reviving the moribund shipbuilding industry as well. Few measures have been less successful. The annual cost of the subsidies almost tripled in six years, enriching the shipping lines that held the mail contracts without improving the competitive situation of the merchant marine, while no more than five ships were built—the *Morro Castle* was one—with construction loans.

This state of affairs led to the Merchant Marine Act of 1936, which called for the cancellation of the ocean mail contracts by 1937, substituting direct construction and operating subsidies in order to bring about an American-flag merchant fleet capable of carrying "a substantial portion" of the nation's foreign commerce in peacetime and of meeting defense needs in wartime. The act permitted the government to build ships for lease to private operators if necessary. All officers on board subsidized vessels had to be American citizens, as must 90 percent of the crew members in passenger ships and 100 percent in cargo vessels. In unsubsidized American-flag ships, all officers and 75 percent of the crews were to be American, although their operators were not compelled to meet the minimum wage and manning scales required by the subsidy contracts.[20]

Initially, the only provision of this act that affected the Coast Guard directly was the requirement that all lifeboat certificates held by merchant seamen be surrendered for replacement by certificates bearing the seal of the local inspectors. Within a few years, however, the Coast Guard's responsibilities became much heavier.

In 1938, the five-member Maritime Commission, appointed to oversee the functioning of the 1936 act, was authorized to establish the United States Maritime Service in order to improve the efficiency of licensed and unlicensed merchant mariners. Those entering the Maritime Service received ranks or rates based on those of the Coast Guard and were required to serve a three-month training period with pay. After completing this course satisfactorily, they were to have a month's refresher training each year with retainer pay in addition to their normal compensation. Since this training was intended to promote the safety of life at sea, the Maritime Service was obviously a somewhat belated result of the *Morro Castle* disaster—and of Coast Guard efforts to gain a closer relationship with the merchant marine.

Administration of the Maritime Service became a Coast Guard responsibility on 1 September 1938. Merchant mariners reported to one or another of three training stations—New York's Hoffman Island, New London's Fort Trumbull, and Government Island at Alameda, California—while shipboard training was conducted on board a former merchant steamer renamed the *American Seaman*, the 125-footers *Kimball* and *Yeaton*, and for a time, the *Northland.* Within ten months, fifty-three commissioned and warrant officers and 125 enlisted Coast Guardsmen together with 197 members of the Maritime Service were involved in the training program, and the demand was such that a further increase in facilities seemed desirable. Additional training ships were acquired during the next several years, among them the sailing vessels *Joseph Conrad, Tusitala,* and *Vema,* the former gunboat *Annapolis,* New York's schoolship *Empire State,* and the *American Sailor,* a sister of the *American Seaman,* while training facilities were established at Boston, St. Petersburg, Florida, and Port Hueneme, California.

The original purpose of the Maritime Service—to provide supplementary training for experienced personnel—had to be altered somewhat as the result of the vast expansion of shipbuilding activity in the United States at the beginning of the next decade. More ships required more seamen, yet increasing numbers of the latter were leaving the sea to seek employment in the shipyards. Thus, the Maritime Service had to expand its training program to include completely inexperienced men, the first of whom were selected from the Civilian Conservation Corps. The initial three-month course was obviously too advanced for these, so a six-month course, of which half the time was to be spent in one of the training ships, was begun for apprentice seamen. A ten-month course for radio operators was added as well.

More than 5,000 merchant mariners completed training during the first three years of the Maritime Service's existence, and by 30 June 1941, eighty-four commissioned and warrant officers and 257 men of the Coast Guard were assigned to this duty, as were forty-seven merchant marine officers and 303 unlicensed personnel. On that date, 1,591 men, almost all apprentice seamen, were being trained—thus, the administrative and instructional staff consisted of more than one-third the number of men enrolled for training. It is only fair to note, however, that this was a time of expansion, with facilities for the training of 1,000 licensed officers and 6,000 men each year then being planned.[21]

Even as the Coast Guard was expanding its activities to include the training of merchant seamen, the continuing increase of recreational boating, which attained unprecedented popularity during the 1930s, made greater demands on the service's personnel and equipment. Regulating small craft activity was the more difficult because many of those operating boats for pleasure or profit did so on inland waterways and lakes, including those that had been created by the construction of dams for flood control and hydroelectric power generation. The Coast Guard had no units on most of these bodies of water, and Admiral Waesche had no desire to disperse his forces further, yet if the Coast Guard did not assume this responsibility, another group was likely to do so. The Power Boat Squadron, an organization composed principally of yachtsmen, was thought to be seeking official recognition, and regulation of recreational boating would be a logical role for it.

The solution was to make the more experienced of the small craft sailors responsible for regulation of boating activity under the general supervision of the Coast Guard. Congress passed the requisite legislation, and the Coast Guard Reserve came into existence on 23 June 1939, although its first members were not enrolled until 5 October. In the meantime, Lieutenant Commanders Merlin O'Neill and Alfred C. Richmond, the latter the Coast Guard's first legal specialist, and John Myers, a civilian with the lifesaving branch, drew up regulations for the Coast Guard Reserve. Several problems emerged, most notably those of payment for damages sustained by privately owned vessels on duty with the Reserve and of compensation of employees on board the larger craft while so serving—members of the Reserve served without pay, but their yacht crews could not be expected to do so.

These difficulties overcome, the enrollment of Coast Guard Reserve personnel began. Applicants and their boats had to meet certain requirements, the former passing an examination on the rules of the road, aids to navigation, boat handling, and navigation laws, while their vessels were inspected to assure proper condition and equipment. Nothwithstanding these requirements and the lack of compensation, there was no dearth of applicants, and on 30 June 1940 the Coast Guard Reserve numbered 2,600 men and 2,300 boats. There would have been more had Headquarters not deferred further applications until an effective organization could be established.

The reservists were organized into flotillas under the Coast Guard districts within the continental United States, aiding the service by helping to patrol regattas, of which there were 481 in 1939, assisting in search-and-rescue missions, and inspecting small craft in their various areas. In order to increase their proficiency, the Coast Guard set up a training program under which reservists attended lectures on subjects relevant to their duties and were eligible to take correspondence courses through the Coast Guard Institute. These men in turn became mentors for other small boat sailors, and Admiral Waesche noted their instructional activities with approval.[22] Organization of the Coast Guard Reserve proved to be an effective solution to a potentially troublesome situation; it was not the least of Waesche's contributions to the service and the country.

Even as O'Neill, Richmond, and Myers were drawing up regulations for the Coast Guard Reserve, the service confronted an organizational challenge of greater magnitude—that of absorbing the Lighthouse Service. This agency was the oldest in governmental service, dating from 7 August 1789, when Congress created the Lighthouse Establishment, giving it jurisdiction over existing lighthouses and other aids to navigation. Like the Revenue-Cutter and Life-Saving services, the Lighthouse Service expanded rather unsystematically under somewhat sporadic Treasury Department control. Indeed, private contractors virtually administered the service until the 1840s, and after several proposals as to the proper means of administration had been considered, the Lighthouse Board was established in 1852. Although the Lighthouse Service remained under the Treasury Department, it was administered largely by the military services, for the board was composed of two officers from the Army's Corps of Engineers, two from the Navy, and two scientists from civil life, with junior officers of Army and Navy as secretaries. Moreover, each of the twelve lighthouse districts into which the country's coastlines were divided had an Army or Navy officer assigned as lighthouse inspector. Control of the Lighthouse Service was transferred to the newly created Department of Commerce and Labor in 1903, but the Lighthouse Board continued to administer it until 1910, when it gave way to the Bureau of Lighthouses under Commissioner George R. Putnam.

Although the responsibilities of Coast Guard and Lighthouse Service with regard to the safety of navigation were closely related, cooperation between the two was very limited. Cutters and stations had standing orders to retrieve errant buoys, other duties permitting, and to notify the Lighthouse Service of defects in aids to navigation, while lighthouse keepers were expected to inform the Coast Guard of suspicious vessels or activities in their vicinities. Revenue cutters had transported supplies and personnel to isolated stations on occasion in the past, but since 1903 that function had been performed almost entirely by the Lighthouse Service's own fleet of tenders.

In 1936, the Lighthouse Service described itself as perhaps the most decentralized of the government services, for less than 1 percent of its personnel were stationed in Washington.[23] That statement, which was probably intended to emphasize that the service was remarkably free of bureaucratic inefficiency, may have had the opposite effect by implying that the seventeen lighthouse district superintendents enjoyed a considerable degree of autonomy, with resultant lack of uniformity and economy. This was unlikely to be important so long as Commissioner Putnam headed the service, for like Sumner I. Kimball somewhat earlier, he was a respected figure in Washington. But Putnam had retired in 1935 and his successor, Harold D. King, had little time to prove himself and gain support in Congress before 9 May 1939, when President Franklin D. Roosevelt announced his Reorganization Plan II, under which the Bureau of Lighthouses was to be transferred from the Department of Commerce to the Treasury Department for consolidation with the Coast Guard.[24] With the approval of Congress, the transfer became effective on 1 July 1939.

In effect, a military service numbering 10,164 officers and men was to incorporate an organization comprising 4,119 full-time and 1,156 part-time employees, all of whom were civilians. Most of these were occupied in manning or maintaining some 30,000 aids to navigation, ranging from the more than 400 lighthouses and 30 lightships to the myriad unlighted buoys and shore marks, some of which were to be found in almost every harbor and navigable waterway in the United States and its possessions. A number manned the service's sixty-four tenders, which varied in size from the 72-foot *Alder* and *Elm* to the 200-foot *Cedar*. The process of incorporating

U. S. L. H. S. Cedar

The lighthouse tender Cedar, the service's largest.

these civilians into the Coast Guard would not be the easier because few of them seem to have had any desire to accept military discipline and customs; indeed, the Lighthouse Service had its own traditions and was looking forward to the celebration of its sesquicentennial on 7 August 1939 when the president made his announcement.

Transfer of the staff and equipment of the Bureau of Lighthouses to Coast Guard Headquarters was completed within a week, and Admiral Waesche appointed boards composed of three officers in each of the districts to decide which Lighthouse Service employees should be permitted to volunteer for induction into the Coast Guard and to recommend ranks and rates for them. Foreigners and those who had been convicted of felonies were excluded, as were men who would have less than thirty years of service at age 64. These and others who chose not to become Coast Guardsmen could be retained as civilian employees. Light keepers generally became chief or first class petty officers, junior officers in tenders were offered warrant appointments, and most of the tender masters and chief engineers were commissioned chief boatswains and chief machinists.

One exception was recommended. Captain John W. Leadbetter, who had commanded the big Cedar since her completion in 1917, had unlimited master mariner's papers with pilot endorsements for the waters of Oregon, Washington, southeastern and southwestern Alaska, and Bristol Bay. Moreover, he was said to enjoy "a social status in the Territory of Alaska comparable to that of a commissioned officer and is held in high esteem throughout the Territory."[25]

The board's recommendation that Leadbetter become a lieutenant commander was rejected by Headquarters, presumably because senior officers feared that a single exception would cause discontent on the part of others. So "Cap" Leadbetter also became a chief boatswain; he was reputed to be the only one who wore the gold oak leaves denoting command rank on his cap visor with his chief warrant officer's uniform. One doubts that Leadbetter was unduly perturbed by this seeming injustice, if he was aware of it, for with nearly forty years of service, he was eligible for retirement, and he could reflect that few Coast Guard officers, whatever their rank, could equal his professional attainments.

Some Lighthouse Service men did become officers. Former district superintendents were commissioned commanders or lieutenant commanders, according to their length of service, and others who had held administrative positions became lieutenants or lieutenants (junior grade). Fifty-nine officers were thus added to the *Coast Guard Register,* as were forty-four chief warrant officers and ninety-six warrant officers. All were junior to the Coast Guard officers holding their respective ranks, in order to minimize dissatisfaction among the latter. Most of the newly commissioned officers were assigned to district staffs with continuing responsibility for aids to navigation.[26] Commissioner King himself accepted the rank of captain and a position at Coast Guard Headquarters, but within a short time he decided that retirement was more attractive.

On the whole, Admiral Waesche and his subordinates seem to have made a genuine effort to treat the personnel of the former Lighthouse Service fairly. Yet there is little doubt that many resented the transfer and the abolition of their own service. Only 466 of them accepted petty officer ratings, and almost ten years later a retired lighthouse keeper wrote: "how the Commission had the heart to think we civilian personnel would ever blend with 15 & 16 year old Coast Guard men, 'is a huckleberry away above my persimmon' no good blood ever existed between or with either group. The Coast Guard & Rear Admirals to[o] brassy for we common Sailors, Fishermen Oystermen & what have you."[27] Many of his fellows probably would have agreed.

This was, however, an economy measure, and Commander Frank J. Gorman, chief finance officer, reported that the Coast Guard's incorporation of the Lighthouse Service had resulted in a saving of some $1 million—almost 10 percent of the latter's annual budget—in fiscal 1940. The centralization of administration and the merging of supply depots and stores accounted for much of the saving, and Gorman stated that the Coast Guard was operating and maintaining the system of aids to navigation much more economically than the Lighthouse Service had been able to do, in large part because of the gradual replacement of more highly paid Civil Service personnel by Coast Guardsmen. Thus, he anticipated that further economy would be realized as the process of consolidation continued.[28]

Initially, former Lighthouse Service personnel did most of the work pertaining to aids to navigation, but as time passed Coast Guard warrant officers, some of them recalled from Civilian Conservation Corps assignments, were put in charge of buoy tenders, and erstwhile cutter sailors learned that relieving a buoy was no task for a novice. Buoys frequently marked shoals, rocks, and other dangers that prudent mariners avoided. Tenders, however, had to brave these to relieve the buoys periodically, maintaining position despite wind, current, and sea condition while the new or overhauled buoy, together with its sinker and chain, was carefully lowered in the proper location and that which it replaced and its chain and mooring were hoisted on board and secured. The large lighted buoys were heavy, cumbersome, and fragile—very difficult to handle on the buoy deck of a tender except under ideal conditions, which rarely prevailed in coastal waters. And of course, the larger the buoy, the more massive its sinker and chain. Buoy-tending might be described as combining the more hazardous forms of piloting and stevedoring; it is not surprising that warrant officers commanded most of the tenders initially, for experience was almost the only school in which to learn the special type of seamanship that their work required.

Acquisition of the Lighthouse Service gave the commandant the opportunity to introduce reorganizations of the field service and Headquarters. Quite obviously, Coast Guard divisions, Coast Guard districts, and former Lighthouse districts could not exist without serious overlapping and jurisdictional problems. On 1 July 1940, all of these were abolished and replaced by thirteen districts, each named for the site of its headquarters: Boston, New York, Norfolk, Jacksonville, New Orleans, San Juan, Cleveland, Chicago, St. Louis, San Francisco, Seattle, Juneau, and Honolulu. A captain was intended to command each district, with a commander as his chief of staff, and all of the Coast Guard activities therein, regardless of whether they were cutters, lifesaving stations, or aids to navigation. Stations themselves were redesignated lifeboat stations and together with lighthouses and the like in their immediate vicinities, were put under a single station commander, usually a chief boatswain or a boatswain.[29] Former lifesaving district commanders, who became personnel officers at the new district headquarters, were still able to look after the interests of those of the lifesaving branch to a degree, but this reorganization clearly was a major step toward complete consolidation of the lifesaving branch with the remainder of the service.

Ships assigned to the districts were classed as patrol cutters—cutters and patrol boats 100 feet or more in length—district vessels—tugs, harbor cutters, smaller patrol boats, and tenders—or lightships. The former patrol boats included in the first category were known as Class B cutters, retaining the pale grey color scheme that distinguished them from the larger Class A vessels, which were white with buff stacks, masts, and ventilators. Tenders continued the Lighthouse Service practice of black hulls, white superstructures, and black stacks.

The reorganization of Headquarters was less extensive. The operations office retained its preeminent position, but divisions of personnel, materiel, inspections, and finance were established. Like the permanent board, these reported directly to the commandant. Expansion of the Coast Guard also brought additional flag ranks: Assistant Commandant Leon C. Covell and Engineer in Chief Harvey F. Johnson were promoted to the rank of rear admiral for four-year terms. Admiral Waesche's own term as commandant ended in mid-1940, but no one seems to have questioned his right to head the Coast Guard for another four years.

This period of expanding resources and responsibilities witnessed no diminution of performance of the Coast Guard's traditional duties. Each year of Admiral Hamlet's term as commandant had seen a greater number of lives saved and vessels assisted, increasing from 5,214 reported in fiscal 1933 to 7,510 four years later, and this trend continued under Waesche, reaching a peak of 9,383 in the year ending 30 June 1939 and decreasing slightly to 9,330 in the following year. Appropriations reached a total of $38,446,000 in fiscal 1939, somewhat more than half the reported value of vessels assisted and derelicts recovered during that period.[30]

Hurricanes and floods contributed to the totals of lives saved and assistance rendered. The September 1936 hurricane that skirted the coast from Cape Hatteras to the Delaware River before turning seaward claimed fewer lives because Coast Guard aircraft warned many of those in isolated areas and in small craft off the coast of its approach, while station crews performed a like service to those in their vicinities and ferried all who wished to safer locations, returning these to their homes after the storm had passed. The *Modoc* responded to the distress call of the steamer *El Almirante* south of Cape Hatteras and took her in tow, with four of the cutter's men injured as she did so; the *Mendota* stood by the Chesapeake light vessel, which was thought likely to founder in the heavy seas, and then proceeded to the assistance of a disabled barge; the *Champlain* and the *Mohawk* stood out at the height of the storm to aid distressed vessels; and the old *Apache* dared the turbulent waters of Chesapeake Bay to succor a sailing barge.[31]

Extensive flooding in the Ohio and Mississippi valleys early in 1937 led to the dispatch of the largest Coast Guard relief force that had ever been sent to a disaster scene. Units on the Atlantic, Gulf, and Great Lakes coasts sent 142 officers and 1,706 men to take part in relief operations that continued from 19 January to 11 March. These manned more than 350 small craft, eleven Coast Guard airplanes, and a dozen truck-mounted radio stations. The relief force was credited with rescuing 839 persons, transporting 67,613 refugees to safety, and saving 1,993 head of livestock. In addition, it transported thousands of Red Cross and other officials and relief workers, towed disabled boats and drifting buildings, carried the mails, helped to restore communication lines, and patrolled to prevent looting.[32] The flood that inundated areas in the vicinity of Alabama's Tombigbee and Alabama rivers little more than a year later required less extensive effort—sixty officers and men with twenty-seven boats and one airplane removed 102 persons from dangerous situations and provided other relief services.[33]

The hurricane that battered the Long Island and New England coasts late in September 1938 led to the involvement of all Coast Guard forces north of Norfolk in rescue and relief work. Ten cutters, nine patrol boats, and numerous smaller craft aided 509 vessels in distress, searched for others that were missing, and joined personnel ashore in rescuing 1,011 persons from sinking boats, inundated areas, and other perilous situations. For several weeks after the storm, Coast Guardsmen were employed at the usual tasks of restoring order and services, helping to salvage wrecked vessels and vehicles, and cooperating with federal, state, municipal, and Red Cross officials. Two Coast Guard vessels carried the mails between New York and New England ports until highways and railroads were returned to service, and Coast Guard radio units were active in allaying the fears of relatives and friends of those residing in the stricken area.

Three Coast Guardsmen, members of a party landed from the *General Greene* at Woods Hole, lost their lives while engaged in rescue operations, and as many stations were destroyed by the abnormally high water accompanying the hurricane. The Academy's waterfront facilities were ravaged, the practice schooner *Dobbin* sinking and her sister, the *Chase,* sustaining considerable damage. All of the surviving smaller craft were damaged to a greater or lesser extent. The total loss to the Coast Guard was reported to be $2 million.[34]

Occasionally, the Coast Guard was called on to justify its involvement in rescue efforts. In June 1937, the *Itasca* was engaged in a regular cruise for the purpose of delivering food, water, and other supplies to Interior Department employees on Baker, Jarvis, and Howland islands in the Central Pacific. The cutter remained at Howland for a week longer than usual in order to serve as a radio beacon for the famed aviator Amelia Earhart and her copilot, Frederick J. Noonan, who were making a flight around the world. Their airplane left New Guinea, bound for Howland Island, and the *Itasca* established radio contact with it during the morning of 2 July. Later efforts to communicate with the airplane were unsuccessful, and when it failed to arrive, Commander Warner K. Thompson got the *Itasca* underway to begin a search that was soon joined by a number of naval vessels, including the aircraft carrier *Lexington*. No trace of Miss Earhart's airplane was found, and on 17 July the cutter returned to Howland Island to embark personnel for transportation to Honolulu.

Even before the search had been terminated, some members of Congress were questioning the use of government vessels in that fashion, and Admiral Waesche had to report that the only unusual expense incurred by the *Itasca* was for the fuel she burned in the course of the search, which he estimated to be $2,000. To complaints that the search had interfered with the Coast Guard's performance of its regular duties, the commandant responded that "one of the principal duties of the Service is to answer all calls for assistance at sea. The search from July 2nd to July 17th was strictly in line with the prescribed duties of the Coast Guard."[35]

Admiral Waesche may have remembered this experience when in March 1939 the world traveler and popular writer Richard Halliburton and fourteen companions who were crossing the Pacific Ocean in the junk *Sea Dragon* were reported overdue. The commandant denied press accounts that the *Taney* was on her way from Midway Island to begin a search. That cutter was undergoing turbine repairs at Pearl Harbor, nor would another be sent because almost a month would elapse before she could reach the junk's last reported position, off the Japanese coast. Merchant ships bound to and from the Orient and the Philippines were requested to keep a sharp lookout for the *Sea Dragon,* and beyond that the Coast Guard did nothing.[36] Like Amelia Earhart and her copilot, Halliburton and his companions were never found.

The end of prohibition had resulted in a great diminution of liquor smuggling, but the taxes on alcoholic beverages were sufficiently high to guarantee a market for illegal whiskey; thus the Coast Guard continued to keep suspicious vessels under surveillance, seizing them whenever there was reasonable cause. The popularity of illegal distilling had decreased but little, and Coast Guard aircraft flew numerous missions helping federal and state officials to locate stills. Narcotics smuggling increased during the 1930s, with freighters arriving from foreign ports, especially those in the Orient and Hawaii, the principal means of delivery. Packages of drugs were frequently dropped overboard as these ships neared their destinations or after they had been moored, and small boats retrieved the narcotics from the water. This practice was countered by having inbound merchantmen trailed by Coast Guard cutters or patrol boats, while Coast Guardsmen and customs agents in smaller craft guarded the moored ships' outboard sides until customs and narcotics officials, often assisted by other Coast Guardsmen, had inspected each vessel. The occasional discovery of narcotics on board freighters indicated the effectiveness of this practice, but it was an undertaking of considerable magnitude, for some 4,500 vessels were trailed in fiscal 1938 and the number reached 5,000 in the next year.[37]

With economy continuing to be a governing principle, Coast

Guard Headquarters questioned the employment of the *Northland,* which, during the six months or so of each year when she was not making the Arctic cruise, lay idly at Seattle, her base since 1935, because her low speed and poor handling characteristics made her unfit for service as a cruising cutter. Commander William K. Scammell, who had commanded her for three years, thought that one of the single-screw cruising cutters could perform all of the duties associated with the Arctic cruise except assisting ships caught in the ice. By 1937, however, only three other vessels normally sailed through the Bering Strait into the Arctic Ocean, and two of these, the small motorship *Patterson* and the Bureau of Indian Affairs' *North Star,* were strengthened for ice navigation. The third, the sailing schooner *C. S. Holmes,* obviously could not enter the ice pack. Scammell doubted that the *Northland* would be able to reach the *Patterson* should the latter get into trouble in her usual operating area east of Point Barrow, and the danger to the other two vessels he thought minimal.[38]

Officers of the Seattle Division, including Commander Frederick A. Zeusler, who had succeeded Scammell in the *Northland,* disagreed on the ground that no one could predict when the cutter making the Arctic cruise might encounter ice. Zeusler went on to praise his command as "the ideal vessel for the work that she is to perform." He cited her success in breaking two ships out of the ice four years earlier and stated that since the removal of her useless sail rig and redistribution of her ballast in 1936, she rolled less and was slightly faster.[39]

The *Northland* made the 1938 Arctic cruise, and at its end, despite Zeusler's repeated protests, she was transferred to the Maritime Service for use as a barracks and training ship at Alameda. The Seattle Division's fears notwithstanding, the *Itasca* steamed into the Arctic Ocean in 1939 and 1940, reaching Point Barrow without incident each year. The Lake-class cutters were no longer available in 1941, so the *Haida* was ordered to make the Arctic cruise. She too arrived at Point Barrow, but while there, the 240-footer was thrust against a grounded ice floe by the current and damaged her screw while working free. The *Haida* was able to complete the cruise, the last before World War II, nonetheless.

The *Northland*'s tour of duty with the Maritime Service was interrupted in 1939 when she was returned to the Coast Guard to participate in the U.S. Antarctic Service Expedition being prepared under the direction of Rear Admiral Richard E. Byrd. She departed Alameda for Boston on 22 July and a week later encountered one of the violent storms of brief duration that sometimes occur during the summer months off Mexico's Pacific coast. Thanks to a radio warning from a vessel some 30 miles ahead of her, the *Northland*'s men had a short time in which to furl awnings, cover ventilators, and secure boats, deck lockers, and the like with extra lashings. The storm struck before this work could be completed, the wind reaching hurricane force in less than two hours. Lieutenant Commander William W. Kenner elected to run before the storm, but the *Northland* could not be kept on anything resembling a course in the mountainous seas and her inclinometer registered several 65° rolls. When Kenner brought her about, the cutter refused to head directly into the wind, whose velocity he estimated at 120 knots. With her rudder hard over and her propeller turning at 100 rpm, she rode with the seas almost abeam, rolling a little less deeply and freeing herself readily of the enormous amounts of water that she took aboard. After three hours of this, the wind dropped suddenly and a torrential rain reduced the sea's turbulence markedly. The *Northland* lost one boat and had two others damaged badly, several compartments were partially flooded because of leaking hatches and ventilators, her fore topmast and mainmast worked loose, and her radio equipment was disabled temporarily. Although several men were injured as a result of the ship's violent rolling, Kenner described the *Northland*'s behavior as "most satisfactory in all respects," considering the force of the wind and the tumultuous seas.[40]

But the *Northland* was not destined to make the acquaintance of the Antarctic ice pack. On 1 September 1939, German invasion forces crossed the Polish frontier. Britain and France declared war on Germany two days later, and on 5 September President Roosevelt ordered the Navy to organize a neutrality patrol to prevent belligerent warships and aircraft from operating in American and West Indian waters. A patrol of this extent was beyond the capability of the Navy's small Atlantic Squadron, so four of the Treasury-class cutters were ordered to the Atlantic coast. Their departure necessitated the immediate return of the *Northland* to resume her former duties at Alameda.[41]

The onset of World War II in Europe also presaged additional duties for the Coast Guard and a greater involvement in international affairs. This, however, had actually begun some years earlier.

CHAPTER TWELVE

THE APPROACH TO WAR, 1936–41

What might be described as the Coast Guard's first true involvement in international affairs since World War I—prohibition-related incidents excepted—came in 1936, when the *Cayuga* was making a cadet practice cruise in European waters. A Naval Academy practice squadron—the battleships *Oklahoma* and *Arkansas* and the latter's demilitarized sister *Wyoming*—was providing a similar service for midshipmen, and when the outbreak of the Spanish Civil War necessitated the evacuation of American citizens from northern Spain, the squadron commander ordered the *Cayuga* to San Sebastián on 24 July for that purpose because his warships were too large to enter the harbor. Commander James Pine and the cadets were transferred to the *Wyoming* a week later for return to the United States, their places being filled by five officers and twenty-five men sent out in the destroyers *Hatfield* and *Kane,* which sailed in mid-August. The *Cayuga* remained in Spanish waters, acting under naval orders and serving as a communication center for the American ambassador. When the spread of the fighting caused the temporary evacuation of the summer embassy, the cutter took the ambassador and his staff on board—probably the first time that a Coast Guard vessel had become an embassy.[1]

In mid-September, Squadron 40-T was established to provide a continuing American naval presence in European waters. Initially it was to comprise a cruiser, two destroyers, and the *Cayuga,* and when the cutter's commanding officer learned of this assignment, he asked the senior naval officer to order the *Campbell,* preparing to leave the United States on her shakedown cruise, to relieve the *Cayuga.* This request brought a deserved rebuke from Admiral Waesche, but on the arrival of the USS *Raleigh* at the end of September, the *Cayuga* was detached from Squadron 40-T and ordered home.[2]

The Spanish Civil War ran its bloody course without further Coast Guard involvement, but the imminence of war in Europe brought new duties for personnel of the New York District late in August 1939. President Roosevelt decided that armed foreign-flag merchant vessels in American ports should not be issued clearance papers, so

Coast Guardsmen and customs officials boarded the French liner *Normandie*, the British *Aquitania*, and the German *Bremen* to search for armaments. At the insistence of the British government, which had authorized the arming of merchant ships, Roosevelt ordered that only vessels with offensive armaments should be detained, but he had the search of the *Bremen* carried out very deliberately in the expectation that her departure would be delayed until after the declaration of war, when British warships could capture her as she cleared territorial waters on leaving New York. A very thorough investigation having revealed nothing remotely resembling armament of any type, the *Bremen* was finally allowed to sail on 29 August, and although she was at sea when the war began, the liner ultimately reached a German port safely.[3]

The inspection of merchant vessels of belligerent ownership to determine if they carried offensive armament became a routine matter for the Coast Guard districts on the Atlantic and Gulf coasts for the next two years, with 4,033 ships being boarded for this purpose by 30 June 1941. Regardless of whether or not they were armed, belligerent vessels were not permitted to transmit radio messages while they were in American waters, with the exception of distress signals, requests for navigational information, and reports of arrival and departure. Boarding officers usually enforced this prohibition by sealing a ship's radio transmitters upon her arrival. Again, it was an operation of some magnitude—Coast Guardsmen and customs officials boarded more than 13,500 vessels to this end during the first two years of the war. And district commanders were required to report daily to Coast Guard Headquarters, which maintained a record of the identity, location, and movements of every merchant vessel in the territorial waters of the United States, including the Virgin Islands, Puerto Rico, Hawaii, and Alaska.[4]

The adoption of the "cash and carry" principle in November 1939, whereby belligerent nations were allowed to purchase war materials in the United States, led to a large increase in the embarkation of explosive and other hazardous cargoes in American seaports. This made effective control of cargo-handling procedures and ship movements mandatory, and although the treasury secretary was not empowered to enforce the boarding, anchorage, and ship movement regulations of the 1917 Espionage Act until 27 June 1940, nine Coast Guard officers were serving as captains of the port in major harbors on that date; twenty-eight more were ordered to this duty within the next few weeks.[5]

Just as in 1917, a number of ships of belligerent ownership were interned in American harbors after the war began, and as Allied shipping losses mounted, Secretary Morgenthau suggested that these be taken over by the United States to free other ships for Allied use. He extended this to include Danish ships after the Germans occupied Denmark in the spring of 1940. Reports that the crews of Axis vessels were deliberately sabotaging them finally led President Roosevelt to act almost a year later; early on 30 March 1941, a Sunday, Coast Guardsmen quietly boarded two German, twenty-six Italian, and thirty-five Danish ships and removed their crews. Two months later, Congress authorized the United States to requisition the vessels for use in trade with Latin America.

This rather high-handed action was taken under the internationally recognized right of angary, which allows a belligerent to requisition neutral ships and equipment within its borders in return for compensation. While the United States was not yet formally a belligerent and some of the ships were not neutral, legal experts justified the action on the ground that a sovereign state had the right to commandeer for its own use any vessels within its territorial waters in time of extreme necessity, paying compensation to their owners. It is not likely, however, that the Coast Guardsmen questioned the legality of their action. They simply carried out their orders without untoward incident.

Meanwhile, aircraft, cutters, and coastal stations undertook systematic patrols to prevent violations of neutrality by American-flag vessels or others in territorial waters, while the *Bibb* and the *Campbell* joined the four destroyers of Captain Louis E. Denfeld's Division 18 to establish the northernmost section of the Neutrality Patrol ordered by the president on 5 September 1939. Patrol "Zero," as it was designated, extended from Placentia Bay, Newfoundland, to 40° North latitude and included the most turbulent section of the patrol line. Too turbulent for the destroyers, it turned out—early in November Destroyer Division 18 was transferred to the Gulf of Mexico, and the commander of the Boston Division assumed control of the newly formed Grand Banks Neutrality Patrol, with the six Treasury-class cutters and the Lake-class *Chelan*, *Tahoe*, and *Cayuga* ordered to duty thereon.[6] Their assignment to the offshore patrol left the inshore forces seriously depleted, so Class B cutters were transferred from the Great Lakes to the Atlantic coast and the *Carrabasset* and the *Kickapoo*, both of which had been laid up at Curtis Bay since 1936, were recommissioned.

Announcement of the cutters' assignment to duty with the Neutrality Patrol led Commander Edward H. Smith to suggest that "a group of floating weather stations . . . established at strategic points in the North Atlantic Ocean" might perform the functions of the patrol vessels as well.[7] "Iceberg" Smith's "floating weather stations" would be established primarily for the purpose of broadcasting meteorological information for the benefit of aircraft flying across the Atlantic Ocean. This concept had been stated on a number of occasions since 1919, when on the conclusion of the first successful transatlantic flight, which he had planned and commanded, Commander John H. Towers, USN, told the press that "meteorological stations will have to be set up all over the Atlantic before transatlantic flights will be commercially profitable."[8] He might have added that aircraft would have to be improved markedly as well, but by the mid-1930s multi-engine flying boats with the requisite range had been developed.

Pan American Airways, under the dynamic leadership of Juan Trippe, led the way in commercial transoceanic flying, beginning in the Pacific because of its inability to obtain refueling privileges in Bermuda and Newfoundland. Air mail service between San Francisco and Hong Kong was initiated in 1935, with regular passenger-carrying flights coming almost a year later. Pan American also pioneered the Hawaii-New Zealand air mail route, but on the second flight south, in January 1938, the *Samoan Clipper* crashed, killing her seven-man crew, after leaving Pago Pago, American Samoa.[9]

A report of this disaster attracted the attention of Lieutenant Commander George B. Gelly, who as public relations officer was alert to opportunities for the enhancement of the Coast Guard's role as the protector of life and property at sea. The International Ice Patrol cutters warned shipping of the presence of danger so that it might be avoided; might a weather patrol provide a similar service for aircraft, enabling them to fly around storms? Gelly approached Pan American officials, who quite naturally liked the idea and made the company's correspondence course in meteorology available for use by Coast Guard personnel. The U.S. Weather Bureau, an agency of the Department of Agriculture, showed little interest in weather reporting for aviation purposes, although it agreed to test its weather balloons for possible use from cutters.[10] The tests proved the feasibility of releasing balloons from cutter decks even in inclement weather, and representatives of the Civil Aeronautics Authority, Weather Bureau, and Coast Guard conferred with Pan American President Trippe to discuss means of assisting aircraft flying transoceanic routes. While the conferees differed on many points, they concluded that the Coast Guard should station one or more ships in the Atlantic Ocean for weather observation purposes and that the Weather Bureau should furnish the necessary meteorological personnel and equipment.[11]

Nothing further had been done by mid-1939, when Pan American began regular transatlantic flights on a southern route to Lisbon, Portugal, and a northern route to Foynes, Ireland. The big flying boats relied on weather reports from merchant vessels, and these proved adequate until the imminence of war caused most of these ships to maintain radio silence while at sea. Juan Trippe approached the Coast Guard and the Weather Bureau again, warning that the transatlantic air service would probably have to be abandoned unless the former were willing to station a cutter midway between Newfoundland and Ireland, two others between Bermuda and the Azores, and a fourth between the Azores and Lisbon. The first would be needed only until the end of September, when flights by the northern route would be suspended for the winter, but Trippe wanted the stations on the southern route maintained continuously.

Admiral Waesche was sympathetic, although he thought cutters too small for this purpose, and in any case his service had none to spare. He recommended to Secretary Morgenthau that six of the World War I-built cargo ships laid up in Maritime Commission custody be transferred to the Coast Guard for ocean weather duty, adding that Francis W. Reichelderfer, the recently appointed chief of the Weather Bureau, had promised to give whatever assistance was required.[12] Reichelderfer was an enthusiastic supporter of the ocean weather station concept—as a Navy ensign, he had served as a meteorologist for the *NC-4*'s flight twenty years earlier.

The treasury secretary, however, did not think the importance of the proposed service would justify its expense. Thereupon, Secretary of Agriculture Henry A. Wallace, who had become interested in the project, turned to the Navy. With the Neutrality Patrol demanding all of its available vessels, the Navy Department declined, observing that a weather patrol was properly a Coast Guard function. Pressure also came from the State Department, which like the Navy, found the transatlantic air service very useful in maintaining a close contact with Europe.[13] Despite all of these efforts, the expense of refitting and operating weather patrol ships continued to be considered prohibitive.

President Roosevelt himself ultimately took the initiative in the matter early in 1940. More than thirty years later, Captain George B. Gelly, USCG (Ret.), attributed the president's action to a *New York Times* editorial on the subject, which had resulted from a newspaper story about Pan American's dilemma that Lieutenant Commander Gelly had helped to write. According to Gelly's recollection, Roosevelt held a press conference that afternoon, at which another reporter asked what he intended to do to help Pan American, and the president called Admiral Waesche some hours later, "directing C.G. to provide cutters for Weather Patrol and safety of planes taking personnel to Europe and Africa."[14]

While there seems to be no reason to doubt Captain Gelly's account of the events leading to the president's decision, the latter acted less precipitously than Gelly recalled. At Roosevelt's direction, his naval aide, Captain Daniel J. Callaghan, met with Admiral Harold R. Stark, the chief of naval operations, Rear Admiral Emory S. Land, chairman of the Maritime Commission, and Rear Admiral Waesche to consider the availability of patrol vessels. Callaghan reported that the admirals recommended the withdrawal of cutters from the Grand Banks Patrol for temporary assignment to weather observation duty. The Congress was debating appropriations for the Maritime Commission at the time, and if Admiral Land received a sufficient amount, four of the old cargo ships would be reconditioned and transferred to the Coast Guard to replace the cutters as weather patrol ships. The Navy promised to provide radio equipment on request, and President Roosevelt approved these recommendations.[15]

The Grand Banks Patrol was terminated on 27 January 1940, and within a few days the *Duane* sailed from Boston to embark Weather Bureau equipment and personnel for herself and the *Bibb* at New York. After delivering the latter's allotment at Norfolk, the *Duane* steamed eastward to a station some two-thirds of the way from Bermuda to Fayal Island in the Azores. The *Bibb* took station half the distance between Bermuda and her sister ship, and both cutters began transmitting meteorological information on 10 February 1940, thus starting a service that Coast Guard vessels would continue to provide for thirty years and more.

In view of the international situation, Secretary Morgenthau agreed that it was advisable to ask the State Department to inform foreign governments of the weather ships' stations and mission, identifying the six cutters that would form the patrol force and forwarding a silhouette and description: "each 327-feet in length, 41-foot beam, 2216 tons displacement, hull, bridge, and superstructure painted white; smokestack (black smoke-band at top), ventilators, and mast painted straw color."[16] In mid-March, the commander of the Boston District posed a series of questions pertaining to the proper action to be taken by commanding officers of weather patrol and other cutters in a number of contingencies. After conferring with officials of the State, Treasury, and Navy departments, the commandant informed the service generally that vessels of belligerent ownership suffering storm damage might be taken in tow if necessary, but if the damage resulted from enemy action, the ship must not be towed—those on board should be rescued if they wished. In the event that a belligerent warship interfered with a cutter's salvage activity, the latter's commanding officer was to assent to the warship's demands, under protest if the incident took place within the 300-mile neutrality zone. All such events, wherever they occurred, were to be reported to Headquarters promptly.[17]

Concerned that requests for assistance from surface vessels might lure weather ships from their stations unnecessarily, Admiral Waesche urged that commanding officers consider carefully the circumstances of each request before leaving their stations; were another vessel relatively close at hand, were the distress signal less than urgent, were the ship in trouble a great distance away, the cutter probably would not be justified in leaving her station. Patrol vessels en route to and from the stations, on the other hand, were to respond to distress signals without hesitation.[18]

The Coast Guard commandant agreed to the assignment of the Treasury-class vessels to weather patrol reluctantly, informing Land and Reichelderfer that the use of cutters for such a purpose "is not conducive to economy and precludes their use on other active duties for which they are much better adapted and for which they were designed. . . . I sincerely hope that the four Maritime Commission vessels will be refitted and made available as expeditiously as possible."[19] But the funds necessary to recommission the old cargo ships for weather patrol were not forthcoming, and perhaps with Treasury

Department encouragement, the Civil Aeronautics Authority proposed that it be authorized to establish weather reporting stations in the Atlantic Ocean. President Roosevelt promptly squelched this proposal, ordering "that as long as emergency weather reporting service is required it will be furnished as at present by Coast Guard cutters."[20] Waesche resigned himself to the continuation of the weather patrol, making the seven Lake-class cutters on the Atlantic coast available for duty thereon in addition to the Treasury-class and directing the Boston, New York, and Norfolk district commanders to draw up their own rotation schedules.

The war brought another task to the Coast Guard soon after the German conquest of Denmark on 9 April 1940. Danes in Greenland appealed to the United States for assistance, fearing that German or British forces would attempt to occupy the island. The United States government had some reason to be concerned about Greenland because German bases thereon would be dangerously close to vital shipping lanes and the northeastern part of the country. Moreover, weather stations on Greenland's east coast could provide invaluable meteorological information to German forces fighting the Western Allies, and due mainly to aircraft orders placed with American manufacturers by the latter, the cryolite mine at Ivigtut had assumed critical importance—its product was essential as a flux in smelting aluminum. The State Department, however, thought that the dispatch of American armed forces to Greenland might be considered provocative, so an agreement was negotiated with the Danish minister in Washington whereby a United States consulate would be established at Godthaab. The choice of a Coast Guard vessel to convey the consul to his post was quite natural—the oceanographic cutter *General Greene* had traversed the waters off Greenland periodically in the course of her ice observation cruises, so the presence of another would cause little comment. It would have to be another, for the 125-foot *General Greene* could provide neither adequate quarters for the consul nor much reassurance for the Greenlanders. The *Comanche* was chosen instead; she departed New York on 10 May with the consul, his staff, and the equipment necessary to set up a radio station on board. The cutter reached Ivigtut ten days later, and after ascertaining that the mine was extremely vulnerable to flooding, she steamed on to Godthaab to land the consul.

The *Comanche*'s mission was the beginning of a commitment that would require a considerable portion of the Coast Guard's resources—and of its shipbuilding program—during the next several years. The *Campbell, Duane,* and *Cayuga* joined the 165-footer in the following weeks, operating principally in Davis Strait and Baffin Bay, the *Campbell* landing a 3-inch gun, machine guns, and small arms for use in protecting the cryolite mine. Fourteen of the *Campbell*'s men accepted discharges from the Coast Guard to provide a crew for the 3-inch gun and to train the Greenlanders in the use of the other weapons.[21]

Meanwhile, a telegraphic order was dispatched to the commander of the San Francisco District: "Detail sufficient officers and men except Commanding Officer to NORTHLAND to bring her to New York placing other units except Maritime in reduced commission as may be necessary to accomplish this."[22] That order marked the beginning of a new career for the *Northland*. Heretofore the Coast Guard's ugly duckling, she was about to come into her own as the only ship in American service that possessed the massive hull strength and endurance required for operation off Greenland's east coast, a forbidding region with its polar current flowing southward bearing immense ice flows, while cold winds blowing off the island's ice cap made the weather uncertain and foggy.

On the *Northland*'s arrival at New York, "Iceberg" Smith took command, and while he was preparing the cutter for an extended cruise, the State Department sought permission for her to enter Greenland's territorial waters as necessary and queried the British government as to the danger from mines that the Royal Navy had laid between Iceland and Greenland. Reassured on both points, the *Northland* sailed from New York early in August and spent the next four months gathering information on which to base sailing directions for the coast between Angmagssalik and Scoresby Sound. Ice conditions were normal in 1940, with 100 bergs in sight off Cape Farewell and the ice pack extending some distance southeast of Angmagssalik. Smith forced the *Northland* through a 5-mile coastal ice belt to reach that settlement on the southeast coast and then took her into Denmark Strait, whence he reported an opening through the ice pack into Scoresby Sound.[23] The cutter returned to the United States in December, to find that plans for her employment in 1941 were well advanced.

Not long after the *Northland* had departed New York in August 1940, the *Campbell* and the *Duane* damaged their screws while attempting to work their way through ice off the Greenland coast, demonstrating that twin-screw ships were not practical for maneuvering in pack ice. The damage was more serious than first thought; when the two were ordered home, neither could sustain more than 7 knots, which was the more embarrassing because the *Campbell* was needed elsewhere.

With the Battle of the Atlantic about to reach a critical point in the aftermath of the defeat of France in June 1940 and a new theater of operations opened by the entry of Italy into the war in the same month, President Franklin D. Roosevelt had decided to make fifty old American destroyers available to the Royal Navy, the United States receiving in return 99-year leases on base sites in British possessions in the Western Hemisphere. The first three of the flush-deckers, one of which was the former Coast Guard *Abel P. Upshur*, departed Boston bound for Halifax on 4 September, and soon thereafter someone realized that these ships were almost identical to the two destroyers of Squadron 40-T, based at Lisbon. German aviators and submariners would be hard put to distinguish American vessels from their British near-sisters—indeed, the cruiser flagship *Omaha* was herself a four-stacker and so might be misidentified at a distance or in poor visibility.

The chief of naval operations called Admiral Waesche to inquire about a cutter to replace Squadron 40-T, and the commandant replied that the *Campbell* was the only ship suited to the assignment because she alone had received her wartime gun armament. She was still limping homeward, so Waesche sent the *Ingham* to take her in tow, and the president ordered that the cutter be docked immediately on her arrival at the New York Navy Yard to have her propellers replaced and to have degaussing gear installed for protection against magnetic mines. The *Campbell* was towed into the navy yard on 15 September and the work proceeded apace—perhaps for naught, because the State Department questioned the advisability of keeping any United States vessel in European waters. At the month's end, however, the president decided that the *Campbell* should go to Lisbon, where she was stationed until relieved by the *Ingham* on 25 April 1941.[24]

Since the president had proclaimed a limited national emergency as early as 8 September 1939, it may seem surprising that only the *Campbell* had received a part of her wartime armament a year later. Rearming Coast Guard vessels was not a simple matter to arrange, for the necessary availability had to be worked into the scheduled activities of both the cutters and the shipyards at which the work was to be done—the Coast Guard Depot and private yards for Atlantic and Gulf coast vessels and the Puget Sound and Pearl Harbor navy yards for cutters stationed in the Pacific.[25]

The schedules were completed during the summer of 1940, and thereafter a few cutters at a time entered the specified yards for the installation of more guns, depth-charge tracks and Y-guns—two-barreled depth-charge projectors—degaussing equipment, and sonar gear. In few cases did the rearmament take the form anticipated when the ships were designed, for the additional top weight of antisubmarine equipment had to be compensated for by lighter gun armament—thus, the 240-footers received a second 3-inch gun in lieu of the projected third 5-inch, and the Lake-class vessels fared similarly with two 5-inch and three 3-inch guns. While the necessary magazine capacity had been included in most of the original designs, no one seems to have foreseen the personnel that would be needed to man additional gun, depth-charge, and detection equipment. More bunks were installed where possible; when they had been occupied, hammocks had to be slung for ever larger complements.

By naval standards, however, the cutters were not overcrowded, nor was the quality of life on board affected adversely. For example, the Navy had adopted a cafeteria system of messing for enlisted men in the mid-1930s, but until the entry of the United States into World War II and in some ships thereafter, Coast Guard sailors continued

The Pea Island Lifeboat Station was typical in all but its personnel.

to enjoy meals served to them by mess cooks at tables set up on lower decks that were sufficiently spacious to serve as motion picture theaters and reading and gaming rooms. Gambling, of course, was strictly forbidden—but the enforcement of the prohibition was not strict. And the meals were good. A senior officer observed in 1939 that "good food . . . probably [does] more for contentment of crew than any other item," and the service acted on this premise.[26]

Additional personnel had been authorized for the Coast Guard to meet the needs of vessels on Neutrality Patrol and tending aids to navigation. "Special temporary" three-year enlistments were initiated in 1939, more recruiting stations were opened, recruiting petty officers visited small towns and rural areas in trucks fitted for the purpose, and Coast Guard units were permitted to enlist men. Nearly 20,000 volunteered, of whom 4,262 were accepted. The recruits were sent to temporary training stations established at Ellis Island, New York, and Port Townsend, Washington, and to the Curtis Bay Depot and the Fort Lauderdale base for outfitting and training before assignment to active units. Supplementary national defense appropriation legislation in 1941 authorized the enlistment of another 2,500 men, and again recruiters had little difficulty meeting their quotas. The Burke-Wadsworth Act of 1940, which instituted conscription, was a contributing factor—many young men seem to have found a three-year enlistment in the Coast Guard more attractive than the prospect of one year of Army service, possibly continued for a longer period.

With an ample supply of volunteers, the recruiters had no reason to turn to one source of manpower, the country's black population, despite President Roosevelt's letter of 3 September 1941, in which he stated that "in the Federal Service the doors of employment are open to all loyal and qualified workers regardless of creed, race, or national origin." To be sure, the president referred directly to "the employment and assignment of negroes in the Federal Civil Service," but three weeks later the Treasury Department required all of its divisions, including the Coast Guard, to conform to his directive.[27]

Mainly as a legacy from the Life-Saving Service, the Coast Guard did have some black personnel in 1941, but they were very few, most of whom were assigned to the Pea Island Lifeboat Station on North Carolina's Outer Banks. In 1880, little more than a year after the station had been established, Richard Etheridge, a black surfman at the Bodie Head Station, had been appointed keeper at Pea Island, and within a short time the station was manned entirely by black men. Under Etheridge, the Pea Island Station gained a reputation for smartness and discipline, and his successors, also blacks, strove to maintain it. By 1915, the tradition that the Pea Island crew must be composed of black men was firmly established, so it was continued by the Coast Guard.[28]

The station retained its reputation for efficiency for a time; on an inspection visit in 1930, Admiral Billard noted in its log: "A well-kept station and a fine looking, snappy and alert crew."[29] By mid-1937, however, rumors of a less satisfactory situation at Pea Island led Assistant Commandant Covell to order an investigation, and after receiving the inspector's report, the commandant put a white petty officer in charge of the station. Congressman Lindsay Warren learned of this from a confidant, R. Bruce Etheridge, who feared that this development implied a complete exclusion of blacks from the service and wrote, "everyone regardless of color, should have [a] goal to strive for—every colored man in eastern North Carolina desires a place in the Coast Guard at Pea Island."[30] Warren took the matter up with Admiral Waesche, who attributed the decline in efficiency and morale at Pea Island to the frequent absences of the black petty officer in charge, who had been ill for some time. If one of the station crew could demonstrate his ability to take charge in a reasonable length of time, the white petty officer would be transferred to another unit.[31]

A black successor was chosen after some months, so Pea Island remained a black enclave in a service that otherwise was almost entirely white, until the station was closed in 1947. A few blacks were enlisted for mess duty during the next several years, and the acquisition of the Lighthouse Service brought into the Coast Guard a number of others who were serving at lighthouses and on board river buoy tenders. Only World War II, however, caused any significant change in the service's policy in this regard.

The rapid expansion of American military forces is usually effected in part by ordering members of their reserve organizations to active duty. But the Coast Guard Reserve had been established for one purpose only—that of assisting the service with certain of its peacetime duties—and there was no provision for ordering its members to active duty. They simply served a few hours or days at times that suited their schedules. This situation was changed by legislation of 19 February 1941, which repealed the Coast Guard Reserve Act of 1939 and established a new Coast Guard Reserve similar in organization and purpose to the military services' reserve forces. Its members, men between the ages of 17 and 64, were appointed or enlisted for three-year terms, during which they could be called to active duty in time of war or national emergency. The former Coast Guard Reserve was replaced by an almost identical organization known as the Coast Guard Auxiliary, with the provision that whenever any vessel therein was used by the Coast Guard, those owning and manning her, if qualified, would serve as temporary members of the Reserve during the period of her service. By 30 June 1941, regular and temporary members of the Coast Guard Reserve numbered 101 officers, of whom thirty-four were regular chief warrant and warrant officers who had accepted reserve commissions, and ninety-six enlisted men. Admiral Waesche expressed his satisfaction with this modest beginning, noting that the rate of growth was determined mainly by the availability of training facilities and the need for the reservists' services.[32]

Neither the transfer of the fifty old destroyers during the autumn of 1940 nor expanded warship production had satisfied the Royal Navy's requirement for escort vessels, and when the U.S. Navy indicated its unwillingness to give up any more of its smaller ships, Secretary Morgenthau, one of the cabinet members most insistent on further aid to Britain, began to consider the possibility of making Coast Guard cutters available. The British need of long-range ocean escorts might be met in part by the Lake-class cutters, nine of which could steam more than 6,500 miles at economical speed—the *Cayuga* alone was capable of only 6,050 miles.[33] Prime Minister Winston Churchill expressed interest in the vessels, and on 28 February 1941, Headquarters ordered district commanders to "relieve all 250-foot cutters from further patrols and cruising schedules."[34] A week later, Morgenthau wrote the president to list as alternatives to the Lake class "certain other vessels of the Coast Guard, some of which may be found suitable for the purpose intended." These were the old *Unalga, Ossipee,* and *Tallapoosa,* the four 240-footers, and the seventeen 165-foot Class B cutters. He recognized that the first three would be of little use to the British and that the Class B cutters were too small for ocean escort duty. The 240-footers the secretary thought nearly the equal of the Lake class.[35]

This is a curious letter. Purporting to list alternatives, Morgenthau made it clear that none existed in sufficient number. It has been speculated that the letter was written at the insistence of Admiral

The Saranac *on trials after receiving her wartime armament. She became HMS* Banff *less than a month later.*

Waesche, who probably was not enthusiastic at the prospect of losing nearly half of the Coast Guard's effective cruising cutters and wished to substitute older vessels.[36] But the information indicating that this was impossible is not likely to have been provided the secretary without the commandant's knowledge, and even if it were, the latter was well aware that only the seven Treasury-class cutters could realistically be offered in place of the 250-footers because the *Tampa* class lacked the endurance necessary for long-range escorts. The omission of the 327-footers and the 165-foot Class A cutters is also interesting. One suspects that Admirals Stark and Waesche chose to give up the somewhat older, slower, and less maneuverable Lake-class in order to retain the Treasury-class, while even such indifferent icebreakers as the *Escanaba* and her sisters could be employed more profitably in that role in American waters than on convoy duty, for which they were too small, too slow, and too "short-legged."

Transfer of the 250-footers did not follow immediately, mainly because the necessary legislative authority was still being debated by Congress. Even after the passage of the Lend-Lease Act on 11 March 1941, a number of details had to be worked out, and some at Coast Guard Headquarters must have hoped that the ships would be retained, for all ten were included in a memorandum of 18 March, which listed cutter assignments for the spring and summer.[37] By that time, however, most were at or en route to the navy yards where they were to be prepared for transfer, and on 2 April 1941, Assistant Secretary of the Treasury Herbert Gaston informed Waesche that the Lake-class cutters were to be transferred to the Royal Navy without delay.[38] Three days later, Franklin Roosevelt signed the official order, noting that "it would be in the interests of our national defense to transfer the defense articles set forth in the annexed Schedule," the "articles" being ten 250-foot cutters. The president directed Secretary Morgenthau to make the necessary arrangements with the head of the British Supply Council in North America.[39]

Admiral Waesche issued three pages of instructions for effecting the transfer on the same day, and on 9 April he assured Gaston that everything was going smoothly under the joint direction of Captain Ralph W. Dempwolf, commander of the New York District, and Captain F. L. Palliser of HMS *Malaya,* a British battleship being repaired at the New York Navy Yard. Crews for the cutters were obtained from the personnel of Royal Navy vessels being refitted or repaired in the United States. Coast Guardsmen remained on board to instruct their foreign counterparts, and Coast Guard commanding officers retained full responsibility until the ships were formally transferred. Following practice runs in Long Island Sound, the first four of the vessels, stripped of all identification including their lake names, painted in British war color, and fully supplied and fueled, hoisted the Royal Navy's white ensign on 30 April. The remainder were transferred in May.[40]

Although the British were disappointed at not receiving the Treasury-class cutters as well, they welcomed the 250-footers, which Winston Churchill ordered renamed for coastguard stations in the United Kingdom. The prime minister had agreed with Secretary Morgenthau that the ships should be based at Iceland for service on the North Atlantic convoy routes, but the British Admiralty did not—the former cutters escorted convoys running between Londonderry, Northern Ireland, and Sierra Leone on the west coast of Africa. They had some victories—HMS *Totland* (ex-*Cayuga*) sank the German *U-522* in February 1943, and almost three months later the *Sennen* (ex-*Champlain*) joined HMS *Jed* in destroying the *U-209.* Only the *Culver* (ex-*Mendota*) became the victim of a German submarine torpedo, in January 1942, but the *Hartland* (ex-*Pontchartrain*) and the *Walney* (ex-*Sebago*) were lost in an ill-conceived operation in November 1942. Crowded with American soldiers and flying large American ensigns with their British colors, they attempted to run the gauntlet of alerted Vichy French warships and shore batteries to land the troops on the waterfront at Oran, Algeria. Both were sunk with heavy loss of life, without completing their mission. Six of the seven surviving cutters were returned to the United States at the war's end.

While the Royal Navy welcomed the 250-footers, 30 April 1941 can hardly have been a joyous occasion for Admiral Waesche and the other Coast Guard officers and men who witnessed the transfer of the former *Saranac, Pontchartrain, Tahoe,* and *Mendota.* In their decade of service, these ships and their sisters had established themselves in Coast Guard tradition, and their departure was felt keenly. To be sure, the president had assured the commandant that replacements for them and for the three oldest cruising cutters would be forthcoming—thirteen 250-footers and one 230-foot "ice protected cutter" were authorized—of which the last, tentatively named the *Arctic*, was to be completed in little more than a year, while five of the larger vessels would be ready within two years. Waesche was well aware, however, that the nation's shipbuilding facilities were already overtaxed, so he must have found small comfort in Roosevelt's promise. Nor was the president's directive, relayed by Gaston on 2 April, to acquire "some old, slow coastal type freighters" from the Maritime Commission for weather patrol, of any help, for no money was appropriated for the purpose.[41]

Even as the diminution of the cutter force was being discussed, the commandant had attempted to free the Coast Guard of one of its traditional responsibilities. Citing the prevailing radio silence on the part of merchant shipping as a principal reason, Waesche urged that the International Ice Patrol be discontinued in 1941: "the Patrol cannot be properly and effectively conducted without the cooperation of shipping in furnishing ice information by radio. The Ice Patrol area is approximately the size of the State of Pennsylvania, and it is impossible for one cutter . . . to define the limiting lines of ice."[42] Moreover, ships using the North Atlantic routes would follow tracks specified by their naval authorities regardless of the Ice Patrol's recommendations, and foreign governments might consider the broadcasting of ice and meteorological information for possible use by a belligerent a breach of neutrality. The Interdepartmental Board agreed that there should be no Ice Patrol in 1941, but it wished the *General Greene* to continue her oceanographic work in the region.

When Acting Secretary Gaston presented this recommendation at a cabinet meeting, the president demurred, pointing out that the International Ice Patrol would be a useful cover for American activities in Greenland, for which there was as yet no legal sanction. Gaston replied that the Coast Guard had no intention of abandoning these in any case, but Roosevelt insisted that the Ice Patrol be conducted as usual.[43]

Planning for the Greenland activities had begun in the autumn of 1940, when a group of officers met with Admirals Covell and Johnson to consider the matter. They recommended that three cutters be made ready for duty in Greenland waters by 1 April 1941, of which the *Mohawk* would cruise on the west coast north of Ivigtut, the *Comanche* between Ivigtut and Angmagssalik, and the *Northland* on the east coast from Angmagssalik to 77° North latitude. The last was to carry an airplane "for short flights to locate radio stations (German) and see what is going on."[44]

The decision to operate an airplane from the *Northland* was based on Lieutenant Commander Rutherford Lank's assurance that the cutter could embark one, which seemed somewhat doubtful in view of her size and propensity for rolling heavily. The cradle for a

The Northland *as refitted for Greenland patrol. Note the seaplane on her after deck.*

Curtiss SOC-4 single-float seaplane was installed abaft the cutter's mainmast, which received extra stays and a boom to handle the aircraft, for which 1,500 gallons of aviation gasoline had to be carried in drums lashed on deck. The replacement of the *Northland's* original 4-inch battery by a pair of lighter dual-purpose 3-inch 50-caliber guns and the removal of her heavy foremast compensated in part for the additional top weight, but extra ballast had to be stowed as well, and successive commanding officers were cautioned about her stability.

The possible use of patrol aircraft in Greenland also received attention. Commander William J. Kossler and Lieutenant Commander Frank A. Leamy studied the reports of the *Duane's* seaplane operations in 1940 and concluded that while the Coast Guard's latest flying boats, the big Hall Aluminum twin-engine biplanes, had insufficient range and other deficiencies, the Navy's Consolidated PBY-5 might be able to operate from bases on Greenland's west coast, flying across the island to patrol the east coast—when the weather permitted.[45]

Although the Coast Guard's plans for operations in Greenland waters were on a modest scale, other governmental agencies had more ambitious projects in mind, among them the establishment of air fields for refueling lend-lease aircraft being ferried to Britain—the

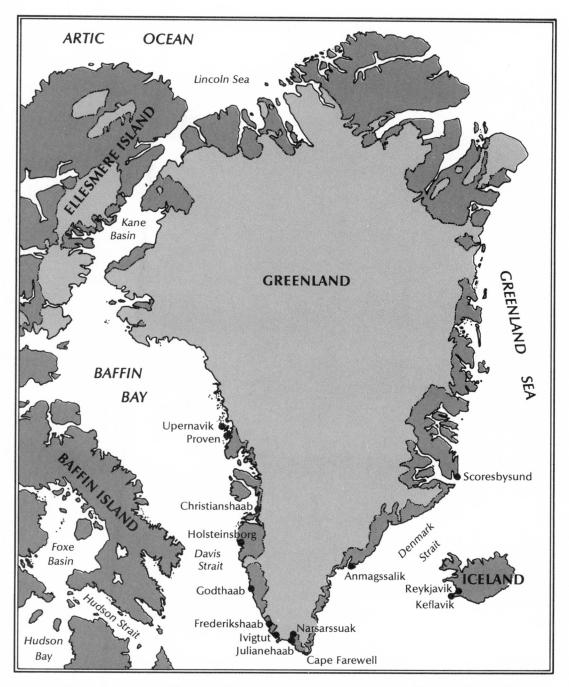

ARTIC OCEAN

Lincoln Sea

ELLESMERE ISLAND

Kane Basin

GREENLAND

GREENLAND SEA

BAFFIN BAY

BAFFIN ISLAND

Foxe Basin

Upernavik
Proven

Scoresbysund

Christianshaab

Holsteinsborg

Davis Strait

Denmark Strait

Anmagssalik

ICELAND

Reykjavik

Keflavik

Godthaab

Hudson Strait

Frederikshaab

Narsarssuak

Ivigtut

Julianehaab

Cape Farewell

Hudson Bay

great circle track between Newfoundland and Scotland passes just south of Cape Farewell—and radio and meteorological stations. The South Greenland Survey Expedition, composed of Army and Navy officers with a Canadian observer attached, was organized to locate suitable sites, and the *Cayuga* was designated to embark the group

Greenland and adjacent areas.

in Boston in mid-March, conveying it to Julianehaab, Sondre Stromfjord, and such other places as might be required.[46]

In the event, Commander Smith in the *Northland* provided some of the most useful information. Knowing the native custom of selecting place names that described the physical characteristics of sites, Smith was immediately interested when told that Narsarssuak was at the head of Julianehaab Fjord. The *Northland* investigated and found that there was indeed a "flat place," a gravel plain some 3 miles long and 1 mile wide. It soon became the location of Greenland's major air field.

Construction of the air base at Narsarssuak and other facilities was sanctioned by an agreement signed by the Danish minister to the United States and Secretary of State Cordell Hull on 9 April 1941. The culmination of months of negotiation, this document placed Greenland temporarily under American protection, authorizing both the South Greenland Survey Expedition and the establishment of American bases on the island. Quite clearly, more vessels would be needed, especially since Franklin Roosevelt considered reported German flights over Greenland's east coast the precursors of an attempt to establish a base there.

Two iceworthy ships became available when Admiral Byrd's Antarctic expedition returned to the United States in the spring of 1941—the old *Bear* and the Bureau of Indian Affairs' *North Star*. Admirals Waesche and Byrd quickly worked out the means for the Coast Guard's reacquisition of its most famous cutter—she would be chartered by the Maritime Commission for one dollar per annum— and after arranging for insurance, the Maritime Commission would transfer the *Bear* to the Coast Guard. But the Navy seems to have had no intention of allowing Greenland to become entirely a Coast Guard theater of operations. A week later Waesche had to inform Byrd that the *Bear* would be manned wholly by naval personnel.[47] The Coast Guard did take over the *North Star*, a nine-year-old wooden 225-footer powered by a 1,500-horsepower diesel that could drive her at 13 knots. Her 9,000-mile endurance at economical speed and her ability to carry a seaplane made her a useful acquisition.

While these vessels were fitting out, the *Northland, Modoc,* and *General Greene* found themselves uncomfortably close to one of the major sea battles of 1941. The three cutters were searching for survivors from merchant ships torpedoed southeast of Cape Farewell when warships and aircraft of the Royal Navy engaged the German battleship *Bismarck* nearby on 24 May. The *Modoc* was mistaken for their target by a squadron of British Swordfish torpedo bombers, which recognized their error in time, and then German antiaircraft projectiles splashed near her. Later that evening, HMS *Prince of Wales* identified the *Modoc* as the *Bismarck*, but again the cutter's luck held—the damaged battleship's men perceived their mistake and she did not open fire. Having had her fill of narrow escapes, the *Modoc* steered northwest toward less dangerous waters. The *Gen-*

eral Greene's men sighted four British warships heading northward the next day, and later they observed the signs of renewed battle—dense smoke and the sound of heavy gunfire. These, however, must have been an illusion, for the *Bismarck* had eluded her pursuers, and 25 May passed without any firing by either Germans or Britons. The latter regained contact on 27 May; when they finally brought the *Bismarck* to bay far to the southeastward, no Coast Guard cutters were in the vicinity.

The cutters' mission on this occasion—rescuing survivors of torpedoed vessels—was completed by the end of the month, the *Northland* having found none while the *Modoc* removed the crew of a sinking ship and transferred it to a Norwegian freighter. The *General Greene,* whose Chief Boatswain Chester L. Jordan joined the search without orders, rescued thirty-nine men from two boats of the torpedoed SS *Marconi.*

As the United States moved closer to belligerent status, the subject of the Coast Guard's possible transfer to the Navy Department naturally attracted attention. Biservice planning committees had discussed this periodically during the interwar period, but in June 1940 Admiral Stark decided that existing plans were not adequate. Asking Admiral Waesche to assign two or more Coast Guard officers to meet with a committee of naval officers headed by Captain Alexander Sharp, Stark explained that he "desired that the contemplated plan be acceptable to the Coast Guard Administration and insofar as conditions of emergency will permit, fulfill the obvious desirability of ready reestablishment of the Coast Guard as a peacetime administrative entity."[48] The Coast Guard commandant designated Captains William H. Shea and Lloyd T. Chalker and Commander Frank J. Gorman to join Sharp and his fellows, and in due course they agreed on detailed plans for close liaison between Coast Guard district commanders and the commandants of naval districts and "for the prompt and orderly transfer of the Coast Guard from the jurisdiction of the Treasury Department to the Navy Department." Actually, there were two plans, the first for transfer of the entire service and the second for assignment of individual units to Navy control. Districts were the key elements in the first plan; Coast Guard districts were rearranged slightly to accord more closely to naval districts, and their staffs were reorganized to facilitate transfer. Upon receipt of the order "Plan One," each Coast Guard district commander would report to his naval counterpart, who would assume command of personnel and units attached to the Coast Guard district, although for geographical reasons sections of some districts might be "divorced" from their erstwhile administrative units. Coast Guard Headquarters would remain as an administrative division under the chief of naval operations, carrying out its logistic functions in close cooperation with the various bureaus of the Navy Department.[49]

Among the points obviously intended to reassure the Coast Guard and Treasury Department were a statement that "the identity of

Coast Guard personnel will be maintained," and the section on demobilization, which read in its entirety: "Upon receipt of the order to demobilize, the entire Coast Guard will resume its former status under the Treasury Department."[50] But some were not convinced. When Admiral Stark wished to implement Plan One in January 1941 and again when he and Secretary of the Navy Frank Knox tried to do so two months later, Assistant Secretary of the Treasury Herbert Gaston suspected another attempt by the Navy to gain permanent control of the Coast Guard in order to provide employment for its "second and third grade officers."[51] Gaston was probably on sounder ground when he warned that the American public would consider the transfer an indication that United States entry into the war was imminent, and probably for that reason the Treasury Department retained control of the Coast Guard.

Some units, however, were assigned to duty with the Navy. The 165-foot *Galatea, Pandora, Thetis,* and *Triton* reported to the Atlantic Fleet Sound School at Key West late in March to serve as training vessels for sonarmen. Within the next two months ten more cutters were put under the Navy's operational control, among them the *Modoc,* the *Comanche,* and the icebreaking tug *Raritan.* These composed the South Greenland Patrol, which was commanded by the *Modoc*'s Lieutenant Commander Harold G. Belford. On 1 July the *Northland* and the *North Star* joined the Navy's *Bear* and the veteran Arctic exploration schooner *Bowdoin* to establish the Northeast Greenland Patrol under Commander Edward H. Smith.

The transfer of the fifty old destroyers to the Royal Navy in 1940 had made earlier plans that the Coast Guard man some of these ships in wartime meaningless, but soon after the Lake-class cutters had been accepted by British crews, the Navy found other employment for personnel of the smaller service. The War Department had acquired several large passenger liners to use as troop transports, and after some difficulty with their civilian crews, the ships were turned over to the Navy. Hard-pressed to find men for its rapidly expanding fleet, the latter looked to the Coast Guard, and on 3 June, President Roosevelt signed an executive order that made some 2,100 Coast Guard officers and men available to man four transports entirely and to serve in twenty-two ships manned by the Navy.[52]

The USS *Leonard Wood, Hunter Liggett,* and *Joseph T. Dickman,* 535-footers of World War I design, were commissioned within a week, and the *Wakefield* followed on 15 June. The last, the former liner *Manhattan,* which had been chartered for naval service, was one of the three largest vessels of the American merchant marine, and at 705 feet and 22,800 tons light displacement, she was the biggest ship ever manned by the Coast Guard.

While most of those assigned to the transports were sailors from the cutter branch of the service, the Navy needed surfmen as well. Amphibious warfare—the landing of troops, arms, and equipment on enemy-held beaches—had fallen into disfavor after the unsuccessful

British assault on the Gallipoli Peninsula in World War I. Nonetheless, the U.S. Marine Corps insisted on developing an amphibious capability during the interwar period, and the Navy hesitantly accepted the responsibility for putting the troops ashore. With Marine Corps encouragement, the New Orleans boatbuilder Andrew J. Higgins designed effective landing craft, but running these ashore successfully on open beaches required boat-handling skill that few other than experienced surfmen possessed.

Rumors that surfmen might be ordered to duty in Navy transports circulated during the spring, and in mid-April Lieutenant Commander Christopher J. Sullivan, a former lifesaving district commander and confidant of Lindsay Warren, addressed a "Confidential and secret" communication to Warren's successor, North Carolina Congressman Herbert C. Bonner: "At present time the station men are jitterie with moral[e] at a low ebb from rumors that the rating of surfman is to be abolished leaving them all subject for a duty onboard ships that they are not acquainted with. Of course these boys will . . . give a good account of themselves in defense of Our Country on any duty assigned them, especially landing troops thru the surf or thru rough and broken water sections including patrol duty on small boats and along our coasts."[53] The rumors were all too true; most of the Coast Guardsmen assigned to duty in the twenty-two Navy-manned transports were surfmen, who would serve as landing craft crews and train others for the same role. Their contribution to the war effort was fully as important as any made by their fellows, and they amply justified Sullivan's faith in them.

The officers and men ordered to duty in naval vessels and the fourteen cutters serving with the Navy in June were but the beginning in Secretary Knox's view. Pointing out the necessity for "the immediate employment on naval duty of all large units of fully trained enlisted men of the Coast Guard," he urged Morgenthau to augment the Coast Guard's training programs to the fullest extent in order to keep pace with the steadily increasing demand. "Particularly, the Coast Guard must be in a position to furnish thousands of enlisted men fully trained in the specialties peculiar to the Coast Guard. These specialties include the operation and handling of small boats, including the operation, repair and maintenance of diesel engines, propelling plants, radiomen, radio and telephone maintenance men, machinists' mates, and enlisted men in any other technical ratings."[54] The treasury secretary responded laconically that the Coast Guard would enlarge its training programs to the limit of its facilities and would seek funds to expand these.

He might have added that training men to meet the Navy's requirements was not the Coast Guard's sole purpose. Preparation for war had increased the service's responsibilities in a variety of areas, some of them of importance to the Navy. Thus, in mid-April Knox had requested that Coast Guard patrols in large seaports be augmented in order to minimize the danger of sabotage that might hamper the construction of warships and the movement of strategic cargoes. Accordingly, some 270 power boats of the Coast Guard Auxiliary were called into active service and while reservists helped to man these, some regulars had to be assigned to them as well.[55]

The construction of new military and naval bases and the extension and improvement of navigable channels by the Army Corps of Engineers increased the Coast Guard's aids to navigation obligation, for each new or altered waterway had to be marked before it could be used regularly. As an example, the commandant cited the 30-foot channel dredged to connect Louisiana's Calcasieu River to the Gulf of Mexico, for which fifteen buoys, forty-two shore lights, almost 100 unlighted beacons, a radio beacon, and a set of range lights had to be installed. In all, nearly 1,500 new aids to navigation were established and almost 900 were discontinued in fiscal 1941.[56]

As if this were not enough, Army, Navy, and other governmental agencies frequently requested that tenders assist them in other ways. The sixty-eight vessels taken over from the Lighthouse Service were unequal to all of the demands, so Admiral Waesche instructed district commanders that nothing should be allowed to interfere with the tenders' work on aids to navigation.[57] He also had the *Kickapoo*, ten 125-footers, and the three remaining 100-footers converted to buoy tenders during the summer of 1941. The conversion consisted of strengthening the vessels' plating below the buoy ports cut in the bulwarks on either side and the provision of a boom with the necessary hoisting machinery on the forward deck. The 100-footers *Nansemond* and *Petrel* became the *Phlox* and the *Pine* respectively, but their sister *Forward* retained her name, as did the *Kickapoo* and the 125-footers, which were intended to perform their usual duties in addition to servicing aids to navigation.

The conversion of existing vessels did little to ease the general need for cutters, and Coast Guard constructors were already preparing the design for a new class of buoy tenders. The Lighthouse Service had generally designed each tender for service in a specific locality, with the result that the only true "classes" of tenders were the eight 190-footers of 1908, which had been built to a design prepared by the Navy, and the six former Army minelayers acquired after World War I. The lack of economy inherent in this practice came to be criticized, and in 1939 the 177-foot *Juniper*, intended to be the first of a class of general-purpose tenders, was laid down. Completed in 1940, she embodied the characteristics the Lighthouse Service had considered most desirable for a buoy tender—shallow draft to facilitate work amid rocks and shoals, twin screws for maneuverability, and diesel-electric drive for endurance and quick response. But the Coast Guard desired ships that could perform the duties of cutters as well as servicing aids to navigation, so the new design bore relatively little resemblance to that of the *Juniper*, principally because of the decision, for which Edward H. Thiele later claimed much of the credit, to make these vessels icebreakers.[58]

Thus, they would draw 13 feet of water, 4 feet more than the *Juniper*, and they sacrificed the maneuverability provided by twin screws to gain the greater immunity from ice damage offered by a single propeller. Indeed, the hull design was based on that of the 110-foot tugs of 1939. Contracts for thirteen of these 180-foot vessels, known as the *Cactus* class, were let to the Marine Iron and Shipbuilding Corporation and the Zenith Dredge Company, both of Duluth, Minnesota, in 1941, but none was completed before the autumn of 1942.

The 180-foot buoy tender Papaw *working a buoy after World War II.*

Yet another problem was that of providing a training vessel for cadets. One or two of the Lake-class cutters had made the cadet cruise each year, and with their departure imminent, Admiral Waesche had begun to consider alternatives. While on an inspection tour in Florida in January 1941, he had noticed the Danish government's sail-training ship *Danmark* moored at Jacksonville and directed officers to inquire about her suitability. Discussions with the Danish legation and Captain Knud L. Hansen of the *Danmark* began in earnest some months later, but by mid-August an impasse had been reached, Hansen considering the Coast Guard's offer for the vessel inadequate and the legation fearing that her sale would bring German reprisals against Denmark. Later efforts by the State Department to deal with the Danish government were similarly unsuccessful, but on 8 December 1941, Captain Hansen placed the ship and her crew at the disposal of the U.S. government, which promptly assigned her to the Coast Guard Academy.[59] There she joined the three-masted schooner-yacht *Atlantic*, which had been donated to the Coast Guard by her owner in April 1941.

The American drift toward war continued as the spring of 1941 gave way to summer. The president declared an unlimited state of national emergency on 27 May, and with United States-Japanese relations deteriorating, the Coast Guard's entire Honolulu District, with its personnel and vessels, was transferred to Admiral Stark's jurisdiction. The *Taney* had been operating with forces of the Fourteenth Naval District for several months, so the only vessels involved were the 125-footers *Reliance* and *Tiger,* the tenders *Kukui* and *Walnut,* and two 78-foot patrol boats. The *Redwing* was the next to go—her Coast Guard crew delivered the former minesweeper to the New York Navy Yard in mid-August for return to the Navy and conversion to a salvage ship.

Most of the cutters remaining under Treasury Department control adopted a warlike guise in September, after the *U-652* and the USS *Greer* had exchanged unsuccessful torpedo and depth-charge attacks southwest of Iceland. Following President Roosevelt's "shoot on sight" order, Coast Guard Headquarters addressed a dispatch to all cutters on the Atlantic and Gulf coasts: "REDUCE USE OF RADIO TO MINIMUM X PAINT ALL VESSELS WAR COLOR X DESTROY ANY GERMAN OR ITALIAN SUBMARINE OR AIRCRAFT SIGHTED WEST OF LONGITUDE 26 REPEAT 26 WEST X TAKE SUCH ACTION AGAINST HOSTILE SURFACE CRAFT AS MAY BE DEEMED PRACTICABLE AND CIRCUMSTANCES WARRANT X TRAIL ALL MERCHANT VESSELS IF SUSPECTED OF ACTING AS SUPPLY VESSELS FOR GERMAN OR ITALIAN NAVAL VESSELS OR AIRCRAFT AND REPORT MOVEMENTS AND CIRCUMSTANCES TO HEADQUARTERS"[60]

The big cutters on weather patrol were a source of concern, remaining as they did in specific localities and transmitting radio messages at regular intervals. They were ordered to darken ship at night and to cruise at the maximum speed consistent with their patrol schedules, steering random courses to stay within 100 miles of their stations. Only in the event of attacks on merchant vessels within a reasonable distance by Axis submarines or aircraft were they authorized to "seek out and destroy" the raiders.[61]

For most of the cutter sailors, this dispatch made the executive order of 1 November 1941, by which Franklin Roosevelt transferred the Coast Guard from the Treasury Department to the Navy Department, almost superfluous. Their service's involvement in World War II can properly be dated from 12 September 1941.

CHAPTER THIRTEEN

WARTIME EXPANSION: PERSONNEL AND DUTIES

*E*xecutive Order 8929, by which the Coast Guard was transferred to the Navy on 1 November 1941, brought a significant reinforcement to the larger service. Four months earlier, the Coast Guard had numbered 613 officers, 764 chief warrant and warrant officers, 17,450 enlisted men, and 199 cadets. Additional enlistments were authorized thereafter, and by the year's end nearly 25,000 officers and men were wearing Coast Guard uniforms.[1] These were the equals of their Navy counterparts on the whole—while naval personnel generally had more experience of a purely military nature, many of the Coast Guardsmen were more versatile because of the diversity of their service.

The Coast Guard's ships and aircraft, on the other hand, were much less important to the Navy. With the exception of the seven Treasury-class vessels, which were admirably suited to ocean escort duty, the cutters were useful mainly for antisubmarine patrol in coastal waters. To be sure, the four 240-footers and some 165-footers did escort convoys, but the former were too slow and unhandy to be very effective, while the latter were too small and lacked endurance and speed. Tenders were useful in a variety of roles besides maintaining aids to navigation—they served on occasion as antisubmarine net layers, small cargo vessels, and salvage ships—but they did relatively little to enhance the direct military force of the Navy.

The Coast Guard had fifty aircraft operating from nine air stations in 1941. Of these, the forty amphibians and seaplanes were the most important. Its fifty-nine commissioned pilots and nineteen "aviation pilots" (petty officers) had received the same training at Pensacola that their Navy and Marine Corps counterparts had, but there seems to have been no thought that Coast Guard aviators be assigned to anything other than antisubmarine patrol and search-and-rescue duty.

As in World War I, the Coast Guard was probably most important in the 1941–45 conflict in its performance of a variety of noncombat duties, especially those grouped under the general heading of "captain of the port activities." These included such familiar responsibilities as port security, explosive-cargo supervision, and the control of merchant ship movements and anchorages. With the passage of time, the Coast Guard was also charged with the patrol of beaches and the manning of lookout stations, while the maintenance of aids to navigation and icebreaking to facilitate ship movements in home waters gained importance in wartime.

These and other duties required increasing numbers of officers and men, a need that was met in a number of ways. The enlistment of regular Coast Guardsmen continued until 1 February 1942, after which men were accepted in the Coast Guard Reserve only, because the service did not wish to find itself encumbered by too many enlisted men at war's end. This short-sighted policy would cause problems later, for the war lasted longer than those at Coast Guard Headquarters seem to have anticipated. By 1943 most of those added were draftees inducted under Selective Service, with only men below or above the latter's age limits being permitted to volunteer for the Coast Guard Reserve. This practice was continued with few exceptions until the end of the war.[2]

Recruits received basic training at a number of stations, of which the most important were the facilities established on Government Island, Alameda, California, and at Manhattan Beach, New York. The former, which ultimately could train 3,500 recruits at a time, was dwarfed by Manhattan Beach with its facilities for 8,500 in addition to schools for various petty officer ratings. By the war's end, Manhattan Beach would have trained more than 43,000, of whom some 38,000 were apprentice seamen.

The Manhattan Beach Training Station became the site for training the first significant number of blacks enlisted in the Coast Guard. This was the result of a presidential order in January 1942, in response to which Admiral Waesche produced a plan to enlist about 500 blacks for general service, 300 for sea duty, and the remainder for service with captain of the port detachments. He wished to begin with 150, and after evaluating their performance at the training station and on active duty, to continue with the program if it seemed feasible. The idea of assigning black seamen to patrol boats and buoy tenders, vessels too small to permit segregated quarters, encountered some opposition among senior naval officers, but Waesche's plan was implemented nonetheless. By late summer, some 300 blacks had completed their training and begun active service. Meanwhile, even more had been recruited for duty in the more traditional role of officers' stewards. Enlistments virtually ended in December 1942, after which the Coast Guard met its personnel requirements principally by accepting draftees, blacks among them, according to a quota system set up by the Selective Service Act. Since the Coast Guard inducted a relatively small number of men, the fact that 13 percent were blacks had little impact on the service as a whole. Only about half could be assigned duty as stewards, so the remainder had perforce to be assigned to general service.

Integration of black personnel into the Coast Guard was facilitated by Carlton Skinner, a reserve officer who considered the service's racial policies to be counterproductive. While on duty at Headquarters in mid-1943, Lieutenant Skinner proposed that a group of blacks be integrated into the crew of a large cutter in order to test the concept of integration of seagoing personnel generally. Admiral Waesche agreed, and Skinner was ordered to the *Sea Cloud*, a 316-foot converted yacht assigned to weather patrol duty in the North Atlantic. The number of blacks in her 173-man company was gradually increased; ultimately she had four black officers and about fifty black petty officers and seamen. Due in large part to Skinner's efforts—he became her commanding officer in 1944—the integration experiment was successful, and it was repeated in the frigate *Hoquiam*, of which Skinner assumed command after the *Sea Cloud* was decommissioned in November 1944. While Lieutenant Commander Skinner's two commands were the only Coast Guard-manned vessels with significant numbers of blacks in their complements, black petty officers were regularly assigned to other ships as the war went on, while their fellows served in a variety of capacities ashore, some of them as instructors at Manhattan Beach.

The latter group furnished the first of the Coast Guard's black officers, Joseph C. Jenkins, who became a reserve ensign after completing the four-month officer-training course at the Academy in April 1943. Clarence Samuels, a warrant officer stationed at Manhattan Beach, was commissioned a lieutenant (junior grade) later in 1943. Like Jenkins and several other black officers, Samuels served in the *Sea Cloud;* he then commanded, in turn, *Lightship #115* and the 180-foot buoy tender *Sweetgum.*

The Coast Guard's record with regard to integration during World War II was probably better than that of any of the other armed services. Army, Navy, and Marine Corps alike tended to form completely segregated units, most of which were assigned to the more menial noncombat duties. The Navy did not commission its first black officers until almost a year after Joseph Jenkins had donned his ensign's uniform, and only late in 1944 were the crews of selected auxiliary vessels integrated. The Marine Corps reluctantly accepted its first black officer candidates as the war ended.[3]

Quite clearly, officers with the attitudes of Admiral Waesche and Commander Skinner deserve much of the credit for the Coast Guard's relatively enlightened racial policy. One must note, however, that blacks composed only 2.1 percent of the service's total wartime personnel, compared with 9.6 percent of the Army, 5.37 percent of the Navy, and 4 percent of the Marine Corps. Moreover, 63 percent of the Coast Guard's blacks served as stewards, in itself a form of segregation. And the degree of integration that was achieved was due in part to the fact that segregation was impractical in most of the Coast Guard's ships and stations.[4] No blacks received regular commissions during World War II; indeed, none became cadets at the Coast Guard Academy until President John F. Kennedy, perturbed because the unit of cadets marching in his inaugural parade in 1961 was composed entirely of white men, ordered their admission.[5]

While the enlistment of men in the regular Coast Guard was halted early in 1942, regular officer procurement continued throughout the war, with cadet training at the Academy differing only in its curtailment to three years instead of the now traditional four-year course. The Academy had been accredited as a degree-granting institution in 1940, so the graduates received bachelor of science in engineering degrees as well as regular commissions in the rank of ensign. Their number remained very small, however, and the considerable enlargement of the officer corps came about principally through the commissioning of reserve officers. Although some of the latter entered the service with senior ranks, most became ensigns on completion of a four-month Reserve Officer Training Course at the Academy. The initial requirement that these men have baccalaureate degrees had to be relaxed as time passed, because the Coast Guard was competing for officer-candidates with the three larger services. By the autumn of 1942, the Academy was unable to accommodate all of the reserve officer-candidates, so the training station at St. Augustine, Florida, assumed a part of this responsibility as well as providing an indoctrination course for those commissioned without service experience. Several hundred enlisted men were commissioned after attending college under the Navy's V-12 program, and others competed for regular appointments to the Academy after completion of the course offered by the Academy Preparatory School established at the Groton, Connecticut, training station in September 1943.[6]

Temporary promotions during 1918 had resulted in an officer corps consisting largely of captains by the end of World War I, a situation that Admiral Waesche wished to avoid. He appointed a board headed by Captain Philip F. Roach to study the problem in September 1941, and after rejecting its first report, the commandant met with the board to develop an acceptable plan. They agreed that promotions in the Coast Guard should be based on the same amount of service as those in the Navy, maintaining a standard proportion of four captains for every eight commanders, fifteen lieutenant commanders, thirty lieutenants, and forty-three lieutenants (junior grade).[7]

The Coast Guard established a women's reserve force late in 1942, following the examples of the U.S. Army and Navy. Admiral Waesche chose Lieutenant Dorothy C. Stratton of the Navy's Women Accepted for Volunteer Emergency Service (WAVES) to head this force as a lieutenant commander. The former dean of women at

Purdue University, she coined the name SPAR, an acronym from the Latin and English versions of the Coast Guard motto, for her new command.[8] At the suggestion of Commander Mildred H. McAfee, who headed the WAVES, the SPARs adopted the same uniform, substituting the Coast Guard shield for the Navy insignia. This uniform had been designed by the noted fashion designer Mainbocher, so its adoption was an aid to recruiting. Women transferred from the WAVES in December 1942 became the first SPARs, and a joint recruiting drive was begun by the Navy, Coast Guard, and Marine Corps, which accepted the first women Marines in February 1943.

Initially, SPARs were trained at naval facilities, but in mid-1943 the Coast Guard withdrew from the joint recruiting and training agreement to establish its own training station at Palm Beach, Florida. Some SPARs, however, continued to receive advanced training at naval schools until the end of the war. SPAR officers, trained in naval facilities until mid-1943, thereafter attended the Coast Guard Academy, although the Navy provided training in special areas for some.[9]

Captain Dorothy C. Stratton, USCGWR.

Like most of their counterparts in the other services, the SPARs were employed in a variety of administrative and clerical positions ashore, in the continental United States only, until September 1944 when they were permitted to volunteer for service in Alaska and Hawaii. Members of the women's reserves were intended to replace men, making the latter available for duty at sea or in other areas not open to women. This they did, although not always on a one-to-one basis largely because of restrictive regulations, a number of which revealed a degree of continuing antipathy toward women in the armed forces.

Reservists, male and female, were to be found in all of the nation's armed forces during World War II, but only the Coast Guard had a Temporary Reserve. This was made up of individuals who for one reason or another were excluded from full-time service in the armed forces and who desired to contribute at least twelve hours each week to duty in one of a variety of activities. Early members of this group were often men of the Coast Guard Auxiliary who volunteered the services of themselves and their boats for local patrol duty. As time passed, the need for guards to protect moored vessels and wharves and other harbor installations from sabotage and natural dangers became apparent, so the Volunteer Port Security Force was established as a part of the Temporary Reserve. Those serving a similar function in shipyards and factories engaged in war industry were taken into the Temporary Reserve as well, as were Civil Service employees involved in a variety of activities relevant to the Coast Guard's responsibilities. The navigational problems associated with the sailing of large convoys from American ports led the Navy to suggest that pilots be brought under military control while so engaged, and the simplest manner of accomplishing this was to make them members of the Coast Guard's Temporary Reserve. Still others, formerly in the Bureau of Marine Inspection and Navigation, were employed full time as merchant marine inspectors, the duties of the bureau having been divided between the Coast Guard and the Bureau of Customs by an executive order of 28 February 1942.[10]

Thus, the Temporary Reserve came to comprise six distinct categories, all of whose personnel had full military status, with all the rights, privileges, and responsibilities thereof, while on active duty. Most of those serving part-time did so without recompense, while factory police, pilots, civil servants, and inspectors were paid by their regular employers or from the Coast Guard's civil service fund. For this reason, obtaining personnel for activities such as the Volunteer Port Security Force was something of a challenge, but the support of the press and of merchants in specific localities helped recruiters to enroll sufficient numbers. At its peak in 1943, the Coast Guard Temporary Reserve had some 50,000 officers and men.[11]

Pilots, inspectors, and policemen of course required little instruction in duties they were accustomed to perform, but few of those volunteering to guard harbor facilities had any familiarity with firefighting or other emergency equipment—nor with the care and use of small arms, in which even veteran members of the Auxiliary had little experience. Training was an important aspect of the Temporary Reserve at its inception, as indeed it must be of even a quasi-military force.

The rapid expansion of the Coast Guard required some reorganization at Headquarters as well, in which Rear Admiral Lloyd T. Chalker, assistant commandant since Covell's retirement in December 1941, had an important role. Admiral Waesche also obtained the services of several civilians, among them Joseph Pois, a management specialist from the Bureau of the Budget; Lawrence J. Bernard, a legal adviser from the Treasury Department; and Robert T. Merrill, a Naval Academy graduate whose experience with a shipping line enabled him to act as a consultant in merchant marine matters. All became reserve captains, while Halert C. Shepheard, former chief of the Bureau of Marine Inspection and Navigation, continued to direct its activities as a regular Coast Guard captain, later attaining flag rank.[12]

While the immediate reason for the Coast Guard's assumption of most of the licensing and inspecting duties of the Bureau of Marine Inspection and Navigation was probably the Navy's desire for a measure of control over these important functions, it is likely that Admiral Waesche had some part in bringing it about. Soon after becoming commandant in 1936, he had initiated meetings with the commissioner of immigration and the chiefs of the Army's Corps of Engineers, the Bureau of Fisheries, and the Bureau of Navigation and Marine Inspection, as it was then known, seeking a better understanding in those areas where the interests of each coincided with those of the Coast Guard. All responded cordially except the last, who left the commandant with the impression that he resented "the plan of having the Coast Guard enforce the laws on the seas over which [his Bureau] had administrative jurisdiction."[13] Since Waesche was said to have proposed the transfer of the Bureau of Navigation and Marine Inspection to the Coast Guard at about this time, the bureau chief's reaction to his overtures is understandable. Nothing came of the commandant's proposal at the time, but there is no reason to think that his interest in gaining control of the bureau waned during the following years.[14]

Some of the commandant's subordinates questioned his decision to offer Coast Guard commissions to all marine inspectors who desired them, citing rumors that some had accepted bribes in the past.[15] Waesche, however, recognized that these men were essential to the fulfillment of the service's new responsibilities, which may be enumerated as follows: Approval of designs and equipment for merchant vessels; regular inspection of such ships to ensure their adequate stability, fire-proofing or fire resistance, fire-fighting and life-saving equipment, and proper observance of load line rules; issuance of inspection certificates; examination and licensing or certification of merchant mariners; supervision of signing on, discharge, and living conditions of merchant vessel crews; investigation of maritime casualties; formulation and publication of regulations to protect those sailing in American merchant ships; and the enforcement of laws pertaining to the numbering, equipment, and operation of motorboats. Quite clearly, the personnel of the former Bureau of Marine Inspection and Navigation were too few to provide all of these services for the rapidly expanding U.S. merchant marine; Coast Guard officers, both regular and reserve, had to be assigned to inspection duties as well.

After three months of experience in the area of merchant marine inspection and certification, Admiral Waesche formed the Merchant Marine Council at Headquarters. Composed of leading individuals from almost every facet of maritime endeavor, including some Coast Guard officers, this group evaluated the Coast Guard's performance of its duties in this area and recommended additional measures to further the cause of safety at sea.

The rapid expansion of the U.S. merchant marine inevitably led to some personnel problems, and reports of misconduct in the war zones caused the Coast Guard to review the Bureau of Marine Inspection and Navigation procedures for dealing with breaches of discipline. While adequate for the peacetime situation for which they had been developed, these were too deliberate and time-consuming to suit the accelerated sailing schedules of the war years. A revised system was introduced in New York during the summer of 1943, whereby a Coast Guard officer boarded each incoming American-flag merchant vessel to interview her company and scrutinize her log. If either revealed any problems of sufficient magnitude, an examining officer was summoned to take evidence and to decide whether a formal hearing should be held. If so, the examining officer served as prosecutor while a third officer heard the case and determined the punishment, which ranged from temporary suspension to permanent revocation of the individual's certificate or license. Those so "beached" had the right of appeal to the district Coast Guard officer and ultimately to the commandant.[16]

As Admiral Waesche assured the National Maritime Union Conference in July 1943:

> . . . we mean business and . . . we are going to do our utmost to maintain discipline. We are going to act quickly and decisively. However, we are also going to act fairly. While no man who should be punished will escape if we can help it, neither will any man be punished without a full opportunity to defend himself. Every man against whom charges are filed will be told exactly what he is charged with, he will be given reasonable notice of the trial, he will be permitted to have counsel, to call witnesses, and to cross-examine witnesses who appear against him. The trial will be fairly and impartially conducted by a qualified officer who had nothing to do with investigating the case and the decision will be made on the facts alone. Furthermore, licensed officers and unlicensed men will be treated alike in all respects.[17]

The New York merchant marine hearing unit having proved successful, similar groups were established in all the major U.S. ports and Captain Halert Shepheard led a mission to Britain to determine the desirability of having units there. By 1945, merchant marine hearing units were functioning in the United Kingdom and in ports in Africa, the Persian Gulf, and Ceylon.

On the whole, this seems to have been a satisfactory solution to a potentially serious problem. There were occasions when the examining officer had also to hear the case, which of course was open to objection, but those concerned generally maintained a sufficient degree of impartiality to escape any major complaint. The success of the merchant marine hearing units would be one of the reasons for the permanent assignment of the Bureau of Navigation and Marine Inspection functions to the Coast Guard after the war.[18]

Even as the Coast Guard was gaining a closer relationship with the merchant marine through its temporary assumption of these duties, its administration of Maritime Service training was being terminated. The War Shipping Administration, created by presidential order on 7 February 1942, was given cognizance over all phases of merchant marine activity, and almost seven months later, on 1 September, it assumed responsibility for the training programs heretofore administered by the Coast Guard. Exactly why this transfer occurred is not clear—one suspects that Rear Admiral Emory S. Land, the dynamic retired naval officer who headed both the Maritime Commission and the War Shipping Administration, did not wish the Coast Guard to gain too much authority over the merchant marine. Indeed, Land may have intended only that the Coast Guard help to organize the training program for merchant mariners. At any rate, the loss of this responsibility was clearly a disappointment to Admiral Waesche, although not all of his fellows shared his feeling. Commander Alfred C. Richmond, who had commanded the training ship *American Sailor* since her commissioning, thought that continued association with merchant marine training would have led the Coast Guard to be identified too closely with such activity, to the exclusion of a more active role in the war. Richmond himself was pleased to exchange his unarmed training ship for the *Haida*, escorting convoys in the Gulf of Alaska, although he soon recognized that the safety of the convoys owed more to the absence of Japanese submarines than to his new command's inconsiderable anti-submarine capability.[19]

During World War I, personnel attached to Coast Guard stations and lighthouses had been put to use as coast watchers, and that function came to be a part of the Coast Guard's responsibility in 1942. This development stemmed from the landing of saboteurs on the Atlantic coast from German submarines in June. The first of these were encountered by John C. Cullen, a seaman of the Amagansett Station on Long Island, in the course of his beach patrol on the night of 13 June 1942. Meeting four men on the beach, Cullen engaged their leader in conversation in the course of which he was threatened and offered a bribe. Accepting the latter, he continued his patrol until hidden by fog, when he returned to the station in some haste. The armed party dispatched immediately found no trace of the Germans, but a further search the next morning unearthed the heavy cases they had been carrying. Their content—explosives, detonators, etc., of German origin—left no doubt of the saboteurs' mission, so the Federal Bureau of Investigation was informed and soon apprehended the Germans. Four more saboteurs were put ashore south of Jacksonville, Florida, a few days later; reported by fishermen, they too were quickly arrested.[20]

Conferences on the subject of coastal surveillance and defense followed, and the Army and the Navy agreed that the Coast Guard should establish a comprehensive system of armed beach patrols on the nation's coasts. The Navy's Sea Frontier commanders were so notified on 30 June 1942, and a Beach Patrol Division under Captain Raymond J. Mauerman was established at Coast Guard Headquarters. By the year's end, additional stations, lookout towers, and a beach patrol communications system were being constructed, the last under the supervision of Captain Edward M. Webster, who returned to active duty as chief communications officer in 1942. A year later, about 24,000 Coast Guardsmen were involved in a patrol extending over some 3,700 miles of Atlantic, Gulf, and Pacific coasts in addition to areas kept under surveillance from lookout towers.

Patrols were maintained continuously in regions thought most likely to attract saboteurs or invasion forces; elsewhere, they were conducted at night and during periods of low visibility. Initially, each

Mounted beach patrolmen in the uniform adopted for "shoregoing" Coast Guardsmen in 1943.

patrol consisted of two men, armed with rifles or sidearms and responsible for two miles or less of coastline, depending on the terrain. Using portable telephones plugged into jack boxes along the way, the patrols reported to their stations at regular intervals, and the absence of a report led to an immediate investigation.

Men were required for other duties, however, so a dog was soon being substituted for one of the men on night patrol, and dog patrols became quite popular. Almost 2,000 dogs, mostly German shepherds, Doberman pinschers, and Airedales, were employed before Headquarters decided to phase dog patrols out gradually late in 1943. Horse-mounted patrols were begun on the East and Gulf coasts in November 1942, and these were continued in certain areas until the Beach Patrol itself was curtailed in 1944. By September 1943, more than 3,200 horses, almost all furnished by the Army, were in Coast Guard service. Members of the Temporary Reserve also took part in Beach Patrol activity wherever possible, but much of the coast that had to be patrolled was too remote from population centers to permit the use of any other than regular or reserve personnel.

Beach patrol duty might be quite arduous—the patrols endured climatic conditions ranging from the humid, mosquito-ridden heat of southern summers to the icy rain and snow of northern winters, to traverse terrain of almost every description, from swamps to cliffs, often densely wooded. Those assigned to isolated stations frequently had less liberty than many of their fellows on sea duty. For most, of course, conditions were somewhat better, but at best the work of the patrols was monotonous with little prospect of an exciting incident.

As to the effectiveness of the Beach Patrol, one can only note that no enemy invasion of the continental United States was attempted during World War II, and the saboteurs encountered by Seaman Cullen were the sole enemy agents whose apprehension was due to the Coast Guard. On the other hand, the patrols served a very useful purpose in reporting and assisting the crews of downed airplanes and vessels in distress; detecting forest fires, especially in the Pacific Northwest; and providing innumerable forms of aid in times of natural disaster. In addition, they helped to keep unauthorized persons away from restricted zones, investigated countless reports of unusual occurrences, and generally served in a variety of ways not unlike those traditionally associated with the Coast Guard.[21]

Work somewhat similar to that of the Beach Patrol was performed by the Coastal Picket Patrol, a force organized by the Coast Guard at the Navy's request to help to deal with German submarines that were enjoying their second "happy time" during the spring of 1942, torpedoing shipping in the Western Atlantic with impunity. Despite its experience during the autumn of 1941, the U.S. Navy was utterly unprepared to cope with this submarine offensive, and the sinking of unescorted merchant vessels—twenty-eight in March alone, often within sight of people ashore, with another fifteen sunk in the Gulf of Mexico—led to extraordinary defense measures, the Coastal Picket Patrol among them.

For almost a year, the Cruising Club of America had sought to convince the Navy that some of the vessels owned by its members might be useful as patrol craft, and in March 1942 the club offered the services of thirty motor sailers between 50 and 90 feet in length, each with an experienced master and a nucleus crew. Other vessels were added to the list, to no avail until a press campaign forced the Navy to take notice. On 4 May, Admiral Ernest J. King, who combined the positions of chief of naval operations and commander in chief, U. S. Fleet, directed that the Coast Guard Auxiliary organize the little ships into a patrol force. The Auxiliary was obviously incapable of performing a duty of this magnitude, so district Coast Guard officers on the Atlantic and Gulf coasts received the responsibility, acting under the Sea Frontier commanders.[22]

When it became apparent that the vessels volunteered by the Cruising Club of America were too few for the role envisioned by the Navy, Rear Admiral Chalker informed the district officers on the Atlantic and Gulf seaboards that it was "mandatory that as many small boats as practicable capable of operating 40 to 50 miles offshore be obtained as early as possible. Boats may be taken into Reserve for periods of from one week to duration of war and may be inducted with or without personnel in either Temporary or Regular Reserve." These craft were to be equipped with radio, machine guns and small arms, depth charges and tracks, and sound gear, although none should be detained for want of any of this equipment except radio. Fishing boats and other suitable commercial vessels were to be obtained, by requisition if necessary, and Coast Guard craft operated by captain of the port detachments would be ordered to the patrol if their absence would not jeopardize port security. Chalker concluded his directive: "The important mission at this time is to get boats out on patrol at the very earliest date practicable."[23]

The order to obtain fishing boats soon had to be modified because these craft had an important economic function and the acquisition of a large number would affect the nation's food supply adversely. Thus, only those whose owners offered them for purchase or charter were taken over by the Coast Guard, and in the latter case some were chartered only for use during the off season.[24] There was no restriction on the acquisition of pleasure boats, of course, and by December 1942 more than 2,000 small craft had been acquired by the Coast Guard, most of them for the Coastal Picket Patrol.

Coast Guard participation in coastal patrol also included increasing numbers of 83-foot patrol boats, of which 230 were built at Brooklyn by the Wheeler Shipyard, Inc., from 1941 to 1944. The design of these craft had evolved from the nine 80-footers of the prohibition era. Like the earlier patrol boats, these were twin-screw wooden craft powered by gasoline engines. They made 20 knots on trials, a speed that fell considerably after the boats had been fitted with radar, sonar, and armament—a 20-millimeter gun, four depth charges, and the antisubmarine rocket launcher called mousetrap. Although they were dubbed "sub-busters" by the press, none of the 83-footers sank a submarine, and their heavy fuel consumption and liveliness at sea limited their usefulness. Their most noteworthy service was as rescue craft during the Normandy invasion.

The operation plan issued by Vice Admiral Adolphus Andrews, commander of the Eastern Sea Frontier, in mid-July required the employment of the pickets on "antisubmarine, rescue and information duties" to supplement the work of larger vessels. The patrols were based on the Army Interceptor Command's grid chart, which divided the waters off the coast into 15-nautical-mile squares. Each vessel was assigned to patrol one of these squares during a specified length of time, in the course of which she was to "observe and report the actions and activities of all hostile submarine, surface and air forces," attacking and destroying the first if her armament were formidable enough to justify it.[25]

Admiral Andrews had little doubt of the value of the Coastal Picket Patrol, but late in October he noted the undesirable state of some of its five task groups: "Inspections in some areas have shown a very satisfactory condition, while others have shown a deplorable condition. In certain areas, there have been evidences of no training, no discipline, improper uniforms, little equipment, and inadequate provision made for paying the crews and granting shore leave, all so essential to the efficiency of this force." While Andrews recognized that this situation was an inevitable result of the haste with which the force had been formed, he emphasized that its proper organization was of paramount importance to the Eastern Sea Frontier and urged the task group commanders to do their utmost to bring this about.[26]

Achieving a proper state of discipline and efficiency in a force of part-time sailors, some of whom were unfit for active service of a strenuous nature, would obviously be difficult, and in the event the effort was not made. During the following weeks, the crews were replaced by regular and reserve personnel; the Temporary Reserve's involvement in the Coastal Picket Patrol ended officially in December 1942.

The patrol itself might well have been discontinued at that time, for any usefulness it had possessed had already passed. In fact, that usefulness was extremely limited, for the German submarine campaign off the U.S. Atlantic coast had reached its peak in May 1942, just as the Coastal Picket Patrol was being formed. Thereafter, the establishment of a convoy system for coastwise shipping led most of the U-boats to seek victims in other areas. Even had they continued to frequent American waters, there was little that the pickets could have done except to report sightings, for without adequate speed, armament, and detection equipment, they could hardly have attacked submarines with any prospect of success. The little ships, on the other hand, were very vulnerable to attack by surfaced submarines. In short, the Navy's early disinclination to become involved seems to have been based on sound judgment. Nonetheless, the Coastal Picket Patrol in somewhat curtailed form was continued until the autumn of 1943.

Yet, however slight their contribution, one must recognize that those manning the pickets did what they could with the means at hand. Most of them seem to have accepted the discomfort incidental to life at sea in small craft cheerfully enough, nor did the possibility of attack by a much more formidable enemy deter them. And some few of them participated in rescue activity, picking up men from sunken ships and downed aircraft, which was certainly in the Coast Guard tradition.

Although the incidence of airplane crashes offshore increased markedly during the war, in large part because of the rapid expansion of military and naval aviation, the Coast Guard was surprisingly slow in developing an air-sea rescue organization. This seems to have come about at the instance of the Eleventh Naval District commandant, who became concerned at the number of losses of pilots engaged in training flights off the California coast. Commander Watson A. Burton, commanding the Coast Guard Air Station at San Diego's Lindbergh Field, recommended the formation of a squadron designed for this purpose. Owing to the small number of its aircraft, the Coast Guard had never had squadrons as such, but late in 1943 nine Consolidated Catalina amphibians under the command of Lieutenant Commander Chester R. Bender, a future Coast Guard commandant, became Air-Sea Rescue Squadron 1.[27]

A Coast Guard aviator had evaluated the experimental PBY—the forebear of the Catalina—in 1936, and while he recognized its suitability for naval use, he recommended that it not be acquired by the Coast Guard, in large part because of its expense—the crash of one PBY would be a serious blow to the service's aviation allotment![28]

Although one PBY-5 was obtained late in 1940, the Coast Guard continued to prefer smaller aircraft. By 1943, however, the Catalina had established a reputation in search and rescue in the Pacific war zone, and it was the logical aircraft to equip a squadron created for that purpose in American waters. The amphibious PBY-5A was chosen because it could take off from an airfield, thus saving the time necessary to launch a flying boat before takeoff. On the other hand, the retractable landing gear added considerable weight, which was a handicap for sea landings.

To reduce the need for these, Air-Sea Rescue Squadron 1 also had AVR-boats, small high-speed craft that could be directed to the downed aircraft by the Catalina that sighted it. This use of search aircraft and rescue boats was not original with the Coast Guard; the Royal Air Force's Coastal Command had developed the concept during the Battle of Britain in 1940, and some Coast Guard personnel had since attended the air-sea rescue school at Blackpool, in Lancashire. Indeed, Bender stated later that the Coast Guard's air-sea rescue techniques owed much to the British experience.[29]

Squadron headquarters remained at San Diego, with detachments usually consisting of two PBY-5As and attached AVRs stationed at various points along the Southern California coast and on islands offshore. These were rotated according to a regular schedule, both to provide some opportunity for all personnel to enjoy the amenities of San Diego and to enable the squadron commander to keep a close check on the level of training and readiness.

In 1944, Lieutenant Commander Bender was ordered to Coast Guard Headquarters to prepare an air-sea rescue manual, and Commander Burton also went to Washington to help to organize the Air-Sea Rescue Agency, which was established in March 1944 at the request of the Joint Chiefs of Staff to analyze rescue techniques and provide information relating to equipment, facilities, and methods. Although all of the armed services were represented among the agency's personnel, its administration became a Coast Guard responsibility. The formation of the Office of Air-Sea Rescue at Coast Guard Headquarters followed in December 1944—somewhat belatedly, it would seem. This comprised the divisions of planning and coordination, shore and vessel rescue, and aviation, and its chief became assistant coordinator of the Air-Sea Rescue Agency.[30]

Meanwhile, air-sea rescue units were formed at other Coast Guard air stations, and Coast Guard officers were assigned to various naval commands in both the Atlantic and Pacific theaters of operations to coordinate rescue activity. These officers, however, had to utilize vessels and aircraft of the commands to which they were attached, for no Coast Guard air-sea rescue units were based outside the continental limits of the United States. Those commanding these ships and aircraft were often senior to the Coast Guard officers and usually had some combat experience as well; thus, the rescue activity coordinators had to use a good deal of tact in performing their duties.[31]

Reporting on Coast Guard air-sea rescue activity in fiscal 1945, Fleet Admiral King noted that a total of 165 aircraft operating from nine air stations had rendered assistance in 686 airplane crashes, saving 786 lives. In addition, 5,357 persons requiring emergency medical treatment were transported.[32] Most of the latter were removed from ships at sea, which is the more notable because this was usually a manifestation of the "flying lifeboat" concept developed a decade earlier. The Catalinas could respond to calls for assistance at distances far beyond the limited endurance of the AVRs, which lacked sea-keeping ability in any event, while cutters were too slow to render assistance quickly. So the PBY-5As, and later Martin PBM-5G Mariners, with their usual four-man crews augmented by a third pilot to serve as navigator, a second radioman, and sometimes medical personnel, flew lengthy missions of a type not originally associated with the air-sea rescue concept.

More important for the future was the Coast Guard's role in helicopter development. Interest in aircraft that could take off from and land on a small area and that had the ability to hover antedated the war, of course, and the apparent potential of the autogiro, a stubby-winged airplane that obtained lift from an unpowered overhead rotor, led to the formation of an interagency board in 1938 for the purpose of conducting research into rotary-wing and other aircraft. Lieutenant Commander William J. Kossler represented the Coast Guard on this board, which by 1941 was seriously interested in the helicopter, a wingless aircraft that utilized variable-pitch rotor blades for both lift and propulsion. The Russian-born aeronautical engineer Igor Sikorsky produced the most successful early helicopter, a single-rotor type with torque controlled by a small vertical tail rotor. He had a military version ready for demonstration in the spring of 1942.

Monday, 20 April 1942, was a cold gusty day, and few of the board members appeared at Stratford, Connecticut, to witness the test. Kossler was there, accompanied by Lieutenant Commander Watson Burton, then commanding the Brooklyn Air Station. Both were impressed, and when the helicopter hovered 25 feet from the ground while a man ascended the rope ladder dangling from it, pulling the ladder up after he had entered the cabin, the Coast Guard officers agreed that this was the type of aircraft that would meet their service's rescue requirements.[33] Their recommendation that at least three be acquired for further tests was approved by Commander Frank A. Leamy, aviation officer at Headquarters, but Rear Admirals Harvey Johnson and Lloyd Chalker thought the cost—$250,000—too high, especially since rescue aircraft were not essential to the war effort. One of them was reported to have explained their refusal to Commander Kossler: "Hell, Bill, the Navy is not interested in life-saving! They just want to get on with the business of killing the enemy!"[34]

Lieutenant Commander Frank A. Erickson, newly appointed executive officer at the Brooklyn Air Station, had that in mind when he wrote the commandant after witnessing another Sikorsky demonstration several weeks later: "The life saving and law enforcement possibilities of the helicopter have heretofore been especially stressed. However, this machine can fulfill an even more important role; that is in providing aerial protection for convoys against submarine action, an important function of Coast Guard Aviation."[35] Erickson went on to describe the possibilities: A platform 30 feet square on the deck of a merchant ship would be sufficient to operate a helicopter from, and it could be refueled by a vessel as small as a patrol boat while hovering overhead. Helicopters ordered by the Army would be able to carry radio, a depth charge, and fuel for four hours of flight, during which their two-man crews could keep a large area under surveillance, hovering just above suspicious objects to permit closer inspection, which no conventional aircraft could do. In addition to reporting and attacking submarines, the helicopter might spot and destroy drifting mines, and it could rescue men from torpedoed vessels more quickly than small boats.

Forwarding the letter with their approval, Burton and Kossler noted that while the Army had thirteen helicopters on order and the British would obtain some by lend-lease, the Navy seemed unenthusiastic. Thus, if helicopters were to be acquired for naval use, the Coast Guard must take the initiative. Kossler thought that the Army might be willing to transfer a few of its helicopters on order to the Coast Guard, and Headquarters agreed that four—one HNS-1 trainer and three HOS observation craft—should be requested. Thus, the Coast Guard's helicopter program began on a modest scale in mid-1942.[36]

It received further impetus six months later when Rear Admiral Stanley V. Parker, a World War I aviator and senior Coast Guard officer of the Third Naval District, became interested. His reaction to a Sikorsky demonstration in December 1942 was similar to those of Kossler, Burton, and Erickson, and his enthusiasm led Admiral Waesche to investigate the matter in person. Accompanied by several of his senior officers, the commandant went to Connecticut on 13 February 1943. After watching two helicopters perform precision maneuvers, Waesche returned to Washington to urge Admiral King that the helicopter be developed for naval use. Thereupon, King ordered the Coast Guard to assume responsibility for doing so.[37]

Accordingly, twenty-one HOS-1 helicopters were ordered from Vought-Sikorsky, and pilot training began at the Brooklyn Air Station for British as well as American officers. The old coastal steamer *Governor Cobb* was acquired from the War Shipping Administration, and with superstructure cut down and a "flight deck" added aft, she was commissioned as a helicopter test ship. The 37-year-old *Cobb*,

the first steam turbine-propelled merchant vessel built in the United States, was plagued by machinery problems and spent most of her Coast Guard career in Long Island Sound, where on 29 June 1944 Commander Frank Erickson landed a helicopter on her flight deck to initiate shipboard use of rotary wing aircraft. It was not the first such landing, however, for an Army pilot had touched down on a tanker almost fourteen months earlier.[38]

Although the Coast Guard purported to be concerned more with the helicopter's antisubmarine capability than with its use in rescue activity, the latter was demonstrated first. Early on the morning of 3 January 1944, the destroyer *Turner,* anchored off Sandy Hook after escorting a convoy from Gibraltar, was rent by a series of explosions. She sank with heavy loss of life, and 160 survivors, 156 of whom were picked up by Coast Guard craft, were rushed to the Sandy Hook hospital, which quickly exhausted its supply of blood plasma. Snow squalls and sleet driven by a 20–25-knot wind had closed all air fields in the New York vicinity, so Admiral Parker asked if a helicopter

Commander Frank A. Erickson congratulating Ensign Walter C. Bolton on the completion of a successful rescue mission in an HNS-1 helicopter in 1944.

from Brooklyn might fly blood plasma from the Battery to Sandy Hook. Erickson undertook the mission in an HNS-1, in visibility so poor that he had almost to "feel" his way between vessels at anchor in Gravesend Bay. Landing at the Battery was difficult because of the high buildings that contributed to the wind's turbulence, but Erickson was equal to the task. After loading two cases of blood plasma, which required that his copilot be left on the ground, he backed the helicopter into the air and delivered the plasma to the Sandy Hook hospital, where it was credited with saving a number of lives.[39]

Some fifteen months later, a Royal Canadian Air Force aircraft crashed in an inaccessible area of Labrador. The nine survivors were located by air search, supplies were dropped, and two ski-equipped airplanes were sent to rescue them. One crashed on landing; the other flew two injured men out and and returned, only to be trapped when thawing snow prevented takeoff. With nine men still to be rescued and conventional methods unavailing, the Canadians requested helicopter assistance from the Coast Guard. The smallest helicopter available, the HNS-1, was hastily dismantled at the Brooklyn Air Station and loaded into a C-54 transport, which took it to Goose Bay, Labrador. The helicopter was reassembled there, and Lieutenant August Kleisch flew it 150 miles to the nearest rescue station, and then 35 miles farther to the disaster scene, returning with the first crash victim before dark. The helicopter's engine froze that night, necessitating a delay while a defroster was brought from Goose Bay, but during the following two days Lieutenant Kleisch flew all of the survivors to safety.[40]

But these were rescue missions, and in the absence of dramatic successes against submarines, the Coast Guard's helicopter development program progressed rather slowly. One obstacle seems to have been the naval aviators' fear that helicopter production would delay that of the Vought-Sikorsky F4-U Corsair, which was one of the most successful of World War II fighter aircraft. In addition, early helicopters were difficult to fly—one observer noted that the pilot really needed three hands!—and some of those accustomed to fixed-wing aircraft doubted that the helicopter's inherent lack of stability could ever be overcome.[41] Nonetheless, the enthusiasts persisted, and by the war's end Coast Guard aviators had prepared the way for the further development of the helicopter for use by the Navy and the Marine Corps. Equally important, Frank Erickson and his fellows made it impossible for their own service to ignore the type of aircraft that would one day be described as "the most versatile item of rescue equipment operated by the U.S. Coast Guard."[42]

Among other uses for the helicopter, Commander Erickson anticipated that it might be flown from an icebreaker to reconnoiter leads through the ice. While the seaplanes carried by the larger vessels had proven invaluable for this purpose, they could be operated only if there were enough clear water to permit takeoff and landing. Further, the necessity that they maintain flight speed made them less than ideal for reconnaissance. With neither of these handicaps, the helicopter would obviously have an important part in ice navigation.

The Coast Guard's interest in icebreaking had been stimulated by the war, in part because of the need to keep the Great Lakes and the Mississippi River system open to navigation for the longest period possible each year. A list of commercial vessels suitable for icebreaking had been compiled late in 1940, and the Canadian naval attaché was asked to provide information regarding such ships of Canadian registry. None of these vessels were acquired, however, until 1942 when three ferries, all about 161 feet in length, were purchased for conversion to icebreaking buoy tenders. Renamed the *Almond, Arrowwood,* and *Chaparral,* they served on the lakes until the war's end, and smaller craft were leased for short periods.[43]

More vessels probably would have been purchased but for the availability of ships built for the purpose in 1942 and 1943. Among these were the 115-foot *Fern* and the 80-foot *Lantana,* which pushed ice plows on the Illinois and Mississippi rivers, and the seven 180-foot buoy tenders that were completed during the autumn of 1942—the first, the *Cactus,* was commissioned on 1 September. Although most of these vessels were not intended for duty on inland waters, they could be pressed into service there until ice conditions permitted their transfer to the Atlantic coast, whence they were assigned to a variety of stations and roles.[44]

Soon after the *Cactus* was completed, her builder, Duluth's Marine Iron and Shipbuilding Corporation, received a contract for five slightly more powerful tenders, while the Coast Guard Yard at Curtis Bay laid the keel of a sixth, which was christened the *Ironwood* when launched in March 1943. These "Class B" 180-footers were followed by twenty almost identical "Class C" ships, of which Marine Iron and Shipbuilding built ten while the Zenith Dredge Company, which had built seven of the original 180-footers, constructed the remainder. The last, the *Woodrush,* was commissioned in September 1944.

The Coast Guard's ability to have these tenders built at a time when the nation's shipbuilding facilities were strained by the increasing demands for warships of all types, including landing craft and cargo vessels, was due in part to the Navy's recognition that they would be very useful ships. Neither of the principal builders was deeply involved with other construction, and the heavy-duty diesel engines that powered the 180-footers were not suitable for use in most naval vessels. Thus, all thirty-nine were completed in reasonably good time and armed with a 3-inch gun, 20-millimeter machine guns, and depth-charge tracks and projectors. Several were assigned to the Pacific Fleet's service forces while some others broke ice and escorted convoys off Greenland.

The 230-foot "Arctic" that had been authorized in 1941 took longer to complete—her keel was laid by the Toledo, Ohio, Shipbuilding Company in July 1941, and she was commissioned in September 1942. As she neared completion, this ship's name was changed to "Eskimo," whereupon the State Department objected that natives of Greenland might find the name offensive.[45] So she became the *Storis,* the Danish word meaning "big ice." The *Storis* was an enlarged 180-footer, intended to serve as a light icebreaker and supply ship in Greenland's waters. Like eight of the smaller tenders, she was strengthened for ice navigation; unlike them she could accommodate a seaplane on her after deck.

In a sense, designing these vessels was a preliminary exercise before undertaking design work on true icebreakers—ships whose sole purpose would be to work in sea ice. President Franklin D. Roosevelt seems to have been directly responsible for this development. Forty years later, Rear Admiral Edward H. Thiele, USCG (Ret.), remembered that in March 1941 he had obtained orders to the *American Sailor* as executive officer, believing that too much Washington duty might affect his career adversely. While the ship was fitting out at Baltimore, he was recalled to Coast Guard Headquarters by Engineer in Chief Harvey Johnson, who took him to the commandant's office. There Waesche handed him a note that the president had written to Treasury Secretary Morgenthau: "I want the world's greatest icebreakers." Thiele speculated that these ships were to be utilized in the construction of an air field at the head of Greenland's Sondre Stromfjord and to aid in the shipment of lend-lease supplies to Archangel, the Russian White Sea port.[46]

Before design work had really begun, Secretary Morgenthau attempted to obtain one or more units of the Soviet Union's icebreaking fleet. The Russian government offered to loan the 323-foot *Krassin,* then near the Bering Strait, to the United States for eight months, adding that she required repairs. Admiral Waesche held that the icebreaker could hardly be useful to the Coast Guard unless she were made available for a least a year, and while negotiations to this end were being carried on, the *Krassin* arrived at Seattle. Lieutenant Commanders Rutherford Lank, Dale Simonson, and Edward Thiele were ordered west to survey her, and it was rumored that she would be manned by the crew of the *Haida,* then being overhauled at the Puget Sound Navy Yard. In the event, however, the icebreaker steamed to Curtis Bay under the Russian flag, and before her repairs had been completed, the Soviet government withdrew its offer, explaining that the *Krassin* was needed at Archangel.[47]

So the Coast Guard failed to obtain a Russian icebreaker for even a year, although its constructors may have learned something about icebreaker design from their examination of the *Krassin.* Thiele denied even this: "But, good lord, it was a 1917 design. . . . this was ancient history at its best." Indeed, he thought that neither the Russians nor the British, who had built the *Krassin* for them, really knew anything about modern icebreaker design.[48]

The information that Thiele had obtained in Europe a few years earlier was undoubtedly much more important than any influence the *Krassin* design may have had. Admiral Johnson later wrote that the Swedish *Ymer* was the prototype for the Coast Guard's Wind-class icebreakers, providing "the closest approximation to the problem in hand, in that considerable power was installed in a ship of relatively short length . . ."[49] While the new vessels would be slightly larger, more heavily constructed, and more powerful, the major difference between the two designs was one of draft, the *Ymer* operating only in the shallow waters of the Baltic Sea.

Even with additional draft, it was not possible to provide a single screw capable of utilizing the desired 10,000 shaft horsepower, so the *Ymer*'s screw arrangement was adopted as well. Twin propellers of massive strength were located as far inboard as possible to minimize the likelihood of ice damage. The propulsion machinery consisted of six 2,000-horsepower Fairbanks Morse diesel engines that turned as many generators, producing the direct current to drive the main motors, each of which was rated at 5,000 horsepower.

The Swedish vessel also had a bow propeller, which presented a perplexing problem. Contrary to frequent assertion, this was not a propulsion unit per se; instead, it had important functions in breaking ice. When reversed, it threw water ahead of the ship, clearing the ice surface of snow that otherwise would cushion the bow effect, and when turning normally, the bow screw sucked water from under the ice, making it easier to break, and its current helped to disperse the broken ice. For ice of uniform thickness, like that usually found in the Great Lakes and the Baltic, the bow screw was quite useful. On the other hand, it would be extremely vulnerable when working in ocean ice. Reports that ice of uniform thickness existed off Greenland's west coast led the designers to incorporate a bow propeller that could be removed and its shaft tube capped when the ship was ordered to other Arctic areas, although the removal of a propeller weighing almost twenty tons was not likely to appeal to many except in a properly equipped shipyard. When the bow screw was in use, each of the three motors produced 3,300 shaft horsepower.

Trim tanks like those of the *Ymer* were also included in the Coast Guard specifications, which required pumps capable of shifting 220 tons of water ballast rapidly from one side to the other, causing the ship to roll 10° in one and a half minutes to help to free herself from the ice. Her longitudinal trim would be altered by transferring water ballast between the forward and after peak tanks, a feature useful in obtaining the most advantageous angle for icebreaking and for lessening the draft forward to facilitate backing off the ice. Trim and peak tanks could also be used for fuel stowage, increasing the already extensive endurance.[50]

Final designs were prepared by Gibbs and Cox, the New York naval architectural firm responsible for much of the Navy's design work, with Simonson and Thiele as reviewing constructor and engineer. Finding a builder was another challenge, for only major

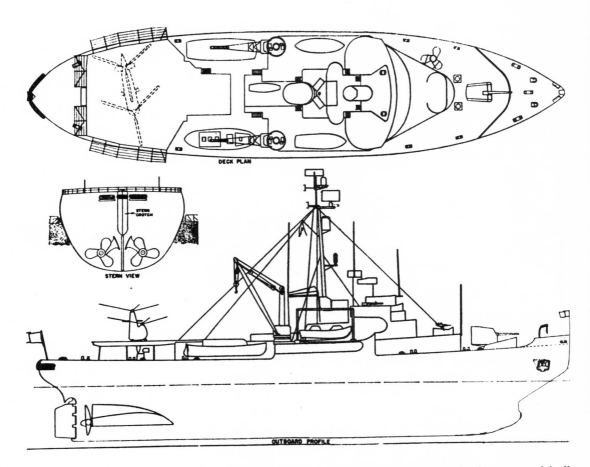

DECK PLAN

STERN
CROTCH

STERN VIEW

OUTBOARD PROFILE

Deck plan and outboard profile of a Wind-class icebreaker with armament reduced and a helicopter deck added after the war. The bow form may be compared with that of the Northland on p. 112.

shipyards possessed the capability of shaping the heavy steel hull plating, which had a maximum thickness of 1⅝ inch, and all of these yards were fully occupied with naval construction. The Western Pipe and Steel Company had the necessary equipment—in Los Angeles—while its shipyard was in San Francisco. On assurance of receiving a contract for icebreaker construction, the company purchased land in San Pedro and established a new yard. Western Pipe and Steel also undertook to develop welding techniques for high-tensile steel, of which the icebreaker hulls would be built.[51] The keels of four of these ships were laid during the summer of 1942, with construction requiring almost two years.

Since these would operate in waters where hostile forces might be encountered, armament had an important part in the design—as Thiele explained: "When you are in the ice, you [have] to have a terrific firepower capability because you are a sitting duck."[52] Thus, the ships were completed with two twin 5-inch 38-caliber dual-purpose mounts, three quadruple 40-millimeters, and six 20-millimeters in addition to depth-charge tracks and projectors. There was not sufficient deck space for a helicopter platform, but a seaplane was almost literally squeezed between the stack and the after 5-inch mount.

When completed, these were not the largest icebreakers in the world, but they were undoubtedly among the best. So, too, thought the Soviet government, which indicated an interest in acquiring them by lend-lease. The request was relayed to Admiral Waesche in mid-September 1943 by Harry L. Hopkins, administrator of the lend-lease program, and following a conference of Navy and civilian officials, the commandant was informed that the lead ship, which had been christened the *Northwind*, would be taken over by the Russians on completion in February 1944.[53] Her sisters, the *Eastwind*, *Southwind*, and *Westwind*, were all commissioned as Coast Guard cutters, but the two latter vessels were transferred to the Soviet Union early in 1945. Like the former *Northwind*, they were stripped of secret equipment and rearmed with 3-inch and 40-millimeter guns obtained from the U.S. Army before transfer.

While some Coast Guardsmen deplored the loss of the icebreakers, others thought that they were too large for Coast Guard purposes generally and that their service would never be permitted to operate such expensive vessels in peacetime.[54] In partial compensation for their loss, one of three identical ships laid down by Western Pipe and Steel in 1944 was assigned to the Coast Guard and named the *Northwind*, her sisters going to the Navy as the *Burton Island* and the *Edisto*.

The building of the Wind class inevitably led to the consideration of such a vessel for use on the Great Lakes, where depth of water had to be taken into account. The result was the *Mackinaw*, which Admiral Thiele described as one of the Wind-class "squashed down and pushed out to meet the requirements of the Lakes."[55] Thus, she was 290 feet long, 74.3 feet abeam, and 19 feet maximum draft as compared with the Winds' dimensions of 269 feet, 63.5 feet, and 25.7 feet. Like them, the *Mackinaw* was massively constructed, but she was not likely to encounter extreme ice pressures, so the Toledo Shipbuilding Company built her hull of mild steel. Her engineering plant was identical to those of the Winds, and like them, she had pneumatic pilothouse engine controls for rapid maneuvering in the ice. The *Mackinaw* was commissioned in December 1944, and a number of Russians joined the ship soon thereafter for engineering instruction before reporting to one of the Wind-class.

Design of the vessels authorized to replace the Lake-class cutters proceeded concurrently with that of the big icebreakers, with which they had something in common—Congress specified that all should be "of heavy construction to permit of working in waters where ice may be encountered," which obviously excluded additional vessels of the Treasury class. Although the belief persists that Congress also limited the length of these ships to 250 feet, preventing the Coast Guard from building 316-footers to the design prepared by Frederick

A. Hunnewell in 1933, neither the original bill nor Public Law 178 of the 77th Congress made any mention of the vessels' size, stipulating only that they be "of the usual Coast Guard type."[56] Apparently the Coast Guard itself decided the dimensions, presumably choosing to build shorter cutters because they could be maneuvered in pack ice more effectively than longer ships and because the Lake-class had been deemed so successful. For reasons of economy, the three improved 327-footers authorized earlier as replacements for the old *Unalga, Ossipee,* and *Tallapoosa* were also built to the new design.

Rather than being "cut down" 316-footers, as some have asserted, the new ships were to be improved versions of the 250-footers, 4 feet longer with a foot greater beam and a foot less maximum draft.[57] Their hulls would be unusually strong, combining longitudinal and transverse framing and having an "ice belt" of heavier plating at the waterline. Like the Treasury-class and all subsequent cutters, they would be entirely welded.

The decision to revert to turbo-electric drive in these cutters is interesting. Quincy B. Newman had thought it the most practical for Coast Guard purposes, but his successor as engineer in chief, Captain Robert B. Adams, had chosen geared turbines for the *Escanaba* and Treasury-classes. Engineer in Chief Harvey Johnson, however, shared Newman's preference for electric drive, so these vessels— called the *Owasco*-class after the lead ship—became the last turbo-electric cutters; indeed, they would be the last steam-powered vessels built for the Coast Guard.

The propulsion machinery was an improved version of Newman's "central power plant" type, developing 4,000 shaft horsepower with pilothouse control. That worked well in ships with diesel-electric drive, but the boilers for the *Owasco*-class had to be redesigned to permit remote control, and many came to believe that the system was unduly complex.[58] Unlike earlier cutters, these had all machinery—boilers, turbines, condensers, auxiliary turbine generators, and other auxiliaries—in a single compartment. This resulted in greater efficiency because shorter steam lines minimized heat loss due to radiation, but it also led to overcrowding. Paul G. Tomalin, one of those involved in the design work, put it succinctly: "As always in the development of a plant, some items grow in bulk from the original designs and sprout various appendages at embarrassing locations. Hitherto neglected items suddenly assert themselves, and new items and requirements are added."[59]

Tomalin's statement, applied to the design as a whole, explains the basic problem of these ships. They had low priority—the first two were laid down at Curtis Bay in July 1943, and the Coast Guard Yard required two years to complete them, while Western Pipe and Steel built the other eleven at San Pedro in somewhat shorter time, laying the keel of the first in November 1943. During this lengthy "gestation period," the design was altered repeatedly to incorporate new de-

The 255-foot cutter Mendota *running her trials.*

velopments. Thus, it was decided that the so-called 255-footers should carry almost the same armament as the Wind-class, on hulls that were 15 feet shorter and 20 feet narrower, and space had to be found for a combat information center and a variety of types of unanticipated electronic equipment, including fire-control radar. Additional equipment required additional personnel for operation and maintenance—ultimately 276 officers and men were to be accommodated in the already crowded cutters! Overcrowding was normal in World War II warships, but this must have approached the upper limit. Small wonder that they were unable to embark the seaplanes originally intended for them or that their stability in severe weather conditions depended on ballasting empty fuel tanks with sea water. At least their living spaces were air-conditioned, hardly a luxury under these circumstances.

The Coast Guard attempted to hasten the construction of the 255-footers, emphasizing "the rugged hull characteristics . . . which make [them] particularly adapted for convoy and other duty in northern latitudes . . . and the towing qualities of these vessels which no doubt will be in demand during advances in the Pacific."[60] The Navy was not impressed; the first, the *Owasco,* commissioned in May 1945, too late for service in World War II.

The *Owasco*'s initial performance was hardly reassuring, for she vibrated so badly when approaching full power that the trial had to be terminated. The designers, anticipating difficulties with her three-bladed screw, had had other types tested at the Navy's David W. Taylor Model Basin, and since a five-bladed propeller had attained similar efficiency, one of these was fitted to the next to complete, the *Mendota,* which attained full power and somewhat more with little vibration.[61]

After witnessing her trials, Captain Philip B. Eaton wrote, "I believe we will have thirteen cutters that we can be proud of when they are afloat."[62] Eaton and the others associated with the 255-footer program had some reason to be pleased, for the new ships were nearly as fast as the 327-footers although they had only two-thirds the shaft horsepower, and they had greater endurance. Unfortunately, neither their heavy armaments nor their ability to maneuver in pack ice would be in demand in the postwar Coast Guard.

Unlike icebreaking, which was clearly a Coast Guard responsibility, the development of the electronic aid to navigation that came to be called loran began as a private endeavor. Interest in such systems antedated American entry into the war, and reports that the British had developed a type of radio navigation to guide bombers to continental targets in 1940 led scientists from the Radiation Laboratory at the Massachusetts Institute of Technology and the American Telephone and Telegraph Company's Bell Laboratories to visit Britain. Returning to the United States, these men set out to devise a system of their own, with the support of the National Defense Research Committee and the cooperation of the War and Navy departments.

The system was based on the fact that radio ground waves travel along the earth's surface at a known constant speed. If pulse signals from two stations some distance apart were transmitted with a constant interval between the first and the second, they would provide a line of position for navigational purposes. Ships and aircraft fitted with receivers and charts that showed these lines of position would be able to obtain fixes as accurate as those by celestial navigation and much more rapidly simply by tracing the lines from two sets of signals to the point at which they intersected.

The Coast Guard's involvement began in the spring of 1942, when Admiral Waesche was asked to recommend an officer to direct a project involving radio and electronics. On the advice of Captain Charles A. Park, the senior officer from the old Lighthouse Service, he chose Lieutenant Commander Lawrence M. Harding, who had worked on radio aids to aerial navigation while employed by that service.[63] Harding learned that experimental transmitters had been installed at inactive Coast Guard stations near Montauk Point on Long Island and on Fenwick Island, Delaware, but the scientists had not been able to synchronize signals from the two with any degree of regularity. Indeed, some had come to believe that resources should be diverted from the project to further the improvement of radar. Harding soon concluded that the principle was sound and that the problem was caused by the choice of a part of the spectrum already in use for other transmissions. Declining an invitation to take control of the work at the Radiation Laboratory, he undertook to represent the Navy at Cambridge and to assure continuing support from that service, a task made the easier by the interest of several high-ranking naval officers.[64]

Lieutenant Commander Harding's assignment to the project brought rapid progress; the scientists developed a reliable, all-weather system in a relatively short time. Fenwick Island and Montauk Point became the first operational stations, the "master" transmitting the first signal and triggering the delayed transmission from the "slave" station. The next pair of stations was established in Nova Scotia with the cooperation of the Royal Canadian Navy, and when the Coast Guard weather ship *Manasquan* returned from a month on ocean station in mid-July to report that she had received the signals at distances of 680 miles by day and 1,300 miles at night, when sky waves were reflected from the ionosphere, few doubted that the system was practical.

It was considered to be highly sensitive—an enemy learning of the project might be able to jam the signals or use them to the detriment of the United States—so a high degree of secrecy was maintained. Harding suggested the name "loran," an acronym for "long range navigation," to conceal the nature of the project, and it was quickly adopted.[65]

While the *Manasquan* was still at sea, loran station sites were being chosen in Newfoundland and Labrador, after which Harding visited Greenland to select a site near Cape Farewell. Weather conditions during the Greenland winter were a formidable obstacle to construction of the last, but in mid-July 1943 it followed the others into regular service. Meanwhile, Commander Harding helped the Royal Navy to set up stations in Iceland and in the Faroe and Hebrides islands to provide loran service for convoys traversing more northerly waters.

Loran's success in the North Atlantic led to its establishment elsewhere, first in the Aleutian Islands-Bering Sea area and later in the Central and South Pacific. The rapid expansion of the loran network obviously required trained personnel in numbers beyond the capacity of the Radio Laboratory to provide, so the loran school at Cambridge was taken over by the Navy and enlarged. By this time, the Coast Guard's connection with the project had increased considerably; officers and petty officers trained at Cambridge had been involved in almost every stage of the North Atlantic system's development. Thus, it followed almost as a matter of course that Coast Guardsmen constructed and manned the Pacific Ocean and Bering Sea loran stations, and when the loran school at Cambridge became inadequate because of limited space, it was relocated at the Coast Guard Training Station in Groton, Connecticut.

Loran's contribution to the Allied war effort was very considerable. It was the first virtually all-weather navigational system, and the network of loran lines of position, extending over a third of the earth's surface that included major theaters of military operations for the Western Allies, enabled ships and aircraft in unprecedented numbers to be navigated with an equally unprecedented accuracy during the latter part of the war.[66] Thanks to Lawrence M. Harding's role in the development of loran and to the fact that the vast majority of the stations were manned by Coast Guard personnel, the Coast

Guard was the logical agency to assume responsibility for the continued operation and further improvement of this electronic aid to navigation in the postwar period.

While Coast Guardsmen of every description—regular, reserve, and temporary reserve—were employed in the multiplicity of duties and endeavors delineated in this chapter, many others—regulars and reserves—were involved more directly in military operations, manning ships of the Army and the Navy as well as those of their own service. The Coast Guard's prized identification with the nation's armed forces was enhanced immeasurably by their service in World War II, which must now be considered.

CHAPTER FOURTEEN

"TO EUROPE AND FAR EAST"[1]

If one accepts the Japanese attack on the U.S. Pacific Fleet at Pearl Harbor on 7 December 1941 as the beginning of American belligerency in World War II, the *Taney* was the first Coast Guard cutter to be engaged in that conflict. Alongside a pier in Honolulu harbor that morning, she fired on formations of aircraft without effect at 9 A.M. and again a little later. These must have been Japanese; not so the airplanes that approached from the south-southwest just before noon. But anything flying that day was an enemy so far as American antiaircraft gun crews were concerned, and the *Taney* opened fire again: "Bursts from the 3 inch guns appeared short, but the planes were observed to be rocked by the blasts. Machine gun tracers were observed to be passing through the leading plane. All planes immediately swerved away and upward without dropping any bombs."[2] So neither foe nor friend suffered much damage as a result of the Coast Guard's engagement on that fateful day.

But a more significant Coast Guard involvement had already begun far to the northeastward. Expecting that the Germans would establish weather stations in Greenland, President Roosevelt had directed Admiral Stark to maintain a patrol off the island's east coast. Accordingly, the Northeast Greenland Patrol, consisting of the *Northland, North Star,* and *Bear* was established under Commander Edward H. Smith, who earlier had organized a Danish and Eskimo sledge patrol to keep the northeastern coast under surveillance.

Early in September 1941, members of the sledge patrol informed the *North Star* that a strange vessel had landed men in Greenland. The *Northland* was closer to the reported position, so she investigated and sighted a small Norwegian sealer on 12 September. Commander Carl C. von Paulsen took the cutter alongside, sent an armed officer on board, and soon learned that the vessel was the *Buskoe,* manned by Norwegians and carrying an unusual amount of radio equipment. Interrogation revealed that she had put a party ashore not long before, so a prize crew was sent on board the *Buskoe,* which was left in the *Bear*'s care while the *Northland* sought the shore

The converted trawler Ar-luk.

party. It was located at a trapping station two days later, and an armed detachment, achieving surprise, captured the three Norwegians, one a radio operator in German employ, without resistance. Like their fellows in the *Buskoe,* they were sent to Boston—not as prisoners of war because the United States was not at war, but as illegal immigrants.[3]

The Northeast Greenland and South Greenland Patrols were combined in October 1941 to form the Greenland Patrol under "Iceberg" Smith's command, and when Germany declared war on the United States some two months later, Smith applied to Admiral Waesche for additional vessels for escort and patrol. Ten trawlers were acquired in Boston, and with blue and white camouflage, Eskimo animal names, and light armament, they were commissioned during the summer of 1942. These rugged craft, little over 100 feet long and capable of 9 or 10 knots, were hardly ideal, but they were seaworthy and possessed adequate endurance, the qualities essential for service with the Greenland Patrol. One—ironically, she was the newest—was lost. The *Natsek* was last seen off Belle Isle Strait on 17 December 1942, en route from Narsarssuak to Boston. An air and sea search ordered when she became overdue at Boston found no trace of the trawler, and since the *Nanok*, which had accompanied her until they were separated in a snowstorm, had encountered severe icing conditions not long afterward, it was thought that the *Natsek* capsized because of the accumulation of ice topside. Twenty-four men were lost with her. The remaining nine trawlers were returned to their erstwhile owners in 1944, by which time more suitable vessels were available.[4]

The Greenland Patrol performed its varied duties throughout the war, under Commodore Earl G. Rose after November 1943, when Rear Admiral Edward H. Smith became commander of the Navy's Task Force 24, which included the Greenland Patrol. Its vessels helped to establish radio and loran stations and other base facilities ashore, cooperated with Army detachments to destroy German radio stations and capture their personnel, and thwarted other enemy efforts to institute a weather-reporting service in Greenland. The *Northland* ferried equipment and personnel to Jan Mayen in November 1943, and her company spent an arduous three weeks installing a high-frequency radio direction-finder station on that volcanic island well to the north of Iceland. In addition, there were occasional encounters with enemy aircraft, none of which caused any loss to either combatant, and a few supposed submarine contacts led to depth-charge attacks, again without result.[5]

The escort of convoys bound for Greenland and Iceland required the services of most of the vessels assigned to the Greenland Patrol, among them the 240-footers *Modoc, Mojave,* and *Tampa,* the 165-footers *Algonquin, Comanche, Escanaba, Mohawk,* and *Tahoma,* and the 125-foot *Active, Faunce, Frederick Lee,* and *Travis.* None was really suitable for this purpose: Even the fastest were considerably slower than surfaced U-boats, none was equipped with radar until 1943, and while all had sonar and depth charges, their officers and men were inadequately trained in antisubmarine warfare, as indeed were those of most American escort vessels until midway through the war.[6] Thus, the cutters were more effective as rescue ships, after disaster had befallen their charges.

Rescue operations were the more difficult because many had to be conducted at night—the submarines' favorite time to attack convoys—often in rough seas, and even in summer months the water temperature was likely to be so low that survivors were numbed by the cold and unable to help themselves. The knowledge that any vessel that slowed to pick up men from a torpedoed ship might find herself the U-boat's next victim was hardly reassuring to cutter crews, although none was sunk while so engaged.

Notable examples of rescue activity include the twenty men picked up by the *Escanaba* after the *Cherokee* had been torpedoed in a night attack on 15 June 1942 and the *Mojave*'s rescue of 293 from

225

The 240-foot cutter Mojave *off Greenland in 1943.*

the troopship *Chatham*, torpedoed off the Strait of Belle Isle on 27 August 1942. The *Chatham's* sister *Dorchester* became a submarine victim south of Cape Farewell early on the morning of 3 February 1943 while the *Tampa, Comanche,* and *Escanaba* were escorting her and two smaller vessels. She made no distress signals, and the cutters were unaware of her plight for some time. When it became known, the *Tampa* took the remainder of the convoy on to its destination while the 165-footers sought to locate the U-boat before turning their attention to rescue work. When they did so, it was too late for many—the *Dorchester's* abandonment had been very disorderly, and relatively few got away in her boats. Most of those in the water were paralyzed by cold when the cutters reached them, so Coast Guardsmen introduced a new "retriever" rescue technique—clad in rubber suits, they swam to survivors to secure lines to them so that they could be hauled on board. The *Escanaba* saved 133, one of whom died later, while the *Comanche* was credited with ninety-seven. But more than 600 of those on board the *Dorchester* were lost, including sixteen Coast Guardsmen.

The *Dorchester* rescue was the last for the *Escanaba*. Little more than four months later, the 165-footer sailed from Narsarssuak in company with the *Mojave, Tampa, Storis, Algonquin,* and *Raritan,* escorting a convoy bound for St. John's, Newfoundland. She exploded at 5:10 A.M. the next day, 13 June, and sank within three minutes. The *Storis* and the *Raritan* picked up two enlisted men; Lieutenant Commander Carl U. Peterson and 100 men of her crew were lost. At the time, the cause of the *Escanaba's* sinking could not be determined, for she sank too rapidly to make any signal, and none of the other cutters reported a sonar contact. Her loss was subsequently attributed to a U-boat torpedo.

Not all of the ships that sank in the Greenland Patrol's area were torpedoed. The British steamer *Svend Foyne* collided with an iceberg off Cape Farewell late in March 1943, and her crew abandoned ship. The *Algonquin, Frederick Lee,* and *Modoc* and the Coast Guard

The Escanaba *not long before she was sunk.*

trawler *Aivik* were among the rescue vessels, picking up 128 survivors from small boats and rafts. In mid-December 1943, the *Comanche* was detached from the escort of a Greenland-bound convoy to assist the small freighter *Nevada,* which was foundering in the gale-whipped Labrador Sea. She was abandoned before the cutter could reach her, but the *Comanche* sighted a boat, from which twenty-nine men and a dog were removed despite the handicaps of darkness and heavy seas. The *Modoc, Tampa,* and *Storis* joined the search for additional surviors the next day; none was found, and the *Nevada* sank before the gale moderated.[7]

Some of the most notable rescues were performed by aircraft, among which that attempted by Lieutenant John A. Pritchard, Jr., and Radioman Benjamin A. Bottoms was unsurpassed in gallantry. A B-17 bomber was forced down on the Greenland ice cap late in 1942, and when it became apparent that its crew had survived, the *Northland* made her way through the ice as far as possible, with Commander Francis C. Pollard intending to send a rescue party overland. Pritchard had led such a party to rescue three Canadian airmen from the ice cap a few days before, and on this occasion he thought that he could land the cutter's Grumman J2F amphibian on the snow-covered ice. Signals from the B-17's partially repaired radio guided the J2F to the bomber, whose men advised against landing. Nonetheless, Pritchard put the amphibian down safely about 4 miles away, and leaving Bottoms to look after it, he helped three injured men across the ice to the Grumman. Only two could be taken on board; with them, the J2F returned to the *Northland* after dark, the cutter's searchlights providing illumination for the landing. Pritchard and Bottoms repeated their flight the next day despite a light snowfall, taking off successfully with the third injured man. Soon afterward, the *Northland* lost radio contact with the J2F, which disappeared in a snowstorm. A search party was sent ashore when the storm abated, to no avail. The Grumman's wreckage was later sighted by Army aircraft, one of which joined a Navy PBY to rescue the remaining B-17 survivors, but Pritchard, Bottoms, and Corporal Loren H. Haworth were never found.[8]

Army and Navy squadrons flew most of the aviation missions in the Greenland vicinity until October 1943, when Commander Donald B. MacDiarmid commissioned the Coast Guard Patrol Bombing Squadron 6, which was based at Narsarssuak. Consisting ultimately of twelve PBY-5As with 29 officers and 156 enlisted men, this squadron undertook search-and-rescue missions, provided air cover for convoys, and advised shipping of ice conditions. Its Catalinas, flying in some of the worst weather conditions imaginable, were invaluable in locating aircraft that crashed or were forced down en route to Britain, dropping medical supplies and food to survivors and guiding rescue parties to them. Their ice information broadcasts were very useful as well; indeed, the squadron spent most of its time performing traditional Coast Guard duties, notwithstanding its "Bombing" designation.[9]

The need for meteorological information led the Germans to send three small expeditions to northeastern Greenland in 1944. One of these established a weather-reporting station near Shannon Island, some 600 miles north of Iceland, which was reported by the sledge patrol in July. The *Northland* and the *Storis* transported a small Army detachment to destroy it, only to find the station abandoned and its equipment smashed. After completing the destruction, the *Northland* found a German trawler, thought to be the *Coberg*, a few miles away, crushed in the ice and gutted by fire.

A second expedition was thwarted on 1 September, when the *Northland* encountered a strange vessel in the ice off Great Koldewey Island, to the northward of Shannon Island. A seven-hour chase ensued, and with the range closing and his challenge unanswered, Lieutenant Commander Reginald W. Butcher ordered the cutter's gunners to fire. Although they scored no hits, the Germans scuttled their trawler and were captured by the *Northland*, which was not unscathed—she had damaged her rudder in the ice during the chase.[10]

Meanwhile, the *Eastwind*, the first of the Wind-class icebreakers that the Coast Guard was permitted to commission, had completed her shakedown cruise and was en route to Greenland from Boston. She reached Scoresby Sound early in September, where Captain Charles W. Thomas, who had been Butcher's predecessor in the *Northland*, lost no time in trying his new command in the ice. Her performance made him confident that Wind-class ships would be able to work farther to the north later in the year than any other, although the bow propeller proved to be a useless encumbrance for work in pack ice.[11]

Soon after Captain Thomas assumed command of operations in northeastern Greenland, the rapid southward movement of the polar ice pack led him to order his smaller ships, the *Storis,* the *Northland,* and the 180-foot buoy tender *Evergreen* to Iceland, after exchanging the *Eastwind*'s storm-damaged J2F for that of the *Storis* and repairing the *Northland*'s jury steering rig. He had been notified that the new *Southwind* was on her way to join him, but before she could report for duty, her sister's aircraft sighted a ship to the northward, standing out to sea. Although nightfall and a heavy fog prevented further contact, aerial reconnaissance the next day revealed that building materials and supplies had been landed on North Little Koldewey Island. The *Eastwind* cleared a way through the ice, her small boats put the landing force ashore early the following morning, and it forced the twelve Germans to surrender without firing a shot.

Captured documents indicated that their supply ship was the 178-foot *Externsteine,* a new vessel designed for ice navigation, which Thomas was sure must still be in the vicinity. She was located in the ice off Shannon Island on 14 October, and although both the *Eastwind* and the *Southwind* sustained screw damage in closing her, the former got within range late that night. With her after mount illuminating the target with star shells and the *Southwind* training a searchlight on it, the *Eastwind*'s forward guns bracketed the *Externsteine,* which thereupon blinked a surrender signal. Confident that their ship could never be freed from the ice, the Germans had made no attempt to scuttle her; to their chagrin, the *Eastwind* broke her out the next day and put a prize crew on board. The *Externsteine*'s new company promptly christened her the *Eastbreeze,* and since she was in good condition and equipped with radar, Captain Thomas added her to his patrol force. Her evaporators defied efforts to make them function, however, so she had to be detached and sent to Boston by way of Reykjavik and Argentia, Newfoundland, a week later. There she was taken over by the Navy, which unimaginatively renamed her the *Callao* and used her as a test ship for the next five years.[12]

Capture of the *Externsteine,* the only German surface naval vessel taken at sea by the U.S. Navy during World War II, really ended hostile activities in the Greenland area, which helps to explain the transfer of the *Southwind* and the *Westwind* to Russia. By the time the arctic winter had given way to spring, the war in Europe was nearing its end, and there would be no more German efforts to establish stations for any purpose on Greenland's forbidding shore. Routine patrols were continued into May 1945, however, and since aircraft continued to be ferried to Britain, search-and-rescue missions had to be carried out as well.

More than any other in World War II, Greenland was a Coast

Guard theater of operations. To be sure, the Army and the Navy had personnel and equipment there, and the former's detachment far outnumbered the Coast Guardsmen. But the Coast Guard was first on the scene, and it provided services essential for the establishment of Army installations. Coast Guard units of the Greenland Patrol, commanded successively by Edward H. Smith, Earl G. Rose, and Charles W. Thomas, had the major part in thwarting German efforts to set up meteorological and radio relay stations, whose work could have facilitated German military operations in Europe and especially the U-boats' prosecution of the Battle of the Atlantic.

Like its involvement in Greenland, the Coast Guard's participation in the Battle of the Atlantic antedated the nation's official belligerency, but on a smaller scale. United States destroyers had begun to escort fast convoys from a rendezvous off Newfoundland to a mid-ocean meeting point (MOMP) south of Iceland, where British escort groups took over, in mid-September 1941. Little more than a month later, four of these destroyers brought an old oiler, the USS *Salinas,* and four cargo ships from Iceland to the MOMP where they relieved the British escort of a westbound convoy, to which their charges were added. U-boats made contact several days later, and the *Salinas* was hit by two torpedoes during the morning of 29 October. Contrary to expectation, the old oiler did not sink, nor was the *U-106* able to hit her with a second salvo of torpedoes. Thereafter, a destroyer sent back from the convoy kept the submarine occupied sufficiently to allow the *Salinas* to get under way at slow speed. Meanwhile, the *Campbell* and the fleet tug *Cherokee* had been ordered to her assistance and joined her on 31 October, the day before the *Salinas* reached St. John's, Newfoundland. The new destroyer *Kearny* had been badly damaged by a torpedo almost two weeks earlier, and soon after midnight on 31 October, the old flush-decker *Reuben James* was sunk with very heavy loss of life. Thus, the U.S. Navy was deeply engaged in the Battle of the Atlantic by the time the entire Coast Guard was transferred to its control.[13]

Having helped the *Salinas* to safety, the *Campbell* became the first cutter to escort a convoy in World War II when she joined five destroyers to screen the thirty-three ships of eastbound HX 159 on 10 November. The convoy was turned over to a British and Canadian escort group at the MOMP ten days later, by which time the *Campbell* had proved herself far superior to the destroyers in fuel economy, maneuverability, and sea kindliness, while her speed and armament were quite adequate. Despite this demonstration of their suitability for ocean escort duty, the other ships of the Treasury class were not ordered to battle immediately. The *Ingham* was next; with four destroyers, she took a forty-six ship convoy eastward on 10 December. Again, the passage to the MOMP required nine days, on the last of which the convoy was scattered by a gale. All of the ships reached their destinations nonetheless.

The *Campbell* also had the opportunity to become the first U.S.

warship to sink a U-boat. She was steaming independently from Halifax to Boston on 22 January 1942, when her lookouts sighted a submarine. It submerged before the cutter could attack and surfaced again some distance away an hour later. This time the *Campbell* got off several shots, to no avail, and her sonarmen failed to make contact after the U-boat disappeared. The torpedoing of a tanker that night brought the cutter to the attack once more, and two depth-charge patterns caused the submarine to broach before apparently sinking. Like so many crews inexperienced in antisubmarine warfare, the "Campbells" accepted signs of injury as proof of death; had they waited for daylight, oil oozing from the submarine's damaged tanks could have guided their ship in for the kill. Instead, the *Campbell* went to assist the tanker, whose crew had already been removed and which sank in flames as she approached, while the U-boat escaped.[14]

The *Alexander Hamilton* joined the ocean escorts on 15 January 1942—she had resumed her original name three days earlier to avoid confusion with the USS *Hamilton*, a high-speed minesweeper. Her passage to the MOMP screening convoy HX 170 with three destroyers, was uneventful, and then she was assigned to tow the disabled storeship *Yukon* to Iceland, with the new destroyer *Gwin* as escort. Some 10 miles off Reykjavik on 29 January, the British tug *Frisky* took over the tow, and the *Alexander Hamilton* began to work up to 15 knots as she headed for a screening position off the *Yukon*'s port bow. At that moment, the *U-132*, undetected by the *Gwin*, fired a spread of torpedoes at the storeship. All missed their target, but one passed ahead to hit the cutter's starboard side near the bulkhead between the fireroom and the engineroom. Seven men were killed in the explosion and others were burned or otherwise injured. The four surviving boats were lowered to ferry the casualties to the *Gwin*, which removed the last of the 213 "Hamiltons" with the assistance of an Icelandic fishing boat an hour later. The final death toll was twenty-six, of whom six died later of burns.

The *Alexander Hamilton*, however, remained afloat, and the *Frisky* attempted to save her after towing the *Yukon* into Reykjavik. Rising seas and darkness thwarted her efforts that day, and the abandoned cutter was driven seaward during the night. The *Frisky* tried again on 30 January, only to have the hawser part after the stricken vessel began to list heavily. Five minutes later, the *Alexander Hamilton* capsized and sank. No less than fourteen destroyers from the nearby base at Hvalfjordur sought her assailant; the *U-132* eluded them all.[15]

The *Spencer* took her sister's place late in February, and the *Bibb* and the *Duane* were assigned to escort duty as well. By the spring of 1942, all were fully involved in the Battle of the Atlantic, serving on occasion as escort group flagships, a role for which their relatively spacious quarters fitted them. Based at St. John's or Argentia, Newfoundland, and operating much of the time out of Hvalfjordur, which offered little more than a poorly protected anchorage, they worked with a few old American flush-deckers, several British destroyers, and British and Canadian corvettes, escorting convoys between a west ocean meeting point and ports in the United Kingdom.

These convoys were generally routed along the great circle track between Newfoundland and northern Ireland in order to gain maximum protection by aircraft based in Iceland and to conserve the escorts' limited fuel supplies. This route, however, had the disadvantage of extremely bad weather in winter months, and those involved in the Battle of the Atlantic, regardless of their nationality, found service in northerly waters the most arduous of all. The mid-ocean escorts were severely taxed by the gale-force winds, heavy seas, and cold, because they were so few that there was little time for the necessary maintenance for ships and rest for their men between convoys. Too frequently, they had to sail with some or all of their detection equipment—radar, sonar, and high-frequency direction-finders (HF/DF)—operating at less than full efficiency or not at all simply because no other escort vessels were available.[16] As might be expected, losses to the convoys were heavy; they would have been heavier had the German U-boat Command concentrated its efforts against those sailing the northern track.

November 1942 was the worst month of the Battle of the Atlantic for the Allies, with the U-boats sinking over 700,000 tons of shipping and 160,000 tons lost to aircraft and other causes. This was a loss rate that could not be sustained for many months. It fell considerably in December, however, because a number of submarines were diverted from the North Atlantic convoy routes to counter the Allied invasion of North Africa and because weather conditions and evasive routing kept wolf packs from locating their prey.

Mid-December brought the big cutters their first victim. The *Ingham*, escorting convoy SC-112, dropped depth charges on a sonar contact on 15 December and made two more such attacks two days later. Although there was no indication that any of the attacks had inflicted damage, Commander George E. McCabe was confident that his cutter's last depth-charge pattern had sunk a submarine. After the war, German records confirmed that the *U-626* had been sunk in that locale, but apparently by the *Ingham*'s 15 December attack.[17]

The weather remained extremely bad—indeed, it deteriorated even more as 1943 began—so the convoys remained relatively immune from U-boat attack through January. This situation changed in February, by which time the enemy had 100 submarines at sea, over a third of them patrolling in the area off Greenland where air cover could not be provided for the convoys. Only three ships of convoy HX-224 were sunk, but a survivor of one was picked up by the *U-632* and he informed his captors that a slow convoy was following on the same route. This confirmed an intercepted message to the same effect, and the submarines gathered for the kill.

Nonetheless, the sixty-three ships and nine escorts of convoy SC-118 might have eluded the enemy had not a merchant seaman carelessly fired a "snowflake" rocket early on the morning of 4 February, illuminating the convoy and attracting the attention of the *U-187* 20 miles away. The submarine closed the convoy and began to transmit a contact report, which was detected by the HF/DF-equipped SS *Toward,* the convoy's rescue vessel. Two British destroyers responded to the alarm and sank the *U-187,* but by that time twenty-one other U-boats were headed for the convoy. These used their radios frequently, and radio operators in the cutter *Bibb* and the *Toward,* the two ships with HF/DF, were kept busy reporting bearings, against the closest of which the British escort commander directed attacks that kept the submarines fully engaged. Only one straggler was lost from the convoy that night, while several U-boats were damaged or severely shaken by depth charges. Dodging attacks and with visibility diminishing as the weather deteriorated, the Germans lost contact with the convoy during the night, and the escort group was strengthened by the *Ingham* and two old American destroyers that had been ordered from Hvalfjordur. The next day, 6 February, brought air cover from Iceland. The aircraft joined the escorts in harassing the U-boats, sinking none but keeping them at a distance from the convoy, where one sank another straggler.

The submarines regained contact soon after dark that evening. Again, the escort vessels engaged them effectively, although the *U-262* got into the convoy and sank one ship before exhausting her torpedo supply. During the night, however, escorts running down contacts astern of the convoy left it exposed, and the *U-402* sank the rescue vessel *Toward* and a tanker, while the *U-614* torpedoed a freighter. After reloading her torpedo tubes, the *U-402* sank another tanker early the next morning and a cargo ship somewhat later, before encountering the American troopship *Henry R. Mallory,* which was unaccountably straggling astern of the convoy at 7 knots. Hit by one torpedo, the *Mallory* remained afloat for more than an hour, but she was abandoned in similar fashion to the *Dorchester,* sunk only four days before. No distress signals were sent, relatively few got away in boats and rafts, and swimmers could not survive for long in the icy waters. More than three hours later, the *Bibb* sighted a boat, and when closing it, found the area strewn with men floating in life jackets. Commander Roy L. Raney called for help, only to be told to rejoin the convoy as quickly as possible. He chose to ignore the directive; the *Bibb* lowered boats and picked up 202 survivors while the *Ingham,* which joined her sister later, found a few more still living. Almost two-thirds of those who had sailed in the *Henry R. Mallory* perished.[18]

After torpedoing the troopship, the *U-402* sank another freighter, whose thirty-three survivors the *Bibb* rescued, and the submarine finished her day's work by torpedoing a seventh vessel—the *Ingham* picked up her few survivors. Ireland-based aircraft were over the convoy on 9 February, and the U-boats withdrew.

In what Admiral Karl Doenitz, commander in chief of the German navy, called "perhaps the hardest convoy battle of the whole war," SC-118 had lost twelve ships to U-boat torpedoes and one sunk as the result of collision.[19] German losses amounted to three submarines, and two others were badly damaged. Although neither the *Bibb* nor the *Ingham* was directly responsible for the destruction of a U-boat, the former's HF/DF provided invaluable information as to the enemies' proximity, and the commanding officers of both cutters repeatedly stopped to pick up survivors, fully aware that their ships might be torpedo targets at any time.

Soon after SC-118 had reached its destination, Ocean Escort Unit A-3, the *Campbell* and five corvettes under Captain Paul R. Heineman, USN, in the *Spencer,* was ordered to screen westbound convoy ON-166. Gales limited the convoy to 4 knots during the first part of its passage, but there were few stragglers and no submarines were reported until 21 February when several were sighted by aircraft. The *Spencer* made radar contact that night and closed it at full speed. Her lookouts sighted a U-boat's conning tower, which disappeared as the cutter's forward guns opened fire, but she soon had sonar contact, and Commander Harold S. Berdine ordered a nine-charge pattern dropped. The exploding depth charges marked the end of the *U-225.*

Although aggressive action by the escorts kept most of the submarines away from the convoy, one ship was torpedoed that night and another the next morning. The latter's men took to their boats, but she was still afloat when the *Campbell* approached to take them on board. Not long afterward, the U-boat put another torpedo into the abandoned vessel and then fired one that exploded in the cutter's wake. Sighting smoke from the submarine's diesel exhaust, the *Campbell* turned to ram and as her opponent crash dived, dropped a pattern or depth charges, inflicting enough damage to force the *U-753* out of the battle. On her way to rejoin the convoy, the *Campbell* detected another submarine by sonar and made three depth-charge attacks without apparent result before losing contact.

That evening the *U-606* torpedoed three ships before being attacked in turn by a corvette and the Polish destroyer *Burza,* a late addition to the screen. The latter's depth charges forced the submarine to the surface, where the *Campbell* made radar contact. She ran in, opening fire, and when the *U-606* turned to avoid being rammed, her diving rudder cut a lengthy gash in the cutter's hull plating below the waterline. As the submarine fell astern, she was jolted by two more depth charges, and the *Campbell*'s after guns continued the fight until the cutter lost all power as her engine room flooded. Thereupon Commander James A. Hirshfield and his men turned their attention to saving their own ship, lightening her as much as possible and shifting weight to the port side in order to bring the gash above the water. The *U-606* was still afloat, so a boat was sent to remove her crew. Only five men chose to leave her; seven more were taken off before she sank by the *Burza*, which had been detached to screen the *Campbell*. With her fuel almost exhausted, the Pole had to depart for Newfoundland a day later after taking on board half the *Campbell*'s crew and the fifty survivors that the cutter had picked up. A corvette screened the cripple thereafter, and a tug finally towed her into St. John's nine days after her encounter with the *U-606*.

With its escort screen depleted even further by the detachment of a corvette that could not be refueled because of rough seas, the convoy was subjected to continued attacks, losing eight ships while the *Spencer* nearly claimed another U-boat. Her depth charges damaged the *U-454* to the extent that the German tried to surface, only to find the cutter awaiting her. After two hours, flooding reached the point that the submarine could no longer remain submerged, but by the time she surfaced the *Spencer* had had to rejoin the convoy. In all, ON-166 lost fifteen of its ships, while its escorts sank two U-boats and damaged several others.[20]

A considerably weakened Ocean Escort Unit A-3 had four days at St. John's before sailing to screen SC-121, which was beginning to scatter in a gale as the group approached. Captain Heineman rounded up his charges, but the weather got worse during the next few days, with the wind blowing heavy snow. When HF/DF indicated that U-boats had made contact with the convoy on 6 March, the *Spencer* and the American flush-decker *Greer* made offensive sweeps, leaving three corvettes to screen fifty-four ships. The convoy's course was changed after dark, despite the heavy seas and poor visibility, in an attempt to evade the U-boats. Nonetheless, a ship was sunk early the next morning, and a straggler was torpedoed later that day. The *Spencer* forced a U-boat to submerge ahead of the convoy and made several attacks on sonar contacts—these were inconclusive, but the weather thwarted the submarines.

The *Bibb* and the *Ingham* were ordered from Iceland to join SC-121, which was further reinforced by another old destroyer and a corvette. The U-boats persisted, however, and when the convoy was turned over to the local escort force off Ireland, it numbered only thirty-six vessels. Some stragglers made port later, but SC-121 had lost thirteen ships, and its escorts had failed to sink any U-boats, in part because the sonar of three and the radar of four were inoperative much of the time. The lack of effective sonar was the more serious for the submarines had begun to attack submerged in an effort to cut their own losses.[21]

Following convoys fared little better—forty-one ships were sunk by U-boats during the first ten days of March and forty-four in the next ten days. To add to the problems of escort vessels overworked and run down because they were so few, the German navy had increased the number of rotors in its Enigma coding machines,

The Spencer *as she appeared as a North Atlantic escort.*

depriving the British of the ability to decipher messages regarding U-boat dispositions. In truth, March 1943 seemed the darkest month of the entire Battle of the Atlantic, and some officials even began to question the feasibility of the convoy system, implying that cargo ships might have a better chance of survival steaming independently.[22]

Before this counsel of despair could gain support, however, the outlook changed dramatically. British cryptanalysts were able to solve the problem of the four-rotor cipher in three weeks, apparently by using computers in unprecedented number; more very long range aircraft, especially the invaluable B-24 Liberators, were made available to provide air cover for convoys; and support groups of antisubmarine vessels were formed to reinforce the screens of convoys threatened with attack. One of these included the U.S. escort carrier *Bogue,* the first of a number of ships whose aircraft could fly air cover for convoys in the area south of Greenland, weather permitting.

The convoys sailing during the last ten days of March escaped serious loss, and on 11 April, Ocean Escort Unit A-3, which had steamed into St. John's only three days before, stood out to screen convoy HX-233. The group now included the *Duane* and a Canadian destroyer as well as the *Spencer* and five smaller vessels. All radar, sonar, and HF/DF sets were operating properly, and the convoy was routed farther south than usual, presaging better weather for the passage. Five days out, the *Spencer* made the first contact; although the U-boat escaped the cutter's depth-charge and mousetrap attacks, she had no opportunity to transmit her own sighting report before submerging. The *Spencer* was pursuing another contact the following morning, 17 April, when a ship was torpedoed in the convoy. A corvette was ordered to rescue survivors, and while screening her, the big cutter made another inconclusive attack on a sonar contact. By this time, a British support group composed of modern destroyers was available to investigate distant contacts, so the *Spencer* returned to her regular station.

Almost at once, her sonarmen reported a contact 5,000 yards ahead, and Commander Berdine rang up full speed. Dropping an eleven-charge pattern, the cutter regained contact, dropped eleven charges more, and then pursued the *U-175* into the convoy, firing a mousetrap salvo when the range was clear. The submarine surfaced some distance astern and her men opened fire with a deck gun even as the *Spencer*'s ready guns were scoring the first hits. The *Duane* raced in with guns blazing, and naval gun crews in nearby merchant ships added their contribution, one of them hitting the *Spencer* in the excitement. Within a short time, Germans were seen jumping into the sea, leaving the *U-175* still making way slowly. The *Spencer* bore in to ram, but Commander Berdine decided that the U-boat had been abandoned, so she turned away and lowered a boat to take possession if possible. The submarine was too badly damaged, however, and although Lieutenant Ross P. Bullard entered her conning tower, he had to depart hurriedly as she sank. The *Spencer* picked up nineteen survivors, and the *Duane* rescued twenty-two. The former had sustained slight damage from enemy and friendly fire. Eight of her men had been wounded, one fatally, and others had been slightly burned and deafened by the muzzle blast of one of the cutter's guns.[23]

HX-233 soon came within the range of aircraft based in northern Ireland, and during the night of 18 April, one of them reported a U-boat submerging some distance ahead. The *Spencer* made sonar contact and followed it into the convoy, dropping depth charges to keep the submarine down. That was the last contact with the enemy—HX-233 made port having lost but one ship, for which the sinking of the *U-175* was ample recompense.

There were convoy battles yet to come, but the tide of war had definitely turned. After losing thirty-one U-boats in the first three weeks of May, Admiral Doenitz recalled the others from the North Atlantic pending the development of new tactics and armament. Although they returned to the offensive in the autumn of 1943 and Allied cargo ships were forced to sail in convoy until the war in Europe ended, the submarines were never again a serious threat.

The British and Canadian navies assumed principal responsibility for the more northerly routes in the late spring of 1943, so the Treasury-class cutters escorted convoys to the Mediterranean with an occasional run to the Caribbean Sea into 1944. By that time, a plenitude of new escort vessels had become available, and with the prospect of numerous amphibious landings in the Pacific theater, the big cutters were ordered to navy yards for conversion to amphibious force flagships, over the objections of the commander in chief of the Atlantic Fleet and other naval officers who thought them unmatched as escort group leaders.[24] The conversions entailed the replacement of most of their antisubmarine armament and equipment by heavier antiaircraft batteries, extensive communication facilities including as many as thirty-five radio receivers and twenty-five transmitters, and quarters for generals, admirals, and their staffs. Upon completion, the *Duane* took part in the invasion of Southern France in August 1944, while her sisters, including the *Taney*, which had been transferred to the Atlantic early in 1944, served in the Philippines and at Okinawa and Borneo.

While the big cutters were serving in mid-ocean escort groups, some of their smaller fellows were fighting the Battle of the Atlantic in waters closer to the United States. The 165-foot *Icarus* drew first blood for the Coast Guard when she encountered the *U-352* off Cape Lookout, North Carolina, on 9 May 1942. The submarine fired a torpedo and then ran aground while submerged. The cutter's depth charges exploded close enough to bring the *U-352* to the surface, whereupon her crew, deterred from manning the submarine's deck gun by the *Icarus*'s 3-inch and 20-millimeter fire, abandoned ship, followed by the commanding officer after he had scuttled the U-boat.

This was the second German submarine sunk by a U.S. warship, and another of the 165-footers accounted for the third little more than a month later. The *Thetis*, assigned to a task group stationed at Key West, was ordered to search for a submarine sighted by an aircraft in the Old Bahama Channel on 13 June. The cutter made sonar contact and dropped a seven-charge pattern, after which her five consorts attacked in turn. They continued the sonar search until the next morning without success, and the group retired after recovering evidence that the U-boat had at least been damaged. The *Thetis* subsequently received credit for sinking the *U-157*.[25]

It is interesting to note that the *Icarus* was commanded by Lieutenant Maurice D. Jester, a former chief boatswain with more than twenty-five years of Coast Guard service, while the commanding officer of the *Thetis*, Lieutenant (junior grade) Nelson C. McCormick, had left the Academy near the bottom of his class in 1935, receiving only a temporary commission that was made permanent more than two years later.

By mid-1943, U.S. warships had sunk only eleven U-boats, and six of those had been destroyed by Coast Guard cutters. The smaller service, however, could claim but one of the twenty-four German submarines sunk by American aircraft during the same period. Chief Aviation Pilot Henry C. White was patrolling an area of the Gulf of Mexico south of Terrebonne Bay, Louisiana, on 1 August 1942 when he sighted a submarine on the surface. He planned to attack from astern, but the U-boat submerged before his Grumman J4F could attain the necessary position. Putting the twin-engine amphibian into a shallow dive, White dropped his one depth charge and scored a direct hit, sinking the *U-166* with all hands.[26]

Several other 165-footers escorted coastal convoys and dropped depth charges on suspected contacts, but postwar examination of German records failed to confirm any of their claims. They were more important in their traditional rescue role, picking up survivors from merchant vessels torpedoed off the Atlantic coast during the U-boats' second "happy time" in the spring of 1942. After the belated adoption of the coastal convoy system, the Germans sought their prey in the Gulf of Mexico and the Caribbean Sea, providing employment for the small cutters stationed in southern waters. Weather conditions off the Atlantic coast and in the Gulf were usually better than those endured by the larger cutters farther to the north, and it was never as cold, yet the danger to any vessel that stopped to recover men from a torpedoed ship was always present, especially if the cutter were silhouetted against the flames of a tanker burning at night.

The only Coast Guard submarine victim in southern waters, however, was the 172-foot buoy tender *Acacia*, shelled and sunk in the Caribbean by the *U-161* without loss of life on 15 March 1942. She was one of only two tenders lost during the war; the other, the forty-year-old *Magnolia*, was sunk in collision off Mobile Bay on 25 August 1945 with the death of one man.

The Coast Guard's most serious loss in home waters, which occurred in mid-September 1944, was only indirectly caused by a U-boat. The 125-footers *Bedloe* and *Jackson* and the Navy salvage ship *Escape* were ordered out of Norfolk to assist a torpedo-damaged cargo ship off the North Carolina coast. Despite the strong wind and heavy seas heralding the approach of a hurricane, the *Escape* got a hawser on board the SS *George Ade* and headed for the capes of the Chesapeake, escorted by the two cutters. Wind and sea increased during the night, slowing the tow to less than 2 knots, and the full force of the hurricane buffeted the four vessels early on the morning of 14 September. With visibility almost nonexistent and radar rendered useless by sea return, the cutters became separated from the larger ships and from each other, struggling to keep their heads to the sea while they were being tossed about like chips. They entered the eye of the storm around noon; then the wind backed northwesterly, gusting to 125 knots, and the swells continued from the northeast. Sturdy sea boats though they were, the 125-footers could not cope with the resulting cross sea. The *Jackson* capsized just before 1 P.M., and her sister rolled over and sank a few minutes later. The former's thirty-seven officers and men all reached life rafts that floated free when their ship sank, as did thirty of the *Bedloe*'s thirty-eight.

Their ordeal, however, was only beginning. With neither food nor water, the exhausted men clung to their rafts for more than two days, those of the *Jackson* further tormented by the venomous tentacles of Portuguese men-of-war, which had been blown westward from the Gulf Stream. A Navy minesweeper rescued the twelve surviving "Bedloes" at nightfall on 16 September, and three OS-2U Kingfisher seaplanes from the Elizabeth City Coast Guard Air Station sighted the *Jackson*'s rafts the next morning. The aircraft landed close by to give first aid after radioing their location, after which a 36-foot motor lifeboat from the Oregon Inlet station braved the heavy surf to ferry the nineteen survivors to a naval vessel where they received medical treatment before being flown to Norfolk.[27]

In addition to the two small cutters and forty-four of their men, the hurricane claimed the destroyer *Warrington*, which sank off the Florida coast with 248 officers and men—only 73 survived—and *Lightship #73*, which was overwhelmed in Vineyard Sound; there were no survivors from her twelve-man crew. The *Escape* and the *George Ade*, however, weathered the storm, although the salvage ship sustained some weather damage. She would become a Coast Guard cutter almost forty years later!

Coast Guard vessels had a much less important role in the Pacific, where only three class A cutters were stationed in December 1941. Following the Pearl Harbor attack, the *Taney* conducted antisubmarine patrols in Hawaiian waters until late January 1942, when she helped to evacuate the few Americans from islands to the southward. Thereafter, the big cutter was unaccountably retained by the Hawaiian Sea Frontier command until she was belatedly ordered to the Atlantic coast at the end of 1943. The *Taney* ought to have joined her sisters in the North Atlantic at least a year earlier.

Meanwhile, the *Haida* and the *Onondaga* together with the class B 165-footers *Atalanta*, *Aurora*, and *Cyane* escorted convoys in the Gulf of Alaska and the eastern Aleutians. Japanese submarines were few in those waters, which was as well because the escort forces of the Alaska Sector, including the gunboat *Charleston* and a few old flush-deck destroyers, were probably even less efficient than those escorting convoys to Greenland. In mid-1943, the *Haida* was assigned to weather patrol on Ocean Station Able, some 1,500 miles west of Vancouver Island, and the smaller cutters were utilized mainly as patrol craft in Alaskan waters for the remainder of the war.[28]

Most Coast Guardsmen who served at sea during World War II did so in naval vessels. Although some had to be assigned to Navy-manned ships as landing craft crews, Admiral Waesche was determined to keep the mixing of Coast Guard and Navy personnel, such as had occurred in World War I, to a minimum. Hence the Navy provided only torpedoman's mates and aerographer's mates, ratings the smaller service did not have, to Coast Guard-manned ships, and before the war ended, some Coast Guardsmen had attained those rates as well.

The first naval vessels manned by the Coast Guard were the big transports commissioned in June 1941. Three of these, the *Wakefield*, *Joseph T. Dickman*, and *Leonard Wood*, and as many Navy-manned transports formed convoy WS-124 in which more than 20,000 British troops were to be ferried from Halifax to the Near East by way of the Cape of Good Hope during the autumn of 1941. The convoy arrived at Capetown on 8 December, and Japan's entry into the war caused them to be diverted to Bombay and Singapore. The *Wakefield* had disembarked her troops and was refueling at Singapore on 30 January 1942, when Japanese bombers attacked the waterfront facilities. She was struck by a bomb that exploded in her sickbay, killing five men and wounding nine. Nonetheless, the transport evacuated some 500 women and children to Bombay, where she received temporary repairs before returning to the United States.

The *Wakefield*'s career very nearly ended in the autumn of 1942. She was bound from Scotland to New York in Convoy TA-18 when fire broke out on board during the evening of 3 September. It spread rapidly, so a cruiser and destroyers of the escort removed her crew and put a special salvage detail on board. The *Wakefield* was towed to Halifax and intentionally grounded; by the time the fire had been extinguished, she was judged a constructive total loss. Completely rebuilt at the Boston Navy Yard, she was recommissioned by a Coast Guard crew in February 1944 and spent the rest of the war transporting troops in the Atlantic and Pacific theaters.[29]

Coast Guardsmen manned twenty-one other transports, most of which were new ships commissioned in 1944 and 1945. Like the *Wakefield*, these were not combat vessels. They carried troops and cargoes from one port to another, having no capability to land men and supplies directly onto beaches.

Some Coast Guard-manned vessels, however, were fitted for this purpose. In 1942, the *Hunter Liggett*, *Joseph T. Dickman*, and *Leonard Wood* were converted to attack transports by the addition of small landing craft carried in davits and on deck. Six new ships of the same type were later commissioned by Coast Guard crews, as were five smaller attack cargo ships that performed the same functions. These vessels took part in amphibious operations in every theater of war, with the *Leonard Wood* and the attack cargo ship *Aquarius* among the most active—each participated in eight assault landings.

The *Hunter Liggett*, ordered to the Pacific early in 1942, was the only Coast Guard-manned vessel taking part in the first American offensive of the war, the invasion of Guadalcanal on 7 August 1942, although eighteen of the twenty-two transports sailing with her had Coast Guardsmen in their Navy crews. The Marines embarked in the *Liggett* were among those scheduled to go ashore later in the day, so her boats began the operation by helping to land those of the first wave from other ships. When Japanese aircraft attacked the transports the next day, Coast Guard gunners shot several down, and on the morning of 9 August, the *Liggett* picked up survivors of the one Australian and three American cruisers sunk in the Battle of Savo Island. The big transport continued to support the American advance in the Solomon Islands for the next year and more, ending her combat service with the Bougainville invasion in November 1943. The *Hunter Liggett* then ferried wounded men to San Francisco, and after overdue repairs, she spent the remainder of the war as an amphibious training ship operating out of San Diego.

The attack transport *Arthur Middleton* had one of the more trying experiences. Her first mission was to land troops on Amchitka Island in the western Aleutians on 12 January 1943. In the course of the operation, the destroyer *Worden* lost power after being holed on a pinnacle rock and was driven ashore, where she began to break up. Small boats from the destroyer *Dewey* joined the *Middleton*'s landing craft in rescuing 175 men, but fourteen were lost in the frigid water. The transport dragged her anchors in a williwaw that night and went aground. There she remained for eighty-four days, enduring several attacks by Japanese fighter planes operating from Kiska; neither their light bombs nor the *Middleton*'s antiaircraft guns scored any hits. The transport was finally floated and towed to the Puget Sound Navy Yard for repairs.[30] After this unpromising beginning, the *Arthur Middleton* went on to earn seven battle stars for her participation in as many assault landings.

Of the others, the attack transport *Callaway* was hit by a Japanese suicide plane on 8 January 1945 while steaming to Lingayen Gulf in the Philippines with the invasion force. Although twenty-nine men of her crew were killed and twenty-two wounded, she kept her position in the formation and landed her troops the next day as scheduled. Three weeks later, her sister ship, the *Cavalier,* was damaged by a torpedo off Subic Bay; she was fortunate to escape with only ten men wounded.

Some of the other vessels had casualties among their landing craft crews, who of necessity were exposed to fire from the shore. The most notable of these was Douglas A. Munro, signalman first class, one of a small party that Lieutenant Commander Dwight H. Dexter took ashore from the *Hunter Liggett* to improvise an operating base at Lunga Point on Guadalcanal. On 27 September 1942, two weeks before his twenty-third birthday, Munro was in charge of ten landing craft that put a small force of Marines ashore in an attempt to encircle enemy troops in the Matanikau vicinity. Within a short time, it became apparent that the Japanese were more numerous than had been anticipated, so the Marines had to be evacuated. Munro volunteered to take them off with five landing craft, and when these came under fire from heavy machine guns, he engaged the enemy with his boat's light weapons, ordering the other craft to complete the evacuation. This they did, shielded by Munro's boat, but he was fatally wounded by Japanese fire.[31] Douglas Munro was awarded the Medal of Honor posthumously, the only Coast

Douglas Albert Munro,
the Coast Guard's only
Medal of Honor winner.

Guardsman on whom the nation's highest decoration for combat gallantry has ever been bestowed. He might be said to have died in the Coast Guard tradition, while conducting a rescue operation.

To obviate the necessity of transshipping personnel and equipment, especially tanks, from oceangoing vessels to landing craft off exposed beaches, the British Admiralty had conceived the idea of ships that could run themselves aground and discharge their cargoes directly onto the shore. Several types were developed, of which the LST—landing ship, tank—and the LCI(L)—landing craft, infantry (large)—were the most important and the most numerous. Both were designed and built in the United States; the former were flat-bottomed ships 328 feet long, fitted with ballast tanks that could be emptied to reduce their draft by 5 feet for beaching and with bow doors that opened to permit vehicles to be driven off the tank deck. The "large slow targets"—diesel engines drove them at 11 knots—were surely among the ugliest ships of their time; they were among the most useful as well. Indeed, the strategy of the Western Allies in 1944 and 1945 was determined in part by the availability of LSTs.

The U.S. Navy retained most of the more than 1,000 LSTs built during the war, and in January 1943 it sought the assistance of the Coast Guard in finding crews for some. The manning section recently established at Coast Guard Headquarters agreed to provide officers and men for sixty-one ships initially, but owing to changes in the construction schedules, only thirty-seven of the early LSTs were manned by Coast Guardsmen. Thirteen of these served with Navy flotillas in the European theater, while twenty-four went to the Pacific. Beginning with the Tunisian landings in July 1943 and the

The LST 831 *beached at Okinawa.*

occupation of Finschafen in eastern New Guinea two months later, one or more Coast Guard-manned LSTs participated in almost every amphibious operation involving American forces. Two of these vessels were lost: the *LST 203* grounded in the Ellice Islands on 1 October 1943, and the *LST 69* was one of six destroyed by explosion and fire while loading ammunition at Pearl Harbor on 21 May 1944, a disaster that Admiral King attributed to negligence on the part of a Navy LST crew. In addition, the *LST 167* was damaged beyond economical repair by Japanese bombers off Vella Lavella in the Solomon Islands on 25 September 1943.

In March 1944, the Coast Guard undertook to man the thirty-six LSTs of Flotilla 29, providing a flotilla commander and his staff as well. Captain Clarence H. Peterson was assigned to command the flotilla, whose officers and men spent ten weeks at the Atlantic Fleet Amphibious Training School before reporting to their ships, the last of which was commissioned on 8 November 1944. Vessels of the only Coast Guard LST flotilla participated in the Iwo Jima and Okinawa invasions in 1945. Three more LSTs were manned by Coast Guardsmen in June 1945, bringing the total number to seventy-six. Completing their training too late to have a part in World War II, these ships returned to the United States in December 1945 after serving with occupation forces in the Far East.[32]

Twenty-eight of the smaller LCI(L)s had Coast Guard crews. These were 160-foot vessels with a ramp on either side of the bow to permit troops to disembark after beaching. Eight diesel engines and better hull lines than those of the LSTs enabled them to cruise at 14 knots, but they were very uncomfortable at sea with some 200 soldiers on board, and crews required careful training to lower and raise the heavy ramps safely.

The first twenty-four, a "bob-tail" flotilla under Commander Miles H. Imlay, went to the Mediterranean, where they participated in the Sicily and Salerno landings without loss. Ordered to England thereafter, they trained for the Normandy invasion. Imlay, by then a captain, described the events of 6 June 1944 succinctly: "Our flotilla was in the early attack and received a pretty thorough going over. We aren't the group we were before."[33] The *LCI(L)s 85, 91, 92*, and *93* did not survive the invasion, the first three becoming mine victims while the last was abandoned after receiving ten direct hits from German shore artillery. The *LCI(L) 83* was also mined and abandoned, but when the ebbing tide exposed the hole in her hull, her crew patched it well enough so that her pumps could keep flooding under control, and she limped back to England for repair. Each of these vessels succeeded in landing most of her troops despite the damage, while their sisters put men ashore and performed a variety of other tasks, including salvage of damaged ships and landing craft, for several weeks after the invasion.[34] The veteran Coast Guard LCI(L)s returned to the United States in the autumn of 1944, and after overhaul and further training with four replacement vessels, the flotilla was sent to the Pacific, where its ships took part in the Okinawa campaign and in duties incidental to the occupation of Japan.

Those planning the Normandy invasion anticipated heavy casualties among the transports and beaching craft and recommended that small fast vessels be obtained in some number to serve as rescue ships. With wooden hulls and gasoline engines, the Coast Guard's 83-foot patrol boats were hardly ideal for this purpose, which would probably require that they remove men from burning ships and come under enemy fire themselves. There was no alternative, however, so sixty of them were ordered to New York where they were stripped of part of their antisubmarine armament and loaded on board merchant ships for conveyance to England. On arrival there, the 83-footers' crews received intensive first aid instruction while special rescue equipment was designed and fitted to the boats. Their five-digit hull numbers were apparently considered too cumbersome for effective communication; the craft were renumbered, with the *CG 83300* becoming the *USCG 1* and the *83516* the *USCG 60*.

Lieutenant Commander Alexander Stewart, USCGR, commanded Rescue Flotilla 1, half of whose boats were assigned to British invasion beaches. All distinguished themselves on D-Day and later, being credited with the rescue of 1,438 persons during the invasion. Their crew members frequently went over the side or on board sinking vessels to aid survivors, and neither gunfire nor the blazing oil surrounding some of the mine victims deterred the rescue

245

An 83-foot rescue boat off Normandy.

craft. Only two 83-footers were lost off Normandy, both in the "great storm" that reached its peak on 21 June—one ripped her bottom open on a submerged obstruction and the other was unable to extricate herself when an LST forced her onto the beach. For months after the invasion, ships continued to hit mines in the English Channel, and 83-footers picked up survivors from many. Some served as dispatch boats, carrying messages between England and France.[35] The success of Rescue Flotilla 1 led to the organization of similar groups for use in the Pacific. Thirty 83-footers were sent to the Philippines and twenty-four to other Pacific islands, but none had the opportunity to rival the exploits of Rescue Flotilla 1 off the Normandy beaches.

Coast Guard cutters' performance as convoy escorts made it natural that the service should be asked to provide crews for some of the mass-produced antisubmarine vessels when these were built in large numbers for both the U.S. Navy and the Royal Navy beginning in 1943. Of these, the most numerous were the DEs (destroyer escorts), of which the Coast Guard manned thirty, all of the long-hull (306 feet), FMR (geared diesel) type. Armed with three 3-inch 50-caliber, 40-millimeter, and 20-millimeter guns and torpedo tubes as well as heavy antisubmarine armament—hedgehog, eight K-guns, and depth-charge tracks—these ships could make 21 knots and had twin rudders, which made them very maneuverable. They were also extremely lively; the commanding officer of a British DE reported that "it is difficult to describe with reticence the nauseating movement of these vessels in the open sea."[36] Americans were generally less critical, considering the DEs tough, seaworthy ships, albeit exhausting for their crews.

The U.S. Navy had finally established a proper antisubmarine training program by mid-1943. The Coast Guard DE crews went to the Submarine Chaser Training Center at Miami for instruction before commissioning their ships, which then had shakedown training at Bermuda. The thirty DEs formed five escort divisions—20, 22, 23, 45, and 46—and escorted convoys to the United Kingdom and to the Mediterranean, losing very few of their charges to enemy attack.

One of the thirty was lost. The *Leopold* was investigating a contact some 400 miles south of Iceland during the night of 9 March 1944 when she was struck by an acoustic torpedo from the *U-255*. Seas were running high as she was abandoned, and her sister *Joyce*, under Lieutenant Commander Robert Wilcox, twice had to interrupt rescue efforts to evade torpedoes. Thus, only twenty-eight men were picked up; the 171 lost with the *Leopold* included Lieutenant Commander Kenneth C. Phillips and all of her other officers. The *Joyce* obtained a measure of revenge a few weeks later. Soon after taking thirty-one survivors off a blazing tanker on 16 April, she made sonar contact and dropped a thirteen-charge pattern that forced the *U-550* to the surface. The *Joyce*, the *Peterson*, and the Navy-manned *Gandy* immediately opened fire, and the last also rammed the submarine, whose men scuttled her and abandoned ship.[37]

Convoys passing through the Mediterranean during the spring of 1944 had to be prepared for both air and submarine attacks. When German torpedo bombers hit convoy UGS-38 on the night of 20 April, the *Menges* and the *Newell* contributed to the convoy's air defense and then spent four hours picking up 234 survivors of the torpedoed destroyer *Lansdale* and two German flyers, whose aircraft had probably been shot down by one of the DEs. The *Menges*'s turn came next. When the *U-371* was detected closing convoy GUS-38 on 3 May, the DE headed in to attack, only to have her stern blown off by an acoustic torpedo. Thirty-one men were killed and twenty-five wounded, but Lieutenant Commander Frank M. McCabe refused to order her abandoned. The *Menges* was ultimately towed to New York, where the stern of another salvaged torpedo victim, the Navy-manned *Holder*, replaced that which she had lost. Following a second shakedown cruise, she returned to service in the autumn of 1944. Her assailant was less fortunate. After assisting the crippled *Menges*, the *Pride* and the Navy-manned *Joseph E. Campbell* turned their attention to the *U-371*, making contact repeatedly and losing it each time. Other vessels joined them the next day, and the U-boat finally had to surface, damaging a French DE with an acoustic torpedo as she did so. The German crew then scuttled the submarine and abandoned her as she sank.

The *Menges* and her division mates *Pride*, *Mosley*, and *Lowe* later formed a task group under Commander Reginald H. French, that spent two weeks in March 1945 seeking a submarine reported to be off Newfoundland. On 18 March, five days after the initial contact, the *Lowe* detected the *U-866* east of Sable Island and dropped two depth-charge patterns that produced evidence of damage. The other DEs attacked in turn with depth charges and hedgehogs, and although the U-boat was almost certainly destroyed by these attacks, the *Menges* regained contact the next day and fired a final hedgehog salvo. Postwar evaluation attributed the *U-866*'s destruction to the *Lowe.*

Ships of the task group joined the escort carrier *Mission Bay* in further antisubmarine activity during the spring of 1945, while the other Coast Guard escort divisions continued to guard convoys until the war's end and for a month thereafter. Most of the Coast Guard DEs went to the Pacific in the course of the summer, too late to have an active role in the war against Japan.[38]

Other escort vessels manned by Coast Guardsmen for the Navy were corvettes and frigates, both British ship-types. The former were 205- or 208-foot, 16-knot ships of the Flower and Modified Flower classes that were built in large numbers in Britain and Canada early in the war. Eighteen were transferred to the U.S. Navy by reverse lend-lease. Coast Guard precommissioning details took over two at Quebec in March 1943, and six more were commissioned in June. Like the ten Navy corvettes, they escorted coastal convoys, mainly between New York, Key West, and Guantánamo Bay, Cuba, with an occasional run to Newfoundland or Greenland.

With the Battle of the Atlantic going badly in June 1942, Admiral King had urged the utilization of merchant shipyards, especially some of those on the Great Lakes that would soon complete existing contracts, to build antisubmarine vessels. These could not be DEs, because merchant yards were thought incapable of building ships to naval standards—hence, another design would have to be adopted. King seems to have had corvettes in mind, although he must have recognized that they were too small and too slow to be very effective. But the Royal Navy had progressed beyond them to frigates—ships similar to the DEs in most respects. Gibbs and Cox adapted the British River-class design to permit prefabrication and mass production, and President Roosevelt ordered the Maritime Commission, under whose direction the merchant yards worked, to award contracts for sixty-nine frigates in December 1942. Interestingly enough, the largest numbers were initially ordered from California yards—eighteen from the Consolidated Steel Corporation of San Pedro and twelve from the Kaiser Cargo Corporation of Richmond. Six Great Lakes yards were to build the others, whose numbers ultimately increased to 100, twenty-one of which, all products of the new Walsh Kaiser yard at Providence, Rhode Island, were transferred to the Royal Navy, while four others were cancelled.

As an emergency measure, the frigate-building program was a fiasco. Delay followed delay—Kaiser, whose cranes could handle 40–50-ton loads, was made responsible for obtaining materials and preparing detail specifications and working drawings, many of which had to be changed because cranes in the Great Lakes yards could lift only 10 tons. Turbine reduction gears were in short supply, so the American frigates, like the River-class, were powered by triple-expansion reciprocating engines—which were almost as scarce. The ships built in coastal yards could at least be turned over to commissioning details on completion; those launched from Great Lakes ways could not traverse the locks leading to the St. Lawrence River, so they had to be taken to the Mississippi River by way of the Chicago Drainage Canal and the Illinois River, with masts lowered to pass under bridges and pontoons reducing their draft by 5 feet. Only twelve frigates had been completed by the end of 1943, by which time well over 200 DEs were in commission.

This disparity would have been more acceptable had the frigates been markedly superior to the DEs; they were not. Their dimensions, detection systems, and armaments were almost identical—the frigates had no torpedo tubes, but most of the DEs landed theirs late in the war—and at 20 knots the frigates were little slower than diesel-powered DEs. They had single rudders, however, and so were much less maneuverable than DEs.[39]

Given the availability of DEs and the delays that plagued the frigates, it is not surprising that the Navy showed little interest in the ships produced under the Maritime Commission contracts; indeed, the only frigates manned by Navy crews were two of the River class built in Canada in 1942. The Coast Guard manning section had to provide officers and men for seventy-five warships—more than 14,000 officers and men in all. To do this and to meet other manning commitments to the Army and the Navy, the Coast Guard had to reduce its shore establishment considerably; more than 200 shore units had been closed by mid-1944 to make their personnel available for sea duty. That, however, was a simple matter compared to the problems caused by the vagaries of the frigate commissioning schedule. In mid-May 1944, twenty-six crews—4,200 officers and men who had completed four months of training—were waiting at the Manhattan Beach Training Station, and some 3,000 more were standing by as their ships were fitted out in Gulf coast yards.[40] The last of the frigates, the *Alexandria*, was finally commissioned on 11 March 1945.

The California-built frigates were the first to be completed. Those from Kaiser were assigned to training and patrol duties in the eastern Pacific and Alaskan waters, while the Consolidated Steel frigates all went to the southwest Pacific to join the escort forces of the Seventh Fleet, as did several of the Great Lakes vessels. Escorting convoys, making antisubmarine "ping patrols," and occasionally providing fire support for minor amphibious operations, the ships accompanied American and Australian forces as they "leapfrogged" westward along the north coast of New Guinea and captured offshore islands. Two of them, the *Bisbee* and the *Gallup*, were a part of the force that

The frigate Knoxville *on weather patrol after V-E Day. Her bridge was painted yellow to make her more visible to aircraft.*

put Rangers ashore on islands commanding the approaches to Leyte Gulf preliminary to the Philippines invasion, and eight other frigates helped to escort the first three reinforcement convoys, all of which reached Leyte early enough to qualify as part of the invasion force. For the remainder of 1944 and into 1945, the frigates shepherded convoys to the Philippines, but when faster steam-powered DEs armed with dual-purpose 5-inch guns joined the Seventh Fleet, the Coast Guard-manned ships were detached for duty elsewhere.[41]

Most of the Great Lakes frigates served in the Atlantic, several escorting convoys bound to and from the Mediterranean and most becoming weather patrol ships, which entailed the replacement of the after 3-inch gun by a deckhouse for inflating weather balloons. Two ships so converted took part in one of the last antisubmarine actions in the western Atlantic. Early in April 1945, intelligence indicated that a U-boat was lurking off Cape Cod, whereupon Commander Ralph R. Curry, commanding Escort Division 30 in the *Knoxville,* was ordered to head a task group composed of the frigate *Eugene,* a Leyte veteran, and the Navy DEs *Gustafson* and *Micka,* all of which were engaged in refresher training at Casco Bay, Maine. Curry and the *Knoxville* had been part of the force that sank the *U-869* off Morocco on 28 February 1945, with the Navy DE *Fowler* and a French vessel receiving the credit; on 7 April it was the *Gustafson* that made the initial sonar contact and fired the hedgehog salvo that destroyed the *U-857.*[42]

Almost a month later, the *U-853* torpedoed a small collier off Narragansett Bay. A destroyer, the Navy DEs *Amick* and *Atherton,* and the frigate *Moberly* were ordered to the scene, and while awaiting the senior officer in the first, Commander Leslie B. Tollaksen of the *Moberly* directed the search. The *Atherton* made the first contact on 5 May and attacked with hedgehog and depth charges, followed by the *Moberly.* The escorts' attacks continued into the next day, probably more because of sheer exuberance than necessity. The

Atherton was credited with sinking the *U-853*, with the *Moberly* assisting.[43]

Many of the frigates were clearly superfluous by the spring of 1945, so twenty-eight were designated for transfer to the Soviet Union. They were stripped of secret equipment and steamed to Cold Bay, Alaska, where the Coast Guard crews trained their Russian successors before turning the ships over to them in July and August.

The frigates have not fared well in postwar studies, most of which compare them unfavorably with the DEs. To a degree, this treatment is justified, for the frigates were inferior in certain respects, and the reciprocating engines in some proved to be very temperamental. Their great advantage over the DEs was their sea kindliness; indeed, they were probably the most comfortable antisubmarine vessels built for the U.S. Navy.[44] But they had little opportunity to display their ability as rough-water escort vessels and so they were largely unappreciated. This quality, however, made the frigates desirable for weather patrol, for which the Coast Guard continued to be responsible.

Five of the long awaited Maritime Commission cargo ships fitted for weather patrol had been manned by the Coast Guard in 1942. These vessels made three-week patrols out of Boston, steaming about their stations at slow speed—they could make only 10 or 11 knots at best—and transmitting meteorological reports at regular intervals, thus informing listening U-boats of their positions. Only one was lost. The *Muskeget* made her last report from her station 450 miles south of Cape Farewell on 8 September 1942 and then went missing with all hands—117 officers and men and four meteorologists. After the war, German records revealed that the *U-755* had torpedoed an American auxiliary vessel in that vicinity a day later; she was probably the *Muskeget*.[45] The others continued to make patrols through the winter, which was very trying for small—250 or 261 feet long—elderly ships. By mid-1943, only the *Manhasset* was fit for service. The other three were relegated to gunnery training duty in Chesapeake Bay, while as many 180-foot buoy tenders became weather patrol ships in their stead.

Transatlantic air traffic increased steadily as the war went on, with a concomitant requirement for more weather patrol vessels. By the spring of 1944, nine ships—the *Manhasset,* the former oiler *Big Horn,* three buoy tenders, three converted yachts, and a 180-foot minesweeper—were assigned to regular ocean stations in the Atlantic, while the *Algonquin, Comanche, Mohawk,* and a minesweeper alternated on temporary stations in Davis Strait. Surveying the situation, a member of Admiral King's staff pointed out that none was really suitable for the purpose and most were needed for other duties. An earlier suggestion that the Treasury-class cutters be returned to weather patrol had been negated by the decision to convert them to amphibious force flagships, and the staff officer recom-

The USS Serpens *as she appeared at the time of her loss.*

mended that at least twelve frigates be assigned to this duty, for which they seemed quite suitable.[46] So they were, but of course they did not become available until 1945.

Coast Guardsmen manned a variety of other naval vessels, including the *Pontus,* which was an LST fitted to tend motor torpedoboats, sixteen cargo ships, eighteen small gasoline tankers, ten submarine chasers, and a number of district patrol boats. Several came under enemy attack in the course of the Pacific war, and one, the Liberty-type cargo ship *Etamin,* was torpedoed by a Japanese aircraft while at anchor in Aitape Roads, New Guinea, on the night of 27 April 1944. Prompt action by her damage control parties saved the ship, apparently with only three men burned seriously, but two bodies were later found in a hold. The crippled vessel was towed to Finschafen and then to Cairns, Australia, where she was decommissioned.[47]

Two of these ships were lost, neither as a result of enemy action. The *Etamin*'s sister *Serpens* had spent nineteen months transporting supplies between New Zealand and the Solomon Islands, when she exploded and sank while loading depth charges in Lunga Roads off Guadalcanal on 29 January 1945. There were only two survivors

from the 198 men of her crew and the fifty-seven members of an Army stevedore unit working on board at the time, although her commanding officer and seven others were ashore when the explosion occurred.[48] The *Serpens* disaster was the Coast Guard's greatest single loss. Those on board the gasoline tanker *Sheepscot* were more fortunate when she ran aground in a storm off Iwo Jima and capsized on 6 June 1945.

The FS 177 *was one of 188 similar vessels manned by Coast Guardsmen for the Army.*

The Army Transportation Corps had its own fleet of service craft and vessels, manned mostly by civilians. On 14 March 1944, the Joint Chiefs of Staff decided that Coast Guardsmen should replace civilian crews in certain tugs, tankers, cargo boats, repair ships, and FS (freight supply) vessels, which ultimately numbered 288 in all. These were either in the southwest Pacific area or nearing completion in the United States, and the directive required that crews for the former be shipped out by 1 May. Transport space was not available, however, so the manning section turned its attention to the vessels fitting out in American yards, and the Army Transportation Corps agreed that as many of these as possible should be taken over before they sailed. The task required improvisation at nearly every step of the way, but by the end of 1944 almost 7,000 officers and men were on board Army ships and Captain Frank T. Kenner, Coast Guard-Army manning detachment commander at Finschafen, was handling pay and administrative matters for the entire force.

Like service craft generally, the Army vessels were unglamorous workaday ships, of which the 188 FS "island hoppers" were the most numerous. These 180-foot cargo vessels drew 9 feet of water at the most and so could ferry supplies, mail, and personnel to islands and atolls that larger ships could not approach, sometimes returning with bodies of men who had died in obscure combat and were to be interred in temporary cemeteries in New Guinea. They had neither radar, gyrocompasses, nor fathometers, yet their commanding officers, reserve lieutenants for the most part, took them into poorly charted, reef-strewn waters as a matter of course with few mishaps. Four became typhoon victims, and another sank off New Guinea.

They were not combat vessels, but a number of them came under air attack, and the *FS 255* was torpedoed with the loss of four men.[49]

Too little attention has been given the activities of the Coast Guard-Army manning detachment; indeed, Lieutenant Malcolm F. Willoughby's semi-official *U.S. Coast Guard in World War II* makes passing mention of only two FS vessels without explaining how they happened to be Coast Guard-manned. Nonetheless, the service of these ships was fully as important as that performed by most of the vessels and craft manned by Coast Guardsmen during World War II, and it should be recognized as such.

The foregoing account of Coast Guard activities in World War II makes it clear that the service was by no means unimportant in the greatest conflict yet known. To be sure, Admiral Waesche was not a member of the Joint Chiefs of Staff, and neither he nor any other Coast Guard officer had a significant part in determining strategy and policy. Thus, the Coast Guard's wartime function in large part simply consisted of satisfying the Navy's requirements. Thanks to Waesche's insistence that his service's identity be jealously preserved, Coast Guard-manned vessels are easily identified, and without exception, their performance seems to have compared favorably with that of their Navy-manned sisters. One must note, however, that only a small proportion of the Navy's amphibious and escort vessels were manned by the Coast Guard and that most of those ships' companies were composed of reservists, whose familiarity with their service and its traditions was obviously limited. On the other hand, the larger vessels—transports, cargo ships, LSTs, DEs, and frigates—were usually commissioned by regular commanding officers, whose ability largely determined their commands' effectiveness. Nor should the importance of the former warrant and petty officers who donned the uniforms of commissioned rank be overlooked; but for their years of prewar experience many of the smaller vessels could hardly have operated as efficiently as they did. And of course the surfmen who served as mentors to landing craft crews while the Navy was learning the techniques of amphibious warfare made a contribution far out of proportion to their number.

Admiral King concluded his final annual report by stating that the various components of the Navy "—the Fleet, the Shore Establishment, the Marine Corps, the Coast Guard and the Seabees—each . . . contributed its full share to victory," and when the Coast Guard was returned to Treasury Department control, Secretary of the Navy James V. Forrestal stated: "During the arduous war years, the Coast Guard has earned the highest respect and deepest appreciation of the Navy and Marine Corps. Its performance of duty has been without exception in keeping with the highest traditions of the naval service."[50]

While such official pronouncements may often be discounted, these were confirmed by Admiral King's deputy, Admiral Richard S.

Edwards, who wrote Waesche on the occasion of the latter's retirement: "No one knows better than I do how much the Navy owes to the Coast Guard in general and you in particular, not only for the outstanding achievements in the war but also for the painstaking preparation in the years leading up to the war. . . . I salute the lowering of your flag with a heartfelt 'Well Done'."[51] Russell R. Waesche had certainly earned that praise, the highest a naval officer could bestow, and so had the service he headed.

CHAPTER FIFTEEN

POSTWAR PLANNING AND REALITY, 1943–50

*D*espite the pressure of wartime responsibilities, Vice Admiral Russell R. Waesche—he had been promoted in March 1942—gave a good deal of attention to the Coast Guard's postwar future. He wished especially to assure the service's prompt return to Treasury Department control and its retention of certain of the missions acquired during the war.

The commandant remembered well the post–World War I struggle to have the Coast Guard retained permanently by the Navy Department, and he was aware that some officers, who were sharing the excitement of operations in the war zones with their fellows of the Navy, would be reluctant to return to the comparative monotony of their service's peacetime duties. Moreover, the old belief that the Coast Guard would be of greater value to the Navy in wartime were it permanently under Navy Department control was still held by some naval officers. To counter this sentiment as far as possible, Waesche directed the division of administrative management at Headquarters to prepare a document on the "Function of the Coast Guard and its place in the Scheme of Government" in June 1943, with particular emphasis on reasons why the service should not be retained by the Navy Department in peacetime.[1]

Thus, when Admiral Harry E. Yarnell, the retired officer who headed the Navy's demobilization planning section, requested information on the Coast Guard's plans in September 1943, Rear Admiral Frank J. Gorman responded promptly that a postwar planning committee was drawing up a comprehensive statement of "postwar activities of the Coast Guard, which are almost in their entirety civil functions in connection with law enforcement and safety of life and property at sea and on the navigable waters of the United States."[2]

Early in 1944, Congressman Carl Vinson invited Waesche to appear before a meeting of his naval affairs committee and Schuyler Otis Bland's committee on the merchant marine and fisheries for the purpose of discussing the Coast Guard's adminis-tration and operation. The commandant took this opportunity to gain congressional support for his service's early return to the Trea-sury Department, restating the arguments put forward by his pre-decessors in 1918–19 and 1933 and receiving a generally sympa-thetic hearing. He next presented his case to the Navy's General Board, a policy-advising body composed mainly of senior officers. Waesche was a persuasive speaker, and possibly fearing that the Navy might have to assume some of the Coast Guard's more mun-dane duties should it retain the smaller service, the General Board recommended that the Coast Guard be transferred to the Treasury or another of the civil departments as soon as practicable after the war.[3]

Meanwhile, Rear Admiral James Pine, the Academy superinten-dent, had joined the commandant and the planning committee to prepare a statement of the "Mission of the Coast Guard":

> To enforce all applicable Federal laws upon the navigable waters of the United States and its possessions and upon the high seas; to develop and promulgate safety requirements for the construction, manning and operation of vessels (other than public vessels) under the jurisdiction of the United States; to develop, establish, maintain, and operate aids to navigation and rescue facilities to promote safety on the navigable waters of the United States and on and over the high seas; and to maintain a military readiness to function as a specialized service with the Navy in time of war.[4]

This de-emphasis of the Coast Guard's military role had been stated more specifically in the planning committee's first comprehensive report, which contained a recommendation "that by every possible means the Service be brought to appreciate the scope and effect of its non-military functions and the need for excelling therein, at a sacrifice, if necessary, of a purely naval efficiency. In a subsequent war the Coast Guard should accept the corollary that it will enter the naval jurisdiction as a body of experts in its special field, rather than as a body of expert naval officers." The report went so far as to suggest that the Coast Guard's military organization was deleterious to the execution of some of its duties.[5] This clearly did not accord with Waesche's views; as rewritten, this section emphasized the importance of military organization to the service's performance of its non-military duties, and it made no mention of sacrificing naval efficiency.

By mid-1944, the planning committee had developed a compre-hensive description of the functions the Coast Guard expected to perform in peacetime, loran and ocean weather stations and Bureau of Marine Inspection and Navigation duties prominent among them, and of the personnel and equipment required for their execution. Drafts of the necessary legislation, including a recodification of the organic act of 1915, and a postwar budget were also prepared. Both the Navy and the Treasury departments signified their tentative approval.[6]

World War II ended with Japan's capitulation on 14 August 1945, and a few days later Coast Guard Headquarters promulgated a detailed demobilization plan. Separation centers in the various districts were to process some 800 officers and 13,000 enlisted men for release from the service each month, beginning in September, and by 30 June 1946, the Coast Guard would reach its tentatively approved peacetime strength of 3,500 officers, 1,400 warrant officers, and 30,000 enlisted men. This plan, however, was based on the assumption that Coast Guard personnel manning Army and Navy vessels or otherwise under the Navy's control—some 73,000 in all, most of whom were serving overseas—would no longer be needed by those services.[7] When the commandant made application for their release, he was informed that reliefs were not available; hence Coast Guard crews would have to decommission their ships, when those could be spared. The vessels no longer required wartime complements, of course, so officers and men eligible for release from the service generally were sent home whenever the opportunity offered.

For the remainder of 1945 and on into 1946, Coast Guard-manned transports ferried troops and other personnel home from the erstwhile war zones, while frigates continued to spend monotonous weeks on weather patrol and other vessels were employed in a variety of tasks associated with the occupation forces. Perhaps the most unusual duty was that assigned the DEs *Hurst* and *Pettit,* which spent the autumn of 1945 searching islets of the southeastern Pacific for possible survivors of wartime airplane crashes. None was found, but a memorable liberty in Papeete, Tahiti, would not soon be forgotten.

The commandant's service was also nearing its end in the autumn of 1945. Although he had been appointed to a third four-year term in 1944, his health had begun to decline thereafter and exploratory surgery in March 1945 revealed cancer of the stomach. That same month brought his promotion to the rank of admiral, with which he might have retired. Waesche, however, insisted on continuing as commandant until the war ended, after which he asked to be permitted to retire on 31 December 1945, the day before the Coast Guard would revert to Treasury Department control.

The matter of choosing a successor required careful consideration, for while Rear Admiral Lloyd T. Chalker, the assistant commandant, was nearing retirement age, Rear Admirals Joseph F. Farley, Frank J. Gorman, and Robert Donohue at Headquarters were obvious contenders for the position, and the Navy was said to favor Rear Admiral Edward H. "Iceberg" Smith. Admiral Waesche seems to have believed that extensive experience at Coast Guard Headquarters was necessary for anyone aspiring to succeed him, so the choice was really between Farley and Gorman. Farley had ranked above Gorman when they were commissioned in 1912; the latter, on the other hand, had attained flag rank earlier, and some thought him the most brilliant senior officer in the Coast Guard—"the crown prince." Gorman, however, was reputed to be a heavy drinker, and that apparently led Admiral Waesche to recommend to the president, through the secretaries of the navy and the treasury, that Farley be appointed commandant.[8]

But the matter was not settled so easily. President Harry S Truman, whose knowledge of the Coast Guard must have been limited at best, returned the nomination without any indication of his attitude. Considerably perturbed, Admiral Waesche invited a group that included Secretary of the Treasury Fred Vinson and Comptroller General Lindsay Warren to his room in the Bethesda Naval Hospital.[9] All agreed that Farley should be nominated again, and on 20 December 1945, the president, presumably prompted by Vinson and Warren, announced his selection of Rear Admiral Joseph F. Farley to be the commandant of the Coast Guard.

Russell Randolph Waesche is recognized as the outstanding commandant of the Coast Guard. He directed an unprecedented expansion of the service, which, due largely to his foresight, was truly unified before it acquired the Lighthouse Service and the Bureau of Marine Inspection and Navigation; but for that, these might well have continued to exist as separate organizations within the Coast Guard, leading to an impossible degree of decentralization. Waesche's role in the acquisition of these services has been noted, and he was directly responsible for the formation of the Reserve and the Auxiliary. He worked very effectively with the Navy Department during the war, carefully preserving the Coast Guard's identity as a separate service, and he prepared for an uncertain future to the fullest extent possible. Perhaps not least, he was the first commandant to appreciate the importance of public relations—with his encouragement, Captain Ellis Reed-Hill, who succeeded George Gelly as public relations officer in 1941, brought a number of able photographers and artists together to provide some of the outstanding illustrations of the war.

Admiral Willard J. Smith, who served twice as Waesche's aide, remembered him as a "very down-to-earth, warm, human person," who inspired a fierce loyalty in his fellows.[10] He had an unusual ability to select able lieutenants, to whom he delegated responsibility freely. Himself a tireless worker until illness took its toll, he demanded much of these subordinates, who, according to Rear Admiral Gorman, occasionally worked twenty-four hours a day to meet Waesche's requirements. Yet most would probably have agreed with Captain Dorothy Stratton, who wrote the retired commandant: "To me, you are the Coast Guard."[11]

Joseph Franklin Farley must have seemed an unlikely successor to the personable Waesche. Twenty of his fifty-six years had been spent on sea duty, and he acted the part of the gruff, uncommunica-

*Joseph Francis Farley,
commandant, 1946–50.*

tive sea dog, apparently unconcerned about his lack of popularity. He disliked public appearances and depended on subordinates to present the Coast Guard's needs to Congress, although he was a friend of some members of Congress who shared his enthusiasm for hunting and fishing. A close associate considered Farley a sound thinker, not given to quick decisions, and a capable administrator. Above all, he was known for his absolute integrity, which occasionally resulted in time devoted to accounting for miniscule sums of money.[12]

Rear Admirals Lloyd Chalker and Harvey Johnson both reached statutory retirement age in 1946, and Rear Admiral Frank Gorman chose to retire prematurely. Thus, Farley lost his predecessor's principal lieutenants within a few months after becoming commandant. The first was succeeded as assistant commandant by Commodore Merlin O'Neill, and Ellis Reed-Hill became engineer in chief. Captain Alfred C. Richmond had the unenviable task of replacing Gorman when budget hearings had just begun; he survived the ordeal to present the Coast Guard's budget requests to Congress in each of the next sixteen years. Five other division chiefs also retired because of age in 1946, so Admiral Farley had almost to appoint an entirely new Headquarters staff.

The task confronting the new commandant was gargantuan. He had to see the Coast Guard's demobilization to its conclusion, and he had to supervise the renewal of traditional peacetime activities without neglecting duties that had accrued to the service during the war. The first was probably easier, although a number of those involved in wartime functions showed a natural reluctance to have their positions phased out. The second was complicated by the desire of many officers and men, regulars as well as reservists, to leave the Coast Guard as quickly as possible, and by the fact that all wartime promotions had been temporary. Admiral Waesche had foreseen the problems associated with mass demotions and to minimize the effect on morale, he had arranged that an individual's permanent rank or rate would be the next lower than that he held at the war's end. This, of course, resulted in a service composed almost entirely of officers and petty officers, so a recruiting program to obtain seamen had to be started. Yet another problem was that the postwar plans anticipated numbers of officers and enlisted men far in excess of prewar levels, and in the case of the former, beyond the ability of the Academy to prepare the required quantity. Selected reserve officers had to be offered regular commissions, while others were allowed to remain on active duty. The Treasury, the Bureau of the Budget, and Congress helped to ease this problem by declining to authorize the desired numbers of personnel in the immediate postwar period.

In mid-1946, by which time demobilization had largely been completed, 2,443 officers, 797 warrant officers, and 22,983 enlisted personnel were on active duty. A year later, the service reached its postwar nadir with 2,195 officers, 532 warrant officers, and 15,730 enlisted men, little more than half the number thought necessary to carry out the postwar program drawn up by Admiral Waesche's planners. Quite obviously, not all of the intended peacetime missions could be undertaken in these circumstances; beach patrols were discontinued and lifeboat stations were either placed in caretaker status or operated with severely reduced complements, and a number of cutters were decommissioned temporarily, among them several of the new 255-footers that were consigned to reserve after completing their post-commissioning trials. Members of the Auxiliary volunteered to augment the crews of some stations and patrol boats, but they could serve for only a few hours at a time. No vessels could be assigned to Bering Sea Patrol in 1946 and 1947, nor was it possible to provide trained personnel for the oceanographic cruise in connection with the International Ice Patrol in 1946.

Several officers later asserted that the Coast Guard would have fared better during the immediate postwar years had it remained under the Navy Department for a longer time, principally because neither the Treasury Department nor the congressional committees responsible for Coast Guard support in peacetime had any recent knowledge of its expanded role and attendant requirements.[13] Perhaps they are correct, yet such stalwart supporters as Congressmen Bland and Herbert C. Bonner, both of whom had retained an active interest in the Coast Guard during the war, were still on the merchant marine and fisheries committee, while Assistant Secretary of the Treasury Edward H. Foley, Jr., a close personal friend of Admiral Farley, is unlikely to have been ignorant of the service's situation. Moreover, the Navy's own future was somewhat uncertain immediately after the war in light of the proposed unification of the armed forces, and one doubts that either the Navy Department or the committees responsible for naval affairs would have been greatly concerned with the plight of a service only temporarily under their jurisdiction. Admiral Waesche thought that the longer the Coast Guard remained under Navy control, the more difficult the transfer would be. He was probably right.

Personnel problems notwithstanding, the matter of most immediate concern to the new commandant was retention of the Bureau of Marine Inspection and Navigation duties temporarily assumed by the Coast Guard during the war. This was opposed by the maritime labor unions and by others who felt that a military organization ought not to be given such authority over a privately owned and manned merchant marine. In the spring of 1945, a congressional committee had reported that only the permanent transfer of those responsibilities would enable the Coast Guard to perform them efficiently and suggested legislation to this end, but nothing further had been done. A year later, Commodore Halert C. Shepheard persuaded Admiral Farley to accompany him on an extensive tour to convince the shipping industry that it would benefit were the Coast Guard to continue its inspection and licensing functions. Despite his aversion to public speaking, the commandant proved an effective emissary, and in May 1946, the president informed Congress of his intention to abolish the Bureau of Marine Inspection and Navigation, making the Coast Guard permanently responsible for exercising most of its functions. This depended on congressional approval, which Admiral Waesche helped to gain in a series of hospital room conferences. It was his last service to the Coast Guard; the transfer became effective on 16 July 1946, three months before his death.[14]

Logical though this development may seem to have been in retrospect, not everyone within the service was pleased. Some Bureau of Marine Inspection and Navigation inspectors serving as Temporary Reserve officers had hoped to revert to civilian status after the war. Instead, they found themselves added to the permanent roster of Coast Guard officers, to the predictable dismay of those junior to them, whose prospects for promotion were adversely affected. Others doubted that the Coast Guard could expand into such diverse areas as loran, ocean stations, and merchant marine inspection and licensing without slighting one or another of the functions. Commodore Shepheard did not share these misgivings; he became head of the Office of Merchant Marine Safety at Headquarters, assuming control over all of the Coast Guard's functions relating to the merchant marine. Promoted to rear admiral in 1948, Shepheard continued in this position until he retired early in 1956.

Perhaps it was as well that Waesche, Farley, and Shepheard had moved quickly in this matter, for the attitude of congressional appropriations committees toward the Coast Guard soon began to reflect the normal postwar public insistence on economy in government. Even after the service's budget proposal for fiscal 1948 had been trimmed considerably by the Treasury Department and the Bureau of the Budget, it came under attack by congressmen, who pointed out that the amount requested was almost five times the Coast Guard's 1940 appropriation. They were especially critical of the growth of the officer corps, noting that there had been three rear admirals in the prewar service while the Coast Guard now wished to have eighteen officers holding that rank, with a somewhat smaller proportional expansion of numbers in the lower ranks.

The explanation that the increased size and responsibilities of the service required a greater number of officers did not satisfy Congressman Everett M. Dirksen of Illinois, who called attention to the anomalous situation of the Coast Guard and demanded a resolution of its purpose:

> What we have got to determine is this: Is it going to be one of those expansive agencies to work all over the world, or is it going to be a coast guard? . . . It is considered to be a civilian agency, but its program makes it appear as an auxiliary navy. I want to know whether it is a coast guard or whether it is a miniature navy. If it is going to be navy, then let the Navy take care of them. If it is a

coast guard, it has no business running loran stations out in Guam and away up in Alaska and all over the blue water of the seven seas.[15]

Everett Dirksen would never be numbered among the champions of the Coast Guard, yet he had done it a great service by focusing attention on a crucial defect. Most of the legislation drafted at Coast Guard Headquarters in 1943 and 1944 had never been enacted, leaving the service to carry on a number of its functions without any specific authority to do so and making it vulnerable to charges that it had "grandiose schemes" for expansion.

To deal with this situation and to ascertain the extent of "waste" and "extravagance" in the Coast Guard's operations, Congress decided that a thorough investigation of the service should be made by a private management consulting firm. At Treasury Secretary John W. Snyder's direction, Coast Guard Headquarters drew up a list of the companies it thought capable of undertaking the study, forty in all, only to have Snyder and the appropriations committees' chairmen select a forty-first, Ebasco Services, Inc., of New York.[16] All Coast Guard activities were ordered to cooperate in the study, and Commander Irvin J. Stephens was assigned to work with the consultants, who began their investigation in September 1947 and submitted their final report on 21 January 1948.

Although this bulky volume contained 193 recommendations for improving the efficiency of Coast Guard operations, the service had no reason to be discouraged by its conclusions, which began:

> The survey findings . . . show that all of the duties performed by the Coast Guard are in the public interest. Also, each duty is a proper part and responsibility of the Federal government. The performance of these duties represents a necessary item of expense to the public, and they are now logically classified or grouped for performance by one government agency.
>
> No evidence has been noted that any other agency of the Federal Government could perform these functions at lower cost or with greater efficiency and better adequacy of service than does the Coast Guard.[17]

The Ebasco recommendations, which ranged from minor administrative and clerical improvements to such major points as a "concise mandate for the Coast Guard, and specific direct authority and funds to maintain a base operating plan and program," were grouped under three headings: those that could be effected by the service itself; those that the Treasury Department could implement; and those that required congressional action. The report was turned over to a steering committee composed of Treasury Department officials with Captain Alfred C. Richmond as chairman. This group considered each recommendation and suggested the action to be taken on it. Admiral Farley reviewed the committee recommenda-

The 133-foot buoy tender White Sage.

tions before forwarding them to the Treasury Department with his favorable endorsement, and Assistant Secretary of the Treasury Foley approved the Coast Guard's reactions to the Ebasco report in toto.[18]

The Ebasco study was not a panacea; nonetheless, it was extremely important for the Coast Guard. It led to the enactment of legislation to authorize a variety of the service's activities, culminating in the passage of the recodified organic act in 1949; it revealed little evidence of waste; and it stated unequivocally that the Coast Guard was "under-manned and under-equipped to perform efficiently and adequately all of the duties now assigned."[19]

While the personnel shortage was undeniable and many shore installations were obviously in need of repair or replacement, the situation with regard to floating equipment was less serious. Most of the vessels acquired during the war had been returned to their former owners or sold, and the oldest cutters and buoy tenders were decommissioned for disposal in 1946. These included the *Pamlico* and the *Unalga*, which were the last of the sometime revenue cutters, the *Ossipee*, *Tallapoosa*, and *Northland*, and the older seagoing tugs. The four 240-footers, condemned by their inadequate endurance, were decommissioned in 1947 and sold the next year; they were soon followed by the surviving Class A 165-footers, while most of the latters' Class B fellows and a number of the 125-footers, ten of which were sold, were laid up in reserve moorings at Curtis Bay and Kennydale, Washington.

To replace some of the vessels disposed of, the Coast Guard turned to the Navy, which transferred two 311-foot motor torpedoboat tenders and a sister that had served as a small amphibious force flagship. These 18-knot diesel-powered ships became the *Gresham, McCulloch,* and *Dexter,* while two 213-foot salvage vessels were renamed the *Acushnet* and the *Yocona.* The 205-foot fleet tug *Cherokee* retained her Navy name as a Coast Guard cutter; her sister became the *Tamaroa.* The eight diesel-propelled 133-foot lighters and five 189-foot steam-powered former Army mineplanters that became buoy tenders received the usual plant, shrub, or tree names, those of the ex-lighters prefixed by "White." A sixth former mineplanter, renamed the *Yamacraw,* was converted to a cable ship, replacing the old *Pequot.*

Although none of these vessels had been designed for Coast Guard duties, they proved to be useful acquisitions. With the exception of the *Yamacraw,* which was returned to the Navy in 1959, all served the Coast Guard for more than twenty years. Indeed, the salvage ships, fleet tugs, and seven of the 133-footers remained active Coast Guard cutters or tenders almost forty years after they were acquired, which casts some doubt on the traditional inferiority of wartime construction.

Britain returned six of the seven surviving Lake-class cutters in 1946. Two, the former *Cayuga* and *Saranac,* were refurbished and recommissioned as the *Mocoma* and the *Tampa* in 1947, while the *Itasca* was retained in reserve at Curtis Bay until 1950, when she was sold. The others, prematurely aged by their arduous wartime service, were listed for disposal soon after their return.

The *Danmark* was turned over to the Danish government in September 1945, ending sail training for cadets until 1947, when the *Eagle* made her first practice cruise. The former *Horst Wessel,* this handsome three-masted bark with auxiliary diesel power had been built as a German navy training ship in 1936 and awarded to the United States after the war. She too is still in commission, perhaps the best-known Coast Guard vessel of them all.

Coast Guard cutters had their armaments greatly reduced for peacetime service, the Treasury and *Owasco* classes mounting a single 5-inch 38-caliber gun and several smaller weapons. Other vessels, including the two Lake-class cutters, had a 3-inch 50-caliber, while smaller patrol boats were armed with 40-millimeter or 20-millimeter guns. Most of the wartime antisubmarine armament was removed as well. Reduced armaments permitted smaller complements; the 255-footers, for example, were manned by 120 officers and men, less than half the number assigned to them in wartime. All cutters, including the smallest patrol and lifeboats, were painted white with buff masts and stacks. Tugs and tenders differed only in having black-painted hulls, much more practical for their activities.

To supply loran stations west of the Hawaiian Islands, the Coast Guard obtained two 339-foot diesel-powered cargo ships of the C1-M-AV1 type. Drawing more than 20 feet of water, the *Kukui* and the *Unalga* could not approach a number of insular stations, so they

The training cutter Eagle.

carried sizable landing craft on deck to ferry supplies and personnel ashore. Three Army FS vessels, which became the *Nettle*, *Spruce*, and *Trillium*, provided a similar service to less distant loran stations.

The Coast Guard was operating forty-nine of these stations in 1946. They were located in the northwest Atlantic, on the East and West coasts of the United States, and on islands in the various areas of the Pacific Ocean. All were of wartime construction, most consisting of Quonset huts or similar buildings that provided relatively little in the way of comfort for some twenty technicians and support personnel, commanded by a junior officer, who manned each station. Few electronics technicians were likely to find the isolation of an island loran station more attractive than the opportunities open to them in civil life, so the Coast Guard would soon face a serious manning problem. This was solved by offering technicians a two-year course of instruction in electrical engineering at the Radio Corporation of America Institute as an incentive to reenlistment. Although such advanced training had heretofore been available only to officers, the enlisted technicians proved their competence in academic work and in subsequent assignments.[20]

Meanwhile, the Coast Guard had made the relocation and modernization of eight loran stations a matter of the first importance in its 1947 budget—the sum required for this purpose amounted to 57 percent of the total request for construction projects. This commitment to loran was something of a gamble at the time, for its primacy over rival systems had not yet been established. Yet loran receivers and charts were available to airlines, shipping companies, and fishermen soon after the war's end, and with its increasing use, the future of loran was soon assured. Whether it would continue to be operated by the Coast Guard was another matter; that was decided by the legislation resulting from the Ebasco study.

Support for the continuation of the loran system came from a number of organizations, prominent among them the Provisional International Civil Aviation Organization (PICAO), which had been founded in 1944. Two years later, eleven member nations agreed that transoceanic aircraft should be guided by loran and should also receive meteorological information relevant to their routes from ocean station vessels. Facilities for the first existed; those for the second did not.

At the peak of wartime activity, there had been twenty-two ocean weather stations in the Atlantic Ocean and twenty-four in the Pacific, for all of which the U.S. Navy was responsible except the nine in the Atlantic patrolled by British and Brazilian vessels and one maintained in the Pacific by Canada. When the Navy announced its intention to relinquish responsibility for the Atlantic and eastern Pacific stations during the spring of 1946, Coast Guard Headquarters inquired of the Weather Bureau whether their continuation was desirable. Francis W. Reichelderfer, still the bureau chief, responded that ocean stations were "essential for meteorological protection of transocean air commerce . . ." and that a minimum of twelve stations in the Atlantic and six between the U.S. Pacific coast and the longitude of Hawaii should be maintained permanently. He hoped that eventually the cost of the ocean stations would be borne by all of the nations benefitting from their service; until that could be arranged, "it should be considered part of the cost of successful air commerce. The United States is committed to transocean air commerce as a national policy and the weather patrol service is therefore necessary."[21]

Nineteen frigates were transferred to the Coast Guard for ocean station duty in the spring of 1946. Obviously too few to maintain stations on the scale Reichelderfer desired, they patrolled two stations in the Atlantic and three in the Pacific. Even this degree of activity could not be supported, however. Lacking personnel to man the frigates, the Coast Guard returned the last of them to the Navy in September 1946, and the *Bibb* and the *Spencer,* operating out of Boston, alternated on Ocean Station Charlie, located in the mid-Atlantic Ocean east of Newfoundland.

This diminution of service did not escape the notice of the nation's commercial aviators, many of whom had become accustomed to the information and assistance provided by ocean station vessels while they were piloting military and naval aircraft during the war. The matter was brought before the PICAO, which was determining transatlantic air routes early in 1947, and it recommended that thirteen stations be established in the Atlantic Ocean. At the Ocean Weather Observation Station Conference held in London in September 1947, representatives of Belgium, Britain, Canada, France, Ireland, the Netherlands, Norway, Sweden, and the United States adopted this recommendation, with the last agreeing to accept responsibility for seven stations, sharing another with Canada.[22]

Agreement by members of an international organization did not assure rapid action by the governments involved, but a dramatic incident less than a month later helped to bring about the ocean station program's implementation. The incident began on 14 October 1947 with a message from the American-owned flying boat *Bermuda Sky Queen,* en route from Foynes, Ireland, to Gander, Newfoundland. The aircraft wished the cutter *Bibb* on Ocean Station Charlie to provide a position check and information on winds aloft. These were transmitted at 2:05 A.M. Three hours later, a celestial observation revealed that the flying boat's progress had been slowed considerably by gale-force winds; she did not have enough fuel either to reach Newfoundland or to return to Ireland. Pilot Charles Martin decided to fly back to the *Bibb,* 310 miles to the eastward, and land alongside. Two aircraft in the vicinity joined the *Queen* to help with communications and navigation; the three were sighted by the cutter's lookouts just before 8 A.M.

The landing would hardly be routine, however, because a moderate to fresh gale had been blowing on Ocean Station Charlie for more than two days, lashing the surface into steep, confused, 30-foot waves. Captain Paul B. Cronk informed Martin of sea conditions and suggested that the *Bibb* try to smooth the seas somewhat by circling at high speed. Instead, the pilot selected a relatively smooth area and put the aircraft down with little damage.

Then the operation became interesting, for there were sixty-two passengers in the *Bermuda Sky Queen,* said to be the largest number on a transatlantic flight to that time, in addition to the seven-member flight crew. Transferring these from the fragile flying boat to the cutter rolling 30 to 35 degrees would obviously require a good deal of ingenuity and skill—and luck. This phase began ominously, for as the *Queen* taxied toward the *Bibb*, she became unmanageable in the cutter's lee and crushed her bow against the latter's side. The *Bibb* sustained damage to a boat davit and her superstructure aft before she could back away. Cronk then sent a Monomoy pulling boat that attempted in vain to find a way to approach the flying boat. After an hour, the oarsmen were tiring, so the captain decided to recover the boat, an operation not without hazard in that sea condition, and seek another rescue method. Several hours were spent determining the relative rates of drift of cutter and aircraft and in experimenting with rubber rafts streamed from both.

At 3:30 P.M., Pilot Martin advised Cronk that the flying boat's condition was deteriorating; passengers and crew should be removed before dark if possible. With only two hours before sunset, the *Bibb* spread an oil slick downwind from the *Queen* before crossing her bow to provide a lee while three of the strongest passengers attempted to paddle a small rubber raft to the cutter. They could make no headway against wind and sea, so the *Bibb* drifted down and picked them up by means of lines thrown over the side. The small raft was obviously impractical; the cutter's motor surfboat towed a fifteen-man raft over to the flying boat, which launched another small raft to float a line to the surfboat. This provided the means for getting the larger raft to the aircraft, and just before sunset the rescue operation began in earnest. Passengers jumped from the *Queen* into the crazily bouncing raft, which was allowed to drift to the surfboat; when they were in the boat, the raft was pulled back to the aircraft. With four adults, two children, and a baby embarked, the surfboat returned to the *Bibb*, where all were passed on board by men hanging onto scrambler nets over the side.

Ten were rescued on the second passage and eleven on the third, during which the wind and sea increased to an extent that endangered the entire operation. The surfboat had to be refueled before making a fourth trip, and its flotation tanks were damaged when heavy seas slammed it against the cutter's side repeatedly. Meanwhile, the flying boat drifted some distance to leeward, losing the raft in the darkness. The latter was finally located, partially deflated; the surfboat got it to the aircraft; and sixteen passengers jumped onto it—too many to be taken into the slowly foundering boat. With three Coast Guardsmen and three passengers on the raft, the surfboat began to tow it to the *Bibb*, only to be disabled, probably by a line fouling the screw. The cutter reached them just in time to pull all twenty-one on board before both sank.

Having lost the surfboat, the *Bibb*'s men had to use a Monomoy to remove the twenty-two remaining in the flying boat. A volunteer crew towed another raft from the cutter, manning only six oars to leave more room for survivors. They passed the raft painter to the *Queen* with a shoulder line-throwing gun; the raft was pulled over,

The Bibb, *heroine of the Bermuda Sky Queen rescue.*

but it failed to reappear. The *Bibb* picked up the Monomoy an hour later, and after discussing the situation with his officers, Captain Cronk concluded that no further effort should be made that night—should the flying boat sink, those on board could cling to the raft until the *Bibb* reached them. This decision was passed to Pilot Martin by the cutter's bull-horn, he concurred by blinker light, and Cronk ordered half his men below for badly needed rest.

When the sun rose at 6:45 A.M. on 15 October, the gale had diminished to a fresh breeze and the seas had gone down somewhat. The *Bibb*'s remaining power boat, the captain's gig, was thought capable of coping with the nasty swell still running, so it was lowered and returned with eight passengers. On its second passage, however, the gig's engine broke down; only two men got on board before it drifted away from the raft. Four men rowed a hastily lowered Monomoy over to complete the rescue, which it did in two trips, the rescued passengers and flight crew members manning oars to speed their way to the *Bibb*. Meanwhile, the gig's engine had been started again, and when it too had been hoisted on board, Cronk turned his attention to the derelict aircraft. He had no desire to risk lives in a salvage attempt and Pilot Martin agreed that she could not be salvaged, so with the owners' concurrence the cutter sank the *Bermuda Sky Queen* by gunfire before heading for Boston.[23]

The *Bibb* received a heroine's welcome on her return—vessels sounding their whistles, fireboats spouting water, innumerable small craft circling her, and unfortunately, reporters and photographers swarming on board as she stood into President Roads. These zealous representatives of the news media had slight regard for the passengers' state of exhaustion, which was not improved by equally insensitive television crews when the cutter was moored, after bumping the pier rather rudely.[24]

The mishandling of the public relations aspect could not detract from the *Bibb*'s achievement, which seemed even greater a few days later, when a French commercial airplane was forced down in the

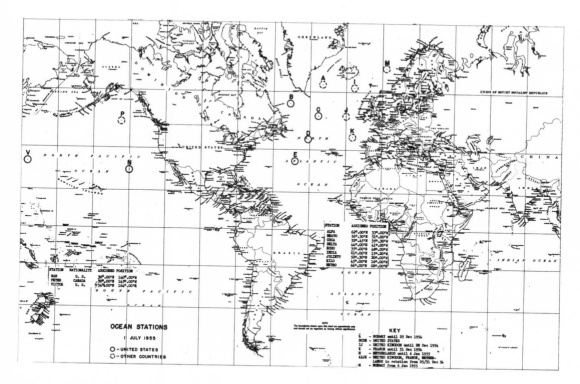

The principal ocean stations.

Mediterranean Sea with the loss of more than forty lives; only two persons were rescued. Other aircraft would come down at sea near ocean station vessels during the next decade, and while the cutters saved all of their occupants, none had to overcome such unfavorable conditions of wind and sea and none had so many persons to pick up. The *Bermuda Sky Queen* incident must rank with the Coast Guard's outstanding rescue feats.

Maintenance of ocean stations on the scale planned in 1947 turned out to be unnecessary. The number varied during the first few years of the expanded program, with the United States ultimately providing vessels for four, known by the Alfa code names Bravo, Charlie, Delta, and Echo. Station Hotel, midway between Norfolk and Bermuda, was also patrolled on occasion, while November and Victor were the regular Pacific Ocean stations. Each was located on a transoceanic air route, approximately halfway between land termini, and consisted of a 100-square mile area measuring 10 miles on each side. A cutter normally stayed near the center of the square, drifting when possible to conserve fuel, transmitting meteorological information to the Weather Bureau at regular intervals, and providing advice on weather conditions alow and aloft and position checks for passing aircraft. Patrols lasted twenty-one days, not including the travel from home port to ocean station and return, so that cutters sometimes spent more than half of their time at sea.

The ocean station program required more large cutters, and since the three 311-foot vessels obtained from the Navy in 1946 had

The 311-foot cutter Half Moon *on Ocean Station Delta.*

proven "their economy of operation and excellent seaworthy characteristics," the Coast Guard obtained fifteen near-sisters from the Navy's reserve fleets.[25] These small seaplane tenders were acquired on loan, so they retained their original bay, inlet, and strait names, which in any event seemed quite suitable for Coast Guard cutters. With their aviation gasoline tanks converted to bunker diesel fuel, the 311-footers could cruise 20,000 miles at economical speed, and their officers and men enjoyed quarters intended to accommodate more than twice their number. Thus, they seemed well suited for ocean station duty.

The newly acquired vessels shared the ocean station assignments with the 327-foot and 255-foot cutters, with the latter probably the least popular because of their size and behavior in a seaway. Like the Treasury class, however, the 255-footers were strongly built ships that could endure heavy weather with little damage. The ex-seaplane tenders, on the other hand, had been designed to spend much of their time riding at anchor in sheltered waters whence their patrol squadrons could operate effectively; these shallow-draft vessels with relatively flat bottoms forward found themselves pounding into heavy seas for weeks on end, sometimes icing up badly as well, with consequent strain on their hull structures. Occasionally a 311-footer had to be relieved early when her hull plating cracked due to metal fatigue.[26] Nonetheless, most spent nearly twenty years on ocean station duty, and while the last of the 255-foot cutters was decommissioned in 1974, the 311-foot *Unimak* continues to operate out of New Bedford more than a decade later.

More ships required more sailors, so recruiting quotas were increased to 700 men per month. The reduction of enlistments from four years to three and permission for ex-Coast Guard and Navy petty officers to reenlist with their former rates helped to entice men, but the ease with which the service met its personnel requirements must be attributed in large part to the extension of conscription by the Selective Service Act of 1948—as usual, many young men found a three-year enlistment in the Coast Guard more attractive than a shorter period in another of the armed forces.

Some may have regretted their choice, for the ocean stations in the Atlantic were described collectively as 400 square miles of bad weather. Bravo and Charlie were undoubtedly the worst—the former had the greatest likelihood of severe icing conditions, and a seemingly endless succession of gales, often laden with snow, swept across Charlie in the winter months. Life thereon was a trial for men and ships alike, as the following terse statement reveals:

> Gales to 73 knots, snow squalls, and 40–50 foot seas turned a January [1951] patrol on Station Charlie into a nightmare for *Coos Bay* crewmen. It was necessary to keep her screws turning 90% of the time to maintain position, and occasional rolls of 50° were reported. A number of men were injured in falls against bulkheads . . . and on separate occasions heavy seas twisted a heavy companionway door on the starboard quarter, pushed in a port side hatch, bent stanchions, and buckled steel plates.[27]

Nor did the end of the patrol bring quick respite, for while the 311-footer was returning to Portland, Maine, she was diverted to assist the fishing vessel *Gudrun*, which was reported sinking 400 miles away. The latter disappeared before the *Coos Bay* or any other ship could reach her; there were no survivors.

The Coast Guard estimated the cost of keeping a cutter on an ocean station at $5,000 per day, high enough to make possible alternatives seem attractive. The construction of non-self-propelled seadromes for this purpose had been suggested in 1940, and when the war ended, the Air Coordinating Committee designated the Coast Guard as the agency to determine the feasibility of the concept. This had to await statutory authority for the ocean station program as a whole; when that was obtained in 1948, the service requested funds to construct a model. Advantages claimed for the seadrome were that it would possess greater stability than a ship, its position would be assured, it would require fewer men, and it could remain on station for years at a time. Its disadvantages included a lack of mobility for search and rescue—the *Bermuda Sky Queen* had drifted more than 100 miles while her passengers and crew were being taken to the *Bibb*—the difficulty of towing it to port for periodic maintenance, and the effects of isolation on its complement's morale. Perhaps its greatest disadvantage was the initial cost—$5,670,000 for the smallest feasible experimental model—which the Congress declined to appropriate.[28] One suspects that the failure to fund this

273

project was not unwelcome to the Coast Guard, which seems to have given only minimal support to the non-self-propelled seadrome.

By 1949, the service's requirements for seagoing units had generally been satisfied. The situation with regard to aircraft was less satisfactory. On 30 June 1946, the Coast Guard had 195 fixed-wing airplanes and thirty-one helicopters, with eleven air stations. This number obviously could not be maintained in peacetime; by early 1948, there were seventy-nine operational aircraft, of which only eight were helicopters. They flew from nine continental air stations or with air detachments in Alaska, Hawaii, Guam, the Philippine Islands, and Newfoundland.

Perhaps the most interesting of these aircraft were a number of Boeing PB-1Gs, Coast Guard versions of the famous B-17 Flying Fortress, which were called "Flying Lifeboats" because they were fitted with detachable keels in the form of motorboats that could be parachuted for use by survivors of maritime disasters. This was a popular concept for a time, and several PBY-5As carried smaller boats for the same purpose.[29] Some pointed out, however, that those who had experienced the trauma of an aircraft ditching or shipwreck were not likely to be able to navigate well enough to reach the nearest haven. Thus, it would be far better for survivors to await rescue in a known location. The development of rubber rafts that would inflate on hitting the water led to the abandonment of aircraft-carried lifeboats, which were heavier, bulkier, and much more vulnerable to damage.

The small number of helicopters in service in 1948 is surprising in light of their rescue feats during the preceding four years—in September 1946, for example, Coast Guard helicopters had removed eighteen survivors, eight of them seriously injured, from a Belgian airliner that had crashed in a Newfoundland muskeg bog.[30] But the helicopter remained a difficult aircraft to fly, and its operational range was very limited. To make it more useful, the Rotary Wing Development Unit, headed by Commander Frank A. Erickson, was established at the Elizabeth City Air Station in June 1948. During the two years of its existence, the unit developed flotation gear and a hydraulic hoist for use by helicopters, and in January 1950 Commander Erickson assured the American Helicopter Society that stabilized flight would soon be realized. Almost a year earlier, Erickson's executive officer, Lieutenant Stewart R. Graham, had flown a Sikorsky HO3S-1 from Elizabeth City to the Port Angeles Air Station by way of San Diego, a total of more than 3,900 miles, in 57.6 hours flight time. Meanwhile, Erickson himself made numerous demonstration flights to popularize the helicopter.

Most of the Coast Guard aircraft were twin-engine flying boats and amphibians, with the Martin PBM-5G Mariner and the smaller Grumman HU-16 Albatross the most numerous. The predominance of these types was due in part to the work of Commander Donald B. MacDiarmid, who conducted extensive experiments landing cross-

A Grumman Albatross—the Coast Guard's first.

wind and downwind with PBM-5Gs flying out of San Diego and finally concluded that seaplanes could land in rather rough water if they paralleled the swell system rather than landing into the wind and sea. MacDiarmid's method required careful preliminary evaluation of sea conditions, for a pilot might easily decide that relatively unimportant wind waves were swells, only to find too late that his landing paralleled the wrong system. As a sometime subordinate wrote later, "Largely as a result of MacDiarmid's work, seaplane rough water landings after 1945 became safer—not safe—but safer."[31] The ability of seaplanes to take off after such landings was enhanced by the wartime development of "jet assisted take off"—JATO. Auxiliary jet units attached to the aircraft were used to provide a short burst of additional thrust, enabling it to take off with a heavier load or in a shorter distance than would be possible with only its own power.

Nonetheless, landings at sea under any but the best of conditions might result in damage to the seaplanes, which caused an economy-conscious service to require that its pilots radio district headquarters for permission to make such landings. Only if no surface vessels were within reasonable distance of those requiring assistance were they allowed to do so. On occasion, this resulted in a seaplane of another service making the rescue, while the frustrated Coast Guard airmen circled overhead. In due course, the seaplane pilot received permission to make his own decision about landing at sea—and he was held responsible for damage incurred as a result.[32]

Many of the aviators agreed that the Coast Guard was devoting too little attention to search and rescue and to aviation generally. In the absence of an effective representative at Headquarters—none of the flag officers was an aviator—they sought support elsewhere.

Congressman Herbert Bonner was already concerned about the Coast Guard's apparent lack of interest in aviation developments, fearing that the Navy might take over the search-and-rescue duties performed by Coast Guard aircraft, and when he became aware of the aviators' discontent, he informed Treasury Secretary Snyder that his subcommittee on the Coast Guard would undertake an investigation of the aviation situation. Snyder responded that the service was deeply interested in aviation, but in the absence of adequate funding, it was unable to expand that branch. Subcommittee hearings he thought likely to provide a forum for "scattered dissentious views," contributing nothing to improve the situation.[33] So the matter rested until 1956, when the Congress demanded a thorough study of Coast Guard aviation and its requirements. In retrospect, it seems unfortunate that this had not been made when Bonner addressed Snyder, early in 1949.

Coast Guard aviation had got another mission when the International Ice Patrol was reactivated in 1946. While the cutters *Tampa* and *Modoc* conducted the patrol in the prewar fashion, they were assisted by aircraft of the former Patrol Bombing Squadron 6, now the North Atlantic Air Detachment. These proved so useful that aircraft participated in the patrol each year thereafter, flying from the U.S. Naval Air Station at Argentia, Newfoundland, and assuming a greater share of the responsibility as it became apparent that their radar was more effective at detecting ice than radar in ships.[34]

Experiments with radar as an ice detector had begun in 1945, and in 1946 the *Mojave* was assigned to continue these while she was making the oceanographic cruise. The personnel shortage forced the cutter's detachment in May, but by that time she had determined that ice was a poor radar target, reflecting "radar waves 60 times less than a ship of equivalent cross-sectional area." Fog and sea clutter, both likely to be encountered on the Grand Banks in the spring, reduced the effectiveness of radar even further—"in summary, while radar is the second best aid a mariner can have, it cannot be relied upon to assure safe transit through ice-infested waters."[35]

The Coast Guard was required by international agreement to renew the ice patrol, but no such obligation existed with regard to the Bering Sea Patrol, which was not reinstituted until 1948 and then by only one cutter, the icebreaker *Northwind.* She had gone to the Arctic as flagship of the Navy's Operation Nanook in the summer of 1946, after which Captain Charles W. Thomas took her to the Antarctic during the antipodal summer of 1946–47 as part of the task force supporting Operation High Jump, the expedition seeking scientific and geographic information about the southernmost continent. In the course of the latter, the *Northwind* towed the naval storeship *Merrick,* disabled in the Antarctic ice pack, nearly 1,000 miles to New Zealand despite hurricane force winds and mountainous seas.[36]

The icebreaker was not merely the sole unit of the Bering Sea

Patrol in 1948, she was also undermanned to the extent that only one of her three engine rooms could be manned continuously, and she carried neither a seaplane nor a helicopter. Nonetheless, she supplied light and loran stations and provided legal, medical, and dental services to the inhabitants of native villages, even entering the Beaufort Sea north and east of Point Barrow.

Although deemed a success, the 1948 cruise showed that the *Northwind* was not an ideal vessel for the Bering Sea Patrol—she touched bottom on several occasions in the shallow waters of Bristol Bay and Norton Sound, and her propensity for rolling heavily made it difficult to disembark fuel and supplies in poorly protected anchorages.[37] For want of a more suitable cutter—or to provide employment for the icebreaker—she returned to the Bering Sea and Arctic Ocean in 1949 and subsequent years, on occasion assisting the Navy's Arctic expeditions.

The Coast Guard suffered several grievous losses during the immediate postwar years. On 1 April 1946 a tsunami swept away the Scotch Cap lighthouse on Unimak Island in the Aleutians and its five-man crew perished. Three months later, on 9 July, sixteen officers and men returning from assignments in Greenland were killed when their Army Air Force transport crashed near Westover Field in Massachusetts.

These deaths reflected no discredit on the Coast Guard; not so those resulting from the collision of the tanker *Gulfstream* with the icebreaker *Eastwind* in fog off the New Jersey coast on 19 January 1949. The tanker, on passage from Philadelphia to the Persian Gulf, was not equipped with radar, but she continued to proceed at 15 knots after entering a fogbank at 4:30 A.M., although she did begin to sound fog signals. Meanwhile, the *Eastwind,* bound for Chesapeake Bay from Boston, was steaming at 14 knots when her radar operator reported the *Gulfstream* 9 miles on her starboard bow. Subsequent reports made it clear that the two ships were on collision courses, and the tanker's bearing remained constant after the minor course change ordered by the officer of the deck. On entering the fog, the *Eastwind* neither slowed nor sounded fog signals. Radar contact was lost in sea return as the vessels closed, and neither sighted the other's running lights until they were close aboard. The icebreaker's rudder was put hard left and the *Gulfstream* turned hard right almost simultaneously—and at 4:37 A.M. the tanker's bow smashed into the *Eastwind* just abaft her bridge. Fire broke out in both ships; that in the tanker was confined to the forepeak—fortunately, for her empty cargo tanks were not gas free—but that in the icebreaker spread rapidly, engulfing the chief petty officers' quarters, the radio room, and the bridge, killing eleven men and burning twenty-one others more or less seriously. Two of the merchant vessels that answered the *Gulfstream*'s distress signal embarked the *Eastwind*'s injured men for transportation to the Staten Island Marine Hospital, where two more died. The buoy tenders *Gentian* and

Sassafras helped to extinguish the *Eastwind*'s fires and then towed the badly damaged icebreaker to New York, stern first, while the tanker made port under her own power.[38]

Although the Board of Inquiry noted the *Gulfstream*'s excessive speed in the fog, the major responsibility for the disaster clearly rested with the *Eastwind,* the burdened vessel under the Rules of the Road. Her officer of the deck had ignored standing orders with regard to reduction of speed in fog, sounding fog signals, and informing the captain when a radar target approached within 3 miles. Nor did the commanding officer escape blame; reviewing the board's findings, the commandant charged him with negligence in that he had permitted an officer and a seaman "of insufficient experience and competence" to serve as officer of the deck and lookout in a busy shipping lane.[39]

The *Eastwind* returned to service eighteen months later, after repairs costing more than $1,000,000. And since the Coast Guard was still plagued by personnel shortages, the loss of thirteen enlisted men, nine of whom were chief petty officers, was the more serious.

More typical of Coast Guard operations was the *Bibb*'s rescue of the *Gaspar* crew under adverse circumstances. The 327-footer, assigned to ocean station duty, was approaching Argentia on 1 September 1948 when her radiomen copied a distress call from the Portuguese fishing schooner foundering in heavy seas 300 miles east-southeast of Cape Race, Newfoundland. Captain Donald G. Jacobs changed course and increased speed, maintaining 20 knots through the night despite the 40-knot wind and 40-foot seas. A Coast Guard PBY-5A sighted the *Gaspar* the next morning and guided the cutter to her. The schooner's master reported that she would have to be abandoned, so the *Bibb* lowered two boats, which towed a pair of rubber rafts alongside, hardly a simple task in the heavy swell and torrential rain, although the wind had diminished somewhat. After a slight delay—the Portuguese seamen declined to board the rafts until the Portuguese-speaking chief radioman in the cutter had assured the master that it was safe to do so—the boats and rafts removed forty men and a dog from the sinking *Gaspar* in three trips, and the *Bibb* headed for Argentia, having completed her second notable rescue feat in less than a year.[40]

The following summer a Military Air Transport Service (MATS) C-47 had to ditch at night on Ocean Station Delta and the 255-footer *Sebago,* Commander Eugene A. Coffin, Jr., picked the four crew members up without incident. Like the *Gaspar* rescue, this operation was conducted so efficiently that it attracted little notice, but it provided further evidence that those in aircraft ditching near ocean station cutters had an excellent chance of survival.

Admiral Farley retired on 1 January 1950, at the end of a very trying term as commandant of the Coast Guard. He had not attained great popularity either within the service or without, but his accomplishments were considerable. Among them, one must note the

relatively orderly completion of the demobilization process, the confirmation of the Coast Guard's responsibility for Bureau of Marine Inspection and Navigation duties, the loran system, and the ocean stations, and perhaps most important, the statutory definition of its many missions, both in peace and in war. Personnel problems had been largely—not entirely—overcome; the period of "confusion drill," as one of Farley's subordinates termed it, had ended. To be sure, the admiral's great predecessor had charted the course to many of the objectives, but it required a helmsman of some ability to carry out his intentions. Joseph Francis Farley had justified Admiral Waesche's faith in him.

The Sebago *on ocean station. The 255-foot cutters were rather uncomfortable in rough weather.*

279

CHAPTER SIXTEEN

THE KOREAN WAR AND AFTER, 1950–54

*I*n September 1949, Congressman Herbert C. Bonner informed the secretary of the treasury that he had discussed the matter of Admiral Farley's successor with a number of Coast Guard officers and found that Rear Admiral O'Neill, the assistant commandant, would have a good deal of support within the service.[1] Bonner himself believed that O'Neill should become commandant, as did Secretary John W. Snyder, who recommended him to the president not long afterward.

Merlin O'Neill, a 1921 graduate of the Coast Guard Academy, had had the usual variety of assignments, including twelve years at Headquarters, during which he had helped to organize the Coast Guard Reserve (later the Auxiliary) and had become its first director. His wartime service included command of the attack transport *Leonard Wood* in 1942–43, for which he had been awarded the Legion of Merit. Unlike his predecessor, who had held the rank of admiral, O'Neill was promoted to vice admiral when he became commandant on 1 January 1950. His sometime associate in organizing the Reserve, Captain Alfred C. Richmond, assumed the duties of assistant commandant as a rear admiral a few weeks later, and Captain Kenneth K. Cowart attained flag rank to succeed Rear Admiral Reed-Hill as engineer in chief.

Vice Admiral O'Neill took command of a Coast Guard comprising 2,073 commissioned officers, 833 chief warrant and warrant officers, and 19,988 enlisted men. These people manned 177 cutters, 50 patrol boats, 41 harbor tugs, 37 lightships, 170 lifeboat stations, 12 bases, 429 lighthouses, 30 loran stations, and a variety of other activities. Aircraft numbered seventy-nine fixed and rotary wing types flying from nine air stations and eight air detachments, the latter outside the continental United States.[2] In short, the service had not changed a great deal since the end of the demobilization period almost four years earlier. Considerable expansion, however, would soon be necessary.

This came about as a result of the Korean War, which began when North Korean forces unexpectedly crossed the thirty-eighth parallel of North latitude on 25 June 1950. Exactly what this presaged for the U.S. Coast Guard was temporarily unclear, for in the absence of a declaration of war, its transfer to Navy Department control required an executive order, and that was not forthcoming. For a few Coast Guardsmen the war had special meaning—a small Coast Guard detachment headed by Captain George E. McCabe had been sent to South Korea in August 1946 to organize and train a Korean coast guard service, which in turn became the nucleus of the Republic of Korea Navy.

Although the Coast Guard remained under the Treasury Department throughout the Korean conflict, its role therein was that which the chief of naval operations had outlined to the commandant in 1946–47. This was based on the premises that "war time functions and duties assigned [to the Coast Guard] should be those which are an extension of normal peacetime tasks," and that "Coast Guard personnel, ships, aircraft and facilities should be utilized as organized Coast Guard units rather than by indiscriminately integrating them into the naval establishment."[3] Thus, there would be no repetition of the World War II experience insofar as manning warships and providing landing craft crews were concerned. Instead, the Navy wished the smaller service to assume responsibility for port security and for additional ocean stations and search-and-rescue capability in the Pacific, both of the latter necessitated by the increased air traffic between the United States and the Orient.

Merlin O'Neill, commandant, 1950–54.

The first was most pressing. The potential for disaster should an explosion occur in a seaport had been demonstrated on the morning of 16 April 1947, when a fire on board the French-owned Liberty ship *Grandcamp*, loading ammonium nitrate at Texas City, Texas, caused an explosion in which more than 500 died, thousands were injured, and millions of dollars worth of property damaged. And in 1949 the Soviet Union had exploded its first atomic bomb. With the cold war intensifying, it seemed quite possible that Russian nuclear devices might be brought into American harbors surreptitiously, for detonation at some subsequent time. The Magnuson Act of August 1950 authorized the president to implement the Espionage Act of 1917 whenever he deemed it advisable to ensure the safety of the country, naming the Coast Guard as the agency to carry out the port security program. President Truman issued the necessary executive order on 20 October 1950.[4]

This should have been the occasion for calling the Coast Guard Reserve to active duty—had there been an effective Reserve. Congress, however, had repeatedly refused to fund a Reserve training program since the end of World War II, and although Admiral Farley had appointed Reserve directors to the various Coast Guard districts in 1949, with orders to establish volunteer training units where feasible—elsewhere Coast Guard reservists might train with Naval

Reserve units—the absence of pay for drill periods hampered the effort considerably. On 30 June 1949, the Coast Guard Reserve had 4,098 commissioned and warrant officers and only 252 enlisted men.

The events of July 1950 led Congress to appropriate $1,000,000, one fourth the amount requested, for Coast Guard Reserve training, and within a year thirty-five Organized Reserve Training Units, Port Security, were established in the larger seaports, while Boston and Washington, D.C., had similar units for "Vessel Augmentation"—to train officers and men for assignment to duty in cutters should their complements have to be enlarged. On 30 June 1951, the Coast Guard Reserve numbered 8,300, of whom more than half were enlisted men.[5]

The immediate need, however, was for men who could undertake port security duties without extensive training. To obtain these, the petty officer complements of ships and stations had to be reduced considerably; to provide replacements, the classes at petty officer schools were expanded to maximum size and larger numbers of men were sent to Navy schools. Coast Guardsmen were trained in explosives loading at the Port Chicago Naval Magazine on San Francisco Bay, while others prepared for waterfront security and patrol duties at the Army's military police school at Camp Gordon, Georgia. Like the other armed forces, the Coast Guard was authorized to extend enlistments one year if time-expired men did not reenlist immediately; it chose instead to permit them to join the Coast Guard Reserve when discharged, which did little to alleviate the immediate problem but assured a stronger Reserve and less resentment. Meanwhile, an intensified recruiting program attracted more than 26,000 applicants, less than a third of whom were enlisted and sent to Cape May, Groton, or Alameda for recruit training. The officer corps was expanded by appointment of some of the temporary wartime officers who had returned to warrant or enlisted status after World War II and by commissioning recent graduates of universities and merchant marine academies.

The fear of subversive activity had led to the denial of licenses to merchant marine radiomen suspected of disloyalty to the United States as early as the autumn of 1949, and the Korean War caused this prohibition to be applied to merchant seamen generally. In the absence of statutory procedures for identifying subversives, the Treasury Department arranged a conference with representatives of shipping companies and maritime labor unions. The conferees agreed that an individual's union activity could not be deemed evidence of subversive sympathies and that those denied security clearances should have the right of appeal to a three-member board representing management, labor, and the Coast Guard. During the next two years, the Coast Guard screened about 500,000 merchant seamen, denying clearance to some 3,700. More than a third of these denials were reversed on appeal.[6]

The Coast Guard's efforts to ferret out subversives in the mer-

chant marine brought the service the greatest unpopularity it had known since Prohibition. Protest movements across the country involved sporadic picketing of Coast Guard offices, and two Pacific coast labor organizations—the International Longshoremen's and Warehousemen's Union and the Marine Cooks and Stewards—refused to accept the 1950 agreement under which the screening was carried out. The latter contested it in the federal courts and even filed a protest with the United Nations.[7]

The 95-foot patrol cutter of 1953. The 95301 became the Cape Coral *a decade later.*

In retrospect, it is clear that the Coast Guard exceeded its authority in this instance, as the courts ultimately decided. However understandable its course may seem in light of the anti-communist hysteria of the day, it had the unfortunate effect of making the service suspect to many merchant mariners and to others who came to consider it an agency suppressing individual rights, not without reason.

Meanwhile, port captains assigned to thirteen major seaports reinstituted a number of the security measures that had become familiar during World War II, with special emphasis on the prevention of sabotage to ships carrying military cargoes to the Orient. It quickly became apparent that additional small craft were needed for harbor patrol duties, so the Coast Guard Yard undertook the construction of 100 diesel-powered, steel-hulled, 40-foot utility boats that could reach 18 knots. And because the remaining 83-footers were approaching obsolescence by 1952, the Yard laid down the first of twenty steel 95-footers intended for harbor entrance patrol. Although these 21-knot diesel-propelled vessels were officially de-

The DE Chambers *as refitted for ocean station duty. But for a modified bridge and the balloon "hangar" abaft her stack, she differs little from her World War II appearance.*

scribed as "seagoing patrol cutters," they were not assigned names on completion; all were later named for North American capes.

The handling of Coast Guard patrol boats did not escape criticism. In mid-1953, the commandant cautioned those in charge of the craft against maneuvering in such a fashion as to endanger larger vessels. The most serious incident reported involved an empty tanker standing into a harbor in poor visibility. When a red light on her starboard bow, subsequently identified as a patrol boat's port side light, began to cut across her course, the tanker, as burdened vessel, had to reverse her engines to avoid collision and in doing so almost drifted onto a breakwater. As Admiral O'Neill noted, such incidents did not reflect credit on the Coast Guard.[8]

The augmentation of ocean station activity in the Pacific necessitated the acquisition of more weather ships, and since the Navy was unwilling to relinquish any more of its small seaplane tenders, twelve of the FMR-type DEs, including nine that had been manned by Coast Guardsmen during World War II, were transferred from the reserve fleet at Green Cove Springs, Florida, in 1951 and 1952. After conversion for weather patrol at the Norfolk Naval Shipyard, eleven of the DEs sailed to the Pacific, while the *Chambers* was stationed at New Bedford. The choice of these notoriously rough-riding vessels for ocean station duty can only be explained by the fact that sea conditions in the Pacific Ocean are usually less severe than those in the North Atlantic.

The Navy and the Air Force desired more extensive loran coverage in the Western Pacific as well, and since there was neither time nor adequate shipping to permit the construction of permanent stations, the Coast Guard designed large trailers in which the electronic and communications equipment and power plant were housed. When several of these had been specifically sited and their antennae erected, a new loran chain began operating. Within a relatively short time, loran coverage was extended to the area from the Philippines to Korea.[9]

Air search and rescue units, each consisting of an aviation detachment, one or more cutters, and a command post with the necessary communication capability, were assigned to Sangley Point in the Philippines and to Guam, Wake, Midway, and Adak islands. The first of these was among the busiest—in January 1953, it sent a PBM to rescue the eleven-man crew of a Navy P2V patrol plane shot down by gunfire from a small island just off the Chinese coast. Lieutenant John Vukic put the seaplane down in 12-foot seas and got the P2V crew on board, but on take off one of the PBM's engines failed, causing it to crash. Four Navy men and five Coast Guardsmen died; the survivors, including Lieutenant Vukic, were rescued after spending a freezing night on a liferaft.[10] Another Sangley Point seaplane was more fortunate. When a Navy aircraft was forced down 100 miles west of Luzon, the PBM made an open-sea landing, picked up the five Navy airmen, and took off without difficulty.

So went the Korean War for the Coast Guard. It was the second of the nation's wars in which no cutters took part as combat vessels, the first being the Tripolitan War of 1801–06. While the big cutters went to naval shipyards or the Coast Guard Yard in turn to have their antisubmarine armaments reinstalled, there was no need to escort convoys so none was sent to the war zone. Henceforth, however, Coast Guard ships and aircraft would carry out regularly scheduled exercises to prepare them for military service, with the larger vessels reporting to the Navy's fleet training commands for this purpose.

The Korean War officially ended after the signing of the armistice on 27 July 1953. The effect on the Coast Guard was not long delayed. Its officer and enlisted complement, which on 30 June 1953 had numbered 34,491, had been reduced to 29,154 a year later. The additional air search-and-rescue detachments in the Western Pacific and Aleutians were discontinued, all of the ocean station DEs were decommissioned and returned to the Navy during the spring of 1954, and port security activities were reduced by the elimination of "shore side patrols" of waterfront areas in the major seaports. The armistice brought no diminution of Russo-American tension, however, so other port security measures were continued.

The cold war had led to another mission for the Coast Guard in 1952. The State Department wished to enhance the ability of its Voice of America programs to reach listeners in Balkan and Soviet-bloc nations by stationing a ship equipped to relay radio broadcasts in an eastern Mediterranean port. The use of a naval vessel for this purpose was undesirable in the prevailing state of international relations, but as Captain Earl K. Rhodes explained, "No one could take offense at the Coast Guard in an area where there were touchy political difficulties because we had no record of being spies, or were not pugilistic in any way, but were more like the Red Cross. We went in wherever somebody needed help."[11] Another of the 339-foot cargo ships was obtained from the Maritime Commission, fitted as an oceangoing radio station, renamed the *Courier,* and anchored in the harbor of Rhodes on the Greek island of the same name in September 1952. For the next twelve years, this vessel, manned by ten officers and eighty men, with a program coordinator and three radio engineers from the U.S. Information Agency, relayed Voice of America broadcasts, and no one seems to have objected to the Coast Guard's involvement in propaganda activity. The *Courier's* duties were taken over by a shore radio station on Rhodes in 1964.

The only other large cutter acquired by the Coast Guard during this period was one of the three icebreakers loaned to the Soviet Union during World War II. After repeated requests for their return, the first, the former *Southwind,* was turned over to the United States at Yokosuka, Japan, in April 1950, and the other two were returned at Bremerhaven, Germany, in December 1951. The Navy took the *Southwind* and the original *Northwind,* naming them the *Atka* and the *Staten Island* respectively, leaving the *Westwind* for the Coast Guard. Captain Edward H. Thiele, who visited the latter two vessels when they touched at a British port en route to the United States, reported that they were in "horrible shape . . . holed in on either heavy ice or on the rocks and [they] had been patched up with cement since [the Russian crews] couldn't get them to dry docks. It was just fantastic that these things were running!"[12] It was the more fantastic because Fairbanks, Morse and Company had refused to sell spare parts for the main engines to the Russians after the war, so that the ships' crews had had to improvise their own. The *Westwind* was recommissioned in the Coast Guard after a seven-month overhaul costing $1,200,000. She and the second *Northwind* would be the longest lived of all the Wind-class icebreakers, serving into the 1980s.

Despite more rigorous standards for merchant ship construction and maintenance and such sophisticated aids to navigation as radar and loran, maritime casualties continued to occur. On 25 August 1950, for example, the Navy's hospital ship *Benevolence,* brought out of the reserve fleet for Korean War service, collided with the SS *Mary Luckenbach* in a fog 4 miles off the Golden Gate and sank in fifteen minutes. The 36-foot lifeboat from the Fort Point station was first on the scene, picking up survivors and ferrying them to the *Mary Luckenbach,* which was standing by. Other Coast Guard and private craft joined her, and the cutter *Gresham* coordinated rescue activities. In all, 407 persons were saved, of whom Coast Guard boats rescued "a substantial number."[13]

Another naval vessel, the small seaplane tender *Valcour,* was standing out of Chesapeake Bay on 14 May 1951, when she suffered a steering casualty and crossed the track of the oncoming collier *Thomas Tracy.* The latter's bow struck the tender's starboard side, igniting the contents of an aviation gasoline tank, which set both ships afire. The blaze in the *Tracy* was kept from spreading and she returned to Newport News, but the fire in the *Valcour,* together with the collision damage, forced her abandonment. Thirty-seven sailors died; the remainder were rescued by other vessels, including the cutter *Cherokee,* which picked up forty men and then joined the submarine rescue ship *Sunbird* in bringing the fire under control and towing the *Valcour* to the Norfolk Naval Shipyard for repair.[14]

Welded hulls had split on occasion during World War II, due in part to poorly trained welders and to limited knowledge of stresses caused by the welding. Postwar research led to the strengthening of many such vessels, but the problem continued in some. On 9 January 1952, the American cargo ship *Pennsylvania,* a week out of Seattle bound for Yokohama, reported that her hull plating had cracked as she labored in heavy seas. Next came a distress signal, followed by a message that her forty-six man crew was taking to her boats because the *Pennsylvania* was foundering. Cutters were ordered to her position, 665 miles west of Cape Flattery, but since it was late afternoon and a gale was blowing, no aircraft were sent until the next morning. By that time, the freighter was gone, and although the ensuing search ultimately involved fifty-one aircraft and eighteen ships of the U.S. and Canadian armed forces, only a capsized lifeboat and some debris were sighted; there were no survivors.[15]

Little more than a month later, another incident—more accurately, two incidents—of the same sort had somewhat less serious consequences. A 50-knot gale was whipping snow onto the Massachusetts coast on 18 February when the T-2-type tanker *Fort Mercer* reported that her hull was splitting in heavy seas southeast of Cape Cod. The *Eastwind* and the *Unimak,* proceeding to the assistance of another vessel, were diverted to the tanker's aid, the 311-footers *McCulloch* and *Yakutat* were ordered out of Boston and Provincetown respectively, and soon after noon several stations were directed to send lifeboats.

As the afternoon wore on, the radar installed experimentally at the Chatham Lifeboat Station detected two objects off the Pollock Rip Lightship, which were identified visually as the bow and stern sections of a tanker, although they were 20 miles farther west than the *Fort Mercer* should have been. This mystery was cleared up when those manning the lightship read the name *Pendleton* on the bow. Learning from that tanker's agent that she had failed to arrive at Boston the day before, the Coast Guard rescue coordinator realized that two T-2 tankers had split at almost the same time in the same vicinity. Thereupon, the *Eastwind, Unimak,* and *Yakutat* were assigned to the *Fort Mercer* while the *McCulloch* saw to the bow of the *Pendleton.* The stern section of the last seemed likely to ground, and the Chatham Station crew prepared beach apparatus for the rescue.

When it became apparent that the *Pendleton's* stern would be driven clear of the shore, Boatswain's Mate First Class Bernard C. Webber, who had only three years experience in lifeboats, took the Chatham Station's second 36-footer through the 10-foot seas surging over the bar, one of which smashed the boat's windshield and tore the canopy. Coast Guard aircraft from Salem dropped flares to provide illumination in the evening darkness, and Webber worked his lifeboat under the *Pendleton*'s stern section, maneuvering close aboard for forty-five minutes while thirty-three men dropped from a rope ladder. Three fell into the sea, from which two were rescued; the third was crushed between the boat and the tanker. With thirty-six on board, the 36-footer was dangerously overloaded, and the driving snow and spray made it difficult to decide the way back to Chatham. Fortunately, the station radar watch had tracked the boat during the entire operation and provided directions by radio that enabled Webber to bring her back safely.

The *McCulloch* and the other Chatham boat reached the *Pendleton* bow section later that night. One man jumped into the turbulent sea as they approached, but could not be located. Although there was no further sign of life, the cutter and two lifeboats stood by until daylight.

The *Yakutat* sighted the *Fort Mercer* bow not long after midnight and attempted to effect the rescue with rubber rafts. Heavy seas thwarted her efforts, so soon after dawn the cutter lowered a 26-foot motor whaleboat. It was stove against the *Yakutat*'s side almost at once but managed to reach the tanker, from which several men jumped, two of whom were picked up before the sinking boat had to return to the cutter. Two more were removed by rubber raft just before the bow capsized, and cutter sailors, some without exposure suits, brought the nearly frozen survivors on board.

The *Eastwind* came up with the *Fort Mercer* stern at noon on 19 February and took three men off in a balsa liferaft as the *Acushnet* reached the scene from Portland. Lieutenant Commander John M. Joseph took the handy ex-salvage ship alongside the wreck, so that men could jump onto her low afterdeck. Five made it before the *Acushnet* had to pull away; she returned to take thirteen more on board while a like number elected to remain in the *Fort Mercer* stern. A commercial tug took that section in tow and got it into port three days later. The bow section, which could not be salvaged, was sunk by cutter gunfire. And on 24 February, the Chatham Station crew removed one body from the *Pendleton* bow.[16]

Thus, the combined rescue operation ended with six lives having been lost while seventy-one were saved, although the thirty-four in the *Fort Mercer* stern might have survived without Coast Guard assistance. Nonetheless, it was a job well done, and even veterans of the old Life-Saving Service must have admired Boatswain's Mate Webber's handling of his 36-footer in such adverse conditions.

These mishaps led to an extensive study of the fractures occurring in welded ships. This indicated that the problem was limited almost entirely to those of wartime construction, with the T-2 tankers especially susceptible to hull fracture. Their owners were required to have structural alterations made to increase longitudinal strength, and the American Bureau of Shipping collaborated with the Coast Guard to produce a manual on recommended loading and ballasting in these vessels. A year later, the commandant reported that there

The former salvage ship Acushnet. *The* Yocona *was her sister.*

had been no serious structural failures in T-2 tankers during the past winter season.

The third rescue of an aircraft crew by an ocean station vessel occurred on 2 March 1953, when a Navy P2V flying from Bermuda to the Azores lost power on one of its two engines after passing Station Echo. Radarmen on board the cutter *Coos Bay* guided the aircraft back to Echo, where its pilot skillfully ditched. The cutter's surfboat crew quickly hauled the fourteen men out of the rough water, and after picking up the boat, the 311-footer headed westward to rendezvous with her sister *Barataria,* which embarked the rescued men for transportation to New York. Commander John P. Latimer took the *Coos Bay* back to Station Echo to complete her patrol.[17]

Rotary-wing aircraft demonstrated their versatility on a number of occasions in 1953. A helicopter from the San Francisco Coast Guard Air Station patrolling off the Golden Gate on 22 February sighted a fishing boat breaking up in the surf and used its hoist to rescue six men from the water. In May, the Traverse City, Michigan, Air Station offered the services of an HO4S when an air and ground search failed to locate a two-year-old child lost in the woods near Menominee. It required only fifteen minutes to find the child and pick her up unharmed. Probably with this success in mind, state police asked for Coast Guard assistance when six convicts escaped from the Marquette state prison a day later. Two HO5S helicopters maintained a circular patrol around the area, and when the convicts were recaptured, they blamed the helicopters, which had made it impossible for them to travel by day. In mid-September, the 6,000-ton ore carrier *Maryland* grounded off Marquette during a rainstorm, and despite weather so turbulent that the efforts of both pilot and copilot were required to steady the helicopter, the *Maryland*'s twelve crew members were taken off safely in an unusual operation combining helicopter and breeches buoy.[18]

Fixed-wing aircraft continued to have an important role as well, not only in normal search-and-rescue operations, but in assisting "numerous" transoceanic airplanes, military as well as commercial, which reported navigational difficulties or engine problems. Directed to intercept positions by radar and very high frequency direction finders, Coast Guard multi-engine aircraft escorted those in trouble to safety, or in the event the airplane went down, summoned surface vessels in the vicinity to the spot and guided them to survivors in the water. While the Coast Guard aviators could not, of course, provide in-flight repair service or anything of that sort to keep another airplane flying, the mere presence of an aerial escort helped to reassure passengers and flight crews alike.[19]

Cutter sailors, however, sometimes had to make repairs to ships at sea. When the American fishing boat *Jeanne M.* reported that she was foundering off the Campeche Bank in the Gulf of Mexico in July 1953, the elderly 125-footer *Cartigan* proceeded to her assistance. Using a portable pump and buckets, the Coast Guardsmen freed the fishing boat of water and then patched her so effectively that her master decided to continue fishing rather than heading for port! Two months later, the *Yakutat* left Ocean Station Delta to assist the Spanish freighter *Marte,* which was drifting 750 miles southeast of Argentia with a hole in her side at the waterline. Boarding the disabled steamer, the cutter's repair and salvage party erected a temporary concrete bulkhead to control the flooding and then pumped her out, after which the *Marte* was able to make St. John's at slow speed.[20]

Cutters, of course, had to be prepared to tow vessels when necessary, which continued to concern commercial tugboat operators. The Coast Guard's policy in this regard was restated in 1954: Its vessels would not compete with commercial tugs, but if none was available or if the cutter commanding officer thought the tug incapable of handling the disabled ship or if he considered the towage charge unreasonable, the cutter would tow the vessel to the nearest port at which emergency repairs could be made. Should commercial towage be available therein, the cutter would merely tow her charge to a safe anchorage. Private enterprise, however, could not be relied on in "low order" cases; therefore, the Coast Guard could not wait until a vessel was in extreme jeopardy before intervening.[21]

The degree of responsibility assumed by the Coast Guard when a cutter took a vessel in tow was also a matter of concern. Thus, while the *Yocona* was towing the fishing vessel *Kalle P.* after she had run out of fuel off the Pacific coast, the boat sprang a leak and sank. Her owner filed suit, charging that the *Kalle P.*'s loss was attributable to the cutter's excessive speed while towing. The judge dismissed the suit in May 1953, observing that the owner had no case—he had put himself and his boat in a perilous position voluntarily by failing to assure that she had sufficient fuel before sailing and by neglecting to keep track of her position. Moreover, he had not requested that the *Yocona* stop when the *Kalle P.* began to leak, although she was equipped with radio telephone. The judge cited the opinion of a Massachusetts jurist to support his decision: "There is a statutory duty which requires the Coast Guard to risk their lives and government equipment in order to assist people that are in difficulty, but there is no duty created toward the person who is in the difficulty. Under the law there can be no liability without a duty, and the statute, by indicating that the Coast Guard should risk its personnel and government equipment in order to help people out, does not create any duty."[22] Nonetheless, Coast Guardsmen could ill afford to ignore the legal opinion that "salvors are responsible for the reasonable care of the property which they take in charge."[23]

There was no cause for complaint when the SS *Aristotelis* ran out of fuel in the North Pacific Ocean late in January 1954. The *Yocona* and the Canadian *Salvage Chief* responded to her call for assistance, the former towing the freighter to a rendezvous with the salvage vessel. Despite heavy seas, the tow was transferred without incident. The cutter remained in company in case further assistance should be required, which it was when the *Salvage Chief*'s port main engine broke down. At her master's request, the *Yocona* put a hawser on board and towed salvor and salved into Victoria, B.C.

Not least of the Coast Guard's postwar problems was that posed by the rapid increase in recreational boating. Reporting the deaths of nine people when a 12-foot outboard motorboat capsized on Hauser Dam Lake in Montana on 3 May 1954 and of eight more when an 18-footer turned over on Lake St. Clair, Michigan, two weeks later, Admiral O'Neill noted that while fatal accidents of this magnitude were unusual, "casualties involving outboard motorboats with the loss of one to five lives have been frequent."[24] Many of these were attributed solely to ignorance or carelessness, which the Coast Guard Auxiliary had been created to combat, but its membership numbered fewer than 13,000 during O'Neill's term as commandant, while more than 20,000,000 people were sailing in some 5,000,000 boats in American waters each year. The Auxiliary's efforts at conducting educational programs and inspecting small craft were invaluable—

and necessarily inadequate. To alleviate the problem without incurring additional expense, the Coast Guard "inspired" the American Boat and Yacht Council, incorporated as a nonprofit organization under New York law in 1954, for the purpose of instructing those owning or using boats in proper practices and standards for small craft operation and maintenance.[25]

Two Coast Guard cutters were lost to the service during this period. In March 1950, the *Mocoma* went to the assistance of the tanker *Fort Mims,* which had run aground near Fowey Rocks, south of Miami. After helping to refloat the tanker, the cutter herself went aground, sustaining such damage that she had to be towed back to Miami by the 165-foot *Ariadne.* The *Mocoma* was later towed to the Coast Guard Yard, where her damage was assessed at $60,000, more than the old Lake-class vessel was thought to be worth. Her crew was ordered to prepare the laid-up 255-foot *Androscoggin* for service, and upon recommissioning, she took the *Mocoma*'s place at Miami. Meanwhile, the *Tampa* was sent from Mobile to join the *Acushnet* and the *Evergreen* on ice patrol in the *Mocoma*'s stead, and en route to Argentia, this last of the Lake-class cutters sprang a leak and had to put in at New York for emergency repair. The damaged *Mocoma* failed to attract a reasonable offer when advertised for sale, so after a year at Curtis Bay she was redesignated a Coast Guard barge and towed to permanent moorings at Houston, Texas, where a port security unit was quartered on board.[26] She was sold for scrap in 1955, by which time the *Tampa* too had been decommissioned.

While the cause of the *Mocoma* stranding is not apparent—neither her log nor the investigation report can be located—the grounding of the *Iroquois* four years later was attributable to pilot error and the poor judgment of her commanding officer. The cutter approached Midway Island during the morning of 29 June 1954 while on passage to Ocean Station Victor. Weather and visibility were excellent, but the commanding officer, who had assumed command just before leaving Honolulu five days earlier, was unfamiliar both with 255-foot cutters and Pacific Ocean atolls. He requested a pilot, whereupon a Navy chief boatswain came on board and took the conn. The *Iroquois* stood northward into the entrance channel at standard speed, and although the prevailing wind and current set to the westward, her log reads: "Pilot gave command left 5° rudder, followed 5 seconds later by left 10° rudder followed immediately by left 15° rudder, then by engine back full . . ."[27] The cutter's turbo-electric plant responded promptly, but the 1,900-ton ship steaming at 13.5 knots could not be stopped quickly—the *Iroquois* crunched onto the coral reef to the left of the channel. There she stayed until the afternoon of 1 July, pounding heavily when the swell increased, grinding a hole in the coral and sustaining serious structural damage. The cutter was finally refloated by the combined efforts of a Navy salvage ship, a district tug, and her own capstan heaving around on beach gear.

This occurrence seems intelligible only if the *Iroquois* had swung suddenly to the right, causing the pilot to order left rudder, although the log entry gives no indication that this occurred. In any event, it is likely that his lack of familiarity with *Owasco*-class cutters led to the grounding. This was the more unfortunate because the *Iroquois* did not actually need a pilot. The lieutenant commander who had commanded the ship temporarily was still on board to assist with exercises carried out while she was en route to Midway. This officer was thoroughly acquainted with 255-foot cutters and North Pacific atolls and fully competent to have taken the *Iroquois* into Midway Harbor. But the new commanding officer elected to utilize a pilot— who put his ship on the reef, ending her career and providing Waikiki bars the opportunity to introduce a drink called "*Iroquois* on the rocks"![28]

On receiving news of the *Iroquois* grounding, the *Winnebago* left San Francisco to take her sister's place on Ocean Station Victor, and another 255-footer, the *Chautauqua*, which was on her way from the Pacific coast to the Coast Guard Yard for inactivation, was ordered to Honolulu in her stead. The *Yocona* towed the badly damaged cutter to the Panama Canal, whence the *Cherokee* brought her to Curtis Bay. The *Iroquois* remained at the Yard until her sale in 1965.

It is interesting to note that cutters to replace the damaged *Mocoma* and *Iroquois* were available almost immediately, indicating a plenitude of vessels that was quite unusual for the Coast Guard. The service also had surplus shore stations when Admiral O'Neill became commandant in 1950. As always, local populations opposed the closing of light and lifeboat stations in their vicinities, perhaps somewhat less adamantly than in the past because the old practice of recruiting station personnel locally had been ended by World War II. Nonetheless, their opposition was often echoed by senators and congressmen, some of whom threatened to retaliate when it came to voting appropriations for the Coast Guard were their wishes not heeded.[29] But technological developments, especially the increasing use of loran and helicopters, had obviously made some stations redundant, as the Bureau of the Budget pointed out, and its opinions were of more immediate importance.[30] Admiral Farley had appointed Rear Admiral Joseph Greenspun to head the Board of Survey of Lifeboat Stations, Light Stations, and Lightships in 1949, and the board undertook a study of these installations in each of the Coast Guard districts "to recommend specific units which could be disestablished in the interest of economy without increasing maritime hazards."[31] As a result, the number of lifeboat stations fell to 144 by mid-1954, twenty-six fewer than four years earlier; there were 311 manned light stations as compared with 429 in 1950— discontinuing a light station had smaller economic impact on its locale—and one lightship had been removed, leaving thirty-six of these vessels. The number of cutters and patrol boats, on the other hand, had increased from 227 to 257, due mainly to the addition of twenty-four patrol boats for duties in connection with port security.[32]

Admiral Farley had also begun a reorganization of Coast Guard Headquarters that was completed under his successor. Put into effect in May 1951, this included a "comptroller-type system" for supervising and coordinating financial matters and a new statistical division to centralize reports, forms, and record-keeping. The positions of chief of staff and deputy chief of staff were created; these officers became responsible "for general administration, for the initiation, development, and review of basic policies and programs, and for functioning as management advisers to the Commandant." Perhaps to minimize the further expansion of Headquarters personnel, Rear Admiral Richmond, the assistant commandant, assumed the additional duties of chief of staff, a number of which he had had before the reorganization.[33]

Merlin O'Neill's term as commandant ended in 1954, and although he would not reach the statutory retirement age until 1960, he elected to retire on 1 June 1954. Under his leadership, the Coast Guard had attained its highest peacetime strength to that time— 29,154 military personnel and 4,963 civilian employees. Although the problems that had confronted him during the past four years may seem to have been relatively minor when compared with those his predecessors had had to face, Vice Admiral O'Neill had overseen the unexpected expansion of his service's personnel, equipment, and responsibilities during the Korean War and their diminution thereafter in competent fashion. The Coast Guard continued to be fortunate in the caliber of its commandants.

CHAPTER SEVENTEEN

THE RICHMOND YEARS, 1954–62

Merlin O'Neill had been the obvious choice to succeed Admiral Farley in 1950; Alfred Carroll Richmond was an even more obvious successor to Vice Admiral O'Neill four years later. Since academy days, members of the class of 1924, an unusually close group, had looked to him as their leader, and his selection to become the Coast Guard's first legal specialist had enhanced that position. Richmond's service organizing the merchant marine hearings and heading the one in London, the most important of those abroad, had merited praise, and he had had collateral duty as senior Coast Guard officer on the staff of the commander, U.S. Naval Forces in Europe. Assigned to Headquarters in May 1945, he held a number of positions, most notably those of chief of the budgets and requirements division and chairman of the Ebasco Study steering committee. In the former capacity, he had to present the Coast Guard's annual budgets to congressional committees and soon gained a reputation as an excellent witness.[1] Some may have noted that Richmond had had only eight years of sea duty—less than any of his predecessors—but he had proved his competence in command of the Maritime Commission training ship *American Sailor* and the big cutter *Haida*.

Richmond's place as assistant commandant was taken by his classmate James A. Hirshfield, who had received the Navy Cross for commanding the *Campbell* in her fight with the *U-606,* and Rear Admiral Cowart, who had been decorated for his service as the *Campbell*'s engineering officer on that occasion, remained as engineer in chief.

Within a few weeks after becoming commandant, Vice Admiral Richmond was startled to learn that President Dwight D. Eisenhower had suggested to the secretary of commerce that the Merchant Marine and Coast Guard academies be merged in the interest of economy. This proposal led Richmond to appoint a committee to study its feasibility. This group considered two possibilities—separate courses of instruction in one location and a completely integrated curriculum for both Coast Guard and merchant marine cadets. Predictably, it found neither attractive, citing the problems of merging

Alfred Carroll Richmond, commandant, 1954–62.

civil and military institutions, the dissimilar purposes of the Coast Guard and the merchant service and hence of their academies, the budgetary difficulties that would result from a single academy serving two departments' agencies, the probable opposition of the New York or the Connecticut congressional delegation should either the King's Point or the New London institution be closed, and the potential difficulty of obtaining candidates for admission to a combined academy. The report concluded:

> Summarizing, then, it is strongly held that consolidation of the U.S. Coast Guard Academy and the U.S. Merchant Marine Academy in any form and to any extent whatsoever would be most impractical and undesirable; could not be expected to yield economies of any significant order; and would most certainly result in a substantial lowering of the efficiency and effectiveness now separately obtaining at the two Academies as presently constituted.[2]

Although Eisenhower's suggestion was apparently prompted by the financial plight of the Merchant Marine Academy, which had had its appropriations reduced repeatedly, the commandant could hardly have forgotten that in 1949 the Hoover Commission's proposals for reorganization of the executive branch of the government had included a recommendation that the Coast Guard be transferred from the Treasury Department to the Department of Commerce. The Coast Guard's response on that occasion had been written by the chief of its planning and control staff, Captain A. C. Richmond, who "strongly recommend[ed] against the transfer to the Commerce Department on the grounds that there [was] no clear showing of any gain in economy or efficiency."[3] In 1953, former President Herbert C. Hoover had been appointed to head a second committee to study matters of organization and policy, and Richmond probably sensed that the proposal for merger of the academies was a first step toward transfer of the Coast Guard itself.

Whatever the president's motive may have been, the objections raised by the Coast Guard committee were clearly valid, and there was no change in the Academy's situation. The Coast Guard's case for retaining the Academy, however, might have been weakened considerably had there been an inquiry into the service's officer procurement practices, for only eighty-eight cadets had become officers on graduation from the Academy in May 1954—and that was the highest number for the decade!—while ten merchant marine officers and 247 graduates of the Officer Candidate School at the Academy were commissioned during the fiscal year. The procurement of merchant marine officers had begun in 1949 as the result of Admiral Farley's commitment to a congressional committee that half of the Coast Guard's marine inspection officers would have merchant service experience, and the Officer Candidate School had been established in 1951 to give selected university graduates and Coast

Guard warrant and enlisted men four months of indoctrination be- *The 311-foot cutter* Coos
fore they became officers. Owing to the resignation or retirement of Bay *on ocean station.*
regular officers and the release to inactive status of reserve officers,
the number commissioned through the Officer Candidate School far
outnumbered the Academy graduates throughout the decade, ranging from 187 in 1955 to 377 in 1959. Thus, the Coast Guard could
hardly claim that its Academy was the essential source of officers,
although as might be expected, most of those reaching high rank
continued to be Academy graduates.[4]

In 1956, the president's Air Coordinating Committee promulgated the National Search and Rescue Plan, which was intended to
fix responsibility for the coordination of search-and-rescue activities
in areas of the United States and contiguous thereto. The Coast Guard
was already required "to develop, establish, maintain, and operate
. . . rescue facilities to promote safety on the navigable waters of the
United States and on and over the high seas";[5] therefore, it logically
became responsible for coordinating search-and-rescue operations
in the "Maritime Region," which included navigable inland waters,
while the U.S. Air Force's Air Rescue Service was made coordinator
of such activities in the "Continental Inland Region." The armed
forces, on the other hand, would continue to be responsible for
search and rescue in support of their own activities, making their
equipment and facilities available to meet civil needs as well, whenever they could do so without interfering with military missions.[6]
Since this only confirmed the Coast Guard's traditional role, it had
little immediate effect, although it helped to justify further development of search-and-rescue techniques.

Several rescues by ocean station vessels during this period demonstrated the effectiveness of established procedures. The first oc-

297

curred on Station Echo on 26 January 1955. The *Coos Bay*, now under Commander William S. Vaughn, had completed a week's refresher course in aircraft assistance with the Coast Guard Air Detachment, Bermuda, before sailing to Echo, so her crew was well prepared when a MATS C-54 had to ditch because of fuel and oil leaks. With a southwest wind blowing at 40 knots and 13-foot seas, the situation was hardly promising, especially since it would soon be dark. The aircraft, flying on only two of its four engines, was barely able to maintain flight speed, so it was necessary for the cutter to steam into the heavy seas at flank speed, taking green water over her bow and an occasional sea over her bridge—small wonder that a later commanding officer noted that the *Coos Bay*'s bottom plating resembled a washboard.[7] As ship and aircraft closed, the cutter's air control officer advised a crosswind ditching to parallel the swells, and the *Coos Bay* laid a line of electric float lights to mark the landing path, thereafter taking a station to windward with boats lowered to main deck level, scrambler nets over the side, and rubber-suited swimmers ready. When her radar indicated that the C-54 was 5 miles away, the cutter's 5-inch gun and mortars fired starshells and flares at maximum elevation. Heading for these illuminants, Captain Paul S. Evans in the C-54 soon sighted the float lights and made his final approach into the wind, turning to parallel the swells just before touching down very gently. Four crew members and the one passenger got away in a rubber raft, but the three men forward could not get their raft through the small hatch and so climbed atop the airplane to await rescue. The *Coos Bay*'s searchlights provided illumination as her motor surfboat approached the C-54; with heavy seas preventing the boat from coming alongside, the three aviators were directed to slide back to the tail and jump into the water. They were picked up quickly, and then the five men were removed from the raft. All were on board the *Coos Bay* in little more than a half-hour after ditching.[8] With the exception of the *Bermuda Sky Queen*, this was the most difficult air crew rescue by an ocean station vessel, and thanks to the skill of all concerned, it was carried out in exemplary fashion.

By comparison, the rescue of the twenty-one passengers and crew members of a Navy P5M that ran out of fuel and came down 100 miles from Bermuda on 17 February 1956 was simplicity itself. The *Coos Bay*'s sister *Casco*, on standby status before going to Echo, took them on board and then towed the flying boat to the Naval Air Station, Bermuda.

Rescues of military aircraft passengers and crews attracted little attention, in part because of the small numbers of people involved. When a commercial air liner went down, however, it was widely publicized. The second such ditching occurred in the Pacific Ocean, midway between Honolulu and San Francisco, on 16 October 1956. The *Pontchartrain* had spent an uneventful two weeks on Ocean Station November when a Pan American Clipper, Flight 943, about

38 miles from the cutter, reported a runaway engine. A few minutes later the airplane, which was on the last leg of a transpacific flight with twenty-four passengers and a seven-member flight crew, notified the *Pontchartrain* that another engine was out and it would have to ditch. Commander William K. Earle called his men to rescue stations and informed them of the situation, ordering float lights laid on the ditching heading while the motor whaleboat was manned and the ship's searchlights and mortar flares provided illumination. After some experimentation, Pilot Richard Ogg found that the clipper's altitude could be maintained by use of maximum power on the two remaining engines—thus, it could wait until daylight to come down. During the next five hours, the airplane circled November while Ogg and Earle discussed its evacuation plan, going over every possible contingency, and the *Pontchartrain*'s men shifted her motor gig outboard of the pulling boat normally rigged out so that two power boats would be available immediately.

It was fully light by 7 A.M., but Ogg decided not to ditch until his fuel was virtually exhausted. Notified that the airplane would come down at 8:25, the *Pontchartrain* laid a 2-mile line of foam to mark the ditching path, but before she could reach her desired position and heading, the clipper made its final approach, bouncing once and then plunging into a low swell with tail breaking off and nose smashed. As the cutter came up at full speed, backing down close aboard and putting her boats in the water, members of the flight crew climbed

The Pontchartrain. *One of her young passengers complained, with some reason, that "this hotel moves around too much."*

299

onto the wing to launch liferafts and help passengers into them. The motor whaleboat took fifteen people from the airplane, after which one of the gig crew inspected its interior to ensure that no one remained. The gig then picked up the sixteen in the rafts, returning to the *Pontchartrain* as the clipper sank, twenty minutes after ditching. All were got on board without difficulty, and the hospital corpsman, joined by a doctor who had been a passenger, treated the five with minor cuts and bruises. Meanwhile, those in the two boats examined the debris left floating when the airplane sank and retrieved a considerable amount of registered mail, luggage, and other things of value.[9]

The 255-foot cutter lacked adequate quarters for so many guests, a number of whom were women and children, so the commander of the Coast Guard's Western Area ordered her to San Francisco, leaving Station November temporarily unattended. Off the Golden Gate, the *Pontchartrain* met the *Gresham*, which transferred thirty-one suitcases, each bearing the name of a passenger or flight crew member and containing clothing purchased by Pan American Airways in accordance with information radioed by the cutter. Thus, those rescued were properly garbed when they went ashore. Nor was the experience of the *Bermuda Sky Queen* survivors with representatives of the press repeated. No reporters were permitted to board the *Pontchartrain* as she stood into San Francisco Bay, and when the thirty-one left the cutter after she had been moored, they went immediately to a section of the pier reserved for relatives and friends, with whom they talked before facing the press and television cameras.[10]

The success of this operation owed much to the fact that on taking command of the *Pontchartrain* two months earlier, Commander Earle had requested refresher training to familiarize himself with his crew and with techniques introduced since he had left the 311-foot *Matagorda,* which he had commanded on ocean station duty in the Atlantic from 1950 to 1952. And the clipper crew had gone through ditching drill at the Coast Guard Air Station, Alameda, less than a week before, with special emphasis on getting passengers out of a partially submerged airplane fuselage.[11] The rescue operation had been conducted almost flawlessly, as indeed it should have been, considering the favorable wind and sea conditions and the time available for preparation.

Seven months later, an Air Force fighter en route to Hawaii ran short of fuel and returned to Ocean Station November, where the pilot and the navigator bailed out. The 255-foot *Wachusett* picked the first up quickly and then a Northwest airliner directed her to the navigator, who was also rescued. On 8 November 1957, a Pan American Clipper flying from San Francisco to Honolulu with forty-four persons on board, informed the *Minnetonka,* another of the 255-foot cutters on Ocean Station November, that it was in trouble. Nothing further was heard from the airplane, and an eight-day search involving 131 aircraft and thirty-eight surface vessels under the general direction of the Coast Guard's Central Pacific Search and Rescue Coordinator resulted only in the recovery of nineteen bodies from a position 60 miles north of the clipper's track.[12]

Ocean station vessels assisted ships as well as aircraft when necessary; indeed, after 1957 surface vessels were the principal beneficiaries of their rescue activities. On the morning of 15 August 1955, for example, the *Mendota* on Ocean Station Delta received a relayed "Mayday"—the voice radio equivalent of SOS—from the Portuguese fishing schooner *Ilhavense Segundo* afire to the northward. As the cutter headed toward the reported position at flank speed, occasionally rolling her lee rail under in the rough sea, her radiomen queried other Portuguese fishing vessels in the vicinity as to the schooner's whereabouts and condition. The replies, which left much to be desired in the way of clarity because of the lack of a common language, seemed to indicate that her men had taken to their dories and that the schooner had sunk. With 12-foot seas running, the chances of locating the small boats seemed poor until a Coast Guard aircraft reached the scene from Argentia. Almost an hour later, it sighted a three-masted schooner burning and thirteen dories clustered nearby. Guided by her radarmen, the *Mendota* headed for the airplane, which was orbiting above the dories, and sighted them fifteen minutes after sunset. Steaming up to windward, the 255-footer rigged scrambler nets on her lee bow and amidships and stopped as the Portuguese fishermen pulled their dories alongside, two at a time. Rubber-suited swimmers stationed on either side of each net assisted those who required it, and bowlines were dropped for men who were injured or completely exhausted. Although the cutter rolled heavily as her bow fell away from the wind and she took the seas on her quarter, only ten minutes were required to get the forty-six men and one dog on board. Thereafter, the *Mendota* attempted to extinguish the fire in the *Ilhavense Segundo* by holding her bow against the schooner's quarter and playing streams from her fire hoses on the blaze. The fire aft was put out after a time, but another flared up under the well deck, which could not be reached because of the danger that the schooner's masts would fall. Thus, the cutter had to back away, and the *Ilhavense Segundo* disappeared from her radar screen early the next morning. Two days after, the 311-footer *Cook Inlet* took the fishermen and the dog on board for transportation to Boston and the *Mendota* continued her patrol.[13]

On 30 October 1956, the *Chincoteague* on Ocean Station Delta picked up a distress signal from the West German freighter *Helga Bolten* 150 miles to the northwest, which was feared to be foundering after heavy seas stove in her forward hatches. The cutter relayed the signal, and when no other vessel responded, Commander Raymond G. Miller elected to leave the station to assist the *Bolten.* As the 311-footer slammed into 25-foot seas, the Cunard liner *Mauretania* radioed that she had the freighter in sight, and her amended position report enabled the *Chincoteague* to reach the *Bolten* in twelve hours, by which time the wind had increased to a full gale. Lowering a boat was out of the question, so the cutter's men prepared two fifteen-man rubber rafts while Commander Miller maneuvered her close aboard the distressed vessel. Five times the *Chincoteague*'s line-throwing gun shot a projectile toward the freighter, and each time the gale carried it wide of its mark. The cutter's equipment included six of these projectiles and their shot lines—the sixth shot passed directly over the *Bolten,* whose men lost no time in hauling a heavier line and the rafts to their ship. All thirty-three of the German seamen crowded onto the rafts; when they were brought alongside the cutter, her men descended the scrambler nets to help them on board.

The *Helga Bolten* did not sink, however, and when the gale moderated the next day, the *Chincoteague* lowered a boat to put the master and chief engineer back on board. Salvage tugs reached the scene, and after six days of effort the *Bolten* was taken in tow for the Azores while the *Chincoteague* brought the German crew to Norfolk, her passage prolonged by orders to join the search for survivors of a Navy P5M that had crashed.[14]

Almost a year later, the West German sail-training bark *Pamir,* with a crew of ninety including fifty-four naval cadets, foundered in the turbulent seas on the periphery of a hurricane 500 miles west of the Azores. The *Absecon,* another of the ex-seaplane tenders, left Station Delta on receiving the distress signal and directed a week-long search-and-rescue operation by sixty merchant vessels from thirteen nations and Portuguese and American aircraft. The *Absecon* and another ship picked up six survivors.

On occasion, cutters on ocean station had to request assistance themselves. When an epidemic of mumps developed suddenly on board the *Bibb* on Station Bravo in March 1955, a PB-1G of the Coast Guard Air Detachment, Argentia, flew medical supplies to the cutter. It was typical Bravo weather—a 400-foot ceiling and a 40-knot wind blowing snow that limited visibility to $1/8$ mile, but the *Bibb*'s radar-men conned the aircraft to the proper position, where five containers were parachuted; four were recovered, and the cutter's Public Health Service surgeon later reported that their contents had been invaluable in controlling the outbreak. With thirty-four men stricken, the *Bibb* was ordered to Argentia whence the sick men were flown to Boston for treatment. Meanwhile, the *Spencer* patrolled Bravo until the *Campbell* could be sent from Bermuda to replace her sister. Similarly, the *Casco* had to relieve the *Escanaba* on Ocean Station Delta in October 1957 because more than half the latter's crew were suffering from Asian flu. Their recovery was more rapid, however, and the 255-foot cutter returned to Delta a week later.[15]

Smaller cutters had a part in distress cases as well, among them the *Yocona,* which began 1955 by getting a hawser on board a disabled tug off the Columbia River mouth despite a full gale and heavy seas. For two days, she steamed seaward, keeping the tug and the barge it had in tow from destruction on the rugged Oregon coast. In mid-November, the 213-foot cutter left Astoria to assist the tuna clipper *Ocean Pride,* reported leaking in stormy seas 50 miles west of Cape Lookout. By the time the *Yocona* reached her, the fishing vessel was awash. With winds gusting to 70 knots and 30-foot seas, neither boats nor rafts could be used, so the cutter was eased alongside, and despite the violent motions of both vessels, all thirteen men jumped to the *Yocona's* low fantail from the doomed *Ocean Pride,* which sank thirty minutes later.

As the *Fort Mercer* rescue had shown earlier, an ex-salvage ship could risk occasional contact with another vessel under such circumstances, but a relatively fragile 165-footer could hardly be expected to do so. Almost a year later, however, the *Aurora* was towing a disabled shrimp trawler off the Georgia coast. When the towline parted in seas too high to permit the use of a small boat, the *Aurora* worked in close enough for the two-man crew to jump on board and then stood by until the gale abated, when she took the trawler in tow once more.[16]

Just before midnight on 25 July 1956, the Swedish liner *Stockholm,* steaming eastward from New York in a dense fog, collided with the much larger Italian *Andrea Doria* about 55 miles south of Nantucket Island and 205 miles from New York. When news of the disaster reached the Coast Guard Eastern Area commander some time later, he ordered the cutters *Campbell* and *Yakutat* of the Cadet Practice Squadron, the New York-based *Tamaroa,* and the 180-foot buoy tenders *Evergreen* and *Hornbeam* at Boston to proceed to the damaged vessels' assistance. Fog kept Coast Guard aircraft grounded at Brooklyn, so the area commander requested that the Quonset Point, Rhode Island, Naval Air Station send an airplane. More than an hour later, the *Andrea Doria,* which had listed heavily before most of her boats could be lowered, radioed that she needed medical assistance and lifeboats for more than 1,500 passengers and crew members. The *Stockholm* was in sight, but her bow was crushed and her forward hold flooded, so her master declined to send boats to the Italian until he could be sure that the 750 people for whom he was responsible would not need them. Nearby vessels changed course to assist, and soon after the first, the American SS *Cape Ann,* appeared, the *Stockholm's* twelve boats were sent to the *Doria.* Additional Coast Guard cutters got under way from Boston and Portland, Maine, in the event that salvage should be feasible; meanwhile, other ships, among them the French liner *Ile de France,* the *Private William H. Thomas* of the U.S. Military Sea Transport Service (MSTS), and the USS *Edward H. Allen,* a DE, came up and lowered their boats. Some eight hours after the collision, the *Ile de France* reported that all *Andrea Doria* survivors had been picked up—the master and eleven crew members remained on board the sinking ship—and that she was heading for New York with 760 of them. Others departed as well, the *Cape Ann* with 129, and the *Thomas* with 156, while the *E. H. Allen* stood by the *Andrea Doria,* from which she took the master and seamen when they abandoned ship—the DE rescued a total of seventy-six. The *Stockholm,* with 533 survivors on board and escorted by the *Tamaroa* and the *Owasco,* made her slow way back to New York. The *Andrea Doria* sank ten hours after the collision; forty-seven were lost in her, and five crewmen died in the *Stockholm.*[17]

Owing to the distance, none of the ten Coast Guard cutters ordered to assist reached the disaster scene in time to take part in the rescue work, although they made the final search for survivors, marked the place where the *Andrea Doria* sank, and destroyed flotsam that might have been hazardous for shipping, while Coast Guard and Air Force helicopters removed five seriously injured survivors from the *Stockholm* before she arrived in New York. Since neither liner was an American-flag vessel, the Coast Guard had no responsibility for investigating the collision. Yet a service concerned with maritime safety obviously had to reevaluate the standards for watertight integrity, ballasting, and stability set by the 1948 International Convention on the Safety of Life at Sea in view of the fact that the *Andrea Doria,* built in 1953 with eleven watertight compartments, any two of which supposedly could be flooded without affecting her stability, had listed heavily—fatally—when only one compartment filled. And Congressman Bonner's committee that investigated the collision recommended that the deck officer examinations administered by the Coast Guard emphasize the interpretation of data provided by radar.

By no means all rescue activity had to do with maritime disaster. Despite extensive flood-control programs in various parts of the United States, flooding occurred quite frequently in low areas. Thus, the Coast Guard joined other federal and state agencies to assist flood victims in the upper Middle West in 1951 and 1952 and in western Oregon in 1953 and 1954. When flood waters inundated river valleys in Connecticut and Massachusetts in August and October 1955, Coast Guard units rescued more than 300 people and removed 1,000 others from endangered areas. But these were relatively minor occurrences compared to the California floods of late 1955. Just before Christmas, 100-mile gales brought unprecedented torrents of rain to the northern part of the state, swelling rivers over their banks and breaking levees. Tens of thousands of residents were forced to leave their homes, thousands of which were destroyed, and about 100 people died in the flood waters. Coast Guard units involved in the rescue activities included six aircraft, twenty-one cutters and boats, and twenty-nine vehicles, while the on-scene commander coordinated the operations of twenty-one aircraft, mostly helicopters, of the other armed services.

The Yuba City-Marysville area, where the Yuba flows into the Feather River, was one of those worst stricken. It was inundated when a dam broke during the night of 23 December, and a Coast Guard HO4S helicopter piloted by Lieutenant Henry J. Pfeiffer with Petty Officer Joseph Accamo as hoist operator, was the first rescue unit to arrive. Accamo began hoisting flood victims into the helicopter at 4:35 A.M., and for the next twelve hours, the HO4S, flown alternately by Pfeiffer and Lieutenant Commander George F. Thometz, Jr., with Victor Roulund relieving Accamo periodically, shuttled between the disaster area and the nearest airport, ferrying a total of 138 people to safety.

But mere numbers are inadequate to describe this rescue operation. The first fifty-eight were picked up while the helicopter hovered in the darkness amidst trees, chimneys, and television antennae, the only illumination being that provided by an Aldis lamp held by the hoist operator. In these conditions, Roulund was lowered to a trailer into which he had to chop his way to free a paralyzed woman. While he was so engaged, Pfeiffer descried four people on a nearby roof and picked them up before returning to retrieve the petty officer and the woman from the trailer. After flying that load to the airport, they detected another woman lying on a roof with a man standing beside her. A tall television antenna hampered the helicopter's approach; its main rotor blades had already cut a wire inadvertently without apparent damage, so Pfeiffer severed the guy wires and toppled the antenna with the rotor's downwash. He then eased the HO4S down so that Accamo and the woman's aged husband could lift her on a stretcher into the aircraft; a polio victim, she too was paralyzed. Learning later that a Navy helicopter lacked the means to recover a mother and her baby from the rubber raft onto which Coast Guard Lieutenant Charles R. Leisy had placed them, Pfeiffer located the raft and Accamo lowered the basket. Leisy lifted the unconscious woman into it, but there was no time to remove her from the basket after it had been hoisted on board. The pilot descended until the helicopter's wheels were immersed, enabling Leisy to hand the baby to Accamo before clambering into the aircraft. On the way back to the airport, they picked up a man who was nearly frozen, standing neck-deep in the water. Thometz then took over and spotting a number of adults and children huddled in a cupola on the side of a building, he hovered within a few feet of a tall antenna while Roulund squeezed three women and eleven children into the helicopter, perhaps a record for an HO4S.

In all, Lieutenant Commander Thometz flew ten missions, rescuing sixty-six, while Lieutenant Pfeiffer picked up seventy-two in thirteen missions. As the commandant noted, theirs was truly an outstanding performance. They and their fellow Coast Guardsmen saved a total of 550 persons and 351 head of cattle, while personnel of the other services rescued about 1,000, mainly with helicopters.[18]

Meanwhile, the Coast Guard's non-emergency responsibilities continued, among them the Bering Sea and International Ice Patrols. Each year, the *Storis* from Kodiak or one of the Seattle-based 255-

The Storis *(left) and the* Spar, *as seen from the* Bramble. *Note the helicopters on the former's after deck. The weight suspended from the* Spar's *boom was moved from side to side to cause her to roll, facilitating her passage through the ice.*

footers—the *Klamath, Wachusett,* and *Winona*—provided legal, medical, and dental services to the inhabitants of Alaska's northwest coast and carried supplies to light stations and to installations operated in the region by other governmental agencies. Cruising from 6,000 to 12,000 miles in the course of a four-month patrol, these cutters also protected seal herds and other wildlife from poachers and collected oceanographic, hydrographic, and meteorological information.

During most of this period, so few icebergs presented a hazard to North Atlantic shipping that no surface ice patrol was necessary. The *Evergreen* made the customary oceanographic cruises, as she had each year since 1948, while several PB1Gs flew aerial reconnaissance patrols from Argentia. Although the 1957 ice season was as bad as any on record, the *Acushnet* was the only cutter assigned to ice patrol duty—the *Evergreen* relieved her as necessary for replenishment of fuel and supplies. In 1959, another severe ice season, the *Androscoggin* alternated with the *Acushnet* making surface patrols. Increasingly, however, aircraft bore a greater portion of the responsibility for the International Ice Patrol.

Establishment of the Distant Early Warning (DEW) line of radar stations and other military bases in the Canadian north occupied the

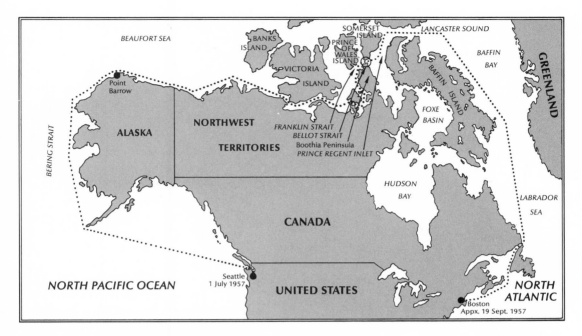

Navy's icebreakers and the Royal Canadian Navy's modified Wind-class *Labrador* after 1955, with the *Northwind* and the *Eastwind* assisting them regularly. Resupply of these stations was an MSTS responsibility, and since the unpredictable movements of pack ice in the vicinity of Point Barrow limited the time during which its vessels could be unloaded in the Beaufort Sea, an alternate departure route was desired. In July 1957, the *Storis* and the 180-foot buoy-tenders *Bramble* and *Spar,* both of which had hulls strengthened for ice navigation, sailed through the Bering Strait and into the Arctic Ocean as the Hydrographic Survey Unit of the MSTS Western Task Force, to determine the feasibility of the Northwest Passage as a route for cargo vessels. Their track skirted the coast of Canada's Northwest Territories for much of the distance, but after traversing Simpson Strait, the three ships had to turn northward through the Rae, James Ross, and Franklin straits to Bellot Strait, which HMCS *Labrador* had just surveyed. The Canadian icebreaker led them through this strait and into the ice-free waters of Prince Regent Inlet, whence they steamed through Lancaster Sound, Baffin Sound, and Davis Strait to the Labrador Sea. Off the coast of Newfoundland, the cutters were diverted to search for survivors of an Air Force B-47 that had been forced down, after which they replenished fuel and provisions at Argentia before proceeding to their home ports—the *Spar* to Bristol, Rhode Island, the *Bramble* to Miami, and the *Storis* to Kodiak by way of the Panama Canal, through which the two buoy-tenders had passed four months earlier.

Although it became apparent almost at the beginning of the cruise that the Northwest Passage could hardly be practical as a route for MSTS ships—strong winds and the resulting ice pressure had

The Northwest passage traversed by the Storis, Bramble, *and* Spar.

307

forced the *Spar* dangerously close aboard the *Storis* while they were icebound in Amundsen Gulf—the Coast Guard vessels' surveys and soundings helped to resolve some of the uncertainty about the 4,525 miles of semi-charted waters through which they sailed. The *Storis, Bramble,* and *Spar* were the first American ships to make the passage from the Pacific Ocean to the Atlantic to the northward of the North American continent, and the *Spar* was the first to circumnavigate the continent within one year.[19]

A number of important developments were under way during Vice Admiral Richmond's first term as commandant, among them greater use of non-Coast Guard resources in oceanic distress situations and Loran-C, a type providing increased range and accuracy over the original, which had been designated Loran-A. In part to ensure continuity to these, in part because of his rapport with administration and Congress, Richmond was appointed to a second four-year term in 1958. Rear Admiral Hirshfield continued as assistant commandant and chief of staff, while Rear Admiral Edward H. Thiele succeeded Rear Admiral Cowart as engineer in chief.

Richmond took the oath of office on 1 June 1958, and a month later the first of these developments was put into effect. Known as the Atlantic (or Automated) Merchant Vessel Reporting System (AMVER), it was an arrangement whereby domestic and foreign merchant ships routinely sent position reports, courses, and speeds to Coast Guard ocean station vessels and radio stations. These relayed the information to a ships' plot center in the New York Rescue Coordination Center, where it was stored in a special computer memory bank. When a request for assistance was received from a vessel in the AMVER area, the ships' plot center informed the rescue coordination center having control of the names and positions of ships in that vicinity and whether any possessed medical facilities. The rescue coordinator then directed those that could assist the distressed vessel most effectively to the scene, making it unnecessary to divert every ship within a large area.[20]

AMVER was, of course, a voluntary system, but it quickly attained popularity—during the first year of its operation, 3,993 merchant ships flying the flags of forty-six nations took part, and by 1962, 90 percent of all U.S.-flag vessels plying the North Atlantic and 65 percent of those using that ocean under foreign flags were participating. Initially, AMVER was used only in the North Atlantic area for which the Coast Guard was responsible under the National Search and Rescue Plan, but in 1963 it was extended to include the entire North Atlantic Ocean.

While AMVER was a means of providing assistance to ships experiencing any type of difficulty, it had obvious limitations in that merchant vessels generally were not equipped for rescue work in high winds and heavy seas, nor were most maneuverable enough to close a distressed ship in those conditions. Its role in providing medical care for ill or injured seamen, however, was especially important. Thus, in November 1961 a man fell into a hold of the SS *Conde de Fontanar,* suffering serious head injuries. Advised by AMVER, the rescue coordinator directed his ship to steam to a rendezvous with the SS *Jerusalem,* the nearest vessel with a doctor on board, and the physician determined that neurosurgery was required as quickly as possible. Not long afterward, an amphibian from the Coast Guard Air Detachment, Bermuda, landed alongside the *Jerusalem,* whence the injured man was flown to a hospital where surgery was performed. And in April 1964, the cutter on Ocean Station Charlie relayed a message from the MV *Margarita,* which reported one man dead and several others ill with similar symptoms. AMVER identified vessels in the vicinity that had doctors on board, and the *Margarita* closed the SS *France,* whose surgeon diagnosed their illness as typhoid fever. These and others who owe their lives to AMVER would probably agree with Admiral Willard J. Smith, who thought it "one of the most effective things the Coast Guard has done since the war" to assist merchant ships and those sailing in them.[21]

While the extension of AMVER to the Pacific Ocean occurred after Admiral Richmond's retirement, a system called Shipboard Air Sea Rescue Plan Alfa was instituted by the Coast Guard's Western Area commander on 1 December 1958. Intended to enable transoceanic aircraft to establish radio contact with the nearest surface vessels in times of need, it required knowledge of the positions, courses, and speeds of ships in the vicinity of the air routes between the United States and Hawaii as well as their radio capability and the type of radio watch each maintained. A ships' position plot established at the San Francisco Rescue Coordination Center satisfied this requirement, but arranging direct radio communication between aircraft and merchant vessel was more difficult because the former no longer carried radio operators, relying instead on voice radio, which many merchant ships did not have. The latter might receive voice messages, but they could respond only by keyed transmissions that could not be copied by the aircraft. The solution was to fit all ships and aircraft with radio equipment capable of utilizing 2182 kilocycles, the international voice radio distress frequency. This, of course, was beyond the Coast Guard's means; it could, however, encourage the installation of this equipment through seminars conducted for interested aircraft and shipowners and operators, while the Federal Communication Commission required that vessels licensed to use voice radio have the 2182 kc frequency. Pan American Airways complied first, and during the summer of 1958, United Air Lines and the MATS Western Air Force provided their airplanes flying across the Pacific with the necessary capability. On 10 December, two United aircraft and the SS *Matsonia* carried out a communications and a radio direction-finding "Homing" exercise, the first involving commercial aircraft and a merchant vessel.[22]

The implementation of Plan Alfa did not result in any dramatic ditchings alongside merchant ships. As Rear Admiral Russell E. Wood, the Western Area commander, pointed out, however: "Any ditching at sea is a hazardous and expensive operation. There is more probability of survival of passengers and crew and, incidentally, of saving a valuable aircraft if it touches down on an airport runway than on the smoothest of waters. The most vital decision in a pilot's life may be whether to ditch alongside an ocean station vessel or risk a run for the nearest airport. The possibility of rescue along the course to an airport runway is a vital consideration in hoping for the right decision."[23] Plan Alfa provided that possibility of rescue, but its importance was soon diminished markedly by increased use of jet-propelled commercial aircraft on transoceanic routes. These had a much lower incidence of engine problems than their propeller-driven counterparts, and their chances of ditching successfully in the event of engine failure were also much lower. Thus, neither ocean station vessel nor merchant ships could provide much assurance to them.

Other examples of international cooperation included the Intergovernmental Maritime Consultative Organization (IMCO), which was established under United Nations auspices in March 1958 and the 1960 Conference on Safety of Life at Sea. The former, of which Captain Robert T. Merrill had been an early advocate, had been proposed at a U.N. conference in 1948 for the purpose of facilitating the exchange of information pertaining to maritime matters and of bringing about agreements thereon. Ten years later, the last of the required twenty-one governments ratified the convention creating IMCO, and it began to function as a U.N. agency based in London. The Coast Guard, designated to represent the United States on this organization, undertook "to encourage adoption of the highest practicable standards for safety and efficiency of navigation" among its member nations, which numbered 106 by 1979.[24]

The 1960 conference was held at the suggestion of the British government, and on receiving the proposal from the British Embassy, the State Department turned to the Coast Guard, one of whose committees was then considering revised standards for watertight subdivision, ballasting, and stability of damaged vessels. This group developed American proposals relating to ship construction, while the commandant appointed other committees to draw up reports on lifesaving appliances, safety of navigation, nuclear power, radio, and load lines. The conference, to which Admiral Richmond led the U.S. delegation, approved broader application of the compartmentation requirement for passenger vessels and established more effective standards of fire prevention and protection for passenger and cargo ships alike. Recognizing the inflatable raft as an important lifesaving device, the delegates drew up rules for its use, and they made provision for the admission of nuclear-powered vessels to foreign ports.[25]

The Coast Guard's involvement with aids to navigation, which was recognized in 1960 when Admiral Richmond was chosen to preside at the sixth International Lighthouse Conference, was enhanced by the further development of electronic devices. A lower frequency type of loran had been tested during the waning days of World War II, and although the then-standard type later known as Loran-A had won approval for postwar use, experimentation with the former was continued with the support of Captain Loren E. Brunner and Commander Helmer S. Pearson of the electronics engineering division at Coast Guard Headquarters. The launching of the first man-made satellite, Russia's Sputnik, in October 1957 led to a demand for a long-range, highly accurate radio-navigation system for use with the satellites and missiles the United States was planning. There were three contenders—the Navy's Omega, Loran-C, and Britain's Decca. The first, operating on very low frequency, had a range of 5,000 miles and provided positions accurate to from 1 to 2 miles, compared to Loran-C's 1,200-mile range and 0.1-0.5 mile accuracy. Decca, the most accurate of the three, was limited to 100–150 miles at night and so was the first to be eliminated. When Navy technicians failed to improve Omega's accuracy significantly, Loran-C was chosen, and the Coast Guard was authorized to build transmitting stations as necessitated by the nation's military requirements. The first of the chains of Loran-C transmitting stations, that on the U.S. Atlantic coast, went into full service in mid-1962, and thereafter additional stations were established, until ten years later Loran-C chains provided service in strategic areas around the world.[26]

The commercial use of Loran-C was retarded by the complexity and expense of its receiver, so after the transmitter had been perfected, the electronics engineering division turned its attention to the development of a simpler, cheaper device, which it achieved some years later. Meanwhile, advocates of Loran-A argued successfully that that system was providing an essential service to merchant mariners, fishermen, and those flying light airplanes; thus the economy to be expected from discontinuing the older system could not be realized immediately.

The commandant's success in obtaining funding for Loran-C was due almost entirely to its military importance, for not least of the ironies of the time was the inability of this most accomplished and experienced negotiator with congressional committees to obtain adequate financial support for his service. The principal reason seems to have been the Eisenhower administration's effort to balance the federal budget, which George Humphrey, Treasury secretary during the president's first term, championed. While his successor, Robert B. Anderson, was more responsive to the Coast Guard's situation, the economic recession that began late in 1957 continued to limit funding to an extent. Thus, the service had to meet pressing material needs as they occurred, to the detriment of long-range planning.

Since the Korean War, the Coast Guard's aircraft had numbered between 125 and 128, mostly acquired from the Navy and the Air Force, with replacements requested as necessary. For fiscal 1958, however, Congress declined to authorize the acquisition of any aircraft at all in the absence of a comprehensive program for the systematic development of Coast Guard aviation. A committee of senior officers was even then working on such a proposal, an earlier plan drawn up by a similar group in 1951 having been shelved. The *Joint Report on the Requirements of Coast Guard Aviation* was submitted to Congress early in 1957 and after some revision, it was implemented a year later. Briefly, this document defined Coast Guard aviation's primary role as the support of search-and-rescue missions, specified the types of aircraft necessary for that purpose, and indicated the number of each type that should be acquired during each of the next six years. It established the service's aviation requirement at 195 aircraft, of which one-third should be helicopters, and provided for the ultimate reduction of the number of types from fourteen to six. These figures proved to be somewhat optimistic; in 1965, the Coast Guard had 152 aircraft, including fifty-six helicopters. By any standard, however, the *Joint Report on the Requirements of Coast Guard Aviation* was an important document.[27]

Budgeting a fixed sum for aircraft procurement had the unfortunate corollary of depriving the service's ships and shore installations of funds, which was even more unfortunate because vessels and stations of prewar and wartime construction were beginning to be in need of replacement or extensive repair. No new cutters were planned; if any were needed, they might be found in the Navy's reserve fleets, which provided two more of the 205-foot fleet tugs, the *Avoyel* and the *Chilula,* in 1956. Seeking to avert the block obsolescence that would inevitably occur in a few years, Assistant Secretary of the Treasury David W. Kendall suggested that long-range plans be drawn up for renovation of the cutter fleet and the stations. A committee thereupon began to consider the missions and condition of the cutters, completing its report in 1959.[28]

By that time, some of the smaller vessels had deteriorated to the extent that immediate action was necessary. Announcing a "structural restoration" program for the old 125-foot and 165-foot cutters, Admiral Richmond added that one ship of each class, the *Bonham* and the *Pandora,* had had to be stricken because of her condition. They were replaced by two of the Navy's auxiliary ocean tugs, 13-knot 143-footers of wartime construction that served the Coast Guard as the *Modoc* and the *Comanche* for the next twenty years.[29]

Kendall left the Treasury Department before the cutter report was finished, and it had no direct result. Nonetheless, some small buoy tenders for river service were added, and additional 95-foot patrol boats were planned to replace the surviving 83-footers. In these vessels, however, antisubmarine and surface weapons took precedence over more traditional Coast Guard capabilities, such as rescue and towing, so only fifteen more were built before the program was terminated in favor of 82-footers designed specifically for inshore patrol, rescue, and salvage work. Forty-one of these twin-screw steel-hulled boats entered service during the next few years, eleven of which could reach 22 knots with 1,600 brake horsepower diesels, while twenty-nine others had less powerful engines and were capable of 18 knots. Gas turbines with controllable-pitch propellers powered the *CG 82314;* she would evaluate this type of propulsion, which was gaining favor in some foreign navies. With eight-man crews, the 82-footers were more economical to operate than the 95-footers, which required fifteen men, and the smaller craft proved their ability in rough water, an early patrol report concluding, "These boats are well built and could probably weather almost anything."[30] The 82-footers received geographical "Point" names in 1964.

Meanwhile, the first postwar cutters were being designed. Intended to replace the aged 125- and 165-footers, these were to be capable of conducting search-and-rescue operations more than 500 miles offshore, with an endurance of 5,000 miles at 15 knots and a maximum sustained speed of 18 knots. Inclusion of a helicopter platform required a 200-foot waterline length, so the new vessels would be considerably larger than those they were to supersede. Contracts for the first two of thirty ships planned were let to Houston's Todd Shipyard in 1961; the *Reliance* and the *Diligence* were commissioned in 1964.[31]

The condition of the Coast Guard's lifeboat equipment also received consideration. Construction of 36-footers had continued after World War II, with the last of the fifty-eight postwar boats joining the service in 1956, by which time a number of the earlier units were more than twenty-five years old and in need of replacement. Before ordering more 36-footers, Headquarters sought the opinions of experienced lifeboat station personnel on Atlantic and Pacific coasts and on the Great Lakes. These criticized the Coast Guard's standard lifeboat for its difficulty of control while towing, its low speed, and the poor visibility from its steering station. None of these deficiencies could be remedied easily, so an alternative had to be found.

The two 52-footers of 1935 had achieved fine reputations, and two improved versions with steel hulls were built in 1957. A year later, "an initial record of spectacular rescues [had] proved the excellence of the design and construction of the new 52-foot motor lifeboat"[32]—but each cost nearly $250,000! Quite understandably, only two more were built.

Instead, an entirely new design was developed, following a study of the Coast Guard's requirements. This boat, a 44-footer, had little in common with its venerable predecessor except in its self-righting and self-bailing capabilities. Two diesel engines drove twin screws to provide a maximum speed of 15 knots; twin rudders with power-assisted steering gave admirable handling characteristics, even

313

One of the postwar 52-foot motor lifeboats heading into a breaker off Yaquina Bay, Oregon.

when towing because of the relocation of the towing bitts; and the raised steering station amidships afforded the helmsman excellent visibility. The hull was built of steel, with both transverse and longitudinal framing, enabling the boat to work in ice, and a double bottom forward offered additional protection against grounding. Provision of a fire and salvage pump powered by the port main engine enhanced the 44-footer's ability to assist damaged vessels, while a radio direction-finder, radar, and a depth sounder contributed to its safe navigation. Crew and passenger facilities were considerably improved as well.[33]

Extensive model testing preceded the construction of the first 44-footer at Curtis Bay in 1962, and after some modifications, the *CG 44300* was put through her paces at stations from Hatteras Inlet to Maine. Her final test came at Yaquina Bay, Oregon, which was noted for its heavy, breaking surf. "Boat performance was outstanding in all types of seas from large ground swells offshore to strong ebb chop, moderate breaking seas and large extremely dangerous seas on the bar and reefs."[34]

With this evaluation, the Coast Guard Yard was directed to undertake the construction of twenty-five 44-foot motor lifeboats, each of which would take six months to build and cost $115,000. In 1980, when 105 were in service, the 44-footer was described as "probably the finest rescue boat in the world."[35]

Recreational boating continued to be a problem, especially because of the disregard of elementary safety measures and practices by many of the continually growing number of small boat operators.

A 44-foot motor lifeboat exercising with an HH-52A helicopter.

The Federal Boating Act of 1958 addressed this problem by requiring the registration of all boats powered by motors of 10 horsepower or more on the country's navigable waters. The sheer numbers of craft involved led the government to encourage states to undertake this responsibility so long as they adopted standards similar to federal requirements, and the Coast Guard remained the principal regulatory and educational agency. This, of course, was a natural role of the Coast Guard Auxiliary, which received added support from the parent service, and to supplement its work, mobile boarding teams were organized within the Coast Guard. Each consisted of several carefully selected enlisted men led by an experienced petty officer and equipped with a vehicle that pulled a trailer carrying an outboard motor skiff. Visiting the most popular boating areas for a week or so at a time, the mobile boarding teams inspected boats and conducted programs in boating safety education. The teams achieved such success that their number was increased from twenty to thirty-five in 1961 and thereafter to fifty.[36]

Increasing maritime traffic in major harbors also attracted attention to the delays and hazards incidental to periods of impaired visibility. Shipborne radar was less effective in confined, congested waters, and some European seaports had developed a radar control system that enabled its operators to inform vessels of ship movements in their vicinities and to recommend courses and speeds to them. While these were not mandatory, American master mariners were thought likely to resent the implication that they could not decide such matters for themselves. Therefore, the Radar Television Aid to Navigation (RATAN) installed experimentally at Sandy Hook in 1961 was intended only to provide ships in the Lower Bay with the information necessary to permit their masters or pilots to determine the proper courses and speeds. Basically, RATAN consisted of a surveillance radar set located ashore and a television station to transmit a picture of the radar scope. Thus, any vessel with a television set could receive a view of herself, the craft and buoys near her, and the shoreline if it were close enough to be a factor.[37] A second RATAN system installed at Bayonne, New Jersey, in 1963 extended the service to the Upper Bay. Despite RATAN's seeming promise, however, technical difficulties led to its termination a few years later.

Development of the 44-foot motor lifeboat came none too soon, as an incident at the Columbia River mouth revealed. Thursday, 12 January 1961, began with light winds and a low swell on the bar, but a southerly gale was predicted by nightfall. At 4:15 P.M., the Cape Disappointment Lifeboat Station received a report that the 38-foot crab boat *Mermaid,* with a crew of two, was disabled and drifting toward the breakers on Peacock Spit. The motor lifeboat *CG 36454* was dispatched at once, and because she probably could not reach the disabled crabber in time, an 18-knot utility boat, the *CG 40564,* was sent out as well. Although the 40-footer was not intended for work in rough water, with luck she might be able to keep the *Mermaid* out of the breakers until the lifeboat came up.

But the visibility was worsening and the crab boat was nowhere to be seen when the *40564* reached her reported position. After receiving another misleading position report, the Cape Disappointment station succeeded in making radio contact with the disabled vessel and directed the utility boat to her. An hour after leaving the station, the *40564* took the *Mermaid* in tow. By that time, heavy rain squalls were sweeping in from the southward and wind and sea alike were getting up. The Point Adams Lifeboat Station had already been asked to send the *CG 52301,* one of the two 52-foot motor lifeboats built in 1935, to take over the tow, which she did at 7:30 P.M. Considering the Columbia River bar too dangerous to cross again with the wind reaching 63 knots and 30-foot seas running, the officer in charge at Point Adams directed her to take the *Mermaid* out to the Columbia River Lightship to await better conditions.

The *CG 40564,* however, could not long survive in those seas, so she and the *36454* eased cautiously in toward the bar to ascertain if a crossing was possible. It was not; at 8:25 huge breakers flipped the utility boat over, and her three crewmen clung to the capsized hull until the 36-footer picked them up, a notable rescue under the circumstances. But the same breakers damaged the lifeboat as well; her after compartments were filling as she struggled out toward the lightship. Coming alongside, her men secured a line to the sinking *36454,* after which rescued and rescuers clambered on board the larger vessel. The motor lifeboat sank early the next morning.

Even as the *36454* was rescuing the 40-footer's men, the Cape Disappointment station received the startling news that the *CG 52301* had capsized and sunk—the *Mermaid* radioed that she had picked up one man, who thought himself the only survivor. Telephoning a request that the Point Adams station send its two 36-footers out, Cape Disappointment also asked the Seattle Rescue Coordination Center to order the *Yocona* and any other units available to participate in the rescue operation. At 9:15 P.M., the *CG 36535,* one of the Point Adams lifeboats, reported that sea conditions made it impossible for her to remove the three men from the *Mermaid,* so she had passed a line to the crab boat and was heading for the lightship. But the *Mermaid* and those in her were not destined to survive the night. Forty-five minutes later, the *36535* reeled under the impact of several heavy breakers, and when her men cleared the salt water from their eyes, the towline had parted and the crab boat had disappeared. Searches by the lifeboats, the *Yocona,* and two aircraft from Port Angeles were fruitless, but one survivor of the *52301* was found crawling out of the surf near Cape Disappointment's North Head Light Station.[38]

So two crab fishermen and five Coast Guardsmen lost their lives during that wild night off the Columbia River bar, as the sea claimed the *Mermaid* and three Coast Guard vessels—the line securing the *CG 36454* to the lightship having parted, she could not be located and refloated after the storm. The causes of the disaster, the service's worst in more than a decade, were several. Sending a 40-foot utility boat to sea when a gale was known to be approaching was a calculated risk; it should be noted that the *40564* did manage to keep the crab boat out of the surf until an abler vessel relieved her of the tow. An accurate position report initially might have enabled her to seek shelter before the bar became impassable. It is, perhaps, surprising that the 40-footer lasted as long as she did. The loss of the *36454* is also surprising, for 36-footers were designed to work in such sea conditions. She was one of the older boats of that type and her hull apparently could not withstand the buffeting by a series of breakers. The newer *36535,* on the other hand, endured a similar battering without serious damage. The twenty-five-year-old *52301* was reputed to be one of the most capable lifeboats in the service, but she was not self-righting, so capsizing inevitably resulted in her loss.

The *CG 52301* was, however, the veteran of a number of successful rescue operations in the vicinity of "the graveyard of the North Pacific," and her failure to survive this one would seem to require further explanation. That may have been provided by an editorial writer for the *Portland Reporter,* who wrote:

In 25 years the tenure of lifeguards at the Point Adams, Ore., and Cape Disappointment, Wash., stations which carry out more difficult rescues than any in North America, had been much reduced. Before World War II both boat commanders and lifeguards served for years, some of them for life, at the mouth of the river.

It is not posssbile [*sic*] to get valuable "combat experience" on the Columbia bar in a year or two because rescuing lost Portland yachts during nice Astoria Regatta weather doesn't add to more proficiency at rescuing crab boats in storms. Most of the young lifesaving crewmen who were lost had spent less than three years at either station.[39]

This situation, of course, was not unique to the two Columbia River stations. Like Coast Guard personnel generally, those manning the lifeboat stations were transferred quite frequently during the postwar years, to the detriment of the local hydrographical knowledge that had enabled their predecessors to carry out their rescue missions in similar conditions of wind, sea, and darkness.

The writer might also have noted that officers in charge of lifeboat stations no longer took boats out on rescue missions as a matter of course. Instead, they usually remained at their stations, directing operations by means of radio. No doubt certain advantages resulted from this practice, yet one suspects that most of the old lifesaving station keepers would have found it difficult to stay ashore when the surf was crashing on the bar and a vessel was reported in distress "outside."

One week after the tragedy off the Columbia River bar, John F. Kennedy was inaugurated as president of the United States. He appointed a friend, C. Douglas Dillon, to the Treasury Department and a sometime fellow torpedo boat officer, James A. Reed, became assistant secretary. Kennedy himself was deeply interested in ships and the sea, and the nation had recovered from the economic recession of the late 1950s—thus, the future seemed somewhat brighter for the Coast Guard.

Secretary Dillon soon became aware of the service's plight with regard to obsolescent equipment and facilities, and when he learned that more than $1 billion would have to be spent to rectify this, Dillon decided that an appropriation of that magnitude should not be sought without a thorough study of the Coast Guard's roles and missions to ascertain the limits of the service's responsibilities. Unlike the Ebasco Study, this was to be made by a group composed of representatives of the Treasury and Defense departments and the Bureau of the Budget. A project staff so constituted, with Lieutenant Commander John B. Hayes—a future commandant—as secretary, began the study during the autumn of 1961 under the direction of a four-member steering committee, on which the very capable Captain Walter C. Capron represented the Coast Guard.[40]

Admiral Richmond—he had been promoted to four-star rank on 1 June 1960 as a result of legislation "to increase the efficiency of the organization of the Coast Guard"—was nearing the end of his second term as commandant when the roles and missions study began. Richmond recognized that it was important for his successor to be closely acquainted with it, and when Vice Admiral Hirshfield retired on 31 January 1962 to accept the presidency of the Lake Carriers Association, Rear Admiral Edwin J. Roland, erstwhile commander of the Eastern Area and the Third Coast Guard District, was ordered to Washington as assistant commandant. Roland assumed responsibility for coordinating the Coast Guard's cooperation with those conducting the study, and he also had five months in which to familiarize himself with the situation at Headquarters.[41]

Yet another portion of the 1960 legislation abolished the statutory position of engineer in chief, "a relic of the days when the Coast Guard had an engineering 'staff corps.' "[42] This was opposed by the incumbent, Rear Admiral Thiele, and more strenuously by his predecessor, Vice Admiral Cowart, on the ground that it would affect the morale of engineering personnel adversely.[43] The commandant, however, held that the engineer in chief was in fact only the chief of the office of engineering and as such was no more important than the chiefs of the offices of operations, personnel, merchant marine safety, and comptroller, none of whom held a statutory appointment.

The Act to Increase the Efficiency of the Organization of the Coast Guard had the effect of strengthening the position of the commandant, who together with the treasury secretary, selected officers to hold positions at Headquarters and determined the length of their tours of duty. Only the commandant and the assistant commandant had statutory appointments thereafter, and the provision that the latter hold vice admiral's rank clearly distinguished him from the chiefs of the various offices, who were rear admirals.

Admiral Richmond's four-starred flag was hauled down on board the *Campbell,* moored at the Washington Navy Yard, on 1 June 1962, marking the end of his eight years as commandant of the Coast Guard. Since that time, no officer has served as commandant for more than one term, and Richmond later averred that four years should be enough time for anyone to get his ideas accepted and implemented. Nonetheless, he thought that the service had not retrogressed during his second term.

Clearly, it had not. With new cutters, patrol boats, and lifeboats already built or planned, a rational program for aviation development being implemented, shore establishments undergoing renovation, such innovations as AMVER proving their value, and the personnel situation attaining some stability after the fluctuations incidental to the Korean War, the Coast Guard would bear the impress of the Richmond years for the next generation and more. Although Alfred C. Richmond, a quiet and rather austere officer, seems not to have attained the popularity of Frederick C. Billard and Russell R. Waesche within the service itself, he deserves to be ranked with them and with Ellsworth P. Bertholf.

319

CHAPTER EIGHTEEN

THE LAST YEARS UNDER THE TREASURY DEPARTMENT, 1962–67

*U*nlike most of his predecessors—and successors—Admiral Edwin John Roland had had relatively little duty at Coast Guard Headquarters when he became commandant. Well known for his interest in service athletics—he played football, basketball, and baseball at the Academy before graduating in 1929 and two years later he was captain of the Coast Guard football team that won the President's Cup in competition with teams representing the Army, Navy, and Marine Corps—Roland helped to coach all three sports during the four years he spent as an instructor at the Academy. His wartime service included command of Destroyer Escort Division 45, and in December 1944 he commissioned the *Mackinaw*, earning a commendation for the "Big Mack's" icebreaking that permitted the passage of ships and cargoes important to the war effort. After the war, Roland commanded the *Taney* and the corps of cadets at the Academy, completed a course at the National War College, and served as commandant of the First and Third districts as well as Eastern Area commander.

The roles and missions study begun before Admiral Roland became assistant commandant was completed in June 1962. In its report, the project staff identified the Coast Guard's ten major functions—port security, military readiness, aids to navigation, oceanography, law enforcement, search and rescue, ocean stations, merchant marine safety, Reserve training, and icebreaking—and recommended changes that it thought would enable the service to perform its missions more efficiently. The staff report contained eighty recommendations in all, of which Secretary Dillon ordered that seventy-six be implemented.[1]

The recommendation that the ocean station program be continued was somewhat surprising, for as noted earlier, the increased use of jet aircraft made the meteorological information that the ocean station vessels provided less important and more than five years had passed since the last aircraft crew rescue. But the staff felt that "such an obviously essential component of the overall national and international effort in communications, safety of air and sea travel, scientific data, and national Defense . . . should be continued,"[2] while Captain Capron wrote that most transoceanic aircraft, both commercial and military, still utilized the services of the ocean station vessels.[3] Perhaps Captain Louis K. Bragaw was correct, however, in his later assertion that "one major reason for [the ocean station program's] retention was that it was the primary justification for maintaining a fleet of large cutters whose command was deemed the capstone of a seagoing officer's career."[4] Although Bragaw was not alone in his belief that the ocean stations had outlived their usefulness by the 1960s, Secretary Dillon agreed with the recommendation that the program be continued, which it was for another decade.

Edwin John Roland, commandant, 1962–66.

And it should be noted that ocean stations were not the sole reason for keeping the large cutters in commission. In 1962, for example, greatly increased numbers of Japanese and Russian fishing and whaling vessels seeking their prey in the North Pacific Ocean and the Bering Sea necessitated the assignment of the *Wachusett, Winona,* and *Klamath* to fishery conservation duty in Alaskan waters. The three 255-footers made six-week patrols in turn from mid-April to mid-September. Within two years, the number of cutters so employed had to be doubled.

Meanwhile, the situation in Cuba, where Fidel Castro had overthrown the unpopular Fulgencia Batista early in 1959, led discontented Cubans to flee their homeland. The craft in which they fled were usually overcrowded and frequently unseaworthy, quite unsuitable for the often turbulent waters of the Florida Straits. Thus, Coast Guard patrols had to be increased considerably, with 82-footers bearing the brunt of the work, although large cutters and aircraft of the Seventh District did their share as well.[5]

Ocean station vessels had no more opportunities to save passengers and crews from ditched aircraft, but they continued to prove their worth by assisting those embarked in vessels that encountered difficulty. Two of the more notable rescues occurred in 1964, the first in February, when heavy seas stove in a hatch of the grain-laden British motorship *Ambassador* 1,200 miles east of New York. AMVER identified the nearest ships, six of which were diverted to her assistance while Royal Canadian Air Force and Coast Guard aircraft headed for the scene. As the Italian liner *Leonardo da Vinci* approached, fourteen of the freighter's men abandoned her in boats and rafts, only to be flung into the sea when these were overturned. The Coast Guard aircraft dropped rafts; none could reach them, nor could they hold onto the lines dropped by the Italian seamen. All fourteen men were lost. The Norwegian ore carrier *Fruen* then maneuvered alongside the foundering vessel and got a line to her. Nine men from the *Ambassador* got on board the *Fruen* before the line parted, leaving twelve yet to be rescued.

By this time a cutter had reached the scene and assumed responsibility for the rescue operation. The *Coos Bay* had been en route to Portland, Maine, after completing an ocean station patrol when her radiomen received the request for assistance from the *Ambassador,* 450 miles away. Commander Claude W. Bailey drove the 311-footer into the seas, and her lookouts sighted the freighter the next afternoon. Assured that the *Ambassador* could not last through the night, the *Coos Bay* stood up to windward and floated a fifteen-man raft down to her. Five men jumped into the raft, but they failed to get under its canopy and four were swept off by the heavy seas—which deposited them back on the *Ambassador*'s deck! Swimmers from the *Coos Bay* brought the fifth man to the cutter.

With the use of the raft clearly impractical, Commander Bailey decided to remove the men one at a time by shooting a line over with a life jacket attached. A man donned the life jacket and jumped into the sea, the shot line was cut, and the cutter dropped down to leeward of the *Ambassador* to haul him on board. The first man was picked up with little trouble, but it was obvious that the day would end before the remaining ten could be removed by this method. The *Coos Bay* closed the freighter's bow again, fired another line, and sent two life jackets. Two men were recovered on this and on each of the next two approaches. Once more, the cutter stood in toward the *Ambassador,* shot a line over, and the freighter's men hauled the two life jackets to her deck. Apparently they concluded that there was too little time left for the evolution to be repeated; all four abandoned ship, each of those in a life jacket grasping a shipmate in his arms. The *Coos Bay* sought the relatively less turbulent water in the *Ambassador*'s lee and got the four on board, but one—the master, who had been injured the day before—died while he was in the water. The other eleven were little the worse for the ordeal.[6]

Despite their belief that the *Ambassador* was sinking even as they left her, she was still afloat the next day, which the *Coos Bay* and aircraft spent searching for any of the first fourteen men who might have survived. Commander Bailey called off the search at nightfall, and the cutter resumed her interrupted passage to Portland. Wind and sea had diminished somewhat, so a Dutch salvage tug put men on board the *Ambassador* to make temporary repairs before taking her in tow. The salvage effort was in vain, however, for the freighter sank two days later.

The *Coos Bay* received a hearty welcome when she moored in her home port, and Commander Bailey gave full credit to her men and to those of the *Fruen* for saving twenty of the *Ambassador*'s thirty-five men. Bailey himself deserved much of the credit. His handling of the *Coos Bay* was little short of superb—on five occasions she closed within 60 feet of the *Ambassador* with the anemometer registering a full gale, in seas the master of the *Leonardo da Vinci* described as the worst he had ever seen. To be sure, the method of rescue was practically a measure of desperation, and as Commander Bailey observed, few of the eleven would have survived had the temperature been appreciably lower—it was 61° during the rescue operation. Nonetheless, the rescue was successful—but for the master's earlier injury, the *Coos Bay* would probably have saved all twelve.

December 1964 brought a distress signal from the American freighter *Smith Voyager,* some 800 miles east-southeast of Bermuda. Her grain cargo had shifted as she labored in heavy seas, causing a 30° list, a crack in her hull, and the loss of power. The West German *Mathilde Bolten* was not far distant; AMVER directed her, two other merchant vessels, and three Coast Guard cutters to the scene. When the *Bolten* neared the *Smith Voyager,* most of the latter's crew abandoned ship in her boats, one of which was swamped almost alongside the German vessel while another capsized close aboard, crushing four men between boat and ship. The remaining thirty-four were picked up by the *Bolten*'s crew. The four men still on board the *Smith Voyager* were taken off by a Monomoy surfboat from the 311-foot *Rockaway,* no mean feat although the sea conditions were better than those the *Ambassador* rescuers had had to cope with.[7]

This may have been the last rescue by a cutter's pulling boat, for all of these were removed from cutter allowance lists during fiscal 1965. Many were in need of repair or replacement, and the commandant reported a saving of $856,000 by dispensing with them.[8] Nor were they replaced by power boats—the larger prewar cutters had carried as many as eight small boats, and those in the postwar period had at least four; their allowance henceforth would be but two, usually self-bailing surfboats powered by diesel engines. While this drastic reduction was made possible in part by the increased reliability of small diesels, it was due mainly to the surfboats' diminished importance in rescue operations. Inflatable rafts were more practical and less costly, and the cutters under construction would have the ability to dispatch helicopters for rescue purposes, albeit not in unduly bad wind and sea conditions. Thus, the surfboats' principal role would be the conveyance of boarding parties to inspect ships at sea.

The importance of helicopters was increasing, although the procurement program anticipated in the 1957 report suffered a check in 1961 when two of those selected to replace the HO4S crashed while hovering over water. The Navy had lost several helicopters of the same type in similar mishaps, so a more suitable replacement had to be found. Meanwhile, six more HO4Ss were borrowed from the Navy to maintain the Coast Guard's rotary-wing aircraft strength at thirty-seven. Two years earlier, four Sikorsky S-62s had been ordered for evaluation. Modifying this aircraft, the first gas turbine-powered helicopter certified for commercial use in the United States, to Coast Guard specifications took longer than expected, but the four were delivered in 1963, by which time their designation had been changed to the HH-52A. Superior to the service's earlier helicopters in almost every regard, this was an amphibian, with a boat hull that

An HH-52A performing a medical evacuation from a U.S. Coast and Geodetic Survey ship off the Massachusetts coast.

enabled it to alight on the water. Captain John M. Waters, Jr., a veteran seaplane and helicopter pilot, explained its superiority over the fixed-wing aircraft: "The amphibious helicopter can land in seas that would be impossible for a seaplane. The forward speed at touchdown is zero, and the pilot can control the helicopter on the water by varying the lift of his rotor. If the seas are rough, he keeps most of the weight of the hull on the rotor blades, and the hull rides lightly over the swells."[9]

A month after the first HH-52A had been delivered, Waters, then a commander, demonstrated its worth by rescuing a man who had fallen overboard from a naval vessel just off Newport, Rhode Island. Semiconscious and near death in the icy water, the sailor could not be hoisted into the helicopter in the usual fashion, so Commander Waters eased the HH-52A down alongside him and then joined the hoist operator to drag him into the aircraft. This and a number of other rescues in the next several months led to the procurement of forty-six of these helicopters within two years; ultimately ninety-nine HH-52As were purchased by the Coast Guard, which was the only service to use them. Years later, Admiral Roland stated that "the helicopter was never accepted by aviation in the Coast Guard until I became commandant."[10] The admiral claimed no credit for its acceptance; that seems to have been due in large part to the HH-52A, also called the Sea Guard.

An HH-52A was one of forty helicopters, military and commercial, that lifted people to safety during a severe storm that struck the northern coast of California in December 1964. Piloted by Lieutenant Donald L. Prince, with Sub-lieutenant Allan L. Alltree of the Royal Canadian Navy as copilot and James A. Nininger, Jr., as hoist operator, the Coast Guard helicopter rescued eighteen, some of them hoisted while the HH-52A hovered between high tension powerlines in winds gusting to 60 knots. Just before dark, Prince took four adults and a baby on board and headed for the Arcata airport, flying on instruments because of the low clouds and heavy rain. The Arcata radio beacon failed before the helicopter reached the field, and while attempting to come in on radio direction-finder bearings, it was set to the eastward by the storm wind and crashed into a mountain, killing the seven on board.[11]

That tragedy could hardly be attributed to the HH-52A, but the new helicopter's single engine was a serious handicap—should it malfunction on an offshore mission, the aircraft would go down at sea. Thus, a fixed-wing escort was assigned for such missions, usually a Grumman HU-16 Albatross, a twin-engine amphibian that had been acquired in increasing numbers since 1951, first to supplement and then to replace the larger and more difficult to maintain seaplanes, the last of which were returned to the Navy in 1961. The HU-16, the "Goat" to those who flew it, became the Coast Guard's principal medium-range aircraft. Like the HH-52A, it remained in service into the 1980s.

The HH-52A's limitation was not shared by an Air Force Sikorsky helicopter modified for use by the Navy and the Coast Guard. Powered by two engines, the latter's version, the HH-3F Pelican, was larger and faster than the HH-52A, and it had a longer cruising range. These advantages, of course, came at a price, so only thirty-nine were acquired. Development took some time—first ordered in 1963, the HH-3F did not become operational until 1969.

Long-range missions, whether search and rescue, ice patrol, or other, were entrusted to the Lockheed C-130 Hercules, which was also used by the Navy, Air Force, and Marine Corps. The first of these four-engine giants was acquired by the Coast Guard in 1960, and a decade later sixteen were on the inventory. Fast, rugged, and extremely reliable, the C-130 was well suited to Coast Guard service because of its range—over 3,300 nautical miles with maximum fuel load—and its ability to cruise on two engines when on patrol, thus extending its endurance. This was especially useful for the International Ice Patrol, which was taken over almost entirely by C-130s. Two of the big airplanes and the oceanographic cutter *Evergreen* have composed the patrol force since 1963. And while replacements for the Sea Guard and the Albatross had been selected by 1980, the Hercules continues to be the service's principal long-range aircraft.

By 1965, the Coast Guard had 153 operational aircraft of all types, including fifty-seven helicopters. This relatively modest growth had made it possible to establish some additional air stations, which in

A Lockheed C-130 Hercules.

turn led to a further diminution in the number of lifeboat stations, for each helicopter could provide search-and-rescue service over a much greater area than several lifeboats. With the exception of those attached to icebreakers, all of the Coast Guard helicopters had to be based ashore because the only cutters fitted with flight decks, the new 210-footers, were too small to have hangars. Helicopters were assigned to them only temporarily, for specific missions.

The 210-footers, three of which were in commission by mid-1965, marked a considerable departure in cutter design. A high forecastle, intended to keep the decks dry in heavy weather, extended seven-eighths of the ship's length, with its after section forming the helicopter deck. A large bridge, which included a helicopter workshop immediately forward of the flight deck, was the only superstructure; the engine exhaust was vented through the transom stern in order to avoid the turbulence that stack gases would cause above the flight deck. Although an engineering review board had recommended in 1947 that henceforth the Coast Guard should eschew experimental machinery designs,[12] these cutters had the first combined diesel and gas turbine drive (CODAG) ever installed in American vessels. Each of the twin controllable-pitch propellers was powered by a 1,500-horsepower diesel engine and a 1,000-horsepower gas turbine, either separately or together. A single 3-inch 50-caliber gun of World War II vintage constituted the cutter's armament, although the design provided space for the installation of antisubmarine weapons and sonar in wartime. Eight officers and sixty-six enlisted men formed the 210-footer's complement; it is interesting to note that a much more heavily armed 240-foot cutter of 1921 had had but eight officers, one of whom was a Public Health Service surgeon, and eighty-one men. Considerable automation and all manner of labor

The 378-foot cutter Morgenthau.

and maintenance-saving devices had not yet reduced personnel requirements to any extent!

Initial reports on the performance of the new cutters were quite favorable. Their habitability set a new standard for the Coast Guard, and they had good seakeeping qualities for vessels of their size. Twin rudders and inward-turning screws made them very maneuverable, and their propeller blades could be shifted from full ahead pitch to full astern within ten seconds. On the other hand, mating a diesel engine turning at 1,000 rpm with a turbine making 22,300 rpm to drive one propeller shaft proved to be more difficult than the designers had anticipated. By the time this became apparent, the *Reliance, Diligence, Vigilant, Active,* and *Confidence,* all of which had CODAG propulsion, were either in commission or nearing completion. The *Resolute* and subsequent ships of the class were powered by two 2,500-horsepower diesels, somewhat heavier but simpler and more reliable. Less crowded engine rooms and a cost reduction of $1,724,000 per ship were additional benefits of the abandonment of CODAG.[13] Despite this saving, only sixteen of the thirty 210-foot cutters originally planned were built, the last entering service in 1969.

These ships were described as medium-endurance cutters (WMEC) under the classification system adopted on 1 January 1966, by which time the first new high-endurance cutters (WHEC) were under construction at Louisiana's Avondale Shipyards. Originally intended to be 350-footers, these ships "grew" on the drawing board to an overall length of 378 feet. Flush-decked, with sharply raked bow and transom stern, the Coast Guard's largest cutter to date would have aluminum superstructure and side-by-side stacks set well aft with the helicopter hangar between them. The design featured diesel engines and gas turbines, but unlike the early 210-footers, the new ship would cruise on the former and shift to the turbines to reach her 29-knot top speed. With a 5-inch 38-caliber dual-purpose gun, 40-millimeter mounts, hedgehogs, antisubmarine torpedoes, and so-

The 157-foot buoy tender
Red Wood.

nar, she was clearly intended to be a true multi-mission cutter.[14] No less than thirty-six of these vessels were planned, but the curtailment of the ocean station program and the unexpected longevity of the old 327-footers limited the number to twelve, the first nine named for secretaries of the treasury and the others for three of the service's heroes, David H. Jarvis of Point Barrow relief expedition (1897–98) fame, John A. Midgett, and Douglas A. Munro. The first, the *Hamilton,* was placed in service in February 1967 and the last five years later.

The Coast Guard received its first seagoing buoy tenders of postwar design in 1965 when the *Red Wood* and the *Red Beech* were completed at Curtis Bay. Twin-screw, diesel-propelled 157-footers drawing only 6 feet of water, with low bows that would not impair visibility when approaching buoys, these ships were much closer to the Lighthouse Service ideal than the only other large tenders of Coast Guard design, the 180-footers of 1942–43. These vessels also had bow-thrusters, propellers recessed into their hulls forward to push the bows to either side without necessitating headway or sternway. The bow-thruster's benefit when relieving a buoy or coming alongside with the wind blowing off the pier was obvious; the 378-foot cutters were fitted with it as well. These concessions to buoy-tending notwithstanding, the new ships and their later sisters, the *Red Birch, Red Cedar,* and *Red Oak,* had their hulls strengthened for light icebreaking.

Icebreaking brought the next significant increase in the Coast

Guard's vessel inventory, albeit not in the form of new ships. Congress had passed a bill authorizing the construction of a nuclear-powered icebreaker in 1958, only to have President Eisenhower veto it, largely because neither the Navy nor the Coast Guard felt that such a vessel was necessary. Congressman Herbert Bonner, one of the bill's sponsors, tried again the next year, substituting three conventionally powered icebreakers—while hoping that one of them would have nuclear propulsion. This time Admiral Richmond could attest to the need for new ships, the *Eastwind* and the *Westwind* both having suffered ice damage, which seemed to indicate that the life expectancies of the Wind-class would be considerably less than the thirty-five years originally anticipated. The Navy thought the need for vessels of other types more pressing, however, and the president's attitude had not changed, so the matter was dropped.[15]

The informal arrangement whereby Coast Guard icebreakers operated in the Arctic and the Antarctic in support of Navy missions concerned Secretary of the Treasury Douglas Dillon, and the roles and missions study contained a recommendation that the Treasury and Defense departments arrive at a clear understanding in this regard. A Navy-drafted memorandum of agreement specifying the responsibilities of the two services was amended by the Coast Guard and signed in March 1963. This confirmed the existing bi-service approach to icebreaking, which apparently would be continued indefinitely.[16]

Less than two years later, however, the Coast Guard liaison officer in the office of the chief of naval operations reported an inquiry as to the smaller service's interest in acquiring the Navy's icebreakers. This reflected a growing belief in the Navy Department that naval personnel should be assigned primarily to ships performing military functions, with civilian or other crews manning many of the auxiliary vessels. The Coast Guard, of course, was interested in this opportunity for expansion, and after a Navy study indicated the feasibility of the proposed transfer, Secretary of Defense Robert S. McNamara signified his approval on 7 May 1965. The earlier Treasury-Defense agreement was revised accordingly, and a board of Coast Guard officers met to draw up a schedule for the transfer of the five icebreakers. This required some consideration, for the Coast Guard would have to recruit an additional 1,000 men, make available the necessary number of officers and petty officers, and arrange the assignment of additional doctors and dentists with the Public Health Service. Thus, the board recommended that at least four months elapse between the final signing of the agreement and the transfer of the first ship, with the remainder to follow at intervals to be determined by operational schedules and the convenience of personnel. The Coast Guard did not have enough helicopters and pilots for five vessels, so the Navy would have to provide these until more aircraft had been acquired and their pilots trained.

Further delay occurred when Secretary of the Treasury Henry H.

The 310-foot icebreaker Glacier *after transfer to the Coast Guard.*

Fowler decided that the transfer should be approved in advance by the chairmen of the congressional subcommittees on Coast Guard appropriations and when Assistant Secretary James A. Reed became concerned about the potential cost. The final agreement was signed on 9 July 1965, and the first of the ships, the *Edisto,* hoisted the Coast Guard ensign on 20 October, followed by the *Staten Island, Glacier, Atka,* and *Burton Island* in February, June, October, and November of 1966 respectively. All retained their Navy names except the *Atka,* which had been christened the *Southwind* when launched in 1943 and reverted to that name.[17]

So the Coast Guard became the nation's sole icebreaking service, a development that was undoubtedly overdue for reasons of economy and efficiency. And it seems only proper that the service to which President Franklin D. Roosevelt had assigned primary responsibility for icebreaking in domestic waters "to meet the reasonable needs of commerce" thirty years earlier and for which the country's first polar icebreakers had been built, should have assumed this role. To be sure, the acquisition of four more Wind-class vessels, which by the Coast Guard's own account were approaching obsolescence, may have seemed a doubtful benefit, especially since funds for new construction were not likely to be voted for some time to come. To forestall this problem, the commandant approved an ice-breaker rehabilitation program, to extend the service lives of the Wind-class for ten years. The *Westwind* was the first to be renovated, then the *Edisto* and the *Southwind,* with the others scheduled to follow during the next several years. The fifth ex-naval vessel, the *Glacier,* could not be criticized on the ground that she was obsolescent, for she had been commissioned in 1955. This 310-footer embodied the lessons of almost a decade of experience with the Wind class, including a better power-displacement ratio—her diesel-electric propulsion plant delivered 21,000 shaft horsepower, more than twice that of any of the smaller ships. Although the crews of the latter were reluctant to acknowledge the *Glacier*'s superiority, she was the most capable American icebreaker for more than twenty years.

Two other vessels were acquired from the Navy during this period, both for reserve training. The 221-foot minesweeper *Tanager* was assigned to the Officer Candidate School at Yorktown, Virginia, while the 184-foot escort *Lamar* provided training afloat for reservists on the Pacific coast. The radio relay ship *Courier,* which ended her twelve years of duty with the U.S. Information Agency in 1964, also went to Yorktown to serve "as a floating, simulated captain of the port/port security facility."[18]

Meanwhile, U.S. armed forces were becoming involved in yet another war, this time in Vietnam. By late 1964, their military assistance and advisory activities had given way to combat operations, and as 1965 began, it became apparent that junks and other small craft were being used to supply Viet Cong forces ashore, leading the South Vietnamese government to ask the U.S. Navy to conduct offshore surveillance patrols to detect these. Operation Market Time, as the naval interdiction campaign was called, began on 12 March, with radar picket destroyer-escorts (DERs) and minesweepers initially assigned. These vessels, however, drew too much water to operate inshore, and the Navy had few craft that could do so. To meet this need, fifty-four "Swift" boats—aluminum-hulled 50-footers drawing only 5 feet and capable of 25 knots—were ordered, and on 16 April the secretary of the navy queried the Treasury Department about the availability of Coast Guard vessels.

Admiral Roland had been trying to devise a way to get the Coast Guard involved in Vietnam, fearing that if his service were limited entirely to a support role as it had been during the Korean War, its prized status as one of the nation's armed forces might be jeopardized.[19] The idea of using Coast Guard craft may well have been his; at any rate, he responded promptly that 82-foot patrol boats and 40-foot utility boats could be provided, and on 22 April Coast Guard and Navy agreed that seventeen of the former would join the Market Time forces, with the Navy to provide support in the form of two LSTs that had been converted to repair ships.

The seventeen patrol boats, ten from the Atlantic and Gulf coasts

The 82-footer Point Banks, *ready for transportation to Subic Bay.*

and seven from the Pacific coast, received heavier armament in the form of five .50-caliber machine guns, one of which was paired with an 81-millimeter mortar on a centerline mount forward, and enlarged food freezers to increase their operating endurance. By mid-May, the 82-footers were being hoisted on board merchant vessels for transportation to the U.S. naval station at Subic Bay in the Philippines.

Despite the commandant's anxiety lest the Coast Guard be denied a combat role, he acknowledged later that some Coast Guardsmen were less than enthusiastic about going to Vietnam. Those of the patrol boat crew members who wished to be excluded, whether because of family responsibilities or for other reasons, were reassigned; Admiral Roland insisted, however, that there had been no policy of exempting conscientious objectors.[20] There was no lack of volunteers to replace these men, and on 27 May Coast Guard Squadron 1 was commissioned at the service's Alameda base. After special training at Coronado under naval instructors, the 47 officers and 198 men were flown to Subic Bay to join their vessels.

There, shakedown and final training exercises were carried out under the Navy's operational control, and on 15 July the eight boats of Division 12 departed for Da Nang on South Vietnam's northeast coast. The remainder, Division 11, headed for An Thoi in the Gulf of Thailand five days later. By the end of July, just three months after the initial decision to commit Coast Guard patrol boats to Operation Market Time, the first of them reported to the DERs and minesweepers of the outer patrol, under whose direction they worked.

Those manning the 82-footers soon found that they were indeed engaged in a war. Division 11's *Point Orient* came under fire from the shore during her first night patrol, an experience that caused the Coast Guard boats' white hulls to be painted dark grey to reduce their visibility. On 19 September, the *Point Marone* was the target of small-arms fire and grenades from a junk she was about to inspect; her machine gunners killed eight Viet Cong, after which the junk and one surviving crew member were captured. On the same day, the *Point Glover* narrowly escaped being rammed by a much smaller boat, one of whose armed crewmen was taken captive.

Closing suspected vessels entailed some risk, but there was no alternative, for the patrol areas teemed with junks, sampans, and other craft, mostly small, whose identity could not be determined without boarding or at least examination from close aboard. There were so many of these that a priority list had to be established: those passing through the area were examined first, followed by craft fishing or otherwise engaged in restricted zones, and finally, fishing boats elsewhere, those at anchor with no nets out receiving close attention. This examination duty was shared with South Vietnamese naval junks, many of such shallow draft that they could enter waters too shoal for the 82-footers. Even with their assistance, however, this was tedious duty, especially in the enervating heat and humidity. Fortunately, the Coast Guard vessels were air-conditioned; but for that their crews could hardly have spent 70 percent of their time on patrol duty. Nor did the arrival of the Navy's Swift boats, the first two of which reached Vietnamese waters at the end of October, lighten their burden significantly, for the newcomers were little more than day boats, with limited endurance and unable to keep the sea in heavy weather.

With DERs, patrol boats, and junks carrying out their mission aggressively, small craft attempting to supply the Viet Cong ashore were thought to have only a 10 percent chance of slipping through the interdiction forces, while the larger steel-hulled trawlers, which were more easily detected by radar, were given no chance at all. So Market Time was achieving some success—but only where its vessels were operating. Between the patrol area in the Gulf of Thailand and that off the northeastern coast of South Vietnam, regions adjacent to the southeastern coast, which included the riverine approaches to Saigon, were controlled in part by the Viet Cong. The need for Market Time patrols in this area was obvious, and on 29 October 1965, Admiral Roland ordered that nine additional 82-footers be prepared for this service. A month later, all were en route to the Philippines to form Squadron 1's Division 13, which sailed from Subic Bay in mid-February 1966 to operate out of Vung Tau, northeast of the Mekong Delta. Until a riverine patrol force was established early in 1967, Division 13 had to patrol the rivers of the delta, which brought its boats under fire frequently and led to some spirited small-scale engagements.

Market Time forces had their first opportunity to intercept a significant arms shipment on 10 May 1966. The *Point Grey* was patrolling near the southwest tip of South Vietnam under the operational control of the DER *Brister,* when her men sighted two fires on the beach during the night of 9 May. The Viet Cong had earlier used fires to guide arms-laden craft to the beach, so the *Point Grey* remained in the vicinity and some two hours later her radarman reported a vessel heading inshore. The patrol boat turned to an intercepting course, and when the radar target was in sight, she made the visual challenge. Receiving no response, the *Point Grey* stood inshore until the stranger stopped about a mile from the beach. The lieutenant commanding the 82-footer considered a boarding attempt in an area of frequently shifting shoals too hazardous at night, so the vessel was illuminated by mortar flares to prevent any unloading before daylight.

The next morning, she was identified as a steel-hulled trawler about 120 feet long, aground and being forced inshore by the flood tide. The *Point Grey* stood in, encountering automatic weapon fire from the mangrove-covered shore, to which she replied with her mortar and machine guns. The 82-footer was hit repeatedly, so the *Brister* ordered her to withdraw to await reinforcements. Thereafter, the patrol boat kept the grounded trawler under surveillance for several hours, periodically spraying her with machine gun fire to deter off-loading attempts. That afternoon, the *Point Grey* was ordered to send a boarding party, and as she closed the beach, the Viet Cong opened fire once more, wounding three men at her forward mount. Air strikes and supporting fire from the *Brister,* the minesweeper *Vireo,* and the *Point Cypress* brought an end to the fighting, but darkness prevented another boarding attempt, so the vessel was destroyed along with an estimated 50 tons of arms, ammunition, and other supplies.

A somewhat similar engagement occurred on 20 June, when the *Point League* drove a 98-foot trawler aground 80 miles south-southwest of Saigon. The *Point Slocum* and the *Point Hudson,* aided by air strikes, helped to silence Viet Cong guns; while doing so, the *Slocum* was hit by a mortar shell that wounded two men. The arms-laden trawler was refloated and towed to Vung Tau.[21]

The 82-footers and their men having proved their ability, it was quite natural that the Navy should turn to the Coast Guard again when its few Market Time DERs required relief. To provide this, the 311-footers *Barataria, Half Moon,* and *Yakutat* were ordered from the Atlantic coast to Pearl Harbor, where they joined their sisters *Bering Strait* and *Gresham.* The five former naval vessels returned to the Navy's operational control as Coast Guard Squadron 3, which sailed for Subic Bay on 26 April 1967. The desirability of ships whose

main armament was a single 5-inch gun might seem surprising, but except for its destroyers, which were obviously "over-qualified" for interdiction duty, the Navy had few gun-armed ships available.

The vessels of Squadron 3 were initially assigned to the Gulf of Thailand, where the *Barataria* executed the squadron's first fire-support mission on 22 May. For the next seven months, the 311-footers performed surveillance duties and related missions and also provided support for the 82-footers and Swift boats operating with them. To keep the latter on station longer, extra crews were sometimes embarked in the cutters to provide the frequent reliefs those in the rough-riding craft required. On occasion, Coast Guardsmen sailed in the Swift boats to vary the routine of "big ship" life. The cutters were enabled to extend their already considerable endurance by replenishing fuel, provisions, and ammunition at sea, so opportunities for their men to leave the ships were few.

The 311-footers were relieved at the end of 1967 by the *Campbell, Duane, Androscoggin, Minnetonka,* and *Winona.* On 9 February 1968, the three 255-footers had a major role in defeating an effort to run four trawlers through the Market Time patrols and land their cargoes in as many different locations on the northeastern coast. Aircraft made the first sightings, and when it was clear that the supply vessels were headed for the coast of South Vietnam, they summoned surface forces. The *Winona* trailed the first trawler, challenged, and then fired warning shots. The trawler jettisoned her cargo and returned the fire, whereupon she was sunk by the cutter, with 82-footers and Swift boats also firing at her. No cutter was available to intercept the second trawler, so she was dealt with by three Vietnamese naval vessels and five Swifts; one of the latter scored a mortar hit, and the trawler ran ashore. The third was shadowed so effectively by the *Minnetonka* that she returned to Hainan Island without attempting to land her cargo. The fourth was

The original Coast Guard Squadron 3 alongside the Navy repair ship Jason *in Subic Bay. From left to right: the* Half Moon, Yakutat, Gresham, Barataria, *and* Bering Strait.

335

engaged by the *Androscoggin, Point Welcome, Point Grey,* and two Swift boats while helicopters provided illumination and additional machine gun fire—surely a force adequate to oppose a lightly armed trawler! She exploded after a direct hit by the *Androscoggin*'s 5-inch gun had forced her aground. The thwarting of this Viet Cong supply effort was hailed at the time as "the most significant naval victory of the Vietnam campaign," which seems a sufficient commentary on the sort of war this was.[22]

The cutters of this second deployment returned home in the autumn of 1968, their places taken by the *Bibb, Ingham, Owasco, Wachusett,* and *Winnebago.* These were relieved in 1969 by as many of their sisters. So it went—by mid-1971, when the last of the big cutters, except four 311-footers that were transferred to South Vietnam, returned to the United States, thirty of the Coast Guard's high-endurance cutters had participated in Operation Market Time. These included seven of the new 378-footers, which did not return unscathed—the *Morgenthau* struck an uncharted rock pinnacle in the Gulf of Thailand in February 1971 and had to be towed to Subic Bay for repair.

Coast Guard vessels clearly made a significant contribution to the success of Operation Market Time, which, according to the senior American officer in Vietnam, forced the Viet Cong and North Vietnamese forces to rely on the tortuous Ho Chi Minh trail for most of their supplies, to the detriment of their military operations. By the time the last of the 82-footers had been turned over to South Vietnam and Squadron 3 had been disbanded, the Coast Guard claimed credit for the destruction of almost 2,000 vessels while killing or wounding 1,827 Viet Cong and North Vietnamese.[23]

It is somewhat ironic that a service identified with the saving of life should have cited the number its vessels had killed or wounded as evidence of their effectiveness, but in that strange conflict "body count" was judged to be an important part of action reports. One wonders, however, if the effects of machine gun and mortar fire directed into wooded or relatively distant areas could be assessed so accurately.

In fairness, one must note that the crews of 82-footers and large cutters alike were involved in "civic" activities when the opportunity offered. These ranged from providing medical treatment to civilians ashore to rebuilding schools, hospitals, and churches, from distributing food and clothing donated by communities in the United States to raising money to send a blind girl to an American school. Projects such as these were not unique to the Coast Guard—all of the U.S. armed forces made similar contributions—but it may be doubted that any did more proportionately than the relatively small number of officers and men serving in the patrol boats and the cutters.[24]

Seven Coast Guardsmen were killed and fifty-three wounded in Vietnam. The most grievous loss occurred on the night of 11 August 1966, when three U.S. aircraft illuminated and then strafed the *Point*

Welcome while she was on patrol, hitting her bridge several times and starting a gasoline fire. The 82-footer was beached and abandoned, with her commanding officer and one man killed and five wounded, one of whom was the Vietnamese liaison officer and another a *Life* magazine reporter. To prevent a recurrence of this unfortunate incident, the U.S. commander in Vietnam restricted the conditions under which aircraft were allowed to attack small vessels. The *Point Welcome* was refloated and returned to service.[25]

Another of the fatalities was a helicopter pilot, one of three Coast Guard officers regularly assigned to duty with the Air Force's 37th Aerospace Rescue and Recovery Squadron at Da Nang. Lieutenant Jack Rittichier, USCGR, had made several rescues under fire, but in June 1968 his helicopter was hit by ground fire while attempting another and crashed in flames.[26]

The contribution of the Coast Guard support forces to the American war in Vietnam was probably as important as that of its combat forces. The greatly expanded merchant vessel traffic in the area necessitated a more effective system of aids to navigation, the establishment and service of which was far beyond the capacity of South Vietnam's lone buoy tender. The 180-footers *Planetree, Ironwood,* and *Basswood* were sent to Vietnam for varying periods, and in 1967 the *Blackhaw* was stationed at Sangley Point in Manila Bay, whence she made regular deployments to Vietnam. The crews of these tenders helped to train Vietnamese lighthouse service personnel while servicing buoys and beacons. By no means all of the work on aids to navigation was performed by the tenders; for whatever their official duties, other Coast Guardsmen in Vietnam were called on to repair buoys damaged by passing vessels or used as targets by troops in the vicinity. The batteries in lighted buoys proved to be very useful to the local population, necessitating their frequent replacement, and in the absence of a tender, the senior Coast Guardsman present was expected to decide on the desirability of additional marks requested by master mariners or the other services.

Monsoon weather often made celestial navigation a matter of chance in the South China Sea and the Gulf of Thailand, making an electronic navigational system highly desirable. Late in 1965, the Coast Guard was asked to establish a Loran-C network to serve vessels in Vietnamese waters. Ten months later, the Con Son station, located south of Saigon and paired with a station in Thailand, was commissioned, and in 1969 another was set up at Tan My in the northeast, to provide better service in the South China Sea.

The movement of military cargoes in South Vietnam came under the U.S. Army's logistics command, which relied on military police and Vietnamese harbor patrols to maintain order in the crowded ports. These functioned adequately, but cargo-handling was beyond their ken. It was performed for the most part by Vietnamese stevedores of both sexes, whose methods of handling explosives were an invitation to disaster. This was a matter of port security—a Coast

Guard mission—so two explosives-loading details, each consisting of a lieutenant and seven senior petty officers, were formed and sent to naval facilities in California for further training before reporting to the logistics command for duty in August 1966.

This port security detachment, later enlarged by two more explosives-loading details sent from the United States—men detached from the original four details subsequently formed a fifth—was one of the most useful groups in South Vietnam. Never numbering more than fifty officers and men, its details ultimately supervised the off-loading of more than four million tons of explosives from over fifty ships in one year, a feat that required men to work twelve-hour shifts seven days a week—they often worked for thirty days at a time without a day off. As word of their expertise spread, masters of ships laden with hazardous cargoes requested that Coast Guardsmen of an explosives-loading detail be assigned to them, for they had the authority to enforce all regulations pertaining to the discharge or loading of cargo, an authority that occasionally did not endear them to Army men considerably their seniors. As with other Coast Guardsmen in Vietnam, those of the explosives-loading details also had a training role, instructing American and Vietnamese personnel in small-boat handling and maintenance, fire-fighting, and pier maintenance. In January 1971, they began to train Vietnamese as their replacements, and within a year the latter were assuming some of the supervisory responsibility.[27]

Support for the U.S. forces in Vietnam was largely provided by merchant vessels chartered by MSTS, and as their number increased, so did personnel problems. Many of these were similar to the incidents that had led to the establishment of merchant marine hearing units by the Coast Guard during World War II, and in August 1966 MSTS requested that a merchant marine detail be sent to Saigon. A Coast Guard marine inspection officer went out in December to become shipping advisor on the staff of the commander MSTS, Far East. He and two assistants traveled widely, boarding some 500 ships in the first years and investigating 263 serious offenses, including sabotage, assault with deadly weapons, narcotics use, drunkenness, gross immorality, and desertion. Merchant seamen were likely to become involved in trouble ashore as well, sometimes as the result of soldiers' dislike of well-paid civilians. The Army's provost marshal helped to obtain an embassy decree making merchant seamen in Vietnamese ports subject to the armed forces' Uniform Code of Military Justice, which made the prosecution of those charged with serious offenses much easier, while the cooperation of union representatives enabled the Coast Guard officers to cope with lesser cases of misconduct with some celerity.[28]

The Coast Guard's part in the Vietnam war ended gradually, with the "Vietnamization" of some units and activities and the withdrawal of others. The twenty-six 82-footers were transferred to South Vietnam, the last two in mid-August 1970, while Squadron 3 was disestablished early in 1972, soon after its last two cutters, the *Castle Rock* and the *Cook Inlet,* joined their sisters *Bering Strait* and *Yakutat* under the South Vietnamese naval ensign. Coast Guardsmen stationed ashore—those of the merchant marine detail and the port security detachment, the helicopter pilots, and the loran station crews—departed somewhat later, and the post of senior Coast Guard officer, Vietnam, established in 1970 to coordinate the service's activities ashore and to serve as liaison with the Vietnamese government and the other armed forces, was discontinued on 11 February 1973.

Whatever the final verdict of history on the American involvement in Vietnam, the Coast Guard had obviously justified its status as one of the nation's armed forces. To be sure, relatively few of its officers and men went to Vietnam—not many more than 1,000 at the most were there at any given time. Some 8,000 Coast Guardsmen served in Southeast Asia during the war; nonetheless, their performance of varied duties, often under difficult conditions, demonstrated their service's versatility.[29] Most of those duties, of course, were among the Coast Guard's many missions; even Market Time was primarily an anti-smuggling operation. Not least, the celerity with which Admiral Roland and his successor responded to the requests of the larger services for assistance indicated that *Semper Paratus* was no empty boast.

Like earlier wars, that in Vietnam brought an immediate expansion of the Coast Guard's personnel, from 31,776 officers and men in 1965 to 35,289 a year later. This rate of growth, seemingly excessive in view of the small number of Coast Guardsmen initially sent to Vietnam, was due largely to the increased port security activity necessitated by the expansion of war-related shipping. Nor were the service's other responsibilities diminished significantly. The Florida Straits patrols, for example, which had been augmented earlier to prevent Florida-based Cuban exile groups from raiding their erstwhile homeland, had to be maintained at full strength to cope with the steadily increasing exodus of refugees from Cuba and to keep Cuban fishing boats out of American territorial waters. The acquisition of the Navy's icebreakers has already been noted, and the extension of U.S. fishery jurisdiction 12 nautical miles offshore by a law enacted in October 1966 required that the larger cutters and C-130 aircraft spend additional time on fishery protection patrols.

Even the loss of a foreign-flag vessel on the high seas could involve the Coast Guard. Thus, when the Panamanian cruise ship *Yarmouth Castle*, bound from Miami to the Bahamas, burned and sank on 13 November 1965 with the loss of ninety lives—370 were rescued by merchant vessels in the vicinity—the government of Panama requested that the Coast Guard investigate the disaster. A special session of the Intergovernmental Maritime Consultative Organization was convened to consider passenger-ship fire safety, and just before the Coast Guard's recommendations on more stringent regulations were considered, the Norwegian cruise ship *Viking Princess* burned in the Caribbean Sea, fortunately without loss of life. She was a much newer ship than the elderly *Yarmouth Castle,* so her loss was the more disturbing, causing the Coast Guard's merchant marine safety office to make even greater efforts to evolve the standards necessary for a "fire-safe" passenger vessel.[30]

Maritime disasters were instrumental in bringing about more effective legislation in another area as well. The Coast Guard had shared with the Army's Corps of Engineers and the Bureau of Customs the responsibility for investigating violations of the Oil Pollution Act of 1924, which forbade the discharge of oil into American coastal waters. This act had several defects, among them the lack of application to inland navigable waters and the Great Lakes—the Refuse Act of 1899 had to be interpreted broadly to protect these—the necessity to prove willful or gross negligence on the part of the offender, and the cumbersome enforcement procedure that often allowed ships of foreign registry to sail before legal action could be taken against them.[31] The first reference to oil pollution in the commandant's *Annual Report* appeared in that for fiscal 1939, when Coast Guard units reported forty violations of the 1924 act. The number rose to forty-seven the next year, and during World War II, investigation of pollution became a responsibility of captain of the port detachments. These, conducting regular patrols of harbors and adjacent waters, noted that as tanker traffic increased during the postwar years, so too did pollution. This alarming situation was not limited to American waters; it led to an international conference in London in 1954, with the commandant and several other Coast Guard officers being members of the U.S. delegation. The resulting Convention for the Prevention of Pollution of the Sea by Oil became the basis for the Oil Pollution Act of 1961, which neither replaced the 1924 legislation nor remedied its worst defects. The 1962 Roles and Missions Study contained a recommendation that both acts be amended to provide more adequate application, more efficient administration, and more severe penalties for violators, to no avail until the large tanker *Torrey Canyon* grounded on the Seven Stones, off Land's End, England, in mid-March 1967. The pollution resulting from this and subsequent tanker wrecks in Puerto Rico and the Bahamas and from the blowout of an oil well in the Santa Barbara Channel, just off the California coast, in 1969 led to executive and legislative action that increased the Coast Guard's responsibility considerably.[32] Its expanded role in this area, however, is beyond the scope of this chapter, which ends with an event of 1 April 1967.

This event had its immediate origin more than a year earlier when, in his State of the Union Message, President Lyndon B. Johnson announced his intention to seek legislation creating a cabinet-level department that would oversee all of the government's transportation-related activities. Not long thereafter, Admiral Roland was summoned to a meeting at the White House, and as he remembered later, "we opposed [the inclusion of the Coast Guard] pretty violently."[33] Roland's successor, Admiral Willard J. Smith, attributed the principal opposition to Secretary of the Treasury Henry H. Fowler, to whom the president replied: "I don't know that I'm going to really insist that you let the Coast Guard be involved in this proposed legislation, but I'll tell you that I don't even need legislation to transfer any functions of the Coast Guard that are related to transportation safety to the new department, if it is formed."[34] According to the account prepared at Coast Guard Headquarters, Under Secretary Joseph W. Barr presented the Treasury view at the meeting, in the course of which the organization of a Department of Transportation along functional lines was discussed.[35] Whether Fowler or Barr voiced the opposition to the proposed transfer is unimportant, for President Johnson's supposed response summed up the danger facing the Coast Guard—that it would be stripped of its most important roles and remain with the Treasury Department as a sort of latter day Revenue-Cutter Service.

Recognizing that continued opposition to his service's transfer to the new department would be likely to bring about its dismemberment, Admiral Roland decided to accept the inevitable, seeking only to assure that the Coast Guard would retain its identity as a military service under the new Department of Transportation. Coast Guardsmen on every level indicated their concern about the service's future, and one of them, Captain Harry L. Morgan, suggested that a group of officers be assigned to attend congressional committee hearings and provide information pertaining to the Coast Guard's desired place and role within the proposed department. Rear Admiral Paul E. Trimble, the chief of staff, agreed and appointed Morgan and four other officers, representing as many offices at Headquarters, to the Task Force on the Department of Transportation. Soon afterward, Captain Mark A. Whalen, newly selected for promotion to flag rank, became the task force commander.[36]

In his first report to Trimble, Whalen contrasted the danger inherent in a passive attitude with the opportunity offered by a positive approach:

> In this jungle of government, agencies can be swallowed up by grasping Administrators or by the stroke of a pen in an Executive Order. If we enter this arena of DOT [Department of Transportation] with a completely defensive attitude and with the sole objective of protecting what we have, we will find ourselves being nibbled at on all sides. . . . I feel our approach should be that we have expertise, loyalty, ability and military professionalism which a DOT must have to operate effectively, and that with the above we can perform certain functions of other agencies forming the DOT better than they now do and should acquire such functions. *All levels of Coast Guard personnel should be directed to at all times reflect this attitude.*[37]

Willard John Smith, commandant, 1966–70.

Rear Admiral Whalen urged that support be sought from the Department of Defense and the Navy Department, both of which could attest to the value of the Coast Guard's services in past wars and in Vietnam, and he listed six senators and congressmen who should be kept fully informed of the Coast Guard's intentions and desires. Further, timely information releases to "that area of the civilian populace where support lies. . . . the Reserve, the Auxiliary, the Temporary Reserve, and the Retired Coast Guard Officer Corps" would win valuable support.[38]

With such a realistic approach and enthusiastic leadership, the Coast Guard's future as a military service was hardly in doubt; indeed, the major concern came to be the provision for a National Transportation Safety Board that would ascertain the causes or probable causes of transportation accidents. This seemed likely to reduce or eliminate the Coast Guard's responsibility for investigating maritime disasters, and the relationship between the service and the board was the subject of lengthy discussion before being resolved to Whalen's satisfaction.[39]

Meanwhile, Captain Warner K. Thompson, Jr., chief of the Public Information Division, recognized the importance of assuring Coast Guard personnel generally that they had nothing to fear with regard to the future of the service or to their own careers. Such assurance obviously had to be given by the commandant, and since it was impractical for Admiral Roland to visit each unit personally, Thompson suggested that he do so by means of a short motion picture film that could be distributed widely. The commandant agreed, and this film appearance, which seems to have been quite effective, was in a sense his valedictory address to the Coast Guard, for he retired on 1 June 1966.[40]

Although the actual transfer of the Coast Guard from the Treasury Department to the Department of Transportation occurred under his successor, Admiral Edwin J. Roland deserves much of the credit for the ease with which the transition was made and for the fact that the service lost nothing in the process. The decision not to oppose the transfer was his, and while subordinates formed the task force that contributed so much to the Coast Guard's ultimate place in the Department of Transportation, the commandant provided the necessary support and counsel. Moreover, he was personally responsible for bringing about the state of military readiness that made possible the rapid response to the Navy's request for assistance in Vietnam, which in turn helped to maintain the Coast Guard's integrity when it left the Treasury Department.

Admiral Willard John Smith, a member of the Academy class of 1933 and the first aviator to become commandant, hoisted his flag in the *Campbell* at the Washington Navy Yard, and a month later Paul Trimble relieved Vice Admiral William D. Shields as assistant commandant, being succeeded as chief of staff by Rear Admiral

Whalen. Thus, the change of leadership had little effect on the preparations for the transfer.

As drafting of the legislation progressed, it became obvious that certain functions of the Corps of Engineers would come under the Department of Transportation. An interagency task force directed Captain Harry Morgan to recommend their disposition, and he concluded that those with any maritime connection—the regulation of bridges spanning navigable waters, the designation of anchorage areas, and the enforcement of oil pollution laws—should become Coast Guard responsibilities, as should the Great Lakes Pilotage Administration.[41] His arguments were persuasive; thus, the opportunity for expansion foreseen by Rear Admiral Mark Whalen was not lost. Meanwhile, other officers represented the Coast Guard on the various task forces drawing up plans for the formation and operation of the new department, which was formally established when Public Law 89-670 was enacted on 15 October 1966.

There was still much to do, and early the next year the matter of providing personnel to staff the transportation secretary's office was discussed. Captain Morgan, with Vice Admiral Trimble's approval, proposed that the Coast Guard be well represented, and subsequently Alan S. Boyd, the first secretary of transportation, appointed a number of officers, active and retired, to positions of responsibility in the department.

When the Coast Guard was formally transferred to the Department of Transportation, on 1 April 1967, it was noted that the service had been a part of the Treasury Department for almost 177 years.[42] One might observe that this was the more impressive because the Coast Guard itself was little more than fifty years old! But since 1922, 4 August 1790 had been celebrated as the date of its founding, and the 6½ years it had spent under Navy Department control seem not to have counted.[43] Whatever its age, however, the reader will surely agree that the U.S. Coast Guard had proved itself a worthy successor to the Revenue-Cutter, Life-Saving, and Lighthouse services and to the other agencies whose missions it had assumed.

CHAPTER NINETEEN

THE COAST GUARD SINCE 1967

*A*lthough the Coast Guard's transfer to the Department of Transportation was largely an administrative move, substantive changes followed: The termination of the service's involvement in Vietnam and the end of the ocean station program; the implementation of the 12-mile offshore fishery zone in 1967 and the adoption of a 200-mile economic resources zone ten years later; expanded efforts to cope with pollution and hazardous cargoes; the interdiction of refugee traffic between West Indian islands and the United States; and especially the development of a "drug war" that might be likened to the rum war of the Prohibition era. The inaccessibility of records, most notably those relating to the service's anti-drug smuggling activities, makes a thorough study of the Coast Guard during the period since 1967 impossible; thus, this final chapter can be no more than a hasty survey, a postscript of sorts.

The winding down of the Vietnam War has been described. One need only add here that a number of cutters were soon found superfluous to the service's needs, which were becoming fewer as a result of the seemingly overdue termination of the ocean station program. The development of large buoys that could be moored in deep water and could transmit meteorological data automatically led to the gradual discontinuation of the ocean stations. The last was Station Hotel, off the Maryland-Virginia coast, on which the *Taney* was relieved by a 40-ton buoy in 1977. Somewhat similar buoys, with powerful lights, fog signals, and radio beacons, replaced the lightships during the next few years. The 311-foot cutters had been decommissioned between 1967 and 1973 and all save the *Unimak* disposed of, while the *Winona* and the *Minnetonka,* the last of the 255-footers, were placed out of commission in 1974. Older vessels also departed: the surviving 165-footers; all of the old 125-footers except the *Cuyahoga,* retained as a training cutter for the Reserve Training Center at Yorktown, Virginia; and the *Spencer,* which was decommissioned to become a stationary training facility at Curtis Bay in 1974. The icebreaker ranks were thinned gradually as well; by 1979 the *Northwind* and the *Westwind,* both re-engined in the mid-1970s, were the only representatives of the Wind class.

Other ships received a new lease on life. The 95-footers, except for nine sent to South Korea in 1968, were slated for replacement in the mid-1970s; they were given extensive overhauls instead and kept in service, while several of the older 180-foot buoy tenders, scheduled for decommissioning in 1978, were treated similarly. Two of the latter, the *Clover* and the *Citrus,* exchanged their booms and other buoy-handling gear for white coats and a pair of 40-millimeter grenade launchers to become medium-endurance cutters, replacing the equally aged tugs *Comanche* and *Modoc* in 1979.

The use of these grenade launchers—light weapons that could be brought topside on need—reflected a change in armament policy generally. The maintenance of permanently mounted guns was expensive, and they were seldom needed in peacetime; thus, in the icebreakers and all but the larger cutters these were generally replaced by .50-caliber machine guns or similar weapons. Vessels operating on inland waters usually had only small arms.

Admiral Chester R. Bender, commandant 1970–74.

Transfer to the Department of Transportation brought no immediate changes with regard to the appearance of Coast Guard units and personnel, but these were forthcoming. After considering several alternatives, Headquarters decided that the now familiar insignia—orange and blue hull stripes, with the Coast Guard emblem superimposed on the former, followed by COAST GUARD in block letters—should be painted on the bows of every Coast Guard vessel and on aircraft. Only the *Eagle* was excepted at first, for aesthetic reasons, but ultimately she too had to be similarly adorned, to distinguish her from foreign sailing ships visiting the United States for the nation's bicentennial celebration in 1976. The white hulls of cutters and lifeboats and the black-painted buoy tenders and tugs could accommodate the diagonal stripes without undue offense to the sensitive, but when icebreaker hulls were painted red for enhanced visibility in ice fields, the broad insignia orange stripe did little for their appearance.

In 1968, Rear Admiral Chester R. Bender suggested to Admiral Smith that Coast Guardsmen should wear a uniform that would distinguish them from naval personnel. The commandant seems not to have been interested, but when Bender succeeded him in 1970, a board to consider uniform changes was established. Senior officers were generally unenthusiastic; nonetheless, the board's deliberations resulted in an officer uniform of "Coast Guard blue"—closer to royal blue than to any other—with a single-breasted coat. Admiral Bender also felt that the traditional bluejacket uniform was demeaning for older enlisted men and that it detracted from the authority of petty officers engaged in law enforcement duties. Thus, the board recommended a uniform similar to that proposed for officers, with appropriate insignia, for all enlisted men. With the uniform design decided on, the commandant circulated photographs and a questionnaire throughout the service. The reaction was not entirely favorable, although the new uniform for enlisted personnel was widely supported. That was enough for Admiral Bender; with the approval of Secretary of Transportation John A. Volpe, he ordered all Coast Guardsmen into "Bender blues," which some older officers would continue to lament a decade and more afterward.[1]

As it turned out, women as well as men were soon wearing "Bender blues." Responding to the women's rights movement that was gaining momentum when Admiral Bender became commandant, the Coast Guard began to offer appointments as officer candidates to qualified women in 1973, and at the same time four-year enlistments were authorized. The other sea services had adopted similar policies, but all three limited the numbers of women recruited and the positions to which they could be assigned. In 1977, Coast Guard women went to sea as crewmembers in the large cutters *Gallatin* and *Morgenthau,* and a year later, all restrictions based solely on sex in training, assignment, and career opportunities for Coast Guard personnel were removed; henceforth, crews consisting of both men and women would be assigned to any unit, ashore or afloat, that could afford the requisite privacy and sanitary facilities.[2]

When Lieutenant (junior grade) Beverly Kelly read her orders on board the 95-foot *Cape Newagen* at Honolulu on 1 April 1979, she became the first woman ever to command a U.S. warship. Others soon followed, among them Lieutenant Susan I. Moritz, whose *Cape Current* seized the cabin cruiser *David* with 3,000 pounds of marijuana 75 miles southeast of Miami on 4 July 1979. Almost four months later, Cadet First Class Linda Johansen became the first woman to command the cadet corps at a service academy; she and several classmates who received their commissions in June 1980, were the Coast Guard Academy's first female graduates.

By 1982, the Coast Guard had 130 female officers and nearly 1,700 enlisted women, about 3 percent of the total number of officers and 5 percent of the enlisted personnel. Some 10 percent of the cadets at the Academy were women. Coast Guard women could apply for flight training, and three were pilots. In short, the principle embodied in the 1978 directive seemed to have been adopted generally. Women had made gains in the Navy and the Marine Corps as well, but neither of these services permitted women to be assigned to combat vessels. And while the Navy had female officers of flag rank, the senior Coast Guard woman was a lieutenant commander.[3]

Admiral Bender's tenure as commandant also witnessed expanded activity in environmental protection and vessel traffic control. This stemmed principally from the increasing importation of oil and was a further development of the response to such disasters as the *Torrey Canyon* stranding. The Council on Environmental Quality, established in 1970, had Coast Guard representation, and under its plan for coping with oil pollution, the service became one of the principal agencies responsible "for the coordination and administration of cleaning up oil spills on the high seas, coastal and contiguous waters, and coastal and Great Lakes port and harbor areas."[4]

To meet this responsibility, Admiral Bender established the office of marine environment and systems at Headquarters, with Rear Admiral William M. Benkert as its first chief. As Captain Sidney A. Wallace, one of Benkert's subordinates, wrote, the creation of this office actually indicated a new approach: "Emphasis traditionally had been given to protection of vessels, cargoes, and people from the environment. Now emphasis was to be placed on protecting the environment in which marine commerce operates; i.e., the navigable waters of the United States."[5]

In the event of an oil spill, the Coast Guard had to ascertain its origin, if possible. This was facilitated by new techniques for matching samples of spilled oil with that remaining in the vessel suspected of polluting and by electronic detection of oil spills from the air. The polluter was generally liable for the cost of the cleansing operation, which might be carried out by the Coast Guard or by a contractor working under its supervision. Devices for limiting the dispersion of spilled oil and for removing it were developed, including booms, skimmers, vacuum trucks, and the air-deployable anti-pollution transfer system (ADAPTS), which was a pump designed to transfer oil from a stranded or damaged tanker to other vessels or into rubber tanks. Men trained in the use of these were assigned to the Atlantic, Gulf, and Pacific strike teams that made up the National Strike Force established in 1973. Each consisting initially of seventeen officers and men, these were based at Elizabeth City, N.C., Bay St. Louis, Miss., and Nevado, Cal. Should a serious oil spill be reported, the strike team responsible for the area was flown to the site with its equipment. On arrival, the team took whatever action was necessary, utilizing local Coast Guard units and personnel, engaging contractors, renting boats, buying booms to contain the oil, etc. Within a few years, the strike teams' reputation led to requests for advice or assistance from countries as far distant as Argentina, Norway, and Japan.[6]

Cleaning up oil spills was not as desirable as preventing them, which could be done in part by harbor traffic control to prevent strandings and collisions. The RATAN system introduced in New York in 1962 had had to be discontinued a few years later because of technical difficulties, but in January 1970, the Coast Guard began the San Francisco Harbor Advisory Radar Project on an experimental basis. Development required some time, but in August 1972 the San Francisco Vessel Traffic System, which had two radar sets designed especially for marine traffic surveillance and control, became operational. A somewhat similar system in Puget Sound was put into service a month later, and Houston-Galveston, New Orleans, and New York were designated to receive vessel traffic systems in the next few years. Unlike earlier attempts at harbor control, these have proven very successful.

The pollution problem was not limited to American waters, especially because tanker crews were wont to clean their ships' cargo tanks after leaving the ports in which they had offloaded. The oily residue was simply pumped overboard, and in Admiral Bender's opinion, "Far more oil [went] into the ocean through tank-cleaning than through accidental spills."[7] This contamination, as well as that caused by pumping oily ballast water into the sea, ordinarily occurred beyond American territorial waters, and most of the tankers were registered in foreign nations; therefore, international agreement was necessary to cope with it. The U.S. delegation to the International Conference on Marine Pollution, which met in London under IMCO sponsorship in October 1973, included Admiral Bender as vice chairman and several other Coast Guard officers, Benkert and Wallace among them. The convention drawn up at this conference included the prohibition of oil discharges within 50 miles of the shore and limitation on those farther out. These and other provisions of the agreement were to be enforced by the nations in which the tankers were registered, although each signatory might punish violations by foreign-flag ships within its waters and it could detain vessels that did not comply with the convention's construction requirements. The chairman of the U.S. delegation described the conference as a "historic milestone in the control of marine pollution."[8]

Oil spills would continue nonetheless. One of the potentially more serious occurred when the Liberian tanker *Argo Merchant* grounded on a shoal 28 miles southeast of Nantucket, on 15 December 1976. The cutters *Sherman* and *Vigilant* removed most of her crew and put damage control personnel, members of the Atlantic Strike Team among them, on board. Arrangements to pump the tanker's 7,500,000-gallon cargo into lighters came to nought, however, when heavy weather forced the evacuation of the Coast Guardsmen and the remaining crew members. The vessel broke up, but most of the oil was driven seaward by northwesterly winds, minimizing the ecological damage.

The *Argo Merchant* stranding and the fact that fourteen more tanker accidents in or near American waters were reported in the next ten weeks caused great public concern. Ten of these involved Liberian vessels, and the Coast Guard was criticized for its supposed laxity in enforcing existing regulations with regard to the condition, equipment, and manning of foreign-flag ships bound for American harbors. The Tanker and Vessel Safety Act of 1977 strengthened these requirements, authorizing the Coast Guard to force ships not meeting its standards to leave U.S. waters and establishing a 200-mile pollution control zone. Perhaps equally important, American and foreign companies that owned ships of Liberian registry began to enforce regulations with regard to tankers.[9]

American concern about oil spills was the greater because the shipment of oil from Alaska's North Slope was scheduled to begin during the summer of 1977. The oil would be pumped from the Prudhoe Bay oil field to Valdez through the Trans-Alaska Pipeline. Having filled their cargo tanks at Valdez, large tankers would have

The Argo Merchant *aground on Fishing Rip Shoal, with the cutter* Vigilant *in the foreground.*

to traverse Valdez Arm and Prince William Sound before steaming into the Gulf of Alaska en route to terminals on Puget Sound. Increased vessel traffic in the restricted waters at both ends of the route meant even greater danger of collision and pollution. By the time the shipments began, the Coast Guard had Marine Safety offices and Vessel Traffic systems operating in Valdez and the southern terminus, and Loran-C stations provided navigational guidance for the entire passage. The *Arco Juneau* brought the first cargo of oil south without mishap, nor have any serious accidents involving tankers on this route been reported subsequently.

Tanker traffic between Valdez and Puget Sound would have been considerably lighter had the shipment of North Slope oil through the Northwest Passage been economically practical. Recognizing that the principal market would be on the U.S. Atlantic coast and in the Middle West, the Humble Oil and Refining Company decided to test the feasibility of using large tankers on this route. After consultation with people knowledgeable about arctic conditions and icebreaking, including representatives of the Coast Guard, Humble chartered the 100,000-ton tanker *Manhattan,* the largest vessel built in the United States—she had been operated under the Liberian flag for a time!— and had her fitted with an icebreaking bow, an ice belt, and a helicopter deck.

Two Coast Guard officers sailed as advisers in the *Manhattan* on

The John A. MacDonald *(left) and the* Manhattan *in* McClure Strait, September, 1969.

24 August 1969, and she was accompanied by the *Northwind* and the Canadian icebreaker *John A. MacDonald,* which were to render assistance should she get into trouble. When the *Manhattan* was beset by ice in McClure Strait, however, the *Northwind* could do little because of an engineering casualty, so the newer, larger, and more powerful *MacDonald* had to break the tanker out. The *Manhattan* reached Point Barrow late in September and returned to New York with a large hole in her plating under the ice belt, despite which the voyage was considered a success.

The big tanker undertook a second voyage, routed farther north in order to test herself in more severe ice conditions, in April 1970. By that time, however, Humble executives were beginning to question the entire concept. It was clear that tankers capable of traversing the Northwest Passage in mid-winter would be very expensive to build and operate, and the Canadian government had some reservations about the potential pollution should one of them be stranded or suffer serious ice damage.[10] The use of the Northwest Passage by icebreaking supertankers ended, as it had begun, with the *Manhattan.*

Humble's experiment had yielded a good deal of information on the use of a big ship in the ice, and the Coast Guard was gratified by the success of the *Manhattan*'s bow, which had been rebuilt to a modified design developed by the service's engineers. Whereas the Wind-class bow struck the ice at nearly a 45° angle, the modified form eased onto it at 15°, reducing the impact considerably. The latter design also provided a longer overhang, increasing the weight applied to the ice surface. The *Manhattan* bow would be duplicated, obviously on a much smaller scale, in the Coast Guard's next icebreaker.

The Lockheed Shipbuilding and Construction Company of Seattle laid the keel of WAGB 10 in May 1972, and the vessel was commissioned in January 1976. At 13,000 tons and 399 feet, the *Polar Star* was the Coast Guard's largest ship, and with gas turbines producing 60,000 shaft horsepower, its most powerful. The turbines were for use in heavy ice; normally she would be propelled by diesel engines driving generators that provided current to turn a 6,000-horsepower motor on each of her three propeller shafts. The use of gas turbines required controllable-pitch propellers, and the thought of these milling ice led some old icebreaker hands to predict trouble.

Trouble there was, from the beginning. The *Polar Star*'s shakedown in Puget Sound and the Strait of Juan de Fuca revealed a number of formidable problems, and she even ran aground, fortunately without being damaged. Her screws functioned properly, however, so when steering system, fuel transfer, and main propulsion control difficulties had been overcome, the *Polar Star* headed for the Chukchi Sea, north of Bering Strait, to test her icebreaking capability. Initially, this was outstanding, and when the starboard shaft malfunctioned, her commanding officer attributed it to a faulty stern tube bearing. Using turbines on the other two shafts, he extricated the ship from the heavy ice, but as she stood southward, the port shaft exhibited similar symptoms and also had to be locked. With cutter escort lest the center shaft fail, the *Polar Star* limped back to Seattle.

The cause of the difficulty became apparent when the propellers were removed—the pitch-changing mechanisms in the starboard and port propeller hubs had almost literally been destroyed. Damage to the center screw was less serious, probably because of its more sheltered position. The three propellers, which had been manufactured in Pennsylvania under license from a West German designer, were shipped back to the factory for major redesign and rebuilding, to make the mechanisms as strong as possible.[11] This process required more than a year, during which the big icebreaker lay alongside a Seattle pier.

Reinstallation of the propellers was finally completed early in November 1977, and the *Polar Star* departed for the Antarctic a week later. In past years, two icebreakers had been assigned to open the channel to McMurdo Station, the principal U.S. base in Antarctica. On this occasion, the *Polar Star* was to do so alone, while testing her screws and determining the limits within which Polar-class ships could operate. The initial channel-breaking was accomplished handily, but when she began to widen the channel, the screws striking broken ice caused "awesome" vibration. Then, instruments monitoring the propeller-pitch mechanisms indicated contamination of the hydraulic fluid, and higher pressures were required to change pitch, which became increasingly sluggish. Leaving the *Glacier* and the *Burton Island* to complete her assigned tasks, the *Polar Star* returned to Seattle.[12]

The second ship of the Polar class, the *Polar Sea,* had been delivered to the Coast Guard in January 1977, and after a preliminary

The Polar Sea, *foreground, and the* Polar Star *in the Strait of Juan de Fuca.*

shakedown cruise to San Francisco, she returned to her builder's yard to have her screws removed and modified. After a year of inactivity, the *Polar Sea* went to the Bering Sea in February 1978 for a month of icebreaking, during which she experienced vibration and propeller problems like those reported by her sister. She too returned to Seattle for further modification, which as in the *Polar Star,* included stiffening the thrust-bearing foundations to reduce vibration.[13]

The *Polar Star* went south again late in 1978, and again the problems of contaminated hydraulic fluid and slowing of pitch change leading to loss of pitch control appeared. The *Polar Sea,* operating in Arctic waters, had a less serious case of "propelleritis," and completed her assigned missions successfully.

Since that time, the propeller and other problems that relegated the two big icebreakers to the status of "Buildings 10 and 11" at the Coast Guard Support Center in Seattle for protracted periods of time seem to have been overcome to the extent that the ships can complete Arctic and Antarctic deployments regularly. The superiority of their design was never in doubt. One Polar-class vessel can do the work of two Wind class—each of the former operates two helicopters—and the newer ships are much more sea kindly. Despite their size, they are manned by smaller crews than the older vessels, thanks to extensive automation. This, however, necessitated the establishment of the Icebreaker Support Facility, which provides engineering maintenance, logistic, and personnel services that the ships' crews are unable to perform.[14]

The next additions to the Coast Guard's icebreaker force were 140-foot tugs intended to replace the 110-footers built before and during World War II. Nine were planned, with the Tacoma Boatbuilding Company of Tacoma, Washington, as builder. For budgetary

reasons, they were ordered over a considerable period of time; thus, the first, the *Katmai Bay*, was commissioned early in 1979, and the eighth, the *Thunder Bay*, followed in 1986. With the usual diesel-electric engineering plant providing 2,500 shaft horsepower, the 140-footer could make 14.7 knots, but full power was likely to be used only in icebreaking because the ship could reach 12 knots with one of the two diesel engines and generators in operation. A hull air lubrication ("bubbler") system, housed in a temporary deckhouse on the fantail, enhanced the vessel's icebreaking capability; it also proved to be a useful shiphandling device, a "poor man's version" of the bow thruster. Extensive automation permitted manning on a minimum level—three officers and fourteen men.

A 140-foot Bay-class tug, probably the Katmai Bay. *She and the* Bristol Bay *had black hulls; most of their later sisters were painted white on completion.*

With conventional single-screw propulsion, the 140-footers experienced none of the problems that bedeviled the Polar class. Indeed, the lack of accommodation for temporarily assigned personnel seemed their most serious deficiency, although their low freeboard and large superstructures would probably make them very vulnerable to icing in heavy weather with freezing temperatures.[15]

Tacoma Boat also received the contract for four medium-endurance cutters in fiscal 1977, with the first to be commissioned in 1980. These 270-foot vessels would be powered by two 3,500-horsepower diesels, each driving a controllable-pitch propeller. A helicopter deck and a hangar large enough for an antisubmarine

The Bear—*a "small, hump-backed hybrid" or a "highly capable platform"?*

helicopter were dominant features of the design, which included a single rapid-firing 76-millimeter gun of the type fitted in the Navy's latest frigates, with provision for additional armament and sonar to be installed in time of need. Again, minimum-level manning—ten officers and eighty-six men—was achieved, in part by the inclusion of a highly sophisticated computerized Command, Display, and Control System (COMDAC), which enhanced the ships' mission capability—and added to their cost.

The 270-footers were called the "Famous class," because each was to be named for a famous cutter of the past, with the first four christened the *Bear, Tampa, Harriet Lane,* and *Northland.* When nine more of these vessels were authorized, the Coast Guard awarded the contract to Tacoma Boat, after disqualifying two lower bidders because neither had submitted a proper bid. A federal judge, however, held that Tacoma Boat's contract was invalid, whereupon the Coast Guard cancelled it and after further investigation, awarded the contract to the original low bidder, Robert Derecktor of Middletown, Rhode Island, who has completed several of the cutters to the Coast Guard's apparent satisfaction.

The *Bear* was finally commissioned in February 1983, more than two years behind schedule, and her appearance brought considerable comment, much of it adverse. The new ship's 19.7-knot speed, her limited endurance, her lack of space for adaptation to future mission requirements, and her over-reliance on "black-box technology" were held to be serious deficiencies. A member of the design team, agreeing that the design left something to be desired, explained that it had been evolved primarily for patrolling the 200-mile economic resources zone, with special emphasis on ability to conduct helicopter operations throughout a two-week patrol.[16] In short, the 270-footers were not really multi-mission cutters, which was the more surprising because they were intended to replace the venerable Treasury-class vessels, perhaps the most versatile—and successful—Coast Guard cutters of them all. And the Treasury-class cutters were handsome ships, quite unlike the "small, humpbacked hybrids" of the Famous class.[17]

The critics did not go unanswered. One of the *Bear*'s officers asserted that the 270-footer "can and will perform any Coast Guard mission assigned as well or better than any WMEC or WHEC in the fleet."[18] Defense of one's ship comes naturally to sailors—yet experience may prove the critics wrong, at least in part.

The delay in completion of the first Famous-class cutters caused the Coast Guard to turn to the Navy once again, and in 1980 the salvage ship *Escape* and the fleet tugs *Lipan* and *Ute,* all nearing their fortieth birthdays and recently relegated to the reserve fleet, were acquired on loan. After minimal conversion, they were commissioned as medium endurance cutters, retaining their original names.

Admiral Owen W. Siler, commandant 1974–78.

These veterans were assigned to the Seventh District, which had become the Coast Guard's busiest, largely because of drug smuggling. While none of the nation's coasts appear to be completely free of smuggling activity, proximity to Latin America and Caribbean islands makes the Southeast the immediate destination of many drug cargoes. Some are flown in; obviously the Coast Guard can do little to interdict clandestine aerial traffic, but bulk cargoes can still be brought in more economically by sea, and the prevention of maritime smuggling remains one of the service's primary missions.

Whether Admirals Owen W. Siler, John B. Hayes, and James S. Gracey, who served successively as commandant during the twelve years beginning in 1974, developed anti-smuggling tactics similar to those implemented by Rear Admiral Frederick C. Billard to deal with rum-runners is not clear. Apparently the principal counter-smuggling activity consists of patrolling waters most likely to be frequented by smugglers. Unlike the Prohibition era, when interception outside the 12-mile limit would almost certainly result in the rum-runner's release by the courts, Coast Guard personnel fifty years later can board a ship on the high seas with the consent of either the master or the country of registry. A radio message seeking the latter's permission is relayed through the State Department, with the time required for a response varying from a few hours to a week or more. A similar delay can be expected should there be reason to doubt the validity of a suspect's registration, in which case Headquarters must determine if the vessel is legally "assimilated to statelessness" and so subject to U.S. jurisdiction on the high seas.[19] In either event, of course, permission to board may not be forthcoming, leaving the cutter commanding officer to decide whether to stay with the suspicious vessel until she enters U.S. waters or continue his patrol.

Admiral John B. Hayes, commandant, 1978–82.

Admiral James S. Gracey, commandant 1982–86.

As in the Prohibition era, identification of smugglers is difficult, because almost any vessel sighted may be carrying an illicit cargo. Many of those seized had simply been engaged for that occasion by agents of the anonymous drug owner or buyer. And when a vessel has been seized, the captor usually has to escort or tow her into port, thereby opening the way for others to reach the point at which their cargoes are transferred to smaller craft for landing.

In 1984, it was estimated that about 20 percent of the drug-runners in waters patrolled by Seventh District cutters were being intercepted.[20] The percentage would undoubtedly be higher were there more Coast Guard vessels. The drug war, however, has not led to an increase in the number of units and personnel even remotely comparable to that of the Prohibition era, which is the more remarkable because many would agree that the widespread use of hallucinogenic drugs is a greater danger to American society than that of alcoholic beverages. The absence of a Coast Guard Destroyer Force is not surprising; the Navy no longer has many destroyer-type ships in its reserve fleets, and if it did, they would be too large and too expensive to function effectively in an anti-smuggling role. But there has been nothing analogous to the "six-bitter, buck, and buck-and-a-quarter" building program that added almost 250 patrol boats to the service's strength during the 1920s. The closest equivalent would seem to be the three fast 110-foot surface-effect vessels and the sixteen 110-foot Island-class cutters authorized since 1980.

The critical shortage of cutters was emphasized when in April 1980 the Cuban government permitted numerous Cubans to embark at Mariel for passage to the United States. It quickly became apparent that this would be an exodus of some magnitude, and Admiral Hayes proposed that a cutter be stationed at Mariel to process would-be immigrants, or if the Cuban government would not permit this—it would not—that cutters pick up refugees just outside Cuba's territorial waters for transportation to the nearest U.S. port. This proposal was not implemented; by that time privately owned vessels were flocking to Mariel, where they embarked Cuban passengers with little regard for capacity or seaworthiness. Predictably, many found themselves in difficulty when they stood into the turbulent waters of the Florida Straits, and Coast Guard cutters had to abandon their quest for drug smugglers to become lifesavers. They were too few to meet the demand, so President James E. Carter diverted naval vessels—five amphibious warfare ships and six minesweepers—and antisubmarine aircraft from exercises in the Caribbean Sea to assist. Other Coast Guard districts on the Atlantic coast sent seventeen cutters, five boats, and sixteen aircraft to augment the Seventh District's forces, leaving themselves extremely short-handed as recreational boating activity swelled with the coming of summer to their waters. To alleviate this paucity in part, President Carter authorized the commandant to order 900 reservists to active duty in those districts for six weeks.

Exactly when the Cuban exodus ended is not clear. President Carter ordered that the sea lift of refugees be terminated in mid-May. But termination was not that simple. A number of vessels were in the Bahia del Mariel at the time, and these would not lose money by sailing without immigrant cargoes. Coast Guard cutters were patrolling the Florida coast and straits to prevent direct passage to Cuba, so other boats steered evasive courses through the Bahamas before heading for Mariel. After 30 June, by which time some 115,000 Cubans had been ferried to Florida, the traffic fell off markedly; only 10,000 more came during the next four months, most likely because the Cuban government decided to limit the number of departures.[21] The "blockade patrol" designed to stop the influx of refugees, reinforced by three Navy patrol boats and four minesweepers, continued into the autumn.

Once again, the Coast Guard—with Navy assistance—had carried out an unanticipated mission quite successfully—at a price. Long periods underway with little pierside availability left insufficient time for cutter crews to carry out engineering and other maintenance, and the effects of this unavoidable neglect would become apparent in weeks and months to come. Drug smugglers had enjoyed a "happy time," running their noxious cargoes in with little fear of apprehension. Nor had the refugee problem ended in 1980. For years to come, some Cubans would seize any opportunity to escape to the United States and Coast Guard cutters would be drawn to less familiar

The White Alder *on the lower Mississippi River, where she spent her entire Coast Guard career. She was sunk near White Castle, La.*

The Jarvis *(foreground) almost became the third cutter lost in Alaskan waters. She and the* Mellon *are shown refueling from the Navy's oiler* Ponchatoula.

waters to intercept boatloads of Haitians fleeing their unhappy homeland.

The period after 1967 witnessed several incidents that did not reflect as favorably on the Coast Guard, among them the loss of three vessels and the near-loss of another. The 133-foot buoy tender *White Alder* was sunk in collision with the Taiwanese freighter *Helena* one clear December evening on the Mississippi River in 1968. Only three members of her twenty-man crew survived, none of whom had been on watch, so the buoy tender's failure to respond to the *Helena*'s whistle signal and efforts to establish radio contact could not be explained, nor could the reason the *White Alder* suddenly and fatally turned directly across the freighter's bow be determined.[22]

The next mishap did not result in loss of life, and investigators were able to ascertain the causes of the grounding of the new cutter *Jarvis* and of her subsequent near-loss. Encountering heavy weather in the Bering Sea in the course of a November 1972 fishery patrol, the 378-footer sought shelter in Dutch Harbor. The wind increased during the night, and inexperienced watchstanders, relying on a single radar bearing, failed to note that the ship was dragging her anchor. Belatedly summoned to the bridge, her captain elected to weigh the anchor instead of slipping the chain. Heaving in 75 fathoms of anchor chain with the wind gusting to 70 knots required thirty-five minutes, and since the anchor detail neither hosed off the chain so that marks on its links could be seen nor determined the way the chain was tending, no one was aware that the anchor was aweigh until it was actually in sight. Only then were the *Jarvis*'s diesels backed, too late to keep her from striking a reef, shearing off the sonar dome, damaging the starboard propeller, and holing the shell plating under the engine room before she cleared it.

Prudence would seem to have dictated that the damaged cutter remain in even a less than adequate anchorage under the circumstances, especially since the location of the ruptured plating made it difficult to ascertain the nature and extent of the damage. Nonetheless, temporary repairs had reduced the leakage to 150 gallons per minute the next afternoon, and when the weather forecast indicated that intense storms were expected north and east of Dutch Harbor, her captain requested permission to depart for Honolulu. Assured that the repairs were adequate and that no escort was needed, the Seventeenth District operations officer in Juneau agreed, and the *Jarvis* put to sea.

With two pumps keeping the water level down, the cutter traversed Akutan Pass without difficulty, but when she left the shelter of the land, her hull began to work in the seaway and the leakage grew worse. Temporary use of a third pump coped with this, and the *Jarvis* held her course. Wind and sea conditions deteriorated steadily, the rate of flooding increased, and two hours later the cutter attempted to come about. She rolled heavily in the trough, however, and fearing that she might capsize, her captain headed southward once more, hoping to find smoother water beyond the 100-fathom curve. It was a vain hope; progressive flooding soon caused the main engines to be stopped, and the southwesterly gale drove the *Jarvis* inexorably toward Akutan Island.

Two Japanese fishing vessels were among those responding to the crippled cutter's distress signal. One of them, the *Kogo Maru No. 3,* got a line to her early the next morning, by which time the *Jarvis* was within 3 miles of the rocky shore.

Towed back to Dutch Harbor, the big cutter received more adequate repairs. She then made the passage to Honolulu under her own power, with the *Winona* as escort. Her damage was made good at a cost of $400,000. Not surprisingly, her captain was relieved of his command, retiring soon afterward, and two junior officers received letters of reprimand for their inept performance of duty.[23]

Almost ten years after the *White Alder* tragedy, another Coast Guard vessel became a collision victim with tragic consequences. The training cutter *Cuyahoga*, with sixteen officer candidates and a crew numbering thirteen, of whom four were temporarily assigned, stood out of the York River on 20 October 1978. The elderly "buck-and-a-quarter," the oldest active commissioned vessel in the U.S. service, was on a weekend training cruise to Baltimore, from which the Argentinian motorship *Santa Cruz II,* laden with coal, had just sailed.

The two ships closed on nearly reciprocal courses in Chesapeake Bay, meeting off the mouth of the Potomac River, in which the *Cuyahoga* was to anchor for the night. Visibility was excellent, and each vessel sighted the other's running lights almost twenty minutes before the collision. While officer candidates were manning a number of stations on board the cutter, her commanding officer, a chief boatswain, was on the bridge as senior deck officer. He reportedly saw only a masthead light and a port sidelight, and the radar contact

The Cuyahoga. *Her appearance had changed considerably in the course of her long career.*

appeared quite small. Assuming that the *Santa Cruz II* was another small vessel standing in to anchor in the Potomac, he turned the *Cuyahoga* across her bow, which struck the cutter amidships at 9:07 P.M. The 125-footer rolled on her beam ends, flooded rapidly, and sank in two minutes. Those of her company who could, took to the water, supporting themselves on pieces of flotsam because they had been unable to get life jackets. Then the *Cuyahoga*'s 14-foot utility boat broke free and floated to the surface. The senior petty officer removed the boat cover, and under his direction, the boat was bailed out and the injured men helped into it. The *Santa Cruz II* picked up the eighteen survivors, while her motor lifeboat searched for others. None was found; eleven had died, of whom five were officer candidates, including one of the two Indonesian naval officers who had sailed in the *Cuyahoga*.

In the investigation that followed, the cutter's commanding officer declined to testify or to answer questions. A general court-martial found him guilty of dereliction of duty; and he received a letter of reprimand and lost 200 numbers on the seniority list. The sentence would probably have been more severe but for the fact that the minimal size of the *Cuyahoga*'s crew required that the senior deck officer divide his attention between navigating the vessel and instructing officer candidates. This and some equipment deficiencies had been pointed out repeatedly during routine biennial inspections, but none of the recommendations for improvement had been acted on.[24]

Little more than a year later, collision claimed another Coast

Guard vessel, with heavier loss of life. The 180-foot buoy tender *Blackthorn*, which had just completed a lengthy overhaul at Tampa, Florida, was outward bound during the evening of 28 January 1980, while the American tanker *Capricorn*, laden with oil, was standing into Tampa Bay. Again, the visibility was excellent, but there was a considerable amount of vessel traffic in the relatively narrow channel, including the outward-bound Russian passenger ship *Kazakhstan*, which overtook the *Blackthorn* almost a half-hour before the collision. After leaving the channel temporarily to let the Russian pass, the buoy tender continued almost in mid-channel. Her commanding officer was on the bridge, as were several other officers, but the officer of the deck, an ensign, had the conn.

Soon after the *Blackthorn* passed under the Sunshine Skyway Bridge, which spans the entrance to Tampa Bay, her executive officer called the conning officer's attention to the lights of an approaching vessel hitherto obscured by the brilliantly lighted *Kazakhstan*. This was the *Capricorn*, which did not sight the buoy tender until after the Russian vessel had passed close aboard. There was still time to avoid a collision, but both vessels were approaching a bend in the channel, and when the tanker began to turn left, they would not be able to pass port to port. Unable to establish radio contact with the buoy tender, the *Capricorn*'s pilot blew two short whistle blasts to indicate that they should pass starboard to starboard. There was no reply; as the tanker's whistle sounded the danger signal, the *Blackthorn* began to turn right, still almost in mid-channel, as was the *Capricorn*.

The buoy tender's officer of the deck erroneously assumed that

The damage caused by the Capricorn's *anchor is clearly visible in this photograph of the* Blackthorn *after she was raised.*

361

a port to port passing had been arranged by radio—standing orders did not provide for whistle signals if radio communication was in use—and his attention was diverted by the necessity to negotiate the bend in the channel. The commanding officer, emerging from the chartroom, recognized the danger and shouted "Right full rudder" followed by "Stand by for collision," and backed the engines full speed. Meanwhile, the *Capricorn* was turning hard left, and as the two ships collided port bow to port bow, her engine was stopped and then went full speed astern.

The collision probably would not have been fatal had not the *Capricorn*'s port anchor, ready for letting go, become imbedded in the *Blackthorn*'s side after ripping through a length of plating. Both ships' engines were backing, but their combined speed had been about 25 knots at the time of impact, and as the tanker's port anchor chain ran out, she towed the much smaller buoy tender stern first for some distance. As the *Capricorn* slowed, the chain sagged to the bottom and the *Blackthorn*, with the anchor still imbedded in her side, swung over it; then the chain tightened, capsizing the buoy tender in a matter of seconds. Off-duty personnel, who had mustered on the mess deck in response to the collision alarm, found themselves trapped in darkness. For six enlisted men, the situation was the more terrifying because they had just reported on board and had had little opportunity to familiarize themselves with the ship. Some of them apparently "escaped" into the engine room, from which there was no further exit. Most of those who had been on deck or on the bridge were quickly picked up by *The Bayou,* a shrimp boat that had been following the *Blackthorn* to sea. She rescued twenty-three survivors, a few of whom had managed to make their way out of the lower deck spaces. A Coast Guard utility boat picked up four men soon afterward. The *Capricorn,* which had been run aground to avert collision with the Sunshine Skyway Bridge, sent a lifeboat to search for survivors, while Coast Guard and police helicopters, a variety of small craft, and civilian divers joined in the search. To no avail—twenty-three "Blackthorns" had died; there were twenty-seven survivors.

For the second time in less than two years, Coast Guard investigators had to determine why a ship of their service had collided with another on a clear night in an area traversed safely by countless other vessels. After reconstructing the events of the period just before and immediately following the collision, they found that numerous factors had contributed to it, with the immediate cause being "the failure of both vessels to keep well to the side of the channel which lay on their starboard side." "The failure of the persons in charge of both vessels to ascertain the intentions of the other through the exchange of appropriate whistle signals" was considered the primary contributing cause.[25] With regard to the former, one must note that the *Capricorn* drew more than 31 feet of water, the *Blackthorn* less than 14 feet. Quite clearly, the primary responsibility rested with the buoy tender's commanding officer, who had permitted an inexperienced junior officer to conn his ship in a heavily traveled and unfamiliar waterway at night with little supervision, and with the junior officer, whose performance had been far short of what reasonably might have been expected.

The *Blackthorn* was raised three weeks later, but the cost of repairs was considered prohibitive, so she was formally decommissioned. To take her place, the Coast Guard re-acquired her older near-sister, the *Cowslip,* which had been sold out of the service in 1976. After thorough refurbishing, the *Cowslip* resumed her career as a buoy tender in 1981.

The final incident that must be related here had much less serious consequences, yet it brought the Coast Guard more unfavorable publicity than even the *Blackthorn* sinking. On 23 November 1970, a Lithuanian radio operator serving in the *Sovietskaya Litva,* the "mothership" of a Soviet fishing fleet operating off New England, defected to the cutter *Vigilant* while she was alongside the Soviet vessel, on board which a meeting between an American fisheries delegation and Russian officials had just ended. The defector, Simas I. Kudirka, had indicated his intention to seek asylum some hours earlier, leading the *Vigilant* to request advice from First District Headquarters in Boston. The district commander was on sick leave, so the chief of staff, acting in his place, relayed the request to Coast Guard Headquarters, which sought guidance from the State Department. The response, to the effect that nothing should be done to encourage a potential defector and that no further advice could be given until he was actually on board the *Vigilant,* was of little assistance. Meanwhile, the convalescent district commander had been informed of the situation. Although he had no responsibility in the matter, he advised the acting commander that to offer asylum would jeopardize the fishery talks and possibly endanger the U.S. delegation on board the Soviet vessel.

By the time Kudirka boarded the *Vigilant,* it was late afternoon, and too many officers and officials seem to have been more interested in returning to their homes at a timely hour than in arranging to monitor a potentially difficult situation. Thus, the acting district commander could not be reached until some time after the defector suddenly appeared on the cutter's bridge; instead, her commanding officer talked with the district commander, who asserted that Kudirka should be returned if the Soviets made a formal request. Subsequent efforts by the acting commander to obtain guidance from Coast Guard Headquarters and the State Department were thwarted by apparent misunderstandings and the fact that senior officers and officials were not immediately available. Ultimately, he accepted the district commander's advice and directed that the defector be returned. Efforts to persuade Kudirka to leave the *Vigilant* voluntarily failed, so five Soviet sailors boarded the cutter with her commanding officer's permission. After a chase around the

Vigilant's decks, the sailors overpowered Kudirka, with whom they were returned to the *Sovietskaya Litva* in one of the cutter's small boats.[26]

When it became known that Russian sailors had boarded a U.S. Coast Guard cutter only a mile off Martha's Vineyard, well within U.S. territorial waters, and forcibly removed a would-be defector while the cutter's crew made no effort to interfere, American reaction was predictably bitter. President Richard M. Nixon was reported to be outraged, and demonstrators in several major cities protested the incident. A congressional subcommittee investigated, as did the State Department and the Coast Guard.[27] Three of the service's officers were held to have acted wrongly: The acting district commander had failed to keep the commandant informed and had failed to order the defector held until he had been advised by proper authority. The convalescent district commander had offered advice that had the force of orders, on a subject on which he was ill-informed, and had assumed an authority beyond that of any officer of the service. The commanding officer of the *Vigilant* had allowed Soviet crewmen to remove the defector from his ship without any attempt at restraint. Reviewing the investigation report, the commandant recommended that the first two be tried by general court-martial unless they requested immediate retirement, and that the third receive an administrative reprimand and be relieved of his command. The secretary of transportation disallowed the court-martial recommendations on the ground that the two officers had already been subjected to severe criticism; both were permitted to retire with punitive reprimands.[28]

Five unfortunate incidents in little more than eleven years may leave the impression that the Coast Guard's level of performance had declined markedly. Many other occurrences might be cited to counter this impression, for units and personnel have demonstrated repeatedly that the Coast Guard under the Department of Transportation has continued the exceptional record that they and their predecessors had established before 1967. One operation, which was described at the time as "one of the largest and most successful maritime rescues in modern times," will suffice to epitomize these.[29]

On 30 September 1980, the Dutch cruise vessel *Prinsendam* sailed from Vancouver, British Columbia, bound for Singapore, touching at Ketchikan, Alaska, and several Japanese and Chinese ports en route. The seven-year-old, 472-foot ship was manned by a crew numbering 205, and she had 319 passengers on board, most of whom were middle-aged or elderly Americans.[30] After leaving Ketchikan and cruising through scenic Glacier Bay, she headed out into the North Pacific Ocean.

Soon after midnight on 4 October, an Indonesian greaser noticed oil spurting from the low-pressure supply line on one of her main diesel engines, and by the time he had reported it, contact with a hot exhaust duct had ignited the oil. The duty engineers failed to recognize the cause of the fire immediately and to cut off the flow of oil; thus, the fire spread with some rapidity. Almost forty-five minutes later, the engine room was closed and carbon dioxide released to smother the flames. The *Prinsendam*'s master used the public address system to notify passengers and crew members, asking the former to assemble in a lounge on the promenade deck. At 1:08 A.M., a radio message was sent, giving the ship's position, about 120 miles west of Sitka, and stating that she was afire. With the main engines stopped and efforts to start the auxiliaries unsuccessful, there was no water pressure in the fire hoses. The fire, which had not been quenched by the carbon dioxide, continued to spread, so the *Prinsendam* sent an SOS.

Her earlier message had alerted Coast Guard commands, and the North Pacific Search and Rescue Coordinator in Juneau requested that the service's air stations at Kodiak and Sitka send suitable aircraft to evaluate the situation. Each launched two HH-3F helicopters, and Kodiak sent two C-130s, one of which became on-scene commander. The 378-foot cutters *Boutwell,* at Juneau, and *Mellon,* on her way from Seattle for a fishery patrol, and the 180-foot buoy tender *Woodrush,* at Sitka, were directed to the *Prinsendam*'s assistance as well. In little more than an hour, the *Boutwell* was on her way at 25 knots, while the buoy tender headed for the scene at about half that speed.

Merchant vessels also received the *Prinsendam*'s messages, and the closest, the *Williamsburgh,* steered for the burning ship at 17 knots. Laden with oil from Valdez and drawing 65 feet of water, the 1,095-foot American tanker would be most important in the rescue operation, for she had two helicopter pads, her size and draft made her unusually stable, and she could offer a reasonable degree of comfort to some hundreds of people.

With the fire spreading and no means of fighting it, the *Prinsendam*'s master decided that she must be abandoned, and at 5:15 A.M., the passengers and most of the crew climbed into the six open lifeboats, a motor launch, and some life rafts, which were lowered into 5-foot swells without incident. Many of the passengers were extremely lightly clad, some in night dress, so the prospect of spending hours in unheated small boats was hardly encouraging. A Coast Guard helicopter had lowered a portable pump and a chief warrant officer to the *Prinsendam*'s deck, and the master and fifty volunteers stayed on board to try to bring the fire under control.

The *Williamsburgh* made radar contact with the distressed vessel just before dawn, and by 7:00 A.M. she was maneuvering to provide a lee for the first lifeboat, no easy matter for a 225,000-ton tanker. The first passenger came on board twenty minutes later. Helping elderly people up the Jacob's ladder was a time-consuming process as well, and the weather was deteriorating. Thus, a better way had to be found.

The helicopters provided it. Assisted by a helicopter from Elmendorf Air Force Base near Anchorage and two Canadian Armed

Heroines of the Prinsendam *rescue: An HH-3F hoisting a survivor aboard and the* Williamsburgh *with a helicopter on her deck. (Courtesy U.S. Coast Guard)*

Forces helicopters, they hovered over the boats while hoisting their occupants in rescue baskets, then flew to the *Williamsburgh* to touch down while the passengers descended to the tanker's deck, to be plied with hot coffee and soup and wrapped in dry blankets. When a helicopter had to be refueled, it took its load of survivors to Yakutat, where medical personnel—four doctors, seven Canadian paramedics, and ten medical technicians and hospital corpsmen— had been assembled. Medical supplies and blankets were flown to the *Williamsburgh* from Yakutat, as was an Air Force doctor, and some

Air Force para-rescuemen were lowered into lifeboats to care for passengers until they could be removed to the tanker.

Two other merchant vessels, the *Sohio Intrepid* and the *Portland,* joined the rescuers soon after noon and stood by to assist as needed. At 1:45 P.M., the *Boutwell* approached, to be informed that those remaining in the *Prinsendam* were unable to control the fire and wished to be evacuated. They were removed without incident, which was as well because the wind and sea were getting up and the temperature was falling. Not everything went as smoothly—a Canadian helicopter lost all except main propulsion power and had to be escorted to Yakutat, and the Air Force helicopter had to make an emergency landing on the *Sohio Intrepid*'s deck late in the afternoon.

The rescue operation was apparently completed by 6:30 P.M., and with the approval of her owners' agent, the *Williamsburgh* was ordered back to Valdez so that the survivors could be disembarked as soon as possible. The other vessels were released, while the *Boutwell* remained with the *Prinsendam,* fortunately as it turned out, for at 9 P.M., the Elmendorf Air Force Base radioed that two para-rescuemen who had been lowered into a lifeboat could not be accounted for. Most of the survivors aboard the *Boutwell* were sure that they had been picked up by a Canadian helicopter, but there was enough uncertainty to justify a search. More than an hour later, the *Sohio Intrepid* reported that the two Air Force men had been left in a boat with twenty survivors, which had last been seen just before the Air Force helicopter had landed on board the *Intrepid.* The *Boutwell* continued her search in 25-foot seas with 25–35 knot wind and rain showers, aided by a C-130 that provided illumination with a "night sun." The boat was sighted four hours later, and its twenty-two occupants, some wearing only pajamas, were hustled on board the *Boutwell,* which immediately headed for Sitka, leaving the *Woodrush* to check all drifting boats and rafts for anyone who might have been overlooked and to act as on-scene commander until the *Mellon* assumed that role. This time, the rescue operation had been completed; all the *Prinsendam* passengers and crew members had been accounted for, and all were in surprisingly good condition despite their ordeal.

There was still hope of salving the *Prinsendam.* Her owners engaged the Canadian tug *Straits Commodore* to tow her to Portland, Ore., for survey and possible repair, and while awaiting the tug, the *Mellon* attempted to put fire fighters on board the still-burning ship. Intense heat forced that effort to be abandoned, but on 7 October a Coast Guard helicopter ferried the vessel's chief engineer and some others to the *Prinsendam* to rig a towing bridle and assess the fire damage. A rising wind made it inadvisable to remove them before nightfall; they spent an uneasy night, and the *Mellon* summoned the helicopter from Yakutat when the fire flared up again the next morning. The *Straits Commodore* continued the tow for several days, but the *Prinsendam* began to list heavily and to settle by the bow. She sank on 11 October, a week after she had been abandoned.[31]

Considering the number of those in the *Prinsendam,* her position, and the advanced age of many of the passengers, it seemed almost miraculous that all on board could have been rescued without apparent lasting ill-effects. The presence of the *Williamsburgh* was one of the most important factors in achieving this success; she provided a refuge for most of the survivors, and some of her men had manned a lifeboat that removed people from life rafts, which might have been capsized by the helicopters' rotor wash.[32] Flying the survivors directly to Yakutat, as originally planned, would have required a much longer time. The *Boutwell* reached the scene more than six hours after the rescue operation began, and whether the helicopters could have touched down on her flight deck to discharge survivors in the prevailing wind and sea conditions is not clear. At best, the rescue would have taken a much longer time, and some of the more infirm passengers would undoubtedly have died had the *Williamsburgh* not been present. The Canadian and U.S. Air Force contributions had been important as well. Nonetheless, one must agree with the survivor who wrote: "Some may call the rescue effort a miracle, but it was only accomplished because of the experience and dedication of the Coast Guard."[33]

With serious budget constraints, a 1981 congressional committee report to the effect that the service was no more than "*Semi-Paratus,*" and repeated assertions that its many missions could be carried out more economically were they divided among various other governmental agencies and private contractors, the Coast Guard of the mid-1980s faces an uncertain future. The situation is somewhat reminiscent of that faced by Captain Commandant Ellsworth P. Bertholf in 1912; and those who would diminish markedly or terminate the Coast Guard should consider carefully the record of more than seventy years of meritorious service that it has provided to the nation and to those who use the sea, since President Woodrow Wilson signed the Act to Create the Coast Guard.

NOTES

CHAPTER ONE

1. Quoted in 62d Congress, 2d Session, House of Representatives Document 670, p. 285.
2. Stephen H. Evans, *The United States Coast Guard, 1790–1915: A Definitive History*, p. 7.
3. Quoted in *Annual Report of the United States Coast Guard, 1915*, p. 63. Hereafter cited as *Annual Report* with relevant year.
4. Irving H. King, *George Washington's Coast Guard: Origins of the U.S. Revenue Cutter Service, 1789–1801*, pp. 162–65.
5. 62 Cong. 2 Sess. H. Doc. 670, 299–349.
6. 60 Cong. 1 Sess. H. Rept. 1057; Yellow Fever Patrol, 1905, Entry 177, Record Group 26, Records of the United States Coast Guard. This collection hereafter cited as RG 26.
7. 62 Cong. 2 Sess. H. Doc. 670, 290.
8. Robert F. Bennett, *Surfboats, Rockets, and Carronades*, pp. 1–2, 19–20.
9. Ibid., 67–75.
10. Evans, 100–101.
11. Ibid., chapter 9.
12. Ibid.
13. Ibid., 111–15; William R. Hunt, *Arctic Passage: The Turbulent History of the Land and People of the Bering Sea, 1697–1975*, pp. 227–33.
14. Evans, chapter 9.
15. Ibid., 147–48.
16. 62 Cong. 2 Sess. H. Doc. 670, 361.
17. *Annual Report of the Secretary of the Treasury, 1865*, pp. 32–33.
18. Ibid., *1873*, xxix.
19. *Annual Report, 1915*, 55–60.
20. King, chapter 2 and p. 153.
21. Evans, 28, 55; 62 Cong. 2 Sess. H. Doc. 670, 310–11.
22. *Annual Report of the Secretary of the Treasury, 1872*, p. xiv; Evans, 93.
23. Evans, 95–96; 76 Cong. 1 Sess. S. Doc. 81, 16, lists eight cadets in the original class.
24. 62 Cong. 2 Sess. H. Doc. 670, 321–22.
25. 76 Cong. 1 Sess. S. Doc. 81, 17–18.
26. Truman R. Strobridge, The Public Works of the Coast Guard: A Historical Survey, 1790–1976, copy in Reference Collection, U.S. Coast Guard Headquarters.
27. 76 Cong. 1 Sess. S. Doc. 81, 18.
28. Quoted in 59 Cong. 1 Sess. S. Rept. 129.
29. 59 Cong. 2 Sess. S. Doc. 399, Part 2.
30. Quoted in Evans, 36.
31. Ibid., 53, 59, 63–64.
32. Ibid., 90–94, 103.
33. Ibid., 199–200; 62 Cong. 2 Sess. H. Doc. 670, 365–67.

CHAPTER TWO

1. John F. Murphy, *Cutter Captain: The Life and Times of John C. Cantwell,* pp. 138, 141.
2. Bertholf to Carden, 22 Jan. 1909, and reply, 6 Mar. 1909, Godfrey L. Carden Collection.
3. Record of General Court-Martial, 3 and 4 Sept. 1884, copy in Bertholf Record as a Cadet. Bertholf was found guilty of having looked on while a fellow midshipman ordered fourth classmen to leave their hammocks and stand on their heads after lights out. The punishment for such a minor transgression would undoubtedly have been less harsh but for the fact that hazing had resulted in the death of a midshipman not long before.
4. Murphy, 130.
5. Ibid., 135–36.
6. 62 Cong. 2 Sess. H. Doc. 670, 269.
7. Nagel to Taft, 10 Jan. 1912 and 8 Feb. 1912, quoted in ibid., 379–81.
8. Meyer to Taft, 7 Feb. 1912, quoted in ibid., 381.
9. MacVeagh to Taft, 26 Feb. 1912, quoted in ibid., 382–89.
10. Bertholf to MacVeagh, quoted in ibid., 389–97.
11. Bertholf to G. L. Carden, 1 July 1912, Carden Collection.
12. MacVeagh to Taft, 26 Feb. 1912, quoted in 62 Cong. 2 Sess. H. Doc. 670, 384.
13. Kimball to MacVeagh, 25 Mar. 1911, quoted in ibid., 281.
14. Telegram, L. P. Leheurier to Taft, undated copy in Subj. Class. 601, Operations of units, RG 26. This obviously was sent soon after the *Titanic*'s loss.
15. *Annual Reports of the Navy Department, 1912,* pp. 147, 197.
16. Bertholf to Allen, 4 Jan. 1913, copy in Ice Patrol File, Box 1871, RG 26.
17. MacVeagh to Bertholf, 10 Jan. 1913, personal, ibid.
18. Bertholf to MacVeagh, 18 Jan. 1913, copy in ibid.
19. Meyer to MacVeagh, 28 Feb. 1913, copy in ibid.
20. Instructions to the *Scotia*'s master and Bertholf's testimony before House Committee on Appropriations on Deficiency Bill for Fiscal Year 1913, copies in ibid.
21. Copies of this correspondence, 5 and 8 Apr. 1913, and Bertholf's reply to all, 11 Apr. 1913, ibid.
22. Clipping from *London and Liverpool Journal of Commerce,* 9 Oct. 1913, ibid. The British delegation to the International Conference on the Safety of Life at Sea later admitted that the *Scotia*'s work had not been "as thorough as was desired." 63 Cong. 2 Sess. S. Doc. 463, 80.
23. *Annual Report of the Secretary of the Treasury, 1913,* pp. 9–10.
24. International Convention Relating to the Safety of Life at Sea (translation), 63 Cong. 2 Sess. S. Doc. 463, 79–80.
25. Ibid., 9–10, 79–80.
26. *Annual Report of the Secretary of the Treasury, 1914,* p. 37.
27. Charles Hocking, *Dictionary of Disasters at Sea during the Age of Steam, 1824–1926,* 1:156.
28. *International Conference on Safety of Life at Sea, London, April 16–May 31, 1929,* pp. 70, 72, 74.
29. Crisp to comdr., Bering Sea Fleet, 7 Oct. 1914, quoted in *Annual Report, 1915,* 114–18.
30. Ibid., 94–95.
31. Ibid., 27–28.
32. Ibid., 119.
33. Ibid., 121.
34. Ibid., 122, 276. It should be noted that the foregoing account of the

Hanalei disaster differs markedly from that given in James A. Gibbs, Jr., *Shipwrecks of the Pacific Coast,* pp. 235–38.

CHAPTER THREE

1. 63 Cong. 2 Sess. S. Rept. 300; *Congressional Record,* Vol. 2, Part 2; Evans, 214–16.
2. Bertholf to Mrs. L. H. Crisp, 12 Feb. 1915, Bertholf Correspondence, 1912–21.
3. The full text of this act is printed in *Annual Report, 1920,* 45–47.
4. Ibid.
5. Ibid., *1915,* 45.
6. Ibid., 37.
7. Newton, memorandum for the secretary, 8 Feb. 1915, copy in Ref. Coll., USCGHQ.
8. *Annual Report, 1915,* 45–53.
9. Carden to Thomas M. Moore, 27 Feb. 1915, Carden Collection; Bertholf to Mrs. L.H. Crisp, 12 Feb. 1915, Bertholf Corr., 1912–21.
10. Quoted in *Annual Report, 1915,* 43.
11. Quoted in ibid., 18.
12. Ibid., *1917,* 104–14.
13. Special Order No. 15, 2 Apr. 1917, quoted in ibid., 28–31.
14. Ibid., *1916,* 12.
15. Secretary of Commerce William C. Redfield to McAdoo, 10 Mar. 1915; Newton to Redfield, 15 Mar. 1915, Subj. Class. 627, Examination of lifeboatmen, RG 26.
16. *Annual Report, 1916,* 16–17.
17. Ibid., 29. Evans, 189, is obviously in error in stating that six officers were so assigned.
18. Bertholf testimony to General Board, 20 May 1919, quoted in memorandum of 10 May 1945, copy in Philip B. Eaton Papers; see also Bertholf, memorandum for secretary of the treasury, 20 Apr. 1918, copy in Woodrow Wilson Papers.
19. *Annual Report, 1915,* 20; ibid., *1916,* 15.

CHAPTER FOUR

1. An Act to create the Coast Guard, quoted in *Annual Report, 1915,* 43.
2. Bertholf to secretary of the treasury, 20 Mar. 1915, Subj. Class. 631, Cooperation with the Navy: Plans and orders, etc., RG 26.
3. Ibid.
4. Newton to secretary of the navy, 12 Jan. 1917, Mobilization of the Coast Guard when Required to Operate as a part of the Navy, ibid.
5. Charles E. Johnston and Richard O. Crisp, *A History of the Coast Guard in the World War,* 1:48–49 and 2:209A–09B.
6. Ibid., 1:27–29; Bertholf to chief, Bureau of Navigation, 11 May 1917, Subj. Class. 631.
7. Bertholf to chief, Bureau of Navigation, 22 July 1918, ibid.
8. Bertholf to Capt. W. V. Pratt, 26 July 1917; chief of naval operations to Bertholf, 30 July 1917, ibid.; Bertholf to R. O. Crisp, 13 Aug. 1917, Bertholf Corr., 1912–21.
9. Bertholf to Crisp, 27 Sept. 1917, Bertholf Corr., 1912–21.
10. Johnston and Crisp, 1:28–29; Bertholf to chief, Bureau of Navigation, 11 May 1917, Subj. Class. 631; Bertholf to Crisp, 6 July 1917, Bertholf Corr., 1912–21.

11. Cantwell to Bertholf, 18 June 1917, Subj. Class. 606, Collisions, accidents, etc., RG 26.
12. Reports of investigations of the *McCulloch*'s loss, Subj. Class. 123, Boards of inquiry and investigation, RG 26.
13. Engineer in chief and constructor for hulls to commandant, 20 June 1923, with enclosure, ibid.
14. Johnston and Crisp, 1:66–67A.
15. Quoted in ibid., 1:68–71; Hocking, 2:481–82.
16. Johnston and Crisp, 1:39–40; *Dictionary of American Naval Fighting Ships*, 4:437. Hereafter cited as *Naval Fighting Ships*.
17. Report of the U.S. Coast Guard, in *Annual Report of the Secretary of the Navy, 1918*, p. 1618.
18. Riley Brown, *The Story of the Coast Guard*, pp. 74–76.
19. Records of Proceedings of Boards of Investigation to inquire into Charges preferred against Captain G. L. Carden, U.S. Coast Guard, 9 Sept. 1918 and 20 Aug. 1919, copies in Carden Collection.
20. Johnston and Crisp, 1:36.
21. Bertholf to Navy Department (Operations), 9 Feb. 1918, Subj. Class. 631.
22. Ibid.; *Naval Fighting Ships*, 3:473. She was replaced in 1922 by a former Army mineplanter that was renamed the *Pequot*. This steel-hulled 166-footer was sold in 1947.
23. Reports of the U.S. Coast Guard, in *Annual Report of the Secretary of the Navy, 1918*, pp. 1618–19; ibid., *1919*, 2654–55.
24. Brown, 76–77; Johnston and Crisp, 2:221–26.
25. Report of Keeper John A. Midgett, copy in Philip F. Roach Papers.
26. Ibid.; Oliver M. Maxam, "The Life-Saving Stations of the United States Coast Guard," *U.S. Naval Institute Proceedings* (May, 1929), p. 378. This periodical is cited hereafter as *USNIP*.
27. Henry Newbolt, *Naval Operations*, 5:161–62.
28. U.S. Coast Guard's Service with the Navy during the World War, 4 June 1920, Josephus Daniels Papers; William J. Wheeler, "Reminiscences of World War Convoy Work," *USNIP* (May, 1929), p. 385.
29. Wheeler, 388 *et. seq.*
30. Ibid.
31. Ibid., extract from N. R. van der Veer to Robert H. Dunn, 1 Oct. 1918, Roach Papers.
32. *Naval Fighting Ships*, 7:30; Wheeler, 392.
33. USCG Service with Navy, Daniels Papers.
34. Johnston and Crisp, 3:329.

CHAPTER FIVE

1. Bertholf to Secretary of the Navy, 6 Dec. 1918, and reply, 12 Dec. 1918, Subj. Class. 631.
2. Daniels to Sen. Carroll S. Page (Vt.), 4 Nov. 1919, Daniels Papers; Murphy, 178.
3. Austin to Philip B. Eaton, 10 Feb. 1919, Eaton Papers; Murphy, 176–78.
4. 65 Cong. 3 Sess. S. Rept. 788, 4.
5. Ibid., 1.
6. Ibid., 7–14.
7. P. H. Harrison to commissioned and warrant officers of the U.S. Coast Guard, 19 Apr. 1919, copy in Glass to Daniels, 24 June 1919, Daniels Papers.
8. 65 Cong. 3 Sess. S. Rept. 788, 9.
9. Bertholf to Crisp, 18 Apr. 1919, Bertholf Corr., 1912–21.
10. Secretary of the navy to secretary of the treasury, 27 June 1919, Daniels Papers.

11. Glass to Daniels, 24 June 1919, with enclosures, ibid.
12. Executive Order 3160.
13. Letters to Daniels from Winthrop L. Marvin, manager, American SS Owners Assoc., 27 Dec. 1919; J. B. Bonning, Jr., secretary-treasurer, Pacific-American SS Assoc., 10 Mar. 1920; *et al.*, Daniels Papers.
14. Murphy, 179–81.
15. Houston to secretary of the navy, 27 Jan. 1921, Subj. Class. 63, Cooperation with Navy, RG 26.
16. E.g., G. L. Carden to Thomas M. Moore, 27 Feb. 1915, Carden Collection; and Bertholf to Mrs. L. H. Crisp, 12 Feb. 1915, Bertholf Corr., 1912–21.
17. Daniels to Sen. Page, 4 Nov. 1919, Daniels Papers.
18. Bertholf to secretary of the treasury, 20 June 1919, copy in Frederick C. Billard Papers.
19. Johnston and Crisp, 1:29.
20. 66 Cong. 1 Sess. S. Rept. 181.
21. *Annual Reports, 1920–23, passim.*
22. Secretary of the treasury to secretary of the navy, 28 Feb. 1922, and reply, 1 Mar. 1922, Subj. Class. 63.
23. Billard to Reynolds, 24 Mar. 1920, Subj. Class. 601.
24. Commandant to Admiral Benson, 24 Apr. 1920, ibid.
25. Commandant to paymaster general, 20 Apr. 1921, with enclosures; secretary of the treasury to secretary of the navy, 15 July 1921, Subj. Class. 63.
26. *Annual Reports, 1920–22.*
27. Papers and notes relative to Hunnewell inspection of Norway-Pacific Construction and Dry Dock Co., July 1919, Cutters No. 36–40, Subj. Class. 2039, Construction of Vessels, RG 26.
28. R. R. Waesche, "Armaments and Gunnery in the Coast Guard," *USNIP* (May, 1929), pp. 382–83; Robert L. Scheina, *U.S. Coast Guard Cutters and Craft of World War II*, pp. 32–34. Information on armaments in the latter must be accepted with caution.
29. Q. B. Newman, "Electric Drive Applied to Coast Guard Cutters," *Marine Engineering and Shipping Age* (Jan. 1922), pp. 15–22; and "First Electric Coast Guard Cutter Completed," ibid. (Nov. 1921), 825.
30. Wheeler to Roach, 11 May 1929, Roach Papers.
31. *Annual Report, 1924,* 38.
32. Richard K. Smith, *First Across! The U.S. Navy's Transatlantic Flight of 1919,* p. 51 *et passim.*
33. Commandant to CO, Aviation Station, 12 Oct. 1920, Subj. Class. 601.
34. Andrew W. Mellon to W. F. Durand, 3 Oct. 1925, ibid.

CHAPTER SIX

1. *Annual Report of the Secretary of the Navy, 1919,* p. 2651; *Annual Report, 1920,* 10–11; *1921,* 10–11; *1922,* 9–10; *1923,* 1–2; *1924,* 1–2.
2. *Annual Report, 1924,* 29–30. The practice of referring to Coast Guard stations by number was discontinued in 1922.
3. *Annual Report of the Secretary of the Navy, 1919,* p. 2656.
4. *Annual Report, 1920,* 25–30.
5. Ibid., 21–22.
6. Ibid., 17–19.
7. Ibid., 16–17.
8. Ibid., *1922,* 24–25.
9. Ibid., *1928,* 57–58.
10. Patrick to Billard, 28 May 1924, and reply, 3 June 1924, both in ibid., *1924,* 20–21.

11. Ibid., *1925*, 16–17; *Haida* Bering Sea Cruise Report No. 1, 1924, copy in John F. Hottel Papers.
12. *Algonquin* Bering Sea Cruise Report No. 2, 1924, copy in ibid.
13. *Haida* Bering Sea Cruise Report No. 2, 1924, copy in ibid.
14. *Annual Report, 1925*, 17.
15. Ibid.; *Haida* Bering Sea Cruise Report No. 3, 1924, copy in Hottel Papers.

CHAPTER SEVEN

1. McAdoo to Glass, 17 June 1919, Carter Glass Papers.
2. Lt. Comdr. LeRoy Reinburg to Mr. Kilpatrick, 31 July 1924, Prohibition File, U.S. Coast Guard Academy Library.
3. Laurence F. Schmeckebier, *The Bureau of Prohibition: Its History, Activities, and Organization*, pp. 5–7.
4. Malcolm F. Willoughby, *Rum War at Sea*, p. 17.
5. Reynolds to Haynes, 17 Feb. 1922, Subj. Class. 601.
6. Willoughby, *Rum War*, 33; circular letter to Light-House Superintendents, 26 Apr. 1922, Light-House Service Circulars, 3 Ser., Entry 12, RG 26.
7. *Annual Report, 1924*, 27–28.
8. 68 Cong. 1 Sess. S. Rept. 294; Billard to commanding officers and others concerned, 2 May 1924, Subj. Class. 011.
9. Billard to all commissioned officers of the Coast Guard, 29 Mar. 1924, copy in Eaton Papers.
10. Commandant to Bureau of Navigation, 9 Apr. 1924, Subj. Class. 63.
11. Commandant to Bureau of Navigation, 22 Aug. 1924; to chief, Bureau of Navigation, 25 Sept. 1924; to CO, Naval Training Station, Hampton Roads, 28 Aug. 1925; ibid.
12. *Annual Report, 1925*, 31.
13. Mellon to Sen. Wesley L. Jones, 19 Dec. 1925, Subj. Class. 012, Legislative—Vessels and Stations, RG 26.
14. Willoughby, *Rum War*, 47–48; CO, *Cassin*, to Comdr. H. G. Hamlet, 15 Jan. 1925, confidential, copy in Roach Papers.
15. Commandant to Lt. Comdr. P. F. Roach, 28 July 1924, Roach Papers.
16. DOCTRINE FOR PREVENTION OF SMUGGLING, confidential, p. 2, copy in Subj. Class. 601.
17. Ibid., 9.
18. Ibid., 6, 10.
19. Ibid., 12. Italics in original.
20. Ibid., 13–14.
21. Willoughby, *Rum War*, 24–25.
22. C. John Colombos, *The International Law of the Sea*, pp. 130–31.
23. Schmeckebier, 15 n. 18.
24. CO, *Cassin*, to Comdr. H. G. Hamlet, 15 Jan. 1925, confidential, copy in Roach Papers.
25. R. O. Crisp, acting commandant, to all section base commanders, 11 July 1925, Subj. Class. 800, General Communication Matters, RG 26.
26. Commandant to comdr., New York Div., 14 Apr. 1925, Subj. Class. 601.
27. Comdr., Sqdn. One, Offshore Patrol Force, to commandant, 22 Mar. 1927, copy in Roach Papers.
28. DOCTRINE FOR OPERATION OF OFFSHORE PATROL BOATS (125-Footers and 100-Footers), Subj. Class. 601.
29. Report of conference at the U.S. Coast Guard Academy, 21 Sept. 1927, p. 2, ibid. Hereafter cited as Report of conference, 1927.
30. Board on policy and methods regarding seized boats to commandant, 9 May 1929, Subj. Class. 0031, Committees and Boards—Coast Guard, RG 26; Willoughby, *Rum War*, Appendix A has a list of these.

31. Report of conference, 1927, p. 3 *et passim*.
32. Ibid., 65–67; Willoughby, *Rum War*, 108.
33. Commandant to comdr., Eastern Div., 1 Dec. 1930, confidential, Subj. Class. 601; Willoughby, *Rum War*, 109–14.
34. John Bentley, Yearly Count of New Types of Aircraft Owned or Used by the Coast Guard since Flying Became an Integral Part of its Duties (1915–1971), pp. 1–2, Ref. Coll., USCGHQ.
35. Report of conference, 1927, 2.
36. Commandant to Asst. Attorney General G. A. Youngquist, 25 Jan. 1933, Subj. Class. 601.
37. Information from Subj. Class. 123, Boards of Inquiry and Investigation—Units Only, RG 26.
38. Wheeler to commandant, 4 Jan. 1930, Billard Papers.
39. Wheeler to commandant, 4 Dec. 1929 and 4 Mar. 1930, ibid.
40. Philip B. Eaton to Geo. F. Lawley & Sons, 13 Dec. 1929, Eaton Papers; Construction and Repair Topics, 22 Mar. 1930, Subj. Class. 2038, Technical Publications originated by Construction and Repair, RG 26.
41. Frederick A. Hunnewell, "United States Coast Guard Cutters," p. 26, advance copy of paper presented at annual meeting of Society of Naval Architects and Marine Engineers, 18 and 19 Nov. 1937.
42. Report of Coast Guard Anti-Smuggling Activities for the Fiscal Year Ending 30 June, 1933, Subj. Class. 601.

CHAPTER EIGHT

1. List furnished Emmet Dougherty, secretary, Assoc. against the Prohibition Amendment, 12 June 1930, Subj. Class. 601.
2. Asst. Secretary of the Treasury Seymour Lowman to Rep. Frank Crowther, 6 June 1928, copy in Prohibition File, Ref. Coll., USCGHQ; B. M. Chiswell, acting commandant, to Lowman, 2 July 1928, Subj. Class. 011.
3. This account is based on the transcript of the *Wolcott* log and the *Dexter* patrol log, Subj. Class. 607, Reports pertaining to operations of service units, RG 26.
4. Quoted in Colombos, 156.
5. Quoted in ibid., 157.
6. Willoughby, *Rum War*, 148–50.
7. Billard to Rep. Lindsay C. Warren, 13 Jan. 1930, L. C. Warren Papers.
8. Willoughby, *Rum War*, 150.
9. Board of Investigation to Inquire into Supervision by Commissioned Officers over Unloading of Liquor from Seized Vessel Flor del Mar on 29 Dec. 1929, Subj. Class. 123.
10. Comment and action by reviewing authority, ibid.
11. List furnished Emmet Dougherty, 12 June 1930, Subj. Class. 601.
12. Willoughby, *Rum War*, 126–27; Brown, 147–60; Kensil Bell, *"Always Ready!" The Story of the United States Coast Guard*, pp. 241–43.
13. *Annual Report, 1927*, 9; Edward F. Sullivan, "The Coast Guard Florida Relief Expedition," *Our Navy* (Mid-Oct., 1926), clipping in Radio, 1904–1935, Coast Guard Academy Library.
14. Board of Investigation, Foundering of Coast Guard Patrol Boat 238, Subj. Class. 123.
15. Ibid.
16. Logs of the *Tuscarora, Paulding, Jouett*, and *Redwing*, Subj. Class. 607; CO, *Redwing* to commandant, 24 Feb. 1927, Subj. Class. 606; F. J. Birkett, *A Manual of Coast Guard Vessels*, Art. 752.
17. Board of Investigation, Foundering of . . . 238. Henry Beston, *The*

Outermost House, pp. 84–90, has an interesting contemporary account of the storm and the *238*'s loss.

18. CO, *Paulding,* to commandant, 24 Dec. 1927, Subj. Class. 123.
19. Ibid.
20. U.S. Navy Court of Inquiry into the loss of the *S-4,* copy in ibid.
21. Board of Investigation, collision between *Paulding* and *S-4,* ibid.
22. Testimony to Senate Subcommittee on Naval Affairs with Regard to the *S-4,* ibid.
23. Birkett, Art. 406.
24. Brown, 217–22.
25. L. C. Covell, acting commandant, to Asst. Attorney General Roy St. Lewis, 22 Mar. 1932, Subj. Class. 601.
26. Comdr., Destroyer Force, to commandant, 19 Aug. 1925, ibid.
27. Birkett, Art. 410.
28. Adams to inspector in chief, 8 Mar. 1929, Subj. Class. 123.
29. Adams to inspector in chief, 3 Apr. 1929, Subj. Class. 606.
30. Statement of number of cases of individuals (noncommissioned officers and enlisted men) in the Coast Guard who were found guilty, during the fiscal year ended June 30, 1926 . . . and from July 1, 1926, to Nov. 24, 1926, Subj. Class. 601. Italics in original.
31. Wheeler to commandant, 7 Mar. 1930, ibid.

CHAPTER NINE

1. *Annual Report, 1926,* 27.
2. Ibid., *1924,* 34–35.
3. Ibid., *1927,* 35.
4. Ibid., *1929,* 50–51.
5. Ibid., *1925,* 36.
6. Ibid., 1931, 54; "The Beginning: Academy Opens Doors 50 Years Ago At Present Site," U.S. Coast Guard Academy Alumni Association *Bulletin* (Sept.–Oct. 1982), pp. 10–11. This publication hereafter cited as Alumni *Bulletin.*
7. Reminiscences of Rear Admiral Edward H. Thiele, USCG (Ret.), p. 196.
8. Report, 31 Dec. 1919, quoted in superintendent, Construction and Repair, and engineer in chief to commandant, 23 Feb. 1924, Subj. Class. 012.
9. Cochran to Headquarters, 22 Nov. 1923, quoted in ibid.
10. Ibid.
11. Cochran to commandant, 17 Mar. 1924, ibid.
12. *Annual Report, 1925,* 16, 19–20.
13. Ibid., *1927,* 26–27.
14. Record of suggestions for characteristics of *"New Bear,"* Subj. Class. 20211, Development of design, RG 26.
15. "Bids Asked for Coast Guard Cutter for Arctic Service," *Marine Engineering and Shipping Age* (Mar., 1926), pp. 133–38. This article includes the plans to which the *Northland* was built.
16. Ibid., 135.
17. The author of A Brief History of Coast Guard Icebreakers, prepared in the Public Affairs Div., USCGHQ, disagrees with this evaluation of the *Northland*'s performance, but Thiele, 10–13; Reminiscences of Capt. Earl K. Rhodes, USCG (Ret.); Hyman R. Kaplan and James F. Hunt, *This is the Coast Guard,* p. 135; Charles W. Thomas, *Ice is Where You Find It,* p. 115 *et passim;* and her reputation as reported by some of my older shipmates seem more convincing. Hunnewell thought that there was "a good deal of psychology" in early reports of her performance. Hun-

newell to Newman, 11 July 1928, Subj. Class. 2039, Informal correspondence, etc., RG 26.

18. Mellon to Rep. James S. Parker, 4 Jan. 1926, Subj. Class. 012.
19. Scott to Charles S. Haight, 31 Dec. 1925, ibid.
20. This clause was taken verbatim from the 1907 Revenue-Cutter Service *Regulations.*
21. Hunnewell, 19.
22. Quincy B. Newman, "USCG Cutters *Chelan, Pontchartrain, Tahoe, Champlain,* and *Mendota," Journal of the American Society of Naval Engineers* (Nov., 1928), p.673.
23. Ibid.
24. "Lectures on Streamlined Rudders Given at Webb Institute," *Marine Engineering and Shipping Age* (Dec., 1928), p. 691; *Chelan* folder, Subj. Class. 20213, Trial trips and trial inspections; behavior in service, RG 26.
25. Ralph W. Dempwolf, "The First Voyage of the New Turbo-Electric Cutter Chelan," *The Bugle* (Feb., 1929), copy in *Chelan* folder, Subj. Class. 20213.
26. Crapster to commandant, 6 May 1929, *Mendota* folder, ibid.; Jack to Hunnewell, 11 June 1931, *Shoshone* folder, ibid.
27. Hunnewell to Newman, 26 Nov. 1928, and reply, 28 Nov. 1928, Subj. Class. 2039.
28. Hunnewell, 15.
29. Commandant to chief of naval operations, 2 Jan. 1926, Subj. Class. 63.
30. *Annual Report, 1922,* 11.
31. Ibid., *1926,* 7.
32. Noble G. Ricketts, "The 'Marion' Expedition to Davis Strait and Baffin Bay," *Coast Guard Bulletin* No. 19, Part 1, p. 49. The foregoing account of the expedition is based on this narrative.
33. Ibid., 52.
34. Edward H. Smith, "Arctic Ice with Especial Reference to Its Distribution to the North Atlantic Ocean," ibid., Part 3.
35. Edward H. Smith, Floyd M. Soule, and Olav Mosley, "The Marion and General Greene Expeditions to Davis Strait and Labrador Sea," ibid., Part 5, 6–12.
36. "Report of Ice Observations made on the Aeroarctic Expedition with the 'Graf Zeppelin,' 1931," *Coast Guard Bulletin* No. 21, pp. 44–51.
37. *Annual Report, 1920,* 61.
38. Ibid., *1921,* 45.
39. Ibid., *1928,* 47–52.
40. Commandant to Gus B. Lofberg, 9 Aug. 1928; Report of Board to consider Boat Equipment at Coast Guard Stations, 23 Aug. 1928, Subj. Class. 0031.
41. *Annual Report, 1929,* 56.
42. Ibid., *1930,* 63.
43. Commandant to Ridgely, 9 Jan. 1931, Subj. Class. 601.
44. Commandant to Sands, 10 Feb. 1931, ibid.
45. Proposed Plan for Reorganization of Coast Guard, ibid.
46. Sands and Rasmussen to Ridgely, 10 Mar. 1931, ibid.
47. Ibid.

CHAPTER 10

1. Chiswell to Waesche, 22 May 1932, Russell R. Waesche Papers.
2. Waesche to Judge Dan Cronin, 21 May 1932, copy; Chiswell to Waesche, 27 May 1932, ibid.
3. *Annual Report, 1933,* 7; commandant to secretary of the treasury, 7 Feb.

1933, and commandant to all Headquarters section heads, 9 May 1933, Subj. Class. 601.

4. Woodin to Secretary of the Navy Claude Swanson, 4 May 1933, copy in Subj. Class. 011.

5. Pratt to secretary of the navy, 5 May 1933, copy in Subj. Class. 020, Organization (of service and Headquarters), RG 26.

6. Hamlet, memoranda for secretary of the treasury, 5 and 6 June 1933, copies in ibid.

7. Hamlet to secretary of the treasury, 11 Nov. 1933, copy in Subj. Class. 011.

8. Report of Committee on Transfer of Coast Guard from Treas. Dept. to Navy Dept., 2 Jan. 1934, copy in ibid.

9. Report of Committee on Transfer, 23 Jan. 1934, copy in ibid.

10. American Steamship Owners' Assoc. to President, 2 Jan. 1934, Subj. Class. 011. This collection has a sizable file of letters and telegrams opposing the transfer.

11. Felix Riesenberg to LeRoy Reinburg, CGHQ, 8 Dec. 1933, ibid.

12. Warren to Rep. F. T. Maloney, 10 Jan. 1934, and memorandum dated 12 Jan. 1934; Warren to Isaac W. Hughes, 15 Jan. 1934, Warren Papers.

13. E. M. Webster, "On Research and Facts," *U.S. Coast Guard Magazine* (Mar. 1930), pp. 14–15.

14. A. Statom to Webster, 19 June 1933, and reply, 15 July 1933, copies in Radio, 1904–35—Coast Guard-Navy Communications Controversy, Coast Guard Academy Library.

15. Subcommittee report to Rear Admiral Cole, 16 Jan. 1934, and Webster to Cole, 19 Jan. 1934, copies in ibid.

16. Hamlet to secretary of the treasury, 10 Apr. 1934, and Acting Secretary of the Navy H. L. Roosevelt to secretary of the treasury, 21 Apr. 1934, Subj. Class. 011.

17. Morgenthau to H. L. Roosevelt, 27 Apr. 1934, copy in ibid.

18. Covell to secretary of the treasury, 24 July 1934, and commandant to Sen. Jesse H. Metcalf, 10 Aug. 1934, copies in ibid.

19. Kenner to F. J. Birkett, 27 July 1934, Birkett Collection. See also W. H. Munter to secretary of the treasury, 2 Aug. 1934, Subj. Class. 011, which Hamlet provided to Metcalf as an example of Coast Guard officers' reaction.

20. Covell to secretary of the treasury, 24 July 1934, Subj. Class. 011; Ridgely to P. F. Roach, 27 Aug. 1934, Roach Papers.

21. Waesche to Roach, 9 Nov. 1934 and 29 Sept. 1935, Roach Papers.

22. Commandant to division comdrs, *et al.*, 8 Oct. 1936, Subj. Class. 011.

23. Freeman to chief of naval operations, 1 Nov. 1933, copy in Subj. Class. 63; Swanson to Woodin, 8 Nov. 1933, copy in Subj. Class. 601.

24. Brown, 105–15.

25. Statement of operations of the U.S. Coast Guard in connection with the AKRON Disaster, 11 Apr. 1933, Subj. Class. 63; Edward Arpee, *From Frigates to Flat-Tops*, pp. 246–47.

26. Brown, 126–37; Karl Baarslag, *Coast Guard to the Rescue*, pp. 198–204.

27. Statement of fact, *Morro Castle,* Subj. Class. 651; Coast Guard Participation in the S.S. *Morro Castle* Disaster, 8–10 Sept. 1934, ibid. The latter source has these numbers on p. 2, while on p. 1B the figures are 318 and 231. Hereafter cited as Participation—*Morro Castle.*

28. Statement of fact, *Morro Castle,* 31–32.

29. Participation—*Morro Castle,* 37–38; Waesche to Asst. Secretary Gibbons, 11 Mar. 1935, Subj. Class. 601.

30. Participation—*Morro Castle,* 13 *et passim.*

31. Ibid., 1B–1C.

32. Quotation from ibid., 38; Board of Investigation Report—Opinion, Subj. Class. 651.
33. William McFee, *The Law of the Sea,* p. 272.
34. CO, *Northland,* to commandant, 11 Feb. 1930; Billard to S. E. Semple, 16 Apr. 1930, and Billard to Sen. Wesley L. Jones, 21 Apr. 1930, Subj. Class. 601.
35. CO, *Onondaga,* to comdr., Western Area, 5 Feb. 1935, ibid.
36. Commandant to secretary of the treasury, 8 Aug. 1933, Subj. Class. 011; commandant to federal administrator of public works, 16 Feb. 1934, Subj. Class. 0034, Executive—Stabilization Board, RG 26.
37. Hunnewell, 17.
38. Commandant to secretary of the treasury, 8 Aug. 1933, Subj. Class. 011.
39. Quoted in Harold C. Reisinger, "The Flying Lifeboat of the Coast Guard," *USNIP* (Jan. 1933), p. 82.
40. Bentley, 1. The General Aviation flying boats are not mentioned in Richard C. Knott, *The American Flying Boat,* which describes the Dolphins, pp. 216–19.
41. Reisinger, 81.
42. Participation—*Morro Castle,* 9.
43. Brown, 186–92.
44. *Register of the Commissioned and Warrant Officers and Cadets, and Ships and Stations of the United States Coast Guard, July 1, 1935,* pp. 82, 138–39; hereafter cited as *Register* with year. *Annual Report, 1935.*
45. Commandant's special order, 28 Aug. 1934, Subj. Class. 020.
46. Commandant to James B. Conant, president of Harvard University, 14 June 1933, and to Ridgely, 19 Oct. 1933, copies in U.S. Coast Guard Academy—Accreditation, USCG Academy Library.
47. Ridgely to Pine, 2 Feb. 1934, ibid.
48. 76 Cong. 1 Sess. S. Doc. 81, 19, 33.
49. Yeandle to Warren, 31 Aug. 1934, Warren Papers.
50. Warren to Gibbons, 1 Sept. 1934, and reply, 10 Sept. 1934, ibid.
51. Warren to Yeandle, 3 Sept. 1934; Yeandle to Warren, 3 Oct. 1934, ibid.
52. Waesche to Roach, 9 Nov. 1934, Roach Papers.

CHAPTER ELEVEN

1. Warren to Pennel A. Tillett, 4 Mar. 1936; Warren to H. Hubert Morton, 13 May 1936; Warren Papers.
2. Bland to Warren, 8 May 1936; Warren to Morgenthau, 19 May 1936; ibid.
3. Raymond L. Jack to Waesche, 24 Nov. 1931; Herman H. Wolf to Waesche, 22 May 1932; Waesche to Jack, 16 Dec. 1931; Waesche Papers.
4. See Henry Coyle to Waesche, 13 July 1936, ibid., for an officer's reaction to one of these visits.
5. Toon to Warren, 6 Feb. 1934, Warren Papers.
6. Warren to Toon, 7 Feb. 1934; Bacon to Warren, 22 Oct. 1934, ibid.
7. Waesche to Warren, 2 Mar. 1937, ibid.
8. Waesche to Warren, 16 Mar. 1937, ibid.
9. CO, *George W. Campbell,* to commandant, 18 Nov. 1936, Subj. Class. 601—*Campbell.*
10. Ibid.
11. Woodin to Sam Rayburn, 5 Apr. 1933, copy in Subj. Class. 012.
12. Commandant to Inland Water Petroleum Carriers Assoc., 28 Aug. 1934, Subj. Class. 601; Kaplan and Hunt, 135.
13. Reminiscences of Admiral Chester R. Bender, USCG (Ret.), p. 52.

14. Kaplan and Hunt, 135; see also Walter C. Capron, *U.S. Coast Guard,* pp. 82–83.
15. Dale R. Simonson, "Bow Characteristics for Ice Breaking," *Journal of the American Society of Naval Engineers* (May, 1936), p. 254.
16. Thiele, 2–11.
17. *Coast Guard Bulletin,* Vol. 1, No. 8, Feb. 1940.
18. Secretary of the treasury to secretary of state, 27 Oct. 1936, copy in Subj. Class. 011.
19. Commandant to all division comdrs., 1 July 1936, Subj. Class. 601.
20. Samuel A. Lawrence, *United States Merchant Shipping Policies and Politics,* pp. 58–67.
21. *Annual Reports, 1940* and *1941.*
22. Ibid., *1940;* Bell, 280–82; Reminiscences of Admiral Alfred C. Richmond, USCG (Ret.) pp. 168–71.
23. Truman R. Strobridge, *Chronology of Aids to Navigation and the Old Lighthouse Service, 1716–1939,* p. 35. See also Thiele, 121–23.
24. 76 Cong. 1 Sess. H. Doc. 288.
25. Proceedings of Boards for Induction of Light-House Employees into the U.S. Coast Guard, Subj. Class. 75, Personnel—Civilian Employees, RG 26. See also Robert H. Macy, "Consolidation of the Light-House Service with the Coast Guard," *USNIP* (Jan., 1940), p. 58.
26. *Annual Report, 1940; Register, 1940, passim.*
27. Gary E. Powell to Herbert C. Bonner, 2 Feb. 1949, Herbert C. Bonner Papers.
28. Gorman to budget officer, Treasury Department, 26 Dec. 1940, Subj. Class. 601.
29. Macy, 58; see also L.C. Covell to C. J. Sullivan, 18 Aug. 1939, Warren Papers.
30. *Annual Reports, 1933–40, passim.*
31. George B. Gelly, memorandum for asst. secretary of the treasury, 23 Sept. 1936, Subj. Class. 601.
32. *Annual Report, 1937,* 1.
33. Ibid., *1938,* 1.
34. Ibid., *1939,* 1; W. E. Chapline, "The Hurricane of September 1938," Alumni *Bulletin* (May–June, 1982), 41; E. G. Rose, memorandum for asst. commandant, 27 July 1939, Subj. Class. 601, mistakenly identifies the casualties as men swept overboard from the *Harriet Lane.*
35. Waesche to Rep. Byron N. Scott, 19 July 1937, Subj. Class. 601, Aviation.
36. Waesche to Rep. Richard B. Wigglesworth, 15 Apr. 1939, Subj. Class, 601.
37. Commandant to comdr., New Orleans Div., 28 Feb. 1936, ibid.; *Annual Report, 1938,* 3; *1939,* 5.
38. Scammell to commandant, 18 Oct. 1937, Subj. Class. 601.
39. Comdr., Seattle Div., to commandant, 8 Dec. 1937; CO, *Northland,* to comdr., Seattle Div., 3 Dec. 1937, ibid.
40. CO, *Northland,* to commandant, 2 Aug. 1939, Subj. Class. 606.
41. Waesche to Byrd, 9 Sept. 1939, copy in Subj. Class. 601.

CHAPTER TWELVE

1. Merlin O'Neill, memorandum for Waesche, 24 July 1936, Subj. Class. 601; chief, Bureau of Navigation, to commandant, 14 Aug. 1936; asst. secretary of state to secretary of state, 26 Aug. 1936, copy, Subj. Class. 63.
2. Commandant to CO, *Cayuga,* 19 Sept. 1936, ibid.
3. Thomas A. Bailey and Paul B. Ryan, *Hitler vs. Roosevelt: The Undeclared Naval War,* pp. 31–33.

4. Memorandum for Mr. Feidler and Mr. Harrison, 3 Jan. 1940, Subj. Class. 601, *Annual Reports, 1940* and *1941, passim.*
5. *Annual Report, 1941.*
6. Patrick Abbazia, *Mr. Roosevelt's Navy: The Private War of the U.S. Atlantic Fleet, 1939–1942,* pp. 65–66, 72; H. E. Gaston to secretary of the navy, 22 Sept. 1939, Subj. Class. 63; E. G. Rose to all officers at Headquarters, Subj. Class. 601.
7. Ed. H. Smith, memorandum for commandant, 14 Sept. 1939, Subj. Class. 63.
8. Quoted in R. K. Smith, 194.
9. Knott, chapter 7.
10. Gelly to Paul H. Johnson, 3 May 1974, MVF 587, USCG Academy Library; Bernard C. Nalty and Truman R. Strobridge, "The Story of the Ocean Stations," Alumni *Bulletin* (Mar.–Apr., 1974), pp. 32–38.
11. Waesche, memorandum for Gaston, 17 Nov. 1939, Subj. Class. 618, Weather patrol, RG 26.
12. Waesche, memorandum for secretary of the treasury, 2 Sept. 1939, Subj. Class. 601.
13. Wallace to secretary of the treasury, 12 Oct. 1939 and 15 Nov. 1939; Acting Secretary of the Navy Chas. Edison to secretary of agriculture, 2 Nov. 1939, copies in Subj. Class. 618.
14. Gelly to P. H. Johnson, 3 May 1974, MVF 587, USCG Academy Library.
15. Callaghan, memorandum for the president, 25 Jan. 1940, copy in Subj. Class. 618.
16. Gaston to secretary of state, 14 Feb. 1940, copy in ibid.
17. Commandant to all units, 22 Apr. 1940, Subj. Class. 601.
18. Commandant to comdrs. Boston, New York, and Norfolk districts, and to COs, weather ships, 14 May 1940, ibid.
19. Waesche to Land, 30 Jan. 1940, copy in ibid. See also Waesche to Reichelderfer, 30 Jan. 1940, copy in ibid.
20. Roosevelt, memorandum to secretary of the treasury, 5 June 1940, copy in ibid.
21. Abbazia, 88.
22. Quoted in commandant to comdr., San Francisco District, 20 June 1940, Subj. Class. 601.
23. Commandant to hydrographer, USN, 28 Aug. 1940, copy in Subj. Class. 63.
24. Waesche, memorandum for secretary of the treasury, 30 Sept. 1940, copy in Waesche Papers.
25. Asst. chief operations officer to engineer in chief, 3 July 1940; commandant to comdrs., Boston, New York, Norfolk, Jacksonville, New Orleans, and San Juan districts, 23 Aug. 1940, Subj. Class. 601.
26. E. G. Rose to chief constructor, 10 Jan. 1939, ibid.
27. Roosevelt to heads of all departments and independent establishments, 3 Sept. 1941, as quoted in W. N. Thompson to heads of bureaus, offices, and divisions, and chiefs of divisions, secretary's office, Treasury Department, 22 Sept. 1941.
28. T. Michael O'Brien and Truman R. Strobridge, "Black Lifesavers: A Brief Historical Survey of Blacks and the U.S. Lifesaving Service," Ref. Coll., USCGHQ.
29. Quoted in ibid., 9.
30. Etheridge to Warren, 31 May 1937, confidential, Warren Papers.
31. Warren to Etheridge, 1 June 1937 and 4 June 1937; Warren to Rep. P. H. Drewry, 10 June 1937, ibid. O'Brien and Strobridge seem to have been unaware of this incident—they indicate a regular succession of black petty officers in charge at Pea Island.
32. *Annual Reports, 1940* and *1941.*

33. Description of 250-foot cutters in Roosevelt to secretary of the treasury, 5 Apr. 1941, copy in Waesche Papers.
34. CGHQ to comdr., Boston District *et al.*, 28 Feb. 1941, Subj. Class. 601.
35. Secretary of the treasury to president, 7 Mar. 1941, copy in Gaston File, Ref. Coll., USCGHQ.
36. Scheina, *Cutters and Craft,* 29.
37. Memorandum for all officers at Headquarters, 18 Mar. 1941, Subj. Class. 601.
38. Memorandum of telephone conversation between Gaston and Waesche, 2 Apr. 1941, Gaston File.
39. Roosevelt to secretary of the treasury, 5 Apr. 1941, copy in Waesche Papers.
40. Commandant to all district comdrs., 2 June 1941, Subj. Class. 601.
41. Memorandum of telephone conversation between Gaston and Waesche, 2 Apr. 1941, Gaston File. See also asst. chief operations officer to chief finance officer, 11 June 1941, Subj. Class. 601.
42. Commandant, memorandum for secretary of the treasury, 5 Feb. 1941, Gaston File.
43. Gaston, memorandum for Morgenthau, 7 Feb. 1941, ibid.
44. Chalker memorandum, 28 Nov. 1940, Subj. Class. 610, Greenland Patrol; minutes of conference, 29 Nov. 1940, Subj. Class. 601.
45. Kossler and Leamy, memorandum for commandant, 11 Dec. 1940, Subj. Class. 610.
46. Commandant to CO, *Modoc,* 1 Mar. 1941, ibid.
47. Waesche to Byrd, 2 May 1941 and 9 May 1941, copies in Subj. Class. 63.
48. Chief of naval operations to commandant, 24 June 1940, Military Readiness Division, World War II, RG 26. Hereafter cited as Military Readiness.
49. Mobilization Plan, General, World War II, ibid.
50. Ibid.; Administration when operating under the Navy, 14; Demobilization, 12.
51. Gaston, memorandum for Morgenthau, 2 Apr. 1941, confidential, copy in Waesche Papers. See also Gaston to Morgenthau, 23 Jan. 1941, strictly confidential, Gaston file.
52. *Annual Report, 1941.*
53. Sullivan to Bonner, 17 Apr. 1941, confidential and secret, Warren Papers.
54. Knox to secretary of the treasury, 18 June 1941, and reply, same date, Subj. Class. 63.
55. Knox to Morgenthau, 15 Apr. 1941, and Gaston to secretary of the navy, 16 May 1941, copies in Gaston File.
56. *Annual Report, 1941.*
57. Commandant to district comdrs., 26 Feb. 1941, Subj. Class. 63.
58. Thiele, 120–27.
59. Department of State, to U.S. Legation, Denmark, paraphrased telegram, 3 Oct. 1941, copy in Gaston File.
60. Quoted in CGHQ (Chalker) to *Bibb, Duane, Hamilton,* and *Spencer,* 12 Sept. 1941, copy in Roach Papers.
61. Ibid.

CHAPTER THIRTEEN

1. *Annual Report, 1941;* Malcolm F. Willoughby, *The U.S. Coast Guard in World War II,* p. 8. Hereafter cited as *World War II.*
2. *World War II,* 15–16.
3. Morris J. MacGregor, Jr., *Integration of the Armed Forces, 1940–1965,* pp. 112–22.

4. Ibid., 33, 98, 111, 116–17, and 122.
5. Ibid., 508.
6. *World War II,* 17–18
7. Roach to Capt. James L. Ahern, 10 Dec. 1941, Roach Papers.
8. Reminiscences of Captain Dorothy C. Stratton, USCGR (Ret.), *passim.*
9. *World War II,* 19–20.
10. Ibid., chapter 6; Rhodes, 264–65.
11. *World War II,* 75.
12. Reminiscences of Admiral Willard J. Smith, USCG (Ret.), p. 97.
13. Waesche to secretary of the treasury, 17 Dec. 1936, Subj. Class. 601.
14. Louis K. Bragaw, *Managing a Federal Agency: The Hidden Stimulus: The Case of the U.S. Coast Guard,* chapter 6, pp. 7–10, unpublished manuscript in USCG Academy Library. This material is not in the book of the same title. See also *Marine Inspection and Navigation Bulletin,* Mar., 1942, pp. 1–3.
15. Reminiscences of Admiral Edwin J. Roland, USCG (Ret.), 2:729–30.
16. *Coast Guard Bulletin,* July, 1945, pp. 1, 7–9. Admiral Alfred C. Richmond remembered later that the same individual served as hearing and examining officer initially. Richmond, 216–21.
17. Quoted in *CG Bulletin,* Sept., 1943, 1978.
18. Ibid., July, 1945, 1, 7–9; Aug., 1946, 233–34.
19. Richmond, 187.
20. *World War II,* 46.
21. Ibid., 47–53.
22. Samuel E. Morison, *History of United States Naval Operations in World War II:* Vol. 1, *The Battle of the Atlantic, Sept. 1939–May 1943,* pp. 268–76. Hereafter cited as *Battle of Atlantic.*
23. Chalker to district CG officers, 16 June 1942, Small Boat Procurement, World War II, RG 26.
24. Waesche to commander in chief, U.S. Fleet, and chief of naval operations, 14 July 1942, Subj. Class. 601.
25. Quoted in Morison, *Battle of Atlantic,* 270.
26. Comdr., Eastern Sea Frontier, to all task group comdrs., 24 Oct. 1942, confidential, copy in Small Boat Procurement, World War II.
27. Bender, 101–13.
28. C. F. Edge to commandant, 8 June 1936, Subj. Class. 63.
29. Bender, 123–24.
30. Commandant's Circular No. 27–44, 20 Dec. 1944, Aviation—Helicopters Box, Entry 279. RG 26.
31. Bender, 144.
32. *U.S. Navy at War, 1941–1945: Official Reports to the Secretary of the Navy by Fleet Admiral Ernest J. King, U.S. Navy,* p. 224.
33. Excerpts from "Fishers of Men: The Story of the Development of Seagoing Helicopters," an unpublished manuscript by Capt. Frank A. Erickson, USCG (Ret.), in *Wrecks, Rescues, and Investigations: Selected Documents of the U.S. Coast Guard and Its Predecessors,* ed. by Bernard C. Nalty, Dennis L. Noble, and Truman R. Strobridge, pp. 281, 283–84.
34. Quoted in ibid., 286.
35. Quoted in ibid., 287.
36. Ibid., 289.
37. Ibid., 290–92.
38. Scheina, *Cutters and Craft,* 4–5.
39. Nalty, Noble, and Strobridge, 293–94.
40. Ibid., 294.
41. Bender, 237–38; Roland, 2:572–73.
42. Nalty, Noble, and Strobridge, 293–94.
43. L. T. Chalker to naval attaché, Legation of Canada, 29 Nov. 1940, Subj.

Class. 601; Scheina, *Cutters and Craft*, 84–87; Brief History of CG Ice-breakers, 7.

44. Scheina, *Cutters and Craft*, 84–85, 90.
45. Ibid., 91.
46. Thiele, 65–75.
47. Scheina, *Cutters and Craft*, 63.
48. Thiele, 79–82.
49. Harvey F. Johnson, "Development of Ice-Breaking Vessels for the U.S. Coast Guard," advance copy of paper presented at the meeting of the Society of Naval Architects and Marine Engineers, 14–15 Nov. 1946, p. 13.
50. Ibid., 7, *et passim.*
51. Scheina, *Cutters and Craft*, 55; Thiele, 47–53; Kaplan and Hunt, 137.
52. Thiele, 88.
53. Transcripts of telephone conversations between commandant and Admiral Horne, between commandant and Admiral Edwards, and between commandant and Captain Martin, all on 22 Sept. 1943, Waesche Papers. See also Thiele, 53–60.
54. Thiele, 47–53.
55. Ibid., 92–93.
56. 77 Cong. 1 Sess. S. Rept. 449, 2.
57. Paul G. Tomalin, "Bridge-Controlled Turbo-Electric 255-Foot Coast Guard Cutter." Paper read at meeting of Chesapeake Bay Section of the Society of Naval Architects and Marine Engineers. Thiele, 113–18, and Scheina, *Cutters and Craft*, 2, assert that they were "squashed" 316-footers, but Tomalin was one of the design team and so in a position to know.
58. Tomalin, 9–10; Thiele, 113–18; Scheina, *Cutters and Craft*, 2.
59. Tomalin, 2.
60. Capt. Charles A. Park to chief of naval operations, 11 Mar. 1944, confidential, Subj. Class. 30, Construction of new vessels, RG 26.
61. Tomalin, 7–8.
62. Eaton to Capt. H. N. Perham, 26 July 1945, Eaton Papers.
63. *CG Bulletin*, Nov., 1945, 79–83; *World War II*, 150–53; Louis K. Bragaw, *Managing a Federal Agency: The Hidden Stimulus*, pp. 94–98. Hereafter cited as Bragaw, *Federal Agency*.
64. Bragaw, *Federal Agency*, 99–100.
65. Ibid., 100.
66. Ibid., 106–7.

CHAPTER FOURTEEN

1. This is the second line of "Semper Paratus," the Coast Guard's marching song, composed by Captain Francis S. Van Boskerck. It begins "From Aztec shore to Arctic zone, To Europe and Far East, The flag is carried by our ships In times of war and peace . . ." Like many other officers of his time, Captain Van Boskerck preferred to emphasize the Coast Guard's exploits in war over its peacetime service.
2. Excerpts from *Taney* War Diary, 7 Dec. 1941–1 Dec. 1942, War Diaries, 1942–45, RG 26.
3. *World War II*, 98, 100; Thomas, xxiii–xxiv; Walter Karig, with Karl Burton and Stephen L. Freeland, *Battle Report*, Vol. 2, *The Atlantic War*, 36–37.
4. Scheina, *Cutters and Craft*, 181–88; *World War II*, 102–3.
5. Robert L. Scheina, "Coast Guard Operations in Greenland, 1941–45," Alumni *Bulletin* (July–Aug., 1981), pp. 18–23; Thomas, *passim.*

6. Scheina, "Coast Guard Operations in Greenland," 20; Morison, *Battle of Atlantic,* 330.
7. *World War II,* 101, 104–8, 201.
8. Karig *et al.,* 45–48; Knott, 221–22.
9. Scheina, "Coast Guard Operations in Greenland," 22; Willoughby, *World War II,* 106–7.
10. Thomas, 171–72; *World War II,* 109–10.
11. Thomas, 176, 179.
12. Ibid., 210–27.
13. Morison, *Battle of Atlantic,* 84–94.
14. Abbazia, 380–81.
15. Ibid., 386–87. Abbazia is incorrect with regard to the "greenness" of the *Hamilton*'s crew; this was her prewar company, old hands by comparison with the destroyer crews.
16. John M. Waters, Jr., *Bloody Winter,* p. 220, notes that the *Ingham* spent eight weeks early in 1943 with sonar gear that was ineffective at speeds above 8 knots.
17. Ibid., 107–12.
18. Ibid., chapter 6; Morison, *Battle of Atlantic,* 334–37.
19. Quoted in Terry Hughes and John Costello, *The Battle of the Atlantic,* p. 256.
20. Waters, *Bloody Winter,* chapter 7; Willoughby, *World War II,* 200.
21. Waters, *Bloody Winter,* 198–99.
22. Ibid., 204–5; Stephen W. Roskill, *The War at Sea, 1939–1945,* Vol. 2, *The Period of Balance,* 367–68.
23. Waters, *Bloody Winter,* 224–26. Waters states that the *Spencer* fired hedgehog patterns, but the photograph of the cutter "bearing in to ram the U-boat" plainly shows mousetrap launchers, and she is unlikely to have had both. See also Capron, *Coast Guard,* 159.
24. E. C. Nussear and A. L. Slover, memorandum for engineer in chief and chief finance officer, 1 June 1944, confidential, Subj. Class. 20.
25. Morison, *Battle of Atlantic,* 143–44, 155.
26. Ibid., 248–49.
27. William E. Ehrman, "Lost in the Graveyard of the Atlantic," *Alumni Bulletin* (Sept.–Oct., 1978), pp. 32–37.
28. "History of the Coast Guard: 17th Naval District, 1941–1944," Appendix G, copy in USCG Academy Library. The comment on the escort force's effectiveness is the author's opinion, based on experience on board the *Haida* at that time.
29. *Naval Fighting Ships,* 8:46–48.
30. *World War II,* 187.
31. "Congressional Medal of Honor Hero—World War II," Public Information Division, USCGHQ.
32. "Activities of Manning Section," pp. 1–2, Ref. Coll., USCGHQ.
33. Imlay to Mrs. M. H. Imlay, 10 June 1944, Miles H. Imlay Papers.
34. Imlay to Mrs. M. H. Imlay, 23 June 1944, ibid.; CO, *LCI(L) 319,* to comdr. in chief, U.S. Fleet, 6 July 1944, copy in Joseph A. Bresnan Papers; *World War II,* 246–47.
35. *World War II,* 250–52.
36. Quoted in Norman Friedman, *U.S. Destroyers: An Illustrated Design History,* p. 159.
37. World War II, 203; Samuel E. Morison, *History of United States Naval Operations in World War II,* Vol. 10, *The Atlantic Battle Won, May 1943–May 1945,* pp. 318–19.
38. Morison, *Atlantic Battle Won,* 256–57, 342.
39. Friedman, 152; Frederic C. Lane *et al., Ships for Victory: A History of*

Shipbuilding under the U.S. Maritime Commission in World War II, pp. 177–80, 614–17.

40. "Activities of Manning Section," 4–5; Taylor B. Glading to Comdr. Overfelt, 23 June 1944, confidential, Military Readiness.
41. *World War II,* 278–82, 287–91.
42. Theodore Roscoe, *United States Destroyer Operations in World War II,* p. 507.
43. Ibid., 514–15.
44. Friedman, 152n.
45. Scheina, *Cutters and Craft,* 59.
46. P. K. Fischler, memorandum for Admiral King, 7 Feb. 1944, secret; A. C. Davis, memorandum for Admiral King, 5 June 1944, secret; copies in Subj. Class. 618.
47. *World War II,* 282.
48. Ibid., 297–98.
49. "Activities of Manning Section," 6–11; E. R. Spencer, Jr., "The Coast Guard in the Army," *USNIP* (Apr., 1946), pp. 569–71; William E. Ehrman, "World War II Memoirs of an 'Island Hopper' Skipper," Alumni *Bulletin* (July–Aug., 1983), pp. 32–35.
50. *U.S. Navy at War,* 232; Forrestal quoted in *Annual Report of the Secretary of the Treasury, 1946.*
51. Edwards to Waesche, 2 Jan., 1946, Waesche Papers.

CHAPTER FIFTEEN

1. Joseph Pois, Notes on a Conference with the Commandant, 7 June 1943, copy in Military Readiness—Demobilization Planning, World War II.
2. Gorman, memorandum for Admiral H. E. Yarnell, 22 Sept. 1943, copy in ibid.
3. Statement of Admiral Waesche before Select Committee on Postwar Military Policy, 12 May 1944, copy in ibid; Robert T. Merrill, "The Role of the Coast Guard within the Navy," *USNIP* (Aug., 1946), p. 1077.
4. Final draft, Mission of the Coast Guard, Military Readiness.
5. Report of Committee on Postwar Planning, 6 Nov. 1943, ibid.
6. Statement of Admiral Waesche before Military Affairs Committee, U.S. Senate, copy in ibid.
7. Waesche to Fleet Admiral King, 10 Sept., 1945, copy in ibid.
8. Richmond, 145.
9. W. J. Smith, 152–55.
10. Ibid., 94–95.
11. Stratton to Waesche, 15 Jan. 1946, Waesche Papers.
12. Richmond, 276–77; W. J. Smith, 175–77.
13. Capron, *Coast Guard,* 170.
14. W. J. Smith, 165–75; Bragaw, *Federal Agency,* 151.
15. *Congressional Record—House,* 11 Mar. 1947, p. 1927.
16. Capron, *Coast Guard,* 176–77; Richmond, 289.
17. Ebasco Services, Inc., *Study of United States Coast Guard,* pp. 4–5.
18. Summary of Comments by Coast Guard and Steering Committee on Review of Ebasco Recommendations, and Foley to Merlin O'Neill, 21 Apr. 1948, bound with it, Ref. Coll., USCGHQ.
19. Ebasco *Study,* 6.
20. Bragaw, *Federal Agency,* 110.
21. Reichelderfer to commandant, 18 Dec. 1945, Subj. Class. 618.
22. *CG Bulletin,* Aug., 1948, 16.
23. Paul B. Cronk, "The Rescue on Station Charlie," *Atlantic Monthly* (July, 1950), pp. 37–46.

24. Reminiscences of Captain Walter C. Capron, USCG (Ret.), pp. 367–73.
25. *CG Bulletin,* Aug., 1948, 16.
26. John M. Waters, Jr., *Rescue at Sea,* p. 176, Bender, 319–20.
27. *CG Bulletin,* Apr., 1951.
28. Rep. C. Millet Hand to Bonner, 14 Mar. 1949; Henry C. Oglesby to Edward R. Armstrong, 6 May 1949, Bonner Papers.
29. *CG Bulletin,* Oct., 1948, 42–43.
30. Ibid., Nov., 1946, 274–77.
31. Waters, *Rescue at Sea,* 105.
32. Ibid., 118–19.
33. Bonner to Snyder, 25 Mar. 1949, and reply, 12 Apr. 1949, Bonner Papers.
34. William S. Ellis, "Tracking Danger with the Ice Patrol," *National Geographic* (June, 1968), p. 791.
35. *The International Ice Patrol in the North Atlantic,* p. 14.
36. Thomas, 303–7.
37. Ibid., 323, *et passim;* Rhodes, 297–300.
38. Marine Board of Investigation, *Eastwind/Gulfstream,* 1949, Subj. Class. 123.
39. Ibid.
40. *CG Bulletin,* Oct., 1948, 37–38.

CHAPTER SIXTEEN

1. Bonner to Snyder, 7 Sept. 1949, Bonner Papers.
2. *Annual Report, 1950.*
3. Policy as to Employment of the Coast Guard under the Navy in Time of War, Appendix A, 8 Oct. 1946, secret, copy in Military Readiness.
4. *CG Bulletin,* July, 1947, 370–72; Capron, *Coast Guard,* 178.
5. *CG Bulletin,* Aug., 1950, 13; *Annual Report, 1951.*
6. Rear Admiral H. C. Shepheard address, 23 Aug. 1952, text in *Supplement to Weekly Report,* 5 Sept. 1952.
7. *Annual Report, 1953.*
8. *Weekly Report,* 10 July 1953.
9. Capron, *Coast Guard,* 179; Bragaw, *Federal Agency,* 113.
10. Waters, *Rescue at Sea,* 117.
11. Rhodes, 318–19.
12. Thiele, 98–100.
13. *Annual Report, 1951.*
14. Ibid.
15. Ibid., 1952; Waters, *Rescue at Sea,* 74.
16. *Annual Report, 1952; Waters, Rescue at Sea,* 198–202; William K. Earle, "[An account of the *Pendleton* and *Fort Mercer* rescues, 1952]," Nalty, Noble, and Strobridge, 109–21. These sources do not agree on the numbers lost and rescued.
17. *Weekly Report,* 6 Mar. 1953; Waters, *Rescue at Sea, 154.*
18. *Weekly Report,* 17 July 1953; *Annual Report, 1954.*
19. *Annual Report, 1954;* Waters, *Rescue at Sea,* is an excellent and readable account of these activities.
20. *Annual Report, 1954.*
21. *Supplement to Weekly Report,* No. 25–54.
22. Quoted in *Weekly Report,* 22 May 1953.
23. Bremen, 111F. 228, 234 (S.D.N.Y. 1901), quoted in Jo Desha Lucas, *Cases and Materials on Admiralty,* p. 673.
24. *Annual Report, 1954.*
25. Ibid.

26. *Weekly Reports,* 31 Mar. 1950, 14 Apr. 1950; and 18 May 1951.
27. *Iroquois* Log, 29 June 1954.
28. Ibid., 29 June–1 July 1954; Capt. W. F. Adams, USCG (Ret.), to author, 1 Sept. 1985.
29. Roland, 2:474.
30. Herbert C. Bonner to Percy Williams, 9 May 1949, Bonner Papers.
31. Merlin O'Neill to S. O. Bland, 25 May 1949, copy in ibid.
32. *Annual Report, 1954.*
33. Ibid., *1951.*

CHAPTER SEVENTEEN

1. W. J. Smith, 178–82, 298–300; Biographical Sketch, Admiral Alfred C. Richmond.
2. Study Concerning the Proposed Consolidation of the U.S. Coast Guard Academy and the U.S. Merchant Marine Academy, p. 19. This study was sent to the secretary of the Treasury on 10 Sept. 1954.
3. Richmond to Mr. Parsons, administrative assistant to the secretary of the treasury, 4 Apr. 1949, Subj. Class. 002, Secretary's office, RG 26.
4. *Annual Reports, 1954–59; Registers, passim.*
5. Mission of the Coast Guard; see p. 257 above.
6. *Weekly Report,* Mar., 1956.
7. Rear Admiral William B. Ellis, USCG (Ret.), to author, 12 Feb. 1984.
8. Waters, *Rescue at Sea,* 155–63.
9. CO, *Pontchartrain,* to comdr., Western Area, with enclosures, 18 Oct.1956, in Nalty, Noble, and Strobridge, 241–55; Capron, *Coast Guard,* 188–90.
10. Capron, Reminiscences, 367–73.
11. Ibid., 373; Capron, *Coast Guard,* 188.
12. *Annual Reports,* 1957–58; Waters, *Rescue at Sea,* 205–6.
13. "[An eyewitness account of the *Ilhavense Segundo* rescue, 1955]," Nalty, Noble, and Strobridge, 239–40.
14. *Weekly Reports,* 9 Nov. 1956 and 11 Jan. 1957; *Annual Report, 1957;* Waters, *Rescue at Sea,* 165–74.
15. *Weekly Reports,* 1 and 15 Apr. 1955, 18 Oct. 1957.
16. *Annual Reports, 1956–57.*
17. Ibid., *1957.*
18. Ibid., *1956; Weekly Reports,* 6 Jan. and 3 Feb. 1956; Waters, *Rescue at Sea,* 129–33, has excerpts from Thometz's and Pfeiffer's flight logs.
19. *Annual Report, 1958;* J. W. Naab, Jr., "Icebreakers and Icebreaking," *USNIP* (June, 1962), 49–50; Capron, *Coast Guard,* 191–92.
20. Roland, 2:488 *et passim.* AMVER is described in Capron, *Coast Guard,* 193; Waters, *Rescue at Sea,* 5–7; and Kaplan and Hunt, 215–16.
21. *Annual Reports, 1961* and *1964;* W. J. Smith, 144.
22. H. M. Anthony, Report on Air Sea Rescue Plan Alfa, copy in Ref. Coll., USCGHQ.
23. Quoted in ibid.
24. *Annual Report, 1959;* Kaplan and Hunt, 76; Bragaw, *Federal Agency,* 210–11.
25. *Annual Report, 1961.*
26. Thiele, 130, 162–74; Bragaw, *Federal Agency,* 114–23.
27. Capron, *Coast Guard,* 199–201.
28. Ibid., 201–2.
29. *Annual Report, 1959.*
30. Quoted in R. J. Carson and W. F. Tighe, Jr., "Development and Problems in Coast Guard Cutter Design," *Naval Review, 1964,* ed. by Frank Uhlig, Jr., p. 187.

31. Ibid., 176–77, 187–91.
32. *Annual Report, 1958.*
33. Robert W. Witter, "Design and Construction of the United States Coast Guard 44-Foot Motor Lifeboat," *Naval Engineers Journal* (Feb., 1964), pp. 93–100.
34. Ibid., 100.
35. John F. Ebersole, "The Lifesavers," *USNIP* (Oct., 1980), p. 129.
36. Capron, *Coast Guard,* 193–95.
37. Walter C. Capron, "The Coast Guard: A Year of Progress," *Naval Review, 1962–1963,* ed. by Frank Uhlig, Jr., p. 287.
38. Report of Assistance, 179–61, Lifeboat Station, Cape Disappointment, 19 Jan. 1961, copy in Ref. Coll., USCGHQ; *The Sunday Oregonian,* 15 Jan. 1961, p. 26. The *CG-52301* had earlier been named the *Triumph;* her sister was the *Invincible.* The 1958 52-footers became the *Intrepid* and the *Victorious;* the names of the 1935 boats were given to the later 52-footers.
39. "Is Another Peacock Spit Tragedy Possible?" *Portland Reporter* (n.d.), reprinted in *The Astoria Columbia Press,* 2 Feb. 1961.
40. Capron, "The Coast Guard: A Year of Progress," 289.
41. Roland, 2:526–30; Biographical Sketch of Admiral Edwin J. Roland, USCG, Public Information Div., USCGHQ.
42. 86 Cong. 2 Sess. H. Rept. 1294.
43. Thiele, 132–41.

CHAPTER EIGHTEEN

1. *U.S. Coast Guard: A Study of Its Origin, Responsibilities, Relationships, and Direction,* p. i.
2. Ibid., 30.
3. Capron, "The Coast Guard: A Year of Progress," 295.
4. Bragaw, *Federal Agency,* 47.
5. Capron, "The Coast Guard: A Year of Progress," 281; Roland, 2:595–96.
6. *Ambassador* file, Ref. Coll., USCGHQ.
7. *Annual Report, 1965;* Waters, *Rescue at Sea,* 167–69, 204.
8. *Annual Report, 1965.*
9. Waters, *Rescue at Sea,* 145.
10. Roland, 2:735–36.
11. Waters, *Rescue at Sea,* 133. Captain Waters placed this incident in 1965, a year too late.
12. Thiele, 85.
13. Kaplan and Hunt, 152; conversation with Captain Bruce Skinner, July, 1981; *Annual Report, 1966.*
14. Carson and Tighe, 179, 191.
15. 86 Cong. 1 Sess. H. Rept. 1057.
16. *Study of Roles and Missions of the United States Coast Guard,* 1:1–22; Edward W. Weeks, exec. secretary, National Council on Marine Resources and Engineering Development, to Subcommittee on Coast Guard, Coast and Geodetic Survey, and Navigation, House Merchant Marine and Fisheries Committee, 19 Feb. 1968, DOT Notebook, Ref. Coll., USCGHQ.
17. Coast Guard Icebreakers, Ref. Coll., USCGHQ.
18. *Annual Report, 1966.*
19. Roland, 2:656–64, 675–77.
20. Ibid., 2:675–77.
21. Eugene N. Tulich, *The United States Coast Guard in South East Asia During the Vietnam Conflict,* 3–15; James W. Moreau, "The Coast Guard in the Central and Western Pacific," *USNIP* (May, 1973), pp. 286–89.

22. Moreau, 289; see also Tulich, 12–13, 16–23.
23. Tulich, 55–56. Kaplan and Hunt, 209, claim over 3,000 enemy junks and almost 2,500 killed in action.
24. Tulich, 41–47.
25. Ibid., 10; *Annual Report, 1967.*
26. Tulich, 39; Moreau, 293–94; Peter B. Mersky and Norman Polmar, *The Naval Air War in Vietnam,* p. 120.
27. Tulich, 24–33; Moreau, 290–92.
28. Tulich, 34–36; Moreau, 291–92.
29. Moreau, 286.
30. *Annual Report, 1966.*
31. Bragaw, *Federal Agency,* 177–78.
32. Ibid., 159–60.
33. Roland, 2:749.
34. Quoted in W. J. Smith, 440.
35. "The United States Coast Guard Becomes Part of the Department of Transportation, April 1, 1967," pp. 2–4, copy in Ref. Coll., USCGHQ. Hereafter cited as "Coast Guard—Transportation."
36. Ibid., 6–7.
37. CO, Task Force, Dept. of Transportation, to chief of staff, private official, 28 Mar. 1966. Italics in original. Copy in DOT Notebook.
38. Ibid.
39. "Coast Guard—Transportation," 13, 16–17.
40. Ibid., 10–11.
41. Ibid., 18–20.
42. *Coast Guard History* (CG-213), p. 20.
43. Asst. Secretary of the Treasury Edward Clifford to Coast Guard personnel, 17 July 1922, Miscellaneous Reference Materials, Entry 279, RG 26.

CHAPTER NINETEEN

1. Bender, 475–79.
2. Georgia Clark Sadler, "Women in the Sea Services: 1972–1982," *USNIP* (May, 1983), p. 142 *et passim.*
3. Ibid., 143.
4. Bragaw, *Federal Agency,* 181.
5. Quoted in ibid., 182.
6. Ibid., 193–95; Bender, 525–27; James A. Atkinson, "VLCC Aground: Everybody's Problem," *USNIP* (Mar., 1976), pp. 96–97.
7. Bender, 531.
8. Quoted in Bragaw, *Federal Agency,* 190.
9. Ibid., 209, 215.
10. W. J. Smith, 633–50.
11. Norman C. Venzke, "*Polar Star*—Sitrep One," *USNIP* (Oct., 1978), pp. 103–6.
12. Robert G. Moore, "*Polar Star*—The Second Time Around," ibid., 107–12.
13. Mark Clevenger, "The *Polar Sea's* Story," ibid., 112–15.
14. D. G. Langrock, "U.S. Coast Guard Icebreaker Support Facility," ibid., 115–17.
15. Lawson W. Brigham and Michael N. Powers, "First Impressions of the New One-Forty Class," Alumni *Bulletin* (Mar.–Apr., 1980), pp. 30–35.
16. Robert G. Moore, "The *Bear* Facts," *USNIP* (Aug., 1983), pp. 112–15. Captain Moore had earlier presented a somewhat more favorable view of the design in "Hip Boots or Blue Water? An Examination of the U.S. Coast Guard and its Future," *USNIP* (May, 1982), pp. 189–90.

17. William K. Earle, "Comment and Discussion: The *Bear* Facts," *USNIP* (Nov., 1983), p. 147.

18. Steven J. Bellona, "The 270′ WMEC, a capable platform!" Alumni *Bulletin* (Jan.–Feb., 1985), p. 2.

19. Christopher Abel, "A Bad Day for *Benny*," *USNIP* (Sept., 1984), pp. 82–83.

20. Ibid., 31.

21. Michael R. Adams and Raymon Fullerton, "The Cuban Exodus Revisited," *USNIP* (Aug., 1981), pp. 91–94.

22. Marine Casualty Report: USCG WHITE ALDER—SS HELENA (Taiwan), Ref. Coll., USCGHQ.

23. Investigation into the Circumstances Connected with the Grounding of USCGC JARVIS (WHEC 725) at Dutch Harbor, Alaska and the Subsequent Flooding and Loss of Power on 15 November 1972, ibid.

24. Marine Casualty Report: USCGC CUYAHOGA, M/V SANTA CRUZ II (Argentine), ibid.

25. Marine Casualty Report: USCGC BLACKTHORN, SS CAPRICORN, ibid.

26. The Kudirka Incident: An Attempted Defection On Board U.S. Coast Guard Cutter VIGILANT, 23 November 1970, ibid.

27. Clyde R. Mann, "Asylum Denied: The *Vigilant* Incident," *Naval War College Review* (May, 1971), p. 4.

28. The Kudirka Incident.

29. Richard D. Brucker, "The Sinking of the Prinsendam," *AMVER Bulletin* (Jan., 1981), p. 4.

30. PRINSENDAM fire and loss: Transcript of Findings of the Netherlands Court of Inquiry, copy in Ref. Coll., USCGHQ. There is some uncertainty about the exact numbers of passengers and crew. The *Prinsendam's* first message indicated 320 and 190 respectively, but apparently some entertainers on board were not counted among the crew members. Other sources vary slightly as well.

31. Peter T. Eisele, "The Miracle that was PRINSENDAM," *Steamboat Bill* (n.d.), pp. 11–12, copy in ibid.

32. Thomas F. McCaffery, "*Williamsburgh* to the *Prinsendam's* Rescue," *USNIP* (Apr., 1981), p. 104.

33. Quoted in Day Boswell, "The Miracle Rescue," *Commandant's Bulletin* (Issue 48–80), p. 14.

BIBLIOGRAPHY

The Records of the United States Coast Guard (Record Group 26) in the Judicial and Fiscal Branch, National Archives and Records Service, in Washington, D.C., which contain records of the Light-House, Revenue-Cutter, and Life-Saving services as well as those of the Coast Guard, are the principal source for this study. Essential guides to this material are the Preliminary Inventory of the Records of the United States Coast Guard, compiled by Forrest R. Holdcamper in 1963, and the Subject Classification for Correspondence, adopted at Coast Guard Headquarters in 1936. Despite this date, a considerable amount of earlier material has been arranged according to the latter system. Unfortunately, Record Group 26 has few records more recent than 1947; those since that date, said to number thousands of boxes, are deposited in Federal Records centers elsewhere. Relatively little has been done to catalog them because the Coast Guard, which retains custody, has never been allotted the resources necessary for this task. Thus, these records are practically unavailable, with few exceptions.

The Coast Guard Academy Library, at New London, Connecticut, has the papers of a number of prominent officers as well as files on various subjects relevant to the service and a complete set of the *U.S. Coast Guard Magazine* and of the Coast Guard Academy Alumni Association's *Bulletin*. The Reference Collection at Coast Guard Headquarters in Washington, D.C., has a good deal of useful material on specific topics and an extensive collection of photographs. The papers of North Carolina Congressmen Lindsay C. Warren and Herbert C. Bonner in the Southern Historical Collection, Library of the University of North Carolina at Chapel Hill, are invaluable for the period from 1924, when Warren was elected to Congress, to 1965, when Bonner, his private secretary and successor, died. The Carter Glass Papers held by the University of Virginia at Charlottesville have little relating to the Coast Guard; most of Glass's correspondence regarding the Navy's efforts to retain control of the Coast Guard is in the Josephus Daniels Papers in the Library of Congress's James Madison Library, which also has the Woodrow Wilson Papers. The relative paucity of material for the more recent period is alleviated somewhat by the reminiscences of Coast Guard officers transcribed under the U.S. Naval Institute's Oral History Program. These include Admirals A. C. Richmond, E. J. Roland, W. J. Smith, and C. R. Bender, and Captains Dorothy C. Stratton, Earl K. Rhodes, and

Walter C. Capron, while the reminiscences of engineers in chief Vice Admiral K. K. Cowart and Rear Admiral E. H. Thiele were prepared at Coast Guard Headquarters.

Senate and House of Representatives reports and documents relating to the Coast Guard and the *Congressional Record* are essential, as are the *Annual Reports of the Coast Guard* and its predecessors. Before 1922, when economy forced their compression, these contain full accounts of notable rescue operations and the like; they became laconic in the extreme after World War II, comprising only a few pages in Treasury Department reports. Similarly, *Coast Guard Registers* before World War II give the assignment of each officer together with essential details of his career, as well as a complete list of stations, cutters, and aircraft. After the war, however, most of this material is omitted from the *Registers.* The *Weekly* and *Monthly Reports* compiled at Coast Guard Headquarters are useful for the post–World War II period. The prewar *Coast Guard Bulletins* dealt mainly with the International Ice Patrol until 1941, when the *Light-House Service Bulletin* was continued and expanded by the Coast Guard.

The Public Affairs Division at Coast Guard Headquarters has published a variety of monographs and booklets on a wide range of subjects, a number of which have helped considerably. Among its most useful publications is the *United States Coast Guard: Annotated Bibliography,* prepared under the direction of Robert L. Scheina in 1982. This is a revised version, in more convenient form, of the work compiled by Truman R. Strobridge in 1972; while it is not exhaustive, it greatly facilitates research in books and periodicals relating to the Coast Guard and its predecessors.

DEPOSITORIES AND COLLECTIONS

U.S. Coast Guard Academy Library

Records and papers of

Ellsworth P. Bertholf	John F. Hottel
Frederick C. Billard	Miles H. Imlay
Frederick J. Birkett	Merlin O'Neill
Joseph A. Bresnan	William E. Reynolds
John C. Cantwell	Philip F. Roach
Godfrey L. Carden	Horatio D. Snow
Philip B. Eaton	Russell R. Waesche
Joseph F. Farley	

Bragaw, Louis K., Managing a Federal Agency: The Hidden Stimulus: The Case of the U.S. Coast Guard. Unpublished manuscript.

History of the Coast Guard: 17th Naval District, 1941–1944.

Murphy, John F., Cutter Captain: The Life and Times of John C. Cantwell. Unpublished PhD dissertation, University of Connecticut, 1968.

Prohibition File.

Radio, 1904–1935.

U.S. Coast Guard Academy—Accreditation.

U.S. Coast Guard Headquarters, Reference Collection

A Brief History of Coast Guard Icebreakers.

Activities of Manning Section.

Anthony, H. M., Report on Air Sea Rescue Plan Alfa.

Bentley, John, Yearly Count of New Types of Aircraft owned or used by the Coast Guard since Flying became an Integral Part of its Duties (1915–1971).

Biographical sketches of Admirals Merlin O'Neill, Alfred C. Richmond, Edwin J. Roland, and Willard J. Smith.

Congressional Medal of Honor Hero—World War II.

Correspondence on certain prewar activities from the personal files of the Assistant Secretary of the Treasury.

Department of Transportation Notebook.

Investigation into the Circumstances Connected with the Grounding of USCGC JARVIS (WHEC 725) at Dutch Harbor, Alaska, and the Subsequent Flooding and Loss of Power on 15 November 1972.

Johnston, Charles E., and Crisp, Richard O., A History of the Coast Guard in the World War. 4 vols. Unpublished typescript.

Marine Casualty Report: USCGC BLACKTHORN, SS CAPRICORN.

Marine Casualty Report: USCGC CUYAHOGA, M/V SANTA CRUZ II (Argentine).

Marine Casualty Report: USCG WHITE ALDER—SS HELENA (Taiwan).

O'Brien, T. Michael, and Strobridge, Truman R., Black Lifesavers: A Brief Historical Survey of Blacks and the U.S. Lifesaving Service.

PRINSENDAM fire and loss: Transcript of Findings of the Netherlands Court of Inquiry.

Prohibition File.

Report of Assistance, 179–61, Lifeboat Station, Cape Disappointment, 19 Jan. 1961.

Strobridge, Truman R., The Public Works of the Coast Guard: A Historical Survey, 1790–1976.

The Kudirka Incident: An Attempted Defection On Board U.S. Coast Guard Cutter VIGILANT, 23 November 1970.

The United States Coast Guard Becomes Part of the Department of Transportation, April 1, 1967.

Library of Congress, James Madison Library

Josephus Daniels Papers.
Woodrow Wilson Papers.

University of North Carolina, Chapel Hill, Southern Historical Collection

Herbert C. Bonner Papers.
Lindsay C. Warren Papers.

University of Virginia, Manuscript Collections

Carter Glass Papers.

394

Letters to author

Captain William F. Adams, USCG (Ret.), 1 Sept. 1985.
Captain William K. Earle, USCG (Ret.), 7 Jan. 1984.
Rear Admiral William B. Ellis, USCG (Ret.), 12 Feb. 1984.
Captain Clifford R. MacLean, USCG (Ret.), 22 Sept. 1984.

BOOKS

Abbazia, Patrick. *Mr. Roosevelt's Navy: The Private War of the U.S. Atlantic Fleet, 1939–1942.* Annapolis, Md.: Naval Institute Press, 1975.

Arpee, Edward. *From Frigates to Flat-Tops: The Story of the Life and Achievements of Rear Admiral William Adger Moffett, USN.* Lake Forest, Ill.: Published by author, 1953.

Baarslag, Karl. *Coast Guard to the Rescue.* New York: Farrar and Rinehart, Inc., 1937.

Bailey, Thomas A., and Ryan, Paul B. *Hitler vs. Roosevelt: The Undeclared Naval War.* New York: The Free Press, 1979.

Bell, Kensil. *"Always Ready!" The Story of the United States Coast Guard.* New York: Dodd, Mead and Co., 1943.

Bennett, Robert F. *Surfboats, Rockets, and Carronades.* Washington: Department of Transportation, n.d. [1976].

Beston, Henry. *The Outermost House: A Year of Life on the Great Beach of Cape Cod.* New York: The Viking Press, 1972 (originally published in 1928).

Birkett, Frederick J. *A Manual of Coast Guard Vessels.* Washington: Government Printing Office, n.d. [1937].

Blum, John Morton. *From the Morgenthau Diaries.* 2 vols. Boston: Houghton Mifflin Co., 1959, 1965.

Bragaw, Louis K. *Managing a Federal Agency: The Hidden Stimulus.* Baltimore: The Johns Hopkins University Press, 1980.

Brown, Riley. *The Story of the Coast Guard: Men, Wind, and Sea.* Garden City, N.Y.: Blue Ribbon Books, 1943.

Capron, Walter C. *The U.S. Coast Guard.* New York: Franklin Watts, 1965.

Carse, Robert. *Rum Row.* New York: Rinehart and Co., 1959.

Colombos, C. John. *The International Law of the Sea.* 5th ed. London: Longmans, Green and Co., Ltd., 1962.

Corbett, Julian S., and Newbolt, Henry. *History of the Great War: Naval Operations.* 5 vols. London: Longmans, Green and Co., 1920–1931.

Dictionary of American Naval Fighting Ships. 8 vols. Washington: Naval Historical Center, 1959–1981.

Ebasco Services, Inc. *Study of United States Coast Guard.* New York: Ebasco Services, Inc., 1948.

Evans, Stephen Hadley. *The United States Coast Guard, 1790–1915: A Definitive History.* Annapolis, Md.: U.S. Naval Institute, 1949.

Friedman, Norman. *U.S. Destroyers: An Illustrated Design History.* Annapolis, Md.: Naval Institute Press, 1982.

Gibbs, James A., Jr. *Shipwrecks of the Pacific Coast.* Portland, Ore.: Binfords and Mort, Publishers, 1957.

Hughes, Terry, and Costello, John. *The Battle of the Atlantic.* New York: The Dial Press/James Wade, 1977.

Hunt, William R. *Arctic Passage: The Turbulent History of the Land and People of the Bering Sea, 1697–1975.* New York: Charles Scribner's Sons, 1975.

Kaplan, Hyman R., and Hunt, James F. *This is the Coast Guard.* Cambridge, Md.: Cornell Maritime Press, Inc., 1972.

Karig, Walter, *et al. Battle Report.* 6 vols. New York: Farrar and Rinehart, Inc., and Rinehart and Co., Inc., 1944–1954.

King, Ernest J. *U.S. Navy at War, 1941–1945: Official Reports to the Secretary of the Navy by Fleet Admiral Ernest J. King, Commander in Chief, United States Fleet, and Chief of Naval Operations.* Washington: U.S. Navy Department, 1946.

King, Irving H. *George Washington's Coast Guard: Origins of the U.S. Revenue Cutter Service, 1789–1801.* Annapolis, Md.: Naval Institute Press, 1978.

Knott, Richard C. *The American Flying Boat: An Illustrated History.* Annapolis, Md.: Naval Institute Press, 1979.

Lane, Frederic C., *et al. Ships for Victory: A History of Shipbuilding under the U.S. Maritime Commission in World War II.* Baltimore: The Johns Hopkins University Press, 1951.

Langer, William L., and Gleason, S. Everett. *The World Crisis and American Foreign Policy: The Undeclared War, 1940–1941.* New York: Harper and Brothers, 1953.

Lawrence, Samuel A. *United States Merchant Shipping Policies and Politics.* Washington: The Brookings Institution, 1966.

Lucas, Jo Desha. *Cases and Materials on Admiralty.* Mineola, N.Y.: The Foundation Press, Inc., 1969.

MacGregor, Morris J., Jr. *Integration of the Armed Forces, 1940–1965.* Washington: Center of Military History, U.S. Army, 1981.

McFee, William. *The Law of the Sea.* Philadelphia: J. B. Lippincott Co., 1950.

Mersky, Peter B., and Polmar, Norman. *The Naval Air War in Vietnam.* Annapolis, Md.: The Nautical and Aviation Publishing Company of America, 1981.

Morison, Samuel Eliot. *History of U.S. Naval Operations in World War II.* 15 vols. Boston: Little, Brown and Company, 1947–1962.

Nalty, Bernard C., Noble, Dennis L., and Strobridge, Truman R., eds. *Wrecks, Rescues, and Investigations: Selected Documents of the U.S. Coast Guard and its Predecessors.* Wilmington, Del.: Scholarly Resources, Inc., 1978.

Roscoe, Theodore. *United States Destroyer Operations in World War II.* Annapolis, Md.: U.S. Naval Institute, 1953.

Roskill, Stephen W. *The War at Sea, 1939–1945.* 3 vols. London: Her Majesty's Stationery Office, 1954–1960.

Scheina, Robert L. *U.S. Coast Guard Cutters and Craft of World War II.* Annapolis, Md.: Naval Institute Press, 1982.

Schmeckebier, Laurence F. *The Bureau of Prohibition: Its History, Activities, and Organization.* Service Monographs of the U.S. Government, No. 57. Washington: The Brookings Institution, 1929.

Smith, Darrell Hevenor, and Powell, Fred Wilbur. *The Coast Guard: Its History, Activities, and Organization.* Service Monographs of the U.S. Government, No. 51. Washington: The Brookings Institution, 1929.

Smith, Richard K. *First Across! The U.S. Navy's Transatlantic Flight of 1919.* Annapolis, Md.: Naval Institute Press, 1973.

Study of Roles and Missions of the United States Coast Guard. 2 vols. Washington: U.S. Treasury Department, 1962.

Thomas, Charles W. *Ice is Where You Find It.* Indianapolis, Ind.: The Bobbs-Merrill Co., Inc., 1951.

Uhlig, Frank, Jr., ed. *The Naval Review, 1962–1963, 1964,* and *1965.* Annapolis, Md.: U.S. Naval Institute, 1963, 1964, and 1965.

Waters, John M., Jr. *Bloody Winter.* Revised edition. Annapolis, Md.: Naval Institute Press, 1984.

——. *Rescue at Sea.* Princeton, N.J.: D. Van Nostrand and Co., Inc., 1966.

Weiss, George. *The Lighthouse Service: Its History, Activities, and Organization.* Baltimore, Md.: The Johns Hopkins University Press, 1926.

Willoughby, Malcolm F. *Rum War at Sea.* Washington: U.S. Treasury Department, 1964.

——. *The U.S. Coast Guard in World War II.* Annapolis, Md.: U.S. Naval Institute, 1957.

Booklets published by the Public Affairs and Public Information divisions, U.S. Coast Guard.

Air Search and Rescue: 63 Years of Aerial Lifesaving: A Pictorial History, 1915–1978. Washington, 1978.

Historically Famous Lighthouses. Washington, 1972.

Strobridge, Truman R. *Chronology of Aids to Navigation and the Old Lighthouse Service, 1716–1939.* Washington, 1974.

The International Ice Patrol in the North Atlantic. Washington, 1969.

Tulich, Eugene N. *The United States Coast Guard in South East Asia During the Vietnam Conflict.* Washington, 1975.

U.S. Coast Guard: A Study of Its Origin, Responsibilities, Relationships, and Direction. Washington, 1962.

PERIODICALS

Abel, Christopher. "A Bad Day for *Benny.*" *U.S. Naval Institute Proceedings,* September, 1984.

Adams, Michael R., and Fullerton, Raymon. "The Cuban Exodus Revisited." *U.S. Naval Institute Proceedings,* August, 1981.

Adams, R. B., and Hunnewell, F. A. "Typical Vessels and Boats of the U.S. Coast Guard." *U.S. Naval Institute Proceedings,* May, 1929.

Atkinson, James A. "VLCC Aground: Everybody's Problem." *U.S. Naval Institute Proceedings,* March, 1976.

Bellona, Steven J. "The 270′ WMEC, a capable platform!" U.S. Coast Guard Academy Alumni Association *Bulletin,* January–February, 1985.

Bennett, Robert F. "The Origins of the Coast Guard's Operational Shore

Structure." U.S. Coast Guard Academy Alumni Association *Bulletin*, May–June, 1981.

"Bids Asked for Coast Guard Cutter for Arctic Service." *Marine Engineering and Shipping Age*, March, 1926.

Boswell, Day. "The Miracle Rescue." *Commandant's Bulletin*, Issue 48–80.

Brigham, Lawson W., and Powers, Michael N. "First Impressions of the New One-Forty Class." U.S. Coast Guard Academy Alumni Association *Bulletin*, March–April, 1980.

Brucker, Richard D. "The Sinking of the Prinsendam." *AMVER Bulletin*, January, 1981.

Chapline, W. E. "The Hurricane of September 1938." U.S. Coast Guard Academy Alumni Association *Bulletin*, May–June, 1982.

Clevenger, Mark. "The *Polar Sea*'s Story." *U.S. Naval Institute Proceedings*, October, 1978.

_____. "*Polar Sea* on Patrol in 1979." *U.S. Naval Institute Proceedings*, December, 1979.

Cronk, Paul B. "The Rescue on Station Charlie." *Atlantic Monthly*, July, 1950.

Dempwolf, Ralph W. "The First Voyage of the New Turbo-Electric Cutter Chelan." *The Bugle*, February, 1929.

Earle, William K. "Comment and Discussion: The *Bear* Facts." *U.S. Naval Institute Proceedings*, November, 1983.

Ebersole, John F. "The Lifesavers." *U.S. Naval Institute Proceedings*, October, 1980.

Ehrman, William E. "Lost in the Graveyard of the Atlantic." U.S. Coast Guard Academy Alumni Association *Bulletin*, September–October, 1978.

_____. "World War II Memoirs of an 'Island Hopper' Skipper." U.S. Coast Guard Academy Alumni Association *Bulletin*, July–August, 1983.

Eisele, Peter T. "The Miracle that was PRINSENDAM." *Steamboat Bill* (n.d.).

Ellis, William S. "Tracking Danger with the Ice Patrol." *National Geographic*, June, 1968.

Langrock, D. G. "U.S. Coast Guard Icebreaker Support Facility." *U.S. Naval Institute Proceedings*, October, 1978.

Larzelere, Alexander R. "'Away the Prize Crew'." *U.S. Naval Institute Proceedings*, January, 1975.

"Lectures on Streamlined Rudders Given at Webb Institute." *Marine Engineering and Shipping Age*, December, 1928.

Macy, Robert H. "Consolidation of the Light-House Service with the Coast Guard." *U.S. Naval Institute Proceedings*, January, 1940.

Mann, Clyde R. "Asylum Denied: The *Vigilant* Incident." *Naval War College Review*, May, 1971.

Maxam, Oliver M. "The Life-Saving Stations of the United States Coast Guard." *U.S. Naval Institute Proceedings*, May, 1929.

McCaffery, Thomas F. "*Williamsburgh* to the *Prinsendam*'s Rescue." *U.S. Naval Institute Proceedings*, April, 1981.

Merrill, Robert T. "The Role of the Coast Guard within the Navy." *U.S. Naval Institute Proceedings*, August, 1946.

Moore, Robert G. "*Polar Star*—The Second Time Around." *U.S. Naval Institute Proceedings*, October, 1978.

————. "The Polar Icebreakers: Breaking Through At Last." *U.S. Naval Institute Proceedings*, December, 1979.

————. "The *Bear* Facts." *U.S. Naval Institute Proceedings*, August, 1983.

————. "Hip Boots or Blue Water? An Examination of the U.S. Coast Guard and its Future." *U.S. Naval Institute Proceedings*, May, 1982.

Moreau, James W. "The Coast Guard in the Central and Western Pacific." *U.S. Naval Institute Proceedings*, May, 1973.

Naab, J. W., Jr. "Icebreakers and Icebreaking." *U.S. Naval Institute Proceedings*, June, 1962.

Nalty, Bernard C., and Strobridge, Truman R. "The Story of the Ocean Stations." U.S. Coast Guard Academy Alumni Association *Bulletin*, March–April, 1974.

Newman, Q. B. "First Electric Coast Guard Cutter Completed." *Marine Engineering and Shipping Age*, November, 1921.

————. "Electric Drive Applied to Coast Guard Cutters." *Marine Engineering and Shipping Age*, January, 1922.

————. "USCG Cutters *Chelan, Pontchartrain, Tahoe, Champlain*, and *Mendota*." *Journal of the American Society of Naval Engineers*, November, 1928.

Odom, Curtis B. "Let's Transfer the Coast Guard to the Department of ————: A History of Proposed Moves." U.S. Coast Guard Academy Alumni Association *Bulletin*, March–April, 1983.

Sadler, Georgia Clark. "Women in the Sea Services: 1972–1982." *U.S. Naval Institute Proceedings*, May, 1983.

Scheina, Robert L. "Coast Guard Operations in Greenland, 1940–41." U.S. Coast Guard Academy Alumni Association *Bulletin*, March–April, 1981.

————. "Coast Guard Operations in Greenland, 1941–45." U.S. Coast Guard Academy Alumni Association *Bulletin*, July–August, 1981.

Simonson, Dale R. "Bow Characteristics for Ice Breaking." *Journal of the American Society of Naval Engineers*, May, 1936.

Spencer, E. R., Jr. "The Coast Guard in the Army." *U.S. Naval Institute Proceedings*, April, 1946.

Sullivan, Edward F. "The Coast Guard Florida Relief Expedition." *Our Navy*, Mid-October, 1926.

"Taps: A Tribute [to Rear Admiral F. C. Billard]." *U.S. Coast Guard Magazine*, June, 1932.

"The Beginning: Academy Opens Doors 50 Years Ago At Present Site." U.S. Coast Guard Academy Alumni Association *Bulletin*, September–October, 1982.

Tighe, William F., Jr. "The New Medium Endurance Cutters," *U.S. Naval Institute Proceedings*, August, 1965.

Van Boskerck, F. S. "The United States Coast Guard: Its Military Necessities." *U.S. Naval Institute Proceedings*, April, 1919.

Venzke, Norman C. "*Polar Star*—Sitrep One." *U.S. Naval Institute Proceedings,* October, 1978.

Waesche, Russell R. "Armaments and Gunnery in the Coast Guard." *U.S. Naval Institute Proceedings,* May, 1929.

Webster, E. M. "On Research and Facts." *U.S. Coast Guard Magazine,* March, 1930.

Wheeler, William J. "Reminiscences of World War Convoy Work." *U.S. Naval Institute Proceedings,* May, 1929.

Witter, Robert W. "Design and Construction of the United States Coast Guard 44-Foot Motor Lifeboat." *Naval Engineers Journal,* February, 1964.

PAPERS

Cowart, K. K. "Development of Vessels Servicing Aids to Navigation for the U.S. Coast Guard." Paper presented at the annual meeting of the Society of Naval Architects and Marine Engineers, 13–14 November, 1958.

Hunnewell, Frederick A. "United States Coast Guard Cutters." Advance copy of paper presented at annual meeting of the Society of Naval Architects and Marine Engineers, 18–19 November 1937.

Johnson, Harvey F. "Development of Ice-Breaking Vessels for the U.S. Coast Guard." Advance copy of paper presented at annual meeting of the Society of Naval Architects and Marine Engineers, 14–15 November 1946.

"Operation of a Small Government Shipyard." Paper presented at meeting of the First Pan American Congress of Naval Architects and Marine Engineering, Rio de Janeiro, June, 1966.

Tomalin, Paul G. "Bridge-Controlled Turbo-Electric 255-Foot Coast Guard Cutter." Paper read at meeting of the Chesapeake Bay Section of the Society of Naval Architects and Marine Engineers, 11 October 1947.

NEWPAPERS

Honolulu Star Bulletin, June, July, 1954.

Miami Herald, March, April, 1950.

New York Times.

INDEX

402

George M. Bibb. See Bibb

George W. Campbell. See Campbell

German Life-Saving Service, 123

Gibbons, Stephen B., assistant secretary of the treasury, 148

Gibbs and Cox, naval architects, 215, 248

Glacier, 310-foot icebreaker, 330–31, 351

Glass, Carter, secretary of the treasury, 58–63, 79, 130

Gloucester CG Air Station, 144, 146

Gloucester CG station, 70

Gorman, Frank J., 151, 164, 189, 256, 258–60

Government Island CG training station, 159, 196

Governor, merchant vessel, 47

Governor Cobb, helicopter training ship, 210–11

Gracey, James S., commandant, 355

Graf Zeppelin, German dirigible, 122

Graham, Stewart R., 274

Grand Banks Neutrality Patrol, 173, 175

Grandcamp, French cargo ship, 281

Grand Marais CG station, 72

Gray's Harbor CG station, 138

Great Lakes Pilotage Administration, 343

Greenland, 22, 111, 122, 177, 185; CG operations in during World War II, 223–30

Greenpoint CG base, 87

Greenspun, Joseph, 293

Greer, destroyer, 194, 235

Gresham, 205-foot cutter (1897), 12, 71–72, 113, 133, 153

Gresham, 311-foot cutter, 265, 286, 300, 334

Groton CG training station, 198, 221

Guarda Costa, 32

Gudrun, fishing vessel, 273

Gulfstream, tanker, 277–78

Gull Shoal CG station, 52

Gustafson, Carl, 98

Gustafson, USN destroyer escort, 250

Gwin, destroyer, 231

Haida, 240-foot cutter (1921), 66–67; and World Flight, 76–77; 78, 155, 169, 203, 214, 240, 295

Half Moon, 311-foot cutter, 334

Halifax, N.S., disaster (1917), 47–48

Hall, Norman H., 42, 145

Halliburton, Richard, 168

Hamilton, Alexander, secretary of the treasury, 1

Hamilton, 327-foot cutter (1937), 155. See also Alexander Hamilton

Hamilton, 378-foot cutter (1967), 328

Hamlet, Harry G., 83, 99; commandant, 127–30, 132, 144, 147–50, 166

Hanalei, merchant vessel, 29–31

Hansen, Knud L., Danish captain, 193

Hanson, Jacob D., 94

Harding, Lawrence M., 220–21

Harding, Warren G., president, 67, 80–81

Hardy, J. H., assistant surgeon, 48

Harriet Lane, revenue cutter, 10

Harriet Lane, 270-foot cutter, 354

Harrison, Paul H., 61–62

Hartland, British cutter (ex-Pontchartrain), 184

Harvard University, 117, 147

Hastings, naval constructor, 110

Hatfield, destroyer, 171

Haworth, Loren H., 228

Hayes, John B., commandant, 318, 355

Haynes, Roy, prohibition commissioner, 80

H. E. Runnels, cargo ship, 72–73

Heineman, Paul R., 235

Helena, Taiwan freighter, 358

Helga Bolten, West German freighter, 301–2

Helicopters, 209–13, 274, 289–90, 323–25

Hemingway, Henry G., 48, 74–75

Henley, CG destroyer, 83, 105–6

Henriques, John A., 14

Henry L. Marshall, British schooner, 80

Henry R. Mallory, Army transport, 233

Herndon, CG destroyer, 104–5

Higgins, Andrew J., 191

Highflyer, British cruiser, 48

Highland CG station, 100

Hirshfield, James A., assistant commandant, 234, 295, 308, 319

Hoffman Island CG training station, 159

Holder, USN destroyer escort, 247

Hoover, Herbert C., president, 296

Hoover Commission, 296

Hopkins, Harry L., 217

Hoquiam, frigate, 197

Hornbeam, 180-foot buoy tender (1944), 303

Hottel, John F., 76–78, 113

Houston, David F., secretary of the treasury, 62, 64, 80

Howard, W. A., 8

Hudson, 110-foot harbor cutter (1934), 157

Hull, Cordell, secretary of state, 188

Humane Society for the Shipwrecked (France), 123

Humble Oil and Refining Company, 349–50

Humphrey, George, secretary of the treasury, 311

Hunnewell, Frederick A., 66, 114–16, 144, 154, 157, 218

Hunt, CG destroyer, 136

Hunter Liggett, transport, 190; attack transport, 241–42

Hurricanes (1926), 99; (1936), 166; (1938), 167; (1944), 239–40

Hurst, CG destroyer escort, 258

Hymer, Melvin M., 140, 142–43

Icarus, 165-foot Class B cutter (1932), 238

Icebreaker Support Facility, 352

Icebreakers, USN, transferred to CG, 328–31

Icebreaking responsibility assigned to CG, 155–58

Ice plows, 157, 213

Ile de France, French liner, 303

Ilhavense Segundo, Portuguese fishing vessel, 301

I'm Alone, Canadian schooner, 95–96

Imlay, Miles H., 97, 245

Imo, Norwegian freighter, 47

Imp, CG patrol boat, 94

Influenza epidemic (1918–19), 70–71

Ingham, 327-foot cutter (1936), 154–55, 179, 230; sinks U-626, 232; 233–35; 336

Interdepartmental Board on International Service of Ice Observation, Ice Patrol and Ocean Derelict Destruction, 116–18, 185

Interdepartmental Radio Advisory Committee, 131

Intergovernmental Maritime Consultative Organization (IMCO), 310, 339–40, 348

International Conference on Marine Pollution (1973), 348

International Conference on the Safety of Life at Sea (1914), 27; (1929), 28; (1960), 310

International Congress of Maritime Coast Life-Saving (1928), 123

International Convention on the Safety of Life at Sea (1948), 304

International Ice Patrol, 25–28, 51,

Mainbocher, fashion designer, 199
Malaya, British battleship, 184
Manasquan, weather ship, 221
Manhasset, weather ship, 251
Manhattan, revenue cutter, 9
Manhattan, 120-foot harbor cutter (1918), 64, 155
Manhattan, tanker, 349–50
Manhattan Beach CG training station, 196–97, 249
Manila Bay, Battle of, 2
Manning, 205-foot cutter (1897), 11, 19, 29, 46; in World War I, 52, 59; 99, 113
Marblehead, cruiser, 71
Marconi, merchant vessel, 189
Margarita, merchant vessel, 309
Marietta, USN gunboat, 127
Marine Cooks and Stewards Union, 283
Marine Corps Institute, 109
Marine Iron and Shipbuilding Corporation, 193, 213
Marine Safety Office, 349
Marion, 125-foot patrol boat (1927), 118–22, 133
Maritime Association of New York, 24
Maritime Commission, 159, 175, 185, 188, 251, 285
Maritime Service, 159–60, 202
Marte, Spanish freighter, 290
Martin, Charles, 268–70
Martin, Frederick L., 76–77
Martin, Samuel, 73
Maryland, freighter, 290
Mary Luckenbach, freighter, 286
Mascoutin, 151-foot cutter, 65
Massachusetts Humane Society, 4
Massachusetts Institute of Technology, 147 220
Matagorda, 311-foot cutter, 300
Mathilde Bolten, West German freighter, 323
Matsonia, passenger vessel, 309
Mauerman, Raymond J., 203
Maul v. *the U.S.,* 158
Mauretania, British liner, 301–2
Maxam, Oliver M., 36, 123, 150
Maxwell, Michael, 31
McAdoo, William G., secretary of the treasury, 24, 26, 32, 34, 40, 44, 58, 79
McAfee, Mildred H., 199
McAllister, Charles A., engineer in chief, 60, 110
McCabe, Frank M., 247
McCabe, George E., 232, 281
McCormick, Nelson C., 238
McCulloch, Hugh, secretary of the treasury, 10–11, 32
McCulloch, 219-foot cutter (1898), 2, 11, 16, 19, 29, 30, 46–47

McCulloch, 311-foot cutter, 265, 287–88
McDougal, CG destroyer, 136
McLane, Louis, secretary of the treasury, 4, 13, 16
McMurdo Station, 351
Meals, Frank M., 90
Mellon, Andrew W., secretary of the treasury, 67, 81, 104, 109, 113, 127
Mellon, 378-foot cutter (1967), 365, 367
Mendota, 250-foot cutter (1929), 115–16, 166, 184
Mendota, 255-foot cutter (1945), 219, 301
Menges, CG destroyer escort, 247–48
Merchant Marine Academy, 295–96
Merchant Marine Act (1936), 159
Merchant Marine Council, 201
Mermaid, crab boat, 316–17
Merrick, USN storeship, 276
Merrill, Robert T., 200, 310
Merritt and Chapman Company, 113, 141
Merryman, James H., 14
Meyer, George von L., secretary of the navy, 20
Miami, 190-foot cutter (1912), 21, 23–27; renamed *Tampa,* 28
Miami CG Air Station, 147
Micka, USN destroyer escort, 250
Midgett, John A., 51–52, 56, 328
Military Air Transport Service (MATS), 278, 309
Military Sea Transport Service (MSTS), 303, 307, 338
Miller, Raymond G., 301–2
Mills, Ogden L., secretary of the treasury, 127–28
Minnetonka, 255-foot cutter (1946), 300, 335, 344
Mirlo, British tanker, 51–52, 56
Mission Bay, escort carrier, 248
"Mission of the Coast Guard" (1944), 257
Moberly, frigate, 250–51
Mobile boarding teams, 315
Moccasin, CG station ship, 99
Mocoma, 250-foot cutter (ex-*Cayuga*), 292–93
Modoc, 240-foot cutter (1921), 66–67, 114, 118, 166; and *Bismarck* chase, 188; 190, 225–27, 276
Modoc, 143-foot cutter, 312, 345
Moffett, William A., 135–36
Mohawk, 205-foot cutter (1902), 23, 47, 49
Mohawk, 165-foot cutter (1933), 116, 143, 166, 185, 225

Mojave, 240-foot cutter (1921), 66–67, 88, 136, 155, 225, 276
Monarch of Bermuda, British merchant vessel, 139, 142
Montauk Point loran station, 220–21
Mont Blanc, French freighter, 47–48
Moore, George W., 14
Moore, John C., 15
Morehead City CG Air Station, 67
Morgan, Harry L., 341, 343
Morgenthau, Henry, Jr., secretary of the treasury, 129, 132; interest in aviation, 146; 148–49, 172, 175–76; aid to Britain, 182; 184, 191, 214
Morgenthau, 378-foot cutter (1969), 336, 346
Moritz, Susan I., 346
Morrill, 145-foot cutter (1889), 47–48, 56
Morris, 125-foot patrol boat (1927), 133
Morro Castle, passenger vessel, 135, 138–43, 146, 159
Mosby, Olav, 122
Mosley, CG destroyer escort, 247
Munro, Douglas A., 242–43, 328
Munter, William H., 124
Muskeget, weather ship, 251
Myers, John, 161

Nagel, Charles, secretary of commerce and labor, 20
Nanok, CG trawler, 225
National Defense Research Committee, 220
National Industrial Recovery Act, 143
National Maritime Union Conference, 202
National Prohibition (Volstead) Act, 79
National Search and Rescue Plan (1956), 297, 308
National Strike Force, 347
National Transportation Safety Board, 342
Natsek, CG trawler, 225
Naugatuck, 110-foot cutter (1939), 157
Naval Academy practice squadron, 171
Naval Appropriation Act (1918), 46; (1902), 62
Navesink, 110-foot harbor cutter (1934), 157
Navy Recruiting Service, 82
NC-4, USN aircraft, 67, 175
Nelson, Erik, 77
Nettle, CG cargo vessel, 266

411